ROBERT PENN WARREN

Books by Joseph Blotner

The Political Novel
The Fiction of J. D. Salinger (with Frederick L. Gwynn)
Faulkner in the University (with Frederick L. Gwynn)
William Faulkner's Library: A Catalogue
The Modern American Political Novel: 1900–1960
Faulkner: A Biography (2 vols.)
Selected Letters of William Faulkner
Uncollected Stories of William Faulkner
Faulkner: A Biography (1 vol.)

ROBERT PENN WARREN

A Biography

JOSEPH BLOTNER

RANDOM HOUSE
New York

To Marnie
quae laetificat meam vitam

Preface

Thirty-three years ago Albert Erskine told me, "You ought to talk with Red Warren." At the time, I was doing research for my biography of William Faulkner. Albert had been Faulkner's editor and Warren's editor, and now, to my great good fortune, he was my editor too. So I wrote Robert Penn Warren to ask his help. I had been reading his work for years; I had first encountered "Bearded Oaks" in an informal reading group of young instructors who met one night a week to renew their souls after regularly teaching course loads of four sections of English Composition. As soon as I was given a section of sophomore literature, I included that poem in my syllabus, and when I was given a course in the novel, I put *All the King's Men* on the list of required reading. Over the subsequent years I read more and more Warren.

Now I looked forward to corresponding with him, asking questions about Faulkner and having the benefit in his replies of the kind of insight and empathy that had made his review of Malcolm Cowley's Viking *Portable Faulkner* a decisive factor in the surge of renewed interest in Faulkner's work. Warren's response was typical of him. He suggested things to read and people to interview and invited me for a visit to the Warrens' summer place in Vermont. That didn't work out, but in December I went to their home in Fairfield, Connecticut. He and his wife, Eleanor Clark, had a gift for hospitality and friendship, and so the visit was doubly rewarding. Warren told me about the few times he and Faulkner had been together. He talked about Faulkner's work as well and about the South, the South he had known all his life, not Faulkner's Deep South but mainly the middle South of Kentucky and Tennessee—though he had also passed years in Louisiana. He was putting together a volume of critical essays on Faulkner, and as I left he asked me if I would provide an introductory essay on Faulkner's life and career. Naturally, there would be remuneration. "The workman is worthy of his hire," he said, smiling. I was afraid of getting sidetracked from the work at hand and said, "I'll take it to the Lord in prayer." He laughed and said, "Good. You do that." Later, I sometimes regretted passing up the chance to work with and for him.

Fortunately, our relationship continued. Once when I visited Albert Erskine in Westport to work on my Faulkner manuscript, the Warrens had invited the Erskines to a party, and the invitation was generously broadened to include me. This happened again in the proof stage, so that there was once more the pleasure of the Warrens' company and the chance to sharpen my ear to Red Warren's dialect and to enjoy the robust humor of his stories and the genuine warmth of his friendship. This process continued when I returned to Westport for work on other Faulkner books. On one occasion I agreed to give a paper at a North Carolina college during a week's program devoted to Warren's work. About to launch into a lecture on *All the King's Men,* to my dismay I saw him enter and seat himself in the back row. Later I learned that often when he was obliged for some reason to sit in an audience, he would employ the time mentally working on poems. I wish I had known that during my lecture.

In the 1980s, casting about for a subject for a new book, I realized that it ought to be another biography, one for which my previous work had somehow helped prepare me and one that would be worth at least five years of my life. I realized that a biography of Robert Penn Warren would meet those criteria. When I first wrote to Warren and proposed the idea, he replied with warm thanks and a reassuring confidence. He regretted that he was not well enough to help me, but he added that he did not object to the project and was in no way trying to discourage me. Still, as we continued to correspond, he began to supply information and suggestions. It was simply accepted that I would write his life.

Then came a series of visits. After one he wrote me that "the buzz of recollection" was continuing, so that, in Connecticut and Vermont, he called up Kentucky and Tennessee and California, then New Haven and Oxford, Memphis and Nashville, Baton Rouge and Minneapolis. I made notes and taped the flow of memory. "Ask me anything," he would say. He would answer my queries directly, often going to the heart of a question I had put in less than explicit terms. And he volunteered information, some of it intimate. Occasionally he would ask Eleanor to verify a point, which she would, as well as supplying breakfast, lunch, afternoon tea, cocktails, and dinner. There was easy, companionable give-and-take along with the lively conversation stimulated at breakfast by reading the *Times*. Opinion and response flowed freely. "You old Agrarian!" Eleanor exclaimed. "You old Trotskyite!" Red shot back.

Work merged into the flow of family life, and my research was deepened and enriched by the occasional company of the Warrens' daughter and son. The outpouring of Red and Eleanor's love for Rosanna and Gabriel made me think of Cornelia, mother of the Gracchi, and her answer to the haughty Roman matron's question, "Where are your jewels?"

Even as Red's vigor waned he provided help, often when he was in pain. And there was still the society of guests and the outing of the daily walk, though finally, as Red's strength fled, it took Eleanor's fond hectoring to make him grasp his cane and venture beyond his door. He was the classic stoic, his daughter said, taking his own old father's silent suffering as a guide through the end of his long life.

America's preeminent man of letters, master of genres, prodigiously creative, heavy with awards and prizes honoring his genius, Robert Penn Warren was also that rare being, a genuinely good man. I am fortunate not only to be able to offer the tribute of a book to his memory but also to have experienced something of his noble life.

Chronology

1905   *Apr. 24:* born, Guthrie, Kentucky.

1908   [*Feb. 20:* sister Mary Cecilia born.]

1911   [*Apr. 8:* brother William Thomas born.] *Summer:* lives on farm of grandfather Gabriel Thomas Penn at Cerulean. *Fall:* enters Guthrie School.

1920   *Spring:* graduates. *Sept.:* enters Clarksville High School.

1921   *Spring:* suffers injury to left eye. *Summer:* spends six weeks in Citizens Military Training Corps at Fort Knox, publishes first poem, "Prophecy," in *The Messkit. Fall:* enters Vanderbilt University.

1923   *Jan.:* moves into Wesley Hall room with Allen Tate, Ridley Wills, and William Cobb. *Spring:* contributes poems to *Driftwood Flames* and *The Fugitive.*

1924   *Feb.:* listed on masthead as member of The Fugitives. *May 19:* attempts suicide, taken to Guthrie by father, Robert Franklin Warren. *Fall:* returns to Vanderbilt and publishes poems in *The Double Dealer.*

1925   *Summer:* graduates from Vanderbilt summa cum laude, Phi Beta Kappa, and Founder's Medalist. *Aug. 8:* enters University of California as graduate student and teaching assistant, meets Emma "Cinina" Brescia. *Dec.:* attempts, unsuccessfully, to transfer to Yale.

1927   publishes poems in *The New Republic,* receives M.A. from University of California. *Fall:* enters Yale University on fellowship.

1928   *Winter:* publishes in *American Caravan* and *The Nation. Spring:* signs contract for John Brown biography. *Oct.:* enters New College as Rhodes scholar.

1929   *June:* returns home with eye trouble. *Summer:* secretly married to Cinina Brescia in Sacramento, California. *Nov. 2: John Brown: The Making of a Martyr* published.

1930   *Spring:* receives B. Litt. *Fall:* accepts assistant professorship at Southwestern College. *Sept. 12:* openly married to Cinina Brescia in Marion, Arkansas.

1931   Novelette *Prime Leaf* published in *American Caravan IV.* "The Briar Patch" appears in *I'll Take My Stand. Sept.:* named acting assistant professor at Vanderbilt.

1934   *Feb. 7:* left eye removed. *Spring:* leaves Vanderbilt and appointed assistant professor at Louisiana State University.

1935   Appointed managing editor of *The Southern Review,* with Cleanth Brooks.

1936   *Feb. 15: Thirty-Six Poems* published. *Sept.: An Approach to Literature* published.

1938   *June:* travels to Italy for the summer. *Understanding Poetry* published.

1939   *March 14: Night Rider* published. *March:* receives Guggenheim Fellowship. *July 20:* departs for Italy.

1940   *May 18:* departs for home.

1941   *Jan.:* visiting professor at University of Iowa. [*Dec.:* LSU to discontinue *The Southern Review.*]

1942   *Apr. 4: Eleven Poems on the Same Theme* published. *Spring:* resigns when LSU fails to meet University of Minnesota offer, and begins teaching there. *Summer:* visiting professor at University of Iowa. *Eleven Poems* receives Shelley Memorial Award.

1943   *Aug. 19: At Heaven's Gate* published.

1944   *Apr. 6: Selected Poems: 1923–1943* published. *July 23:* begins work as Consultant in Poetry to the Library of Congress for one year. *Winter:* "The Ballad of Billie Potts" published.

1946   *Aug. 17: All the King's Men* published. *Nov. 1:* "Blackberry Winter" published.

1947   *Apr. 8:* receives Guggenheim Fellowship. *May 5:* receives Pulitzer Prize for Fiction for *All the King's Men. May 9:* Columbia Pictures buys film rights to *All the King's Men.*

1948   *Jan. 27:* departs for Italy.

1949   *March:* works on film version of *All the King's Men* in California. *Apr. 28: Modern Rhetoric* published. [*May 14:* Cinina hospitalized in New York.] *June 20: World Enough and Time* published. Resigns from University of Minnesota.

1950   *June 17:* elected to National Institute of Arts and Letters. Accepts visiting professorship at Yale University, takes New York apartment.

1951   *Winter:* declines offer from University of California at Berkeley because of their insistence on loyalty oath. Named professor of playwriting in Yale School of Drama. *May 10:* elected to American Academy of Arts and Sciences. *June 28:* granted divorce in Reno from Cinina. *July:* leaves for England.

1952   *Apr. 11:* moves in with Eleanor Clark in New York. *Dec. 7:* married to Eleanor Clark.

1953   *July 27:* Rosanna Phelps Warren born. *Aug. 21: Brother to Dragons* published. *Christmas:* moves into new home in Fairfield, Connecticut.

1954   Travels to Italy.

1955   *July 19:* Gabriel Penn Warren born. *Aug. 22: Band of Angels* published. *Mid-Dec.:* retires from Yale.

1956   *May:* returns to Italy. *Aug. 31: Segregation: The Inner Conflict in the South* published.

1957   *Feb. 8:* departs for home. *Aug. 15: Promises: Poems, 1954–1956* published.

1958   *Mid-Jan.:* receives Edna St. Vincent Millay Prize for Poetry. *March 11:* receives National Book Award for *Promises. May 7:* departs for France and Italy. *June 25: Selected Essays* published. *Aug. 28: Remember the Alamo* published. *Oct. 11:* departs for home.

1959   *Feb.: How Texas Won Her Freedom* published. *Apr.:* elected to American Academy of Arts and Letters. *Aug. 24: The Cave* published. *Sept. 28: The Gods of Mount Olympus* published. *Oct. 16: All the King's Men* produced in New York. *Mid-Oct.:* purchases cottage in West Wardsboro, Vermont.

1960   *Apr. 25: All the King's Men: A Play* published. *Aug.: You, Emperors, and Others: Poems, 1957–1960* published.

1961   *Feb. 27: The Legacy of the Civil War: Meditations on the Centennial* published. *May 1:* departs for summer in France. *Sept. 10:* returns home. *Nov. 15: Wilderness: A Tale of the Civil War* published.

1962   *Spring:* accepts one-term-per-year appointment as professor of English at Yale. *May 27:* departs for summer in France.

1963   Builds vacation home in West Wardsboro, Vermont.

1964   *May: Flood: A Romance of Our Time* published.

1965   *May 27: Who Speaks for the Negro?* published.

1966   *May 27:* departs for France. *Oct. 7: Selected Poems: New and Old, 1923–1966* published.

1967   *March:* trip to Egypt. *Aug. 28:* departs for home.

1968   *Oct. 16: Incarnations: Poems 1966–1968* published.

1969   *Audubon: A Vision* published.

1970   *July 21:* receives National Medal for Literature. *Nov. 24: Selected Poems of Herman Melville* published.

1971   *June 2: John Greenleaf Whittier's Poetry* published. *Aug. 20:* departs for France. *Aug. 27: Homage to Theodore Dreiser* published. *Oct. 4: Meet Me in the Green Glen* published.

1972   Flies home for surgical operation.

1973   *End of spring term:* retires from Yale. *May: American Literature: The Makers and the Making* published.

1974   *Fall:* distinguished professor at Hunter College. *Apr.:* delivers Jefferson Lecture in the Humanities. *Oct. 7: Or Else: Poem/Poems 1968–1974,* published.

1975   *July: Democracy and Poetry* published. *Aug.:* departs for Italy.

1976   *Jan.:* returns home. *Spring:* receives Copernicus Award.

1977   *Jan.: Selected Poems: 1923–1976* published. *March: A Place to Come To* published. *Spring:* sails in the Greek archipelago.

1978   *Sept.: Now and Then: Poems 1976–1978* published.

1979   *Apr. 17:* receives Pulitzer Prize for Poetry for *Now and Then. Sept.: Brother to Dragons: A New Version* published.

1980   *Dec. 6: Jefferson Davis Gets His Citizenship Back* published. [*May 24:* Gabriel Penn Warren marries Ana Maria Flores-Jenkins.] *July: Being Here: Poetry 1977–1980* published. *Oct. 1:* undergoes prostatectomy with evidence of adenocarcinoma.

1981   *May 15:* receives MacArthur Prize Fellowship. *Aug.: Rumor Verified: Poems 1979–1980* published. *Nov.:* travels to Algeria. [*Dec. 21:* Rosanna Penn Warren marries Stephen Scully.]

1982   [*Dec. 1:* granddaughter Katherine Penn Scully born.]

1983   *March: Chief Joseph of the Nez Perce* published.

1984   *March:* travels to Oxford for eightieth anniversary of Rhodes scholarships.

1985   *March: New and Selected Poems: 1923–1985* published. *May 16:* receives American Academy and Institute of Arts and Letters Gold Medal for Poetry. [*July 9:* granddaughter Chiara Scully born.] *Aug. 8:* undergoes surgery for cancer.

1986   *Feb. 26:* appointed Poet Laureate Consultant in Poetry to the Library of Congress. *June:* visits the Orkney Islands.

1987   *July: A Robert Penn Warren Reader* published.

1988   *June 18: Portrait of a Father* published.

1989   *March: New and Selected Essays* published. [*Aug. 24:* grandson Noah Penn Warren born.] *Sept. 15:* dies in West Wardsboro, Vermont.

Contents

Contents

THREE
Marriage and a Career

FOUR
Arrivals and Departures, Acclaim and Anguish

FIVE
Remarriage, Fatherhood, and Renewal

SIX

Recording History: Literary and Otherwise

SEVEN

Honors and Valedictory

ONE

Childhood and Boyhood

1

The Parents

The center of attention—an infantile face. . . .

That center of attention, swathed in a sort of white dress,
Is precious to the woman who, pretty and young,
Leans with a look of surprised blessedness
At the mysterious miracle forth-sprung.

In the background somewhat, the masculine figure
Looms, face agleam with achievement and pride.
—*"Old Photograph of the Future"*[1]

Robert Franklin Warren was born in 1869 in Trigg County, in south-west Kentucky, close to the Tennessee state line. He was the second of six children. His mother, Sarah, died in 1877, when he was eight years old. His father, William Henry Harrison Warren, Jr., remarried two years later. His new wife, Virginia Forrest Elliott, the daughter of a neighboring family, was little more than a girl. Their first child died in infancy, but two years later she produced another son, Ralph, the first of four more children in her husband's second family. Robert Franklin Warren had probably gone to work soon after finishing a sixth-grade education, which must have been mediocre at best. But he may already have begun to cherish a dream: to become a lawyer and a poet.[2]

His twenty-first birthday found him working as a clerk in John McGehee's country store and warehouse in Belleview. There, at about eight o'clock on the windy evening of March 27, 1890, he experienced the most dramatic event of his life. He was standing behind the counter adding a column of figures when a tornado slammed into the frame building. Warren ducked under the big counter just as the second floor came crashing through the ceiling. As he crawled toward the front of the store he saw flames starting from the shattered oil lamps. One man who had been sitting by the stove appeared crushed, moaning in agony. Two others were trapped in the wreckage. Bleeding heavily, Warren crawled toward the side wall. "The hot smoke was now right behind me," he recalled later. As two of the others were burning to death, Warren finally struggled through the wreckage to one corner. He was able to thrust his hand through a break in the wall and call for help. Someone outside was trying to raise the shattered timbers, without success. Then one final effort moved them before the rest crashed down. Grasping an outstretched hand, Warren emerged, discovering that his rescuer was young Sudie Meacham, the daughter of the Belleview blacksmith. He took a few steps, staggered, and collapsed. He was taken to a nearby home and put to bed for twenty-four hours. His cuts and bruises proved to be superficial, so that the next day he was "fully restored." The Hopkinsville *Kentuckyan* found him "still laboring under considerable excitement" but able to give a detailed account of "the most horrible holocaust that has ever occurred in this county. . . ."[3]

Another event that same year must have validated his life in a different way. It was the publication in Chicago of *Local and National Poets of America, with Interesting Biographical Sketches and Choice Selections from Over One Thousand Living American Poets.* There among the works of twelve hundred other versifiers were "Our Pilgrimage" and "The Orphan Girl." In the couplets of the first Warren had written, "We're walking with Jesus, side by side. . . ." In the quatrains of the second he foresaw the final destination of a seven-year-old waif amid the snowflakes. There was no photograph of this author, and only the notation, "Mr. Warren now lives in Belleview, Ky., clerking in a dry goods store. He is a great lover of poetry and occasionally writes short poems, more for recreation than fame." How much of his clerk's wages went toward this debut, only he and the publisher knew.[4]

Three years after these events, W.H.H. Warren died. Robert Franklin Warren's older brother, Nick, was off on his own, and his younger brother, John Walter (called Sam), had left Trigg County for the West and an adventurous career as a mining engineer. Cortez, the youngest brother, was three years Robert Franklin's junior. So at the age of twenty-four, Bob Warren became the principal support of his stepmother, "Aunt Jenny," and the remaining members of his father's two families. Many years later he would tell his elder son that he learned "to take joy in his obligations."[5]

His work took him to Clarksville, twenty miles to the southeast just over the Tennessee line, where the McGehee brothers had another store. He was also trying to acquire the rudiments of a liberal education. He studied Greek with some tutoring from a teacher at Clarksville's little Southwestern Presbyterian College. He joined the National Guard and stood in uniform for a full-length portrait photograph, but his enlistment was up before their call to active duty in the Spanish-American War. So he remained in Clarksville, his stepbrother Ralph with him. He worked and studied, trying, as he put it, to "establish" himself.[6]

A year earlier, in 1892, he had met Anna Ruth Penn at the outdoor dancing pavilion of the Cerulean Hotel, where well-to-do vacationers came to drink the mineral waters at Cerulean Springs in Kentucky. Brown-eyed and auburn-haired, with a thin-faced wistful prettiness, the slim girl must have seen in the young man, six years her senior, something like a counterpart to herself. He too came from English stock, and his coloring was much like hers. His bearing was erect and his manner reserved. But she must have perceived similar bookish interests. They both came from families there in the farmlands of the Red River and Cumberland River valleys. She lived about a mile away in the farmhouse where her younger sister, Sarah Thomas, kept house for their widowed father, Gabriel Thomas Penn. But Ruth Penn did not envision spending her life there in the country seventy-five miles northwest of Nashville. Neither did the serious young man she had met at the dance.

Ruth Penn's life soon enlarged beyond Cerulean and the isolated farm of Gabriel Thomas Penn. She and a younger sister, Mary Mexico Penn, became successful schoolteachers, and in 1894 Ruth Penn began to teach second grade in Hopkinsville, the seat of Christian County, ten miles southeast of Cerulean. Little Emily Kelley would remember Miss Penn's poetic recitations. For "an afternoon treat" she would recite favorites such as "Little Orphan Annie" and "The Raggedy Man." Emily and her friends loved her. So did her fiancé, Robert Franklin Warren.[7]

The McGehees opened another branch of their business in a small town that straddled the Kentucky-Tennessee line twenty miles southeast of Hopkinsville. Todd County provided a good base for growth. It was located almost at the center of "the Black Patch," an oval-shaped area on the map comprising thirty-five Kentucky counties and eighteen in Tennessee and stretching over two hundred miles from the Mississippi River on the west to the Cumberland on the east. Todd County farmers planted various crops, but the money crop was tobacco. It was not the bright leaf of the North Carolina Piedmont but was produced instead with different methods in the yearlong cycle of growth, harvesting, and curing to become "dark-fired" tobacco. Whole families worked the long hours of cultivation. If the fields had enough sun and rain and escaped the worms and hailstorms, the stalks would be ready for cutting sometime between late August and early October. Unlike the barns for the air-cured burley tobacco, the two-and-a-half-story barns that dotted the landscape were chinked tight for the low smoldering fires to dry the leaves for stripping—if no spark set the leaves and the barn ablaze. Then came the sorting, bidding, and buying. In a good year there would be a small profit after the debts were paid.[8]

By 1868 trains of the Louisville and Nashville Railroad steamed through, and the town that sprang up was named for its president, Congressman James Guthrie. Two years later another set of L&N tracks crossed the first from east to west. At that point the character of the settlement began to change. To residents of older places such as the county seat at Elkton, Guthrie was becoming a "railroad town" with a rough-and-ready class of workers and laborers. Some were respectable family men, but others comprised a violence-prone clientele who patronized the bootleggers, cockfights, and other diversions. The business interests looked forward to the day when the L&N would put in a roundhouse to help service the scores of freight and passenger trains that came through every day. Because the two lines crossed there, many passengers stopped in Guthrie to change trains. The forty-year-old Guthrie Hotel, with its beautiful new interior, would welcome as many as two hundred for breakfast on a busy morning, when some of the townsfolk would engage in a favorite pastime, strolling down to the depot to observe the new arrivals.[9]

Robert Franklin Warren had gone along when the McGehees opened their new store in Guthrie, but he had other career plans. Many of Todd County's citizens transacted their business at the Farmers and Merchants Bank in Guthrie. And when they came to town they could choose from among forty or so businesses, including "seventeen grocery and drygoods stores, . . . five saloons, . . . two publishers, . . . an 'opera house' with real plays, two restaurants, and a combination grocery store and undertaker." Mr. Choate, the president and principal stockholder of the bank, was sanguine enough to hire Robert Franklin Warren as clerk and cashier. He had been faithful to his obligations, seeing to his stepmother and the children at significant cost to himself, though he never complained. As the century drew to its close and he edged toward thirty, now a partner, his appearance began to change. Years later he would tell his son that he had been going "seriously bald." His hair, he said, began coming out by the handful. As he retold this long afterward, he made "a sudden unconscious gesture . . . as throwing something to the floor—as though repeating an angry or despairing gesture from all those years before." And his face bore an "angry and despairing expression" the boy never saw before or after. He would tell his son, "I finally realized that it was too late for me. It was doing your mother a wrong, trapped in an engagement that had already been contracted too long."[10]

Anna Ruth Penn and Robert Franklin Warren were married in her father's home at Cerulean on July 6, 1904. The wedding was performed at 6:00 A.M. so they could catch the Illinois Central morning train in Princeton, twenty miles away. At Saint Louis they visited the World's Fair and went on to see the Great Lakes and probably Niagara Falls too. At last the train carried them south, back to Todd County to begin their long-delayed married life and raise a family.[11]

Their first child arrived at seven o'clock on a Tuesday morning, almost exactly a month after his mother's thirtieth birthday. In her clear, flowing, schoolteacher's hand she recorded it in the big family Bible: "Robt Penn Warren   Guthrie, Todd Co Ky   April 24–1905."

2

❖

Childhood

All predictable—lunch, the baby asleep, children gone
But not far, and Father and Mother gone, hand in hand,
Heads together as though in one long conversation
That even now I can't think has had an end—
But where? Perhaps in some high, cloud-floating and sunlit land.

But picnics have ends, and just as the sun set,
My mother cried out, "Could a place so beautiful be!"
And my father said, "My ship will come in yet,
And you'll see all the beautiful world there is to see."
"What more would I want," she now cried, "when I love everything I now see?"

So she swung the baby against the rose-tinted sky,
And a bird note burst from her throat, and she gaily sang
As we clop-clopped homeward while the shadows, sly,
Leashed the Future up, like a hound with a slavering fang.

But sleepy, I didn't know what a Future was, as she sang.

And she sang.

—"October Picnic Long Ago"[1]

The newlyweds had rented a comfortable brick cottage on the corner of Third and Cherry streets one block from Guthrie's main thoroughfare. For a time Ruth Warren taught school in her home. It must soon have become a house full of books, not just the ones from her Clarksville classroom and her own favorites, but also those her husband had carried from one small settlement to another in his journey of thirty-five years and twenty miles from Cerulean to Guthrie. He put his Greek grammar and lexicon on the shelf together with histories of France and Blackstone's *Commentaries*. Their modest library included popular romances as well as sets of Bulwer-Lytton, Cooper, Dickens, and Thackeray. But their son would recall most the way his father was "mad for poetry." His tastes ran to dramatic verse and the Romantic poets. He savored the ring of the lines, and some of his children's earliest memories would be his reciting the ones he loved.[2]

Robert Franklin Warren remained the principal support of Aunt Jenny, though Nick was nearly forty and Cortez was a Todd County storekeeper. But he was managing to support his family and provide a hedge against the future. His work at the bank must have helped him learn what farms and other parcels were available, and he may already have begun acquiring property. One new expenditure had come with the birth of his son.

Following the southern custom, he had hired a nurse. Geraldine Carr was a bright young woman who helped in many ways. But one task Ruth Warren especially enjoyed was bathing the baby. This would be his earliest memory. There was the wet warmth, then the towel's texture as he was dried and dandled, supported by the knees beneath. He looked down at the bright pattern of the tile floor. Years later when he returned to test the accuracy of the memory, the pattern was there just as he recalled it.[3]

Ruth Penn took him out in his carriage and then for walks as soon as he was able. She could not restrain her pride in this precocious child, her blue-eyed boy. One neighbor recalled meeting them on their slow promenade. She and her friends stopped as she bent down to greet the toddler. Ruth Warren bent down too. "Rob' Penn," she said, "tell 'em what color your hair is." He looked up. "Pret-ty red," he said. When he was big enough to play outdoors, neighbors would hear Ruth Warren calling, "Rob' Penn! Rob' Penn!"

There was much to see as the boundaries of his world expanded. A mile from town was the Guthrie Race Track, which local residents had considered one of the finest in the country. It was a mile long, with a large grandstand that had a kind of promenade deck where people had danced to the strains of the band below. Now abandoned, the track was perfect for Robert Warren to practice driving their new "touring car," with the family swathed in scarves and veils against the wind created by the twenty-mile-an-hour speed.

One day, in a field near the depot, Robert Penn's father held him up so he could see the state militia putting up their tents. The governor had sent them to quell the violence of tobacco growers against monopolistic buying practices of the American Tobacco Company. It was a struggle that "pitted neighbor against neighbor" and led to intimidation, shootings, and burnings like nothing since the days of the Ku Klux Klan. It was called the Black Patch War, and though it could mean nothing to the child watching the soldiers, it would be a meaningful memory later in his life.[4]

As Bob Warren moved into middle age his features were becoming more angular, the prominent nose appearing larger—a regular Roman nose in the son's memory. He would watch and remember how, on his father's birthday, February 14, Ruth Warren would stop behind his chair at breakfast, then lean over and kiss his bald pate and murmur, "My comic valentine." He would flush with embarrassment and say, "Oh, shucks." But no matter how reticent he might be, his hazel eyes conveyed his devoted love for her.[5]

On February 20, 1908, she presented him with a daughter. Once again she opened the Bible to the children's page and inscribed a new name, Mary Cecilia Warren. The nurse hired for the new baby was Cecilia Bradshaw, whose black glossy skin signaled her Guinea origins. "Seeley" soon moved into a secure place in the family with a reciprocal love that was to continue for decades. Her voice was one of those that wove a rich pattern in those growing years. Often Mother sang, sometimes with the records on the Victrola in the parlor, and often Father recited poetry. There was one poem the boy would ask for over and over, the first one he could remember. He would sit rapt as his father began,

> Lars Porsena of Clusium
> By the nine Gods he swore
> That the great house of Tarquin
> Should suffer wrong no more.

At last his father had enough of "Horatius at the Bridge." He said, "Never mention that poem to me again. Take that book and go sit in a corner and look at every word and be reciting the poem to yourself while you look at the words. This will be reading." Robert obeyed, "and . . . I was reading. Slow and fumbling—but reading."[6]

The boundaries of Robert Penn's world continued to expand. The family had moved to a stone house on Park Street a block from the railroad. Then they moved again, this time to Third and Locust, while their own house was being built out in the country, a good half mile from the center of town. He and his precocious sister waited expectantly for its completion. Then one day Dr. Robinson paid a visit. Soon he emerged from the bedroom and told Robert Penn to go to the bank and tell his father the baby was about to be born. The two returned home just as the baby arrived. Later Ruth Warren made the last entry in the children's page of the family Bible: "Wm Thomas Warren Guthrie, Todd Co Ky April 8 1911."[7]

Robert Warren rented the wagons to haul everything from Third and Locust out into Todd County. (This was a pattern the Warrens' oldest son—like his parents and his grandparents before them—would follow whenever he could: to live out in the country.) There were woods close by and even a swamp not far away. Robert Penn was small for his age, but he was a lively child and found plenty to occupy him in the country. There were fascinating things to discover, to identify and collect. There was increasing activity in the house, and even though his mother would have help from a cheerful young woman named Savannah, she must still have had her hands full with little Thomas and three-year-old Mary. If Robert Penn had a bit more freedom, there was no lack of care. Seeley Bradshaw was more than a servant. She was a storyteller, a friend, and as he would later say, "a second mother."[8]

The new profusion of riches in his life spread itself amply in another dimension on Grandpa Penn's farm, thirty-five miles to the northwest in Christian County. The ramshackle house stood a mile from the pike, which led to Cerulean Springs. This summer of the boy's seventh year must have seemed just right for an extended visit. Aunt Sarah, ever competent and cheerful, could run a sizeable household and, if necessary, snatch a twelve-gauge from the kitchen porch and blast a chicken hawk out of the sky. In memory it would be "an unchanging summer. . . . an old man with white hair and a rather pointed beard, wearing blue jean pants, with a black tie hanging loose from a collar open at the throat. . . . He is sitting . . . under a cedar tree, propped back against the trunk, and blue smoke from his cob pipe threads thinly upward. . . . I am a small boy sitting tailor-fashion on the unkempt lawn. . . . I would be waiting for the old man to talk." Grandpa Penn might range back to *Napoleon and His Marshals* and sketch the lines at Austerlitz with a stick in the dirt. Or he would talk about his own war, his two years in the infantry and two more in the cavalry. He had seen bitter fighting, like the siege at Fort Pillow under the legendary Forrest, and memory made it all vivid.[9]

Grandpa Penn loved poetry, declaiming with zest for his audience of one. He would recite Burns with a Scots burr, or Byron's "So, We'll Go No More A-Roving." Sometimes he would sing in his old uncertain voice songs such as "Hallie in the Valley," which Forrest's men had sung on the way to Shiloh. For the boy, stories of the war were better even than poetry and song. The sword and rifles he had seen stored in a closet took on vivid significance. Some of what he learned came as a shock: Gabriel Penn had been a Union man before the war. He saw slavery as a doomed institution. "This will break up the country," he said, "and my people helped make it." He didn't want to see his nation "Balkanized" by war. But when the war came he enlisted for the same reason that persuaded Robert E. Lee and countless others: "You went with your people." What he saw left him with anything but a romantic view of warfare.[10]

Six weeks after the firing on Fort Sumter he was mustered into service at age twenty-five as a corporal in the Thirteenth Tennessee Infantry. Almost a year later he was a survivor of the bloody field of Shiloh. Eight months after that he recruited eighty-five men and formed them into Company H of the Fifteenth Tennessee Cavalry, serving as their captain. His stories disabused his grandson of the idea that warfare was a matter of gallant charges and heroic combat. He told how he and his men captured a gang of bushwhackers, marauders who fought for neither side but preyed upon the defenseless. Captain Penn did what the Yankees would have done too. "We gave 'em a fair trial," he told the boy, "and then we hanged 'em." One thing he did not tell was the connection between these events and the fact that he, a Tennessean, was living in Kentucky. After the war relatives of the bushwhackers began to talk of reprisals. So Gabriel Thomas Penn picked up and moved—carrying along all his people, including Aunt Cat, a wizened old pipe-smoking black woman who had been his nurse—out of the state to Trigg County, not to return to Tennessee until his last year.[11]

It was mostly family life on the farm, with few visits from outsiders until Aunt Sarah met a young man named Frank Carmack at a Cerulean Hotel dance and spunkily married him in Ruth and Robert Warren's parlor despite her father's disapproval. Frank moved in, and in a few years they had two little girls. Grandfather called Mary Mex-

ico Penn the beauty of the family, but she never married, and so
when school was out she occupied herself with an enormous ge-
nealogical study the size of a roll of wallpaper complete with appendices and family charts.[12]

The Penn chart extended for eleven generations before it got to
Robert Penn Warren. In a direct line before him came Sir William
Penn the admiral and William Penn the Quaker, who lived until
1718. The American branch included William Penn of Westmore-
land County and, three generations later, another Virginian, John
Granville Penn, who signed the Declaration of Independence. In the
same generation was Colonel Abram Penn, who led the Henry
County militia against Cornwallis and was there for the surrender at
Yorktown. In a familiar migratory pattern, his son, Edmund, married
Mary Ferris and moved from Patrick County in southwest Virginia to
Kentucky, finally settling near Murfreesboro, Tennessee, in 1836.
Twenty years later and 150 miles farther west, their son, Gabriel
Thomas, was born in Trenton, not far from the Mississippi River. (He
would speak with their Virginia accent all his life.) He fell in love with
a Trenton girl named Mary Elizabeth Mitchell. After Forrest's victory
at Fort Pillow he gave leave to many of his troops, and this may have
permitted Gabriel Penn to marry Mary Eliza in Trenton on June 24,
1864.[13]

Robert Franklin Warren once told his son that his family had arrived in Kentucky at the time of the War of 1812, but he added little
more when there was much more to add. William Warren had been
wounded at the battle of Cowpens but fought in two more battles and
then migrated to Kentucky. One of his sons, William Henry Harrison Warren, fought at Shiloh in Forrest's infantry and rose to the rank
of major before being invalided out of the war. His eldest son,
William Henry Harrison, Jr., another veteran of Shiloh, left the Sixth
Kentucky Mounted Infantry before the war's end at the expiration of
his enlistment. It was that son who sired Robert Franklin Warren four
years after the surrender. Did Robert Franklin Warren know about
this family history? Indeed, how could he not know about it? Did
these records of relatively short service in the agonizing four-year ordeal trouble him, with his punctilious sense of honor and responsibility? Could they have seemed to him unworthy of mention beside the
arduous service of Captain Gabriel Thomas Penn?[14]

Robert Franklin Warren's father managed to acquire land and then
lost it. The son's silence suggests that he did not forgive his father any

more than he did the mother who had died leaving him to be raised by a stepmother. Was it because his father left him responsibilities rather than opportunities? Whatever it was, he mentioned his father to his own son no more than a few times, and then but casually. Only many years later did the son learn that his Warren grandfather lay in the Cerulean Springs cemetery. "Why," he asked, "had my father never even mentioned the fact to me?" Once when driving in the car his father told him to look off beyond the road to a large house, yellow with white trim, which looked handsome at that distance. "Your grandmother was born there. A long time ago," he said. "That girl who had lived in that yellow house," Robert Penn remembered decades later, "suddenly became for me a single totally isolated mystery in the big mystery of my father's life."[15]

Far different from Robert Franklin's reticence about his father was his continuing care for Aunt Jenny. He insisted that once a year Robert Penn spend a day and stay overnight in her house in Cerulean Springs. Robert Penn found her dull, but his father said she was a good woman who "did the best she could according to the lights available to her." Prowling in the attic the boy found "some strange-looking books," one by an author whose name he could neither recognize nor pronounce: Dante Alighieri. But he recognized the author of a book called *Paradise Lost*. He took his discoveries to Grandma Jenny, who could read though she could not write. "Oh, those old books, they belonged to your grandfather," she told him. "When he died, I just threw away such stuff with the other old stuff."[16]

Grandpa Penn's daughters put up with his tastes and eccentricities. He didn't like strangers, and he didn't like town people either because he could predict what they were going to say and didn't want to hear it again. He was a prosperous farmer with no mortgage who hired laborers to work the crops. But there was some awareness of a business failure before the move to Kentucky, and there had been another lapse too. He had stored tobacco on consignment, and when a barn burned, it was discovered that he had missed an insurance payment. Over a long term he paid the growers for the loss, but from then on he was regarded as having no head for business. So he oversaw the crops and retreated to books and newspapers in the big wicker chair under the cedar tree. Some nights, after the boy's bedtime, when he would hear Sarah and Frank Carmack singing in the lawn swing under the moonlight, he would see the lamplight from under his grandfather's door. He had heard his aunts say, "Papa is an inveterate reader," and he wondered what a Confederate reader was. They would also say, "Papa is not practical. He is visionary." Like them, the boy loved him.[17]

Each day as the summer waned Robert Penn would sit with his grandfather and then spend time in the woods alone. Being here was a crucial part of what he would later call "a lonely boyhood" but a happy one. "My summers were very happy, anyway," he said. He would later tell his son that his grandfather "was a lot closer to me than anybody." There was a big change ahead now, with the new experience of school to come, but the farm would be there next year. Then one afternoon his father arrived in the touring car with the great acetylene headlights and shining brass rods and creaking leather top, and they said their good-byes and set out for Guthrie.

3

❖

Growing Years

So we had to invent it all, our Bloody Ground, K and I,
And him the best shot in ten counties and could call any bird-note back,
But school out, not big enough for the ballgame,
And in the full tide of summer, not ready
For the twelve-gauge yet, or even a job, so what
Can you do but pick up your BBs and Benjamin,
Stick corn pone in pocket, and head out
"To rally in the Cane-Break and Shoot the Buffalo"—
As my grandfather's cracked old voice would sing it
From the days of his own grandfather. . . .

—*"American Portrait: Old Style"*[1]

At once small and advanced for his age, Robert Penn stood out among the others, particularly the children of the farm families and the railroad families. The Guthrie School was a three-story brick building housing about 175 pupils who were taught two grades to a room. He would look back on it as a place of learning and violence, and it seemed to him that about a third of the pupils had come to avoid learning. The teachers were generally very competent, and his was Miss Lula Choate, the daughter of Mr. Choate, the banker. She worked a few hours every afternoon at the bank, and Robert Penn had noticed there how nice her legs looked in her silk stockings. Miss Lula covered many subjects, including their own state, the "Dark and Bloody Ground." With his quick intelligence and retentive memory he did well from the first, and there was plenty of reinforcement at home for the whole learning process.[2]

Then disaster struck. His father was taken in acute pain to Hopkinsville twenty miles away for gallbladder surgery. He developed both pneumonia and typhoid fever, and his doctors feared he might die. Ruth Warren went there to be with him. While Seeley took care of Mary and Thomas, Robert Penn was taken out of school to stay with the Choates. When at last his father was able to come home, Robert Penn came home too but did not return to school for the rest of the year. It was a time of "uncertainty of all kinds, [a] horrible period, with the nightmare odor of formaldehyde and the squeaks of the rubber soles of nurses' shoes." His father was in bed for a year.[3]

But there was one stroke of good fortune. The son of the neighboring Greenfields must have seemed an unlikely playmate for Robert Penn Warren, but Kent had a capacity for friendship to match his other extraordinary attributes. He was a gifted athlete and a crack marksman. A self-taught naturalist, he could sketch birds and imitate their calls. "He was seven years older and a thousand years older psychologically," Robert Penn would remember. But even so, Kent enjoyed their games of imagination and exploration. Once, picking their way through the marsh, they found a skull with a star-shaped broken place and speculated about what could have caused it. Then, in the shade of a great oak on the hill, they came upon a six-foot-long depression, a trench long overgrown with grass. They wondered about the body that must have lain there, and they created their own image of the Dark and Bloody Ground.[4]

At last the year turned, and it was time for Cerulean Springs again. "The farm was paradise to me," the boy would remember. "I couldn't wait to get there." And so he resumed that other life. There were always new books at the farm. Grandpa Penn would read aloud from James Henry Breasted's history of Egypt. "I remember building a pyramid of clay blocks," Robert Penn would say years later, "very detailed, with rooms and interiors, with mummies, and with gold-leaf or silver-leaf all over the outside . . . then made a discovery of it all the next summer." Grandpa Penn still had his large stock of stories. Sometimes even his irascibility could be amusing. He disliked what was called progress. He said there were only two good things about the present day: window screens and painless dentistry.

But the past was always there, often with something new emerging from it. The boy was fascinated by a painting at Great-aunt Anna's house, a life-sized bust of his grandfather as a handsome young man. It may have been made at the insistence of his wife, who had called him

Telemachus. Robert Penn must have had his own watercolors by now, and on his solitary forays into the surrounding woods he would sketch birds. It may have been easier at the end of this summer to leave the farm, with Kent there in Guthrie and with the first grade behind him.[5]

The pupils would memorize poems, and on Friday afternoons they would recite them. Each evening Robert Warren would sit on one side of the fireplace to hear his son's lessons. When Mary and Thomas were older, their mother would sit on the other side of the fireplace to hear theirs, and afterward Mother or Father would read them a story. It was at this time that Robert Penn formed a habit that seemed strange to his classmates. Called on, he would rise from his seat, face the class rather than Miss Lula, then deliver the answer. "He always knew it," Virginia McClanahan said. "He was never wrong. We'd let him do it and just sit and listen."[6]

But he suffered one dreadful embarrassment. Late one afternoon he started for home, walking slowly down the hill, dawdling at the edge of a pond. Suddenly he slipped and fell into the freezing water. His heavy coat weighed him down as he struggled to get out. When Miss Lula happened to look out her window she saw him thrashing about, ran down to the pond, and pulled him out. She led him, wet and shivering, back into the schoolroom and stood him right next to the big woodstove. Then she made him undress, completely. "Turn around! Turn around!" she said. "It was awful," he remembered.[7]

He grew a little and made a few new friends. He would stay overnight at Jimmy Stahl's house, and they would play with a sling-shot and a pump gun that fired big BB's. With Richard Bourne he played chess and tried a new sport, fencing. Robert Warren bought them foils and masks and a book that explained the rudiments. They shot bullfrogs with Richard's powerful air rifle, and sometimes they gigged them. After one night's catch Richard's mother fried forty frogs' legs for their breakfast. They watched fascinated as the legs jumped about in the skillet.[8]

Kent Greenfield was still his best friend. Kent could put a match between two bricks and ignite it with one shot from his prized Benjamin air rifle. They would practice target shooting with the bows and arrows they made, and they turned up plenty of arrowheads in that rich soil. They took what game they could, and on one occasion Kent's mother confronted them, holding one of her Dominicker hens bloody from BB shot, and asked, "Now, who did that?" They confessed. They had thought it was a buffalo there in the woods. But they were after small specimens as well as big, especially the butterflies they mounted between sheets of glass. They continued their artwork with the birds, whose calls Kent still mimicked expertly, though his voice was changing. When the warm weather came Robert Penn began to swim, passionately. It was Kent who, in spite of strict instructions not to go in the water, taught him the fundamentals in a pond hollowed out where clay had been dug for the nearby brick kilns. In a few years Robert Penn would be swimming in other ponds and streams there in the Cumberland Valley.[9]

He skipped a grade, as later he would skip two more. This reflected not only his intelligence but also the Penn and Warren ethic of work and learning. He would remember Aunt Mary's discipline during summer vacation. Still the beauty of the family to her father, she was the dragon to Robert Penn. After the noon meal he would sneak away, and sometimes he would make it to the woods. But often he would hear her voice following him: "Rob' Penn! Rob' Penn! Time for arithmetic." Wherever and whenever the Guthrie curriculum left off, his mother and aunt could provide informal lesson plans of their own. And though Thomas would present some disciplinary problems as he grew, there were no whippings. Privileges might be suspended, but there were no scoldings. Instead, Robert Penn remembered, "there might well be a detached and rational description of the crime involved. But the real thing was some sense of a withdrawal, not actual, for nothing would actually change, no unusual word, always the usual smile, but something undefinably withdrawn."[10]

Even though Robert Franklin Warren would describe himself as "an old-fashioned free thinker," he joined the Methodist church when his elder son was about seven. Later the boy would conclude that his father had probably made this concession because of social pressure. He remembered his father saying, "The church is a useful social institution." For the boy there was no baptismal sacrament, but he did go to Sunday school for a time. At Grandpa Penn's he had heard the Lord's Prayer said on occasion, but in his own home there were no prayers, no grace before meals. As a grown man, he would often say, "We were not a churchy family." Father knew the Bible, and he would later pay his son to read it through at the rate of three chapters a day. As if to even the score, he later gave him a copy of Darwin's writings.[11]

It was not surprising that neither the church nor the Bible provided emotional support for Robert Franklin Warren. He had taken pride in his brother Sam's mining career, but then, one afternoon when Robert Penn came in from play, he found his father sitting in the darkened parlor, "his head bowed on his chest, and the arm nearer me hanging limply over the chair, with a sheet of paper hanging from the obviously loose grip of the fingers. I don't know how long I stood there before my father slowly lifted his head and stared at me before saying: 'Son, Sam is dead.' " The boy could see the tearstains on his father's cheeks. "I had never seen him weep. It was a real shock to me to know he would weep at all, at anything." Characteristically, Robert helped the penniless widow and sent her son to preparatory school so he could have a career.[12]

Mary Cecilia entered school, proving to be just as bright and precocious as her brother. When Father bought a piano, she practiced faithfully, whereas Robert Penn proved to be utterly unmusical. Outdoors he tried to be the big brother. He excavated under the chicken house and then used wooden boxes to install a large dollhouse. Then he dug a twenty-foot tunnel to it and put a kerosene lamp inside. "We could have been asphyxiated," Mary said. They gradually accumulated a menagerie: a billy goat, a water moccasin, and an alligator. They had a series of dogs too, with collies their favorite breed, a choice probably influenced by the books Robert Penn was reading. *Jerry of the Islands* was one he would never forget. Sometimes he sat in the kitchen and read *Tarzan of the Apes* or another Burroughs novel to Savannah as she worked.

For a time his growing interest in science intersected that in animals. He wired a battery to a tin plate, and his sister would sprinkle grains to entice chickens onto it. Then they would give them a jolt from the battery. In their workhouse he and Thomas had a large doll's chair with brass plates in the bottom. They attached the rheostat they used to run their electric train with power from the house current. When a neighborhood girl named Emma looked in one day, Thomas invited her to sit down and said, "Hold this, will you please, Emma?" It was an electrode, and the electricians promptly threw the switch. For whatever reason, Emma did not report the incident, and Robert Penn and Thomas had a firm pact not to squeal on each other. Mary marveled at her older brother. "He was something," she said.

When Robert Franklin Warren bought him a ten-volume set of electrical handbooks he built a crystal set radio. He had a rudimentary chemical laboratory too. These activities, like his collecting fossil specimens in the woods, were viewed askance by some of the other boys. It was like the regimen that kept him in during the afternoons when others were out playing. He would later realize that "the fact of the routine of study and the wilful reading was generally regarded as, at the best, a little nutty."[13]

His father was impressed by his skill and absorption in drawing and painting. "I'll get you an art teacher," he told him. It turned out that she lived in Nashville and that she was a nun. So in the summer when he was thirteen he went there to stay at the home of one of his mother's friends. He took his lessons from Sister Mary Luke, a small woman in her seventies. He would have lunch at the convent school, aware that everyone was saying grace but him. Some days they would go to the Glendale Park Zoo with a big picnic basket. After their co-pious lunch Sister Mary Luke would repose, her hands folded over her ample stomach as she snored. But he was eagerly absorbing her competent instruction. "It was a big thing in my life," he said. "I was mad for it." The environment provided a chance for his naturalist's interests to flourish. "I painted the whole damned zoo, practically."[14]

At this age he still wanted to know more about his father. There had been glimpses of the past, like scenes suddenly flashing upon a screen and then vanishing. The boy would sit on the bathtub to watch his father shave. Once, cleaning the blade, he directed at the boy a stream of unintelligible words. "That's Greek," he said. "Now you know how it sounds." Another time he mentioned his escape during the tornado in Belleview. When Robert Penn asked him what he had done as a boy, his face took on "a strange intense look," and he did not speak. When the boy asked him again, his father told him about going through a field of young corn with his brother, Sam, spraddling the stalks and bending them down. Pressed for the consequences, he said, "Our father did not like it." When the boy asked about his father's family, the answer was, "There's nothing to know." But once Robert Franklin Warren said that his father had a good deal of land after the war, much of it in timber. Was this part of the land that was somehow lost? There was "some fundamental disagreement" be-tween father and son that had ruptured the bond, dissolving it into perpetual silence.[15]

Later, a local doctor offered to finance Robert Penn's education if he would become a country doctor. He even took him to see a med-ical school, but the dissecting rooms convinced him "that his passion for learning did not go 'that far.' " The boy knew, though, that his father was not squeamish about blood. Waked once in the middle of the night, he had rushed into his parents' room to see his father standing there, breathing hard, his eyes "glittering," an iron bar in his hands. He had waked to see the bathroom doorknob turning. When the intruder's head leaned into the darkened bedroom, he had swung the bar. Glancing off the door, it knocked the intruder into the bathtub. Father had waited, poised to club the man without ruining the tub. Before he could strike, the man leaped through the window and escaped. The next morning they traced his steps and the blood on the snow. Father said that if he had been wearing shoes he would have pursued him and "fixed him."[16]

The son would finally conclude that his father "had written off his early life" and sealed off "his own past." He had also denied himself any verbalization of his emotions. The son could not recall his father's ever saying how he felt, either physically or emotionally. The boy's reaction was never to feel "any need of words from him beyond what an occasion of human pleasantness suggested." Reflecting many years later, he would say in his father's defense, "Our mother was very affectionate to the children and to our father. He was not a demonstrative man, not even to his children. He did not have to be." But as the years passed, his father became "more and more a man of mystery."[17]

The bond between Grandpa Penn and the boy grew even stronger, so much so that "in a way I almost resented my own father's visit to the Penns." As Robert Franklin Warren sat with his father-in-law engrossed in talk, the boy would "appear to be wandering aimlessly past, but I was always trying to hear that mysterious conversation." Always, though, it would stop or change. He finally concluded that "their peculiar bond was based on failure: one who had failed because he was a 'visionary,' the other who had laid aside ambition in favor of another aspiration." The harsh word *failure* was one Robert Penn Warren chose many years later for his summary judgment of these two fathers he loved. He could not have known how much this sense of them was helping to shape one of the strongest elements of his own personality: the drive for success, the determination to be an achiever rather than a failure.[18]

But a satisfaction at the core of his father's life was very clear. His marriage was genuinely what used to be called a "love match." There was never crossness in any words exchanged by this husband and wife in what seemed to be "a continuing private conversation." At night, when the boy drifted off to sleep, he would hear the murmur of their voices, and he would wonder what they were talking about. The emblematic image for him would be their walking off together, as at one of the family picnics, holding hands, their heads "slightly bowed as though they were trapped in an interminable conversation never finished, and always there waiting to be resumed."[19]

What was the meaning of this paradigm? How strong were the boy's feelings of exclusion? How firm and sustaining was this image of love and devotion? He would ponder it all his life, and some of the strongest feelings of his love for them would wait scores of years for their clearest expression. There was certainly the assurance of the integrity of the family unit, so strong that "only years later did I realize how cut off our family had been." He would also say, many times, that their family was "very close, very close." Soon he would need all the sustenance and support that closeness could provide.[20]

4

❖

Humiliation, Ambition, and Despair

> In the South, there is always the possibility of
> violence, just below the surface.
> —*Robert Penn Warren*[1]

When Robert Warren had built their house at the crossroads, a half mile from the center of Guthrie, they had only one neighbor, the Greenfield family diagonally across from them. Later Judge Kimbrough built a house nearby. People said he had killed a man. Homicide was a fact of life in Guthrie. Years later Kent Greenfield declared, "You wouldn't believe the people in my lifetime that have been killed in this town. Shot. Cut up. Doctors come in here and stay overnight and say they've seen more blood than they've ever seen in their life."[2]

The character of the town had changed when the railroad people came in. "I remember some very vile children," Robert Penn Warren said, much later, "who came from that same stock. [This railroad gang] carried on a feud in the early days [with] the country boys, the old stock, and the number of people in my school who died violent deaths of one kind or another, or who went to the dogs, was enormous." A rite of passage for a new principal was single combat with the biggest boy. Robert Penn watched when Charlie Parham, a 180-pound high school freshman, tested Mr. Willett. Charlie threatened him with a piece of stove wood, and Mr. Willett grasped Charlie's upraised hand and then his collar. With a quick turn he tripped the boy and threw him through the glass window a story and a half above the ground. When a bloated 200-pound pupil named Weingarten confronted Mr. Barkler, the assistant principal, with a long, thick iron poker, Mr. Barkler knocked him out with a piano stool.[3]

How would a fellow student fare, particularly a younger and smaller one who always had the right answers and got the best grades? Robert Penn Warren was fortunate again in high school. Mack Linebaugh, a friend eleven years his senior, gave the boy his first tennis lessons and chose him for pickup basketball games. There were baseball games on a diamond Mr. Warren laid out near their house. Because Robert Penn owned a catcher's mitt, he was the catcher, briefly. Part of the reason for his "miserable baseball" was that he had to catch Kent Greenfield, destined to pitch for John McGraw's New York Giants. Robert Penn soon turned over the mitt to another boy.

But he was now on his way to becoming a prodigious swimmer, and he was developing his endurance by walking and jogging. But neither of these activities would make his academic performance more tolerable to some of his fellows. He was generous with his books as with his catcher's mitt, but this too gained him little credit with potential tormentors. And he made no overtures to disarm them. He was polite, but he later said, "I never did suffer fools gladly."[4]

One of his playmates would recall that in Guthrie the Warrens were considered "real aristocrats." Robert Franklin Warren had his position in the bank, and he had interests in several stores, including a dress shop. People would see him holding Mary Cecilia's hand as he collected his rents Sunday morning before breakfast. He had what he called "sidewalk friendships," and he would sometimes stop on his way home from work to play checkers with one or two old men, but the Choates were the only people he and Ruth Penn saw socially. She was severely criticized for not "doing any church work." She had her reasons. She once confided to another woman, "Oh, yes, a happy marriage is simple. Everything outside the front gate is Bob's concern and everything inside is mine." Her concerns with her children, however—especially her eldest—had ramifications outside the front gate. One of Robert Penn's early playmates said his mother "was the most possessive mother I ever saw. He wanted to be like the others. . . . She just wanted everything for him. . . . This made a certain crowd dislike him. It didn't matter to us, who played with him." Her son would later say, "I'm sure that my mother as 'boasting' is a damned lie. She was very reserved, with a lot of natural dignity and some strong streak of ironic humor." Small-town gossip, envy, and malice could account for much of what some people said about Ruth

Warren, as with one woman's assertion that "she choked her young 'uns down people's throats."[5]

Robert Penn was active but still undersized, and he was perceived as frail and bookish. His friend Richard Bourne knew that some of the other boys thought him a sissy. His intellectual achievements were not just a source of pride to the Warrens but a reproach to others. By the time he was fourteen he had read the Bible three times, not for pay, as he had the first time, but because he liked it. He won prizes such as the state-fair award for his painting, and he continued to bring home straight A's.

Some of the bigger boys acted out their jealousy and envy. He must have been only one of many Guthrie children harassed on the way home from school, but there was a pattern of persecution in his trials. Once the bigger boys were going to make him fight a boy who was closer to Robert Penn's size but tough, but the boy moved away. Many years later Warren would tell his son, "I remember having fights on several occasions, as a small boy, with the railroad boys." The most traumatic event, however, was the work of a few whom Mack Linebaugh called "nice boys." First there were threats. They were going to put him in a well. He minded his own business and tried to get along with them, but he could not change his classroom behavior.[6]

"Once some older and bigger boys got me in a deserted building," he would remember, "and put a rope around my neck and started pulling on it. They said they'd teach me about grade-making. They lifted me off my toes two or three times, to scare me. Then one of them, suddenly, got ashamed, or sick of what they were doing, and made them quit. Later one or two tried to apologize, and I said, 'Go to hell.' That is the *one* [true] story of all the persecution stories. I was lucky—I seriously considered shooting the ring-leader to death, then thought of the family trouble." He was clear on the source of such stories: "They arose from evil, from enmity, from pride, from envy." One friend said simply, "The children were jealous of him because of his abilities. You know how little towns are. He was to me one of the finest and most compassionate persons I've ever known." But these experiences had lasting effects, especially taken together with the loneliness of much of his childhood and adolescence. He would sum up succinctly: "I saw Guthrie as a place to be 'from.' "[7]

He recalled his earlier years as "a strange childhood lived in a self-contained world of books." Years later he remembered "an over-whelmingly passionate desire to write a poem when I was twelve

years old and had a fever." His father sat by his bed and took down
the lines. In their galloping rhythm and regular rhyme they followed
a favorite of his, Browning's "How They Brought the Good News
from Ghent to Aix." His father patiently wrote and erased. Finally he
put the pencil down. "If you can't get any better than that," he said,
"I'm going to quit." And he did.[8]

In high school they read Shakespeare along with *The Duchess of
Malfi* and *The White Devil* and poems such as "The Rape of the
Lock." Latin instruction went as far as Cicero and six books of Vergil.
Mathematics went from algebra through plane and solid geometry.
He maintained his usual high level of achievement and inclined further toward a career in science. But when he was assigned *Lycidas* as a
term-paper topic he "simply fell in love with it. And I studied for
three months and tried to find out everything I could about it. . . .
My father had started me off with lots of notes, from books about the
house, so I read all the books I could about Milton, and tried to
memorize the poem."[9]

Mary Warren would recall reading in their parents' library—
French books, novels by Dickens and Thackeray, and even contemporary writing such as Sherwood Anderson's stories. Her brother
read widely too, from the Boy Scout magazine to Prescott's *The Oregon Trail* and Motley's *Rise of the Dutch Republic*. One particular book
opened vistas for him: Henry Thomas Buckle's two-volume *The History of Civilization in England*. "The thing that interested me about
Buckle was that he had the one big answer to everything: *geography*,"
he wrote later. The book also inoculated him against Marx when he
encountered him: "I had previously got hold of one key to the universe. Buckle. And somewhere along the way I had lost the notion
that there was ever going to be just one key."[10]

So he moved on toward his graduation from Guthrie High School,
gradually distanced further from his classmates. Robert Franklin Warren wanted him to study law. Each year he would take his son to
Nashville for a private ritual: their own Thanksgiving dinner and then
afterward the Vanderbilt University football game. And Robert
Franklin Warren would point out the law school. But then the father
of one of Ruth Warren's friends wrote to ask if Ruth would meet his
son, newly graduated from Annapolis, when his train stopped briefly
in Guthrie. Robert Penn was also there at the depot when "there descended a tall young man in summer whites, with epaulets and brass
buttons. He kissed my mother on both cheeks, shook hands with my

father, and gave me a manly handshake. My doom was sealed." The redheaded, freckle-faced boy who looked up at him knew what he wanted: not to be just a midshipman but someday commander of the Pacific Fleet.[11]

In that spring of 1920 he was ready to graduate from Guthrie High School, but even if he obtained the Annapolis appointment and passed the examinations, he could not enter the naval academy until he was sixteen. He would not reach that age for another year, and he would have nothing to occupy him academically in the meantime. Ruth Warren and her son took the train to Clarksville, fifteen miles away, for an interview with Dr. Charles E. Diehl, the president of Southwestern Presbyterian College. He gave them practical advice. "You could register here as a freshman," he said, "but I think that would be a mistake. In the first place, there's a very good school here. I think you should go to Clarksville High School as a special student and take another year. Why rush?" The boy must have been excited at the prospect of an escape from the confines of Guthrie to a larger world in Tennessee.[12]

This was a time of passage in his life. Grandpa Penn's health had been declining, and so he, Sarah and Frank, and their two little girls moved to Fayetteville, south of Nashville, where Grandpa Penn had lived many years before. Robert Penn visited them, but that winter the flu epidemic hit Fayetteville and carried off Grandpa Penn at the age of eighty-three. "A great piece of my life was with him," his grandson remembered.[13]

Even though he was three years younger than his high school classmates, the transition to Clarksville came quickly and easily. Robert Penn took the train for the fifteen-mile trip, feeling a sense of release. A classmate remembered that as the train jerked forward out of the Guthrie station he would shout, "Whoops! Here we go!" The Clarksville Depot, almost in the shadow of the Burton's Dental Snuff factory, was just a short way from the high school and the wide Cumberland River beyond. After four weeks of commuting Robert Franklin Warren decided his son should live in Clarksville with their friend Mrs. Muirhead, "a dragonish old lady," as Robert Penn remembered her, but she presented no problems for him. At home he must have chafed under his mother's discipline, and he did not get on with his precocious sister who wrote "novels" in her school tablets and circulated them among her friends. He would later say that she was "brilliant," but he remembered that "as children she and I would frequently quarrel, aimlessly." His brother, Thomas, a robust eight-year-old who had been a "mad electrician" with him, was growing into a likeable but sometimes mischievous boy. "Father said he'd give him a dollar for reading every book he didn't have to read," Mary remembered, "and he never earned a dollar."[14]

Robert Franklin Warren did not speak about his elder son's passion for a naval career. Self-contained as he had always been, devoted to his wife and children, he was almost a cipher in the emotional life of his son. Grandpa Penn's shadow was there as it would be all his life, but this was only one of the factors in the distancing process that would have complex results later in the boy's life. Over the perspective of years he would say, "After fifteen my life became very full and self-centered, and I never really lived at home again, at the best just making long visits."[15]

Life in Clarksville was significantly different. It was much larger than Guthrie, with the traditional aura of other county seats such as Hopkinsville and Elkton, preserved in a culture whose hierarchies and values were based on ownership of land. There was the hospital, the college, and the large high school, which prepared many students for further education. Robert Penn was enrolled in the regular senior curriculum, which offered very good science courses. He brought with him his strong study habits and intense drive for achievement. Once he got 99 on a history test and took it to Mr. Stone because he thought it should be 100. Mr. Stone refused to change the grade. "You can't always be perfect," he said. He wrote a report on Conrad's *Lord Jim,* and other work in English earned him a degree of acceptance he had not known before. But it was not entirely uncritical. "I picked up the name of 'Bull,' " he wrote long afterward, "[from] 'slinging the bull' (i.e., bullshit) = 'liking to talk or argue'."[16]

He played basketball on pickup teams and swam in the school pool, sneaking in after hours for a fast mile. He made friends among the older boys. One was Harry Lyle. "He was girl-minded and gave me my first hard liquor." There would be parties out in the country where the mothers would provide plenty of food and turn the house over to the boys. Girls were becoming more important to him, but he was timid, still undersized and younger than the rest.

Then it was time to prepare for the year ahead. Robert Warren finally spoke. "Make your own decision," he said. His son promptly reaffirmed his first one. Resigned, Robert Franklin Warren went to their convivial congressman, R. Y. Thomas. (It was said that it took him three tries to get through a door.) He was glad to oblige so that formal application for the Annapolis appointment could be made when Robert Penn Warren turned sixteen in April. He passed the written and physical examinations. Then, just for insurance, he applied for admission to Vanderbilt. He graduated from his second high school with highest honors. More self-possessed now, he enjoyed the graduation ceremonies and celebrations. Finally Congressman Thomas's letter arrived. Robert Penn had been granted admission to the United States Naval Academy. Back home, he was free again—to read, to play amateur naturalist in the woods, to spend time with Kent Greenfield.

One balmy afternoon he lay on the grass, solitary in the sunset, distanced from the house by the high hedge. Ten-year-old Thomas was amusing himself in the driveway strewn with ashes and unburnt lumps of coal. "I was flinging pieces of coal over [the] hedge," he would remember. "I picked up one chunk about baseball-size and let go extra hard." It sailed in an arc and landed directly on his brother's left eye, knocking him unconscious. "I heard a cry and ran over the hedge and there was Red lying on the ground. I'll never forget it." Ruth Warren and Mary ran out to see the blood welling up. They put compresses on the eye, and Robert Franklin Warren drove fast over the country roads to the hospital in Clarksville, where the doctors confirmed the severity of the injury. "That was the most horrible night," Mary Warren said. "I'll never forget it. Mother just went all to pieces. There was his school all gone." They took him to a specialist, Dr. Savage, at the Vanderbilt University Hospital. It was impossible to say yet how much of his vision was lost or how much recovery was possible. But one thing was clear: he could not pass the physical examination again for admission to the United States Naval Academy.[17]

His father had said, "Make your own decision." The son would later say, "God made the decision." He would enter Vanderbilt University in the fall to become, he thought, a chemical engineer.[18]

5

❖

College Boy

... I carry the old Nashville in my head, grateful for the friends
it gave me and for so much else. How remarkably lucky I was to
have been there. I have often thought that for me and my purposes
and aspirations, it was the best place in the world. I couldn't want it
to have been any different from what it was.

— *"Reminiscence"*[1]

So they drove south fifty miles to Nashville. The anticipation, perhaps mixed with some anxiety, must have helped the sixteen-year-
old freshman focus on the future as the old dream of Annapolis
faded into the past. With the city looming ahead his mother had a
parting injunction: "Whatever you do, just don't tell me anything
about it."[2]

Ruth Warren's misgivings probably derived from a view shared by
the university's devout Methodist founders when it opened in 1876.
To them Nashville "always appeared as a modern Babylon. . . ." Not
only were there a few theatres and many saloons but also the racetrack
and brothels—behind the capitol. Fraternity activities gave little reassurance about moral values among some undergraduates, but fully
half the student body were faithful Methodists who shunned dancing
and drinking. The university's first dormitory, Kissam Hall, was an
ornate brick building that housed two hundred men of the predom-
inantly male student body. Its two-man suites comprised two bedrooms and a common study, with baths in the basement. That was
where Robert Penn Warren took up residence in September 1921.[3]

There was some continuity between the new life and the old. Faced with compulsory chapel after his reading in Darwin and the Bible, "I tried to talk myself into some religion in my freshman year," he wrote later, "but no dice. Vice won. But I kept on reading the Old Testament." The basic chemistry course was a disappointment. He was interested in principles and concepts, but it was intended to prepare students for medical school. And one quiz must have reminded him of Clarksville. When it was returned with a low grade he took the course textbook to the section leader and showed him that the grade was incorrect. The instructor promised to change it but never did. "I'll never forget that son of a bitch," the disgruntled student later said. He continued to work at the course assiduously along with the English, French, history, and mathematics.[4]

Freshman English comprised one hour of literature taught by Edwin Mims, the autocratic head of the department, and two classes in composition taught by a young professor named John Crowe Ransom. Mims and Walter Clyde Curry, a Shakespeare and Chaucer specialist, were the department's two Ph.D.'s. Mims wore a neatly trimmed Vandyke, which gave him the air of a kindly Mephistopheles. He played the Victorian paterfamilias, with a special interest in his female students. He indulged his passion for Victorian literature in assigning only work by Tennyson for all of the first term. Like most English professors his age, he emphasized the author's life and times and supplied rather brief impressionistic appreciations of their works. He was also notorious for an inflexible requirement: the students had to memorize seven hundred lines of poetry. He gave a bonus for every additional fifty. This suited Robert Penn, who memorized three thousand.

John Crowe Ransom was, like a number of other Vanderbilt faculty, the son of a Methodist minister, a Vanderbilt graduate, and sometime high school teacher. He had capped his undergraduate record as Founder's Medalist and Phi Beta Kappa with a Rhodes scholarship at Christ Church, where he earned a B.Litt. degree. Having concentrated on Greek and philosophy, he had no graduate training in composition or modern literature, but he taught his course well. He was not systematic, but sometimes, following an idea through with his powerful, logical mind, he would "catch fire and make the class fascinating." To Warren he seemed "a calm, gentle man . . . rather small, but extremely handsome in a kind of benign way." As the boy got to know him and his family, he came to see what a teacher—and a teacher's life—could be.

Then he learned Ransom was also a poet, the first poet he had ever seen. It was like "looking at a camel or something." Yet he used a familiar vocabulary and scenes from life. As an undergraduate, he had been one of a group of congenial spirits who gathered informally to talk about poetry and philosophy. He continued to write poems in wartime France, and Robert Frost recommended them for publication. Using everyday domestic imagery, *Poems About God* employed "a simplicity of language and reference" and, in spite of its title, provided "explorations of the human condition in a world that has moved away from theological certainty."[5]

Warren felt a shock of recognition: "For the first time I saw the world that I knew around me to be the stuff of poetry, because that book was a book with the same background of the upper South. It was strange and even disturbing, that discovery." The compositions he wrote for Ransom and the lines he memorized for Mims must have reminded him of his passion for *Lycidas* and his writing for the student magazine, *The Purple and Gold*. Now he was writing more than ever, and soon he would make the transition from classroom assignments to the verses he would show Ransom privately.[6]

He made new friends, as usual older and bigger than himself. But he made a lasting impression on several of them. William T. Bandy, a sophomore already headed for a brilliant career in French literature, felt a kinship with him. "We both came in at sixteen," he said, "with hayseed in our hair, but I knew the minute I laid eyes on him that here was somebody." Another classmate named Andrew Nelson Lytle was two years older and almost as different from him as Kent Greenfield was. Lytle was interested in drama as well as literature, though his social life took precedence over both. (He was probably the only Vanderbilt undergraduate who owned not just one but two sets of evening clothes.) Warren, so different temperamentally, "needed somebody to talk to occasionally," and they would go for walks, Lytle keeping up with his companion's fast pace as he talked rapidly, his head tilted back and his face turned to Lytle, the ideas and energy pouring out. He was taller now, and to Lytle "an odd-looking boy," freckled, his hair standing up "on top of his head, red as a fireball." Lytle found him "very brilliant, and the smartest boy I knew, extraordinarily alert, knowledgeable in every way."[7]

Lytle and Bill Bandy called him Red. To his family and others in Guthrie he would always be "Rob' Penn." But there in Nashville, though subject to university rules, he was out from under parental authority for most things. Red was more like a man's name. He was still an adolescent, but he was growing and changing. If his hair seemed like a fireball to Andrew Lytle, his academic trajectory seemed similarly bright to his teachers. John Crowe Ransom followed his work closely, and at the end of the fall term he said, "You don't belong in here, so I'll take you to my next class." It was "an advanced writing class . . . the nearest thing to a 'writing course' at Vanderbilt." For that first term he made all A's except for a B in history, and he performed at the same level in the winter and spring terms. His freshman year came to an end with his energy undiminished.[8]

He was seventeen now, and he was saved from spending the whole summer at home by six weeks of barracks life in the Citizens' Military Training Corps at Fort Knox. He loved drilling with a Springfield rifle and fixing the bayonet for combat instruction. In spite of the glasses for his damaged eye he was made point man for his squad and assigned to set the range for firing in the realistic sham battles. And there was more. "I did some boxing," he later told his son. "I got some bruises and flattened noses and banged a few myself, and felt more manly for it. . . . There were several other people, three or four [who] went home from my country, and they all went home after about two weeks, and I stuck it out." And though he had taken up cigarette smoking, his endurance was increasing.[9]

Each summer program was commemorated in *The Messkit* (*Food for Thought*). The day before they left the lieutenant said there had to be a poem. "Warren," he said, "you've been to college. Write the poem." The next day Warren handed him "Prophecy," in three quatrains with a regular rhyme scheme. His fellow trainees found no beauty in the long marches, he wrote, and saw "little beyond the present whirl of circumstance," but when the marching was forgotten, "Then you will reck as paltry small the cost, / And memory will purge the bitter from the sweet." Signed Robert P. Warren and distributed by the Military Training Camps Association, it was his first published poem.[10]

The excitement of discovery that had marked his first year was even stronger when he registered for his courses in September of 1922. It came not from the prospect of beginning courses in economics, German, and history but from the two in English from Ransom and Davidson. In Ransom's advanced composition course he received acute criticism of his writing, and in Donald Davidson's literature course, the chance to broaden his range. He found Davidson "a darkly handsome man with an intense gaze, passions and convictions, though kindly and generous in human relations." Besides the passion and excitement he conveyed, he gave challenging and liberating assignments.[11]

The admiration was mutual. Davidson found it almost intimidating to teach this seventeen-year-old boy whose Latin was almost as good as his own and who knew many of the classics well. Ransom would tell a colleague that "Warren was the brightest student that they had ever seen around there. His daily or weekly themes were the ones that always got read with admiration by the instructor," and "his mind seemed to work with extraordinary speed." Davidson taught by example as well as precept. Like the boy's first reading of Sherwood Anderson's *Winesburg, Ohio,* Davidson's lectures gave him "a great waking up." He was fond of balladry, and this resonated with the folk tales and poems absorbed in those summers on the isolated farm out in Christian County. Then, on November 22, something momentous happened, for Red Warren and many others like him.[12]

A poem by T. S. Eliot entitled *The Waste Land* appeared in *The Dial,* and Davidson loaned the magazine to his student. Its effect was stunning. "I was completely overwhelmed by it," the boy remembered, though he didn't understand it at all, "but we memorized the poem and went around quoting it all the time. We intuited the thing as belonging to us." The poem was for him a "watershed," ushering in—as Joyce's work was doing in prose fiction—the modernist era. On the Vanderbilt campus poetry was not confined to honorary societies, writing clubs, poetry groups, and the student newspaper, *The Hustler.* Looking back, Warren said, "Everybody wrote poems."[13]

His social life continued to change that fall, almost as much as his intellectual and aesthetic life. The progress had begun the previous year: He would remember "a freshman with a hat cocked on one side of his head and a cigar in his mouth [as he] entered a poolroom with a friend and began to chalk his cue." Out in the country was an Italian farmhouse, a kind of café where "four or five students—freshmen and sophomores and I—went out there and sat there and drank Dago Red a good part of the night." He also learned to patronize a bootlegger. His circle broadened to include harder-drinking and tougher-minded students than those at the farmhouse. One was Ridley Wills, a dashing decorated war veteran and published novelist. As editor of *The Hustler* he had been a trial to the administration and an inveter-

ate prankster. Now completing his degree requirements and working
on the Nashville *Banner,* he was "as bright and flippant as ever." One
day he met Warren in Wesley Hall, the Theological School dormitory, whose cafeteria was better than that in Kissam Hall. "He was a
great taleteller and a wonderful comic," Warren remembered, and
one day Wills invited him to share his larger room in Wesley Hall.
Greatly flattered, Warren moved in.[14]

Number 353 was a large suite with two double-decker beds on the
top floor. Wills brought in a graduate student named William F.
Cobb. Another of Wills's friends was John Allen Orley Tate, who described Wills as "small, graceful, ebullient, and arrogant, and one of
the wittiest and most amusing companions I have ever had." Tate too
was returning to complete his degree after six months' recuperation
from pulmonary problems. A slim man who wore three-piece suits
with his Phi Beta Kappa key on a chain strung across the vest, he had
a striking appearance that was emphasized by his penetrating gaze and
disproportionately large head. His manner was courtly, but his quiet
wit had a sharp edge. He used his literary gifts in describing his first
meeting with his new roommate.[15]

Typing a poem in Walter Clyde Curry's rooms one day, Tate became aware of a presence at his back. "Turning round I saw the most
remarkable looking boy I had ever laid eyes on. He was tall and thin,
and when he walked across the room he made a sliding shuffle, as if
his bones didn't belong to one another. He had a long quivering
nose, large brown eyes, and a long chin—all topped by curly red hair.
He spoke in a soft whisper, asking to see my poem; then he showed
me one of his own—it was about Hell, and I remember this line:
'Where lightly bloom the purple lilies. . . .' This remarkable young
man was 'Red,' Robert Penn Warren, the most gifted person I have
ever known."[16]

Tate had known Wills and his cousin Jesse as fellow members of
The Fugitives, who read their poems to one another and in the spring
of 1922 started a magazine called *The Fugitive: A Journal of Poetry.*
They fell easily into their old intimacy. Tate recalled that "to get into
bed at night we had to shovel the books, trousers, shoes, hats and fruit
jars onto the floor. . . ." In spite of the mess, "gangs of people would
come there to argue poetry and read aloud," Warren remembered,
"and so I contributed by decorating the walls with episodes from *The
Waste Land* and [Sherwood Anderson's] *The Triumph of the Egg. . . .*"
Tate and Wills would be out with girls almost every evening, and

Warren would have quiet time to write. He would be asleep in his upper bunk when they returned. "We stuck pins into Red while he slept to make him wake up and tell us his dreams," Tate said. If he had left a new poem on the desk, they might tear it to pieces in a critique the next morning.[17]

There were other informal sessions. Bill Bandy, now a senior, would hold forth in his rooms. "Well, God damn it," he would say, "come in here and let me read you some Baudelaire, and we'll talk about it." Warren said later that Bandy created a one-man Left Bank there on Westside Row. With their animated discussions fueled by a jug of corn whiskey, they would go on until four in the morning. At the end of one session Bandy piled them into his Stutz Bearcat and "undertook to climb the great story-high stone flight of entrance steps to Wesley Hall in the Bearcat. He succeeded, and then made a hair-raising descent . . . leveled off and we sped away." Like many of his friends Bandy wrote verse and sketched. That spring of 1923 he contributed to *Driftwood Flames*, a forty-seven-page book of poems published by the Poetry Guild and dedicated to John Crowe Ransom. The fourteen contributors included Andrew Lytle, Bill Cobb, and Charlie Moss. The largest contributor was Red Warren, with five poems. One was the poem Tate had seen, "The Golden Hills of Hell," in which the poet knelt there "among the purple lilies." Tate and Ridley Wills took him to a meeting of The Fugitives, and before long he would be publishing in their magazine.[18]

The shortest of his poems in *Driftwood Flames* was "Wild Oats." His own apparently consisted mainly of drinking, staying out late, and cutting classes. (In spite of it he would get all A's for the year.) Despite this self-accusation, he sometimes appeared shy and almost withdrawn to his friends, and unlike Lytle and Tate, he had never been much at ease with girls. At fifteen he had dated one girl he later described as "amiable." Another reported that they sat on her front porch swing and "let it go back and forth till we got worn out from swinging" and he went home at nine o'clock. The next year he had several dates with another girl who remembered that he talked "about the sky, the stars, the moon." But she thought he flaunted his smartness so that "she felt that she was in the dark." At Vanderbilt, though, he had begun to seek out female company in a way that even Ruth Warren could not but approve.[19]

Chink Nichol lived in a large house on Twenty-fourth Avenue South, surrounded by university property. Her family was one of three credited with founding Nashville. They had started with a trading post and profited from their friendship with Andrew Jackson. Chink's parents, William Lytle Nichol, Jr., and the former Catherine Dean Hutchison, were hospitable people who entertained often. Chink's cousin, Andrew Lytle, liked her father, whom he called Cousin Will and often visited, though he thought her mother frivolous. Catherine enjoyed the company of creative people, and Allen Tate was one of those who strolled over to their house to join her salon.

Catherine Baxter Nichol got her nickname when her father announced to her mother, "We've got a baby girl, and her name is Chink." At sixteen she had an exotic look, and even though she was considerably overweight, she had a beautiful face. Often shy and silent, she nonetheless enjoyed chattering with Tate and Warren and Moss even though she thought of them as intellectuals. Her parents had sent her to the Ward Belmont Preparatory School for Girls, and she was now a debutante. Sometimes the boys would borrow her mother's car and take Chink for a drive. After Andrew Lytle saw Warren at several of her debutante dances he concluded that she was his first love.

Warren would tell his son many years later that he was then leading a very active life—studying, reading widely, and writing poems and stories. "I had also been drinking very hard. One night a week I would go off on a binge with my friends." On weekends they would see the girls. "I had a girl, most of the time the same girl . . . with a quite beautiful face and a sweet nature." She probably enjoyed his attentions but no more than those of the others. However, he did not go home to Guthrie when the school year ended "because I was stuck on a girl where I was."[20]

Each of the faculty houses on West Avenue had a two-room cottage for servants. Professor Herbert C. Tolman agreed to rent his to Tate and Warren. Later Charlie Moss moved in too. Warren got a job driving a truck for the American Express Company. Once when they moved a big steel safe, the boss made him the "money guard" and hung a .44 pistol and cartridge belt around his waist. Then he laid a sawed-off shotgun on the safe. "All you have to do," he said, "is close your eyes and pull both triggers if anybody sticks his head in the back of the truck." Reflecting on these events many years later, the erstwhile money guard said, "To my eternal disappointment, nobody did."[21]

They celebrated the Fourth of July with a formal party. Mr. Nichol couldn't attend, and so Tate and Warren came to the house to escort Chink and her mother to the cottage. They also invited an able young psychologist named Lyle Lanier. Chink spoke not a word to him, but she would see him again.[22]

In August Warren returned to Guthrie. His leave-taking from Nashville must have been doubly uneasy. He had taken too many cuts in Dr. Mims's course, and he confided to Tate that he was "running about one term behind" in both papers and examinations in other courses. Guthrie must now have seemed more unappealing than ever, but he needed a rest to prepare for the coming year.[23]

6

❖

One of the Group

Down the stair had creaked the doctor's feet
Shuffling. He heard them out thinking it queer
Tomorrow night at nine he would not hear
Feet shuffling out and down and into the street
Past the one murky gas jet in the hall,
Past the discarded chair beside his door. . . .
 — *"Death Mask of a Young Man"*[1]

In mid-September of 1923, a few days before his return to Vanderbilt, Warren wrote Donald Davidson, "I am now working in the bank here trying to rehabilitate my somewhat shattered fortunes. . . ." Davidson had informed him that the New York *Evening Post* had published an enthusiastic review of *Driftwood Flames*. Better than that, *The Bookman*'s columnist had reprinted Warren's "The Golden Hills of Hell" and remarked that it had "a bizarre quality of mysticism that recalls Blake." He was praised at home too. As associate editor of *The Fugitive*, Tate had made up the August-September number and included Warren's poem "After the Teacups." The title seemed an allusion to T. S. Eliot's "The Love Song of J. Alfred Prufrock," and the range of historical references suggested *The Waste Land*. But Tate told Davidson, the editor, that "Warren's poem is a first-rate piece of work; that boy is a wonder, or I'm much mistaken, and deserves election to the Board. I might even go so far as to say the Board deserves to have him."[2]

Back at Vanderbilt, a declared English major and philosophy minor, he signed up for German, Greek, and English courses, and Philosophy 3. But he would later conclude, "My real university did not wind up as Vanderbilt as such. I had the great good fortune of classmates and friends whose intellectual interests and philosophic and literary tastes were sometimes more sophisticated than my own." Chief among these was Tate, who was "really a combination of older brother and tutor" and also his "most powerful critic." The group of poets known as The Fugitives provided another kind of education. Going to meetings with Tate and Wills, Warren saw that "when we sat down together to discuss poetry, we sat as equals. It was one long seminar, and I was getting a priceless education writing boyish poems. I *was* a boy." With Ransom and Davidson there, Warren found it "an exhilarating experience to be suddenly involved in an intellectual interchange with men twice my age." There was no party line; they were "all Southerners, coming together around a common interest—poetry. . . ."[3]

The Fugitives had the life cycle of an organism. The nucleus had formed before the war. An English instructor named Stanley Johnson had introduced Davidson to "a group of Southernized Jews and art-minded Gentiles." Figuratively the keystone and literally the largest of the group was Sidney Mttron Hirsch. After some early success as a dramatist he found himself languishing, feeling that he was not properly valued in Nashville because he was self-educated. When his half-brother, Nathaniel, brought his Vanderbilt classmates to the Hirsch apartment on Twentieth Avenue they would sit on the second-story balcony and Sidney would happily preside over the swirling, wide-ranging discussions. To William Yandell Elliott, a political scientist-to-be, they were "Olympian."[4]

As the group grew, Hirsch's "somewhat undisciplined largeness of thought" was balanced by Ransom's "fine discrimination between ideas" and his Oxford-bred sophistication: "tentative, dry, and incisive." Walter Clyde Curry came from Stanford, grounded in philosophical and historical scholarship but also interested in aesthetics. Davidson invited him to join the group. As Davidson had been the leader in bringing the group together, so Ransom was becoming its intellectual leader. By 1919 he had set another example with the publication of *Poems About God,* which showed some of his characteristic traits: "fascination with domestic imagery, . . . the undercurrent of violence," and his "revolt against poetic diction" together with "simplicity of language and reference. . . ."[5]

Now the group's location shifted and so did its subject matter. Sidney Hirsch had moved in with his sister Rose and her husband, James

Frank, a man of wide culture. In their large redbrick house on Whit-
land Avenue he and his wife would delight to see Sidney presiding, re-
clining on a chaise longue to ease the pain from an injury suffered in
the Far East. He would often talk about the symbolic aspects of ety-
mology, though more and more the others turned to literature and especially poetry. By the time Johnson returned from the army in 1921,
the group was on the verge of new creative activity. Tate, the only undergraduate, remembered that the members gave one another the hon-
orific title of "doctor." At a February gathering Hirsch suggested that
the group publish a magazine. "It seemed to us all," Tate wrote, "a
project of the utmost temerity, if not folly," but they pursued the idea.
What title would they use? Alec Stevenson suggested *The Fugitive*.[6]

They intended the magazine to make its way strictly on its intrinsic
merits. The price would be twenty-five cents per copy, with their
books uncomplicated by advertising income. In Ransom's foreword to
the first issue in April 1922, he said that "a literary phase known rather
euphemistically as Southern Literary has expired, like any other stream
whose source is stopped up. . . . *The Fugitive* flees from nothing faster
than from the high-caste Brahmins of the Old South." The members
solicited subscriptions from persons who, if not Brahmins, might be
sympathetic. Tate tried Dr. J. H. Kirkland, the chancellor of the university, who declined, as did his stalwart supporter, Edwin Mims. This
autocratic head of the English department was a passionate adherent of
the idea of the New South—developed along some northern lines—
which was anathema to most of The Fugitives. Far from being a potential subscriber, Mims "tried to persuade us to desist."[7]

There were, however, new recruits to their pages: Witter Bynner
from New Mexico, William Alexander Percy from the Mississippi
Delta, and Robert Graves from England. Another was Merrill Moore,
who settled on the sonnet as his favorite form and, during a career as
a poet and psychiatrist, would compose no fewer than fifty thousand
of them. Looking back in the year's-end editorial, Alec Stevenson
noted subscriptions from "Canada, California, London, and Berlin,"
and also the addition of two new editors to the staff: Ridley Wills and
his younger cousin, Jesse. *The Fugitive,* he said, looked back "with
some pride and not a little amazement on its initial twelve months."[8]

Ransom had opposed naming an editor—the members chose the
poems to be printed by secret ballot—and was content simply to list all
the names on the masthead. But because he was generally thought to
be the editor, some of the others felt the credit for the work was un-

fairly apportioned. They proposed that Davidson and Tate take over the editorship. At about the same time, Ransom and Tate began a controversy—in print. For Robert Penn Warren the literary combat between his surrogate older brother and the man who would shortly become a surrogate father must have been an uneasy thing, and there would be general satisfaction when the difficulties were resolved and Tate was listed as associate editor alongside Donald Davidson as editor on the *The Fugitive* for August–September 1924. Earlier Robert Penn Warren had been listed as one of the magazine's sixteen publishers. When Ransom had invited him to the meetings it had been the "greatest thrill I'd had in my life." Now, at eighteen, he was a full member. "Ransom was writing his best poems then, and Tate was just finding himself." Red Warren said to himself, "This is what I'm going to do."[9]

In the chill days of March he must have thought back to the golden autumn. One day Warren, Tate, and Lyle Lanier had walked across the campus to the Nichols' house to see Chink. With the trees blazing it was just the kind of a day for a drive out into the country. They enjoyed the crisp air in the changing panoramas and stopped on a hill to gaze at the colors of the valley below before returning. Back at the house, Tate asked Mrs. Nichol to take their picture. Sitting among the men was Chink with a winsome smile on her face—the only smile in the photograph. It was Lanier who had said, after their first meeting, "What they see in that little girl is beyond me," but he apparently changed his mind. He was staying on to do graduate work in psychology at the George Peabody College for Teachers. Chink had a number of callers now, and he was one of them.[10]

In that summer of 1923, Tate and Warren had taken courses, renting a cottage belonging to the faculty house assigned to Herbert C. Tolman, dean of the university's academic department. Tate stayed on until late February of 1924, when he left for a high school substitute-teaching job in West Virginia to earn money for a try at a literary career in New York. In these years when telephone long-distance lines were used mainly for bad news and good news, friends such as these corresponded frequently and voluminously. The Fugitives sent back and forth new poems and critiques of poems, providing an ongoing record of their lives.

Lyle Lanier kept tabs on his friends. On March 18 he informed Tate that "the situation here is little changed, except for the worse. Just on the eve of his Psychology exam, in fact, only thirty minutes before it commenced, Red went to bed with what is most easily described as an attack of nervous indigestion. That was Wednesday; Thursday afternoon, at the instigation of David [Clay] and myself, and following the doctor's admonition; we carried him to St. Thomas' Hospital where he remained until this morning." A behavioral psychologist, Lanier reported in clinical fashion: The problem was caused by "lack of sleep and general irregularity in habits of work . . . and a profound conflict between the conscious habits he has tried to shield himself behind and the general unconscious . . . functioning of his instincts. . . . only two weeks ago he said to me: 'It is pitiful the way I'm losing [my] grip on myself.' "

Lanier went on to say that Warren had left the hospital that morning, but later Lanier had been unable to find him in his room. Often, apparently, he was out late at night. There was only one way Warren could resume an orderly and productive pattern: "It would be for certain persons to cease manifesting their kindness to the point of weakness and to regulate vigorously the habits he refuses to regulate himself. . . . Two nights each week away from his room, and on those never later than eleven-thirty, would change the lad."[11]

"He was a boy," Andrew Lytle said, "and he had been very innocent in kid love affairs," and this was "his first love." Katie Dean Nichol liked having all those boys and girls around the house. And so did Chink. The hours Red spent there were only a part of his current problems. Students were allowed to continue their studies despite numerous class absences, unfinished papers, and missed examinations. Reading his poem "Wild Oats," his instructors may have thought these were wild oats he was sowing. But he was slipping into a serious malaise.[12]

He was still an adolescent, and his body must have been trying to assimilate its growth spurt. The Nashville winters were not particularly harsh, but some of his fellow students remembered his suffering from colds and other ills. When he went home to Guthrie, Ruth Warren must have done her best to nourish him, but there was apparently little emotional nourishment there, and perhaps some gnawing of conscience. His parents had never stinted on the education of this first and favored child. Next year Mary would go off to college. Her record was as good as her brother's, but the quality of her future education would be far below his. There was also the unwelcome parental authority. Robert Penn was not yet nineteen, and at home his parents made the rules.

In Nashville the group had asked him to replace Tate as assistant editor of *The Fugitive,* but he thought it would be "a thankless bit of drudgery of no particular significance" and declined. The group had accepted three of his poems. "You see," he wrote Tate, "writing poetry was about all I did while convalescent, if the sequel to my little flurry of indisposition can be given such a dignified title. I have come to look upon poetry as a sort of escape from a good many things these days. I do not know whether it is due to my physical condition or not, but I find every other aspect of my existence infinitely wearying or worse. . . . The prospect of the work of the next term combined with the six examinations which must be taken between now and June stupefies me. I have absolutely no energy left after my sickness, nothing but a sort of apathy which extends into every phase of my existence, except, as I said, that directly concerned with poetry, and even there I seem to find decided deterioration."

He felt trapped. "If I could go anywhere else except to Guthrie I would drop out this term and get away. Everything connected with Vanderbilt or Nashville seems night-marish to me now. Only Guthrie is worse. . . ." Unburdening himself, he was more direct than Lanier had been. "Things at the N's are as when you left. . . . Little solace there for a weary poetaster—is it not so? You know at one time not so lately past I half-believed myself in love with Chink, but though that has passed or at least subsided, it is unfortunately attended by consequences which are rendered more acute by my obliging tendency to do what is expected of me, at least sometimes."[13]

By early April he was able to report that he had probably passed two of the examinations, one in Greek and the other for Dr. Mims, with whom he was now in bad odor. For a standard assignment Mims gave on students' beliefs, Warren wrote Tate that Charlie Moss "referred to you and myself as a group of debauched aesthetes, whose one ambition was to die before the age of thirty-five with only a poem or two to live after them. . . . Of course he makes no specific mention of names, but what he says is definite enough to justify the wildest suspicion that Eddie's lurid imagination ever conceived. . . ." As for his romance, "The relief in the situation at the N's may be momentary, but it is real." As his birthday approached he was meditating on time as well as love. "Can you conceive of me as nineteen years of age[?] I can only give thanks that it isn't twenty."[14]

When he next wrote Tate there was "a possibility that I may not be able to come back to Vanderbilt next year because of financial conditions." He had been finding The Fugitives' meetings increasingly tiresome, and now they were worse, with "the usual fruitless discussion and wrangling as to how the magazine is to be continued. . . ." His own six-quatrain "Romance Macaber [*sic*]" had been called morbid, affected, and unconvincing. By the time he wrote again on a Saturday morning he was back in the hospital. "I had several [academic] examinations on Monday and Tuesday and consequently was a little strenuous in preparing for them; this time however I finished the examinations before I got sick." But he was exhausted and had to close because "I am already beginning to feel the effects of sitting up."[15]

Very shortly he was hit with another problem. He dated his letter to Tate "Night of Black Friday." The trouble was the cottage they had rented in the summer. Mrs. Tolman had charged her former tenants with sexual misconduct and stealing property. She was holding a trunk that belonged to Tate, and she had appealed to both Dr. Mims and Dr. Sanborn, to whom Warren still owed an examination. Now Warren was afraid that she might write to his parents. "Father has written me some urgent letters imploring my presence next Sunday." Robert Franklin Warren had already paid one bill for the cottage without complaint, and apparently there was no emergency at home.[16]

Tate and Warren had begun using a code word: *albatross*. In a paragraph of allusions, Warren had recalled that Tate had exhorted him to "bury the albatross" but that he had not done so, and that a "specter of the fowl" haunted the rigging "nocturnally." Chink was his albatross not because she pursued him but because she did not. His love for her, unreturned, haunted him. He still visited "the *N's*," though less regularly; it would be desirable but impractical to break off abruptly. And he had experienced a nightmare the previous night that had left him physically ill all day. Lyle Lanier hoped Chink's parents would intervene, and now he could report that "the girl" would be sent away next year. On Saturday, when Warren went home for his birthday, Lanier called and found Mrs. Nichol "somewhat perturbed" that Chink no longer found any pleasure in the company of boys her own age.[17]

On Warren's return from Guthrie, he informed Tate that he had taken four of the six examinations he owed, one with borrowed notes because he had lost his own. But he was concerned because Dr. Sanborn had been postponing his psychology examination for two weeks. On May 6 Lanier sent Tate another of his clinical reports. Warren had suffered another attack, which "assumed the general appearance of a regular organic disorder to a greater degree than . . . last month." The immediate cause was preparation for the examinations because of the time he was still spending at the Nichols' house. But Warren told Tate there was nothing new. "About Albatross," he wrote, "what has been said concerning the fascination of corpses and vampires may be yet applicable. . . . The person is to be kept out of Nashville nearly all summer by her mother to make assurance doubly sure."[18]

He was now attending the Fugitive meetings irregularly. The April number of the magazine carried his "Three Poems." The first began, "Beyond this bitter shore there is no going. . . ." The other two were similarly bleak and filled with imagery of sorrow. In the last poem's sestet a prophetic hooded figure appeared, but then, in the closing couplet, "I awoke and all that hideous night till dawn / Watched the pale world wheel on and faintly on." Tate's confidence in Warren's talent was even stronger now. "That boy's a wonder," he told Davidson, "has more sheer genius than any of us; watch him: his work from now on will have what none of us can achieve—power." But Tate's concern over his welfare was stronger too: "If he can triumph over that hellish environment of his for another year, I have no fears for him."[19]

Warren's opinion of the Fugitive meetings continued to decline. As for his schoolwork, he was to take the psychology exam the next day. "I have it pretty well in hand now," he wrote, "and consequently am not more disturbed than is requisite." He typed a P.S. at the top of the page: "I bought a gem of a stiletto yesterday. Engraved metal hilt and handle, eight inch blade, and leg sheath. You ought to see it. It is an Italian make. I happened to find it at a pawnshop."[20]

Charlie Moss was out of Warren's good graces for several reasons. There were the continuing effects of his unfortunate essay for Mims, and now he was engaged in a love affair that appeared to be leading to marriage and defection from poetry to journalism. Charlie was now working the late shift on the Nashville *Banner*. Sometimes when it was too late for him to go home, he would sleep in Warren's room on Westside Row. On the night of May 20, when Warren wrote Tate about his preparations for the next morning's exam, Charlie finished up early, a little before ten. Normally he would have gone home, but he decided instead to spend the night on campus. Unlike the occasions when Lyle Lanier had tried without success to find Warren in his room, Charlie found him there. He was on his bed unconscious, a chloroform-soaked towel nearby.[21]

7

❖

de profundis

Now has the brittle incandescent day
Been shattered, spilling from its fractured bowl
The so trite dusk upon a street and soul
That wait their own and evening's decay.
Will not a midnight grant deliverance
Of dusk and all its bitter casuistries;
Nor death, nor dawn whose querulous harmonies
Are torn to day and gorgeous dissonance?

Autumn, we know, is twilight of the year.
This bronze and amber rumor of our death
Stains far hills and soon to us will bring
The caverned sleep of winter, when beneath
The fennel's frigid roots we shall not hear
Again the bright amphigories of spring.

—*"Autumn Twilight Piece"*[1]

Tate's friends kept him informed. "Red Warren has done the craziest thing in his career," Jesse Wills wrote. "He tried to commit suicide Tuesday night. As usual his action was entirely futile and in a certain way even ridiculous." Don Davidson was all sympathy. "Poor boy. He has had a wretched time, [he] must be saved from himself. . . ." Lyle Lanier reported that the immediate cause seemed to have been Sanborn's psychology examination, but the root cause involved "nervous (emotional) maladjustment."[2]

On finding Warren, Charlie Moss had run to Dr. Crockett's porch but receiving no response had roused the Mims household and got their friend and classmate, Puryear Mims, to drive them to the Woman's Hospital. When Warren regained consciousness the next morning, the first face he saw was his father's. When Davidson, Wills, and Ransom went to see him that afternoon they were too late, for the Warrens had already taken him home. "I wanted to see Red before they abducted him," Ransom wrote Tate; "we all in fact wanted to laugh with him a little about it." Ransom also wanted to hear more about him. "He's a great fellow," he concluded.[3]

The motive was far from clear. So was the nature of the act itself. Why had he chosen chloroform? Had the towel slipped, or had he knowingly removed it? He would say later that Moss had found him with the pad over his nose and mouth. Another friend, Brainerd Cheney, heard that it had been wrapped around his head. Was it a genuine, if bungled, attempt, or was it instead a symbolic action, a cry for help? He had supplied a motive in several letters left there in the room. (Charlie had taken with him all but the one addressed to himself.) Davidson informed Tate that "Red said he was cashing in because he was convinced he 'would not make a poet.' " Tate hurriedly wrote Warren and received a two-page single-spaced reply by turns angry, arch, and hysterical.

Tate had asked about the motive given in the suicide letter. It was "purely marginal and incidental," Warren wrote. "The real reasons, if such can ever be comprehended by me, resulted from a sort of ennui which had extended, and I almost said is extending, over a considerable period of time." In the note he had left for Tate, "I was merely being logical. At present I am more nearly approaching chaos in my actions and consequently normalcy, as it is generally understood." His parents did not allow him to read or write, except for correspondence. What he wanted most was a visit from Tate, and he enclosed an appeal from his mother. "Somehow I feel he has missed and needed you," Ruth Penn wrote. "We want to keep son from writing or reading as much as possible, and time hangs heavy on his hands in this little town." His own urging was explicit: "You must come to Guthrie for the month of June if not longer. *You must come. I will hear of no other plans.*"[4]

What was his mental state? Loving his parents, he nonetheless resisted any threat of domination. As for the others, if he felt any guilt vis-à-vis his sister's life expectations, how did he feel toward his brother? Had he, at age nineteen, forgiven his brother for the injury that had destroyed all chance for the career he coveted, the injury, scarcely concealed by spectacles, that left him feeling maimed? Would his feelings—with possibly enormous unexpressed rage—have carried this guilt too? His injury came at a time when he was likely moving through normal male sexual development to assert his emerging manhood, and he may well have been experiencing age-appropriate anxiety about his masculinity. The injury was traumatic enough to have an effect like castration. And what he seems to have taken as Chink Nichol's rejection of him could well have reinforced this feeling. If she was his albatross, his unrequited love for her a heavy weight around his neck, his incapacity may have seemed the root cause. Where, then, would he turn for the kind of sustenance she might have provided had she been more than a plump adolescent with a beautiful face? Where other than to his older brother, Allen Tate?

   The intensity of his feeling for Tate had been clear in his letters. They were a warm and close group of friends. Occasionally when writing Bandy, Davidson, and Tate, Warren would sign himself "Affectionately." But most often in writing Tate he would close "with love." The range of emotion included tenderness as well. Looking for a job so Tate could spend the summer in Guthrie, Warren could find only rough manual labor, but he told Tate, "You may wear gloves to preserve the silken texture of your hands; they deserve such protection." His emotional dependence became acute when he was brought home, and his frustration became intense when Tate's promised visit was delayed. "If you don't come on now I shall never forgive," he told him. Correspondence from Tate sustained him. When he finally arrived, Warren's days were full and contented. Was there a homosexual element in his feeling for the dapper, charming, and assiduous ladies' man? If there was, it was most probably latent rather than overt or pathological, and the heterosexual feelings he had manifested toward Chink Nichol would reappear powerfully after he left Vanderbilt, the place where the psychological stresses were greatest in this, his late adolescence.[5]

Not until many years later would Warren reveal the governing dynamic of his inner life in those months leading up to the night of May 20. He remembered that the eye injury "drove me more and more to intellectual pursuits as compensations." At the beginning of his junior year "a feeling of pressure" had begun to set in. He had fought depression and the sense of deprivation and injury with the antidote of work, but that was no longer effective. His course work was now boring, especially his bête noire, psychology. (Was the course intrinsically boring, or did it induce painful introspection?)

He wore his glasses less and less. Then he noticed that the vision in the damaged left eye was beginning to deteriorate slightly. "I felt maimed," he remembered. He had been told that the injury would somehow affect the other eye. Then, "I began to notice after a year or so that the [left] eye was swinging out of orbit. . . . I began to worry about losing vision and going blind, and so I lived with a state of almost chronic depression. . . ." (It was, of course, intensified by Tate's departure.) He saw Chink and other girls too, still feeling "disqualified" and "ashamed." But it was not failure in love that drove him to the attempt. It was, he would say, fear. After brief respites, sometimes as much as a week at a time, "it would come back aggravated. . . ." The left eye was going completely, "and then I tried to see if the other eye was being affected. It was a constant preoccupation. . . . I was watching, watching, watching. . . ."

He made one appeal for help. "I was aware of this change taking place," he said many years later, but "I couldn't persuade [the doctor] of it. I didn't want to talk to my friends about it. I didn't want to talk to my parents about it and alarm them. . . . If I even had a decent kind of sensible medical man to talk about it with . . . or just an older, wiser friend who could have taken charge of the case to see what the situation really was, and made tests and things. I was nursing this fear, more than fear, almost certainty, all the time." Ransom and Davidson had asked him out to their homes "dozens of times," but he had never gone. The disfiguring effect of the injury was seemingly minor at this point, but he could not bring himself to talk about it—appearance or potential consequences—even to so intimate a friend as Tate. His lengthening delinquency in his work must have increased his sense of crisis and guilt. "And then I got in a fit of awful depression," he said. "I felt myself going blind."

When he spoke later of *The Fugitive* and his youth, he said, "It was poetry or death for me then, and some of the others shared that passion." But there was no religious faith to sustain him, no confessor to absolve him of whatever guilt he felt. His hearing was attuned to the voice of one muse. For a poet, strangely, he had no ear for music. There was no comfort there or elsewhere. As the shadows lengthened—in his vision and in his poetry—he drifted toward silence and sleep. His valedictory account, that he feared he would never be a poet, was a cover story. Though some of his work did not please him, he had enjoyed extraordinary success among talented older poets. Maimed, ashamed, he could not live to be a blind poet.

No one but Robert Penn Warren would ever know for certain if his suicide attempt was more than symbolic. Buying the stiletto may have been a symptom or merely an impulse. The purchase of the chloroform was deliberate, and its use planned. If he had a rescue fantasy, he was unlikely to have used enough chloroform to render himself unconscious until the next day, and if he had dislodged the towel himself, the effect would have been weaker. He lived, it seems, by accident. Later he said he could never be sure whether or not he faintly heard Charlie Moss's voice as he was drifting off. But after he awoke he felt shame. "I would never do that again," he said. "I would never *have* done it because it was so wicked, as the results would have been for other people."[6]

His father acted almost as though nothing had happened, but it was not an easy situation. Jesse Wills's first reaction to Tate had been, "I doubt the advisability of Red's staying at Guthrie. Yet his father may be afraid to let him come back here." Apparently his parents never questioned him about his actions. He never tried to explain them to anyone, he said, any more than he had confided to anyone the onset of the acute phase of the illness. He was far less likely to talk to his parents than to Tate or Ransom. "I never talked about anything with my parents, not seriously," he said. "I was totally aware of their affection and concern for me, but we never had any talks." And now he was in their charge again. "I am at home after the sundry vicissitudes of my health and of other aspects of my existence," he wrote Tate, "and unhappily it appears that I am doomed to remain here for the rest of the term."[7]

As it turned out, it was a time of recovery. He was able to report by early summer that he weighed 140 pounds, "eighteen more than I weighed when I began work a few weeks back." It was manual labor for the Litchfield Shuttle Company, "tossing logs about for ten hours each day and sleeping ten more," he told Don Davidson. Later it was cutting lumber: "one man with an axe, one hundred degrees back in the swamps, and a halo of mosquitoes around your head, is not easy work, for about a dollar thirty-five an hour." He wrote Tate—in New York since early June—that the manager had practically promised work for him too about the middle of July.[8]

He had resumed his writing and "surreptitiously completed all of a sonnet except the couplet," and within a few days he would "declare my rights as a freeborn American and secure paper and pencil." He was able to record gleefully the acceptance of new work by *The Double Dealer.* "Portraits of Three Ladies" would appear in the August–September number. *The Double Dealer* would publish two less lusty poems in the October issue, and he intended to send in others. If he had doubts about his ability to produce publishable work, the appearance of eight poems in two magazines over such a short period should have allayed them.[9]

As he worked to rebuild his "tattered constitution," his tattered psyche was also repairing itself. A trip to the doctor in Nashville revealed no problem with his appendix, and he apparently managed to get back to the campus to see his friends. It seems likely that the doctor must have given him at least a cursory examination, which may have allayed his fears about imminent blindness. In any event, Warren later said that his fear of blindness remained with him for a long time, but looking back to that anguished winter and spring of 1924, he could also say, "I never got that down again with it. . . ."[10]

The boredom and monotony of manual labor in exile were relieved when Tate arrived for his promised visit at the end of June. There was no job for him, and Warren quit his. Tate had much to tell about his two weeks in New York. He had met Hart Crane and E. E. Cummings almost as soon as he arrived. He liked them and the way "this gang is much less theory-ridden than we Fugitives." He met others including Kenneth Burke, Edmund Wilson, and Malcolm Cowley. Gorham Munson, who edited a little review called *Secession,* told him how much he liked his work as well as Davidson's and Ransom's. He also said he had noticed progress in Warren's poetry since the previous summer.[11]

Warren was now importuning other friends to visit almost as fervently as he had Tate, "for our solitude becomes more acute daily." Davidson managed to come, but even after he left, as it turned out, Tate had no problem with solitude. One of Ruth Warren's friends was the former Nancy Minor Gordon. When her daughter, Caroline, came to visit, Nancy called Ruth Warren. "I hear you have a guest," she said. "It would be nice if he could come by and see Caroline." When James Gordon encountered Warren and Allen he invited them to come home and meet his daughter, who was, he said, just as "crazy" as they were. She was a teacher, part-time journalist, and fiction writer. Four years older than Allen Tate, Caroline Gordon was remembered by one of her students as small and slim, with a trim figure usually attired plainly in black. To one friend, her appearance was

dramatic, with hair that "gleamed blacker than a raven's wing, matching her eyes set in a masklike face, magnolia white. . . ." The attraction between her and Tate was immediate. He was handsome and
courtly, she, intense and passionate. They went on walks together, at
first with Warren and later without him, giving rise to the story that
they made love in the cemetery.[12]

In mid-August, Tate and Warren went to Nashville, where they attended a few sessions of The Fugitives and Warren talked with some of
his professors about the work he owed them. But then, writing from
Washington on Monday, August 25, Tate told Davidson, "I had to take
Red back home Monday night cutting my visit in Nashville short by
two days." He added cryptically, "Red was in bad condition again because of a severe nervous shock he received while he was in Nashville.
I mention this to indicate that he will bear watching off and on in the
coming year. He couldn't very well have made the trip home alone last
week." Had he learned only then that he owed one paper to Walter
Clyde Curry, five to John Ransom, and a long one to Eddie Mims?
Had the shadow of the albatross fallen over him again? Had he turned
to whiskey to dull whatever shock he had received? Whatever it was,
he had to pull himself together for his return to the parental rooftree.[13]

He did so as the summer drew to an end. He wrote Davidson that
he had worked for a week at the bank and earned forty-five dollars.
He had written thirty typed pages on his religious convictions for Dr.
Mims and finished the papers for Ransom and Curry too. "My own
health is of the best," he wrote Bill Bandy. "I now weigh one hundred and forty-five pounds and feel like a bull." In a week he was returning to Nashville, where, in the winter, he would have a large
room with a bay window in town, "which will perhaps contribute to
my peace and well being."[14]

The registrar had recorded four A's for Robert Penn Warren for the
previous term—and no credit for Sanborn's course. Now he signed
up for a full course load and plunged into extracurricular activities.
Though rooming in town, he still spent most of his time on the campus, often in Kissam Hall in the first-floor suite of his classmate Saville T. Clark. A gregarious Mississippian, he was a political science
major, a labor sympathizer and advocate of social change who had
made friends with students at the neighboring black institution, Fisk
University. Active in YMCA visitations, he made one trip to the
McTyeire School, a small classical academy in West Tennessee, and re-

cruited a brilliant student named Cleanth Brooks. To this young Kentuckian, the slim visitor had the face of an idealist. When Brooks arrived on campus in September of 1924, Clark took him in as his suite-mate. Clark had a wide circle of friends, and when Brooks returned from class he was as likely to find a star football player as intellectuals engaged in animated conversation. For Cleanth Brooks it was a heady freshman year. At the start of the winter term, when Bill Clark moved into an apartment in a house on Grand Avenue with his brother Cannon, he invited Red Warren to join them.[15]

Bill Clark was not only a close friend but a tolerant and independent one as well. On at least one occasion Warren had appeared in Kissam Hall to sleep off a drinking episode. When Bill's girlfriend told her mother that Red drank too much, her mother told Bill that he would have to quit rooming with Warren or quit going out with her daughter. Clark replied, "I'm not having my life run that way." When in the new year a clash developed between students and administration at Fisk University, he brought several of the black students to the apartment to learn what was happening—to the horror of the landlady. Undaunted, Bill invited them back. Though he was uninterested then in politics, Red Warren would later remember "what an eye-opener it was for me. . . ."[16]

This was a better year. Warren now accepted invitations he had declined. He was so much with John and Robb Reavill Ransom that it became "a sort of second home" for him. The life there he found "delicious." His own background, as he would remember it, was "rather lacking in humor." For the beautiful Robb Reavill, onetime Colorado State Golf Champion and a national competitor at bridge, "everything was a game or a joke—everything was fun. . . ." Her husband was not only a crack golfer but also keen at croquet and poker. Every Saturday night they played bridge or poker for small stakes. "They had all sorts of games—volleyball, and bowls, and their whole life was a game. They worked, but work was play too, just a different kind." Robb Reavill, equally adept as player and hostess, made the guests feel at home. Her husband, Warren remembered, "was much like a father to me. . . ."[17]

Guthrie was still no farther than his mailbox, but Bill Clark would see letters from Warren's mother stack up unopened. Her hopes and ambitions were shadowed by worries about his health. Bill described one result to Andrew Lytle. Ruth Warren was making her son take silver for a stomach complaint. But he was taking too much, and sometimes he would draw up his knees spasmodically in the big double bed he and Bill shared, and Bill would have to sit on him to straighten him out.[18]

In spite of the silver, in spite of keeping up with his work, he was writing poetry copiously and broadening his range. (He also agreed to serve as Ransom's assistant editor of *The Fugitive* for all four issues in 1925.) In some of his verse he was taking a new tack, as in the ironic and technically ambitious "Praises for Mrs. Dodd," with its treatment of death only a little less bizarre than Wallace Stevens's "The Emperor of Ice Cream" a few years earlier. He was still writing poems full of angst and despair, but in "Alf Burt, Tenant Farmer," which *The Fugitive* would publish in the December number, he treated death with a tone reminiscent of Edwin Arlington Robinson, A. E. Housman, and even Thomas Hardy:

> Despite that it is summer and the sun
> Comes up at four and corn is rank with weed
> Old Burt is abed and won't see the plowing done
> Nor find a harvest where he laid the seed.

There were other models closer at hand. Among the Fugitives Warren had often been thought of as a disciple of Tate, but in poems such as "Autumn Twilight Piece" he was shaping a directness of his own.[19]

As he approached his twentieth birthday he was making plans. Clearly he was headed for graduate school, but he would need financial support. He tried for a Rhodes scholarship without success, as Ransom warned might happen on his first try, but "as soon as I finished Vanderbilt, I wanted to go as many places as I could." He probably had more than one acceptance, but to his mother's dismay he accepted a seventy-five-dollar-a-month teaching assistantship at the University of California. "So I went to San Francisco first," he said, "as far away as I could get."[20]

The summer of 1925 provided a mixture of backbreaking work and celebration. At commencement time Warren reported to Allen Tate that Nashville was "literally flooded" with gin, and he and Cannon Clark had laid in a store for a final celebration in mid-July. Soon bored after his return to Guthrie, he invited Andrew and the Clarks for the Fourth of July weekend. It was probably about this time that his father made a symbolic gesture. He walked into the kitchen when his son was making drinks. "Why don't you make one for me too?" he said.[21]

They came on Thursday, July 2, for a weekend Warren would remember all his life. Andrew Lytle wrote to his Aunt Mary from
Guthrie. John Ransom had arrived the next week to join in their activities, and "we took many walks together, read much poetry, gam-
bled some, smoked good cigars, swam. . . ." Then, after the others
left on Sunday, Warren and Lytle went to a Methodist revival. "I like
the family very much," he wrote. "His father is quiet, almost taciturn, while his mother is active and lively. [She was a nervous woman
who spoke rapidly, he noted later.] He has a little brother with a
bright eye and rapid talk. His sister, I understand, is exceedingly intelligent, red-headed, and plays [the piano] fairly well."[22]

A few days later Warren sent Allen Tate a brief account of it and
added, "John and Father are a most peculiar pair. . . . However, they
appeared to hit it off splendidly." On Sunday afternoon they had spread
a blanket under a maple tree in the backyard. As they sat there, passing
books of poetry around and taking turns reading from them, there was
suddenly an "absolute moment of transfiguration and vision. . . ."
Ransom opened a volume of Hardy and read "Wessex Heights." Warren had heard him read Hardy in class, but this "absolutely bowled me
over. It was not like any poetry I had ever heard in my life. A whole
new world of poetry!" After that, Warren said, he was never the same.
He would try imitating Hardy only to give up because he felt it was no
good. But there were periods ever after when he would read him every
day and conclude that, for him, "after Wordsworth, there is Hardy, and
then, after that, there is a great question mark. . . ." Another unlooked-
for gift came that Sunday afternoon under the maple leaves when he
chanced to see, sitting on the grass deep in conversation, Robert
Franklin Warren and John Crowe Ransom—his two fathers.[23]

He gave a strangely mixed account of himself. "My health is so
good these days that I need a little reaction to make me realize how
very fine I have been feeling of late." He had put together a manuscript of thirty-eight poems, but he had "few illusions left about
them," and that probably had "a good deal to do with my present
state of general despondency." But he wanted Tate's opinion and
"detailed advice concerning the arrangement of poems and other
matters." Don Davidson was now book-page editor of the Nashville
Tennessean, and Warren had done some "trivial reviews," but "I'm
stale on everything now and I know it. I can neither read nor write
and I lack energy for any great physical activity." But he was sending
along a thirty-six-line poem, with his usual request for criticism.[24]

Before the close of school Warren had sent Tate a poem entitled "Easter Morning: Crosby Junction." In its eight stanzas the poet followed the preacher's voice from inside the church—where he preached of spring and Christ's resurrection as promise of eternal life—through the window to the churchyard, his sermon rejecting "the confutation of the stone. . . ." It was not only the imagery that suggested T. S. Eliot but also the poet's own voice parenthetically contradicting that of the preacher:

> The cedar hath an hungry root and long.
> How may we sing who have no golden song,
> How may we speak who have no word to say,
> Or pray, or pray—who would so gently pray?

The poem was printed on the first page of the June number of *The Fugitive* and followed by three other strong ones he had written.[25]

The Hardy poems he had heard and the service he had attended apparently had given him the impetus for "August Revival: Crosby Junction," the new poem he was sending Tate. It contrasted the boring preacher and pharisaic congregation with Christ in his death agony. It would appear in *The Sewanee Review* for October–December, and it showed how he was now attempting to assimilate what he could from Hardy as well as Eliot.[26]

If the familiar lack of energy was due principally to boredom and his poems' shortcomings, there may also have been an additional cause. "The Albatross was here tonight for a few minutes while on her way to visit some friend in Indiana," he told Tate. "I saw her, discoursed with her, and made the requisite gestures of farewell." He could not but compare his situation with that of Tate, who had all the poetry reviewing he wanted for *The New Republic* and close relationships with not one woman but two: Laura Riding Gottschalk, who had contributed poetry to *The Fugitive,* and Caroline Gordon. "I am pleased by your news of the situation existing in the new homestead," Warren wrote. "Yes, A. Tate, you possess a remarkable facility for weathering sundry disturbances of the elements. . . ." In May of the following year Tate and Caroline Gordon would be married, and in November their daughter, Nancy, would be born.[27]

In spite of the enervation he described, Warren somehow found the energy for "great physical activity." He was working on the road in Guthrie with a pick and shovel. He needed the money, for he would board the train for California in early August.[28]

TWO

❖❖

Graduate School

8

❖

The California Experience

So I stood, and I thought how my years, a thin trickle
Of sand grains—years I then could
Count on few as fingers and toes—had led me
Again and again to this lonesome spot where
The sea might, in mania, howl, or calm, lure me out
Till the dunes were profiled in a cloud-pale line,
Nothing more,
Though the westering sun lured me on.
— *"Swimming in the Pacific"*[1]

The afternoon of August 8, 1925, found Warren writing as the train
rocked along through the Arizona desert. It was in part a thank-you
letter to Andrew Lytle for a party at his home and in part a literary
resolution. "I think that my philosophy of poetry is right, at least for
me, who am a relativist," he wrote, "but my method demands discipline; it is too romantic in essence with too much sarcasm. . . . I have
been too quick to stick to my 'This poem is good' without qualify-
ing the assumption with the phrase, 'but not good enough.' But by
God, I mean business now."[2]

His first impression of California the next day was almost overwhelming. Laura Riding Gottschalk put him up for "a most splendid stay" of three days in a studio cottage in the garden of her
brother-in-law's house atop the highest hill in Los Angeles. The
head of the Little Theatre movement in Los Angeles, he gave a
"party that began about the middle of the afternoon and progressed
until deep into the night. It was one mass of novelists, poets, critics,

et cetera, successful, good, bad, great and small. . . . Laura Riding herself is one of the most delightful people I have ever seen. Peculiarly intense, she has a cast of mind almost fanatic that does not subdue her charm, which is genuine. She is a marvellous talker . . . and our conversations down in the cottage ran through each night until dawn." She was the first of three women in California who would have a powerful impact on him.[3]

His first impressions of Berkeley and the university were generally good, but it was very different from Vanderbilt. The English department placed a strong emphasis on undergraduate composition and an expanding graduate program. Graduate students working as teaching assistants were in the bulging composition courses. Warren would collect his seventy-five dollars a month as one of them.

The graduate course offerings were the staple ones, but his choices were restricted by his duties. "I find that the institution will most probably get value received from the pittance they put out," he told Davidson. As for the faculty, in the five years before his arrival, a total of three books had been published by department members, none of them possessing any scholarly distinction. No book of poetry or fiction had ever issued from the department, in part because such work was not valued there. But his living arrangements were "rather fortunate, for I have room and board with a French family which gives me the opportunity of acquiring a conversational knowledge of the language."

His initial misgivings proved prophetic. Because he was last to arrive, he had been made assistant to Charles H. Raymond, A.B., an assistant professor of English who taught commercial English and journalism. Warren very soon stopped going to class because Raymond's lectures were terrible, and he stopped reading the text because he couldn't bear the writing. Mr. Raymond offered a trade-off: Warren would grade thirty-five papers each week and stop attending class. In 22 Wheeler Hall, with a dozen other teaching fellows, he graded the papers and held conferences with each student. After a series of student complaints about him, his relationship with Professor Raymond went into a steady decline.[4]

The climate for poetry bothered Warren more than the academic situation. The problem was that "they hadn't heard the news." They had no idea what modernism in literature was. "I didn't know anything about Freud, for instance, or Marx [but] when I went to Berkeley, I thought I was among the barbarians, as far as poetic taste was concerned." The only hope must have come from The Poetry Group, comprising faculty and picked students. He accepted their invitation to join and in November published a poem in *The Occident,* a student magazine. It was entitled "To One Awake" and began in a realistic mode but almost immediately shifted into tone and imagery much like those of his dark winter of discontent at Vanderbilt:

> The sifting darkness like the dust again
> Will drift through sockets of the skull, oppress
> The throat, the brain. . . .[5]

Back in Nashville during Christmas vacation he enlisted his Vanderbilt teachers in an attempt to transfer to Yale, trying to give no hint of his intentions in Guthrie. It was a hectic vacation. Andrew Lytle would later observe that what might be a rather ordinary task— packing for a departure in a limited time, for instance—could become one of Red's "crises." This apparently was one such departure with repercussions that lasted into the spring, when Don Davidson was writing to both Lytle and Tate about him. "If you have any influence over Red Warren, you'd better write and advise him to steer clear of Nashville on his return East," he told Andrew. "There are some very angry people here who are likely to have him arrested the minute he arrives, and I am one of them. He carried off (at Christmas time) some books that I value—in fact he made a general haul on his Nashville friends, leaving injured feelings and even a bad check behind. Since he left—not a damn whisper—except a request to write a recommendation. I've written my last one for him."[6]

Tate replied that he was "distressed to death over the actions of Red. . . . It looks as if he has gone wild out there. He has always had a certain weakness—but his present actions appear to have pressed things to the breaking point." Tate had heard complaints "from all sides," including Bill Clark, who had charged both a loan and Red's friendship off "to bad debts." Tate said he would try to see what had come over him. "He has always felt that he is the offspring from God's second son, and with such lineage he evidently feels that he can treat his friends that way, then soothe their wounds with the balm of his smile. However, he has made a grievous mistake and needs a jacking up."[7]

He was heading for trouble on all fronts, just as he had done two years before in Nashville. There at least he had older friends such as

Tate and Lanier to check on him, with a number of others such as
Ransom and Davidson ready to help him and offer a home away from
home. In California he was two thousand miles from them and his
parents. His new sense of freedom was reinforced by his physical
growth, though there was no compensating growth in emotional maturity. He was free to try almost anything he wanted to do. He was
frantically busy as usual with writing, studying, and now teaching,
but there was also an almost wilful carelessness about his obligations—
academic, financial, and social. Well could Tate say it looked as if he
had gone wild.

Tate had already heard one account of misfortune, and the first
sentence was more than just an allusion to *The Waste Land*. "From this
decayed hole among the mountains," Warren began, "I salute you."
He would not be seeing Tate soon "thanks to a piece of well meant
but misdirected maternal interference." He had been awarded a
scholarship and a cash stipend to enter the graduate division at Yale in
the second semester. "I unfortunately transmitted this information to
my mother, mentioning at the same time that I might simply have to
take French leave from the University of California. The ethics of
such a departure troubled the lady and so she wrote to the President's
Office here to ask them if a more regular mode of leavetaking were
possible. The President's office replied in great wrath that the guy
who pulled out as I had intended would be guilty of a grievous of-
fence and could expect no further good will from this dump. In per-
turbation mother then laid the state of affairs before the Yale English
department. You can imagine the consequences. The head of the department there regretted that my valuable services had to be dis-
pensed with for this semester and by way of consolation held out
some enticing prospects for next year. . . . I am terribly disappointed,
for I had hoped to see you and Lyle and Carolyn in New York before
the second semester opened. And I don't like California." He hoped
they could have their reunion next summer and concluded,
"Nothing can hold me here beyond that time."[8]

A series of his letters apparently crossed the others in the mail. In
mid–May he wrote Bill Clark on two successive days recounting almost Hardyesque mishaps. Clark's letters had been delivered to the
wrong offices, and he had moved without leaving a forwarding address. He hadn't sent the twenty-five dollars he owed Clark because
he had been in the infirmary for a week with food poisoning. Moreover, "I have just passed the significant point of the most critical situ-

ation of my life thus far." The whole story was too long and complex to try to tell now and he was not sure he would "care to commit the matter to paper in any case. . . . Indeed Bill, it is a wonder that I even survived as a person." He was desperately sorry. Striking the Hardy-esque note, he hoped that Bill could see that he had been "the victim of a set of circumstances. . . ."[9]

He had meant to earn his M.A. in the extraordinarily short time span of two semesters plus spring and summer work. So, while grading his thirty-five papers a week, he carried four courses and prepared for the M.A. comprehensive examination, which covered "all [the] history of English Literature" and "almost swamped me." He passed it with an A. Except for one B, all his course grades were A's.[10]

Despite the sense of uprootedness and discontent in his letters, he had acquired some friends and a number of acquaintances. One graduate student, Celeste Turner, said her friends "were interested in his growing reputation as a poet," and she liked his "agreeable personality." He got to know the director of the Little Theatre, a lively group that produced a full season. Carolyn Anspacher, the president of Mask and Gown, the dramatics honor society, was the most conspicuous member. Later the subject of a striking portrait by Ansel Adams, she was once described as a woman with a "formidable" style, who "did not so much enter a room as sweep into it, imperious and regal." There were other dramatic women there whom Warren got to know, party-givers whose guests included faculty as well as students.[11]

He had met one exotic woman through two young philosophy professors, David Prall and Stephen Pepper, who were interested in modern poetry and aesthetics. One day when they went to a speakeasy opposite the San Francisco police station, they encountered Emma Brescia. In a letter on February 6, he asked Tate, "Did you receive a mysterious communication, probably couched in terms of studied naiveté from one 'Cinina' Brescia about Christmas time? She is an Italian girl I know pretty well here, the daughter of a composer, who, incidentally, has a mine or something in Peru. I suppose that she is about the cleverest female I have ever known and so I hope you weren't taken in by her letter. I told her about you once and a few days later she asked me where you lived. . . . and some time later she informed me that she had written you. . . ." She had three poems in the same issue of *The Occident* with Warren's "To One Awake," and the next year she would publish two essays on music. He would see more of her.[12]

· · ·

Warren often spent time with three members of the Poetry Guild—
Lincoln Fitzell, Raymond Dannenbaum, and Lewis Russell. When
he found better accommodations he took Lincoln Fitzell in. To Russell's wife-to-be, Ieda "Skilly" Ogborn, Fitzell was "tall, blond and
completely naive," with a fey quality. She thought Warren craggy but
handsome. With his belated growth, he stood just under six feet and
weighed over 170 pounds. His freckled skin and red hair made him
one of those who, Andrew Lytle would say, would "never brown but
always burn." But his adolescent acne was gone, and now, stoking his
pipe or lighting a cigarette, he had clearly passed into young manhood. He still had the racing, staccato speech as the ideas came tumbling out pell-mell, but to Skilly Ogborn he had "lovely manners"
and was even "rather aghast at our free and easy western ways." Lew
Russell was a socially conscious member of the student council opposed to student military training, president of the English Club, and
also editor of *The Occident*. Ray Dannenbaum was an amateur hyp-
notist and writer-to-be.[13]

"Upon my return to these parts after Christmas," Warren wrote
Tate, "I had the good fortune to discover a large and really beautiful
house in the hill district of Berkeley. There was an enormous studio
with unfinished redwood walls, hardwood floor, and excellent furnish-
ing. Aside from that there was a sleeping porch, bath, dressing room, attractive brick-floored kitchen and dining room, and a garden. . . . It
was only a fifteen minute walk down to the campus . . . with a fine
view toward the [Golden] Gate. . . ." They settled in for a winter semester of hard work.[14]

In the previous semester, he wrote Tate, "I had diverted myself in
the city about once every two weeks after the several fashions of diversion especially contrived for young men. . . . I only drank five or
six times during the whole semester. Three of those times were at
pretty wet parties given at our house. The parties were small, about ten
or twelve people. . . . Everybody was out to the eyes, and was more or
less incapacitated for laudable scholastic pursuits the next day. . . ."
Warming to his narrative, he went on: "The real source of my near
ruin sprang from a more personal matter." He had described its beginnings to Andrew Lytle. "The personal quandary," he had written,
"is in the form of an Hebrew female of the Judith of Bethulia type,
who, I am sure, would cut off not only Holofernes' head but any other
noggin with equal zest. She is the Little Theatre's leading lady, spe-

cializing in undraped roles. . . . she burns with a most insistent and consuming flame, is perverse, and possesses the temper of a very Lucifera." This personal quandary, apparently, was whether or not to succumb. "Burn we candles before the virgin," he wrote with a fin de siècle air, "for here there is neither a virgin nor are there candles."[15]

He gave Tate a blasé account of the sequel: "She gave me what in the vernacular of the byway might be termed the 'come-on.' . . . At the end of a week she was coming out to the house in the afternoons; at the end of two weeks I was standing my roomate [sic] to shows to secure his absence for several evenings a week; at the end of a month my roomate was staying more than occasionally with his family in San Francisco. In March I spent a few harried days but the crisis passed quite normally. . . ."[16]

But another crisis was brewing. His friend Professor Guy Montgomery told him he had been reappointed with a substantial raise in salary. Two days later Professor Robert Utter, the head of the department, told him "there was no chance of reappointment here [because] I exhibited an essential lack of enthusiasm for the work of commercial English. I answered with some degree of asperity that he was quite right. . . ." Utter responded angrily that Warren was "a disturbing element and more of a liability than an asset. . . ." When he demanded an explanation, Utter told him "that certain aspects of my private life were not approved by the department." He offered to hand in his resignation and left. Montgomery pleaded his case, arguing that "what counted was the graduate work, not the fellowship work. Furthermore, the university had little concern with my private life so long as it did not get in the papers." A few days later Professor Utter handed him his reappointment "with a nice raise in salary" and "a vague apology." But the respite from trouble was brief.[17]

"Meanwhile," he told his fellow Eliot devotee, "black clouds gathered far distant over Himavant. I took the Master's Comprehensive on April 22, [1926,] and made an A. That night there was the second party at our house. . . . On the night after examinations, there was the third party, a trifle more raucous," with two uninvited guests present. Skilly Ogborn would recall that when the party was at its height Ray Dannenbaum "announced that he could hypnotize people. Red volunteered and amazed us all by lying with his head on one straight chair and his feet on another, remaining while we took turns sitting on his tummy." Lew Russell had made "an enormous pot of spaghetti," and there was plenty of wine, but "no marijuana or dope in those innocent days." One vignette would remain vivid in her memory: "Several ladies were languishing at Red's feet, including the dark lady from San Francisco who became a by-line writer for the *Chronicle* . . . who followed him to New York."[18]

Thanks to one of the uninvited guests, Warren wrote, "by the following Saturday morning a fantastic tale involving every possible breach of the Decalogue was being discussed in Oakland and San Francisco business and social circles. Hell was to pay in the family of the young lady of Hebraic extraction, since her name and mine figured in nine hundred and ninety-nine phases of a revised version of the Arabian Nights Entertainment. I talked to the young lady that night for the last time. She was going to summer school, and her family wanted me to take a vacation. . . ."[19]

But his problems were financial and legal as well as amatory and social. He had deposited seventy-four dollars in his account and wrote several checks on Saturday, and on Monday a small one to a Berkeley shoe store was returned for insufficient funds. He was then moving to San Francisco, and when his landlady told this to the shoe store's proprietor, he turned the check over for collection. Warren made two more deposits and explained at the shoe store. But the check had attracted the attention of the Berkeley police. The landlady had told Inspector Woods about the party and "a complaint made by a neighbor . . . that I had brought a girl up to the house at night and that he (the neighbor) was going to notify the police." He received a notice to report to Inspector Woods.[20]

"I caught hell for about six hours," he told Tate. "I tried the force of logic to which he seemed peculiarly impervious. . . . A young law student, a friend of mine . . . told me for God's sake to give some sort of vague confession to the immorality business without dates, etc. . . . It turned out that the check was not what the Inspector was really interested in, but the other matter. I finally achieved the proper reaction at about nine o'clock at night and was dismissed from the jug with the obligation of making weekly reports as to every move of the week. Furthermore I am debarred from all the proper joys of men in consequence. . . ." It was a worrisome situation, for "they had me up on a variety of charges, actually including the Mann Act, transporting liquor, disorderly conduct, homosexuality (which amounts to a passion with the police here) and the check charge. The contradiction inherent in the first count and the homosexual one somehow did not seem to perturb the illogical official mind; I pointed out that one was probably untrue and got roared at for my pains. So now I am wandering about on probation with no means of diversion except seminars in English. . . . in the name of Christ don't write a word of this whole business to anyone, especially at Nashville. It would certainly blast any chance I have for the Rhodes Scholarship if I ever want it again." If his plans worked out, he hoped to see the Tates the first week in September, "that is if you will receive me despite my criminal record." Just turned twenty-one, he was hardly hardened in debauchery, but he had been proving all the pleasures he could.[21]

By May he was writing Bill Clark from his new address a few blocks from the Embarcadero. "I have an old studio on Telegraph Hill overlooking the bay. This is the center of the Italian Quarter—the part of town that cops patrol in groups if at all. So far I have gotten along with them (the wops, I mean) very well indeed, for I had previous connections with this part of the city and my introduction was favorable." It was a huge second-floor studio as large as the Spanish poolroom below it. There were the simple creature comforts, a fireplace, and windows in the huge living area that gave views all over the bay. Goats often clattered on the roof, and a bear often kept them there. There was a tower, which was fine for writing poems. Good inexpensive food and wine were plentiful, and every month when the landlord came for the rent he would bring a jug of wine for a sociable drink and leave it behind.[22]

A whole other world opened for him in the city with its museums and galleries. But better than that was the world beyond, for "you could leave San Francisco by public transportation early in the morning and be in the deep woods in an hour and a half, and you could cross over on a mile hike and be in wild country." There was good swimming at Fleishaker Beach and even beyond the city, "wonderful dunes and wonderful beaches for miles. It didn't get too cold even in January to swim, if you really meant it. I spent days and days out there, wandering the dunes and swimming."[23]

"I hope to get my degree in August [1926]," he told Bill Clark, "if the wops and their vintage doesn't get me down." But halfway through the May-June intersession a problem arose: one of the three parts of the one-hour M.A. oral examination was devoted to translating Anglo-Saxon, in effect a foreign language. Warren told Davidson that "due to bad advising" he had not enrolled in a reading course in Anglo-Saxon, and so he was trying to get it up on his own by August.

A postponement would mean that he couldn't take the Yale scholar-ship in September even if he could find money to get there and live there.[24]

In the flurry of apologies he had sent in May he had also asked Tate's advice about his book of poems. Tate advised waiting a year, and Warren concurred. "In one sense the year here has been rather sterile. I have written but little poetry, [though] at least now I have an inkling of direction, something which before I lacked." He was also trying to deal with his psyche. "You are right about the quality of ob-session. . . . If it was a function of my age (as you remark and I be-lieve) it will work itself out; if it was not it will end in poetic sterility. . . ." In his critique of his manuscript of poems he told Tate he liked one sequence he was calling "Kentucky Mountain Farm" because "it marks a sort of release, or rather sublimation, of the ob-session of my other work." During this fallow time at Berkeley he had turned in a new direction, reading widely in history, especially American history. In individual poems that made up this sequence, the poet surveyed his land from the arrival of the early settlers to the struggle of the blue- and gray-clad soldiers who fought and died there, all this against the rugged beauty and starkness of the natural world. These poems provided a wide panorama different from the many he had written dominated by the poet's solitary figure meditat-ing on his solitary griefs. It was a rich lode he would mine increas-ingly for the rest of his life.[25]

By the end of summer school he had concluded that he could not manage the Anglo-Saxon and had resigned himself to another year in Berkeley. But before the summer's end there was news to raise his spirits, though he learned some of it only belatedly. In the December 1925 issue of *The Fugitive,* John Crowe Ransom had announced the magazine's suspension because no one was free to edit it, but Donald Davidson had begun efforts to publish a collection of their poetry and proposed an anthology to Houghton Mifflin. For his contribution, Warren provided a ranked list of seven poems. "Within the limits of its intention the 'Letter of a Mother' is easily my most finished poem. 'Kentucky Mountain Farm' is second because it presents a more spe-cialized and perhaps more subtle if weaker treatment of the same at-titude. . . ."[26]

Lew Russell was writing too. Busy taking classes and editing *The Occident,* he had time to publish only a few stories, but six years later he would complete *Vacation,* a novel of graduate-student life in Berkeley. The principal characters were based on himself and Skilly Ogborn, and others on their friends. One called Red is a lean southerner, a former Rhodes scholar good at shooting craps and playing tennis. Carol is an exotic, olive-skinned rabbi's daughter, playing both passionate lover and mother to Red. He is a paid book reviewer and a hard-drinking playwright able to work in the midst of a noisy party. To the poet-protagonist, Mike, Red is a success but a cold intellectual who doesn't know how to enjoy Carol. When last seen, at another party, he sits propped against the wall, bottle in hand, looking contemptuously at the others. Lew Russell was fleshing out imagination with experience and observation. Warren's remarkable concentration could block out the world around him, but a contemptuous attitude toward those close to him would never be one of his traits.[27]

As the fall term of 1926–1927 began, his course load was lighter and his colleagues more congenial. Jack Lyons organized a dinner for the teaching assistants in a speakeasy on San Francisco's North Beach. It was "a noble dinner in a private room with lots of red Italian wine," Fred Bracher remembered. "Jack persuaded Red to recite, from memory, the whole of T. S. Eliot's *The Waste Land.* . . . It was a marvelous performance, and thereafter I viewed Red with something approaching awe." His assistantship was now less onerous, but it still presented problems. Kindhearted Mr. G. Dundas Craig gave all his students A's. When Warren found it impossible to adjust to his standards, he was assigned to yet another instructor. "I was passed around like a hot potato," he would say many years later, or like "fruit with a worm in it."[28]

His emotional life was equally unstable. In early April of 1927 he confided to Allen Tate that Carolyn Anspacher had been replaced by Cinina Brescia. (Carolyn would, however, occupy a singular place in his memory.) Cinina and Gordon McKenzie, "my roommate, were two of the first people I met upon coming to Berkeley. I liked Cinina tremendously from the first, which, on the face of it seemed rather absurd, because she and Gordon McKenzie were engaged to be married. He and I became something of friends and naturally the three of us were a good deal together. . . . After a trip to Los Angeles with Gordon, some of his relatives and myself, she practically broke with him. In the fall, McKenzie, who incidentally was aware of the situation, asked me to share an apartment with him [in Berkeley]. I protested, for obvious reasons, but when he insisted, I agreed to do so. . . . We got along excellently, worked, drank, went to parties together and took a couple of trips, but were never intimate. After Christmas he and I went to the mountains for a while, and when we got back Cinina had a severe attack of pleurisy and has been slowly recovering since. . . . Things were on a slightly strained basis between Gordon and myself after the return from the trip. Not long ago, when it could not be deferred any longer, we had it out."[29]

Fred Bracher recalled that there were "many differing accounts of a 'duel' (fists only) that he fought with Gordon McKenzie . . . on the beach at San Francisco over Cinina." Warren's version was quite different. He told Don Davidson that McKenzie "was awfully decent at the time. . . . We separated and I moved to the city. . . . But hell broke loose a little while later when Cinina told him she was definitely decided. He seems to have lost his head and went to her house and raised an awful stink. . . . and I haven't seen him since."[30]

When Warren first met Emma Brescia (Cinina was a pet family name), she was a sophomore living at the Kappa Alpha Theta sorority house. "She is rather tall," Warren told Tate, "slender, has blue eyes, dark hair, and a bad disposition." Her portly father, Domenico, wore an imperial and resembled a short, plump Joseph Conrad. He had graduated from the University of Bologna, studied music at one of Italy's principal conservatories, and gone on to a career as a composer, teacher, and orchestral director. According to family accounts, he had the bad fortune as a composer somehow to run afoul of the authorities and so left for Ecuador, where Cinina and her brother, Peter, were born. When they were quite young the Brescias moved to Savannah, Georgia, and from there to San Francisco, where Mr. Brescia continued his career as a conductor and headed the music department at Mills College. The brother and sister were much alike, with the family's very dark hair and "the same style, dash, and fire," according to a musician friend. Warren told Tate, "Her father is a perfectly charming man, but her mother is a hellion, when she wants to be. . . ." Once she informed Warren, "My people were in the ruling class in Rome when your people were eating acorns in the forest!"[31]

Warren had apologized for his delay in writing because his time had been "almost equally divided between being in bed with tonsilitis and another matter of greater pith and moment. . . . The engagement of Cinina Brescia and myself is to be announced at the end of May. Things have been in a horrible mess here, but the dust of the tumult has settled and that fact emerges, [and] much to my surprise [her parents] approve the business. But, God, imagine Mother."[32]

As the dust was settling he had received some good news from Tate. He had placed some of Warren's work with *The New Republic.* "Pro Sua Vita" would appear in the magazine on May 11 and "Croesus in Autumn" on November 2. Both might have been written by a much older poet. The cryptic couplets of the first poem, with their reflections on his mother and imagined speeches to both his parents, constituted an ironic statement of loss. Similar in some ways to his earlier "Letter of a Mother," the poem showed him wrestling with his relationship to the parents from whom he had distanced himself. Though "Croesus in Autumn" was tinged with the old melancholy, its five quatrains employed an almost playfully familiar and ironic tone. In it he switched from ancient Rome to his new resource, the Kentucky landscape, and assimilated old models for his own present purposes:

> The seasons down our country have a way
> To stir the bald and metaphysic skull,
> Fuddling the stout cortex so mortally
> That it cries no more, Proud heart, be still, be still.[33]

There was good news too about Davidson's project, *Fugitives: An Anthology of Verse.* It was finally accepted by Harcourt Brace in May for publication in January. It would include fifteen pages of the work of Robert Penn Warren: the two poems in *The New Republic* plus seven others. Tate had read parts of the manuscript to Mark Van Doren, and he "was knocked cold by Red. . . ." A habitual gossip, Tate was nonetheless honest and generous about his friends' work. "You know," he told Davidson, "Red is pretty close to being the greatest Fugitive poet."[34]

As the year moved toward summer his concerns were threefold: his future with Cinina, the completion of his work at Berkeley, and the transition to New Haven. Her pleurisy had hung on so that by mid-April she was only beginning to sit up. Her family's plan was for her to continue her recuperation in Southern California and then go to Europe to study. Warren was eager to spend time with her before her departure, and he enlisted Tate's help. "Cinina is going East a month after I do. . . . The project is this: would it be possible for you and Carolyn to go to the country with Cinina and myself and take some sort of place?" They would all share the expenses. "Naturally [her family] will know nothing of the business since they keep no strict account of Cinina's expenditures." It was an anxious, repetitive letter that often took on a conspiratorial tone. "A visit to an intimate friend of mine, known by my family, would pass. They know you are immersed in eminent respectability with wife and child."[35]

Warren was delighted at their consent, but Cinina had to wait for the doctor's approval. After the Tates' invitation she could "begin the long and necessary process of converting her family to the idea of her crossing the continent alone." A seashore stay was approved, but Mrs. Brescia was still fearful that Cinina would swim, in spite of its being forbidden for two years. So Allen and Caroline were to "make it the country and not the seashore" in the letter "for Mrs. Brescia's benefit." He also asked them to "minutely describe climatic conditions as ideal. . . . All of this makes Cinina out as a sort of invalid, but don't let that alarm you; I can warrant the contrary."

He conveyed a kind of harried optimism. "The struggle here is about won after a number of mother-daughter recriminations, invocations of the Deity and a general display of the latin temperament. But after Cinina ran about seven tenths of a degree of theatrical temperature, victory crowned her standards. God, what a household!" He congratulated Tate on a poem that would become "Ode to the Confederate Dead" but then returned obsessively to the planning: "In the letter to Cinina for God's sake promise to meet her in New York. You needn't of course. One half of the struggle is based upon Mrs. Brescia's wonderful and terrible conception of continental propriety which is outraged daily."[36]

Warren was enjoying his last two courses and feeling academically secure. As for the final M.A. oral examination, "a table was prepared for me in the house of my enemies," but "the marines had the situation well in hand, and are now recuperating while their laurels wither." He would later say of Berkeley, "I thought that I had exhausted the place." Jack Lyons remembered that he had announced early his intention to become "a 'man of letters,' which he defined as a man who had done distinguished work in each of six literary genres: short story, novel, biography, poetry, criticism, and drama." For the present, however, "I was following scholarships. Wherever I got the scholarship, the biggest scholarship, that's where I went." But at the same time, "I was always aiming at the Left Bank."[37]

He would go to Yale and await results of a second application for a Rhodes scholarship. "If that falls through again I shall take my doctor's degree at Yale, unless I decide to . . . follow your path to New York. If I get the Rhodes Scholarship Cinina will remain in Europe, if not she will come back to America after she has finished work for her degree at the University of Florence. So you see, as far as marriage is concerned, the plans are, as they should be, sane and tentative enough." But there were other concerns. "All the family has been sick this spring and much needed money owed Father can't be collected. I don't know how things will turn out there: Father's health is pretty bad. I may leave California about the middle of May if I can get a job on a boat to New Orleans." Promise beckoned, however, in his own life. "I am excited as the time draws near for me to get back East," he wrote in a rapid scrawl. "I'll be in New York this summer despite hell and high water and our long postponed reunion can take place. . . ."[38]

9

❖

New York and New Haven

My brother, brother, whither do you pass,
Unto what hill at dawn, unto what glen
Where among rocks the faint lascivious grass
Fingers in lust the arrogant bones of men?

Beside what bitter waters will you go
Where the lean gulls of your heart along the shore
Rehearse to the cliffs the rhetoric of their woe?
In dreams perhaps I have seen your face before.
—*"To a Face in the Crowd"*[1]

He stopped in Nashville first and set about surveying and mending his fences. He saw Lyle Lanier and learned that he was going to marry Chink Nichol. Mrs. Nichol "told me everything except the date," he wrote Tate. "She said that Chink was going to marry Lyle because he was the only man she knew who was stronger than she. I assented with all the gravity I could muster."[2]

Back in Guthrie he wrote Tate and Caroline Gordon. "Cinina was much improved when I left California and the only letter I have received since my return says that she is even better. The chief inhibitions . . . are that she must go to sleep at nine and can drink no gin." By July, however, the plan for a sojourn in the country looked dubious, and so did their finances. "If we do have to descend on you [in the city] we may have to have [Cinina's] letters from her parents sent to some place in the country and forwarded to 27 Bank Street. Could that be arranged?"[3]

He was trying to borrow money on his insurance to supplement his Yale fellowship, and he was quite willing, even eager, to divert some of the loan for the holiday. He added a postscript: "With great urgency I say, do not let news of the project leak out here. I haven't told my family yet and shan't until everything is arranged and Cinina is on her way."[4]

In June and July he worked on new poems and sent one called "Garden Waters" for Tate's criticism. "Things are drifting along for me at Guthrie in a fashion which you may remember from your summer here. I wish you were here now to help me in doing practically nothing." He did have some good news to report: "I got my loan." He was leaving for New York on August 10. "I've had it out with the family and that's the conclusion," he informed Bill Bandy. "I compromised and agreed to wait a week longer in return for the parental blessing."[5]

News of the impending visit probably evoked something less than enthusiasm at 27 Bank Street. Caroline Gordon Tate was unhappy with her output in New York: one unpublished novel, part of another, and two stories. "It is these young poets from the South," she wrote her friend Sally Wood, "they call us up as soon as they hit Pennsylvania Station and they stay anywhere from a week to a month. I have gotten bitter about it." She had gone through difficult times since their arrival in the fall of 1924. Her relationship with Tate was passionate but vexed. By early winter she had become pregnant, and though he had been reluctant to marry, he did propose—and she refused. He later told their daughter, Nancy, this was "because she had seen him with a beautiful woman in a restaurant as she walked by outside. She was very jealous and very proud." Laura Riding (no longer Gottschalk) had by this time returned to New York. She felt that Tate's attraction to her was another source of his and Caroline's problems, but they were married on May 15, 1925, and when Caroline came home from the hospital after Nancy's birth on September 23, Laura Riding carried the baby.[6]

Their lives were scarcely easier in the ensuing months. When Nancy Minor Meriwether Gordon came to stay with her daughter, she decided immediately that her granddaughter and namesake would be better off with her in Guthrie than with her parents in their Greenwich Village basement apartment. A month later, following the example of friends, they had moved to a remote New York State farmhouse sixty miles north of Manhattan near the Connecticut border. In less than frugal conditions they settled in to their work and invited the charming, volatile, deeply neurotic Hart Crane to share their place. He worked on *The Bridge,* Caroline worked on her fiction, and Allen completed the first draft of "Ode to the Confederate Dead." By March of 1926 the Tates and Crane were communicating by notes slipped under their doors. By late April Crane had left, and by fall Allen and Caroline were eager to move back to Manhattan, where they obtained the apartment at 27 Bank Street in return for Allen's services as janitor for the building.[7]

When Warren arrived at Bank Street, Cinina was with him. He had told the Tates he thought they would like her. She was a striking young woman with large blue eyes and almost black hair parted in the middle and drawn back severely into a bun. Her makeup was applied liberally to her oval face and pouting mouth. She presented a voluptuous appearance, dressed stylishly, and moved gracefully. Cherished in the protected environment of the Brescia home, she expected the attention she received when her father entertained his students and colleagues there. Emotional and voluble, with a high shrill laugh, she enjoyed conversation and particularly the chance to use her flawless and musical Italian.

Living in the midst of another family was new to her but familiar to these southern writers, who were used to having house guests, often for extended periods. This kind of hospitality was the rule, so that in traveling, even in middle life when many of them had moved from the South, they would stay with friends, rarely at hotels. There was a kind of natural intimacy here for Warren. To Tate he was comrade and protégé. To Caroline he was a family friend and fellow townsman. To bright and precocious Nancy Tate he was "Uncle Penn." Cinina, however, was possessive with Red, her cavalier, and called him "baby."

Later Caroline vented her frustration. "Our dear friend Red Warren descended on us this summer with his fiancee and here they stayed for six weeks," she wrote. "I, of course, got nothing done. The fiancee—her right name is Emma Cinina Elena Clotilda Maria Borgia Venia Gasparini Brescia—felt that she must live up to her descent from the Borgias and raised as much hell as she possibly could all the time. It wasn't so much because she is really rather a stolid soul but it was enough to keep either of us from doing a bit of work—except that once I elbowed them all out of the way and wrote a story in two sittings. I would have thrown her out of the window the first week but for my deep affection for Red. . . ."[8]

Warren stayed on in New York as the summer brought the culmination of one of the greatest causes célèbres in American jurisprudence: the Sacco–Vanzetti case. "I was mixed up in all that," he would later say, "because the Tate apartment was the headquarters of the protest committee." One of those who went to Boston to protest the imminent execution of the two Italian-born radicals was Katherine Anne Porter, a slim, petite, thirty-seven-year-old Texas-born writer. When she returned, Warren heard her tell her story of being arrested in the demonstration on the day of the execution. That summer would be fixed in his memory for many reasons, and he would later say that though he knew meeting Katherine Anne was an important event, there was no way for him to know that "the friendship thus beginning was to be one of the most treasured of my life, that her work was to be for me a deep and abiding joy. . . ."[9]

There were other memorable people and times that summer. From Tate's first residence in the city he had enjoyed going out with Crane and Malcolm Cowley and other friends such as Kenneth Burke, John Brooks Wheelwright, and Slater Brown. Cowley had admired Warren's poems and now welcomed him. "Here he was at last," Cowley remembered, "in person: tall, long-necked, angular, with a lot of curly red hair. He made abrupt gestures and seemed self-conscious except when telling a story in his low Kentucky voice." If he was self-conscious among these well-known writers, he was still a fundamentally gregarious twenty-two-year-old who had a talent for friendship. When Ford Madox Ford needed secretarial help he hired Caroline Gordon Tate and came to admire her fiction as well as her typing skills. With her, Ford, and Katherine Anne Porter, Warren found himself in a new kind of group. "I began to have a sense of the inside of fiction," he said later, "and began to get interested in fiction as an art form . . . these people would sit around and talk—the three artists of real quality—and sometimes some others too . . . I had a whole new view of fiction, like the Fugitives talking about poetry. . . . And there were also some big poets who were around, that mixed you up in a way that made you feel the relationship of the two forms. . . . So this was worth money . . . and I was getting it all for free."[10]

His horizons continued to widen. Paul Rosenfeld was a distinguished music and art critic who, with Lewis Mumford, Van Wyck Brooks, and Alfred Kreymborg, had just founded *The American Cara-*

van, which was to be an annual publication of American poetry and fiction. Invited to Rosenfeld's apartment, Warren was excited to hear about two writers he greatly admired—Sherwood Anderson and E. E. Cummings. Warren was struck by "the simplicity and generosity which made Rosenfeld sit up half the night and, without any hint of patronage or boredom, answer the dozens of questions which a boy would put to him." He showed Warren pictures and took him to exhibits, one by Georgia O'Keeffe, whose paintings, together with the photographs of her husband, Alfred Stieglitz, were changing the way people looked at the human form and human sexuality. He also took "At the Hour of the Breaking of the Rocks"—a part of the "Kentucky Mountain Farm" sequence—for *The American Caravan.*[11]

Now Warren was ready for the next step in his plan, to take the Yale fellowship and, if the Rhodes scholarship didn't come through, to stay on for the Ph.D. In early October Tate wrote Don Davidson that Warren was in New Haven in residence to take the Ph.D. in 1929.

It was the farthest north he had ever lived, in this 210-year-old university with its 1,200 teachers and 5,000 students, its 10 schools and almost 2 million library volumes. Perhaps his first reaction was like that of another young writer from the South, almost exactly six years before: "New Haven is beautiful this time of year, especially around the campus, with all the buildings of gray and white and faded pink stone absorbing sunlight, and all the trees scarlet and flame color." (This was William Faulkner, writing home to his mother in Oxford, Mississippi.)[12]

Warren had come at a good time. Seven years before, James Rowland Angell had been elected president. Emphasizing the importance of research, he had supported the appointment of outstanding scholars such as Tucker Brooke, Robert Menner, and Frederick Pottle in English, and George Pierce Baker was hired away from Harvard, where he had made his English 47 Workshop famous as a nurturer of dramatic talent. The recruitment of promising graduate students was also part of Angell's program, and Warren, with his Vanderbilt and Berkeley achievements, was one of them.[13]

Warren's reactions soon became mixed. "Time is at a premium with me," he wrote Don Davidson in late October, "for I am taking a pretty heavy course and have been doing some writing on the side." He would summarize the academic experience there, many years later, as "just a hell of a lot of hard work and two brilliant teachers of the four." Most impressive was the distinguished Tucker Brooke, whose Shakespeare seminar was "a wonderful experience," but there was a big drawback, as Tate relayed it to Davidson. "Brooke told him on sight: 'Now, young man, you must forget your own writing; you can't serve two masters.' Red is determined to stick it out and get his union-card emblazoned *Ph.D.*" But apparently he found no difficulty in disregarding Brooke's advice while admiring his learning. He must have received similar negative views, however, from Andrew Lytle, who had enrolled in the School of Drama the year before to study with Baker in the 47 Workshop, where he wrote and acted in several plays. He was quite ready by the next year to devote his energies to the University Players in Southampton, New York, and to act for twelve weeks in a Broadway play.[14]

Warren must have felt busier than he had been at Berkeley. Though he did not have to teach, he had taken the maximum course load, and he was writing book reviews through the good offices of Cowley and another new friend, Edmund Wilson. What pleased him much more was *The New Republic*'s acceptance, in one week, of "Garden Waters," "To One Awake," and "The Letter of a Mother," which would all appear in the first half of the next year. He was trying to get up enough Latin to pass the language examination, and he was applying himself to his course work.[15]

He kept one of his papers. "Garrick and the Plays of Shakespeare," written for Brooke's English 123, was a thoroughly professional performance. Work at this level had another value: enhancing his chances in another try for a Rhodes scholarship. He would win honors in three of his four courses. When he completed the Rhodes application, he was able to share the waiting process. Allen Tate was going for a Guggenheim Fellowship.[16]

By Christmas recess Warren was more than ready to get away from New Haven. But there was nothing to keep him in Guthrie. His relationship with his sister, Mary, was now more rather than less complicated. He would later say, "She had one of the most brilliant minds I ever encountered." But she was the victim of depleted family resources and contemporary ideas about education for women, and she felt it keenly. (When he was at Vanderbilt, Warren had arranged for Mary to do a review for Don Davidson's book page in the *Tennessean*. When he told her about it, "it was as if I had struck her with a stick.") As for his relationship with Ruth Warren, her possessive love would never alter, and her sense of the independence he was asserting could only have increased the tension of the visit. He later wrote Davidson,

"After being at home for two days [I] got my resolution to the point of catching the train." He stayed in California for three weeks.[17]

The western scene was a welcome change from the New England winter. "I loved that landscape so," he would later say. "I walked over so much of it." It was the only place that moved him so much that he felt the impulse to pick up the watercolor brushes he hadn't touched since his days at the Nashville zoo with Sister Mary Luke. And Cinina was there in San Francisco at the Brescias' home on Octavia Street. She was still studying Italian at Berkeley, and with the time she had lost to illness, it would be almost two more years before she would receive her degree.[18]

Whether or not their engagement had been announced, there was still no imminent prospect of marriage. "I told her from the start," he would later say, "that I wasn't going to consider matrimony until I had run through my list of travels." She had wanted him to stay and teach in California, but he did not want to find himself stuck there in whatever institution would hire him with just his Berkeley M.A. But he had every intention of continuing their relationship. When Andrew Lytle gave a party in a house whose owner was away, it grew so boisterous that a neighbor called the authorities, who responded with a riot squad of seven policemen. Lytle remembered a vignette: Warren sitting there—while the men and women milled about with their glasses of Prohibition gin—oblivious in his concentration, writing a letter to Cinina.[19]

Back in New Haven in early 1928, he answered Andrew's questions bluntly:

> I do not like Yale. . . . I do not feel the need of three-fourths of the stuff the *university* thinks I stand in need of. Yale Grad school is a school for teachers. It is a high-powered Peabody, which runs on the assumption that no one except a student who wants to learn scholarly method belongs here, and that all others are to be coerced into this regime or to be cast out and trodden under the foot of men. Of course it was nothing more nor less than sheer ignorance which brought me up here—and the fact that Vanderbilt cannot boast of a single professor . . . who might have been able to give me some idea of what I was getting into. Of course what I really wanted was to get in an environment where men were actually doing creative writing, but Yale is not the place for that, I learn too late.[20]

His sense of displacement was heightened by his fellow graduate students there in "the tombs of learning." To him they were "retarded." There were only two or three who knew his world. One was a student of literature named Randall Stewart. Another was a Texan named Dixon Wecter, who was "one of the most brilliant men I've ever known in my life." He told Lytle, "I am keeping up my verse writing," and added, "have written eight chapters—about 30,000 words on my novel—which I would like for you not to divulge too freely. . . ."[21]

His new verse continued to show the vitality of two recent poems—"At the Hour of the Breaking of the Rocks" in *The American Caravan* and "Rebuke of the Rocks" in *The Nation*. These dense and difficult poems, with their distanced panoramic view of "the little stubborn people of the hill" and the passage of "the lean men" through this forbidding landscape, were, he would later say, "a pure invention—I had never seen Eastern Kentucky—and little of East Tennessee." In "Pondy Woods" he used imagination again for a scene he had never witnessed: the flight of a black murderer from a posse. The tone and texture as well as the diction were now vastly different from the formal phrases and languid lines he had so often employed. Here,

> Big Jim Todd was a slick black buck
> Laying low in the mud and muck
>
> . . . .
> [until] down your track the steeljacket goes
> Mean and whimpering over the wheat.

The action is framed by the the observing buzzards, one of which speaks to the fugitive in tones both menacing and metaphysical:

> The Jew-boy died. The Syrian vulture swung
> Remotely above the cross whereon he hung. . . .

Writing to Tate, Warren said, "you have placed everything I have ever published; you might as well start an agency. . . . for if they do get printed it will most probably be due to you." Paul Rosenfeld took the poem for the *Second American Caravan*.[22]

It must have been mid–February when Warren learned there was more to celebrate. His Rhodes scholarship had come through. He visited the Tates in early February and often thereafter, celebrating with them. Not only did Allen get his Guggenheim Fellowship, his book of poems was accepted for publication that year. His *Stonewall Jackson, the Good Soldier: A Narrative* was due out in April, and he received a contract for a life of Jefferson Davis. *Fugitives: An Anthology of Verse* appeared to favorable reviews, and Mark Van Doren wrote in *The Nation* that they had "made a permanent contribution to American poetry."[23]

In late spring Warren wrote Bill Bandy that his time was "divided between meeting the demands of local slave drivers with bald heads and beards and making trips to New York." When Tate brought Lytle up to date on Warren he wrote, "Calamities still pursue him." Four months later Warren explained, "I wrecked the car in West Virginia, and bummed in to Nashville." He was leaving for California by way of Texas and could be reached care of Cinina, who was now living in an apartment in San Francisco.[24]

Apart from the time he spent with her in June and July, the summer afforded little letup, but it provided time for a new major project. Tate had recommended Warren to Mavis MacIntosh, a literary agent, and she had obtained for him the offer of a contract for a biography of the abolitionist John Brown for Payson and Clarke Ltd., who had taken chances on other young writers. Accepting it was "in a way, a question of homesickness," he would later say. "As long as I was *living* in Tennessee and Kentucky and knew a great deal about various kinds of life there from the way Negro field hands talked or mountaineers talked . . . I had no romantic notions about it." He had read widely in its past, and he had the vivid oral history provided by Grandpa Penn. "But this didn't seem to apply to the other half of my life, in which my sole passion was John Donne, John Ford, Webster's plays, Baudelaire. Then as soon as I *left* that world of Tennessee . . . I began to rethink the meaning . . . of the world I had actually been living in without considering it." He may not have been consciously aware of one operative element: the plays of John Webster and John Ford were characterized by violence—a taste for it would show increasingly in his own work—and it was there in John Brown's career. There was also a technical challenge: it constituted "an approach to fiction because it presented a psychological problem to deal with and the question of narrative." Moreover, his friends were writing biography. It would be good professionally to have a book in print, and there was also "the itch to write." When the contract was offered, he said, "I grabbed it."[25]

The summer was so busy that he fell behind in his correspondence, and in early July Tate passed the secondhand information on to Lytle that Cinina "gives the impression that she and Red are hunky-dory. I hope not, if I may put it in black and white. I guess my motive in the opposition is personal. We'll lose Red if he marries that girl." (Keenly aware of the bond between the two men, Lytle would later say, "What he meant was '*I'll* lose him.'") Warren's address, Tate added, was Cinina's.[26]

In early September Warren returned from a research trip to Harpers Ferry, Winchester, and Charlestown. (He had rendezvoused there with the Tates, loaded down with a tent and supplies for their own tour of Virginia battlefields. Andrew Lytle was there too in pursuit of Nathan Bedford Forrest.) Warren had spent a long time talking with the last living witness of John Brown's raid on the U.S. armory, and he had worked in the Yale library. Now he could see the shape of the book.[27]

By late September he was in New York, and then he hastened back to New Haven, where sailing time found him packing frantically. Andrew Lytle saw the approach of another of his "crises" and stepped in, and with another student's help, got him packed and onto the boat for England.[28]

10

❖

A Southerner at Oxford

But you, my friend . . . you do not praise at all,
Or praising, stop and seem to cast your eye
Toward some commensurate cold finality
That once you guessed, or dreamed, or read about.
There are some things you do not praise enough;
For instance now, the perilous stuff
Of your own youth. It is not long . . . beneath
The door, the wind . . . the candle gone black out.
It is an arrogance to save your breath
Until the time when, self-possessed, you stand
With measured approbation where await,
In darkling kindliness, the bored and bland
Incurious angels of the nether gate.
— *"For a Self-Possessed Friend"*[1]

Balliol College had a great many applications and was unable to take him, but New College—also one of the oldest and very well endowed—accepted him as a probationary student to come into residence for the new term commencing October 11. He was moving now to a venerable institution whose medieval roots had grown and flowered into the environment that provided what he now most wanted: time to read and write and reflect with as little institutional interference as possible.[2]

Because he was a late arrival in Oxford, he was put with five others in a house for overflow students. They had drafty bedrooms high upstairs where they could see light coming down from the chimney where snow could also descend. But they shared an enormous sitting room downstairs, and there were "scouts" to attend to their needs. He would have to go to the porter at the college gate to get his mail, but because of the location of his residence, he would not have to go through the gate to get out of the college, which would be something of a convenience.

His reactions were mixed. "New College has the temperature of an ice house," he wrote Lytle, "rooms, dining hall, chapel, can, library. The whole institution exists at something approximating the absolute zero." The English beer was making his wits thick, he wrote, like those of most of the gentlemen scholars, but he liked them. As for the women, he thought them so "generally ugly and uninviting" that patriotism must be the reason why men begot sons for the empire. "There is some good company, tobacco (pretty bad), drink, books, and dulness. Great dulness. Rain. There is something like a narcotic effect about the whole dump, which is rather pleasant in its total effect."[3]

He was delighted at the Tates' arrival, but the next morning Allen felt so bad that they took the noon train back to London. "It was the flu," he later explained to Lytle; "the miasmal airs of the place, the moment we got off the train, struck me down." He added that Red "looked disconsolate but stoical. I don't think he likes Oxford, but he will as time goes on. He is already instructing the innocent Britons in the manly art of poker, and I infer that their living will shortly be his." The Tates returned to Oxford at the end of the month, Caroline to try to finish her novel, *Penhally,* already three years in the writing, and Allen to work on his book.[4]

Warren began to learn more about his principal place of residence for the next two or three years, founded in 1379 to replenish the ranks of the clergy. Five and a half centuries later, having weathered the Reformation and civil war, social change and institutional reform, the college had altered greatly. For one scholar New College was "the almost exclusive preserve of the English ruling class, a kind of pheasantry in which the products of the English public schools were reared like game birds." But another graduate remembered how, with "the magic of the college garden enclosed in the ancient city walls, the bookshops, the walks in the town and the country outside, and Bach and Palestrina in the chapel after hall on Sunday evenings, I lived almost as in an earthly paradise and took comparatively little thought for the morrow."[5]

Warren and his fellow Rhodes scholars differed from most other New College students, overwhelmingly undergraduates, for reasons other than nationality. They were a small group. One of Warren's new friends, Herbert Woodman, had come the previous year to study jurisprudence. When Woody sailed, there were only about twenty-five in all, just a handful of American graduate students in the colleges where they enrolled. They wore the commoners' gowns and ate in Hall with their English colleagues, but beyond that and the differing academic programs, the extent of their immersion in English college and university life was much a matter of individual choice. Warren would be more selective than most.[6]

He could go on in stages for the B.Litt. degree if the faculty board found him promising. During the first year the student received instruction in archival and textual research to equip him to read Chaucerian and Shakespearean manuscripts and even to set type. By the end of the first year he would start on scholarly research for a thesis and finally defend it in an oral examination. With the permission of the board he could then pursue the D.Phil. degree with a dissertation that was "an original contribution to knowledge set forth in such a manner as to deserve publication." This would require at least a third Rhodes scholarship year. Tate told Donald Davidson, "Red is curious but not yet happy. . . ."[7]

Though the crucial figure would be his supervisor, another faculty member would also be assigned to him. "I have a moral tutor," Warren informed Lytle. "He's a real person and that's his real title . . . 'moral tutor.' He called me up to him and gave me several items of advice. . . ." The first was "not to run into debt." (Warren would have done well to heed him.) Oxford dons often tended to be eccentric. Some were also witty and generous. Warren had no such luck in his supervisor. He got Percy Simpson. Fellow of Oriel for seven years now and immensely learned, Simpson had published six enormously scholarly studies in drama including one called *Shakespeare's Punctuation.* A sixty-three-year-old expert on archival and textual research, he was a stunningly incompetent thesis supervisor. When Warren arrived at Simpson's rooms he was abruptly asked, "Are you Australian or American?" At his reply, Simpson said, "I must tell you something. No American has ever distinguished himself with us." The harangue went on, Warren remembered, for the rest of the hour. He left with a dim view of what lay before him.[8]

But he settled in to college life. His paneled bedroom, innocent of plumbing, was furnished with a washbowl, a pitcher, a slop jar, and a chamber pot. The pleasant coal fire took the chill off the room, but one had to go down the staircase, out across the quadrangle, and through a passage to the unheated "rears" to reach the baths and toilets. Every morning the scout would make his rounds to each room on his stair, pouring hot water into the pitcher, lighting the fire, and opening the curtains. Far more essential to students than their moral tutors, the scout would clean the rooms, serve lunch or tea for guests in the sitting room, and wait table for dinner in Hall. Like most members of the college, Warren and Woodman donned their gowns to dine in Hall, a magnificent medieval structure with oak linen-fold paneling and long oak tables that often bore silver tankards and platters. Woody would remember "lots of pork and mutton, overcooked vegetables (pale grey Brussels sprouts, cabbage, carrots, potatoes), dreary kedgerees, and some kind of pudding such as a greyish blanc mange." Student guests at High Table might be asked to join the dons for coffee in the senior common room, where a cheerful fire blazed. Warren was occasionally invited to dine at High Table.[9]

Despite his early reaction to the gentlemen scholars, he made friends among them but found no appeal in group activities. Writing and reading a good deal of poetry, he visited the Poetry Society only once or twice. "I just soaked myself in Elizabethan poetry," he remembered, "in sixteenth and seventeenth century poetry." His own new poems showed that influence. And he was still writing John Brown's biography, working from the materials he had brought with him and books in the American history library.[10]

One of his friends, Chaumont Pierre de Villiers, was going to drive to Paris and the Riviera during the Christmas holidays, and he invited Warren to go with him. He gladly accepted, looking forward to seeing the Tates, and there in the quarter on the Left Bank he would learn more about their growing acquaintance among the makers of contemporary writing. Warren had written Lytle that "Allen gave me a detailed account of Eliot and his henchmen; he was greatly impressed by the leader of the gang, more than he expected to be, and likes some of the others."[11]

The Tates were staying in rooms Ford Madox Ford had reserved for them at the Hôtel de Fleurus. For two days Warren would share the second floor with Allen, Caroline, and Nancy. They took him to some of their favorite places—the Dôme, the Rotonde, and other popular cafés. Through Kenneth Burke, Allen had met a West Virginian named John Peale Bishop who had been at Princeton with Edmund Wilson and Scott Fitzgerald. Bishop had succeeded Wilson as editor of *Vanity Fair* and also published his own poems and essays. Now living with his wealthy wife in a château near Paris, he felt uprooted and unfulfilled. Tate went to meet him in the city and took Warren along. They spent a pleasant evening over a bottle of scotch at a café in the Rue Mignard. It was more than that to Bishop. It was from that evening, with their comments on the poems he shyly showed them, he wrote Tate much later, that he began to feel that he could still make his mark as a poet. Tate's aid and encouragement were such that Bishop knew he owed "what is little less than my life to you."[12]

One encounter during that December visit was unexpected and, in its way, shocking. As Warren described it years later, "I had dinner with Mr. and Mrs. John Peale Bishop . . . the Tates, and Scott Fitzgerald (Mrs. Fitzgerald had canceled out for some mysterious reason, half nuts anyway). After dinner we began to go cafe-crawling. I had been having a very fine time talking with Fitzgerald. Finally, he asked me to walk to his apartment and see how Zelda was. I went, but as we approached he became glummer and glummer. He asked me to go upstairs with him to the apartment. No more conversation. We got nearly to his floor, a winding stair, when he turned and ordered me to stand right there. He knocked on the door, and Zelda came out. Then began a ghastly cat-dog fight. I had to witness it, having been ordered to stay there. Finally she slammed the door, and he came down and said, 'Let's go.' No conversation all the way back. But once seated he began to take on a load and became talkative. I got around to saying something that I admired about *Gatsby*. It touched off an explosion, 'Don't even mention that book' (or that's the substance) 'to me again, you bastard'—or son-of-a-bitch or something of that sort. I got up and opined that I didn't have to take that off him or anybody, seized my coat, and stalked out. Next day I got a pneumatique from him full of apologies, begging me to 'understand' the strain he was under, or something like that. Anyway, all friendship. I learned later about his domestic troubles, and that he couldn't write, and the mention of the old success drove him nuts. I never saw him again."[13]

With Warren and de Villiers off to the Mediterranean, Tate resumed work. At four o'clock in the afternoon of the first day of winter, having written twenty-five lines of poetry since breakfast, he began a letter to Lytle as the waiter at the Café du Dôme brought him his first absinthe-based *amer picon avec citron* of the day. He wondered if it was intended "that their friend Warren should be crucified by the necessity to make a living? For such, when I last saw Red a week ago . . . was the lugubrious cast of his mind. . . . Red is, in short, about to toss the sponge high in the air and become a professor. . . . I should be sad for Red's sake were it not for the reflection that his dedication to the Academy has been inspired by the culture of the Far West. . . ." (This was probably an ironic reference to Cinina's hope that Warren would take a teaching job in California.) Meanwhile, de Villiers and Warren had driven east along the Côte d'Azur, stopped briefly at Cannes, and gone on.[14]

It was the end of January 1929 before Tate heard from him again, in a jocular, almost manic letter after one of his extended furious bursts of energy. "I have been to five cocktail parties, two theatre parties, four dinners, one shooting party, five poker games, and to church since my return to Oxford; furthermore, I have written an astonishing amount of J.B., read half a dozen novels, three books on America, *The Demon of the Absolute,* Zola's *Therese Raquin,* and the comic sections of the New York *American.*" But he also said that he had suffered a collapse and "begun to take a certain pleasure in the fact, for, in one sense, it seems to relieve me of any further responsibility. Also, the poker has given me a very pleasant profit of about five pounds, which helps me over an excessively lean term." He mentioned no new poems but confessed that "as the sheets pile up, I become more and more humble and distressed on the subject of biography. I reread and revise and the more I do those things the flatter the thing seems to become. God help me."[15]

He made a two-day trip to London with Dixon Wecter, who was living in Merton College and was "the best company in Oxford and a sterling fellow. . . ." Warren went with him and two hundred other Rhodes scholars invited to the viscountess Astor's ball in spite of feeling "like hell" and being so low on funds that he didn't dare to take a drink. The five weeks between Hilary term and Trinity term would leave him free until late April. "I am staying in Oxford because the library is here and because I can work with absolutely no distraction," he wrote Tate. But there was another reason: "She, also, is remaining in Oxford to work in the library. When the library closes we work elsewhere. I got her over her college gate last night but myself I could not save."[16] He had gotten the unnamed lady into her college after the nine o'clock gate closing, but his own tardiness would cost him a small fine to the porter at his gate to New College. "I expect a notice from the authorities today or tomorrow which will probably cost me something unless I squared things better with the porter than I now believe."

But he had not squared things well at all. "They have me on several counts, I'm afraid, including late entry into college, having an unchaperoned young lady in my rooms and being in Oxford for a night without reporting my presence to the college authorities. . . . I guess they'll stick me some sort of fine. Thank God it didn't occur in term, or I would be in a bad shape. However, I don't think I could get very worried if they sent me down. If they decide to do that I'll give them something to send me down for before I leave."[17]

It was as if he was repeating the pattern that had gotten him into trouble with the Berkeley police and the English department. But what had led him into this escapade with "one of the Daughters of Britain" when he and Cinina Brescia had "an understanding"? At the end of January Lytle had written Tate a letter with a cryptic allusion, apparently to a cooling on Cinina's part. Anything in her letters suggesting a change of heart might have increased the attractiveness of this unusual daughter of Britain.

Two weeks after being summoned to see the college disciplinary officer, he was living in town, "for I had to move out for about a week around Easter and decided when that time was up that it would be more convenient all around for me to remain here." The first college report had pronounced him "widely read" and "respected by a small circle." The second called him "retiring and shy." The warden of Rhodes House declared, "He is not exactly the kind of ideal Rhodes Scholar of whom we sometimes think [but] I think that we may be glad in the future to claim Warren as an old Rhodes Scholar for he is certainly a man of ability and character." But now his Rhodes House file card bore the brief notation "(kicked out of college.)" In any event, he must have wanted his personal life as relatively unfettered as his academic life had been.[18]

Tate was concerned enough to write him in the tones of an older brother, and Warren subsequently reassured him that his remarks "were not presumptuous" and that there was "no idea of the sort you specify in the bottom of my mind; I do my mental and spiritual housecleaning as often as possible and whatever of that sort ever existed has long since found its way into the incinerator."[19]

Warren's new housemates, Evelyn Norie and Jay Birkbeck, were nonintellectual "hearties," athletes and beer-drinkers. To Woodman they were "rowdy and noisy and fun to be around." The sons of well-placed army families, "they were the type that would scale the formidable barbed wire or broken-glass topped walls to get back into college after nine o'clock to avoid being caught." They shared comfortable digs at 3 Wellington Square, ten minutes by bicycle from New College. The bedrooms were upstairs, and downstairs was the big sitting room where they would gather by the fireplace. They played poker, usually in Red's rooms—one-eyed jacks for small stakes—and dined together in Hall. To Woody, Red Warren was quite different from these companions. Lean, with a kind of craggy look, he would often just stand and watch—interested, speculative, and sardonic, making "very sharp comments" on what he saw.[20]

He was working now on several poems. The native materials he was using for the Brown biography may have entered into one of them, which suggested "Pondy Woods" though it focuses on love rather than death. It follows a pair of young Negro lovers to Vinegar Hill, the Negro cemetery, where they spend the night, and their lovemaking even imparts a little spark of warmth to the dead who watch them. (It was unmistakably Squiggtown, where Guthrie's blacks lived.) He continued at his labors steadily. "I work until four every day, then paddle a canoe up the river, have some tea at an inn, and return in time for dinner. I amuse myself in the early hours of darkness and return to college at ten-thirty, and work for two more hours. I am getting an incredible amount of work done under this regime." By April, however, the pace had slowed. "More difficulties about J.B. develop all the time, but I hope to be finished soon." Waiting impatiently for a visit from Warren, Tate told Lytle, "The reason for the delay seems to be, in his own words, 'one of the daughters of Britain.' "[21]

By the time he arrived in Paris, his host was too sick with the flu to read more than a third of the John Brown manuscript, but he wrote Lytle, "I am all applause. It's a great piece of work—very deceptive at first glance. . . . but very soon you are amazed at the subtlety of the presentation. . . . It's going to be a great book." At last, feeling somewhat better, Tate was able to go out with Warren to a party given by Stella Bowen, Ford Madox Ford's ex-wife, where one of the guests was Ezra Pound. Warren knew some of his work and was aware of his reputation, but he derived no particularly striking impression of him.[22]

Warren was no sooner back in Oxford than he was engaged in several tasks, one of them involving another of his periodic crises. He first tried to help Tate, who desperately needed several books—diaries and memoirs chiefly—to "fill in local color and scenes" in his Jefferson Davis biography. A more pressing problem arose from his having disregarded his moral tutor's first injunction: he had gotten into debt. He borrowed from Wecter and other friends and loaned some of the money to Tate. (By his calcuations, he now owed Tate only fourteen shillings.) "I had no idea that my affairs were in such a sad state," he told him. Though he was now studying at his fourth institution of higher learning, he had not yet improved his skills in managing money.[23]

There was one darker bit of information, which signaled a recrudescence of a more serious problem: "My eyes are giving me hell. I read for a bit and everything goes blotto. I'm seeing a specialist some time this week." Apprehensive, he wrote, "Something tells me that I should finish J.B. first—if I'm to do it with a clear conscience." He supplied no information after the medical consultation, but he did change his plans for the summer. He would delay his work toward his B.Litt. thesis and find the money for a return to America. Two notations on his card at Rhodes House summed up his situation: "Eyes bad—Summer 1929" was one. "Home—Long Vac. 1929" was the other.[24]

11

❖

Contracts—Secret
and Otherwise

But, backward heart, you have no voice to call
Your image back, the vagrant image again.
The tree, the leaf falling, the stream, and all
Familiar faithless things would yet remain
Voiceless. And he, who had loved as well as most,
Might have foretold it thus, for well he knew
How, glimmering, a buried world is lost
In the water's riffle or the wind's flaw;
How his own image, perfect and deep
And small within loved eyes, had been forgot,
Her face being turned, or when those eyes were shut
Past light in that fond accident of sleep.

—*"The Return"*[1]

He stopped in New York for two days, hoping to satisfy the option clause in his John Brown contract for his next book with a volume of his poems—being more eager to see the poems in print than to meet his contractual obligation—but Joseph Brewer replied that the present was not the best market for poems. But since the biography of John Brown had been set in type, Brewer authorized a check for two hundred dollars. When Warren tried the Viking Press, they declined the poems too.

His stopover in Nashville was disappointing, for the brethren who made up "the family" were all out of town, and Guthrie was sweltering in mid-July. So he left to spend two months in San Francisco. It was a happy return. "Cinina is bouncing with health now and in good spirits," he would tell Tate when he reported on the summer. "She finished college and has a good job as instructor in Spanish and Italian." She was still writing poetry and fiction, with her sense of self-worth enhanced by her faculty status at Mills College. Moreover, during his absence she had not lacked the male attention that was so necessary to her.[2]

He had changed more than she. He still had the earlier youthful exuberance, the ideas coming out in a rush that taxed the hearer's comprehension, but most of his naiveté had disappeared. He was physically mature, with his capacity for swimming and hiking and ac-complishing more in twenty-four hours than most men could. He would always have the face of the freckled redhead, but it had filled out now to fit his strong skull and bone structure, producing what Woody had called that craggy quality. And if he felt anxious or de-pressed with the recurrent eye problems, there was nothing in his strong-jawed face to make him look maimed.

Any trouble signs such as those in Cinina's letters—the ones An-drew Lytle had feared would be "hard on Red"—had apparently dis-appeared. Their understanding had continued. But his writing income was likely to remain small, hardly enough to finance a mar-riage, though Cinina probably reasoned that she could supplement it as a teacher and translator. But there were other questions. What of a third Rhodes scholarship year? If he married, he would immediately forfeit any possibility. If he continued, he could do all, or almost all, of the work for a D.Phil. Or he could return to Yale, where the En-glish department expected him to complete another year of study. If he stopped with his California M.A. and his Oxford B.Litt., what sort of job could he expect? Ever since Vanderbilt he had felt there was no place more beautiful, and no place more right for him, than middle Tennessee. But Vanderbilt, like most other established universities, was now hiring Ph.D.'s in preference to M.A.'s. He and Cinina would have to wait.[3]

He had now been a college and university student for eight straight years, and he must have felt some impulse toward change. Ruth Penn Warren had been the strongest force in his life until his middle teens. Since then, one of his major psychic efforts had been to free himself from the claims of that relationship. Volatile and emotional, Cinina was obviously different from quiet, firm Ruth Warren. But Cinina shared one thing with her: she too wanted to dominate. He chafed at authority, as his various disciplinary difficulties demonstrated. He was brilliant and analytical but at times emotional and impulsive. This may have been one of those times. With or without planning—only they knew—they went to Sacramento and got married.[4]

When they returned to San Francisco they announced their elopement to the Brescias and he moved in, to stay there with Cinina until it was time for his departure. Why had they done it? When a friend asked, many years later, if there were any special circumstances that led to their marriage, he replied, "Do you mean, was she pregnant?" When the other assented, he said, "No. I was stuck on her." One of his attributes, all his friends agreed, was that he was a gentleman despite the problems with overdue loans and books and violated rules. One person who would come to know him better than anyone else would use a hard-to-translate French word, *pudeur:* a quality encompassing decency and modesty. Like so many others of his generation, especially among his class of southerners, he placed a high valuation on the concept of honor, and he would not complain to others about intimate relationships.[5]

Because the terms of the fellowship prohibited marriage, it would have to be secret at least until he finished the next year and earned his Oxford B.Litt. Then they could have another ceremony. He would have the degree, and no one would ever need know. Allen Tate had faithfully kept Warren's secrets before, but this time, apparently, Warren entrusted the secret to none but Cinina's family. It would be many years before he would confide it, and then only to close friends. He must have known how Tate and Lytle felt about Cinina. Warren's journey west in 1925 was to Lytle "a fateful trip." No one could say that he and Cinina had rushed into marriage, but as with any elopement, questions would remain. Much later Tate would tell Lytle that Cinina got him to marry her by telling him that she was pregnant— when actually she was not. Lytle's version had one variation: the man responsible for the supposed pregnancy was not Warren. But now the newlyweds had the rest of the summer for a secret honeymoon, and then they would have to manage the secrecy and separation for at least another year.[6]

By mid-September he was "getting broker and broker daily." But he regretted the summer's end. "Between Cinina and the Civil War I have had two very agreeable occupations for the past two months," he told Tate. He had put Cinina to work arranging the John Brown bibliography. "In all justice, I must say that she did it very efficiently. There have been some good trips too, back into the mountains. One to a friend's quicksilver mine out beyond hell-and-gone; the mine is on the edge of a tremendous lake—twenty-five miles long—and the mountains all about to break straight down to the water." It was a splendid visit, and he could have stayed there in "perfect happiness."[7]

"The plan, at least at present," was "for Cinina to come to England next June, when we shall be married. Then we'll spend a time in France and Italy, studying the languages of those two countries and Latin, and reading as much of the literature as possible. We'll probably hang about a continental university for a time—though God knows I'm pretty sick of universities. When I finish Oxford in June I'll probably be sicker still." He did not say how they would finance this dream. They seemed caught up in joyful planning and anticipation of a formal wedding. He wished that Lytle and Tate could be present in Oxford to sustain him and "to indulge in the preliminary drinking." He mentioned only one financial consideration at the end of his hopeful letter. It was about library books. He had nineteen charged out, and they were accruing fines every day.[8]

This time when he arrived in Nashville the brethren were there. In 1926, less than a year after John T. Scopes was tried in Dayton, Tennessee, for teaching the doctrine of evolution, Tate had proposed to Ransom a "Southern Symposium" in which they would argue their stand on many of the issues involved. Though the members of the group remained busy with their teaching, studying, and writing, this project occupied much of their correspondence and conversations during the next two years. Lytle had advocated "the formation of a society, something like the *Action Francaise* group," which "should announce a whole religious, philosophical, literary and social program, anti-industrial on the negative side, and all that implies, and, on the positive, authoritarian, agrarian, classical, and aristocratic." Warren was ready to come in with them. "The Nashville brothers," he told Tate, "are on fire with crusading zeal and the determination to lynch carpet baggers."[9]

But then the eye trouble flared up again as he noticed the damaged eye "swinging out of orbit." The doctors concluded that something was "poisoning" his eyes. They reduced the possible causes to his teeth or his tonsils and removed the tonsils. If there was no improvement by winter he would have to undergo a "risky" operation in London, which would involve "cutting on the eye muscles." For the present, there was nothing to do but wait. He was still looking ahead to the year on the Continent, in France and Italy, and this plan had probably helped to wring a future concession from Cinina. "She is at least resigned to the idea of a rural life," he told Tate. "We would like very much to settle in your neighborhood, somewhere south of the M. and D., and watch the seasons, read, write, talk, play cards, and raise vegetables."[10]

In New York he went to dinner with Edmund Wilson, who had written, a year before on the publication of the *Fugitive* anthology, that Warren was "one of the most interesting young poets who have recently appeared on the scene." Another meeting in New York would be more productive. Having published "Kentucky Mountain Farm: At the Hour of the Breaking of the Rocks" two years before in *The American Caravan,* Paul Rosenfeld was interested in seeing more of his work. Rosenfeld listened carefully when he began to talk about other Kentucky materials that might serve as the basis for fiction rather than poetry.[11]

Behind schedule now, Warren made another harried departure on October 5. "I lost my wallet," he wrote Tate, "along with most of my money on shipboard and I thought for a while that I would have to get a job as a dock-hand at Southampton. But the last two days I developed a poker game, and held a *straight flush in spades to the king!* I stepped off the boat with eleven pounds clear profit on the voyage. The limit was low or I would have been a millionaire."[12]

Back in Oxford's mild English autumn, he searched for thesis topics. Crotchety old Percy Simpson rejected the first two he suggested, and he rejected one Simpson suggested. In December they agreed on John Marston, an early seventeenth-century satirist and dramatist. Now he could concentrate on the examinations.

By the middle of the first week of December he had finished all of them and felt more relaxed. He had been able to go shooting with a friend named Karri-Davies on his family's estate at Wytham Abbey. He finished Tate's *Jefferson Davis, His Rise and Fall: A Biographical Narrative* and thought it much better than his Jackson biography. And there were other kinds of relaxation. "I played poker last night and drank too much and I'm quite tuckered out; I won two pounds ten and a sore throat." (The drinking was a part of the public persona he had acquired in spite of a notation on his card at Rhodes House that he had not mixed enough with other students.) Cleanth Brooks, after a year's graduate work at Tulane University, arrived that fall of 1929 to enter Exeter College as a Rhodes scholar from Louisiana. In his room he found a note from Warren telling him to look him up. When he went to Wellington Square, Warren welcomed him warmly in his comfortable digs, where a framed portrait photograph of Cinina stood on his dresser.[13]

By December Warren had eaten enough "blue mutton and pale sprouts" as well as kidney pie and cauliflower. "I shall take the bull by the horns," he wrote Allen Tate, "tell John Marston to go to hell for a time, and get train and boat to Paris shortly before Christmas. . . ." Bill Bandy was there with his bride, Alice, immersing himself in French literature. They were living in a Left Bank hotel apartment in Rue Jacob, and they invited Warren to sleep on their sofa. After feasting on the foods and wines he had dreamed about in Oxford, he would recite poetry, having more by heart than anybody Bill had ever known. At night the Bandys heard him reciting lines until he dropped off to sleep. When he woke in the morning Bill heard him resume right where he had left off.[14]

He saw much of the Tates, who were living in a small two-room suite on the third floor of the Hôtel de l'Odéon. Caroline especially loved Paris. She had gotten a good deal done on her novel, and they had made a number of friends. To Tate's surprise, Ernest Hemingway had proved gossipy and charming. He and his wife Pauline were staying nearby, and the Tates and Hemingways saw much of each other. There was one fine party for which Ford Madox Ford made the punch from his grandfather's recipe at double strength. Hemingway took Warren with him to the bicycle races at the Vélodrome d'Hiver. He also took him home to meet Pauline and their son, Patrick. Hemingway had helped Ernest Walsh with his magazine, *This Quarter*, and now Walsh accepted Warren's "Tryst on Vinegar Hill," to appear in the issue for January-February of 1930. The following July-August number carried his forty-nine-line poem entitled "Empire." These were appearances at decent rates in prominent company.[15]

The Tates were planning to find a spot in the South where they could live and work in the company of their friends, with a place for Warren and Cinina nearby. Donald Davidson had become one of the most enthusiastic planners, and he was still eager to produce the Southern Symposium. With the year about to end and the Tates due to arrive in New York in the first week of 1930, Davidson reported a series of conferences in which he, Ransom, and Lytle were working "on a sort of Credo or Manifesto" that might develop into "a program of provincialism in general . . . and with it all the values that belong to a country life." Warren had agreed to write one of the essays, though it would be the better part of a year before he could join them in the home country where these former Fugitives would take their stand.[16]

When the first review of *John Brown: The Making of a Martyr* had appeared in mid-November, the author was immediately identified as a southern partisan. He had wanted to call the book *John Brown's Body,* but Stephen Vincent Benét took the phrase for the epic poem he published in 1927. Because Warren had attempted to analyze, not mythologize, his subject, his conclusions were much more critical. In his "Bibliographical Note" he wrote that most of the early accounts of Brown's career were defenses by interested parties. Writers such as Oswald Garrison Villard neglected "one of the most significant keys to John Brown's character; his elaborate psychological mechanism for justification which appeared regularly in terms of the thing which friends called Puritanism and enemies called fanaticism." The man would not be understood until the totality of his life was understood, including his last month in prison, "for though he now wielded the 'sword of the spirit' he was still the same man" who committed base acts, "embezzled the money of the woolen mills, [and] slaughtered and stole in Kansas. . . . Such an understanding is the final aim of this book." Moving in his restless life from one failure to another, Brown was characterized by "superb energy, honesty and fraud, chicanery, charity, thrift, endurance, cruelty, conviction, murder and prayer. . . ." This was the complex figure Warren had undertaken to analyze. The bibliography and the rest of the apparatus in the near-five-hundred-page book were scholarly, but the texture of the narrative was more than that, for it involved the invention of dialogue based on historical sources, the imaginative attempt to penetrate the psychological depths of this complex character, and the shaping of the story for maximum dramatic effect and rhetorical persuasion. It was a remarkable performance for a poet who had begun the work at twenty-two and completed it at twenty-four.[17]

When Warren wrote Davidson he told him, "The reviews which I have received so far have been about equally divided between vicious attacks and large praise; and I don't know which is preferable under the circumstances." The verdicts tended to split along regional lines, but Warren might well have felt vindicated by one review in particular. Writing in *The New Republic,* the distinguished historian Allan

Nevins, a northerner, praised Warren's weighing of the evidence and his attempt to render impartial judgment, concluding that "Mr. Warren's book is notable for its interpretation of the last act in the grim fanatic's life." Another comment that must have pleased him came in a review-essay by the editor of the *American Mercury*. "It is a capital piece of work," wrote H. L. Mencken, "careful, thorough and judicious—and its merits are not diminished by the somewhat surprising fact that its author is but twenty-five years old." For Mencken it was also one of the ten best books of the year.[18]

Has *John Brown: The Making of a Martyr* withstood the test of time? Subsequent commentators have been chiefly admirers of Warren's mature work, and so there has been much more agreement among them than there was among the reviewers. These critics have been less concerned, however, with the book as historical biography than with the ways in which it foreshadows Warren's philosophical attitudes toward history and the thematic interests to be elaborated in his fiction. One such link was provided by a tableau: John Brown and Ralph Waldo Emerson together in Concord as the guests of Henry David Thoreau. About Emerson and Transcendentalism Warren wrote, "He spent his life trying to find something in man or nature which would correspond to the fine ideas and the big word. In John Brown, Emerson thought he had found his man." Warren saw the apotheosis of Emerson's wrongheadedness in his characterization of the insurrectionist as "the new saint awaiting his martyrdom . . . who, if he shall suffer, will make the gallows glorious like the cross." For the rest of Warren's life, Emerson would be anathema to him.[19]

The concerns emerging in this book would later surface full-blown: the social misanthrope and the complex interaction of idealism and the temptation of power. This work—which held for him in a foreign land a "sentimental appeal and an attempt to relive something"—was also "an approach to fiction because it presented a psychological problem to deal with and the question of narrative." And as Ransom had told him, it proved something. Looking back later he would realize that "once you sit down and write a long book all the way through . . . you know you can do it. You know you can suffer through it."[20]

12

❖

Fiction, Faction, and an Oxford Degree

Just beyond the bridge the house could be seen, and farther down the sweep of land toward the river, the bulk of the firing barn. The smoke stood up from its roof in thin unperturbed plumes and lay over the fields like the faintest strata of mist. In the middle of the nearest field stood a wagon, deserted after the day's work. Not a breath of wind stirred, and everywhere hung the scent of burning.

— *"Prime Leaf"*[1]

It was a long leap from John Brown to John Marston, and Warren grew bored with the thesis. Then he received a cable from Paul Rosenfeld asking him to write a novelette for *The American Caravan* using stories he had told about Kentucky. He had grown up with the lore of the Black Patch War. Grandpa Penn had dabbled in the tobacco growers' association, but when he saw where it would lead— to burning the crops of men who sold to the buyers instead of holding firm against them—he had said, "No, I will not join." He had received letters threatening to burn his barns, but he had publicly warned that if anybody came out to his place somebody would be killed. He would be ready for them, and he added, "My daughter can shoot like a man." Warren had made all his notes on Marston's plays and Marston criticism, and so he worked on the thesis by day and the novelette by night.[2]

John Brown's life had made Warren look back at his own origins and his homeland. Both that work and this new one carried "great emotional charges" for him. The writing gave him a "free feeling," he remembered, "the sense of seeing something fresh," and he began to feel "a vague nostalgia" for that world he had left behind. "I made up a story about a family," he would recall, "a Southern farm family like my own people. . . ."[3]

They were the three generations of the Hardin family—the grandfather, his son and daughter-in-law, and their son, Tommy—modeled on the family constellation of those summers in Christian County. But the relationship between grandfather Joe Hardin and his son, Big Thomas, foreshadowing future father-son relationships in Warren fiction, is marked by conflict rather than closeness. Powerful and opinionated, Joe Hardin is one of the directors of the tobacco growers' organization, but when its chairman, Bill Hopkins, plans intimidation and barn-burning to compel the farmers to hold to an agreed price for their crops, Hardin declares that he will resign rather than take part in the violence he knows will follow. Big Thomas Hardin, always at odds with his father, has followed him into the association against his better judgment, and now he sees only disaster from his father's resigning but angrily follows his lead once more. When night riders begin burning the barns of recalcitrant growers, the Hardins' is one of the first to go. Big Thomas shoots one of the night riders, who, it turns out later, is Bill Hopkins. Persuaded by his father to give himself up, Big Thomas is ambushed. In the last scene, Tommy is called home from the schoolroom by his grieving mother.

The 25,000-word narrative gave Warren a chance to develop his skills. The physical world of southern Kentucky is evoked with vivid sensory detail and poetic imagery. At the same time, the realistic description encompasses symbolic scenes, as when a cruising chicken hawk is knocked from the sky by a shotgun blast. The dialogue ranges from the colloquial speech of the farmers to the dialect of the black farmhands. Thematically the story prefigures future fiction in the clash of wills, in family dynamics, in the conflict of ideas and groups producing civil discord and violence, and in the exploration of moral and political issues against the background of history. He called it "Prime Leaf." The writing taught him much and affected his attitude toward his future.

As spring came he was ready for a change of scene. He had hiked to the Channel and seen the white cliffs. Now he and Andrew Corry, another Rhodes scholar, took a week and, starting in Cornwall, walked back eastward along that rugged coast, eating in farmhouses and sleeping in inns. But on his return he had to deal with another piece of writing. In January Ransom had written him, "We have been counting on you as one of the faithful. . . . Haven't you a burning message on the subject of ruralism as the salvation of the negro? or this, that, or the other?" A month later, Warren told Davidson he would like to write "the essay on the negro."[4]

But he began with something less than enthusiasm. "The negro is a delicate subject and one which could be most easily attacked," he wrote the Tates, "Consequently, for my own good and the good of others, I can't afford to pull a boner in dealing with it." Warren would remember "the jangle and wrangle of writing the essay and some kind of discomfort in it, some sense of evasion . . . in contrast with the free feeling of writing the novelette." One of the sources of the Southern Literary Renaissance was the impact upon a whole generation of their return home after exposure not just to Europe but also to the whole milieu of the literary avant garde. Friends such as Tate would remain receptive to the experimental, but this openness did not always extend to areas of thought and feeling. On Warren's return home later that year, he would realize that "certain friends of mine, like Davidson, became more *frozen* in their opposition to change, and the issue became drawn for me."[5]

The basic idea that united the group's core members was clear: the agrarian values of the Old South were the best hope not only for the South in resisting the effects of northern industrialism but also for the rest of America as well. *I'll Take My Stand* was the work of twelve southern-born essayists. Four—Ransom, Davidson, Tate, and Warren—had been Fugitives, and two—Lytle and Lanier—had been at Vanderbilt with them. The introduction set forth their "common convictions" in sixteen separate paragraphs.

They stood against industrialism because it attempted to dominate and transform nature and so suppressed the sense of the divine from which religion was derived. The increasing cyclical production of more laborsaving devices would produce "an increasing disadjustment and instability." And there was an ultimate peril: the economic engineering of "Coöperationists or Socialists" would produce "the true Sovietists or Communists" who would finally create "the same economic system as that imposed by violence upon Russia in 1917." What was to be done? The members of the group meant to seek out alliances to produce "a national agrarian movement." In its simplest

formulation, "the theory of agrarianism is that the culture of the soil
is the best and most sensitive of vocations, and that therefore it should
have the economic preference and enlist the maximum number of
workers." Warren would have the most difficult task: locating the position of the Negro in this economic and social order.[6]

The "jangle and wrangle" suggests his ambivalence. He remembered his grandfather's equable relations with his black farmhands and
his father's upbraiding him for his use, as a child, of the word *nigger.*
But he knew well Davidson's inflexibility on the subject of segregation and other aspects of black-white relations, feelings vehemently
shared by most of the other contributors. ("It's up to you, Red,"
wrote Davidson, "to prove that Negroes are country folks . . . 'born
and bred in a briar patch.' ") Warren would later say, "I was just very
uncomfortable with the piece, but it was this. My position was exactly that of the Supreme Court. Equal, you see; 'different but equal'
was the view of the Supreme Court and of 99 percent of the white
people in the country."[7]

Warren's essay was called "The Briar Patch." Between the ex-
tremes of the immediate franchise or permanent servitude "as hewers
of wood and drawers of water," he wrote, "lay a more realistic view
that the hope and safety of everyone concerned rested in the education of the negro. . . ." But for what was he to be educated? Warren
agreed with Booker T. Washington that the most urgent need was vo-
cational education. Opportunity in the professions would require not
just ability but unselfishness and patience. He thought that "the simplest issue, and probably the one on which most people would agree,
is that of equal right before the law. At present the negro frequently
fails to get justice. . . . It will be a happy day for the South when no
court discriminates in its dealings between the negro and the white
man. . . ." And what was required in the area of industrial progress
was that "an enlightened selfishness on the part of the Southern white
man must prompt him to encourage the well-being and possibly the
organization of negro, as well as white, labor." But he concluded,
"Let the negro sit beneath his own vine and fig tree." He told Davidson, "[If] for any reason—such as adjusting one essay to another—
you wish to make certain changes or point up certain arguments
please consider yourself as having a free hand here."[8]

One day he had been called to the porter's lodge when a cable arrived. The Yale English department had been holding his fellowship

open for the fall, but now they needed an immediate decision. He could stay at Oxford for the B.Litt., perhaps go on for the D.Phil., or return home for the Ph.D. His Yale fellowship was a good one, but he knew it would mean spending all of his "time trying to put salt on the tail of the academic albatross." Laboring over his Oxford thesis, he could not bear the thought of starting a Yale dissertation. Standing there at the gate of New College, he crumpled the message in his hand. "I'm going to be a writer," he said to himself. He went inside and sent a cable declining the fellowship.[9]

He had been investigating jobs and declined one at the University of Southern California teaching four sections of freshman composition. He had been in touch with a Princeton Ph.D. named Samuel Holt Monk who taught at Southwestern College in Memphis. Monk wanted to extend his fellowship time in England but needed to find a replacement for Southwestern. He offered Warren a one-year assistant professorship teaching one senior composition course with four other preparations including a Shakespeare course and a senior honors course. The job paid twenty-eight hundred dollars, and Warren thought that he could earn extra money with his writing. "I hope I have chosen wisely," he told the Tates.[10]

He was still beset by uncertainty. He did not yet have a date for the oral examination on the thesis. So Cinina's elaborate plans for a June wedding were scrapped. She had intended to come to England for the summer, "but a week ago," he confided to Bill and Alice Bandy, "I received a cable from her, without any explanation, saying that she had changed her mind. I'm still a bit puzzled about the matter, but a letter ought to be here soon giving the best reasons in the world. Or another cable may come saying that she has changed her mind again."[11]

A sequence of events something like his previous collapses followed. His letter to the Bandys, verging on incoherence, breathed alcohol fumes as well as jocularity. "I appeal to your sympathies," he wrote, "am a cripple, an invalid, and a charge on society. I fell in a ditch, sank a canoe (or was rather in a canoe which someone else sank), walked, ran, and danced on a cracked leg. . . . Nothing worried me much last Sunday night . . . but on Monday morning I found myself a charge on society. X-rays, doctors, masseurs, cold sweat, profanity, elaborate and unconvincing consideration from friends, bedpans: a charge on society." But he thought now that he would be in

New York in July. "I don't know whether Cinina will meet me in New York or whether I shall go to California and hunt her up." He enclosed ten shillings to cover the fifty francs he had owed Bill since Christmas.[12]

In the last days of June he was still waiting for his oral-examination date. A sympathetic reader of "A Study of John Marston's Satires" would understand why, after five years of graduate study, its author did not relish two more years and another scholarly treatise. Here were seventy-three pages of text, almost half of many of them consisting of footnotes in English and Latin. These three chapters analyzed Marston's relation to classical satire, to a rival satirist, and his own standards for satire. The following thirty-five pages held six appendices and listed the ninety-five books used in the study. He praised Marston but declared that his position in English satire was "not a very important one." The examination on the thesis was apparently uneventful, and he received from Oxford University his B.Litt. degree.[13]

Warren asked his landlord if he could lay on a dinner for his English friends who were graduating seniors. The landlord asked what course he would like to start with. Warren said oysters, and the landlord assented. He already knew that Americans liked martinis. When Cleanth Brooks arrived for the party he saw there on the table a big bowl of martinis, with oysters in it. The celebration was successful anyway.[14]

In late June, Warren told Davidson his plans were vague. "I may spend the shank of the summer in California and I may spend it in the east. In any case, I hope to be in Nashville in the latter part of August before I go to Memphis." As far as his friends knew, he was still a bachelor. That was only one of the things he had to work out when he returned in the late summer of 1930 to start his new career.

THREE

❖❖

Marriage and a Career

13

❖

Professor Warren at Southwestern

Among the pines we ran and called
In joy and innocence, and still
Our voices doubled in the high
Green groining our simplicity.

And we have heard the windward hound
Bell in the frosty vault of dark.
(Then what pursuit?) How soundlessly
The maple shed its pollen in the sun.

Season by season from the skein
Unwound, of earth and of our pleasure;
And always at the side, like guilt,
Our shadows over the grasses moved, . . .
—*"Monologue at Midnight"*[1]

In September of 1930 Warren stopped briefly in New York and Guthrie before arriving in Memphis. He stayed with Ridley Wills, and Cinina joined him there. (Preserving the fiction they had created, she later told Harriet Owsley that she had not known until her arrival in Memphis "whether Red was actually going to marry me.") On Friday, September 12, Ridley drove them across the Mississippi to the little town of Marion, Arkansas. Cinina was nominally a Catholic, but a justice of the peace performed the ceremony. Engraved cards were sent out by Mr. Domenico Brescia announcing the marriage of his daughter, Emma Cinina, to Mr. Robert Penn Warren and noting that they were now at home in Memphis. At the end of a fruitless

week of house hunting Warren had been shown an apartment, a
"whited sepulchre," on Poplar Avenue with an exorbitant rent and,
he later discovered, cockroaches. Out of weariness, he had taken it.[2]

They settled in to the housekeeping and teaching as the fall semester began. Memphis was almost as different from Nashville as Southwestern was from Vanderbilt. Here began the flat and rich Mississippi
Delta, where the main crop was cotton, not tobacco. But for Warren
it was still the South. For Cinina, he knew, it was not just a different
world but a wasteland. But she had a flair for decorating, for entertaining, and for cooking, and she set to work to try to make their
apartment attractive and comfortable.[3]

For Warren there was one sentimental link. Southwestern College
had begun as Southwestern Presbyterian University in Clarksville,
where his father had found the professor who tutored him in Greek.
Renamed and moved, it enrolled a thousand students, most of them
in premedical and liberal arts programs. Its small faculty was a good
one, with several members, like Sam Monk, trained at prestigious Ivy
League universities.

So Warren began his heavy teaching schedule: fifteen hours a week
in the classroom, plus student conferences and administrative duties.
The pattern of his professional life would be set here, with his enthusiastic teaching attracting overflow classes. But basic to all was his
writing. And though he would write critical and scholarly articles,
the poems and fiction would almost always have priority. In a trait
that would distinguish him throughout his academic life, he made
friends with students as easily as he did with faculty. One undergraduate would recall, "I passed in the corridors a student, obviously not
a freshman, whom I did not know. . . ." The undergraduate would
later say that the supposed student "was not long unknown, however,
for one day he stopped me to say he had seen me playing chess in one
of the common rooms and suggested that we have a game. Thus
began a chess combat that was to last for years." The student was Albert Russell Erskine, Jr., a tall, slim, handsome economics major who
would eventually become his major editor and lifelong friend.[4]

Warren had to deal with old as well as new business. Donald
Davidson wanted to reject "The Briar Patch" entirely. He thought it
went "off at a tangent to discuss the negro problem in general" and
felt it would dismay the very readership they were addressing by its
" 'progressive' implications. . . ." It didn't even sound like him, so
much that "I am almost inclined to doubt whether RED ACTU-

ALLY WROTE THIS ESSAY!" The others disapproved too but without Davidson's zeal. Tate tried to reassure Davidson. He too regretted the "sociological taint" but thought it "a good essay, A VERY GOOD ESSAY." He admired the closeness of the writing and thought that "in this respect it is far superior to any of the essays that I have seen. . . . I am very envious of Red." Ransom favored including it, and so Davidson invoked Warren's postscript authorization of changes and argued that he could accept or reject them when he read proof. He could not know how "The Briar Patch" would haunt him, or how he would be judged a racist by people ignorant of his later repudiation of the "separate but equal" doctrine.[5]

This was not the last contretemps. Another flared up over the working title *I'll Take My Stand.* Allen Tate suggested *Tracts Against Communism,* which Lytle and Warren both preferred. They composed a letter to Harper & Brothers disapproving *I'll Take My Stand* and urging that another title be chosen. Davidson and Ransom heatedly defended the title's origin in Daniel Emmett's "Dixie" with "the full total of all the associations of the song," arguing defensively that the book's subtitle, "The South and the Agrarian Tradition," would clearly indicate that the preceding phrase "could not possibly occur to a frenzied and uncritical patriot. . . ." Warren and Tate replied, "We admit defeat," though Tate concluded, "My melancholy is profound."[6]

In early November the book was widely reviewed, but Tate was proved right in his forebodings. (The authors were pictured in overalls in at least one cartoon.) Predictably, H. L. Mencken took a critical view of the South, which could "no more revive the simple society of the Jeffersonian era than England can revive that of Queen Anne."[7]

Determined to carry the message beyond the printed page, the group organized a series of five debates. In the years to come Tate and Warren and even Ransom would move on from this cause to other concerns. Only Davidson would fiercely defend it to the end. In a larger sense, however, the thrust of the book was one they could continue to approve, and one that would gain relevance and wide acceptance though couched in different terms. Its admirers would call it a prophetic book asserting humane values in the face of an increasingly mechanized world. Though rejecting the paternalistic attitude in "The Briar Patch," Warren would share the other authors' assessment of the book.[8]

"I'm working like a slave and find it difficult to resign myself to chapel," he wrote Davidson. "Aside from that all is well." His life was nothing if not full. Always susceptible to pulmonary ailments, Cinina would occasionally take to her bed, and so the housework would fall to him. Thomas Warren came to visit, and Robert Penn began to get to know him and arranged for him to attend some classes. And there were visits to friends. Out in the country, Allen and Caroline Tate had found a tall, narrow three-story brick house, which had been built in 1823 by a riverboat captain. Although it was badly in need of repair, the old building set upon a bluff overlooking the Cumberland River appealed to them. Allen's oldest brother, Ben, provided ten thousand dollars, and they bought the place for six and spent the other four making it habitable. Caroline's skeptical father named it Ben's Folly. The new owners rather liked the ring of that, and so the old Whitehall Place became Benfolly.[9]

Allen wrote poetry and played the violin, but he also built cupboards and bookshelves while Caroline saw to plantings. Before long a series of guests arrived including Malcolm Cowley, Mark Van Doren, Ford Madox Ford, and the Warrens. Most of them would work at their writing during the day. After drinks and dinner—which might consist of lamb or country ham with a profusion of garden vegetables—they could sit on the cool gallery looking out over the green countryside stretching north toward Clarksville three miles away. Sometimes they would invite local musicians, and Allen would do his best to play country music with them. More often they would divide up for charades, with Allen heading one team and Warren the other. Twenty years later Caroline would describe them: "The person who had thought of the words would repeat it over and over, shaking with laughter. Sometimes they would laugh so hard they would have to put their arms about each other's shoulders in order to stand up." With their quick minds, with wit and gossip so delightful, there was often an edge to the wordplay. In Caroline's novel, *The Strange Children,* "Uncle Tubby" was based on Warren. Before long, Caroline's references to Cinina would be literal rather than fictional, and they would take on a sharper tone.[10]

The Warrens were back at Benfolly to see in the new year of 1931, and returning to his heavy workload after the holidays was particularly hard. He may have remembered Tucker Brooke's admonition that he couldn't serve two masters. "I've got to do off a little article which I hope to place with one of the so-called subdivisions of limbo which are known in the profession as the 'learned periodicals,' " he wrote Andrew Lytle. "The frivolities must wait, for I must improve my earning capacity in the academic sty. It is a sty. It's a foul, stinking, unsanitary, unhygienic, drug-reeking sty without proper drainage. I like it less and less."[11]

Late winter found him plugging away at reviews and fiction. *The American Caravan IV,* containing "Prime Leaf," had appeared to good reviews. On the strength of them, Isidore Schneider, of the Macaulay Company, *The American Caravan*'s publisher, had approached him about writing a novel. "That is precisely what I want to try instead of a biography," he wrote the Tates. If Schneider refused his novel, perhaps Brewer would take it. Another bit of news was welcome even if it was of only short-term import. John Crowe Ransom had won a Guggenheim Fellowship. With Davidson's enthusiastic concurrence, Ransom suggested Warren as his replacement at Vanderbilt. Mims hesitated. He still thought of Warren as a "radical" undergraduate and asked Lyle Lanier's opinion. He assured Mims that Warren would be a good appointment as an acting assistant professor for one year. "I gravely doubt if there will be any sequel to it," Warren told the Tates, "but I shall get the same money as here and four hours of teaching less a week." In this Prohibition era of bathtub gin, while Cinina baked salt-rising bread in the kitchen, Warren busied himself elsewhere in the apartment. There was "a new bath of beer which ripened today," he wrote, "which is excellent. A glass sits beside me now. Do come to see us and sample our brew. Make it soon."[12]

June saw them installed in an apartment in Oakland in the building where Cinina's widowed father lived. "The typewriter runs in our apartment and the piano bangs in Mr. Brescia's," Warren wrote Andrew Lytle. "Cinina is thrown between pillar and post—or novel and fugue. She seems to be bearing up, however." Cinina was dividing her time between detective stories and Andrew's recently arrived biography of Nathan Bedford Forrest. After Warren got four thousand words done on his novel, they planned a brief change from city life. Cinina's best friend had married the son of a tycoon who owned a quicksilver mine on Clear Lake, eighty miles north of San Francisco, and the Warrens rented a cabin there. To him this wild country, up in the hills miles from the railroad, was perfect for climbing and long walks. He described to Tate the "beautiful lake—mountains and forest fires and all the stage settings. . . ." Seized again with the impulse to catch those rugged scenes in watercolors, Warren found that one of the others painted too. One young woman was rather good, and they made a joint venture of it until, to his amusement, "it somehow didn't seem quite appropriate [to Cinina] when I'd go heading off to the mountains with another painter." Back in Oakland, he kept at the work. "I've managed to get more than a fourth of the novel done so far," he informed Tate. "I stay at the typewriter about six hours a day, and my conscience hurts like hell when I miss. . . ."[13]

Just as he returned from Clear Lake he received a desperate appeal from Tate. Balch needed the manuscript of his Robert E. Lee biography by October, and he hoped that Warren could take a week and write a chapter of about seven or eight thousand words on the campaigns of Antietam and Fredericksburg. He could offer a hundred dollars for the job out of the first royalties due in November, but it would of course have to be kept secret. Having sent off three chapters of the novel to both Schneider at Macaulay and Brewer at his new firm, he set to work on the reading for Tate's chapter. "I've gotten the habit of staying at the typewriter so well formed now," he wrote, "that I doubt if I can do any teaching next year."[14]

About this time he received a letter from his father that told him his mother was not well but did not express any grave concern. He decided, however, that when he did return he would go first to Guthrie rather than Nashville. "As you probably know [Mother] has been pretty sick," he wrote Tate, "and I've been on tenter hooks about her. Her letters recently have been more cheerful, but I suspect her of some well-meaning casuistry on the point of her health." He had been thinking about departures. One poem he may have begun about this time was called "The Limited," picturing lovers as they kiss and part at the Pullman car's step.[15]

He worked on two other poems as the summer faded. One, for the "Kentucky Mountain Farm" sequence, was called "Watershed." There, high above the rivers, ridges, hills, and pastures, the poet looks out over the land. Warren found an image that would become one of his favorites:

> The sunset hawk now rides
> The tall light up the climbing deep of air.
> Beneath him swings the rooftree that divides
> The east and west. His gold eyes scan
> The crumpled shade on gorge and crest. . . .

The concluding poem of the sequence, "The Return," had been published in *The New Republic* a year and a half ago, but he borrowed that
title and an image from "Watershed" for a new long poem. It was
"pure fiction," he would later say, "and a spin-off from the group. . . ."
It was close to finished when Robert Warren wrote that Ruth Penn
was "really ill, but that there was no reason" to speed up his departure.
The title of the new poem was "The Return: An Elegy." Into an early
draft he interpolated a prose paraphrase: "The matter is, roughly, this:
I have been summoned to the funeral of my mother (a fine woman if
I do say so myself) and have departed, dutifully and at considerable expense, the eastern city, where I am engaged in the pursuit of happiness
and profit, and now rest, troubled by insomnia, in lower berth, number five." Images of death—bones and blind eyes—crowd the poem
from the first stanza. The quick shifts in tone and image would not
have been strange to any reader of Eliot, from a corpse holding violets
to a dead fox among the ferns. Another tonal shift follows:

> the old bitch is dead
> what have I said!
> I have only said what the wind said
> wind shakes a bell the hollow head[.]

After another five lines of description comes a single line:

> *does my mother wake*

and then, after five lines of sinister anthropoid imagery,

> *the old fox is dead*
> what have I said

The fox-death motif recurs before the final stanza:

> Over the hoarse pine over the rock
> Out of the mist that furled
> Could I stretch forth like God the hand and gather
> For you my mother
> If I could pluck
> Against the dry essential of tomorrow
> To lay upon the breast that gave me suck
> Out of the dark the dark and swollen orchid of this sorrow.

He would later remember, "I had felt, or hoped, I had made some sort of break-through" in the poem.[16]

What sort of breakthrough did he mean? He had written many poems filled with images of melancholy and death, most often the grief of despairing lovers. He had echoed T. S. Eliot often. In "The Return: An Elegy," however, his style, though still somewhat derivative, was more flexible and daring, and the emotion expressed was more sharp, direct, and personal. It was not, he said, like other early poems, written under the influence of the Metaphysical poets, but rather it "illustrates my experiments and fumbling . . . and . . . it somehow gave me a base for the future." So it was not, apparently, so far as he said, any sort of psychological breakthrough in fathoming the complex relationship with his mother.[17]

He had overstayed his planned time, and so they set about the packing and shipping for their return home. "Just as I was about to leave California," he wrote later, "a letter reported that her illness had taken a turn for the worse."[18]

14

❖

Professor Warren
at Vanderbilt

What were you thinking, a child, when you lay,
At the whippoorwill hour, lost in the long grass,
As sun, beyond the dark cedars, sank?
You went to the house. The lamps were now lit.

What did you think when the evening dove mourned?
Far off in those sober recesses of cedar?
What relevance did your heart find in that sound?
In lamplight, your father's head bent at his book.

What did you think when the last saffron
Of sunset faded beyond the dark cedars,
And on noble blue now the evening star hung?
You found it necessary to go to the house,

And found it necessary to live on,
In your bravery and in your joyous secret,
Into our present maniacal century,
In which you gave me birth, and in

Which I, in the public and private mania,
Have lived, but remember that once I,
A child, in the grass of that same spot, lay
And the whippoorwill called, beyond the dark cedars
    —*"What Were You Thinking, Dear Mother?"*[1]

Warren knew that the last three years had not been easy for his parents. In the year when he had gone off to Oxford, the shareholders had closed the Farmers and Merchants Bank. In time Robert

Franklin Warren had lost the stores where he and Mary Cecilia used to stop every Sunday after church to collect the rents. Now he managed the general merchandise store where he still owned an interest, standing behind the counter and waiting on the customers with quiet dignity. He still owned his home plus two other lots, and he had a few farms in the country, but they were mortgaged. For several years Ruth Penn had taught school in her home to help out. Her husband must have been loath to confide his financial troubles to his son, just as he must have wanted to spare him what he could of her illness.[2]

She had been treated for gallbladder disease, and in mid-September she was taken to the Jenny Stuart Memorial Hospital in Hopkinsville; she was operated on on Monday, September 21. Gallstones were found but also an abscess in the bowel. At first she seemed to improve, but then as she was watched closely during the rest of the week, she grew worse.[3]

Already behind in his academic preparations, Warren drove first to Vanderbilt to report his situation. It was Sunday night by the time he reached Guthrie. He went straight to Hopkinsville "in a state of great agitation. . . ." As he drove he thought of "The Return: An Elegy," which now "seemed a thing of ill omen, tangled with all sorts of emotions and crazily with some sense of nameless complicity and guilt." Why should he feel guilty? Theirs was a close family, and his relationship with his mother was his closest one. He loved her enough to weep when he went off to college, but there was ambivalence too. They were both strong-willed. He was ambitious as well as precocious, and she was proud and protective. He would say that after he was sixteen he never lived at home again—though he spent vacation time there. Those years away completed the distancing process, and his marriage reinforced his psychological independence. But the silver cord was still there in memory even if there was evidence that it had been severed. Were there still emotional claims he resented? Was it sheer coincidence that he was writing "The Return: An Elegy" at about the same time that he learned of his mother's illness? How much of this poem he regarded as a breakthrough was fiction, as he claimed? Did he harbor a death wish? Or was he imagining, in a kind of defense against the possibility of her death, what it would be like for a faraway son to be summoned home?[4]

At the hospital he joined his father in a silent vigil. Thomas was there as well as Mary Cecilia, come from her teacher's job in Whitesburg. Warren was not allowed to see his mother. She had received a blood transfusion preparatory to a second operation. After the long night, when she was wheeled in for surgery, Warren and his father waited wordlessly in the hall. The door opened at last, and the doctor came out. Warren saw that he was "carrying something on a pad of gauze. . . . My father looked studiously at the little blob of something . . . streaked with blood. 'There it is,' the doctor said." Neither father nor son knew what it was. Mary knew that no tumor had been found, and so Dr. Gaither may well have excised tissue involved with the abscess where peritonitis had developed. Warren and his father returned to the hospital parlor, where Mary and Thomas waited. Allen Tate wrote Andrew Lytle, "I've tried to stay with them as much as possible to give them some conversation to support their really pitiful self-control. I've never seen such *character* so uniformly possessed by a whole family." When their mother was returned to her room, she raised her hand for a moment and then it fell back. As the nurses lifted her onto the bed she managed a smile.[5]

Allen Tate and Caroline Gordon had been there since Saturday. "It is really remarkable how she hangs on," Tate wrote. "We've been spending half of every night at the hospital with Red," Caroline wrote her friend Sally Wood. "They kept her going with saline solutions and water injected in the veins and all that. . . . it's been a terrible ordeal. Poor Mr. Warren has had no hope from the first." He was there beside her, holding her hand, doing his best to respond to her smile. Her son would remember one of her efforts all his life. "Son," she said, "I like your new suit." They were her last words to him.[6]

On Thursday, October 1, as the clock ticked toward midnight, the doctor, his fingers on her thin wrist, nodded at last to Robert Warren. He leaned down and kissed her, followed by the children, in order of age. Down the hall in the parlor, sitting in a straight chair, "seemingly unchanged by time," was Grandma Jenny, her head bowed. Robert Franklin Warren sat down on an armless sofa against the wall. Shortly the doctor entered and nodded again. The husband stared at him and then, his back still straight, simply collapsed sideways on the sofa. Grandma Jenny rose and silently rested her hand on his shoulder.[7]

The Todd County *Times,* reporting her death on its first page, noted that she "had a cultivated mind and was a woman who kept abreast of the times in every way." On Saturday morning the minister conducted the Methodist funeral service at home, and then the small procession made its way out to Highland Cemetery. If this death was overwhelming for Robert Franklin Warren and Mary Cecilia, it was devastating for young Thomas. A robust young man with a gift for companionship and a taste for alcoholic beverages, he had been making a troubled transition from high school to the next step in his life. Now he seemed to his brother "totally disorganized." Thomas would later say, "Mother left me just when I needed her most." Robert Penn would say simply, "The light always falls differently after the mother goes." The rest he would put in poems.[8]

There was another family occasion after the funeral. Robert Franklin Warren and his three children walked across the railroad tracks to Squiggtown to visit Seeley Bradshaw, now old and sick. Propped up and struggling for breath, she greeted them with a raised hand and then laid it on Robert Penn's cheek. After a brief time his father placed a gift on the table. Then they kissed Seeley each in turn and left. Walking back in silence under the dark night sky, the father suddenly spoke. His son remembered years later:

> My father says: *Twenty dollars—oh, God, what*
> *Is twenty dollars when*
> *The world is the world it is!*[9]

Every Sunday, Robert Franklin Warren would walk out to the cemetery, and if there was anything blooming, he would carry it in a jar and place it by Ruth Penn's tombstone. Later he planted a bed of zinnias so there would always be fresh flowers to lay upon her grave.[10]

Back in Nashville, Warren found an apartment at 2104½ State Street, in the center of the city, and entered into the life of the university. In this depression year Chancellor James H. Kirkland, still the dominant power at Vanderbilt after nearly forty years, was considering cutting salaries but managed to stave it off. One of his most loyal subordinates was Edwin Mims. To generations of students he was "Eddie" Mims, still assigning his favorite Victorian poets for memorization and often perceived as a kind of paterfamilias to his students and some of his faculty. But many failed to share this view, particularly those who recalled his arguments against publishing *The Fugitive*. His writing clearly aligned him with the New South adherents, not the Agrarians. And they repudiated his teaching techniques, with the predictable poems, memorization, and recycling of timeworn lecture notes. But it could not be denied that he had recruited writers such as Ransom and Davidson as well as Ph.D.'s. And he prided himself on his support of creative writers. One day when Professor Warren was ten minutes late, Professor Mims intercepted the students who began filing out of the classroom. They had a chance to hear a man who would become a great writer, he told them. "Now go back and wait for him." Nonetheless, their opposing ideas about teaching literature would work to sour this relationship.[11]

But Warren found his teaching agreeable in this institution, thought to be the best southern university after Texas and Duke. In his general survey of English literature was a boy with dark wavy hair, dark eyes, and an engaging smile. His name was Randall Jarrell, and he made an unforgettable impression. He had been admitted to this sophomore course "though he was the only freshman, because it was quite clear that no freshman class could hold him. He was so gifted that he terrorized my bright group of sophomores, not out of malice but with the cruel innocence of a baby. Finally I told him that he was scaring them to death. . . . He was already writing extraordinarily beautiful poems." Warren encouraged him. "He would [later] come out to my little whitewashed house and talk poetry and philosophy and brutally criticize my poems. I would listen carefully. He was often right and more often amusing, so amusing that it didn't matter much that it was at my expense."[12]

Warren was doggedly writing reviews for the *Virginia Quarterly Review* when he wanted most to sell them his poems, fiction, and essays. Stringfellow Barr took the reviews and sent the other submissions back. By late November Warren was unable to contain his frustration. He told Barr that "if my prose, whose virtues and defects by any absolute standard can be waived for the moment, is decent enough for you to print, my verse is equally, or more, so." Then he launched into a slashing critique of a poem Barr had recently printed. Barr replied that he had liked Warren's poems but had no time to explain his reasons for accepting or rejecting any submission. In January, Warren's last review for the *Quarterly* would appear.[13]

The Tates had looked forward to his return to Nashville. Caroline told Sally Wood candidly, "I can't hand Cinina much but I adore Red. . . . he is a sweet creature to have around if you have any time at all to play." Andrew Lytle made an effort to welcome Cinina to their circle, knowing that he could not have a cool relationship with her and remain Warren's friend. Cleanth Brooks observed a very different response in the Tates, who "wanted to take over Red. Here was this brilliant, prodigious, precocious young man, with so much talent, and they [wanted] to protect him, steer him. They were furious when he married Cinina." Cinina was difficult, but "Caroline herself could do some pretty terrible things. Caroline was pretty hard to put up with for anybody." She could upbraid a friend in a flash of rage one day and then act as if nothing had happened the next. So Cinina was a natural antagonist and one who irritated even more people than Caroline did. Nonetheless, the two couples would see each other at Benfolly and in Nashville.[14]

The Tates were hospitable in good times and bad. For Christmas that year they had invited a houseful even though Caroline was uncertain where the money would come from, but the Christmas turkey was raised by Caroline's mother, and sorghum, fresh pork, and two guinea hens were brought from Alabama by Lytle. Allen brought in a tree from among their cedars, and they decorated it with candles. They diverted themselves, Caroline wrote Malcolm Cowley, "shooting craps, playing charades, and drinking Hopkinsville liquor." The Warrens and two others stayed for a week.[15]

Another visit from the Warrens gave a better indication of the true state of affairs. An animated discussion turned into a passionate argument, and as Cinina spoke heatedly she began waving her knife. The Tates' cook watched transfixed. She remembered it as "the night Mrs. Warren got loose." Caroline wrote one of her friends:

> While I am on the subject of terrible people I wish to relieve my feelings by saying that Red Warren had taken to himself as wife just about the God damndest woman that ever I saw in my life. It isn't so much that she is selfish and vulgar and always rowing but just that everything that we think important is unimportant to her and vice versa. She is still trying to impress us—Allen and me—with butlers and town cars and things. . . . I thought Allen would burst a blood vessel when he discovered that she has Red typing all her class papers for her. She is taking a master's at Vanderbilt for lack of something to do. I suppose it comes down to the fact that she is ignorant and incapable of ever understanding the way an artist has to live . . . Red is teaching . . . writing reviews to make out expenses and trying, poor devil, to write a novel. . . . I have the most murderous thoughts about her. She is frail and has to stay in bed till noon every day and the whole household centers around the pound or two that she has just lost or gained and I keep thinking

why in God's name don't you die? . . . but I suppose she would just have a lingering illness and do for Red completely before she passed away. . . . He hasn't the kind of guts that it takes to deal with such a situation. . . .

Caroline was the most vehement of Cinina's critics, but her view would come to be shared by nearly all those who knew the Warrens.[16]

Cinina had continued to write occasionally. Warren encouraged her and sent poems to Tate for criticism. His friends agreed that though Tate's conversation might be tinged with exaggeration or malice, his criticism was usually honest and direct. It proved to be too direct for Cinina. On March 22 she typed out a four-page reply. She felt hurt, angry, and misunderstood. The letter provided an opportunity to say things she had wanted to say for some time. Although she did not feel as he and the others did, that one should place writing above all else, she said he had been wrong to say that she cared more for many other things. In spite of seeming hostile she had learned much. His good opinion of her work would stimulate her much more than publication of the poems, but she would accept his kind offer to send two of them on for publication. Then she took her pen and wrote a rather incoherent note along the two margins. The sense of it was that she would never write as well as her husband. She wanted to help him spend more time on his writing but couldn't think how.[17]

The attempted rapprochement did not last a week, as Tate reported to Andrew Lytle almost immediately in two long letters. "I've told Red that he is asking too much of us to bear with her—that it is not immaturity, that it is a fundamental difference in one's feeling for the values of life; that I am willing to go ahead and try to get along with her, but unwilling to pretend that it is a mere conflict of temperament among equals. . . . I finally wrote Red a letter . . . telling him just what I thought about her, what I think of the way her vulgarity, her stupidity, and pretentiousness has corrupted our Community. . . . He admits everything we say *in detail,* but of course he could not admit the abstract words with which we describe our situation entire. . . . Caroline wrote her a long letter cataloguing in detail her faults, but she was evidently so stupid that she didn't get the force of the indictment. . . ." Two weeks later Tate wrote, "Brer Warren come down by hisself two weeks ago and we talked hit all over, and we say he ain't got no right to do like he's been a doin', naw siree, and what do you think, he upped and said he ain't neither. . . . Hits shore done him good, cause when Miss [Caroline] piped up and said his old woman needed a good whupping, he sorta agreed, and said she was a gittin hit."[18]

The Tates were not Cinina's only antagonists. Brainerd "Lon" Cheney had graduated from Vanderbilt in Warren's class and had gone to work for the Nashville *Banner*. Now he was married to a professional librarian named Frances Neel. They had bought a handsome antebellum home in Smyrna, twenty miles southeast of Nashville, changing its name from Cold Chimneys to Idlers' Rest. Warm and witty people, they often entertained there. Lon was a liberal agnostic who had rejected many of the values of his Georgia family and had developed into a talented reporter deeply immersed in the political life of the city and the state. But he also wanted to be a novelist. He and Warren read each other's manuscripts, and Lon would call him "one of the most generous men I know." Lon knew that Cinina was working on a novel that Warren thought "should be taken seriously," but to Lon it was worthless. Worse than that, however, he thought Cinina was competing with her husband the way Zelda Fitzgerald was with Scott. It seemed to Lon that Warren loved Cinina deeply in spite of the way she made demands on him like a perennial adolescent, making him her slave. Albert Erskine would reach Lon's conclusion about Cinina's writing, but he was sympathetic to her.[19]

Fortunately for both the Warrens, there were others like Albert Erskine. He had switched his major from economics to English and won a graduate fellowship at Vanderbilt. He made weekend visits to the Warrens, and soon he would move to Nashville, ready to resume the chess and bridge games. When the hospitable Ransoms returned from a year in England they rented a two-acre place six miles out in the country. (Ransom encouraged Cinina to write, and this was another reason why the Ransoms' home was one of her favorite places.) Harriet Owsley remembered that "one had only to mention the word *charade* and Robb Ransom was up and at it." They would go to her closet full of old clothes for costumes, or they would play Murder. The game began when the lights were turned out and someone was handed the murder card. A district attorney would be appointed to begin asking questions until one of the players was tripped up in a lie and identified as the murderer. When Andrew Lytle drove up from Alabama he would always be asked to perform. He drew upon his experiences as a working farmer, and with his acting talents he was the star in this group of raconteurs. He re-created his stories, constantly adding and changing. Their favorite was "The Weaning of Brother Micajah," built up from a frontier anecdote. Harriet Owsley remembered his account of "how six-year-old Micajah's Mammy had to put lard and quinine on her 'tits' in order to wean him and how Micajah came in with his pappy from a hunting trip and said, 'Mammy, lemme hav it.' He took one swig and spat it out, saying, 'Gimme er chaw er terbaccy, Pappy. Mammy's been eatin' bitterweed.' "[20]

The Owsleys would entertain at their home on the campus and their camp on the Cumberland River. They were warm and supportive friends to the Warrens. In swimming weather they would take a canoe across the river to a good beach. Warren would pack his ears with cotton against infections, pull on a bathing cap, and wade out into the water. Albert remembered one day when he went downstream, then swam back against the current past them and on out of sight until he finally returned to the beach. Those were good times for all of them.[21]

Warren's uncertainty about the future, however, was increased by his conviction that Mims did not want to keep him on. But then Don Davidson was granted a year's leave and Warren was appointed to replace him with his salary raised to three thousand dollars for the 1932–33 school year. At the end of May, when all the term's work was finished, the Tates gave a picnic at Buck Spring. On the way there the Laniers waited for some time while Warren and Cinina quarreled. At last he came out alone and went on without her. A week later he and Cinina packed the car and headed west.

15

❖

Trying to Become
a Novelist

It was almost a mile from the big gate on the pike to
the yard gate, the drive through the cedars thick near the
big gate looking cool to teamsters on the hot pike, then
spreading to a slow sweep of meadow toward the house.
The buggy came bowling up the drive from the west, the
roan pacing fast and royal like the last stretch, the
gravel sputtering, cracking on leather, the roan's feet
thumping—one, one, one—on the gravel, the dust
swirling up in a cloud of rose and gold against the
sunset beyond. Snorting, the roan pulled up to the
hitching post, and for half a mile behind, the long
plume drooped, losing its rose, then its gold, then going
minutely grey on the grass.

—*God's Own Time*[1]

The east-west axis had already figured importantly in Warren's taking
a degree and taking a wife. And though he was glad to leave for the
West and loath to return east to teach, it was a trip he would make
many times, and east-west journeys would be important for characters in his poetry and fiction. Loving the beauty of that western country as he did, he may have come to associate other positive attributes
with it—vacation and freedom from teaching, and time for work in
progress. That was the case now. Through Thomas Mabry, a friend
from Clarksville days and now a Vanderbilt colleague, Warren had
met Edward Donahoe, an aspiring writer who invited him and Cinina to stop at his home in Ponca City, Oklahoma, on their way to

California. While they were there, Warren asked for some paper and typed out the last four pages of chapter twenty-four to complete his first draft of *The Apple Tree*.[2]

From the past Warren borrowed the farm of his childhood and familiar names. It was primarily the story of one family. Martha Campbell Miller, the daughter of a dead Confederate colonel, supplies the actions generating the two plotlines, but they are also prompted in a crucial way by her maternal uncle, Lemuel Telemachus Morden, modeled partly on Grandpa Penn. Troubled romantic and marital relationships are presented together against scenes Warren knew from childhood: the visiting carnival and the railroad depot. Martha concludes that she must leave her husband, and she departs with a tent-show evangelist whose exhortations had already gone into "August Revival: Crosby Junction." Warren sent off five chapters to Harcourt, Brace. When they asked for a summary of the rest of the novel, he sent a "short statment of intention." The last half was to focus on Martha's reasons for her ill-fated elopement and her unhappy younger brother's affair with a pregnant "white trash" country girl. Disasters were to befall in both plotlines, with his violent departure from home and subsequent murder. Harcourt was willing to consider the rest of the novel. Warren completed his revisions in Oakland and sent off the manuscript, retitled *God's Own Time*. On August 26 Harcourt declined it, but he was not ready to give up, and he packed the manuscript with his books when it was time to return to Tennessee.[3]

He would work at it and get on with his poetry and perhaps an essay, but at the same time he had to do the best he could to hang on to his temporary job, his salary now cut back by five hundred dollars to twenty-five hundred. And though in some ways he was gradually distancing himself from the other Fugitives, their friendship and the possibility of collaboration were important in his life. And he was torn, like many young faculty members, between the demands of his career and those of his marriage. But this new semester would be different in some ways. For one, the Tates would not be there. Caroline had received a Guggenheim Fellowship to begin her new novel, and they sailed for France with Sally Wood and the Laniers. Established in a villa near Ford Madox Ford, Caroline was hard at work, but Allen, disillusioned with Robert E. Lee and unable to complete his biography, composed poems and fiction instead. The Warrens meanwhile had determined that there would be another difference this semester.

They were tired of living in the city, and they began to comb the countryside for a place they could afford.[4]

They were unsuccessful until Lucius Burch, a young horseback-riding friend of Warren's, told him, "There's a cabin on our place. Come look at it." The place was Riverwood, the estate of his father, Dr. Lucius Burch, on the Cumberland River twelve miles east of Vanderbilt. "We are to have it for as long as we like in return for putting it in repair," Warren wrote the Tates. "It is a lovely spot. . . . our house is down the hill in a grove with lots of old wistaria and honeysuckle running about. . . . We have worked like dogs putting the place in order, for it was a hovel when we undertook the job." Spending $250 left them nearly broke, but it was worth it. They now owned a baby Austin so small that Albert Erskine had to sit in the backseat, wrapping his legs around the front seat to drive it. After school Warren would leave the city, where the bituminous coal darkened the air with soot that seeped onto windowsills and into shirt collars, and drive into the freshness of the country. He signed the letter "Much love," and wrote at the top their new address: "Pennfolly."[5]

John Ransom welcomed him back warmly. "Red is as good a head and heart as I've known and it's a pleasure to be with him," he wrote Tate, but he had noticed a change in him. After Andrew Lytle spent four days with the Ransoms he told Tate that "John noticed he didn't have his old life and spontaneity." Andrew thought he knew why. "I'm afraid Red is gradually growing more like Miss Emma." Tate would scarcely have gathered this from some of Warren's letters. He had classes at eight o'clock every morning from Tuesday through Saturday, but he was content. "John R. is back and in fine fettle. He and I visit a bit every morning at nine o'clock and talk a little poetry or politics." Ransom had added a social note in his letter to Tate. "Saturday evenings the Warrens, Laniers and Ransoms sit about the Ransoms' green table; with possibly a bachelor or two on hand to furnish the spoils of war. We speak reverently of you all." Warren had told Tate the same thing, adding, "We have been having some good games. I devoutly wish that you all could drop in for the sessions."[6]

Tate's reaction was different from the one his correspondents expected. Writing to Don Davidson, who was hoping for a second Agrarian symposium, Tate told him, "What I hear from Nashville seems to prove that the Agrarian movement has degenerated into pleasant poker games on Saturday night." This kind of disaffection had occurred among this group before and would occur again.[7]

Even though these brethren had their political differences, they continued to bring one another's poetry to the attention of a widening audience, as Warren did in an essay called "A Note on Three Southern Poets," which he had supplied for the southern number of *Poetry* Tate edited. Writing about a 1928 anthology entitled *The Southern Lyric,* he regretted the exclusion of Allen Tate, Merrill Moore, and Conrad Aiken. Turning to Donald Davidson as one who had "stayed at home both literally and spiritually," he praised the "concentrated and personal intensity" of this poetry couched "in terms of his own social tradition." As the issue had been stated by I. A. Richards (whose books Warren had sent to Ransom from Oxford), the poet was today "plagued by the problem of thought and feeling as poets have never been plagued before." The "awakening and agitation" in the South in the past fifteen years had "taken the form of a highly dramatic moral issue: old values implicit in a society have been made explicit, and there has been a testing of the old by the new."[8]

The year of 1933 began with his old susceptibility to illness. In mid-January he started to feel a soreness in his throat, which developed into one of his frequent colds. But he began to feel nauseated too and ached all over. Then, on the twenty-seventh, after abdominal cramps, more nausea, and vomiting, he decided to go to the university hospital. While the laboratory tests were being run, the doctor completed a detailed examination. His patient was a well-muscled specimen just under 160 pounds who presented lingering symptoms of his cold. (The thorough checkup revealed no other problems but his vision: his left eye could distinguish only between light and darkness. The iris was scarred, and a cloudy cataract was forming. The pupil was contracted and fixed. The fundus and reaction of the right eye were normal, and glasses corrected that eye for astigmatism and farsightedness and the tendency of the damaged eye to wander.) That afternoon Dr. Barney Brooks found the middle portion of the appendix swollen and bound down to the large intestine by old fibrous adhesions, and he removed it without difficulty. Under the customary conservative regimen, the patient was discharged on February 5. The Owsleys insisted that he was not ready to go back home to Porter Road out on Route 9, and so he joined Cinina in the Owsleys' guest room. To Harriet they were like members of the family, and she enjoyed preparing food for the recuperating patient. On his trips to the hospital, Dr. Brooks saw that the wound was healing nicely and also noted that his general appearance was better. In early March he and Cinina returned to Pennfolly, now fragrant with budding and blossoming redbud and dogwood.[9]

But March came in with a violence that emphasized life's precariousness. The night of the fourteenth Warren was sitting in bed reading the papers. Suddenly, he recalled later, "I heard a noise like a freight train passing over my head, and then a crash." A tornado had picked up part of a brick barn not far off and carried it through the air. A week later another hurled a tree in front of the baby Austin as he was driving home. Then, "when there was a lull I got out of the car, but the wind returned and literally pinned me against the door. That was one of the most frightening experiences in my memory." His surgery, followed by two brushes with death, could well have deepened his sense of his own mortality, though he was not yet twenty-eight. But he was blessed with sympathetic friends. Don Davidson wrote Allen Tate that "the operation came not a moment too soon. I'm terribly sorry for Red. This has been a hard year for him." By now Mims may have told him that he could expect only part-time teaching in the fall. Writing to Caroline Gordon, Warren told her he felt like he'd been treading water for years.[10]

But there were occasions to keep up their morale. The Tates could not return to Benfolly until the departure of their tenants, and so they went to Merry Mont, Caroline's family's farm near Trenton, Kentucky, fourteen miles northwest of Guthrie. One weekend in mid-May when Warren and Cinina were visiting in Guthrie, Allen and Caroline and two friends saddled their horses and rode over to Guthrie to visit them, returning home by moonlight. When Malcolm Cowley wrote that he was thinking of coming south for a quiet place to work, Allen and Caroline urged him to stay at Cloverlands, the nearby farm of her Meriwether relatives. It was a beautiful time of the year, and it would be cool and lovely until the scorching heat of August. "Guthrie, sacred as the birthplace of Red Warren, has good beer and good food to go with it." (Cowley found Guthrie "a singularly drab and impoverished railroad town." With Warren he walked past the depot and the defunct bank, and then into the general store to meet Warren's father.) One sunny Sunday "the Fugitive group held a picnic on a houseboat moored in the Cumberland," Cowley wrote. "The river was in flood and the current swept past us at a rate to frighten timid swimmers. Red dived from the houseboat, swam arrow straight across the river, and then swam back again as if the Cumberland in flood were a millpond. One of his friends told me that he liked to swim a mile before breakfast every morning. At twenty-eight he was already becoming a somewhat legendary character."[11]

In the heat of August the Warrens made plans for a visit to the Donahoes in Oklahoma and then to California if possible. They set out on the first leg of the journey, a short one to Ponca City. No sooner had they arrived than disaster struck. Warren scrawled a distraught letter to Tate on August 24. "For the last two days Cinina has had a series of very severe hemorrhages . . . five to be exact. . . ." He grew more distraught as he wrote. "At this point I was interrupted by the nurse's calling me. She just had another—the most severe—and protracted. . . . She gets so desperate, Allen. She scarcely gets a hold on herself before there is another one." He broke off at the doctor's arrival and did not resume until midnight. Then he gave Frank Owsley the news. It had been "a severe breakdown," but Cinina was now "on the mend" though "the doctor says that she will have to remain in bed for at least six months. . . ." The next day he told Tate, "The examination showed five spots of infection." In mid-September Warren drove back to Nashville and Cinina followed by plane, pursued by further misery. "She had pneumonia, and now has appendicitis," he wrote Frank Owsley.[12]

In these weeks and months they were riding an emotional roller coaster. The appendicitis subsided, and Warren was able to report that Cinina was much better and looking almost well. "I finished the novel and shall mail it some time this week or early next," he added. "I don't know how I finished it, but I did. Whether it's good or bad as a novel, it represents a moral triumph." Two weeks later John Ransom was able to inform Allen, "Red got off his novel, which I think is very fine." And Cinina continued to improve. Enrollment had held steady, and so "Red will probably get 2 sections of teaching." That meant he could expect eight hundred dollars for October through December. Then, three weeks later, on October 18, Harcourt, Brace informed him that they had decided not to publish *God's Own Time*.[13]

But he was busy with other writing, and the long-meditated second symposium was taking shape. The essayists were to include ten from *I'll Take My Stand*. Robert Penn Warren was to write on "Some English Agrarians." In spite of the manifold demands upon him and headaches that had begun to plague him—severe ones in the left frontal area—he had accumulated enough stories to send several to

Curtis Brown, a prominent New York literary agency where Caroline Gordon knew a member of the firm. One was entitled "When the Light Gets Green." The central character—the young narrator's grandfather—was enough like Grandpa Penn to classify the piece a memoir rather than a work of fiction. Curtis Brown sent back all but that one as unsaleable. Allen Tate liked it well enough to send it to Eliot for *The Criterion,* but no one bought it.[14]

Even so, the situation must now have seemed more hopeful than he had feared. Cinina was sitting up a little each day, and they had "a good and competent servant." John Donald Wade had decided to leave the Vanderbilt English department. Even though Mims saw Red Warren as a young Agrarian who had never turned to him for leadership, it must have been easier to replace Wade with someone already on the scene than to recruit from outside. So Warren would be teaching full-time from January until June at a salary of $1,250.[15]

They went to Benfolly for Christmas, where Cinina had to go to bed after three days. (Caroline's cousin Marion Meriwether said, "The strain of bearing with us was too much for her.") The Owsleys, Laniers, and Ransoms came for a party, and they played dice and poker and drank eggnog. Caroline's Aunt Loulie Meriwether passed out after two glasses but said it was caused by the heat from the fire and then started ringing bells at six the next morning to show she didn't have a hangover. They played charades, with Andrew Lytle as a toreador and Lyle Lanier as a human fly.[16]

Clinging to a precarious livelihood, Warren was full of plans for the future. With the encouragement of Caroline Gordon and John Ransom he applied for a Guggenheim Fellowship for the "completion of a long poem and writing of a novel." Listing his accomplishments, he wrote, "My volume of poems was accepted and announced by Brewer and Warren, but was never published, since I withdrew it and held it until the firm changed hands." He added that he had two poems and two essays forthcoming. His novel, *God's Own Time,* was under consideration by a publisher, and he hoped to report on this in the near future.[17]

He was determined to write, not just because it was his vocation, but also because it promised a better return than teaching. And he was determined to become a novelist. He was also approaching another ride on the roller coaster.

16

❖

Doors Closing
and Doors Opening

Adept, too late, at art of tears he stands
By gravest orchard in diminished light:
And aged eyes, like twilit rain, their effort
Spill gentlier than herb-issue on a hill.
　　　　　—*"Aged Man Surveys the Past Time"*[1]

He was used to waiting for editors' responses to his manuscripts. In the new year of 1934 there were three responses he craved: word on the novel, relief from his headaches, and resolution of his employment problem. As it turned out, they came in that order.

He had submitted *God's Own Time* to the Bobbs-Merrill Company of Indianapolis. The response of D. L. Chambers, the company's vice president, was frustrating and tantalizing. He had read the novel carefully, and in spite of somewhat ambivalent feelings he had voted to publish it. "The novel has the form of a piece of music, and the music is turbulent, insistent; it troubles the reader." And it had "a queer power" from the way "sex has corroded the lives of these people." He thought it was an unusual achievement by a young man who would be worth watching. "It is a book worth rereading. Somebody ought to publish it. And it might even be popular." In a postscript he wrote, "(Alas, that was not the opinion of les autres.)" Their objections were clear: "Ellen Glasgow, William Faulkner, Erskine Caldwell and many others have written of the corruption and disintegration, of the inherent evil strain in widely different elements of Southern society and now Robert Penn Warren adds his able contribution to that field of fiction."[2]

But the response was not totally without encouragement. Chambers hoped that Warren would send him more of his work. He was in fact already into a novel. The setting, borrowed from his time at Southwestern, was a Tennessee town called Charlestown. But it was populated with people, scenes, and impressions from Guthrie. His principal characters were high school seniors, their parents, teachers, friends, and families. As in the earlier novel, family models stood behind main characters. With a memory like his, this material was ready and the imagination was there to flesh it out. What he needed was more time and less pain.[3]

The headaches had been getting worse. One of his riding companions was Tom Zerfoss, the genial one-man student health service at Vanderbilt. He took care of Warren and Cinina and other friends without charge. (When Cinina had told him that she wanted a baby, he had told her that the threat of tuberculosis was too great.) Tom's wife, Kate Savage Zerfoss, was an ophthalmologist in private practice with an office full of modern equipment. She examined Warren on Tuesday morning, February 6. Her diagnosis was clear: traumatic cataract. The history she took from the patient revealed more. About six years ago the vision had begun to dim in the damaged left eye after constant swimming in the ocean. With the persistence of the sinusitis in the aftermath of the respiratory infection at the time of his appendectomy, he had noticed the vision decreasing more rapidly. Then, as the headaches continued, he began to suffer from nausea, and he noticed flecks before his right eye. The conjunctiva started showing signs of infection, which gradually increased. Then, in early February, the sight in his left eye failed completely. Dr. Zerfoss advised that it should be removed immediately.

The general examination at Vanderbilt University Hospital indicated something of the difficult year he had passed. His arms and legs were thin, and his chest was "very thin." By five in the afternoon he was ready for surgery, and at six o'clock he was returned to the ward in good condition. Wednesday morning he received morphia again for pain, but the site of the operation was healing well. On the next day, February 8, wearing a large plaster bandage, he was discharged at noon.[4]

In the years since his suicide attempt, it was as if, far from adopting a defensive posture, he had determined to live as much as he could and challenge fate. He had hiked in the California hills and swum far out into the Pacific. And he had strained his sight at Oxford working on John Brown and his thesis until his eye muscles were threatened with surgery. He had been spared the worst, it seemed—the blindness that had terrified him as a college sophomore—as the infection disappeared in his remaining eye. Whether his now being truly one-eyed made him feel more vulnerable than before, only he knew. But one thing was certain: He would continue to live the strenuous life, physically and mentally, just as he had done before.

It must have been difficult, nonetheless, with the drab shades of winter still on the land, to keep his spirits up. His wife's health remained precarious, and his father's was declining. Warren would later say that Ruth Warren's death had left Robert Warren stunned: "He went through all the motions of life, but his judgment was impaired. He bought farms and overextended himself." Warren's own financial situation could hardly have been more tenuous. He hoped that Dr. Mims could find work for him in the fall term, but he had no reason to believe he would. Warren may have felt a momentary foretaste of spring when Seward Collins took not just one but five poems for the May number of *The American Review.* (One was a wintry poem with the hopeful title, "Aubade for Spring.") But it must have seemed like a sudden hard frost when the Guggenheim Foundation informed him that he had not been awarded a fellowship for 1934–35. So he had been buffeted in all three of his major concerns.[5]

Clearly, he had to keep trying to avoid unemployment six months hence. In downtown Nashville, the Watkins Free Night School provided a full high school and an expanded adult and continuing education program, including art, home economics, and business. For some time, Dr. Mims had taught one of the courses, but he finally decided he had enough to do at Vanderbilt, and resigned. Warren applied to teach the course. It wouldn't bring in much, but it would help in their straitened circumstances. When Mims learned that Warren was in line for the job, he rescinded his resignation. Warren's friend Sam Monk was still at Southwestern to intercede for him. There was also another possibility. When Cleanth Brooks finished at Oxford, he felt that his only possibility for a job was at Louisiana State University. (His family had moved to Louisiana, and he was technically a citizen of the state. One of the members of his Rhodes Scholarship Committee was Charles W. Pipkin. With an Oxford doctorate Pipkin had resigned a full professorship in government at the University of Illinois to become dean of the graduate school at LSU.) Brooks knew that Pipkin was "a brilliant man, rising like a rocket in this university with a lowly rank. . . . It was really a military college, an old-fashioned military college on the banks of the Mississippi, but building a new campus and trying to improve its new faculty."[6]

Two years after his election in 1928 as governor of Louisiana, Huey P. Long began his campaign to make LSU into a first-class university. He appointed James Monroe Smith, a fellow native of Winn Parish, as president. An adept politician, he followed Long's orders enthusiastically. When Pipkin became dean in April of 1931, Smith's mandate was that he was to recruit outstanding scholars for every department, and "money was to be no object." Pipkin invited Brooks to give a lecture in Baton Rouge. While Brooks doubtless benefited from Pipkin's endorsement, he was at the start of a brilliant career, and he was offered an instructorship on the English faculty for September of 1932. Now, in the spring of 1934, he had the opportunity to return the kindness shown him by Red Warren at Vanderbilt and Oxford.[7]

When the Warrens left for a brief trip during spring break, they were still hoping that Dr. Mims would find at least two courses for Warren. But there were other instructors who would be glad of that work. One was Edd Winfield Parks, a Tennessean one year Warren's junior who had a Harvard B.A. and a Vanderbilt Ph.D. When the Warrens returned after Easter they gave a party at their cottage. Trying to bring Cinina up to date on local news, Harriet Owsley told her that Edd Parks said he would be back at Vanderbilt in the fall, and Dr. Mims had already assigned to him the courses he would teach. Cinina wanted to know what the courses were, and when Harriet told her, she went into a fury. She screamed, "Those were the courses he promised to Red!" She called him from among the guests and told him the news. His face lost its color and assumed a look his friends had noticed in times of stress: a look they called "the mask," a face of complete stonelike immobility. He was finished at Vanderbilt.[8]

It was one of the worst traumas of his life. "The place I wanted to live," he would recall, "the place I thought was heaven to me, after my years of wandering, was middle Tennessee. . . . Tom Zerfoss had wanted to buy a farm where I could live, a place where he could keep his horses and I could keep a garden and write. . . . I made a search and did find such a place . . . and he subsequently bought it, but by then I had been fired and my dream of Middle Tennessee country was gone." That was the way he would always think of it, that he was fired, driven out. It was easy to focus his anger. More than fifty years later, when he spoke of the man he saw as his evictor from this demi-Eden, he would call him "that old sonofabitch Mims." To Warren's most loyal friends the epithet was deserved, especially those who said they had heard Mims refer to Warren now as "Cyclops."[9]

They waited, and then A. T. Johnson, the chairman at Southwestern, came through. "Red has a job at Memphis," Caroline Gordon informed Andrew Lytle, "but doesn't want to go there, or else Cinina doesn't, and is going down to see Pipkin on a forlorn hope." As it developed, he did not have to make the trip. When Pipkin wrote that he was coming to Nashville and would like to see him, Warren invited him out to his house for dinner. He did not know that President Smith had been contemplating an effort to increase LSU's scholarly prestige by jointly sponsoring the *Southwest Review* with Southern Methodist University. As Warren later described the visit, "Pipkin asked if [I] had any new poems handy." When he produced one, Pipkin read it carefully and said he would like to print it in the *Southwest Review.* He produced fifteen dollars and completed the transaction. Shortly thereafter, Warren was invited to present an informal lecture at LSU.[10]

At last there was a lift for their spirits, and some of the results gained even Caroline Gordon's half-grudging admiration. She told Andrew Lytle, "Cinina—remains Cinina through thick and thin. They have the place shined up like a new pin. . . . Cinina should be a lesson to us all, I think. Through this distressing time she has kept her flag flying at high mast, has never stopped spending for one moment. She saved three dollars the other day by buying six dollars worth of jelly moulds for three dollars. . . ." Allen Tate's view of his friend's wife was no less waspish. Warren took the opportunity of his summer freedom to visit Guthrie. As Tate later reported to Andrew Lytle, "Red came up last week to spend a week with his father, but Miss Emma was so solicitous for him that she followed him in 24 hours and stayed for the remainder of the visit. Mr. Warren planned a fishing trip for a day with his elder son, but Cinina always did want to try fishing, so she went along, and she said she would have to take it up if Red did because 'we always want to do things together.' "[11]

When Warren arrived in Baton Rouge, Brooks had done his part in paving the way. The chairman, Dr. William A. Read, knew of their friendship. "You know Warren," he said to Brooks. "What's he like?"

This provided a perfect opportunity, for Brooks was a man to be trusted. This Methodist minister's son was a model of probity, rectitude, and decorum. He could well have said to Read what he said of Warren later, how he had always impressed him and Lytle and Lanier "with his talk, the brilliant stream of ideas, also his ability to write poems, to publish books . . . his passion for ideas, his energy, his sheer power and agility of mind, his sensitivity." Even as Brooks answered Read's questions, he knew that Pipkin "wanted Warren on any terms we could get him. We didn't have to debate the matter. It was just a question of, could it be arranged?"[12]

Brooks was there to greet him when he arrived, a pink plaster covering his left eye. He could have chosen any number of subjects for his talk. He had been reviewing fiction as well as poetry, and he chose a current southern novel, probably Caroline Gordon's *Aleck Maury, Sportsman*. It was well received, and the warmth and spontaneity of his informal conversation exerted its familiar charm.[13]

A few days later he was offered an assistant professorship. He would teach three quarters in each academic year at a salary of $2,800, beginning in the fall. "The Old War Skule," as LSU had been affectionately called by generations of students, was not Vanderbilt University, but it was a university on the move, with all the power of Senator Huey P. Long behind it. The use of that power would sometimes run contrary to academic freedom, but in the decade to come the impetus from Long to Smith to Pipkin would help to assemble there on the banks of the Mississippi, especially in the English department, one of the most talented groups of young professors in the country.

After arranging for the job at Southwestern to be offered to Allen Tate, who was burdened with debts too oppressive to bear any longer, Warren made ready to leave middle Tennessee for Baton Rouge and the Deep South. But it was mid-September before they could depart. When they stopped to see the Tates in Memphis they explained the delay. In January, Cinina's handsome, charming, thirty-four-year-old brother, Peter, had paid them a visit. As Caroline Gordon told Sally Wood, "He has been driving a hundred miles a night between orchestra engagements and sleeping in his car and so on and says that he is now going to be a dentist and keep music for his own pleasure." The Warrens found out at the last minute that Peter Brescia had run up a bill of fifty dollars at the gas station and charged it to them. "Peter couldn't be found," Caroline wrote Andrew Lytle, "but his landlady obligingly loaned them some money so they rolled off, leaving the four cats to come by express."[14]

Frank Owsley sold them his 1931 Studebaker for fifty dollars. The "beat-up" green sedan had many rattles but a good engine. Warren said later, "Original Sin is supposed to be indestructible, and the old Studebaker damn near was." So he named it. On the roads cut through cypress swamps they could see "the palmetto-leaf and sheet-iron hovels of the moss pickers, rising like some fungoid growth from a hummock under the great cypress knees, surrounded by scum-green water that never felt sunlight, back in the Freudianly contorted cypress gloom of cottonmouth mocassins big as the biceps of a prize-fighter, and owl calls, and the murderous metallic grind of insect life, and the smudge fire at the hovel door, that door being nothing but a hole in a hovel wall, with a piece of croker sack hung over it." After nineteen hours on roads Warren called "frightful," they finally drove into Baton Rouge and parked the car in Charles Pipkin's driveway at two o'clock in the morning.[15]

At first the house hunting was discouraging. They had loved living on the Burch place, but in the Baton Rouge area, Cinina wrote Harriet Owsley, there were "cardboard effect bungalow suburbs, or there isn't anything at all." But finally they found a house on Park Drive (later Hyacinth Avenue) in Southdowns, south of the city limits and a ten-minute ride from the campus. They had seven rooms plus glassed-in porches on four acres of land, with water and electricity included, for twenty-five dollars a month. Caroline told Andrew, "I can just see it turning into one of those snug Warren retreats. Cinina already has her eye on a Chippendale dining table."[16]

Though the population of Baton Rouge did not exceed forty thousand, it shared something of the same exotic culture as New Orleans—an hour and a half away by train—with its live oaks and Spanish moss, its banana trees and magnolias. Nearby was the soaring new capitol building, on whose twenty-fourth floor Senator Long kept a suite from which he ran the state just as high-handedly as he had done before he left the governorship for Washington. Not far to the south was the university, with its 5,000 acres, 230 faculty members, and more than 5,000 students. It was a land-grant institution, which had long been dominated by the school of agriculture. The Old War Skule heritage was still evident in the cadet corps, which wore uniforms three days a week. But this was changing as the fierce will of

Huey P. Long put in motion the programs meant to make it a major university—a university its football team could be proud of, as one wit put it.

The students were "like students anywhere in the country in the big state universities, except for the extraordinary number of pretty girls and the preternatural blankness of the gladiators who were housed beneath the stadium to have their reflexes honed, their diet supervised, and—through the efforts of their tutors—their heads crammed with just enough of whatever mash was required (I never found out) to get them past their minimal examinations. Among the students there sometimes appeared, too, that awkward boy from the depth of the Cajun country or from some scrabblefarm in North Louisiana, with burning ambition and frightening energy and a thirst for learning; and his presence there, you reminded yourself, with whatever complication of irony seemed necessary at the moment, was due to Huey, and to Huey alone. For the 'better element' had done next to nothing in fifty years to get that boy out of the grim despair of his ignorance."[17]

By any practical measure Warren was better off than he had been a term before, even apart from the salary. As an assistant professor he would teach four courses, and if Pipkin's plans matured, he would be relieved of one of them. Warren had arranged his schedule so that he taught three days a week, clearing the other days for work to provide added income. He had been writing and marketing short stories. And there was the promise that other elements of their new situation would fall into place. Cleanth and Warren succeeded in obtaining a graduate assistantship for Albert Erskine, who was glad to leave his Memphis bookshop to work for a Ph.D. and teach freshman English. But the Warrens were still pressed for money. They took a break from their efforts, however, at the end of September. "We went to New Orleans Friday and spent an exciting week-end there," Cinina wrote Harriet Owsley. "As a matter of fact we had too good a time Friday, and Saturday morning I thought my time had come."[18]

17

Huey's University

It was great Canaan's grander counterfeit.
Bold Louisiana,
The landfall of my soul—
Or then it seemed—
               —*Brother to Dragons*[1]

He was writing new stories and mining earlier manuscripts for others. He had sold "The Unvexed Isles" to a new journal called *The Magazine*. The story was short on action and long on style, revealing the empty life of Professor George Dalrymple, a Nebraskan stuck forever in a dreary Illinois college. Warren had been sending stories to Lambert Davis at the *Virginia Quarterly Review,* and Davis had been rejecting them. He had adapted "The Love of Elsie Barton: A Chronicle" from his novel in progress. Davis liked it better than his previous submission but refused it. When Davis asked for a contribution for the *Quarterly*'s tenth anniversary issue, he sent "Her Own People." The story's major characters are a rancorous newspaper reporter and his wife, both suffering hangovers, and their maid, Viola, whom they have brought with them from Alabama to Tennessee and who has deserted them just before their party the previous night. Davis accepted this story. It would pay seventy-five dollars on publication, six months later. "I wrote quite a few short stories," Warren would say later, "but I never had the same feeling for them as I had for poems or novel[s]. . . . I was very hard up and hoped for the quick buck."[2]

Stories were only a fraction of his output, as he made clear when he sent his new Guggenheim Fellowship application. He was asking for the grant to complete a long poem begun two years before. Part of it, "The Return: An Elegy," would appear in *Poetry* in November. Books in progress included his volume of forty-four poems. And there was the longer fiction. He would also use the fellowship to write a novel "laid in southwestern Kentucky and northwestern Tennessee, the section known as the Dark Fired Tobacco Section. The period involved is from 1890–1914." He wanted to revise *God's Own Time* and complete the still untitled novel in progress.

By now he probably had a first draft of eight chapters. It begins in the classroom with Ernest Griffin, a grotesque mathematics teacher and school principal who might be a latter-day Ichabod Crane. His best pupil is precocious Steve Adams, skinny and greasy-haired. The action is generated through Helen Beaumont, who is stolid and stupid but attractive to Frank Durrett, a flashy railroad detective. Helen's mother is the Elsie Barton whose life Warren had extended in the story he had offered to the *Virginia Quarterly*. Steve's mother, Mary Scruggs Adams, is melancholy and ineffectual but overprotective. Steve's father, the president of the school board, is a lawyer, once Elsie Barton's suitor, whose drab life has never matched his "dwindling" dreams. Steve's wretched schoolfellows treat him with contempt, and he is befriended only by Jim Hawkins, the school's star athlete, who protects him. Guthrie was obviously much in Warren's mind as he spun out his story. But it was as if all his models were rendered in cruel caricature: the steady but uninspiring father, the overprotective mother, the powerful grandfather, and the idealized older friend.[3]

Kent Greenfield still supplied friendship and material for poetry as well as fiction. He pitched for John McGraw's New York Giants for five seasons, and in 1926 he pitched against the legendary Grover Cleveland Alexander and won. But for a man with Kent's energy, McGraw's discipline was harder than Guthrie High School's. He barred physical activity outside the ballpark so Kent would be fresh for the games. So Kent diverted himself with girls who followed the team and by drinking heavily. A few years later he was in the minor leagues with a succession of new teams with smaller ballparks and longer bus rides. Finally he was back home in Guthrie—in the fields with his dogs, on the blacksmith shop bench with the idlers, in the shacks of Squiggtown. On some of Warren's returns he would see Kent when he was well, and the old affection was still there.[4]

The decline of Red's father was not so precipitous, but the distance traversed was also great—from banker to bankrupt. On December 12 the house in Guthrie and two other lots went on the block. Thomas Penn Warren was there among the bidders. In March of 1933 he and his bride, Alice Proctor Bryan, had appeared at his brother's cottage, newlyweds uncertain of their future. Warren had offered what help he could, and the couple had returned to Guthrie. Given to claiming, like Kent Greenfield, that he never read a book, Thomas plunged into the hard work of tobacco farming and showed he had a talent for it. When the property auction ended, the winning bid was $126.50, by Thomas Penn Warren. Robert Penn Warren worried about his silent, stoic father, soon to be sixty-six years old. But he had other worries there at home.[5]

Albert Erskine was aware of them. He had moved in with the Warrens, a welcome boarder as he had been in Nashville. At their convivial, hard-drinking parties he would join in singing the Italian songs Cinina loved. Tall and graceful, he made an admirable dancing partner whereas Warren danced poorly and could hardly carry a tune. Albert was her sympathetic friend, knowing how the Tates hated her. Highstrung, subject to insomnia and depression, she would sometimes take barbiturates. Combined with alcohol they had a powerful effect. One afternoon when Warren came home early he found Cinina drunk, the first evidence that she had become a secret solitary drinker.[6]

The roots of the problem were deep. Cinina's need for acceptance and esteem, the need to exert influence of some kind, had grown. Her writing produced no publishable work. But she hoped she would find employment and satisfaction in teaching Italian at LSU. There was no good text available, she declared, and said she would write one. She had tried to ingratiate herself with Warren's friends, but her tone put people off. She was not shy about asking Harriet Owsley— one of her few friends—for favors, and sometimes with something of a rather grand manner. She assured Rose Bradford, the wife of Caroline Gordon's nephew, Manson, that she would get Mrs. Burch to do a tea for her and introduce her to friends who "really count." She told Manson, "I'm going to do some *real* entertaining at Baton Rouge." Tate commented, "Not one of us doubts it for a minute."[7]

By November both the Warrens had reason to be pleased. Cinina was hired to fill an unexpected vacancy teaching two Italian classes. She found them enthusiastic and organized an Italian club, which grew so well that the next month she had twenty-eight people to supper. Urging the Tates to come down for a visit, Warren told them, "I shan't describe again the paradise we have. . . ." When they did come, it was a memorable time. Afterward Warren wrote, "It has taken me all this time to conquer the impulse to start drinking after breakfast. And even yet the impulse to drink in the middle of the afternoon is recalcitrant." He and Cinina made a trip to Nashville and stayed with the Owsleys. Their money ran so low that Warren had to ask Tate for a thirty-dollar loan. Back home, nursing a cold and about to resume work, he couldn't find the check. After hours of searching they discovered it in one of their trunks. He took up the thread of his story and went on.[8]

Other projects promised a quicker payoff. *Poetry* had published "The Return: An Elegy" in November. Lambert Davis took "John Crowe Ransom: A Study in Irony" at a price of a hundred dollars. Warren sent in three more poems and proposed an essay on Faulkner. The poems showed the growing skill of their thirty-year-old author. "History," couched in language almost biblical, suggests the historical perspective of the first three "Kentucky Mountain Farm" poems. Longest of the seven at just over a hundred lines, it is the account of the arduous journey about to be climaxed by the cataclysmic descent of these hardship-hardened predators upon "the delicate landscape unfurled" whose nameless and peaceful people have created a rich and beautiful land. Davis would use this poem and "Resolution" in the July 1935 issue of the *Virginia Quarterly Review.*[9]

At this same time Warren was beginning to take on editorial duties himself. In early November Charles Pipkin told him more about his plans for LSU's participation in the *Southwest Review* and asked him to help obtain good new material. Warren promptly enlisted Tate and asked Caroline Gordon for new stories. "There is a divided editorship," he told Tate, "but I feel sure that in this instance no difficulty could possibly arise." He was wrong. At Southern Methodist University, Henry Nash Smith and John H. McGinnis saw the magazine's primary focus located just where the title said: in the Southwest. Pipkin on the other hand believed "that rather than Louisiana being part of the Southwest, Texas was part of the South." In the fall of 1933, Pipkin and Professor Read appeared on the masthead as editors, while Cleanth Brooks, Roark Bradford, Lyle Saxon, and John Gould Fletcher became associate editors, joining four from SMU. When John McGinnis learned that Warren was to be appointed too, he wrote Smith that he was concerned about "the foundations of the *Review:* I suspect an invasion of termites—Agrarian termites."[10]

The Warrens must have felt that they deserved a special holiday that year. They joined the Tates at Benfolly for what Caroline called "The

Christmas Debauch." Then the party moved on southward as Andrew Lytle and other friends joined them. "We spent two weeks between Red's house and the hard boards of the Quartier," Lytle
recalled. There in New Orleans "We got up at nine o'clock in the
morning and started the day with absinthe frappé." The days and
nights ran into each other in a way Scott Fitzgerald might have described. Because the depression was still on, the bars were almost
empty. "We took over one, with its piano, square-danced to 'Go In
and Out the Window.' At three o'clock we ate oysters. . . ." In Baton
Rouge Caroline admired the Warrens' "lovely cottage, beautifully
furnished, camellias blooming in the front yard, liquor flowing, people inviting you somewhere every minute." She told Warren that
their moving the party from New Orleans to Baton Rouge and from
gin to whiskey without losing any of the revelers was a memorable
feat. In the early days of the new year of 1935, Allen and Caroline
spent hours just sitting before their fire. The monotony, she wrote
Warren, was broken by the postman bringing, to their amazement,
poems and long articles from Baton Rouge. "How in the name of
God do you do it?" she asked him.[11]

For the Baton Rouge editors of the *Southwest Review* the beginning
of the new year was anything but monotonous. In *So Red the Rose,*
Stark Young presented a kind of apotheosis of southern life. In his review, Albert Erskine praised the novel for its historical accuracy and defense of southern prewar society, including enlightened paternalism.
When Henry Nash Smith wrote that he and his colleagues disapproved
of the review, Warren defended it but asked Erskine to do some rewriting. Smith was ready to see the magazine fail rather than survive as "an
Agrarian sheet," but he finally agreed to publish the review. Meanwhile, back in Baton Rouge, important events were imminent.[12]

The frenetic pace continued. Edward Donahoe came for a week's
visit, followed by Robert Franklin Warren in late January. In his two
weeks' stay they made several trips and attended more parties. Cinina
told Harriet Owsley, "I feel abnormal when I'm completely sober."
When the new term began on February 4, she returned to her teaching and her reading for her M.A. thesis. She also put on a program
honoring the Italian consul. Warren proudly reported to Frank
Owsley, "She has worked like a dog at the business, coaching singers,
coaching grammar, and everything else." Not only was the consul
pleased with the recital, but it appeared that the library might receive
a large gift of books from the Italian government.[13]

With energy that seemed phenomenal to Caroline Gordon—and to Allen Tate, who suffered, often for long periods, from writer's block—Warren kept churning out work: a short story, another chapter of the novel, a revision of his manuscript volume of poems, letters soliciting submissions to the *Southwest Review,* and material for his new courses. For the story "Goodwood Comes Back" he drew directly on boyhood memories of Kent Greenfield, then his fame and fall, but he made the fall more fell than in life. (Warren would later say, "Short stories kill poems," but this material would reappear more effectively in poems.) It was rejected as "unsuitable" at both *Scribner's* and *Esquire.* "I just can't keep bad language out of my stories," he wrote Caroline and Allen, who thought this story perhaps his best.[14]

March brought word that Bobbs-Merrill would publish neither of his novels. They did not like the new novel nearly as well as the first one. (In the ninth chapter he had sent them, his hero, Jim Hawks, seemed implicated in a robbery, and Helen Beaumont and Frank Durrett contracted a secret marriage.) The trouble, D. L. Chambers wrote, was not with his ability but rather with his choice of material in both novels. "Either," he told him, "in our poor judgment, would be a bad beginning." The book market was still depressed. So they advised him to wait. But he was not ready to give up on either of the two novels, and he completed the second book in two more chapters featuring homicide and sexuality in a way that suggested *True Detective* magazine covers.[15]

Asked about these unpublished novels years later, Warren would say, "They were awful! They were terrible! They shouldn't have been published!" But they were part of the learning process. And from *God's Own Time,* by far the better of the two, he salvaged material for three short stories. He had gained experience in plotting a long narrative, and he had sharpened his talent for dialogue, dialect, and the description of his native country, which he had displayed in "Prime Leaf." Caroline Gordon once wrote that she couldn't seem to keep violence and killings out of her fiction. Warren might have said the same thing. And there was a consistency in his vision of life that linked his fiction with his poetry: a sense of the tragic common to human experience.[16]

18

❖

The Southern Review—
and Other Projects

And now
We see, below,
The delicate landscape unfurled,
A world
Of ripeness blent, and green, . . .
— *"History"*[1]

Saint Patrick's Day brought a good omen. On that sunny Sunday afternoon President James Monroe Smith's shiny black Cadillac limousine drew up in front of the Warrens' house. He and his wife had come to show them something of their new surroundings. To Brooks and Warren, Smith was a minion of Huey Long, and his wife was a brash social climber. But Cinina found Mrs. Smith's company agreeable, and she enjoyed the ambience of her status. The Smiths invited Albert Erskine to join them for their ride through the countryside. At a momentary lull in the sightseeing recitals, Smith put a question to Warren. "If I could raise enough money for it, could a quarterly review published at LSU get good contributors?" Warren unhesitatingly replied, "Yes." Smith asked him if they could produce the first issue by June 1, and again Warren said yes. "Who could you get as a business manager?" Warren pointed to Erskine. "He's right here," he said. "All right," Smith said. "Can you let me have the details on the project by Monday afternoon?"[2]

Warren lost no time in telling Tate. "I got Pip and Cleanth Monday morning and by 3:30 P.M. the whole matter had been approved with a minimum guarantee of $10,000; we are instructed to ask for more if we need it." Pipkin was to be editor-in-chief. Brooks and Warren were to be the managing editors, with their teaching loads reduced to three courses, though the magazine would take far more time than the remitted course would have taken. Warren solicited manuscripts from T. S. Eliot and many other American writers including Faulkner, Fitzgerald, and Sherwood Anderson. By the end of the month he had positive responses from a half-dozen writer friends. It was a good start for a journal that *Time,* five years later, would call "superior to any other in the English language. . . ."[3]

Uncertain of his next job less than a year before, Warren was now—though still an untenured junior professor—in a position of some influence. Louisiana State University was celebrating its diamond jubilee, and Warren and Brooks had planned a conference of editors of southern and southwestern magazines, directors of university presses, and writers to be held on April 10 and 11. Cinina was busy with her own preparations. April 12 was to be Italian Day. Augusto Rosso, the ambassador, was to pay an official call on Governor O. K. Allen, watch a military parade, receive a nineteen-gun salute, and speak at the luncheon in his honor. There would be more speeches, and then they would all go to tea at the president's house. Cinina was happy the Owsleys were coming, for "I know your sentiments regarding my well beloved Italy!"[4]

The conference began in midsummer heat Wednesday morning on the top floor of the Heidelberg Hotel. The forty participants numbered among them the two factions that had made the *Southwest Review* collaboration so tenuous. As chairman, Warren led them into the conference topic, "Reading in the South," which soon resolved itself into a debate on the South's cultural heritage. Warren and Brooks took little part in the heated exchanges. The high point for them came at Thursday evening's banquet when they announced the birth of *The Southern Review.*[5]

Warren and Ford Madox Ford were there in the Venetian Room of Foster Hall when Senator Huey P. Long spoke on "Politics and Education." The Kingfish gladly admitted that he had interfered in the operation of the university: he had stepped in to prevent the reduction of teachers' salaries when they were being reduced all over the country. The state appropriation had nearly doubled. "I have had considerable to do with only the last five years and we have done as much in that five as was done in the other seventy," he told his listeners. "If you will come back in the next two or three years we will show you some more." Ford thought the speech "astonishing" and its author "a remarkable man." Warren later called him "a political genius" who played many roles: "vulgarian, buffoon, clown, dude, sentimental dreamer, man of ruthless action, coward, wit, philosopher, orator."[6]

Seeing Long in action must have made Warren wonder about the assurances he had received. "It was Huey's University, but he, I was assured, would never mess with my classroom." Established in the magazine's two adjoining offices in the North Administration Building, Warren, Brooks, and Erskine worked together with little thought of possible political repercussions. The maiden issue contained articles touching much of the political spectrum. John Chamberlain wrote in *The New York Times,* "Huey may dictate to the Louisiana Legislature, but he evidently permits free controversy in the new quarterly published by 'his' university." Warren did not attribute their freedom to Huey's magnanimous large-mindedness. "He was far too adept in the art of power to care what an assistant professor might have to say." The paid subscriptions for the second issue would rise to more than nine hundred.[7]

Now, in the hot Louisiana Maytime as the trees came fully into leaf in the sunny days and the nights grew heavy with the scent of jasmine and magnolia, Warren was able to turn to preparations for their annual alternation between the South and the West. They would be at the University of Montana in June and early July, then at the University of Colorado's writers' conference for three weeks until early August, spending the rest of their time in Oakland and San Francisco before returning home in mid-September. They broke their journey in Oklahoma, where Edward Donahoe welcomed them with his usual hospitality. Cinina reported to Albert Erskine "a fine drinking spell" that knocked her out "for two days after I left Ponca City." They crossed the Continental Divide and on Sunday afternoon, June 9, having put 2,600 miles behind them, they drove into Missoula.[8]

It would be a crowded summer. Warren worked hard for his $300 stipend. His students were generally good, but reading six novels and assorted poems left him little time for much writing other than the lectures for the Colorado conference. There he would earn $250 for his three weeks' work. *The Southern Review* profited too: Warren wrote to Baton Rouge for forty-five copies of the freshly published first number and sold thirty-five of them. He shared the lecturing and

student conferences with Robert Frost, Bernard DeVoto, Whit Bur-
nett, and his old friend Dixon Wecter. Edward "Ted" Davison directed the conference, and he and his wife provided warm hospitality.
Warren quickly formed a friendship with them and their children,
seven-year-old Peter and his sister, Lesley. He would take them to
Baseline Lake on the outskirts of town. Peter was afraid of the water,
and he would observe Warren with something like hero worship as
he inserted nose plugs and ear plugs and pulled on a bathing cap.
Peter was fascinated by the rhythm and relentlessness of his Australian
crawl as his figure grew smaller until he reached the other side of the
mile-wide lake. He was a good companion too, and Peter would always remember that he was not only sweet to them but also terribly
funny. The stay was marred, though, by illness. On a hiking expedition, Cinina suffered a deep puncture in her heel that put her to bed
with pain and fever. Warren developed a case of conjunctivitis that
kept him from working. On August 11 they were glad to set out for
Oakland, where they would be with Domenico Brescia again on Ver-
non Street. Their time went fast, but they made the most of it. Writing Albert Erskine just before their return, Warren told him that he
had typed out a hundred-page novelette, three short stories, and the
revisions of the second novel.[9]

At home Brooks and Erskine were working on the next *Southern Review*. It could not have been in better hands. The sole support of his
parents, Brooks could now finally afford, after a six-year courtship, to
marry a diminutive, wise, and witty New Orleans woman whom
everyone called not by her given name, Edith, but by a childhood
nickname, Tinkum. As lively as Cleanth was courtly, she entertained
generously and with style, playing hostess to faculty colleagues and
nephews and nieces, coping not just with senior faculty but also with
one small kinsman who managed to swallow a class pin while under
their roof. (Though Dr. Carl A. Weiss could not make the house call,
his son, Dr. Carl Austin Weiss, Jr., managed the problem with professional skill and social grace.)[10]
    Cleanth and Tinkum welcomed the arrival of two new colleagues,
Robert B. Heilman, a freshly minted Harvard Ph.D. and Renaissance
scholar, and his wife, Ruth. A week after their Labor Day arrival, the
Heilmans walked the two blocks from their sweltering apartment to
the capitol to observe the legislature in session with the Kingfish,
there from Washington. It was September 8. From the visitors' gallery

the Heilmans did in fact see him giving orders and holding court from a swivel chair on the speaker's rostrum. A few minutes before adjournment, Long left the chamber, his rapid stride outdistancing his aides and bodyguards. "A few seconds later there was a strange outburst of sounds in a rapid but irregular sequence," Heilman would remember. "We were hearing the shots that killed Dr. Carl Weiss [Jr.] and [Dr. Weiss's shot that] fatally wounded Senator Long, who died a day and a half later." A number of hypotheses would be offered to explain the actions of the genteel young healer. His motivation would remain a puzzle for many, including Robert Penn Warren.[11]

The Warrens heard the news at a gas station in Nevada, and it seemed to them that people were talking about it all the way back across the country to Nashville. It was a hurried trip. They had to be back for the start of classes and their other projects. "Red and Cinina blew in Saturday from California," Caroline Gordon reported to Andrew Lytle in mid–September. "They stayed only one night, were pretty exhausted, of course, but full of plans and beans, as usual. Cinina is positively fat and Red looks better than he did this spring. Is starting another novel!!" The comment revealed more than habitual cattiness. It suggested Caroline and Allen's ambivalence about their onetime protégé now outstripping his onetime mentor. Warren also sent two poems to Lambert Davis with the postscript, "I shall greatly appreciate as prompt a decision as you are able to give, because I have recently had a request for some stories."[12]

Other prose projects were also occupying his attention. Besides the novel Caroline Gordon mentioned, he would soon be at work on a textbook. But the most immediate task was an essay he had promised for *Who Owns America?*, the symposium devised by Allen Tate and Herbert Agar as a critique of capitalism. Entitled "Literature as Symptom," Warren's essay began with John Milton and his "search for a worthy theme" and then glanced at other canonical writers from Hawthorne to Hemingway before moving to the "regional" and the "proletarian" writers who were "revolutionary" because "both may be said to be opposed to finance-capitalism and to resent the indignity heaped by that system of society upon the creative impulse, indignity which has succeeded in estranging the artist from society and from the proper exercize [sic] of his function as 'a man speaking to men.' " Any reader seeking a political-literary program would have been disappointed, finding there instead a brilliant discourse on literary history capped by the adjuration to the artist to his own self to be true. After a disappointing reception, the high points of the book's publication would be the parties, one of which, according to Caroline Gordon, went on until "everyone, including John Ransom, reeled with drink."[13]

There was no such cause for merriment in the classroom. Warren and Brooks taught big sections, and they soon found that their students could not read literature. They had no idea how to read a poem or short story. Textbooks provided only biographical and bibliographical facts and the kind of impressionistic criticism Edwin Mims had purveyed for years. One day Warren handed a dozen pages of notes on metrics to Cleanth Brooks, who soon supplied material on metaphor and imagery. The undergraduates threw the mimeographed results away, but one bright graduate student, John Thibault Purser, suggested that they get the LSU Press to publish them. The result, entitled *Sophomore Poetry Manual,* met with opposition—some from faculty—but two terms later, under the title *An Approach to Literature,* the collaborators would provide one text that met all the needs of the introductory courses. One day Frederick Crofts, who traveled for his own small firm, made them a proposition. "Look," he said, "a university press can't sell a textbook. Why not let me make an arrangement, if I can, with the Press to take over the book?" Not long afterward the collaborators were under contract for another version of *An Approach to Literature.* The modest set of mimeographed notes was evolving into what Brooks would call "a matrix" for future collaborations.[14]

Warren sent new poems to Tate, probably "Monologue at Midnight" and perhaps "Bearded Oaks." Scrupulously direct in his judgments, Tate told him, "I imagine these are the best poems you have ever written. . . . There is a closeness of texture in this work that I've never seen in your poetry." In October "The Garden" had appeared in *Poetry.* It was in part Warren's tribute, himself an avid gardener, to one of his favorite Metaphysical poets. In nine eight-line stanzas of "The Garden" Andrew Marvell had celebrated the joys of quiet and innocence as better than the rewards of ambitious striving. Warren's four stanzas followed Marvell's metrics but showed an awareness of love's unease as well as its joys, with an autumnal sense of appetite quite as much as innocence. Another thing the poem showed was a virtuosity with the seventeenth-century idiom as well as the contemporary.[15]

Thirty-six Poems, his gathering from more than ten years' work, was published on February 15, 1936. If the technical influences of the Metaphysical poets and T. S. Eliot were both apparent, the underlying sense of life owed as much to other poets as to Eliot's view of the modern world as a spiritual wasteland. Warren would never lose the deep affinity he had felt for Thomas Hardy's work since that summer day in Guthrie when John Ransom had read aloud as they sat on the lawn. His early preoccupation with death was there in these poems and—perhaps from his late adolescent sorrows if not from poetic convention—something like a death wish. The consolation of religion would never be available to him, nor faith in any kind of transcendence or means of understanding the mysteries of time and change and identity, nor cushion against a harsh awareness of the individual's fate as finite and end-stopped. Man had to live in the harsh world of the Naturalists.[16]

The book appeared to a reception ranging from curt dismissal to encouraging praise. Most reviewers began with lists of influences they saw, but a few saw craftsmanship and growth and a keen intelligence at work. As if in agreement, President James Monroe Smith approved the recommendation for his promotion to associate professor.[17]

He was writing now with the assured fluidity of form he had shown in "The Garden." In "Picnic Remembered" he used rhyming couplets again. And again there is the natural beauty of the quiet day and the suggestion of both innocence and experience. But now there are two lovers in the foreground, and their joy is clearly shadowed and precarious. They are likened to swimmers or, in a passage Donne might have written, to insects:

> We stood among the painted trees:
> The amber light laved them and us;
> Or light then so untremulous
> So steady, that our substances,
> Twin flies, were as in amber tamed. . . .

And as darkness falls on the landscape, the two depart with darkness in their bosoms. *Scribner's Magazine* published it in March, and three months later, in the *Virginia Quarterly Review,* there was another study of a similar situation in "Monologue at Midnight." The lovers are again attended by both innocence and guilt. The mysteries of time and identity shadow them as the failing light had done.[18]

If these were poems posing problematical philosophical and aesthetic juxtapositions with linking imagery that gave them a subtle coherence, they were also love poems arising out of a relationship still passionate if often troubled. Cinina's letters to Harriet Owsley showed concern as well as possessiveness. The previous fall she had written that she thought they should not come up to Nashville at Thanksgiving: "In the first place, I am anxious to have Dr. Kate check Red over. He seems well but I want to be sure." But her own demands upon him had not diminished. One day when he and Albert had been long immersed over the chessboard, she finally walked across the room and kicked it off the table, scattering chessmen all over the floor. She did not resent Albert's place in her husband's life, as she would resent the presence of others, but she wanted his attention, and to be the center of attention herself. These emotions would continue to yield material for poetry.[19]

Five years earlier, Joseph Brewer had liked "Prime Leaf" well enough to offer an advance of three hundred dollars if Warren would expand it. Now Herbert Agar's publisher, Houghton Mifflin, was offering thousand-dollar "literary fellowships" to promising writers. Agar urged Warren to enter the competition. On June 13, 1936, Robert N. Linscott announced that Robert Penn Warren had won one of their two fellowships, from among 836 contestants, for "Prime Leaf." Warren would later say Houghton Mifflin told him, "Make it a novel. We'll give you the prize now." He promised it for January 1938, in spite of his other obligations: summer work in Baton Rouge before another three-week session of the University of Colorado Writers' Conference. That stint of lecturing and teaching sandwiched between the hot dusty trips out West and back was relieved only by the Davisons' hospitality and a brief time in "a cabin up in a canyon with a swift creek outside the door" where it was "cool and very fine."[20]

The conference could have produced awkward moments for Warren. The dominant figure was Thomas Wolfe, who, according to one participant, was "not so much lionized as adored." Gargantuan in stature, exuberance, and appetite for life, the thirty-six-year-old North Carolinian was still riding the wave of popularity of *Look Homeward, Angel* of 1929. Just the year before the conference, however, he had published an even more ambitious but uneven novel called *Of Time and the River.* One of the most critical reviews had come from Robert Penn Warren. When the two men were together bystanders expected fireworks, reckoning without Wolfe's generous openness. As Wolfe's biographer reported it, "He said there was one review of his book which had been by no means favorable, but that he had learned from it and appreciated it."[21]

Back in Baton Rouge there were masses of papers on the desks at *The Southern Review.* ("You occupy externally a much stronger position than you perhaps imagine," Tate had written him. "You *are* the Southern Review. Lest your modesty beguile you, remember that occasionally.") There was an anthology of stories by southern writers he had promised for Houghton Mifflin. And in the classroom he was teaching his sophomores from *An Approach to Literature* at the same time that he had two other texts on his mind.[22]

On July 22, just before they had set out for Colorado, T. J. Wilson, of Henry Holt and Company, sent $150 as an advance against royalties for a poetry text for freshman classes. It would be called *Understanding Poetry.* From Christmas to March, Brooks and Warren spent all the time they could on it. Word got back to Brooks that the Tates thought he was seducing Warren into time on textbooks better spent on poetry or fiction. (That Tate and Warren were anxiously awaiting word on a poetry text they had sent to a publisher sometime before must have added to the Tates' conviction.) But the fact was that the collaboration of Brooks and Warren was as fortuitous and natural as that of others of their time: Rodgers and Hart or Gershwin and Gershwin. Face-to-face across their abutting desks they would thrash things out: the thirty-one-year-old Brooks, short and compact, chubby-faced yet firm-jawed with a direct gaze from behind wire-rimmed spectacles; Warren, a year older, taller and rawboned. One of their best students, John Palmer, later to join the magazine staff, saw them as complementary: "Warren rather grand and expansive and somewhat roughneck, and Brooks always very sort of contained, the prototype of the scholar-gentleman, but my goodness did they strike sparks one upon the other. . . . [Brooks's] criticism is very orderly, logical, persuasive. It's reasonableness itself. . . . Warren's is more intuitive, more gutsy, more dramatic." An editorial session with Erskine joining in was for Palmer not just an intellectual exercise but also "a wonderful sort of social event."[23]

What Warren and Brooks were creating was a text that would translate sophisticated poetic theory into practical application. It would teach a student how to differentiate poetry from prose not only by rhyme and metrics but also by the function of the narrative and descriptive elements, and to go beyond the poet's explicit statement of crucial ideas to apprehend tone and attitude, to follow the function of imagery, and—for the brightest—to savor the operation of ambiguity and irony. What they were writing, as they taught their classes and wrote their poems and essays, would become the most influential poetry text ever printed. But at the moment it had to take its chances. Warren also had to get on with his novel.

19

❖

Getting It Written,
Among Other Problems

The oaks, how subtle and marine,
Bearded, and all the layered light
Above them swims; and thus the scene,
Recessed, awaits the positive night.
— *"Bearded Oaks"*[1]

He had accepted the Houghton Mifflin fellowship with the understanding that he would turn "Prime Leaf" into a novel, but when he
began writing, it became a different story. It was steeped in Tennessee
history up to the recent present. In its full development it would
come to juxtapose two mountain men—one a religion-obsessed
drifter and the other a corrupted war hero—with members of the
upper class: a wealthy entrepreneur and his corrupt daughter, and a
college boy ripe for corruption. Ranging widely in geography as well
as social classes, it may have been more than Warren was ready to handle in spite of his two previous novels. He put it aside to resume it
later as he would often do, nurturing an idea for years before setting
it all down.[2]

"Suddenly I switched to the tobacco war thing," he said later. It
was *not,* he would insist, a historical novel, for he remembered those
times from his childhood. He had resigned from the University of
Colorado Writers' Conference to devote all summer to the novel,
"even if I eat honey and wild locusts." Later that spring, writing a
critique of *The Fathers,* Allen Tate's novel in progress, he told him
he had about eighty thousand words done, but "now I'm not half

through. I'm jittery about the thing, one minute thinking I've got something by the tail and the next thinking it's a bust."[3]

In Nashville that spring a drama was playing itself out. For twenty years John Crowe Ransom had received outside offers, but his love of Tennessee and Vanderbilt had kept him there. Now the reaction against a curriculum-reform review he had chaired left him disillusioned and disgusted. Then he received a generous offer from Kenyon College in Gambier, Ohio. Allen Tate passionately threw himself into a campaign that put a flood of letters and telegrams on Chancellor Kirkland's desk. A university with a twenty-million-dollar endowment should not lose one of its chief ornaments to a small northern school with one-tenth Vanderbilt's endowment. Tate went ahead, arranging a dinner with Warren's help to honor Ransom for his contribution to southern literature regardless of his decision. Though Ransom had gradually made it clear to the Agrarians that he no longer fought under their banner, almost all of them were there on the occasion of what turned out to be his farewell.[4]

By late August, when he had moved four hundred miles northeast, across the Mason-Dixon line to Gambier, his mind was full of ideas with consequences for many others. He took along two of his best students, Randall Jarrell and Robert Lowell, to be joined the next year by another promising writer named Peter Taylor. In less than two years *The Kenyon Review* would appear, to be followed by the Kenyon School of English. In one writer's view, "These two developments brought together more distinguished and soon-to-be distinguished poets, critics, and writers of fiction than almost any other of this century. . . ." A by-product would be a Baton Rouge–Gambier axis that would bridge the geographical gap to reestablish something of what they had known in Nashville.[5]

As the spring term moved along, Warren's manifold activities made increasing demands. "I am trying to finish up my novel," he wrote Katherine Anne Porter in late May, "which Houghton Mifflin, with childish optimism, expects next January." (He was also requesting her "Old Mortality" for *A Southern Harvest,* the anthology he was editing for Houghton Mifflin.) Some of his friends were becoming distressed—by his problems and also his behavior. "Red and Miss Emma came through Middle Tennessee like a bewildered Kansas tornado," Allen Tate wrote Cleanth Brooks from Benfolly on June 24. "It is increasingly impossible to talk to Red. He is doing so many things he can't put his mind on any of them." Ford Madox Ford told Warren he wanted to write something for *The Southern Review,* and Allen was upset when "Red just stared at him vaguely, and at last suggested that he read and review 49 novels for the fall issue. . . . Red didn't mean anything unpleasant; he just didn't know what he was saying." Tate suspected another cause besides distraction and the trip to California: Red "doubtless had one eye on the question: Will Miss Emma take me off to the bedroom before or after lunch?" Tate disapproved of the trip to California. Cinina told them she was getting Red away from Baton Rouge so he could finish his novel. Tate said she "was like a sucking dove, and played a piece of high politics." The sexual dynamics of their marriage must by now have become increasingly complicated. If there were times when Cinina wanted him and he was busy writing, there were probably times when he wanted her and she in turn was unavailable.[6]

Brooks replied immediately. "There are several reasons why Red should have been in a daze when you saw him." One day when Cleanth was invited to lunch he listened as Cinina said, "I've made the decisions, Red, and thought out what we'll do. Now you'll have to see about them." In early June she was feeling ill and was put to bed by her doctor for rest and quiet, where she could eat what she liked and read detective stories. If Warren had consulted a physician he might well have been ordered to bed too. He and Cleanth "had fairly slaved for weeks—night work as well as day—trying to get the manuscript of [*Understanding Poetry*] in shape before Red had to leave." Warren had been suffering from terrible headaches for four days. The Brookses invited Cinina to stay with them so he could take the train for Nashville and the Ransom dinner and get some rest rather than taking the car. To their shock, she insisted that she go too and that they drive through the night to Nashville.[7]

A generous man not given to malice, Brooks wrote principally to explain the erratic and uncharacteristic behavior of one old friend to another. He hoped that his account would not seem too petty and nasty. "You forget how bad Cinina is after you get away from her for a little while, and your conscience begins to worry you a little." But he had been furious, he said, at the "intolerable" behavior that sprang from her jealousy of Red.[8]

In one of love's paradoxes, it was now that Warren put the final touches on "Bearded Oaks." The ten quatrains in iambic tetrameter had not only the Metaphysical echoes of "The Garden" but an even greater facility. Forty-five years later he would gloss the poem at one woman's request. It was written about 1935, he said. "The scene is a broad meadow with a number of the enormous live oaks of Louisiana strung with grey Spanish moss. The people involved are two lovers who have been lying in the shade of one of these trees after the sun goes down. The shadows of the trees now tend to level out as though they were water, as though the lovers were submerged in the water. They compare themselves to a coral growth that has been submerged for thousands of years, as they feel submerged by the human history before them. Though all of us are trapped in time, and live in time, so little time, there are moments, say in love, that seem outside of time—moments in which 'we practice for eternity.' I can't do more to explain it."[9]

If he had tried to do more, it would have taken more than one short paragraph, for the poem sounded many echoes and worked on several levels. As Andrew Marvell's lover in "To His Coy Mistress" tells his beloved that they do not have "world enough and time" as its flight rushes them toward "deserts of vast eternity," so Warren's lover, aware that "we live in time so little time," sees ahead "eternity" in the image of dark and silent sea depths, one of the most powerful images in Eliot's "Love Song of J. Alfred Prufrock." But whatever the influences, Warren assimilated them smoothly in this complex poem, which works on three time levels: the day that progresses from the bright "storm of noon" to the encroaching "graduate dark," the lovers' life span, and finally history, in which they are caught.[10]

At the end of the "Paradiso" in Dante's *Divine Comedy,* a lifelong favorite of Warren's, the poet learns through his beloved Beatrice that "in His will is our peace." There is no such belief or assurance in Warren's thoroughly naturalistic poem. The lovers are simply another order of creation, higher than the polyp and the kelp and the deer but destined nonetheless for decay, death, and dissolution. As the Elizabethan poets often used the words "to die" to signify not just death but also sexual climax, so there is here the linkage of the two ideas. Lying in the grass, the lovers are like the scene of which they are a part as it "awaits the positive night." Experiencing something like postcoital *tristesse,* he silently tells her not that he loves her more but rather that he does not love her less, now that "the caged heart makes iron stroke." And so this death-laden image leads him to see this silent hour's term as practice for eternity. This is hardly the familiar *carpe diem* theme. If the lovers have seized this day for pleasure, it is with the awareness that such pleasure is rigidly limited in duration and ultimately subject to oblivion.

If one were to speculate on personal revelation here, what might one hazard? Almost a dozen years had passed since Warren had met Emma Brescia and seven years since they had married. They had gone from flirtation to infatuation, to passion and love. After separation, illness, and increasing conflict they were still together, though at increasing emotional and physical cost. If Allen Tate was right, she still held him with strong bonds of sexual passion, but her demands upon him and her possessiveness and jealousy had been encroaching ever more strongly, not just upon their own relationship but also upon his relationships with most of his friends. A short consideration of this poem—with its entwined images of light and grass and water, the wavering motions of descent downward to darkness, the dying of the day and the inevitable victory of death over love—can only suggest its richness. One indication of its centrality is the fact that the poet would include it in each of his volumes of collected poems.

With Mamye, their cook, they drove west again. After several days in San Francisco and Oakland they made the trip to Clear Lake, a hundred miles to the north. They were welcomed by Bernard and Mildred Bronson, friends from Berkeley. Mornings were quietly luxurious. "Cinina returned to her bed with her typewriter on her lap," Mildred remembered, "Red to a shady spot with his typewriter—not too far away for Cinina to call him back to hear the last sentence she'd written." Mildred would set out with her paints and big watercolor pad to go farther afield. Warren was seized again with the challenge of getting those mountain colors down, and on occasion he would join her.[11]

In spite of his initial reluctance, the trip was turning out well. The companionable Bronsons brought out Warren's natural gregariousness. Mildred sketched them concentrating over a chessboard, Bronson smoking his pipe and Warren smoking his cigarette, his mop of red hair down over his forehead. After lunch he would swim to the middle of the lake and float on his back for what seemed to Mildred an hour and a half. She thought he was composing whole chapters of his novel. He was working hard, Cinina wrote Albert. "He swims every day and weighs 166 pounds."[12]

The return to Baton Rouge brought a halt to the writing. Charles Pipkin was becoming aggrieved at the increasing dominance of literature in *The Southern Review.* But he was beset by personal problems and did little to bring in manuscripts more congenial to him as a social scientist. Warren and Brooks were obtaining work from established writers such as Katherine Anne Porter and promising new ones such as Eudora Welty. Such coups may have made "Pip" only more resentful. "Tinkum and Albert and I have been working on a parody of *The Waste Land* for extremely private circulation," Brooks wrote Tate. "Our *Waste Land* is the *Southern Review* office, and the dead which has been buried is an MS on social science which we hope will remain interred in the filing cabinet." This was a time when other relationships were also changing. The signs were sometimes small but significant. Warren's letters to Allen and Caroline used to end with love to them both from him and Cinina. Now he signed only himself, "As ever."[13]

As that relationship was cooling further, another was warming. Katherine Anne Porter moved into the lower Pontalba Building in New Orleans's Vieux Carré in September, and she would increasingly become a part of their lives. After their move to Baton Rouge Warren had rented "a pretty good little room on Royal Street" so they could make the seventy-mile drive southeast for weekends. When they saw Katherine Anne shortly after her arrival there, the trip was marred by what Brooks called Cinina's "hell-raising appearance." By the last weekend in October, her behavior had improved. Cleanth told Allen, it was "apparently due to Red's taking her in hand. . . . Red apparently told her that, if her bad manners to her friends came from her drinking too much, she would have to stop drinking. At present she is strictly on beer."[14]

Warren did as much writing as he could. *A Southern Harvest* was finished, and in early November he sent copies to his friends. Late that month he and Brooks finished their final revisions of *Understanding Poetry.* Warren mailed a new long poem to Tate, a practice he would continue all his life no matter what the distance or changing poetic styles and convictions. He had done a few fragments of a play, but he wouldn't get at it seriously until he finished the novel for Houghton Mifflin. "I can't see the end before 155,000 or 160,000 words," he told Tate.[15]

Warren's impact upon his students remained powerful. Cecile Starr said he set higher standards than any other professor she ever had. And he "discussed sexuality and mortality more openly and naturally than I had ever before heard. . . ." During one two-hour session of a seminar Patrick Quinn thought Warren gave "the most brilliant academic exhibition" he ever saw. When a very promising Vanderbilt senior named Leonard Unger had asked John Ransom for advice, Ransom had urged him to go to LSU to study with Brooks and Warren. "Red seemed without any effort, just with perfect naturalness, to develop a comfortable relation with students both graduate and undergraduate," Unger discovered. "I was one of a whole group that I found already calling him Red. . . ."[16]

Robert Heilman advised Norton Girault to enroll in Warren's Shakespeare course, and the first class meeting was unforgettable. "Here came this intense man in his early thirties with red hair and rugged good looks charging in right on the bell, smiling, saying 'Good morning,' then, with the vigor of a finely honed boxer going a series of very fast rounds, launching into a brilliant discussion of what tragedy was. Between brilliant bursts he would pause, head high, chin slightly elevated, giving the effect of a bird dog on the point, maybe call for questions, then resume. He kept that up until the bell, then gave us the assignment and name of the text and went barreling off leaving us in a euphoric daze. And yet, with all his intensity, Warren somehow managed always to communicate a genuine gentlemanliness, warmth and concern, not only to students, but to everyone he came in contact with, on campus and off." The course changed Girault's life.[17]

It was fortunate that Warren found such energizing pleasure in his teaching, for he encountered debilitating tension at home. For some people Cinina fitted the stereotype of the volatile Italian. She must have known this, for she was increasingly convinced that people did not like her. Some were amused at her sedulous attendance upon Mrs. James Monroe Smith. Warren and Cinina arrived early at a party given by Cleanth and Tinkum Brooks but left to go to a lavish wedding reception for President Smith's daughter. When she and Warren returned an hour later, Cleanth saw that she was spoiling for a fight. He knew that his diminutive Tinkum "had a little of the devil in her," but he was with his guests on the other side of the room when Tinkum made a teasing remark about Cinina's going to the president's party. Suddenly there was a scuffle. Later Cleanth told Tate what had happened. "Tinkum gave C. a playful pat on her seat when she leaned over. C. proceeded to kick the hell out of her. Tinkum still suspected nothing, thinking that C. was merely playing and had not realized how hard she had kicked. Tinkum then moved across the room, and C. followed her, and standing over her, dared her to hit her again. Tinkum tried to pass it off by smiling and tapping her on the cheek. C. then proceeded to box her jaws." Warren seized his wife amid murmurs of commiseration with Tinkum. Katherine Anne Porter heard Warren as he rushed Cinina out of the apartment. "If you ever do anything like this again," he said, "I am going to leave you." Cinina telephoned the next day. She explained what had happened: too much liquor and the morbid fear that people didn't like her or understand her. Then she told Tinkum that she actually liked her and Cleanth a great deal. Tinkum simply heard her out, and thereafter she and Cleanth avoided social meetings. "At the moment you begin to think that you could pity her," Brooks wrote Tate, "she does something really revolting."[18]

Tate replied that he and Caroline had not been surprised to hear of the contretemps. At Benfolly Cinina had pointedly asked Caroline why she wasn't liked. Caroline's reply—that they all thought "she ought to treat Red better"—provoked an emotional attack on Caroline. The Tates had no friends, Cinina told them, and Allen was generally hated. "In the scene at Benfolly," Allen wrote, she said that "she and Red were better married than Caroline and I, because it was well-known that the Tates were about to get a divorce. I remember distinctly the horror in Red's face when she said that." Before long Warren would learn to control his facial expression, but when his friends saw what they called "the mask" descend, they came to feel that one of the costs was a kind of general withdrawal in this man they had always known as outgoing, genial, and warm.[19]

It was no wonder that he looked forward to the summer's escape. By early March he and Brooks were "swamped with proof on the Holt book and with the forthcoming issue of *The Southern Review*." They had finally finished reading proof on *Understanding Poetry,* and he was near the end of his novel. It was now 150,000 words long, and he hoped that two more weeks would see it done. Why did he drive himself so? For one thing, he needed the money from the books and the lectures he would give in increasing numbers. But there was probably another motive at work seen more clearly in the poetry: the drive for success and, whether he acknowledged it to himself or not, for fame.[20]

It was nearly three years since they had moved into Southdowns, and it was now too well settled for Warren. A friendly real estate man named Heidel Brown found them some land just across the Hammond Road (later the Old Hammond Highway), five miles east of Baton Rouge, and for a thousand dollars they bought six acres. By the time they closed on June 2, Warren was busy with "an out-of-work carpenter" building a small, five-room clapboard structure set well back from the road. The interior walls were unfinished pine, but there was a fireplace and a big old-fashioned claw-footed tub in the bathroom. He meant to stay there only until they could find a place farther out, but it would be their Baton Rouge home for three years.[21]

It must have seemed to Caroline Gordon that Benfolly never cooled off from the influx of guests when the good weather came. Katherine Anne Porter came for a visit, having just divorced her third husband on April 9. "She made mint liqueur, five gallons of elderberry wine, four quarts of apple butter, and brandied peaches." Her writing had enchanted Warren, Brooks, and Erskine. "She was one of the most fascinating women I have ever met," Andrew Lytle remembered. Caroline enjoyed her brilliant conversation, as did Erskine, twenty-six years her junior. He felt her powerful attraction, and they "sat up most of the night talking on the porch in the light of the full moon" to the annoyance of Allen Tate, who was trying to get to sleep. In New Orleans on April 19, after libations of planter's punch in the bar of the St. Charles Hotel, they were married at the Palace of Justice on Royal Street. They had found a judge after Cinina sought the advice of the Italian consul, and she and Warren served as witnesses.[22]

Back in Baton Rouge, the newlyweds moved into an apartment across the hall from the Brookses. Cleanth said it would be "delightful to have them so near," though he thought "the odds are hopelessly against" the marriage. Tate agreed. "We've known K.A. for going on fifteen years," he wrote Brooks, "and she has gone through this same pattern five [sic] times. She always comes out of it with a kind of moral virginity, ready to try it again because she forgets that she has tried it; but the men lie gasping on the sand." Scarcely a month later Brooks told Tate, "trouble has already broken out between the Erskines and the Warrens. But both sides are keeping mum; and Albert may be depended on to keep silence about it" for he had "a deep loyalty and even a liking" for Cinina.[23]

If Warren thought less than Cinina did about these troubles, he had others to occupy him. He still had not finished his next-to-last chapter, though he now had a title: *Night Rider.* The school term was over, and he would be free for three months. Brooks anticipated his plans. "I thought that Red was going to Italy sometime before he told me that he was leaving," he wrote Allen. "I don't think Red really wanted to go. (I may be quite wrong.) Miss Emma, however, has been vowing to go for a long time, and though I know little of the details I think that she is to do some study while in Italy."[24]

"We up and tore out for Europe on less than a week's notice," Warren wrote Andrew Lytle, "catching a freighter out of Savannah, after a bus ride of a day and a night."[25]

20

❖

Night Rider,
and a New Beginning

History is a process fraught with risks, and the moral
regeneration of society depends not upon shifts in
mechanism but upon the moral regeneration of men.
— " 'The Great Mirage': Conrad and Nostromo"[1]

They enjoyed the crossing as the only two passengers on the freighter. "It is a perfect arrangement if you have to do a little work during the trip—as I had to," he wrote Andrew Lytle, "for the novel required a lot of retouching." Disembarking in Genoa, they were met by John Palmer, now a Rhodes scholar enjoying the long vacation after a year's work toward his B.Litt. Together the three traveled to Perugia.[2]

They had a fine month there, but it was not all vacationing. Palmer was writing poems and Cinina was enrolled in a monthlong course at the University of Perugia. Warren was taking Italian lessons four hours a day, and by the end of the trip he would be speaking it, in Cinina's judgment, "adequately." He finished the revisions on *Night Rider,* and Houghton Mifflin had it by mid-July. Some days when he walked out into the country he would sit under an olive tree in a wheat field to work on a verse play. But that was not all. "A long poem, book-length," he wrote Allen Tate, "is moving now—in what direction I can't be too sure—and I'm trying to get the plans worked out in some detail for another novel."[3]

His pace did not slacken at the end of their month in Perugia. They had stopped in Rome on the way for a few days with some distant cousins of Cinina's. There contemporary history provided material for reflection. In the climate of increasing apprehension over the growing threat of fascism and Nazism and the possibility of American involvement in Europe's troubles, Warren told one friend he was an isolationist. This feeling must have been intensified as he stood one day in the jammed Piazza Venezia while Mussolini harangued the cheering crowd. (The experience also had an effect in Warren's verse play about a dictatorial American governor in a southern state.) They journeyed nearly two hundred miles north to Sirmione, where they had arranged for an apartment on Lake Garda. After three weeks they left Sirmione for Venice, where they stayed with Pier Pasinetti, the young writer they had befriended a few years earlier in Baton Rouge. "His hospitality is unexcelled and Venice is entirely to my satisfaction," Warren wrote Andrew Lytle, "so thus far the trip has been a first-rate success." Near the end of August they sailed from Genoa for home.[4]

When they docked in New York in early September Allen Tate and Caroline Gordon were there, but the reunion proved more than disappointing. It was "a horrible evening," Caroline wrote two friends. "Red is more withdrawn than ever. The mask hardly ever slips now. . . . Cinina is as tiring as ever even though she behaved very nicely." Warren never criticized his wife even to intimate friends, and he never reproved her in the hearing of others except for the time she assaulted Tinkum Brooks. So he wore the stony mask when she lost control. The irony of Caroline's comment was that she too was capable of unacceptable behavior. There was also irony in her servant's recollection of "the night Mrs. Warren got loose." Caroline was capable of murderous rage, and before the end of her second marriage to Allen Tate she would fly at him with a knife in her hand. She had cause, of course, for her anger at this husband she loved passionately, a notorious philanderer capable of betraying her in an affair with her own cousin. Tate's prejudices against Cinina were strong, but she was a sexually provocative woman, and Caroline's animus against her may have been heightened by some frisson of jealousy or insecurity.[5]

The Warrens settled into their little house on the Hammond Highway, a good place to work, with "real quiet and no casual callers." Warren updated his Guggenheim Fellowship application—giving as his project a long novel set in the rural South in the 1920s—and sent Tate the first two scenes of his play while he got on with the third. The pace kept up in the late fall and early winter of 1938. The proofs of *Night Rider* came in November, together with Robert Linscott's suggestion that he reduce the novel by about thirty thousand words. Linscott and Tate both urged him to delete or reduce a long monologue by a frontiersman-farmer interpolated into the narrative. With "grave misgivings" he left it in, though somewhat shortened, because he felt that it bore on the total meaning of the novel. Working before and after Christmas, he managed to cut eighteen thousand words and then fashioned eight thousand of them into a story, entitled "How Willie Proudfit Came Home," for the autumn number of *The Southern Review*.[6]

On March 14 Houghton Mifflin published *Night Rider* in a printing of five thousand copies. In spite of his disclaimer that it was not, "in any sense, a historical novel," Warren had in fact done considerable research. And there were clear similarities and instructive differences between *Night Rider* and "Prime Leaf." There was the clash of ideas and personalities, the conflict of choices in the face of economic oppression, and the ensuing complications in personal relationships. The new work was constructed on a larger scale in every way. Before Percy Munn's death he performs larger actions and affects more lives than does Thomas Hardin, though he is much less stalwart. A successful lawyer and part-time farmer, Munn joins the Association of Growers of Dark Fired Tobacco at the urging of friends. Bit by bit he is drawn in until he becomes a leader of the night riders. His successful defense of a client leads to the execution of an innocent man. He persuades his client to join the night riders only to learn that he had been the murderer. When he is sentenced to death by the leaders for extorting money from a farmer, Munn fires the first shot. That night he rapes his wife in a culmination of a pattern of abuse. When troops hunt Munn for a murder committed by another leader, he hides out at the farm of the frontiersman-farmer Willie Proudfit, one of his foils. Betrayed by Proudfit's nephew, Munn makes only a halfhearted attempt to evade pursuit and slips into an acceptance that amounts to suicide.[7]

Foreshadowings of this novel are clear in *John Brown*. As Brown employed pillage and murder to abolish slavery, so Munn uses the same means in defending the growers against the monopolistic tobacco company. He also suggests comparison with other literary creations. Though his life ends not with a whimper but a bang, he is still clearly a hollow man. In creating a man with a drive toward power yet a fatal sense of alienation, Warren may have thought of classic tragic heroes but imagined his protagonist infected with a kind of modern malaise. Even so, Percy Munn's qualities have suggested to some readers comparisons with Shakespeare's Macbeth and Brutus.[8]

Students of the novel have thought of that modern master, Joseph Conrad. Although Munn's story in some ways recalls that of *Lord Jim*, it is *Nostromo* that provides more intriguing analogues for Munn in the title character and Martin Decoud, a journalist whose skepticism undoes him. Along with these similarities in theme and incident are common elements of technique such as the interpolated story. In *Night Rider* Warren uses the device to point up central meanings. Hiding from pursuit for the murder he did not commit, Munn hears Willie Proudfit's narrative of his thirty years in the West. One of the hunters who slaughtered the great herds of buffalo, he concludes at last that he must return to his poor Kentucky farm for his own salvation even though he may in the end lose the farm.[9]

Proudfit was a lucky find for Warren. Driving through a desolate part of New Mexico years before, he had a flat tire. An old man who noticed his Tennessee license plate told him he was born there but had not been back in seventy years. The life story he told Warren became that of Willie Proudfit, "with some decorations." But Proudfit's greatest importance is thematic. Explaining why he kept the monologue in spite of Tate's advice, Warren gave him four reasons. For one, he wrote, "Proudfit is a man who has been able to pass beyond his period of 'slaughter' into a state of self knowledge. If he is not at home in the world, practically (losing his place, etc.), he is at least at home with himself, has had his vision."[10]

Night Rider is a long novel whose many characters act out violent lives with ethical and philosophical implications against a background of history rendered in a fully realized sensuous physical environment. Years later Warren might have been describing his own practice in his summation of his essay on Conrad: "The philosophical novelist, or poet, is one for whom the documentation of the world is constantly striving to rise to the level of generalization about values, for whom the image strives to rise to symbol, for whom images always fall into a dialectical configuration, for whom the urgency of experience, no matter how vividly and strongly experience may enchant, is the urgency to know the meaning of experience." The quest for self-knowledge—and sometimes the seeming effort to avoid it—would recur. And one aspect of that self-knowledge would involve the search for the father. There were other protagonists to come who, like Percy Munn, have absent or shadowy biological fathers and who enter into often vexed relationships with surrogates. He would examine these psychological situations with increasing penetration as he sharpened his skills. Early notices called *Night Rider* an exciting discovery, a novel both powerful and profound. Robert Penn Warren had arrived as a novelist, not only at home but in England as well.[11]

He had dedicated it "In Gratitude" to Daniel Justin Donahoe, his sometime Oklahoma host, and to Domenico Brescia. In the early hours of March 26 the telephone rang in the Warrens' home. Brescia had died at seventy-three following a sudden heart attack. Still recovering from the lingering effects of an appendectomy in March, Cinina took the train for San Francisco. If she had felt a foreigner in Tennessee and Louisiana, she must now have felt distanced even more from the time when she was the cherished daughter of a close if highly emotional California family. She had no bond with her stepmother, and her charming brother, Peter, was as likely to cause problems as pleasure. If Warren's star was rising, she might have felt hers was in eclipse. She must have longed more than ever for a return to Italy.

On March 16, Henry Allen Moe informed Warren that he had been appointed to a Guggenheim Fellowship for creative writing in the field of the novel at a twelve months' stipend of $2,250. James Monroe Smith approved Dean Fred Frey's recommendation for a sabbatical leave for 1939–40 with a stipend of $2,300. They would hardly be affluent, but barring the unforeseen they should be comfortable. His plans, he told Moe, were "to take a couple of months in Nashville, Tennessee, working on newspaper files and in libraries there to finish up some of the material." Then they might go abroad. He may have taken some further encouragement from a letter from his Berkeley friend Ray Dannenbaum. Now a contract writer at Twentieth Century–Fox, he was trying to sell *Night Rider* to the movies. He was unsuccessful, but thereafter Warren would think of movie sales with each new work.[12]

A possibility more to his taste had come from William Sloane at Henry Holt, which had been enthusiastically promoting *Understanding Poetry*. Would he care to submit his new book of poems for publication? The manuscript, entitled *A Problem of Knowledge*, was already being read at Houghton Mifflin. In the meantime he sent the table of contents for comments to Allen Tate, who was resigning from the Woman's College at Greensboro, North Carolina, to become poet in residence in Princeton's creative writing program. When Houghton Mifflin rejected the volume, Warren would send it to Sloane, who did the same. Still another New York publisher was aware of him, even if he did not know it. A talented young editor named Eleanor Clark wrote to Katherine Anne Porter about a historical and analytical treatment of southern literature being discussed at W. W. Norton & Company. Someone in the office had suggested Robert Penn Warren but thought, rightly, that his Guggenheim would disqualify him. But Warren would see more of Miss Clark, if not Norton.

By late May the Warrens' plans were beginning to crystallize. Dealing with a hip infection caused by scratching a mosquito bite, Cinina wrote Harriet Owsley that she would be happy "to really leave this dreary school year behind." If the Owsleys would be away, they hoped they could rent their house. The Guggenheim Fellowship formally begun, they left Baton Rouge on June 2. A few days later they moved into the Owsleys' home at Vanderbilt.[13]

For the next six weeks Warren scoured newspapers from the First World War to the early 1930s for material about the careers of two Tennessee soldiers: one the greatest modern military hero and the other a spectacular soldier turned mountebank. Warren was retracing the rise of a local banking house to a pinnacle never before attained in the South and its subsequent fall, causing widespread political and economic reverberations. He was fortunate now not just in the files of the *Tennessean* and the *Banner,* but also in having the firsthand information from Lon Cheney.

Looking ahead, Warren was aware of two other problems of differing magnitude. One involved uncertainty at best and danger at worst. On March 15 German troops had marched into Prague, and Neville Chamberlain's offer of British support to Poland brought the threat of war closer. Germany had had no need of Italian aid in absorbing Austria and Czechoslovakia, but further international adventures might well involve Germany's ally in some way. Concern for American citizens was already prompting warnings against some European travel. So even as they prepared to take ship, the Warrens had to confront the possibility that, once there, they might have to turn around and come back.

The other problem was almost insignificant by comparison, but it would recur constantly in Warren's correspondence. When he had accepted the Houghton Mifflin Literary Fellowship he had found that he wanted to write not *Night Rider* but an entirely different novel—

the one he had specified in his Guggenheim application. But now that he had received this new fellowship to write it, he found that what he wanted most was to expand the few scenes he had from the play he had been meditating on for nearly two years. He told Kenneth Burke, "As soon as I got on the boat, July 20, I began again on it—when I should have begun the novel which I'm supposed to do on the Guggenheim—for it seemed pretty ripe to me then and ready to pluck."[14]

So he and Cinina were once again shipboard—for the slow freighter voyage they had enjoyed the year before but now on seas beneath which U-boats prowled. They were embarked upon a journey and a year more uncertain than any they had known.

21

❖

Italy, the Play, and the War

So some, whose passionate emptiness and tidal
Lust swayed toward the debris of Madrid,
And left New York to loll in their fierce idyll
Among the olives, where the snipers hid;
And now the North—to seek that visioned face
And polarize their iron of despair,
Who praise no beauty like the boreal grace
Which greens the dead eye under the rocket's flare.
They fight old friends, for their obsession knows
Only the immaculate itch, not human friends or foes.
　　　　　　　　　　　　　　　　　—"Terror"[1]

The four-week voyage began inauspiciously. "The sea broke on the top deck for two whole days and nights," Warren wrote Frank Owsley. "Suddenly I saw someone had left the outside door of the passage open, and just as I saw that, I saw a wave, say neck-high, come strolling into the passage. I yelled to Cinina to throw suitcases onto the bunks, but she wasn't quick enough—no human could have been. . . . She says, too, that she couldn't see much point in saving suitcases if the ship was already sinking. Then the wave marched over into the dining salon." After drying out they settled into the quiet shipboard routine. "I've been working on my play, on Italian grammar, and on Dante," he reported. (He had read eighteen cantos of the *Inferno* and thought he could finish by Christmas and start over.) As they steamed through the Mediterranean, Cinina jotted a note to Katherine Anne Porter. The French coast was lovely, and the trip had been "better than a Keeley cure [for alcoholism], rest-cure, etc. put together."[2]

They docked at Genoa on August 16 and settled in at Sirmione on the southern shore of Lake Garda. Their little country pensione was very cheap and close to the beach. They had a fine fortnight there before the radio news became increasingly alarming. Then, on the morning of September 1 the German armies rolled into Poland. Forty-eight hours later Britain and France declared war. "For two or three weeks we had a very bad time," Warren told Frank Owsley. "Everybody was running like rabbits into Switzerland. . . . we just sat quietly, and listened to the radio broadcasts, and occasionally had a moral collapse."[3]

They lived with uncertainty and anxiety. The American consuls were ordering citizens out of the country, but when Warren asked in Milan how to get out, they told him, "We don't know. There aren't any boats." So they returned to Sirmione where the fall winds carried the rumble of artillery practice down from across the lake. He wrote Kenneth Burke, "It is probable that we shall clear out of this section, which is too damned near the Brenner Pass for comfort."[4]

The mail was their greatest diversion, and they implored their friends for the latest news. Shortly before his death, Huey Long had predicted, "If anything happens to me, the people who try to wield the powers that I have created will all land in jail." LSU president James Monroe Smith, originally a professor of education, had developed a strong interest in economics. Anticipating wartime scarcities, he forged a million dollars in university bonds for collateral against a purchase of two million dollars in wheat futures. But after the Munich agreement prices plummeted, and his desperate measures led him to a bank swindle and more forgery. On June 25, having resigned from the university, he quietly departed Baton Rouge with portable assets including the presidential plate and silver carefully stowed on the floor of his big black Cadillac. Governor Richard Leche resigned the next day. Smith, like another embezzler—George Hurstwood in Theodore Dreiser's *Sister Carrie*—fled to Canada, where he was soon arrested. When the Warrens had been preparing to take ship from New Orleans, he was lodged in the East Baton Rouge Parish jail. The misdeeds of these subordinates paled in comparison with Long's, and even though his depredations paled beside Hitler's and Mussolini's, these varieties of power politics provided material for reflection for this thoughtful reader of Dante and Machiavelli.[5]

The small world of Sirmione was "one of the best spots on the globe," he wrote Andrew Lytle. "All you have to do to go to work is pick up your typewriter and stroll some ninety seconds away and fall on the grass and go to sleep." For him, however, the fields were not for sleeping. By mid-September he had drafted half of the play. But the world kept intruding. By mid-September no mail was getting through, and they were told there was no ocean passage available for at least a month. When they telephoned Pier Pasinetti in Rome he told them that "under the special circumstances they would find the place peculiarly interesting." When he invited them to stay with him, they canceled their passage, packed their bags, and said good-bye to Sirmione.[6]

Rome was expensive, and there was no reassurance from the American consul there or in Naples. So they boarded the *traghetto* for the two-hour trip across the bay to the island of Capri and rented a little house out in the country. For the first few days, Cinina told Harriet, they thought they were in Paradise. They were near the Emperor Tiberius' villa on the northeast tip of the island two miles from town. Their house was modeled on a medieval castle, and Cinina thought it was beautiful. It was "stuck on the edge of a terrific cliff," Warren wrote Tate. "It's a beautiful spot, but God knows, it is like living in the crow's nest of a ship rounding the Horn, for we catch every wind that blows. . . ." He sent off more pages to John Ransom, who now had all but the last four scenes. Warren was entering the homestretch on the play, and he hoped to get a good deal done there in the next few months. But then the good weather ceased, and it became for Cinina "the windiest place outside of hell and the middle of a tornado." This went on for a week. Then, climbing up the path to their house, she injured a ligament at the base of her spine. That was the end of Capri.[7]

Back in a Roman pensione, Cinina went to bed with her bad back, both of them fighting colds as well as hovering anxiety and occasional depression. When they were able to move into a promised apartment atop the Janiculum Hill, Cinina began again on a novel she had started and attended classes at the university. Working occasionally on the novel he was supposed to be writing, Warren applied for a Guggenheim renewal to carry him through the summer. In December Cinina felt they were in "a disastrous situation." They were worried about money and the Russians, who had rolled into Poland on September 17 and then invaded Finland on November 30. But they learned with relief that their passports could be renewed for six more months. So on New Year's Eve Warren requested the $246 left of the Guggenheim grant. He would have his LSU money—$1,150—for the second half of the 1939–40 academic year. "Unless I get a renewal," he told Tate, "God knows what I'll do next summer."[8]

For the present, he was covering all the possibilities he could think of for his play. On December 22 he sent a copy for his friends at *The Southern Review* and another for Frank Owsley, who was to send it next to Andrew Lytle. If John Ransom declined it for *The Kenyon Review*, his copy was to go to the *Virginia Quarterly Review.* If they returned it too, it was to go to the *Atlantic Monthly.* And he did not intend to stop there.

It now bore the title *Proud Flesh.* When he gave a copy to other friends, one of them saw the title's import immediately. "Proud flesh is that flesh that gets inflamed," she said, "around a nail for instance, produces swelling and discoloration, and looks as if corruption is setting in, and when you get to the point of false pride, it is to the point of corruption." When he had sent the first act to Kenneth Burke, Warren outlined the play.

> The whole thing is to be in five acts, and twelve scenes, each act being introduced by a chorus. The choruses are: highway cops, football players, steel construction workers on the new capitol, the women who are connected with Governor Strong, and the surgeons. The different choruses represent a scale of increasing complexity, it may be said, and the poetry is supposed to reflect this in its style, etc. . . . the play is about power, and the various justifications of power. The main character, Strong, is a man who has the talent for gaining power and has never asked himself the question as to its meaning. Its mere exercise has been sufficient. The play is the story of his attempt to give meaning to power, and the only meaning which seems available to him, in our world, is mere humanitarianism. Needless to say, Strong doesn't survive this attempt, for the meaning which he has built up will not be repudiated.[9]

If he had chosen the dramatic form in part for the promise of larger and quicker rewards than novels normally brought, there was also the challenge of trying his hand at this genre he had studied and taught for so long. He was aware of the dramaturgical approach of George Pierce Baker, whose students included Eugene O'Neill and Sidney

Howard. There was much in contemporary American drama from which Warren could learn, including the work of experimentalists his own age. Sidney Kingsley had won the Pulitzer Prize for 1934 with *Men in White,* in which a young hospital surgeon struggled with the ethical implications of his actions. Maxwell Anderson employed verse drama in work such as *Elizabeth the Queen.* Clifford Odets used contemporary politics in *Waiting for Lefty,* and Warren surely knew Robert Sherwood's *Idiot's Delight,* prophetically set on the eve of war in an isolated Italian hotel close to the Austrian border.

Over the next two years Warren would make many changes. He reduced the five acts to three. Governor Strong would become Willie Talos. The first fragment of the play—nine lines of the Highway Patrolmen's Chorus—would be revised and expanded for the Chorus of Surgeons. But through wholesale revisions the plot and themes would remain unchanged. In this early draft Governor Strong is a master politician who expands his power through coercion and bribery as well as his charismatic appeal to the masses in the southern state he rules autocratically as "the Boss." He attempts to squeeze the powerful financial and industrial interests while dealing with other corrupt politicians and power brokers such as Benet Pillsbury. Divorced from his wife, Clara, he finds his closest relationship with his executive secretary, Sue Parsons, who credits herself with masterminding his rise to power and endures his casual affairs. His main henchman is Tiny Harper, whom he watches warily and treats contemptuously.

Governor Strong's great goal is to build a medical center to serve all the people, but he allows the contract to go to Gummy Satterfield, a lawyer-entrepreneur and crony of Harper's, for a substantial kickback. For director of the center, however, he chooses a dedicated surgeon named Keith Amos, who does not know that his sister, Anne, has become Strong's mistress. Strong's love is expended on his only child, Tom, who is the star of the university football team, which shares Strong's prideful indulgence. When Tom dies from a football injury, Strong decides to repudiate the contract for the medical center and break off with both Anne and Sue. Though Clara Strong refuses to take him back, declaring that his corruption infected the boy through his condoning his immorality, Strong sticks to his renunciations. In revenge, Sue prompts Tiny to plant a newspaper story that Strong is firing Amos because his unsuccessful operation cost Tom Strong his life. But Tiny blunders and inadvertently blurts out Anne's relationship with the governor. Rushing to the capitol, where the legislature is in special session, Amos shoots Strong before he is gunned down by Strong's bodyguards. Act V, Scene ii, is set in a waiting room where Anne Amos tries to comfort Clara Strong. As the curtain falls, Tiny Harper and Jack, a seedy newspaperman, a friend of Keith Amos's youth, are there when a nurse summons Clara Strong for her husband's last moments.

A note at the beginning of the manuscript read, "Just as both realistic and non-realistic elements appear in the style of this play—prose at the level of fact and circumstance, verse at the level of interpretation and dramatic intensity—so the staging involves realistic and non-realistic elements." The text shifts constantly between the two levels. When there is action it moves briskly, but the characters' spoken interior monologues are often lengthy. So are the choruses' passages, which serve as a vehicle for analyses of both character and action as well as general statements about the human condition. In the often difficult imagery there is frequent emphasis upon deterministic, mechanistic, and even chemical bases of human behavior, but the idea of sin in a conventional religious context is there too.[10]

If the disparate elements of the play needed pulling together, it would not be achieved through the diverse modes: blank verse and free verse, standard prose and heavily dialectal speech. In November, as John Crowe Ransom was preparing to send scenes to Allen Tate, he told him, "There's the boldest possible mixture of steep poetic symbolic bits, in Red's own tones, and of very broad satirical jingles; I don't know whether his scheme can carry any real poetry."[11]

The weather did nothing to lift their spirits as 1940 came in. "I'm freezing to death," Warren wrote Henry Allen Moe. "Rome has recently had the worst snow in nearly a hundred years, and though the snow is now melted, the weather is vile." In mid-January both he and Cinina were in bed with colds. They tried to keep warm and wrote. Now that the play was finished, he gave precedence not to the novel but to three long poems. The references in "Terror" range from "the debris of Madrid" to "the Piazza" and the Wilhelmplatz, where "the brute crowd roars or the blunt boot-heels resound," and to "the bomb-sight over bitter Helsingfors." The images suggest Pablo Picasso's *Guernica,* painted four years before. Warren would later say, "I was struck by the thought that the same impulse which had made [volunteers] go to fight Franco had made them go to fight Russia, their recent ally in Spain." A large component of that impulse, he thought, was "the *passionate emptiness and tidal lust* of the modern man who, because he cannot find long-range meaning, seeks meaning in mere violence. . . ." There was one stylistic device he would use increasingly: a kind of direct address to the reader—("You know, by radio, how hotly the world repeats . . .")—as if summarizing a common experience. The seven stanzas written in irregular rhyme and near-rhyme, shifting from iambic pentameter to free verse, may have owed something to *Proud Flesh*. They showed the same kind of compression, ellipsis, and allusion that demanded the reader's closest attention.[12]

The five stanzas of "Pursuit" are very like those in "Terror." Again the poet speaks directly to "you," the reader, while speaking for himself as well. The second and third stanzas are set in a medical clinic where the references range widely in space and time, conjuring up loneliness and despair, where love may be just "a groping Godward, though blind." The other poem, "Love's Parable," is written in Warren's metaphysical mode, with clear echoes of John Donne, focusing on two lovers fallen from grace:

> Are we but mirror to the world?
> Or does the world our ruin reflect. . . .

If this poem is linked to these two, it is mainly by the sense of loneliness and loss, as the poet marks

> . . . how ripe injustice flows,
> How ulcerous, how acid, then
> How proud flesh on the sounder grows
> Till rot engross the estate of men.

He thought that his poetry gained from *Proud Flesh* and told Tate that the second half of the play was "much the best poetry I've done."[13]

At last he got well into the novel and confided to Katherine Anne Porter, "At moments I feel that I see my way through the tangle; then at moments I feel like throwing the whole damned thing into the Tiber, which is high, swift, and muddy like turtle soup." He was a craftsman, an intellectual novelist who tended to see a book in terms of problem solving rather than a process of following ardently where the daemon led. He would often start a novel by scrawling ideas or questions. Then he would draft scenes and passages of dialogue. Finally he would type and elaborate them. Now, in chill February, with hints of spring for encouragement, he was finally creating, on his Roman hill, another tale of his home country.[14]

That he could do it was a testimonial to his toughness, his creative fertility, and his driving ambition in the face of discouragements aplenty. "I took to my bed for a week or so of flu and still feel pretty rotten," he wrote Brooks on March 7. "Cinina fell in the bath and nearly brained herself: cut a great gash across her nose, closed up one eye, bruised herself rather liberally about, and was pretty sick for a few days from shock and loss of blood." With the uncertain mail there could have been disasters at home in Baton Rouge too for all they knew.[15]

Warren wrote Ted Davison that Cinina "has spent eight weeks in bed since the first of December," but by March things seemed to be looking up. The fickle gods even seemed to smile. They went to the races, and a friend took Warren to the Vatican, where he fell in with friendly American priests and played poker with them until late at night. The Ides passed uneventfully, and then the gods turned their backs.[16]

If Warren had been inclined to mysticism, the rest of the month might have seemed like one long dark night of the soul. "I took to my bed with a violent seizure," he told Tate later, "which four doctors finally decided was intestinal flu plus malaria. Anyway, I vomited blood, had the highest kind of fever for five or six days, had the bone-ache, and in general felt like hell." After two weeks in bed, when the fever finally broke, he had shakily arisen for a few hours. He had lost nearly eighteen pounds. He wrote Andrew Lytle that it had been "a mysterious complaint," which brought nights of delirium and vivid dreams. Later the mystery was solved. He had typhus. "And, God, the fool Fascist doctor! He didn't even know it was typhus. I got that diagnosis back home from a record of the symptoms."[17]

While he was in bed a cable arrived from Henry Moe. It read, RE-NEWAL NOT GRANTED. In Baton Rouge on April 3, two days after Warren had arisen from his two-week siege, outgoing department head W. A. Read forwarded to Dean Fred Frey his recommendation for the promotion of Robert Penn Warren and Cleanth Brooks to the rank of professor of English. But whatever happened when the recommendation reached the promotions committee or Dean Frey's office, Brooks and Warren were not promoted.

Even before the typhus he wrote Tate, "I have had of late a sense of increasing pressure." He had gotten stuck in the novel, but then, "In a delirium one night my problem was suddenly solved. I had the most vivid dreams during this fever and went through the whole story. . . ." A whole sequence involving a character like Willie Proudfit came to him and showed the way to a dramatic climax. But it was not all clear sailing. "My novel is moving along," he wrote Andrew Lytle on April 30, "toward what far-off divine event I don't pretend to know, and some days I don't give a damn."[18]

They decided to return to Sirmione, but they reckoned without the war. On April 9 Germany had invaded Norway and then overrun Denmark. Warren had managed to book their passage for late May, but he was concerned too about the precarious situation of Pier Pasinetti. An outspoken antifascist, he had been working as a journalist, and Warren had been trying to aid him in a return to America through the immigration officers in Naples and the consul in Rome. On May 10, the Nazi panzer sweep into France began, and Pier started to pack.[19]

"Then," Warren later told Albert Erskine and Katherine Anne Porter, "the bombshell broke." The immigration officers "called [Pasinetti] in and told him that Italy would [enter the war] on June 8. He promptly brought us the news, and said that the time had come to beat it." On Tuesday night, May 14, they found the Genoa dockside a mob scene of people from Norway, Germany, and elsewhere trying to get out of Italy. "By Thursday noon we had wangled passage, cots, not beds" on the S.S. *Washington*. She sailed on Saturday, May 18. On May 20 the Germans drove to the English Channel. It must have been a day later when the *Washington* steamed past Gibraltar and out into the Atlantic. "We got out by the barest," Warren told Brooks.[20]

22

❖

The Loneliness Artist

On the last day swim far out, should the doctor permit
—Crawl, trudgeon, breast—or deep and wide-eyed, dive
Down the glaucous glimmer where no voice can visit;
But the mail lurks in the box at the house where you live:
Summer's wishes, winter's wisdom—you must think
On the true nature of Hope, whose eye is round and does not wink.
                                                  —*"End of Season"*[1]

The second night out they slept in beds, women and men in separate cabins. "We spent the entire voyage listening to horror stories from Norwegians, Belgians, Germans, and French," Warren wrote Brooks. At last the *Washington* docked in New York on June 3. Cinina told Albert Erskine and Katherine Anne Porter that if she was asked her feelings, she would simply say that she was glad to be home "& probably mean it as few do."[2]

Home for now was North Bennington, Vermont. "I'm struggling along on a revision of the play," Warren told Albert and Katherine Anne, "working with Francis Fergusson, who is a very nice guy and who seems to know his stuff." A year older than Warren, he had taken a B.A. at Queens College, Oxford, in 1926, and then spent four years as associate director of the American Laboratory Theatre of the New School in New York. He had been professor of literature and drama at Bennington College for six years and served as director of the Bennington Theatre. Warren gladly accepted his offer of help with the play. "He is going to put on a couple of scenes experimentally this summer and talks about doing the whole thing next year, if some of the revisions pan out. I despair of ever getting a commercial production."[3]

In late July the Warrens headed west for two writers' conferences. At Olivet College in Michigan he taught with Sherwood Anderson, John Peale Bishop, Glenway Wescott, and Katherine Anne, now separated from Erskine. When that week was over they traveled on to Boulder for Ted Davison's conference, where "the combination of the fun and the routine of the Conference . . . was almost more than the human frame could bear." The Davisons took the Warrens on a mountain picnic, and after a few days of recuperation they headed back east.[4]

By mid-August they were with the Ransoms in Gambier. There were charades again and costumes adorned with beads and feathers. They played croquet with teams of four, games that went on so long they had to turn on the car's headlights to finish. Cinina played some games just because her husband enjoyed them. Once she played jacks with Helen, the Ransoms' fourteen-year-old daughter, and managed to sprain her wrist in the process. Helen was taken with Cinina's looks—her bright blue eyes, her beautiful olive skin, and her good legs. She thought Cinina had an interesting voice too. But one night as she was talking, a strange thing happened. Robb Reavill wore a hearing aid. Suddenly, apropos of nothing, Cinina made a sharp comment about it, and Helen detected a momentary glare in her eye. It left Helen bemused and stunned. It was like something out of a novel. "She looked mad," Helen remembered. Another time, at a cookout, when someone mentioned Katherine Anne Porter, Cinina launched into a tirade of jealousy. Helen's parents were, she thought, naive about Warren's problems and his marriage. She knew she had seen not just abnormal behavior but a real madness.[5]

The last of the summer was crowded. On the twenty-seventh they left for Bennington so that Warren could resume his work with Fergusson. After they blocked out the last act of *Proud Flesh* Warren came down with a sore throat and a terrible cold. At Gambier he went to bed for three days before they could continue on to Nashville.

As the new semester began Warren must have felt a sense of marking time even though he was busy with *The Southern Review* and his teaching. During the Olivet conference he had written acting department head Tom Kirby, "I have just received an invitation from the

University of Iowa to come there for the second term of 1940–41 to give a course [with] only one class meeting a week." From Bennington he had written Brooks, "I hope it will go far enough to give me some sort of a stick to beat the local dog with. I'm pretty damned sore if, after the various promises which have been made to us, we don't get some satisfaction pretty soon." Dean Frey temporized, and acting President Hebert responded with a request that Warren defer his decision until his return. Finally, on November 25, Dean Frey recommended a leave without pay for the second semester, and Warren accepted the Iowa appointment.

There were social as well as professional reasons for departing. Brooks wrote Tate, "We've made a point of trying to get Cinina off to a good start—at least on our side. It's been hard, but has worked so far. C. is obviously on her best behavior—but she nearly got out of control the other night. I'm afraid it can't last." Perhaps Iowa City might be a more congenial place for this high-strung, ambitious, unhappy woman. "We left Baton Rouge in late January," Warren told Katherine Anne later, "somewhat embittered and worn-out by all the confusion about university reorganization. . . . I'm in a state of mind to begin looking around hard for a job, if things aren't on the mend when we get back next fall."[6]

When the Warrens arrived in Iowa City in that January of 1941, they found one friend already there, and Leonard Unger and his former teacher resumed their warm relationship. By mid-February Warren was able to give a full report to Erskine, now working at New Directions in Cambridge. "Austin Warren has been enormously nice to us, and I like him better and better. René Wellek, the learned professor from Prague, has turned out to be very interesting, and we have seen a good deal of him and his wife. Grant Wood has been nice—in fact, since we had to take an unfurnished apartment, he has given us a lot of furniture. . . ." Uncertainty still prevailed at LSU, but the budget prospects were dim at Iowa, so there was little likelihood of leverage for use at LSU. He could do nothing but hope and get on with his writing.[7]

He was able to follow his favorite routine: writing until midafternoon, then exercise, then a drink with friends. Wallace Fowlie, a teacher of French literature at Bennington College, was visiting his friend Austin Warren, who suggested that Fowlie walk over to the Warrens' house at five and introduce himself. When a student appeared for a conference, Warren asked him how many hours he had spent at his typewriter. When the student answered sheepishly, "Only five," Warren reminded him that he had told him to get it up to eight. The young man replied that when he worked that long his novel began to grow stale. "That's because you stay too long with one kind of writing," Fowlie remembered Warren's saying. "When you get tired of the novel, then go to your short story, and after that to your essay. A writer should be working on three or four kinds of writing at the same time." Fowlie knew he had also told other student-disciples, "Long working hours and vigorous exercise—that's the regimen you have to follow if you want to be a writer."[8]

He was following it himself, and by late February he was able to send two scenes to Francis Fergusson, who told Warren they needed "cutting for speed and intelligibility. This I have done fairly roughly. . . ." He was troubled by a lack of character development in Governor Strong's wife and by Anne Amos's becoming his mistress. (Allen Tate would later say Warren could not draw women well because he did not understand them.) Fergusson also had reservations about the chorus and its elaborate irony, and he wanted to have the whole play before him.[9]

After Warren arrived at Bennington with completed revisions, he said he would like to hear a complete run-through. Fowlie was there. Fergusson presided impressively. A tall, somewhat bent figure with abundant dark hair, a white face, and fine eyes, he spoke slowly and quietly. He gathered a group of students and faculty. "Scripts were handed out and we read at sight," Fowlie remembered. "The text, which contained choruses, seemed impressive to us. Francis and Red listened attentively for two hours. When the reading was over, Red thanked us, and turning to Fergusson, said, 'Francis, if you would like to give this play its first production here at Bennington, I would be honored.' It was a dramatic moment for all of us, but Francis replied with words I instinctively felt he was going to say, 'Red, I don't think the text is ready for production.' Red Warren's reply came quickly. 'Perhaps you're right. I'm going to shelve it, and tomorrow morning I will begin to write it over again in the form of a novel.' "[10]

Warren pursued the kind of alternation among genres he prescribed for the student. From time to time he worked at the novel for Houghton Mifflin, and he meditated on an essay on Katherine Anne Porter. But his core identity was that of poet, and there were few times in his life when he was not scribbling lines that would become parts of poems. Now there was an added incentive to assess his current work. Albert Erskine was functioning as editor and man-of-all-work for New Directions in Cambridge and publishing a series of monthly poetry pamphlets. William Carlos Williams was "Poet of the Month" for January, and the others for 1941 would include Josephine Miles, Delmore Schwartz, and Rainer Maria Rilke. Warren's work would be featured for March 1942. He told Erskine that they could draw from *Thirty-six Poems* if they needed to, "But by the time you all are ready to come out, I may have enough new stuff to fill the booklet."[11]

There were elements of uncertainty in the immediate future. What could they afford to do in the summer, and what in the fall? In late June, accepting Warren's essay on Katherine Anne Porter for *The Kenyon Review,* John Ransom added, "Austin [Warren] wrote me most handsomely about your 'magnificent' performance out there, and said they were putting their heads together to see if they couldn't assemble a good offer for you permanently." (In the winter Cleanth Brooks had written Allen Tate about their concerns over the LSU presidency. "The Board of Supervisors has nominated six candidates, including [Paul M.] Hebert but also including a broken down county superintendent of schools and a major general.") In Ransom's last paragraph he had commiserated: "Wasn't it awful what the Board did at LSU in the matter of the new President? I can't imagine that any army man is a real president, or a favorer of literary studies and publications."[12]

Campbell Blackshear Hodges would have been named president of LSU in 1926 if the army had agreed to release him. Now, after serving as military aide to Herbert Hoover and Franklin Roosevelt and commanding the V Army Corps, he was free to accept the presidency of LSU. He began to plan for a staff organized along military lines, and one of his first actions in Baton Rouge was to dissolve the faculty senate and extinguish the reform movement Brooks and his colleagues had struggled so hard to launch. Even before Hodges's appointment Brooks had said, "I can't say that the outlook is too bright."[13]

With summer approaching Warren had to make a choice when he was offered six weeks' teaching at the Bread Loaf Writers' School. He wrote Katherine Anne Porter, "I was wavering, however, when Cinina put her foot down and said 'no teaching' even if we had to do something pretty drastic to get through." By late summer they were heading for Jalisco, on Mexico's Pacific coast. They settled in a pleasant place, "a tiny town, some thirty miles from Guadalajara, on a very large lake—some eighty miles long, in fact—with a perfect climate. We got a native house, but one absolutely new and therefore clean, screened it, furnished it—all for the price of about ten dollars a month." Gregarious as ever, they invited Alexander and Jean Kern and two other Iowa students to join them for two weeks there on Lake Chapala. By good luck the Warrens were there to receive them. "Returning at night from Guadalajara, we saw a cow on the road, got into a skid because of wet brakes," Warren told Tate, "and turned over two or three times, coming to rest, on the side of the car, in a rather deep ditch. Cinina, who was driving back, took a beating on the wheel, and had a rather badly wrenched back and had to stay strapped up for a few days, but I and a friend who was with us escaped with nothing worse than a shaking-up."[14]

It was a good place for work. Warren wrote every morning and then went for a long swim with his friends. There were afternoon excursions to Guadalajara, and Warren would join the Kerns in the evenings on the veranda or in the bar at the nearly deserted Hotel Nido. "I'm on the down grade with the novel I've been working at, on and off, for a long time, and hope to finish it by Christmas," he wrote Tate. He enclosed a poem of six five-line stanzas called "End of Season." Although it was set on the beach of Lake Chapala with vivid visual imagery, it dealt with familiar themes as the poet, contemplating ancestral and collective guilt, meditated on history and time.[15]

When they returned to Baton Rouge in the second week of September, there were signs and portents. There was pressure from the state government to trim expenses. Then, early in the semester, General Hodges wrote *The Southern Review*'s editors that the magazine might be suspended.[16]

The first thing they had to do was to move into yet another house. Although they had liked living in their tiny tin-roofed home amid the tall water oaks and pecan trees on the Old Hammond Highway, they wanted a larger place. They found it in the town of Prairieville, eighteen miles south of Baton Rouge on the Jefferson Highway leading to New Orleans. On twelve acres of land, set well back from the road and concealed by trees and shrubs beyond a broad lawn, was a well-built story-and-a-half bungalow. From the front gallery a steep slope could be seen leading down to the black waters of the bayou. There was a gazebo there, and all around were live oaks festooned with thick cloudy masses of moss. (The scene could have reminded Warren of "Bearded Oaks.") It was September 10 when he signed the agreement to purchase the house and land for $6,750. Here he meant to put down roots at last.[17]

Warren wrote Katherine Anne, "the place, though ugly as sin externally, has very good rooms, enormous ones, in fact, and is well arranged and proportioned. We have installed a gas heating system, have pretty good plumbing in the two baths, and have a working windmill for water. . . . We have been living in the midst of carpenters, plumbers, electricians, and nigger boys for a month." Brooks told Tate, "The Warrens are getting settled. Miss Emma looks well from her trip in Mexico, and Red seems in fine shape from it. All goes pleasantly as a wedding bell—well, almost as pleasantly as that. One doesn't ask too much of some situations."[18]

Warren's capacity for concentration, for seizing even brief stretches of time for work, must have served him well in the din of remodeling and the hovering anxiety about the fate of *The Southern Review.* He told a reporter for the *Daily Reveille* that his new novel would be published in the spring. (Its title, *And Pastures New,* was drawn from the last words of Milton's *Lycidas.*) Speaking through clouds of smoke from the large meerschaum pipe clenched between his teeth, he told the reporter that his poetic drama was temporarily "cooling off." However, a long poem with echoes of childhood called "Revelation" would appear in *Poetry* in January and "End of Season" in *The Nation* three months later. He would soon have more time for poetry.[19]

On December 20, a few days before *The Southern Review*'s Yeats issue came off the press, Brooks informed Tate, "This spring number will be our last. . . . the end came rather suddenly." When he and Erskine had pleaded their case, General Hodges guaranteed them a fair hearing before the nine university deans who reported to him. Anticipating stringencies from America's entry into the war, however, the board of supervisors and the administration were convinced that harsh economies would be necessary. The *Journal of Southern History* and the *Louisiana Journal of Mathematics* were also marked for extinction. An added handicap for *The Southern Review,* though, was the perception among some that its two managing editors were "rebels." And to those English professors who felt that *Understanding Poetry* was inimical to their traditional historical-philological view of literature, the modest subvention afforded the magazine amounted to aid and comfort to the enemy. (Ironically, like many American educational

institutions, LSU would earn millions of dollars from wartime training programs.) When the issue came to a vote, only two of the nine
deans voted against killing what had become probably the most admired and influential literary journal in English.[20]

After many efforts to keep it afloat through grants and mergers, the
magazine's founders tried to look on the bright side. "In a way, the
loss of the magazine will be a relief," Brooks wrote Tate. "Red and I
ought to get some books finished now." They were working on one
for their old publishing associate, F. S. Crofts. To be called *Understanding Fiction,* it was aimed, like *Understanding Poetry,* at the classroom. But they would never lose their valedictory feelings. It had
been a unique situation. When brilliant young Robert Lowell came
to take graduate work at LSU, his wife, Jean Stafford, began work at
the review, typing, filing, and acting as general factotum. Brooks and
Erskine were good bosses, but she was keenly aware of the differences
between her life and that of her husband. She was aggrieved too that
the job left her little time to work on her own fiction and that it was
Lowell, the poet, rather than she who received the benefit of Warren's advice and influence. (Warren would remember how "Cal Lowell took graduate work with me and then Cal and I locked up the
doors several days a week at twelve o'clock and had a sandwich and a
quick Coke and then we read Dante for two hours.") Charles Pipkin
too had his grievances, complaining that Warren and Brooks had
taken the magazine away from him, refusing, however, all the offers
of greater participation as he slipped further into alcoholism. But for
the two managing editors, these were challenging years of exciting
opportunities to set new currents moving through contemporary literature in the company of friends such as Albert Erskine and John
Palmer.[21]

With the exception of *Proud Flesh,* Warren's enterprises were thriving. By mid-February he had completed *And Pastures New* and would
shortly begin revisions. The book of poems Erskine was producing at
New Directions would appear shortly as *Eleven Poems on the Same
Theme.* Warren had a visit from Lambert Davis, who had left the *Virginia Quarterly Review* for Harcourt, Brace and wanted to talk business
with one of his favorite southern authors. Davis would see him soon
in Baton Rouge and again in the spring when, through Allen Tate's
good offices, Warren would lecture at Princeton. Such appearances
increased his academic visibility. Most universities were, like Iowa,

unable to create new positions with the war on, but some still were able to hire in special circumstances. One was the University of Minnesota, and Joseph Warren Beach invited Warren there for the first week in March.[22]

The nephew of Cyrus Northrop, who had left Yale to become Minnesota's most dynamic and powerful president, Beach had arrived from Harvard a slender and sensitive young teacher who swayed before classes and audiences with the intensity of the poetry he read. Beach grew increasingly powerful as a teacher and defender of academic excellence. When he was named head of the department in 1940, he showed himself a champion of American poets, bringing Edwin Arlington Robinson, Robert Frost, and others to the campus. A fine tennis player, swimmer, and hiker, he loved dancing parties, where he and his wife, Dagmar, did the latest steps. They would fill their house with undergraduates. As a man who had reacted bitterly against Edwin Mims and found a model in John Crowe Ransom, Warren could hardly have had a more compatible chairman.[23]

Not long after Warren's return from Minneapolis he received Beach's offer of a full professorship at four thousand dollars. Now, at the end of their current budget period, they could not offer much financial advancement, but Beach said they would take care of him very well indeed later. "On the purely practical side I ought to go," Warren wrote Katherine Anne Porter. "But I hate to leave here because of some pretty strong personal ties—though the personal ties become fewer every year. You and Albert gone, John Palmer going in June, etc." He put his situation more decisively to Tate: "It looks probable that I'll leave LSU. Primarily because I don't think they want me—or Cleanth either for that matter."[24]

In Baton Rouge the administrative process moved with surprising speed. By March 27 Tom Kirby had prepared the recommendation for advancement to full professor. Kirby noted that Warren ought to have the Ph.D. for a full professorship, but he called him one of the most valuable members of the department and wrote that he was "one of the few with a genuinely national reputation." The promotions committee approved the recommendation and added that he "should have a light teaching load in order to have plenty of time for creative writing." Both he and Brooks were proposed for promotion with raises from $3,600 to $4,000. Now, with the basic conditions of his offer met, Warren could stay there among congenial companions to live out his life in the house in Prairieville.[25]

He was in for a shock. They cut the salary offer to $3,800. "I took it as an invitation to leave," Warren would say later. "I left out of pride." Brooks understood. "The truth of the matter is," he said, "they wanted him out." When Bob Heilman learned that Warren was going, he proposed to Cleanth that they try to hire Allen Tate. Kirby made the recommendation, but Brooks cautioned Tate that departmental jealousy or administrative reluctance might kill the deal. "This is a real hell hole," he warned him, "a real sty." Tate received the offer, at a salary of $3,600, and declined it.[26]

The *Daily Reveille* published a story captioned, "Robert Penn Warren—Minnesota's Gain, L.S.U.'s Loss." It pointed up "a question of what values are to prevail in this University. . . . It cannot afford the Southern Review, one real claim to fame and greatness, and apparently it cannot afford Mr. Warren." There was one thing, however, that the university could afford despite wartime economies. As the bulldog was to Yale and the longhorn to Texas, so the Bengal tiger was to LSU. In more than one avatar, sinewy Mike the Tiger had prowled the football field on a leash or reclined in the sunlight in his cage. But now he needed a new cage—and he got one. According to one report, it cost twenty-five hundred dollars, which, if accurate, would have paid for the raises for Warren and Brooks together—four times over.[27]

The Warrens had moved often during his years as a young teacher—out of necessity in finding employment and out of preference in finding sanctuaries conducive to his writing. They enjoyed travel and had a high tolerance for the disruptions it inevitably involves. But this was different. So the artist who had wanted to live out his life in the country of middle Tennessee prepared now to leave this second refuge he had found there in the grove of live oaks by his bayou and his windmill in Prairieville. But he was leaving more than just this place or this university: he was leaving the South. One of his most perceptive critics quotes the protagonist of a Warren novel to come more than three decades later, a southerner finding himself in the West for the first time: "This loneliness was, for me, a new kind. For unlike the bleeding away of the self into distance, the kind of loneliness I had known so well—the Southern, not the Western kind—is a bleeding inward of the self, away from all the world around, into an internal infinitude, like a pit. This was the kind I had been bred up to, and I had taken full advantage of my opportunities. I was the original, gold-plated, thirty-third-degree loneliness artist, the champion of Alabama." Whether or not this is an ironic reference to Franz Kafka's enigmatic story "A Hunger Artist," the critic sees this plight as one shared by other modern literary artists, "the sensibility of exile and deracination," so that Warren's own life, his own story, would become "partly at least that of an exile telling stories about his homeland."[28]

This departure made an even deeper wound than the first. In places far from his native region he would come to love a different land and a different sky. In his poems he would range far beyond the native place from which he felt himself expelled, but this removal now was a great, unpremeditated watershed in his life. He was advancing toward a flowering, toward a pattern of extraordinary achievement, and it seems likely that much of it—with its awards, prizes, and place—must have been, at least on some level, his way of demonstrating to these kinsmen of place, but not of blood or sensibility, the nature of the loss that his departure really constituted.

FOUR

❖❖

Arrivals and Departures, Acclaim and Anguish

23

In the Northland, at Fame's Door

Whatever pops into your head, and whitely
Breaks surface on the dark stream that is you,

May do to make a poem—for every accident
Yearns to be more than itself, yearns,

In the way you dumbly do, to participate
In the world's blind, groping rage toward meaning, and once,

Long years ago, in Minneapolis,
Dark falling, snow falling to celebrate

The manger-birth of a babe in that snowless latitude,
Church bells vying with whack of snow-chains on

Fenders, there I, down a side street,
Head thrust into snow-swirl, strove toward Hennepin.

There lights and happiness most probably were—
But I was not thinking of happiness, only of

High-quality high-proof and the gabble in which
You try to forget that something inside you dies. . . .
—*"Minneapolis Story"*[1]

Warren had little time to brood in May of 1942 with the new book of poems, a new publisher for his fiction, and guest lecturing. *Eleven Poems on the Same Theme* was published on April 4. No reviewer attempted to identify precisely the theme postulated in the title. Actually, there were at least two clusters of poems. One consisted of a generally melancholy treatment of love: "Monologue at Midnight," "Picnic Remembered," "Revelation," "Love's Parable," and "Bearded Oaks." A faculty colleague at both LSU and Minnesota saw these poems as deeply personal, written at a point in his marriage, she thought, when he came to understand "that this was an affair that was going to be tragic for him, and for her, and that there was nothing either of them could do about it." In another cluster—"Crime," "Pursuit," "Terror," and "Original Sin: A Short Story"—theme and descant were blended from violence and guilt, randomness and fatality in human life, and the dominion of history and time. The last of these four poems was the most powerful:

> Nodding, its great head rattling like a gourd,
> And locks like seaweed strung on the stinking stone,
> The nightmare stumbles past, and you have heard
> It fumble your door before it whimpers and is gone: . . .

The poet feels guilt for past and present failures and the impossibility of evasion:

> You have moved often and rarely left an address,
> And hear of the deaths of friends with a sly pleasure,
> A sense of cleansing and hope which blooms from distress;
> But it has not died, it comes, its hand childish, unsure,
> Clutching the bribe of chocolate or a toy you used to treasure.[2]

The book's reception was generally good. John Crowe Ransom wrote Warren, "The eleven poems are brilliant. No important poet in our time ever was so successfully withheld from his natural public. But I see from reviews that you are beginning to get yours." There his poetic craftsmanship was praised along with the poems' range and emotional power.[3]

His Princeton visit was successful professionally but—for the Tates—not socially. "I think he was much more interested in seeing Albert [Erskine] than in seeing Allen," Caroline Gordon wrote. "We decided that Cal Lowell, who is positively saintly since his conversion, was the only one of us Christian enough to associate with Red these days. I really don't think I ever want to see him again. When anybody prefers Albert Erskine to Allen I think they are pretty dumb." Warren had resented Tate's criticism of Katherine Anne Porter, who had decided to divorce Erskine. Caroline's chagrin at

Warren's attention to him rather than Allen was understandable, particularly in the light of Warren's growing reputation, which would be further enhanced in December when he was named corecipient of the Shelley Memorial Award for *Eleven Poems.* But her feelings ranged beyond envy nearly to paranoia, as when she "jumped on" the visiting Cleanth Brooks furiously about the way he and Warren had been turning down pieces she had sent to *The Southern Review.*[4]

The trip gave Warren the chance not only to see Erskine again, now working at *The Saturday Review of Literature,* but also to see Lambert Davis. He had arranged for a thousand dollars from Harcourt, Brace to pay off Warren's advance from Houghton Mifflin, and he drew up a long-term contract with Harcourt, Brace that called for several books plus a guaranteed "annual summer payment to relieve me from the necessity of doing any vacation teaching or lecturing." He spent enough time with Davis to return home with notes for revisions of *And Pastures New.*

In Iowa City the Warrens rented René Wellek's house, and he plunged into another term of teaching. Though Wellek was away, there were others like Norman Foerster who had formed in the previous summer what Wellek called "a group of people interested in criticism and in reforming also the teaching of English and literature away from the purely historical emphasis onto the reading of text and interpretation," professionals who found *Understanding Poetry* right up their critical alley. As Ernest Sandeen would recall, "He gave some lectures but he was best at vigorous free-swinging Socratic-conversations with smaller groups. He associated mostly with young English Graduate Assistants like Charlie [Charles H. Foster] and me. He liked to lead us, his young disciples, on long walks around the countryside . . . all the time talking or leading vigorous discussions. He also gave parties which were mostly long discussions, at his house." He made time for other diversions too. When "a small carnival came to Iowa City a group of us, with Red, went out to see what they had to show. . . . There was one particular contest that involved hitting a punching bag which sent a weight up in the air along a metal slide. . . . Red hauled off and hit the bag so vigorously that we thought it would knock off the top. We were all pleased at this (as was he), but the next day Red found that he had broken some bones in his hand. Somehow this seemed to be characteristic of his behavior at this time."[5]

. . .

With the northern winter looming, with automobile tires rationed and their own worn thin, Warren could see himself "standing in the twenty below three mornings a week at seven-thirty, waiting for his bus with the morning paper wrapped around his torso under his overcoat." It was natural that his thoughts should turn back to his homeland. He wrote Don Davidson to thank him for "your efforts and those of [Richmond Croom] Beatty to bring me back to Vanderbilt. . . . I leave the South with many misgivings and with some sense of irony." He recounted the maneuverings before his departure and concluded wistfully, "I hope, however, to come back South some day—and some day not too distant—if any respectable place will have me."[6]

This would be a new experience, living in a metropolis of nearly four hundred thousand inhabitants. Near the university senior faculty could afford multibedroom English cottage–style houses, and until the war boom there were good purchases and rentals for junior faculty. The city's glory, though, was the park system, which ran from a loop of the Mississippi River at the south for nearly thirty miles to the city's northern rim, with excellent swimming and fishing and bridle paths. Warren could hardly have fared better. And so they settled in on West Calhoun Boulevard, in "a rather pleasant apartment, very small but overlooking one of the dozen or so lakes in the city and with a good bit of greenery."[7]

But they could no longer escape the war as Stalingrad settled into a grim, desperate siege. Suddenly it impinged on him. He told Frank Owsley, "It seems that I shall probably be classified out of 3A this fall. . . . That might mean 1B—limited military service." He was in for a shock three months later. "I have been reclassified into 1A, and have been told that I'll probably get my induction examination this month. I was turned down by the Navy on account of eyes, and by the Army specialists outfit under the Procurement Office." The university had applied for a deferment, but they were not optimistic because the board had made him 1A anyway. So this married, one-eyed, thirty-seven-year-old teacher saw himself adding columns of figures in the Quartermaster Corps. Finally reason prevailed, and he was not called to defend his country at a desk.[8]

At the university everything had been done to smooth his way. "Joseph Warren Beach is a grand old gent," he told Lon Cheney. "We don't see eye to eye on a good many points, but those points have provided some pleasant evenings of argument with the bottle on the

table." One of his courses would be shared. Native son Sinclair Lewis
would teach the graduate class in creative writing in the fall quarter,
and Warren would teach it in the winter and spring quarters. His assistant for his big American-literature course, Mary Wyville, saw both
his professional and social sides. He was a popular teacher who extended the same "exquisite courtesy to some uncomprehending student as to the president of the university." But sometimes, she
realized, he talked over their heads, and it became her job to see that
they understood. When he visited Mary Wyville's home he told stories to her two little girls, who had to be sent off to bed long before
the Warrens left at two-thirty in the morning.[9]

His circle of faculty friends grew quickly. They ranged across the
age spectrum from younger men such as Arnold Stein and Leonard
Unger to Beach, twenty years his senior. Huntington Brown, six
years older than he, was a good friend whose home and family became a second one for the Warrens. A tall, spare, handsome man,
Hunt Brown would walk the paths along Lake Calhoun many mornings swinging a stick or carrying a crowbar to prepare for the approaching hunting season. Some mornings he would walk the three
miles around Lake of the Isles, and often Warren would join him,
talking animatedly about their shared passion for sixteenth- and seventeenth-century literature.[10]

"The walks were very fine indeed," he wrote much later, "but what
remains most vividly in mind is the scene at the dinner table at the
Brown house with three of the flock of Brown children." He listened
especially to Chickie (Elizabeth)—the eldest at sixteen—and to her
two very small brothers, Jonathan and Chris. "This was a new world
to me, for, since my own childhood, I had never been much around
children." He would stop in at the Browns' three or four times a week
on his way home from school. At the center was Elizabeth "Bid"
Brown, a short-haired, brown-eyed brunette, "a rather small woman,
well under average height, but brisk, graceful, energetic and active."
Warren found her witty and charming. Welcoming intimacy whereas
Hunt abhorred it, Bid had a natural flirtatiousness, which was stimulated by Warren's gregarious charm. It was different, though, when
Cinina came along. She was displeased when others diverted attention
from her. Then, as Warren and Joseph Warren Beach became warm
and intimate friends, Cinina grew close to Dagmar Beach, who would
become her only friend, a good friend such as Edward Donahoe had
become, one to share confidences and an early-afternoon drink.[11]

December brought the expected plunge down to ten and twelve above zero. The dry cold seemed not to bother Warren, but with it came auguries of future problems. He liked pickup basketball games, but one day he jumped for a rebound and crashed to the floor. He made a slow recovery. Ordered to exercise his injured shoulder regularly, he took up weight lifting. On Christmas Day he wrote Frank Owsley, "As for news with us, it's not very great. . . . Cinina has been flu–y for the last several days, and so today Huntington Brown, one of my colleagues, and his wife brought a Christmas dinner, complete, over here and set it up in our apartment." Increasingly Cinina would take to her bed, sometimes for months, complaining of lingering back trouble from the auto accident in Mexico. Warren hired the apartment superintendent's wife to take care of her when he was at school. Looking back later, he would remember Cinina's being in bed most of the time.[12]

Professionally things went well. Cinina had helped read proof on the novel, renamed *At Heaven's Gate,* and it was now in New York. He had also been writing twelve thousand words of script every week for three radio talks on "Great Literature" and teaching literature to air-corps premeteorology candidates and modern drama to college juniors and seniors. Then at last he was able to tell Katherine Anne Porter, "Spring has really come and the boys and girls are lying on the grass on the campus and the ice is off the lake under our window at the apartment, and I've turned thirty–eight and am, as a result, momentarily out of the draft."[13]

There was excitement for the Warrens awaiting the publication of *At Heaven's Gate,* but it was dampened by a familiar syndrome. Cinina gave a party with Jean and Alexander Kern for Lambert Davis. He was uneasy though, for he felt that Cinina begrudged him his relationship with her husband, and the emotional crosscurrents became puzzling and distressing. At the party she behaved so angrily for vague reasons that some of the guests were uncomfortable. The Kerns helped with the cleanup and left as soon as they decently could the next morning. They had known that "Red was aware of her tension though he did not witness all of her curious behavior, nor [did] we ever refer to it. . . ." The tension was heightened by delays in publication, but then on August 19, *At Heaven's Gate* appeared.[14]

It was a multilevel novel. In addition to depicting a time and a place while transcending both, it provides a spiritual dimension while chronicling political, economic, and sexual misbehavior. It addresses specific themes: the agrarian world based on a natural order versus the world of commerce based on immoral acquisitiveness, and self-deception versus self-knowledge. In the fictional elaboration of the actual scandals on which the story was based, the range of characters is correspondingly wide: from the empire-building entrepreneur Bogan Murdock (modeled on Rogers Clarke Caldwell) to hill-country religious fanatic Ashby Wyndham, and from former football star and aspiring businessman Jerry Calhoun to the effete yet sinister poet-student Slim Sarrett. Moving into the world of finance, Calhoun is leaving behind the rural world of his father. Young Sue Murdock, his lover, is another seeker who fails to receive from her father the nurturing she needs. Characters are ranged around Murdock or opposed to him: the governor and the war hero Private Porsum (modeled on Sergeant Alvin York) on one side and Slim Sarrett and labor activist Jason Sweetwater, who organizes a strike at Murdock's logging operation, on the other.

When Warren changed his title (borrowing from Shakespeare instead of Milton), he may have meant to emphasize Jerry Calhoun's initially bright prospects as a promising executive and potential son-in-law for Murdock. But gradually Jerry's prospects begin to change. Sue, with her unsympathetic parents, is a neurotic who turns first to Slim Sarrett and then to Jason Sweetwater in her search for love and emotional security. As her father's affairs move closer to a ruinous scandal, her life becomes more and more that of the victim, undergoing rejection, abortion, and finally murder. The fates of most of the other characters are also grim. A murderer who has tried to kill again, Ashby Wyndham awaits trial. Murdock's cat's-paw, Jerry Calhoun, is sentenced and heavy with guilt, forced at last to acknowledge not only that he had wanted to be Murdock's son, but also that he had even wanted to kill his natural father.

Robert Penn Warren had been a boy when the events presaging the greatest southern financial debacle to date were brewing. Rogers Clarke Caldwell—dynamic, persuasive, and endlessly resourceful—established his company to assist southern municipalities in selling their bonds. Gradually, Caldwell and Company expanded into real estate bond operations and industrial securities. A genius at his high-stakes shell game, he diversified his holdings. He had as ally Luke Lea, owner of the Nashville *Tennessean* and also owner, it was said, of Governor Henry H. Horton. When the crash came in 1929, Caldwell and Company went into receivership, and all the major players in the myriad schemes were indicted.[15]

When Lea went into hiding, Lon Cheney, working as a political reporter for the Nashville *Banner,* tracked him down. He knew that one of Lea's friends was an authentic hero. Awarded the highest Allied decorations and amply publicized in the *Tennessean,* Alvin Cullum York had entered into American history and folklore. When Lea took refuge in York's mountain home, Cheney tracked him down and interviewed him. Cheney told Warren about his adventures. Then, Warren said, "I hunted [York] up and got an acquaintance with him, and I read all the stuff about him." The still vigorous hero would serve as the model for one of the characters, as Rogers Caldwell and Luke Lea would serve as models for others.[16]

When a reporter asked Warren about the novel's setting, he told him that it was the South, but "it could be any one of several places." Like *Night Rider,* this new novel reflected other contemporary novels as well as the hostility to finance capitalism in *I'll Take My Stand* and *Who Owns America?* As the values of the Agrarians underlie descriptions of the countryside Warren loved, so a vision of the modern world like T. S. Eliot's informs the depiction of these hollow men exploiting it. This latter element gave the novel a spiritual dimension lacking in *Night Rider.* Like Eliot, Warren found special inspiration in *The Divine Comedy.* It was the Seventh Circle of Hell, in the *Inferno,* that "provided with some liberties of interpretation and extension, the basic scheme and metaphor for the whole novel. All of the main characters are violators of nature." Like Dante, he used real people, though he did not use their actual names.[17]

The writing proved to be exhausting. Still learning his craft, Warren first wrote "a complete outline from start to finish, and it was about eighty pages long. . . . And I spent months doing that and thinking it through . . . and then writing a consecutive narrative for it. And I hated writing the book so much that I threw the outline away. Because it was killing the sense of discovery in the writing of the book. . . ." It was hard going before he reached the climactic actions.[18]

He had earlier moved along the events in the larger world, where Murdock had sent Private Porsum to his Massey Mountain timber operation to quell the strike organized by Sweetwater. Wyndham's jailhouse statement, occupying twelve of the novel's twenty-seven chapters, provides not only counterpoint to the Murdock-Calhoun plot but also the solution to a problem. It was during the troubled

Italian winter of 1939–40, when Warren had gotten stuck, that his undiagnosed typhus helped him burn his way through. "I had the most vivid dreams in this high fever, and went through the whole story of the mountaineer coming down the river and coming to Nashville, and his touch blowing the [impasse] up." Wyndham's life has been a long pilgrimage from his hill-country home with the blood of his brother on his hands finally to the sinful city where, jailed for his assault on Sweetwater, he writes his testament.[19]

Years later, speaking about his work, especially his poems, Warren would say that it constituted a "shadowy autobiography." But he would also tell one interviewer, "The autobiographical stuff is so tangled up with psychological questions and philosophical questions that everybody . . . who tries to make use of things for biographical material is crazy." But the reader cannot miss the recurrent father–son problems, with surrogate fathers supplanting natural fathers who do not measure up to their sons' expectations. In these years Warren visited his father and traveled with him when he could, but even near the end of his life he would record emphatically his strange sense of guilt, as a successful poet, for having somehow appropriated the vocation his father had vainly cherished, living out his small-town life as an unsuccessful banker and stoic storekeeper. The character in *At Heaven's Gate* whose circumstances are closest to Warren's is Slim Sarrett, moving in an academic environment and cherishing ambitions as a poet and critic. If Warren were to have thought in terms of a Jekyll-Hyde relationship, here was his Hyde.[20]

At Heaven's Gate is less controlled than *Night Rider*, but it is more ambitious and interesting technically. The "Testament of Ashby Wyndham" is an extended tour de force that allowed Warren to display his mastery of the hill-country dialect he knew so well. If at length it grows tiresome—a risk Faulkner avoided by using many voices in *As I Lay Dying*—it still provides an effective linguistic and moral counterpoint to the Murdock plot. More intriguing are the patterns of imagery. The most interesting one, echoing early poems and anticipating later ones, is that of geological formations seen from a great height. It is not just compelling imagery. It fits with his fundamental thought—that of a man with a religious temperament but without religious belief, dazzled by the beauty of the world but yearning for more, yearning for a kind of transcendence, for an answer from the constellations in the night sky beneath which a gazing poet often stands.[21]

The reception of *At Heaven's Gate* was mixed. Reviewers praised its vitality and power but criticized its melodrama and sexuality. They tended to like its technical versatility and dislike its content. Nevertheless, it would make more than one list of the year's best books, and for all the censure and disgust, the general reaction probably assured Lambert Davis and his colleagues at Harcourt, Brace that the first printing of five thousand copies would certainly be sold out and that there would be a continuing audience for Robert Penn Warren's fiction.[22]

Some of Warren's friends came down as hard on the novel as the toughest reviewers. It was dedicated to Frank and Harriet Owsley, and it was just as well that Warren did not know Frank's private reaction. Allen Tate wrote Owsley, "I am sorry to confess that I agree with you about Red's novel, certainly about his pushover women. . . . In short, I think it is as a whole inferior to *Night Rider,* though in some respects more expert technically."

John Ransom had strong reservations about the book but expressed them to Warren more positively: "I find myself wishing that you would do a fiction analogous to your fine poetry; in the grand manner, in the magnificent manner. . . . You are the easiest, most flowing, prose artist we have, whether in critical or fictional prose." Although Caroline Gordon would later dismiss Warren's novels while she praised his poetry, she came through on this occasion, writing in the *Weekly Book Review* that "Mr. Warren has provided in *At Heaven's Gate* not only a stirring novel—the account of Private Porsum will stand with the best writing of our times—but one of the most profound interpretations that has yet been made of Southern life."[23]

For his second published novel it was an impressive achievement, a big novel that evoked a whole culture, posed political and ethical problems, and managed a large cast of vividly realized characters. His strong powers of description were enhanced by his adaptation of poetic devices for prose. He showed his fine ear for southern speech even while he displayed an excessive fondness for cynical, wisecracking dialogue. There was as much action and sex as most readers could expect in 1943, even if carried into melodrama—a charge that would be leveled often again. *At Heaven's Gate* would never be rated one of his best novels, but it demonstrated his growing powers and supplied direction signs toward the future.

24

❖

In the Service of
the State

There is always another country and always another place.
There is always another name and another face.
And the name and the face are you, and you
The name and the face, and the stream you gaze into
Will show the adoring face, show the lips that lift to you
As you lean with the implacable thirst of self,
As you lean to the image which is yourself, . . .
—*"The Ballad of Billie Potts"*[1]

If most of his attention had been focused on *At Heaven's Gate* in the
spring of 1943, he was characteristically involved with other prose and
poetry as well. He was putting together a volume of his short fiction,
and he was still writing poems, though the lyric impulse came less and
less often now. Cinina took to her bed with various complaints—chest
problems that brought back memories of her hemorrhages and fears of
tuberculosis, malaise, and lassitude from indeterminate causes. It was as
if his lyric impulse was shriveling along with the husk of the marriage.
But he was still a practicing poet, and in the absence of present inspiration he could draw upon memory.

He thought back to the previous summer, to Chapala, where he
and Cinina had gone when the war prevented a return to Italy. Instead of memories of congenial Italian companions, he recalled now
how "I had encountered a rag-tag and bobtail of the Left Bank, full
of Nazis and homosexuals hiding out at Chapala away from the war."
Working from what he called "scraps of poems" as well as recollection, he re-created not just the exterior sense of place but also an in-

terior sense of vacancy and dessication. With his increasing tendency to write sequences of poems, he put them together as "Mexico Is a Foreign Country: Five Studies in Naturalism." In their two hundred lines his references range from literature to politics to history. There are jibes at Hemingway's bullfight writings, at Henry Wallace, at Baptists, and Standard Oil. The poet gazes afar at "Small Soldiers with Drum in Large Landscape," recalls Wordsworth's delight at his host of golden daffodils, and brooding upon "the done, and the undone," contemplates his own heart's seizing "its hint of pleasure. . . ." But in "The Mango on the Mango Tree" the old sense of guilt is there, for unnamed crimes, shared alike by the poet and the mango tree, by men as a whole, who must suffer "until His monstrous primal guilt be washed away," thus implicating God, the author of "our vicarious sacrifice [for] fault not our own. . . ." So the last of the studies dresses this socio-literary concept in strange garments of original sin. The sequence appeared in *Poetry* in June.[2]

In the first half of 1943 he had continued work on another poem begun the previous year. He recalled that, returning from Italy, he felt dissatisfied with the "metaphysical" poetry he had written under the influence of John Ransom. So he tried his hand at what one writer termed "backwoods and ribald poetry" in "his first frontier and narrative poem. . . ." At first it embodied a philosophy of American history. But then, unconsciously, he began to fuse it with theological concerns. "I remember the very day it came to me," he said. "I was crossing the snow-swept campus of the University of Minnesota and about to open a door, when the first few lines came like a flash, while I tried to get the door open. So I spent ten days or two weeks writing the poem. I was trying to get back, make a tie between modernism and balladry and make them both stack up to a kind of view of American history *and* a kind of interplay of styles." This new poem was twice as long as the sequence of Mexico poems. The rhyme scheme again was irregular, and the poem was broken into verse paragraphs of varying length, but it echoed the ballad form not just in subject matter and treatment but also with devices such as incremental repetition of lines for emphasis.[3]

"The Ballad of Billie Potts" tells how an evil innkeeper not only earmarks guests for robbery and murder but also trains his son in crime. When the hulking boy's bungling puts him in danger, his father sends him west. Returning as a rich man, he conceals his identity as a joke, only to be murdered by his parents. It is a brutal poem of violent action ending with the parents' recognition under the torchlight's glare of a birthmark on the exhumed body. (Warren confirmed one student's speculation that it embodied his concern with the fallacy of human perfectibility.) The poem was taken by the *Partisan Review* for publication in the winter number. It would reappear in subsequent Warren volumes and in a number of anthologies. But it was the last new poem he would publish for more than a decade. The causes for the long drought were several, and they had little to do with the problem of the fallacy of human perfectibility.[4]

Returning to America after the First World War, Archibald MacLeish pursued successful careers as magazine editor, essayist, dramatist, poet, and political activist. Named Librarian of Congress in 1939, he set about modernizing it. He also changed the Chair of Poetry from a permanent appointment to a rotating one and named Allen Tate to it. As his term at the library reached its midpoint, MacLeish had to think about a successor. Tate proposed Warren and got permission to sound him out.

Warren's reply on January 31 of 1944 initiated three months of negotiation. When he came east in late March for a lecture at Harvard and a visit in New York, he also stopped in Washington. Whether anything came of the visit or not, it meant a reunion with Katherine Anne Porter, there to take up residence as a Fellow of American Letters at the library, and with the Cheneys, both now working in Washington. Warren stayed with the Tates, and the day after a cordial meeting with MacLeish, Tate took him to lunch and invited Eleanor Clark along. She thought Tate "an incredible girl chaser" and found him physically unattractive, but she decided to accept anyway. A striking blonde with a classic profile, she was a thirty-one-year-old Vassar graduate, an aspiring writer who had made a precarious living as an editor and a freelance writer until she landed a job with the Office of Strategic Services monitoring French and Italian publications and interviewing refugees. She and Warren enjoyed each other's company at the lunch. Warren left Washington, with assurances that he would hear from MacLeish.[5]

The imminent appearance of his *Selected Poems, 1923–1943* from Harcourt, Brace must have lightened the tag end of the Minnesota winter. The publication date for the fifteen-hundred-copy edition was April 6. The 102-page volume was divided into two parts. First came thirty-one late poems. The twenty-one early poems included favorites in the major styles he had employed: the metaphysical in "Garden Waters," the personal in "The Return: An Elegy," the symbolic in "Kentucky Mountain Farm," and the colloquial with a hint of the incipient ballad style in "Pondy Woods." The early notices in the major opinion-makers were encouraging, with praise for his mastery of modern poetic technique and his exploration of the pathology obscured by the conformity and stultification of modern life. Then, after affirmation of his status as a powerful and important poet, the notices appearing later in the fall would turn wintry, with charges of obsession and indebtedness to Eliot. Nonetheless, the volume would make *The Nation*'s list of the ten best books of poetry for 1944.[6]

In early spring the Minneapolis *Sunday Tribune* reported Warren's appointment as Consultant in Poetry of the Library of Congress, "given annually to an American poet of outstanding accomplishment and reputation in his field." Warren knew it would increase his acquaintance with leading literary figures and his own influence too. And despite his impressive-sounding responsibilities and the business he would have to transact, the job would actually provide more time for his own work than teaching did. By mid-July he was packing manuscripts to take to Washington with him, one of them lengthy. When Douglas Newton asked for new poems for anthologies he was preparing, Warren replied that he would not have any short things soon, "for I am in the middle of a long novel which promises to keep my nose to the grindstone for some months to come. I am also working along on a narrative poem, some seven or eight hundred lines (a ballad and commentary like 'Billie Pott' . . .), but I don't know that I'll finish this before mid-winter." It had come to him as an idea for a novel, but then it had turned into a poem. "I started a poem on Audubon," he said later, "but I got stuck in a trap, a narrative trap. There's no narrative there, as such, to work from. You can't carry him that way, because the narrative doesn't have enough bite to it. I wrote a lot about him." Several winters would pass before he would complete either of these works.[7]

He turned back to *Proud Flesh*, which he considered "a tight little play." He found, however, that he still wanted to tell his story through the voice of a character rather than a third-person narrator. He went to the last scene of the play where he had introduced the newspaperman—identified only as Jack, a boyhood friend of Keith Amos—for purely dramatic purposes to set up the final action. So Jack became the narrator, and "it turned out that what he thought about the story was more important than the story itself. . . . He made it possible for me to control it. He is an observer, but he is involved." Warren soon discovered, however, that Jack Burden presented a problem himself.[8]

He would later say that he came to a stop because he needed something to relate his narrator to the moral issues of the novel. A segment he called "Cass Mastern's Wedding Ring" was his attempt at a solution. It took place before and during the Civil War, whereas the body of the novel was set seventy years later. For readers who knew his poetry, there would be familiar themes. The account began with the efforts of Jack Burden, a graduate student in history at a university very like LSU, to write his dissertation. It was to be an edition of the letters and the journal of Cass Mastern, his great-uncle, together with a biographical essay. In the course of his research, Burden learns how Mastern entered into a liaison with Annabel Trice, the wife of his friend Duncan Trice, and of the consequences, including the overpowering sense of guilt that leads Mastern to seek death in combat. Jack Burden is unable to complete the dissertation because he "realized that he did not know Cass Mastern." What the novel would have to make clear would be the reasons why Jack Burden felt, even after all his scrupulous research, that he did not know his great-uncle. As Warren was leaving Cass Mastern in the land of his imagination, so he was ready to leave Minnesota. He was moving south again, not to the South of his childhood and young manhood, but nonetheless to a place below the Mason–Dixon line, where his professional life would be enlarged once more.[9]

"Today Robert Penn Warren arrives to take up the Chair of Poetry lately vacated by Allen Tate," Katherine Anne Porter informed Barbara Wescott on July 23, "and there is going to be a long lunch at a long table in a very plushy office for him, with no drinks and food brought in from the Senate Cafeteria." The weather was less welcoming, Washington's usual summer humidity turning to driving rain and then extreme heat. But two weeks later Warren could report that things were going pleasantly and that he had just rented a house. One month after his arrival he wrote a full account to Hunt and Bid Brown with reassuring news about Cinina, whose arrival had been unlike her departure from Minneapolis. Bid Brown would later recall her "lying on a stretcher in the middle of our railroad station holding a sort of farewell soiree, like that lady in Trollope. I think her mortal illness was entirely imaginary, but she was having an awfully good

time." Now, Warren wrote Bid, they were residing at 2445 Thirty-
ninth Street, NW, where they had a roof over their heads, "and
everything under it is very ugly and very comfortable." Katherine
Anne Porter wrote Glenway Wescott that "Red Warren has a Japanese servant from a concentration camp, who is very good and faithful up to a point, and then refuses to allow him guests more than so
often, is pertinacious in demanding holidays and overtime, etc."[10]

Warren also gave the Browns a picture of his situation on the top
floor of the old Library of Congress building. Katherine Anne was
lodged in an office across the hall from him "making the resources of
the Library useful to writers concerned with the American past and
the American scene." As for himself, "I'm sitting in a big old office
back of the map room, with a desk and a swivel chair and a big black
horsehair couch on which I recline when in vacant or in pensive
mood. . . . and now and then I see that I'm in the Rare Book Room
to look for holes in the collection of American poets of 1860–1910.
For that is my chore for the year, that and the quarterly. All of this
sounds—and is—pretty unexciting, but I've managed to get some
very exciting reading done. I'm going through the manuscript narratives of ex-slaves, of which the WPA collected thirty-seven or -eight
big volumes. It is really wonderful stuff, full of all sorts of information
and human quality and God knows what." There were journals and
memoirs, and one in particular seized his attention. It dealt with "two
sons of Charles Lewis, who was related to Meriwether and married
to Thomas Jefferson's sister. The sons became involved in a perverse,
violent, and hideous situation, out west in Kentucky."[11]

He remained as outgoing and gregarious as ever. Hugh Cox and
John Peale Bishop were there, and he saw them often. He also formed
a close friendship with Denis Devlin, a poet and friend of Allen Tate
who was secretary to the Irish legation. And he did not allow routine
to disrupt favorite physical activities. At noon he would eat a sandwich in his office and be off to the YMCA. One day when his former student Norton Girault visited him, Warren invited him to come
along. There, with another friend, they lifted weights and jogged
around the track. Then they shot baskets. They got back to the office
before two, "having had a good workout, feeling good," Warren said.
He decided you could do the work in half the time they supposed because bureaucrats spend their time in meetings. "I didn't go to many
meetings or talk in the hall," he said. "I did four hours' hard work a
day—did everything I was supposed to do, and I was writing every

day on my novel in the office." And as he wrote, his secretary kept typing the manuscript.[12]

These recollections scanted the amount he accomplished. He summarized for MacLeish recommendations for the limited number of films that should be preserved of the fourteen hundred made in the country each year. (The range assessed was enormous—from *The Song of Bernadette* to *Curse of the Cat People*.) He solicited nominations for new fellows of the library, himself proposing several distinguished candidates and then fixing on John Dos Passos, Louise Bogan, and Theodore Spencer or Kenneth Burke. By fall he was even busier with administration. As secretary to the fellows in American Letters he had to manage various activities and take part in entrepreneurial projects. He planned a two-day meeting of the fellows, preparing the agenda, obtaining accommodations, and arranging entertainment. They met twice each day on November 16 and 17, finally proposing the issuance each year of five albums of five recordings each. They compiled two long lists of older poets and two of younger poets, the artists themselves to record their works. The program would prove fruitful.[13]

It was a busy holiday season. Cinina had been in bed for most of the fall, and now Warren went from shop to shop, finally settling for a big tom turkey. He wrote Andrew Lytle that they were sharing the Thanksgiving preparations with his secretary, Sheila Brantley, who was providing mince pies, and with John Palmer, who was supplying wine and brandy, "old time, pre-war stuff." As Christmas approached there were occasions with other friends—the Cheneys and the Bandys, the Devlins and the Coxes, Hugh Cox now serving as assistant solicitor general of the United States. Then, a few days before Christmas, Cinina began getting up each day. Robert Warren sent them a twenty-four-pound ham, and Dagmar and Joseph Warren Beach shared it with them and made it a festive Christmas. They finished off the ham at a New Year's Eve party. "The festivities are over, and probably not a minute too soon," Warren told Allen Tate. "I have been able to sit upright today, but I don't know how I have managed it after a long party last night."[14]

January brought snow. "It's miserably cold and gloomy," Cinina wrote. The combination of her mood and his impending out-of-town engagements made Warren uneasy. Sometimes when he returned from trips he could tell Cinina had been drinking. Often their Oklahoma friend Edward Donahoe had been there with a friend of his. Donahoe's father had settled an income on him, and so he was free to do as he pleased. Cinina was attractive to men, and in recent years her attempts to gain their attention had become more overt, almost as if these needs had grown in proportion to the increased attention her husband received. There was no reason for him to suspect sexual dalliance between her and Donahoe, but he was not the sort of company Warren wanted his wife to keep, and there was the constant worry about her illnesses. More and more he took refuge in his work, intensifying her loneliness and craving for attention and dominance.[15]

There was plenty of work for him to do. The narrative poem similar to "The Ballad of Billie Potts" still resisted his efforts, and so he turned to the Bergen Lecture to be given at Yale in April, a close reading of Coleridge's *Rime of the Ancient Mariner.* Most of his writing time and effort, however, went into the novel. More than a year before he had written Tate, "I am suffering the agonies of the damned with it. . . . the problem of carrying the narrative in the first person. . . . I had hoped to make it a fairly compact book, but now it looks like a long, long son-of-a-bitch. I've finished about 80,000 words and haven't neared the halfway mark, God help me." Almost exactly a year later, with Tate teaching at the University of the South, Warren wrote that he had a fifty-page section of the novel, "not as much of a self-explanatory unit as the Cass Mastern section," but one he would send hoping it was not too long for *The Sewanee Review,* which Tate was now editing.[16]

The section was in fact too long for the magazine, and it was so closely knit that Tate did not see how it could be cut. Though the events of the governor's career remained essentially unchanged from *Proud Flesh,* there had been many alterations in emphasis, characterization, and even names. Jack Burden had become not just the narrator but also a foil for Governor Strong, who had become Governor Talos. Anne Amos had become Anne Stanton, once the sweetheart of Jack Burden but alienated from him by the malaise that prevents him from finishing his dissertation on Cass Mastern. Leaving graduate school, he has become a cynical newspaperman married to a delectable empty-headed sensualist he comes to call "Lois the machine." As he has gone to work for the governor, checking his conscience at the door, so Anne too is drawn into the governor's life as his mistress. Tate thought the material on Jack's short-lived marriage overdone, but "up to the Lois episode I'm convinced that you've never done better writing, if as good."[17]

. . .

Warren continued work on his lecture on *The Rime of the Ancient Mariner.* Despite his early prejudice against career-enhancing articles in the prestigious scholarly journals, he was now writing yet another essay whose scholarship could have stood the scrutiny of any journal in the field. Two years before, in "Pure and Impure Poetry," he had written that "pure poems want to be, and desperately, all of a piece," excluding "certain elements which might qualify or contradict [their] original impulse." For him, however, far from being impure, poetry that was more inclusive could be more powerful. "Poetry," he wrote, "does not inhere in any particular element but depends upon the set of relationships, the structure, which we call the poem," and "nothing that is available in human experience is to be legislated out of poetry." He entitled his new essay "A Poem of Pure Imagination: An Experiment in Reading." He drew upon all his study and practice of the art of poetry and upon his deepest convictions of its importance.[18]

His reading of Coleridge's poem continued his attack on "the general theory of pure poetry which says that poetry . . . does make comments on life but that the truths it offers us are not worth listening to." His special target was "a brand of hyperaesthetical criticism" of the poem, the brand that "flourishes in the very citadels of academic respectability, and in the works of some of the most eminent and sober students of Coleridge." He directed his fire at several who argued that Coleridge intended that the poem should be "without a theme, without relevance to life," much less a moral meaning. For them, he wrote, the poem "is nothing more than a pleasant but meaningless dream." He meant to prove that the poem embodied a statement "thoroughly consistent with Coleridge's basic theological and philosophical views as given to us in [his own] sober prose. . . ."[19]

He argued his case with staggering erudition, ranging over Coleridge's life and the whole corpus of his work, over theories of artistic creation from Plotinus to I. A. Richards (Warren's good friend), and over crucial issues about the nature of poetry in the previous two centuries. And as he did so he offered an explication, his own reading of the poem, in the kind of vigorous and lucid prose that had helped make *Understanding Poetry* such a boon to students and teachers. He explained that when Coleridge called his poem a work of "pure imagination," the word was "freighted with a burden of speculation and technical meaning," and not used "in the casual and vulgar sense, as equivalent to meaninglessness or illusion. . . ." He went on to explain the word's complex meanings in Coleridge's theory and its function in embodying the poem's secondary theme of imagination, the primary one being that "of sacramental vision, or the theme of the 'One Life.' "[20]

His comments on Coleridge's work were full of relevance to his own. Coleridge "found peace simply by accepting the idea of Original Sin as a mystery." The Ancient Mariner's lack of motivation in killing the albatross was the significant thing about the act: It "re-enacts the Fall. . . ." This sin of the will issues from "Satanic pride and rebellious self-idolatry," precipitating a crime of betrayal that is symbolically a murder visited upon this symbolic bird, which had loved the man who killed it. The act and the subsequent disasters springing from it leave the Mariner with a burden of guilt that drops from him finally only with an awareness of it and the acceptance of "the sacramental view of the universe. . . ." Warren's new novel would be the story of a great fall shot through with many betrayals and much guilt before a final expiation.[21]

Now, with the cherry trees about to bloom in pink and white in the moist and balmy Washington spring, Warren's thoughts had already turned to other poems and to the author of the loveliest celebration of cherry trees. Textual bibliographer as well as close reader of texts, he had studied the manuscripts of A. E. Housman at the Library of Congress. He wrote Cleanth Brooks, "I even discovered that on the pasted-down backs of the sheets were a large number of earlier versions and had them exposed to the light of the day." They gave "beautiful examples of the approach to a poem, a series of revisions leading up to the finished product." He thought they might use photographs for a revised edition of *Understanding Poetry,* and he had written an essay on a Frost poem they could include along with material he could adapt from his *Ancient Mariner* analysis. He was ready to revise that manuscript and to prepare for departure from the city and the job.[22]

For him the joy at the war's end was tempered by other emotions. In early summer, well into his revisions, he would write Katherine Anne Porter, "It is a sort of relief to turn to something as objective and impersonal as that kind of writing now and then." He was revising his novel—now called *All the King's Men*—and he told her he had "the dumps over it and over everything else I've ever done." It was when he got "too sad about the novel" that he turned to the revision. "But my dumps are a little more general than I have indicated. . . . the news of everything from Europe to San Francisco has been, since the President's death, most monstrously depressing." At home, however, there seemed to be reason for optimism. "Cinina continues to improve," he wrote, "and is now in the kitchen standing on her able pins to get me a lunch." But the best he could summon up was a kind of equanimity. "No great news here," he wrote Allen Tate. "I'm drifting toward the end of the year with a feeling that the time for departure is timed about right."[23]

It brought a return to his peripatetic teaching, first summer school at the Connecticut College for Women and then four days at the University of Iowa. As the Warrens prepared to return to Minnesota he could take some satisfaction from his sojourn in the East. Programs he had implemented at the Library of Congress were running, and his successor, Louise Bogan, would carry on ably. He had served his country and literature, and in the process he had increased his own stature and made influential new friends. There had been happy times with old friends such as the Cheneys and with new ones such as Eleanor Clark. "We liked Eleanor Clark very much," he wrote Katherine Anne Porter. "She is a fine, intelligent, gifted girl, isn't she?" Katherine Anne replied that she was "indeed a lovely gifted person, and having a very hard life of it too, trying to come out on some kind of firm ground in all this. I have liked her immensely for years. . . . The last I heard she was still at Yaddo, fighting it out with [her first] novel. She'll win. . . ."[24]

As usual, the Warrens would have to find a place to live. And there was always the work, past and future. "As for the long poem," he wrote Tate, "it isn't ready yet. I've got some sections, but nothing very consecutive." It would be a long time before it became *Brother to Dragons.* And the short lyrics still would not come. Some future work was embryonic. One morning Katherine Anne Porter had come in from her office across the hall and flung a document down on his desk. It was called *Confession of Jereboam Beauchamp.* "This is for you," she told him. "I'm giving you a novel."[25]

25

❖

All the King's Men—
At Last

By now the literal, factual world was only a memory, and therefore was ready to be absorbed freely into the act of the imagination.
—*"The Matrix of Experience"*[1]

He had to postpone work on the new novel, living in a hotel room until they finally found an apartment "the size of a birdcage over a garage." The fall term of 1945 made another set of demands. The Minnesota *Daily* reported that "sardines who know anything about the University have a joke going around about people. This time it's on the large number of students packed, crammed and crowded into the three English courses taught by Robert Penn Warren." Total enrollment in his three courses ran close to two hundred.[2]

Warren's vitality gave the impression that he was always in a hurry. Much of the time he was. He declined a book review for Allen Tate because "I simply haven't got the time. I am beginning work on a book which is taking all the energy I have." He still had to revise his Coleridge essay for Reynal & Hitchcock publication with the text of *The Rime of the Ancient Mariner.* It would include twenty-five drawings by Alexander Calder, and Albert Erskine, now with the firm, would edit it. Tate's reaction to the essay was all Warren could have wished: "easily the finest work of poetic criticism of our generation. Nothing else touches it. It is simply magnificent."[3]

Meanwhile, the long labor that had begun with *Proud Flesh* was in its final phases. The manuscript Warren had submitted in the spring was a "ragged composite typescript." Lambert Davis suggested alterations in the novel's structure and the character of Jack Burden, and

Warren incorporated many of them in his reworking. Davis spent a weekend reading the revised manuscript. He suggested toning down Jack's language to his mother and approved his reducing "the smart-aleck tone that we both recognized in the earlier version." The conclusion, he thought, was "absolutely right." Five days later, however, he wrote that both he and David Mitchell Clay, Warren's Vanderbilt classmate and now a Harcourt, Brace editor, thought the book needed a scene at the end between Jack and Anne providing resolution, for "Anne has been more deeply involved in the killing of Stark than anyone else, and more deeply affected."[4]

Early in the new year of 1946, Warren visited Davis at his home in Chappaqua, north of New York City. They immediately fell back into their earlier relationship when Davis talked about poems and fiction "with a strange mixture of almost boyish enthusiasm and a hard shrewdness. . . . Davis could early grasp the main idea, the germ intuition, of a work, and nurture your own hope for, and confidence in it, but at the same time he could be only a little short of merciless about the working out of the intuition." For relief they would take long walks to Flag Hill. They would talk about technique, especially foreshadowing in preparing the reader, particularly with the first-person narrator as hero who changes in the course of the novel. Davis told Warren to cut the long first chapter. "Your story begins here, on the highway." Warren saw that "the original opening got off to a very slow start. . . . expository in the worse sense." Davis suggested cutting much of the second chapter as well, and like Lon Cheney, he didn't like the governor's name, Talos. When Warren returned home, Davis wrote him about problems he would continue to encounter, particularly "the necessity to create, by constant implication, the narrator." And he insisted that Warren rewrite one whole section. The author listened carefully to his editor and heeded his advice. Shortly before Christmas, he sent in the finished version.[5]

On the blue-penciled typescript "Talos" was changed to "Stark," and though Jack Burden was still the wisecracking cynic, numerous deletions lessened the abrasiveness and vulgarity in his smart-aleck personality. Occasional portentousness was also cut. The narrator-mouthpiece problems that had surfaced in a windy didacticism were also gone, but his character was also less complex than it had been.[6]

Pier Marie Pasinetti reentered their lives. Edward Davison's wife, Natalie, helped to expedite his passport application, and Warren helped him get a job at Bennington College. They welcomed him in

Minneapolis for a Christmas visit. At the parties he met young writers such as Max Shulman, Thomas Heggen, Sylvia Fine, and Dan Brennan. But there was a mix of other guests. Pier met English-department members ranging from Joseph Warren Beach to a new instructor named Saul Bellow. Dimitri Mitropoulos, the director of the symphony, was there at one party too. To Pier, Minneapolis was a marvelous city, and he enjoyed himself greatly with Red and Cinina and their friends. Cinina was delighted when Huntington and Bid Brown invited Pier to stay in their roomy old house until his teaching began in March. She enjoyed not just the Italian conversation with Pier but also the whole ambience he brought with him, and she glowed under the warmth of his obvious affection. The three recaptured much of their pleasure together before the uneasy days when the Warrens had not known when they would have to sprint for the last boat from Italy. Pier formed another intimate threesome with them, as Albert Erskine and John Palmer had done earlier. It seemed to him that Red loved Cinina very much. And they gave the appearance, he thought, of being very good together in bed.[7]

As usual, the holiday did not prevent work. Warren finished a "novelette" to be called "The Circus in the Attic." Katherine Anne Porter wrote to thank him for a copy of "Cass Mastern's Wedding Ring," for a long essay on Hemingway for a new edition of *A Farewell to Arms,* for the *Rime of the Ancient Mariner* essay, and for "Blackberry Winter." The latter was a new short story drawing on the world of his childhood. With her usual warm affection, Katherine Anne told him, "I am more and more amazed at the tremendous amount of work you get done. And all of it is superb."[8]

    She had not, apparently, seen any of the novel, now being set in type. It had two principal characters, whose stories were intertwined. In present time Jack Burden—former graduate student in history, newspaper reporter, and then assistant to governor-to-be Willie Stark—tells the complex story of his relationship with Stark, who follows his star to dictatorial power until he meets the assassin's bullet. Abandoning his idealism in the rough world of politics, he substitutes pragmatism, slipping further into corruption, betraying his school-teacher wife, Lucy, then his successive mistresses: his secretary, Sadie Burke, and well-brought-up Anne Stanton. A foil for Willie, Jack has found him compelling for his determination and power, qualities Jack lacks, just as he had been unable to commit himself to the same Anne, his boyhood sweetheart, unable to complete his thesis or make himself effectual in the real day-to-day world. At the end they are together, committed to the goals Willie abandoned.

In acknowledging the items Warren had sent Katherine Anne Porter at Christmas, she had listed the *Ancient Mariner* essay first. It had, as a matter of fact, an interesting congruity with the new novel. Coleridge's Mariner, still obsessed with his killing the albatross, expiates something of his crime with each retelling, complexities of tone mixing guilt and self-justification. Recalling his search for the right tone for his narrator in *All the King's Men,* Warren said it "turned on the question of getting a lingo for this narrator. . . . A straight journalistic prose would not do. That is the trap of all traps. There has to be an angularity to any piece of writing that claims to have a person behind it." Although he had not employed a journalist as narrator before, Duckfoot Blake talked in the sardonic, cynical, and slangy mode in *At Heaven's Gate.* Now Warren enlarged upon it to accommodate Jack Burden's reflections on matters philosophical, psychological, and religious as well as the political concerns that dominated Blake's ruminations. Warren would use this racy, worldly-wise mode often again, and his affinity for it could be heard in his own tale-telling. But he had more as a source for Jack Burden's lingo. "I used a model," he said, "but he doesn't know it yet. I know him very well indeed. I even know that he doesn't know what I know about him." But he never revealed his identity.[9]

The source for Willie Stark was at once more clear and more complicated. Huey Pierce Long was the model for the protagonists of three novels already in print. Years later Warren would write, "When I am asked how much *All the King's Men* owes to the actual politics of Louisiana in the '30s, I can only be sure that if I had never gone to live in Louisiana and if Huey Long had not existed, the novel would never have been written." But "for better or for worse, Willie Stark was not Huey Long. Willie was only himself, whatever that self turned out to be, a shadowy wraith or a blundering human being." Warren had heard Long speak on that single occasion at the official luncheon celebrating LSU's seventy-fifth anniversary, but he could not help absorbing a great deal from simply living there. "What I knew was the 'Huey' of the myth," he wrote. But some thought the novel closer to life than Warren acknowledged. He wrote that "Politics merely provided the framework story in which the deeper concerns, whatever their final significance, might work themselves out."

What, then, were those deeper concerns, and how did the characters and events show their working out?[10]

In its earliest embodiment the work "started as the simplest kind of idea. A man who has the gift for power gets his means and his ends mixed up, and gets some power, and there's a backlash on him. He gets killed. It starts with that. Huey Long and Julius Caesar both got killed in the capitol, and there you are. It's as simple as that. It's a germ, an anecdote. And teaching Shakespeare in Louisiana in 1935, you couldn't avoid this speculation." Warren gave his annual lecture on the political background of *Julius Caesar,* and during the two weeks they studied it "backs grew straighter, eyes grew brighter, notes were taken, and the girls stopped knitting in class, or repairing their faces." (One was daughter Rose Long, a bright girl who sat in the back row.) What some reviewers would see as melodrama had actually been conceived on the scale of tragedy. Working on *Proud Flesh* in Rome, he was "hearing the boot heels of the Fascist troops on the cobblestones." He was interested in the dynamics of power, and the provincial world of Louisiana shared in the "airs and aspirations that the newspapers attributed to that ex-champagne salesman Von Ribbentrop and to the inner circle of Edda Ciano's friends." It also manifested something uniquely American because, to the novel's creator, "Long was but one of the figures that stood in the shadows of imagination behind Willie Stark. Another one of the company was the scholarly and benign figure of William James." An American pragmatist himself, Willie was interested in what worked, convinced as he was that man had to be guided by efficacy—not actions based on an absolute scale of morality but rather upon the need to create the good, out of the bad if necessary.[11]

In Warren's narrative strategy, Jack was made to carry the book's meanings just as Willie was. From very early his quests have led him down roads pocked with disastrous failures. His seeming inability to give direction and meaning to his life—which leads to Anne Stanton's alienation from him—ironically constitutes one component of the makeup that also leads him to decline to take her virginity, presumably from some unspecified idealism. One of his ironic sobriquets for himself is the "historical researcher." He is unable to complete his thesis because "he couldn't face the fact that in his own blood there was a man who *had* faced up to a moral problem in a deep way." Not only has Cass Mastern attempted to ameliorate some of the consequences of his sin, he has finally attempted to expiate his guilt in death. Jack, an ironically self-styled "brass-bound Idealist," has reacted to defeat and disillusionment with withdrawal—"The Great Sleep"—and then flight. But at the end, Jack has accepted the idea of consequentiality and responsibility arising out of a genuine, painfully acquired value system. A fragmented modern man, he has achieved at last a kind of reintegration approached by Willie only near the end of his life.[12]

Warren's use of foils or doubles extends beyond the Willie-Jack relationship, though this one is the most emphasized with Jack's assertion that the story of Willie Stark was also the story of Jack Burden. One of Willie's doubles is Adam Stanton, who is the man of ideas, according to Jack, while Willie is the man of action. A similar pattern reinforces one of the novel's central motifs, that of fathers and sons. Ellis Burden, "the Scholarly Attorney," is Jack's father in name only, and Montague Irwin, "the Upright Judge," the surrogate father of his adolescence, is also his biological father. Jack's rejection of individual responsibility by going to work for Willie—who dictates actions for others—in effect casts Willie as a kind of paternal authority figure. Can the reader see, in this recurrence of the pattern of the ineffectual father and the powerful alternate, a reflection of the loved but ineffectual Robert Franklin Warren and the loved and powerful John Crowe Ransom? The grounds would seem to be there even if introduced into the text only unconsciously. But there is also a father-son conflict (between Willie and Tom Stark), and in any case this is but one of the novel's recurring themes.

If the themes are several, so are the patterns of image and symbol. There is incremental repetition of the physical attributes of Willie and Sadie Burke, his secretary-mistress, and the use of character tags and catchphrases: "the brass-bound Idealist" and "the Scholarly Attorney," "the Great Twitch" and "the Spider Web." The book is filled with color—dark and violent hues in skies and waters, fields and bayous—and the pages teem with images of death. More than one commentator has seen imagery of the prenatal as well as birth and rebirth. A dominant image issues logically from the novel's title: that of the fall. When Willie tells Jack that it will not be necessary to frame Judge Irwin because the truth about anyone is always sufficient, Jack jeers at this view of human nature. But original sin is an article of faith for Willie. "I went to a Presbyterian Sunday school when they still had some theology," he tells Jack, "and that much of it stuck" (p. 358).

Every one of the major characters experiences some sort of fall into sin. Cass Mastern, Annabelle Trice, Willie Stark, Sadie Burke, Anne Stanton, Judge Irwin, and Jack's mother are all guilty on the grounds of adultery alone, and almost all of the other characters are guilty of sins ranging from larceny and lust to sacrilege and homicide. The principal characters' sins also take the form of betrayal, of others and of self. Willie, for example, betrays Lucy Stark with his adulteries, Tom Stark (who falls to the turf with a broken neck) with his failure of paternal guidance, his constituents with his malfeasance, and himself with his abandonment of idealism for expediency. His belated awareness of the depth of his fall echoes in his last words: "It might have been all different, Jack," he says. "You got to believe that" (p. 425). The imagery of the fall appears frequently in the text as well as in the nursery-rhyme source of the title. What is the final import of these falls?[13]

On the personal level, the fall is not all. If there is death, there is also rebirth. Willie's rise and fall are contrasted with Jack's fall and rise. At the book's end, he and Anne, now married, care for the dying Ellis Burden at Burden's Landing while Jack completes his book on Cass Mastern. (Warren, however, had not been able to write the scene Lambert Davis and David Clay advised between Jack and Anne to provide "the purgation of the Stark problem.") Finally at peace with both of his fathers and his mother as well, Jack envisions the day when he and Anne will reenter the world, perhaps to join the idealistic former attorney general to pursue some of the goals of the young and idealistic Willie Stark.[14]

"What happened to his greatness is not the question," Jack tells the reader. "Perhaps he could not tell his greatness" (p. 452). Now, in 1939, Jack can recall the Willie Stark of 1922 and then the gubernatorial aspirant who genuinely wanted better medical care, better roads, fairer representation, a fuller life for the inarticulate people who thrilled vicariously to his eloquence. Jack's hard-won understanding of the capacity for evil in Willie Stark and Cass Mastern has led to this bitter but necessary self-awareness, which prepares him for his reconciliation and fulfillment with Anne. Jack cannot achieve the intense if heterodox religious faith of Ellis Burden, but he achieves a kind of affirmation, like that of the novel itself.[15]

On the public level, Jack's new commitment, like his perception of Willie's true greatness, signals a faith in the possibilities inherent in democracy no matter how vulnerable it is to neglect and evil. The attempt to understand Willie's life leads to the attempt to understand history without cynicism or sentimentality. So the Dantean epigraph, with its assertion of human possibility, has as its corollary the possibility of renewal within the body politic, so that Jack can say at last, "Soon now we shall go out of the house and go into the convulsion of the world, out of history into history and the awful responsibility of Time" (p. 464).[16]

It was probably late February when almost six hundred pages of proofs arrived. Warren was fighting off the flu, but on March 5 he finished reviewing them. Ten days later the flu was still hanging on. "Cinina and I have been swapping the job of nursing each other," he wrote. (In a postscript Cinina said that except for that and falls on the ice they were well. She had been having a series of pulmonary X rays, and the last one was fine.) The novel had been scheduled for May, but it was not published until August 19 in a printing of fifteen thousand copies selling at three dollars apiece. On the dust jacket it was called "massive, impressive," and the author was "probably the most talented writer of the South." This came from Nobel Prize winner and fellow faculty member Sinclair Lewis. The initial reactions were good enough for Harcourt to order six thousand more copies. It was also the main selection of the Book-of-the-Month Club.[17]

From the earliest reviews it was characterized as a political novel. An old and honorable form, the political novel had engaged the talents of some of the genre's best practitioners. None, of course, would have wished their novels to be seen in a narrowed category, but actions could gain in power, intensity, and breadth of relevance when played out in that crucial area of history and human experience. The most perceptive reviewers saw *All the King's Men* also as a brilliant novel with philosophical dimensions. Some used superlatives: "the finest American novel in more years than one would like to have to remember," and "For sheer virtuosity, for the sustained drive of its prose, for the speed and evenness of its pacing, for its precision of language, its genius of colloquialism, I doubt indeed whether it can be matched in American fiction." Predictably, there were complaints— about lack of crusading zeal, about melodrama, about coarse language. This latter objection might well have amused the author, like the kind of criticism that saw the book as a eulogy of Long. For others it lacked the militancy needed to fight men like Long.[18]

There were rebuttals. A year after the novel's publication, Robert Heilman skewered some reviewers for "sheer incompetence to read tragedy." A brief one from the author seven years later, to the charge of Long glorification, put it succinctly: "There is nothing to reply to this kind of innocent bone-headedness or gospel-bit hysteria." Several years after that, in an introduction to an English edition, Warren labeled several reviewers as "functionally illiterate and fellow traveling." They were, he told his publisher, "members in good standing of the little Stalinist coven." There is no evidence that they hurt the book's sales, and thirty years after its publication one commentator noted that "almost three million copies have been sold around the world" in twenty different languages.[19]

Now, a half century after its publication, what conclusions can one reach about *All the King's Men*? Although Allen Tate's praise for the novel was genuinely felt, both he and Caroline Gordon, like Katherine Anne Porter, still thought that Warren's primary talent was in poetry. They also thought that he did not do women well, and the character of Anne Stanton has troubled other readers. When Jack Burden asks Anne why she became Willie's mistress, she replies that he was not like anyone she had ever known, and "I love him, I guess." Jack's feelings of guilt over the consequences of his discovery of the crimes of both Judge Irwin and Governor Stanton are deepened when Anne further explains that, after Jack told her about her father, "There wasn't any reason why not then" (p. 345). Anne is also drawn to Willie by her social conscience and her admiration for his wish to change things and his power to do so. As Warren put it, he provides for her "some meaning to life." Aware as Warren was of the problem of credibility, he was unable to solve it and probably hoped that the positive resolution at the end would divert the reader's attention.[20]

The other two characters requiring scrutiny are, of course, Jack and Willie. The former has seemed to some a combination of Sam Spade and Stephen Dedalus. But if Warren were to be charged with employing such models or the stereotyped journalists in Ben Hecht and Charles MacArthur's *The Front Page,* the fact was that Warren knew more than one newspaperman capable of that kind of racy dialogue. As for other sources, a recollection from his colleague Robert Heilman is instructive. There was, he said, "the joyous and laughing Red, whose full face crinkling into merriment meant a fine display of teeth and that long little suck or hiss of breath, an inbound or outbound sibilance, that somehow doubled the sweep of delight." But he could also present "a deadpan, almost stern, mood, a sort of flat withdrawal or uncommunicativeness which could make one wonder, 'What have I done?' Then there was another style that seemed to go naturally with the lined face and hardbitten look which were there early—a skeptically ironic twist of expression and of speech that could effortlessly deflate any foolish ideas. . . . It neither reflected a suspicious nature nor fell into easy sarcasm. . . . Perhaps in his close look at things there was also a touch of that strong wariness which helps toughen up the fiction."[21]

Readers aware of novelists' use of self in creating characters—such as James Joyce with Stephen Dedalus and D. H. Lawrence with Paul Morel—are not likely to be surprised at resemblances between Robert Penn Warren and Jack Burden, even if there is less biographical indebtedness. As for Jack's foil, Cass Mastern, his segment of the novel (reprinted separately four times) has been consistently praised. When Lambert Davis sent out advance copies in the hope of receiving blurbs, William Faulkner wrote back, "The Cass Mastern story is a beautiful and moving piece. That was his novel. The rest of it I would throw away."[22]

Faulkner qualified that verdict: "The Starke [*sic*] thing is good solid sound writing but for my money Starke and the rest of them are second rate." In this judgment, he was very much in the minority. This novel has been one of the most extensively analyzed in modern American literature, and the figure of Stark has elicited most of this flood of commentary. The very vehemence of the attacks on Stark vis-à-vis Huey Long is a testimonial to the portrait's power, and even for most of the readers unwilling to accept Warren's disclaimer of equivalence between the two, Stark takes on a powerful life of his own. Vivid as a protagonist, he is also notable for his symbolic import in the political, philosophical, and ethical realms. And as for the use of a historical milieu, there is the example of Warren's admired Shakespeare.[23]

The novel has sometimes been faulted on familiar grounds in Warren criticism: complexity of plot and abundance of melodrama. (As a simple observation, Warren wrote of the Long years, "Melodrama was the breath of life. . . . in Louisiana people lived melodrama, seemed to live, in fact, for it, for this strange combination of philosophy, humor, and violence.") If the book is judged as a political novel, it is certainly the foremost in American letters and capable of standing with the best in other literatures. Warren rejected this kind of judgment, however, declaring that it "was not intended to be a book about politics." Heilman agreed: "The author begins with history and politics, but the real subject is the nature of them: Warren is no more discussing American politics than *Hamlet* is discussing Danish politics."[24]

In recent years critical opinion has generally concluded that Robert Penn Warren's best work is finally in his poetry, particularly that of his last three decades. But even so, *All the King's Men* seems

likely to remain his most outstanding single work and his most exhaustive effort, his longest travail in trying to achieve what Faulkner
called "the dream of perfection." It is more than his best novel. With
its narrative power and the versatility of its prose, its depiction of a
real and complex world, and the extended relevance of that world in
its philosophical and moral dimensions, it appears likely to remain
one of the major novels in American literature. Its materials held a
continuing fascination for him, and he would return to them again
and again, trying to express their meanings in yet other forms.[25]

26

Prizes
and Performances

. . . he saw folding money for the first time in his life.
He saw quite a lot of it.

—*All the King's Men*[1]

Before the publication of the novel they had managed a trip in mid-
April to Nashville and then Guthrie. Cinina wrote Pier Marie
Pasinetti, "Red's brother and sister-in-law and ourselves have a glorious time together." Life was good for Thomas Warren. His grain
business was thriving, and so was his family. Cinina got on well with
Alice Warren, and she was fond of her two older daughters, twelve-
year-old Vivian Ruth and six-year-old Tommie Louise. But she was
completely taken with the baby, eleven-month-old Sandra Alice.
Cinina may have felt as Red did when he congratulated Andrew
Lytle on the birth of his second daughter, adding, "As for us, alas, no
extra leaves in the dinner table yet."[2]

He was at work on essays as well as *Modern Rhetoric* with Cleanth
Brooks for Harcourt, Brace. But that work had paled beside another.
The subject was a horrendous murder on the wild frontier early in the
nineteenth century. To research it he set out from Guthrie with his
father on the first of several trips. They drove northwest for more
than ninety miles to the spot north of Paducah where Colonel
Charles Lewis brought his family in the fall of 1807. "I spent several
days up at Smithland," Warren wrote Andrew Lytle, "working on
background for my new long poem." Then, "near Smithland I found
the track, not even a path, up the bluff to the site of the terrible

house." While Robert Franklin Warren drowsed in the car, his son clambered up the steep bluff through the thickets and trees to the rubble that was left of Rocky Hill.[3]

He wanted "concreteness." At the top, near the ruin of the great central chimney, he stopped at the edge of a meadow where trees had grown up and cattle now grazed. Then he saw something staring at him from the chimney's stonework. It was an *Elaphe obsoleta obsoleta,* bigger than a black racer—a six-foot snake. He saw it rolling up "about three feet and a half from my face, looking down at me. . . . the very spirit of the demon of the place." On the way to Smithland his father had been silent, even close to the country where he had grown up. But on the way back he began to talk about his own father and his boyhood. No matter what Warren's intention had been when he invited his father on the trip, his company was fortuitous. Bob Warren would be there in the poem's published form with his recollections of his own father. This would be part of an attempt to link the modern world with that of Charles Lewis, and the poet's father would provide it. Moreover, "the special relation with my father that I had is also tied in the poem." This relationship was still changing, and though it would not appear in his poetry for several years, this trip, squeezed in between travels to California and Ohio, would help prepare for other poems besides *Brother to Dragons.*[4]

In July the Warrens settled down for two months in Gambier. "We live in the old Bishop's House, a fine Victorian version of the Castle of Otranto plus a funeral home, set in a woods with a nice rolling lawn. All very pleasant and pastoral and soothing. We have enough work to maintain self-respect, many picnics, lots of conversation and croquet, and sound sleep." Eleanor Clark was traveling west with two friends, and they accepted an invitation to pass the night there. Eleanor was amused that the Ransoms would put up her two male companions while she would stay with the Warrens. (She did not know that the assignments had been Cinina's idea. Helen Forman recalled Cinina's saying, "You can't trust her.") There was moderate drinking—a drink before dinner—and nothing to excess. In that year, Warren would recall, "bad trouble started," but not yet, not in that July and August. The reason, he was sure, was the soothing influence of the Ransoms on Cinina.[5]

They left Gambier for New York in the first week of September for a mixture of business and pleasure, and this time Cinina had an important part. Warren's relationship with Lambert Davis was still good. Southerners of the same age, they were both also "yearners," Davis thought, seekers after a belief system but unable to find one in orthodox religion. But now he felt that Cinina wanted to detach Red from Harcourt, Brace. "She was very jealous of me," he remembered. "She was absolutely alone. She clung to Red. She didn't want him to have any other person close to him, and she felt our relationship was a threat to her." Cinina did have a few friends—Harriet Owsley, Albert Erskine, Pier Pasinetti, and Edward Donahoe—but Davis's assessment was even then being borne out.[6]

One of the bright young people at the powerful William Morris Agency was an attractive young woman named Helen M. Strauss. With the success of *All the King's Men,* she had been recommended to Warren. The New York visit was a whirlwind, so that his only real social moment was a luncheon with Allen Tate. As a result, it was Cinina who visited Helen Strauss. "She asked the obvious questions: what could I do for her husband and how much, and how much commission was charged, and how much Hollywood was offering for best sellers, and whether he could make the transition from scholarly quarterlies to the high-priced slick magazines without compromises. Though the questions and answers were routine, her intense scrutiny of me was not. Clearly she was bright, but also as clearly, insecure, and we were not, it seemed, just discussing a simple business alliance. She was wielding the power of decision in the matter, but she carried it dangerously, with fearful unsteadiness. Her assessment would be wholly personal, focusing on me, not on my reputation or my function."

Helen Strauss combined professional acumen with a keen sensitivity to human relationships and the capacity for genuine friendship. At last Cinina seemed to relax. "I think that I have nothing to be afraid of," she told Helen Strauss. "You are the one woman I can trust Red with." After several years, Helen would come to understand something of her visitor's situation: "The career of her husband, the isolating and introspective existence of a writer, was a challenge, a closed door behind which her husband found fulfillment that she could never fully share. . . . but someone who can share those concerns, particularly if she is a woman, is always a threat, the accomplice, an imagined potential rival to any wife who is not secure within herself and who lacks a comparable fulfillment beyond a limiting role as *Mrs. Writer.*" Helen Strauss felt that she had been granted "the grand housewife's seal of approval," and so she invited Warren to lunch at Toots Shor's.[7]

For her, it was more than an agent's lunch with a potential client; she was a fan with an author she held in awe. His "extraordinarily well-disciplined ego"—in his testimony to having learned from past failures—impressed her immediately, just as his injunction "Call me Red" had put her at ease immediately. The lunch was a professional and a social success. Their subsequent relationship would only reinforce her impressions. She found him to be "one of the most wonderful humans I have known in my life, and that luncheon provided me with insights which I was to carry and share with many another writer throughout my career."[8]

When the Warrens returned to Minneapolis in mid-September, *All the King's Men* was seventh on the *New York Times* best-seller list. A photo spread in the *Sunday Tribune* featured a large picture of him and another showing a smiling Cinina in a large flowered hat. "She is beautiful," ran the text, "and the daughter of a distinguished composer of Italian ancestry. She loves animals and everything about the country, as he does." As for her husband, the news was that he had quit smoking his pipe and was "currently smoking Sanos, which he admits are terrible, though probably healthy." By the time they were back home at Waverly Place after the hectic pace, he was in bed with a cold.[9]

Omnibook bought the rights for a condensed version of the novel in December, and another book-club adoption for February guaranteed the sale of fifty thousand more copies. There was little time for writing now, but he did send Helen Strauss some work he had on hand. It was his sixty-page "novelette" called "The Circus in the Attic" and a story entitled "Blackberry Winter." This latter dated from "the fall or winter of 1945–46 just after the war, and even if one had had no hand in the blood-letting, there was the sense that the world, and one's own life, would never be the same again." He was drawing on a "remembered world." There was probably something personal too in "The Circus in the Attic" if on a deeper, perhaps even an unrecognized, level. "I simply made it up from a verbal account," he explained, "scarcely more than a few sentences, given me years ago by a young man from Hopkinsville." It was about John Wesley Venable, Jr., born in the 1880s in the town where Warren's father had worked as a young man. Dominated by his possessive mother, Venable withdrew more and more from life to create, in his attic, the wooden circus figures that fascinated his imagination. Warren said he didn't know his name or anything about his life, and moreover, "I had more of Clarksville in mind than Hopkinsville when I wrote the story. That is, for me, it was almost purely fiction."[10]

With its leisurely, backward-looking beginning, it shows a fondness for the novelist's method rather than the short-story writer's. So does the familiar preoccupation with time and history, moving from the lives of Bolton Lovehart's forebears (with imagery suggesting "Kentucky Mountain Farm") to his own life, through the First World War, then to the Second and its aftermath. The central fact of that life is the terrible domination by Bolton's mother. After a brief schoolboy flight he runs away with the circus, only to be brought home ignominiously. His real life is led in the attic in the imaginative re-creation, with wood and paint, of that remembered beauty as the months stretch into years and "the passion for perfection grew to torment him" (p. 12). This story of a fettered and frustrated life, with sketches of others made sterile by other forms of isolation, is played out against a contrast between the remembered town of Bardsville and the present one, where factories deface the old farmland in the added disfigurements of wartime industrialization.[11]

How close was Bolton Lovehart to John Wesley Venable, Jr., and how close was he to Robert Penn Warren? An obedient, studious child, Bolton reads omnivorously, collects arrowheads, and treasures his father's cavalry saber. He wins the prize graduating first in the academy and goes on to study at Sewanee and to teach for a time. He works for long years, intermittently and unsuccessfully, to write the history of his native Carruthers County. The son of an ineffectual father who dies early, Bolton succumbs completely to the domination of his proud, possessive mother. Had Robert Penn Warren been submissive rather than powerfully self-assertive, he might have become a historian of Todd County. Little of the early lore he absorbed was lost, however, and there to be turned instead into fiction and poetry.[12]

The arrival of "The Circus in the Attic" was welcomed by Helen Strauss. "I grew very excited once I had read it and promptly sent it to *Cosmopolitan,* which offered five thousand dollars to publish it. Before closing the sale, I grew oddly apprehensive. . . . I did not know if this commercial leap would sit well with Warren's peers, or with Warren himself." She was prescient in anticipating reactions to his commercial successes, but she need not have worried. He "quickly responded that he had not known that such money existed for a short story." When he completed his longtime project of collecting his stories, she sold it to Harcourt, Brace for publication in January 1948, as

The Circus in the Attic and Other Stories. And she got him a thousand-dollar advance against royalties.[13]

He led from strength—following the title story with "Blackberry Winter." Less than half the length of the title story, it deals with a few days in the life of a nine-year-old, marked by an epiphany he remembers vividly now as the forty-four-year-old narrator. A dozen years after Warren wrote the story in the bitter Minnesota winter, he composed a short searching recollection of the process. Eight months past his fortieth birthday, he found himself going "back into a primal world of recollection. I was fleeing, if you wish. . . . that iron latitude where I now lived, [and] I had a vague, nostalgic feeling and wondered if spring would ever come." And he remembered how going barefoot was a kind of assertion of independence, particularly in the time when ripening blackberries might be subjected to unexpected cold.[14]

Though it is June, Seth's mother cautions him against going out barefoot. The appearance of a tramp from the woods, his knife clutched in his hand against the threat of the farm dogs, suddenly changes the whole ambience of the day. The tramp grudgingly does chores for food, gathering drowned chicks. Later, perched behind his father on his saddle, Seth sees other animals drowned in the storm. The emotional tone darkens further when he goes to Dellie's cabin with her son, Jebb, his black playmate. Sick with "woman mizry," she reaches up from her bed to slap Jebb with shocking viciousness. Big Jebb's explanation, "Hit is the change of life and time," explains nothing to Seth, any more than his assurance "Time come and you find out everything." Shivering in the blackberry winter, he is to experience yet a deeper chill. When his father orders the tramp off the place, Seth asks him a harmless question. "Stop following me," he snarls. "You don't stop following me and I cut yore throat, you little son-of-a-bitch" (p. 86). The narrator recapitulates deaths and disasters since that time. Then, in the story's last lines, Seth quotes the tramp and adds, "That was what he said, for me not to follow him. But I did follow him, all the years" (p. 86).

Once into the story and uncertain where it would go, Warren had solved the problem with the appearance of the tramp, at first threatful but finally "a creature altogether lost and pitiful, a dim image of what, in one perspective, our human condition is. But then, at that moment, I was merely thinking of the impingement of his loose-footedness and lostness on a stable and love-defined world of childhood." Had Seth stopped following the tramp? Literally, yes, but figuratively, no: "as later he had grown up" and "recognized this lost, mean, defeated, cowardly, worthless, bitter being as somehow a man." The story would be one of the most praised and anthologized of its time.[15]

There were fourteen stories in all, stories of initiation whose protagonists sometimes were cast in the mold of the Adamic figure. They demonstrated his familiar thematic concerns with the past and personal relationships. Two of the stories have academic settings, but all of the others are unmistakably southern, especially the last, "Prime Leaf." After publication a year later he would tell Andrew Lytle, "I know that the collection is, at the best, uneven, but if I was ever to publish them I reckoned I might as well go ahead and hope for the best." It was indeed uneven, achieving distinction only in the first two and the last story. His range of characters and inventive imagination would be praised along with the atmosphere and continuity of the stories, but there would also be numerous cavils and rather general agreement that in prose fiction he was a novelist rather than a short-story writer. It was to be his first and last collection of stories.[16]

He admired the practice of the short story by the masters, including his friends Katherine Anne Porter and Eudora Welty, but he could not give it the same fealty himself. When he finished "Blackberry Winter," he thought he would never write another. One reason was that "short stories kill poems." These were the years when the short poems still refused to come. Looking back he would say, "Many times the germ of a short story could also be the germ of a poem, and I was wasting mine on short stories. I've only written three that I even like. And so I quit writing short stories."[17]

Helen Strauss empathized with him, finding him sometimes disorganized, "instinctive and emotional," involved in a "chaotic agony" of creation as "each work involved a protracted dredging of the soul and ruthless self-questioning." Eric Bentley thought he suffered from a duality that constituted a major problem: "his combination of critical and creative power." His essay on "Blackberry Winter" suggests much greater control than either of his friends thought, but how much of a duality there actually was, only he could know.[18]

It was another strenuous semester of crowded classes. He was continuing with his part of *The Sewanee Review* issue honoring John Ransom at the same time that he was replying to invitations for lectures in the coming spring. By late December he had sent off the last of the supporting material for his application for a 1947 Guggenheim Fellowship. Earlier that month, his friend Arthur Mizener had provided Allen Tate with an update. He and his wife, he wrote, "saw Red and Company Saturday last. And Company allows you to talk of nothing now except Red's Hollywood offers. . . ." There were in fact bids for film rights in the offing. Unfortunately, the negotiations were the business of Harcourt, Brace rather than Helen Strauss. But she had other plans for him. "My next move was to switch him to a new publisher." Even apart from these business affairs, plus work on the new novel and the text he was writing with Cleanth Brooks, 1947 was going to be a busy year.[19]

The insistent demands on his time were largely his own doing. "I am a one-armed paper-hanger trying to fight off a bear and play the piccolo while carrying on the paperhanging job," he wrote Katherine Anne Porter. "My little charges at the university are too numerous for comfort right now. . . ." But still he agreed to lectures at the Universities of Kansas and Indiana and the Woman's College of the University of North Carolina. (In early March, Lytle told Tate that Warren was "riding the circuit again.") One compensation would be seeing friends—Peter Taylor, Robert Lowell, John Ransom, and Randall Jarrell in Greensboro. Ranging from Carolina to Connecticut, he told Lytle, "I might as well take up carrying a nice little line of hardware on the side and working that as a sideline this spring."[20]

But he had a bad conscience. "I have been very wicked about the text book," he had confessed to Cleanth Brooks in February after having spent Christmas vacation on "The Circus in the Attic" instead of *Modern Rhetoric*. He included a page of comments on the chapter Cleanth had sent him. "Well, it is a grim business," he grumbled, "and I suppose the only thing is to sustain our courage by keeping our eyes firmly fixed on the dollar sign in the sky. . . ." He was now making more money than ever before, but his attitude had been conditioned by several factors. Though his parents had provided generous support within their means for his studies at Vanderbilt, his salary later when he was teaching there and at Southwestern had been far from ample. Though he was better paid than many of his colleagues by the time he left LSU, and though Cinina worked some of the time, he still depended on the outside income to meet bills as well as to pay for a cook and for travel. He would never forget the early experience—

the times when a five-dollar loan might be crucial and its early repay-
ment welcome. Money was the key to doing what he wanted most,
to write without distraction. There may well have been something
else too. He was proud and ambitious, and financial security would be
further evidence of success for the boy who had been teased and
taunted in his Guthrie childhood.[21]

The year had begun with a good augury when the Southern
Women's National Democratic Organization had named him the
winner of the Southern Author's Award for *All the King's Men*. Now,
on April 8, Henry Allen Moe informed him that he had been
awarded a Guggenheim Fellowship with a three-thousand-dollar
stipend for "continuation of creative writing in the field of the
novel." (Another recipient was Eleanor Clark, who had fulfilled the
prediction Katherine Anne Porter had made at Yaddo by publishing
a novel, *The Bitter Box*.) Warren received a second award that year.
On May 5 the Literary Advisory Board of the Graduate School of
Journalism of Columbia University informed him that he would receive the three-thousand-dollar Pulitzer Prize for Fiction for *All the
King's Men*. Together with his sabbatical leave, it would buy sixteen
months of freedom.[22]

He must have felt that when the gods smile they may also scowl.
Replying to Albert Erskine's congratulations, he scrawled, "This letter was dictated some days ago (I have a busted wrist & can't type) &
so its vintage is old & rare." Nor was this the only affliction. In early
summer Cinina would tell Katherine Anne Porter, "I've had a miserable six months—a broken bone in the spine; a breast tumor removal
(*not* cancer); [and] a leg operation." But at least he did not have to
worry about the doctors' bills. On May 9 he was informed that Columbia Pictures had purchased the movie rights to *All the King's Men*
for $200,000. But here too the good fortune was not unalloyed. The
deal had been made not by Helen Strauss but by Maxwell M. Geffen,
acting for Harcourt, Brace. Not only did the publisher own half of
the film rights, but Warren had to take all of his half immediately,
with the result that he would pay more income tax to the state alone
that year than he would receive from the state in salary.[23]

The Warrens traveled to Gambier to spend a quiet summer, but his
thoughts were often elsewhere. By mid-July he had finished a chapter of his new novel set in Kentucky. And *Proud Flesh* was still on his
mind. Eric Bentley had produced it with the University Theatre al-

though his original enthusiasm had waned. "I liked the experimentality of the staging that he proposed and I liked the attempt to use poetry from the stage," he said. "On the other hand, some of the writing wasn't the best language for actors to speak." Then Warren turned up another possibility. He took the play to Erwin Piscator, a fifty-four-year-old director who had worked with Bertolt Brecht employing both classic devices such as a chorus and contemporary media such as film. He offered to work on revisions to produce the play at the New School in New York. Fascinated by the idea of theatrical success, like so many novelists, Warren had his eye on Broadway. His choice, he wrote Katherine Anne, was "whether I want to mortgage a couple of months or more to do the job of prosing the play or want to let the New School go ahead, with a few revisions which I need to make in the verse version."[24]

At the end of July he made a hurried trip to New York for "a pow-wow with HB and my agent," he wrote Allen Tate. "The Broadway producers couldn't get the money for a verse version, and wanted me to prose the thing. . . . But I am too sick of the subject to undertake a project like that. So I shall revise the thing for Piscator at the New School, going up to Lake Placid for a couple of weeks to work with him on the scheme of revision and production." Warren entered into this collaboration with misgivings, which Eric Bentley shared. Piscator seemed to him "rather old and very rigid," and he thought he might not be able to understand the play or the novel, content to see it as an attack on an American Mussolini by a progressive who didn't get the politics quite right and would need correction. Warren, of course, was not looking for ideological correctness but rather the kind of practical dramaturgy he had started learning from Francis Fergusson. By the end of the first week of November they were able to leave for New York. Optimistically he thought the play would be produced in December.[25]

By late December they were in New York at the Hotel Marguery for a hectic month before they sailed for Italy on the trip they had originally scheduled for the fall. They were able to spend time with Albert Erskine and his new wife, Peggy. Later, Bennett Cerf, cofounder of Random House, would recall that "Frank Taylor and Albert Erskine—both experienced editors and officers of the firm of Reynal and Hitchcock, became discontented and resigned. Taylor came to see me and offered their services; since they had performed well together, they wanted to continue to work as a team." Cerf hired both of them. Erskine may have been thinking about other teamwork too. Lambert Davis could regretfully see a move in the offing. Helen Strauss was thinking along the same lines. She did not know Davis well, and he was every bit as southern as Erskine, but "we felt that Erskine would be more attuned" to Red. She did not say who "we" were, but it seems likely that Cinina must have concurred in this opinion. In any case, the "productive realignment" Helen envisioned was apparently only a matter of time as 1947 drew to a close.[26]

Life magazine reported that in the off-Broadway theatre, "Experimental Groups Are Having an Exciting, Successful Season." Two productions had moved to Broadway, but "*All the King's Men* does not enlist Broadway help. It is put on by the Dramatic Workshop of the New School of Social Research directed by Erwin Piscator. His 700 students put on 20 plays every year, all of which get seen, one way or another, by New York's critical audiences." Warren was still working on it after it opened. "I wish you all had seen Saturday night instead of Wednesday," he wrote Cleanth Brooks, "because I did a lot of work on it, dropped two scenes, changed the end, etc." The review in *The New York Times* on January 19 duly noted the experimental techniques. A *Life* photograph showed how Piscator attempted to enlarge the space with a backdrop of the capitol's interior crisscrossed by a pipe-iron staircase below which Willie Stark and Adam Stanton stood. *Time's* reviewer pointed out the drawbacks: "Even Mr. Piscator's dramaturgic know-how sometimes seems to get in his own way." Albert Erskine had a stronger reaction. Piscator began the play with film footage of Adolf Hitler, "so that already puts you into a spot that really doesn't have anything to do with *All the King's Men*." Erskine said it was "one of the worst things I've ever experienced." But the author was by no means ready to quit. If he needed encouragement, he must have found some later when *Life* reported on March 29 that the play was "still off Broadway but attracting a lot of professional interest." Warren would continue work on this play and others for many years.[27]

He must have been glad to turn to research for the novel, and Kentucky was the place to investigate the story Katherine Anne Porter had dropped on his desk that day at the Library of Congress. By mid-November he and Cinina were living in a borrowed apartment in Lexington, where Cinina was happy. They had been having such a fine time, she wrote Pier Pasinetti, that it was hard to get much work done. She had, however, resumed work on her novel that day. Two weeks later he received another enthusiastic letter with more praise for the "best" part of Kentucky with its "white fences, blue grass, horses, horses, horses, and mint juleps."[28]

None of these pleasures kept Warren from the University of Kentucky Library, however, where, she said, he was excitedly surveying its treasures. He was using manuscripts as well as printed materials— letters, maps, and diaries. Cinina was hard at work too on a complete rewriting. This was not her first try at a novel. When she had shown an earlier one to John Ransom, he thought her writing had some elegance, displaying some refinement and sophistication. But he also thought that she might harbor feelings of envy and jealousy toward Warren.[29]

He must have been anxious to leave for Italy. Cinina's needs for ego gratification had, if anything, increased, together with the inability to control her emotions. On the Warrens' last visit to Nashville, driving out to see the Owsleys' new farm, Warren had ill-advisedly invented a game. Sitting in the backseat with little Margaret, he would say, "Margaret, I don't like you—I like your father." And then it was her turn to use the same phrases with a different name. She enjoyed it so much that she remembered it that evening in the dining room. Stopping her tricycle at Cinina's chair, she said, "I don't like you. I like Red." Cinina leaped up, knocking her chair over with a force that broke its back. Then she ran from the room slamming the door furiously. Harriet went upstairs to explain. "No, Harriet," Cinina said. "Everybody loves Red but nobody loves me." She had begun to resent imagined slights. After a convivial cocktail hour at Fanny and Lon Cheney's house, Frank Owsley stepped back to allow her to precede him into the dining room. "What's the matter, Frank?" she snapped. "Are you afraid of me?" As they waited to be seated in the dining room, she asked Richmond Croom Beatty if he was trying not to stand next to her. Unflustered, he replied, "Oh, darling, come on. We'll go upstairs together." Cinina turned on her heel and left the room.[30]

The combination of need and hostility grew. Not only would she interrupt her husband, she would belittle him. Richard Wilbur remembered a moment in Washington when Cinina began speaking about "younger men," with an implied comparison to her husband's disadvantage. There was another kind of embarrassment too, at least to short, dapper Lon Cheney. He found Cinina attractive, and apparently she knew it. "She had charms, all right," he said. "She took out after me. She'd come up and put her arms around me. Well, I damn well knew this was part of a plot." Albert Erskine knew that though its object was to excite Red's emotions, her tactics included others too. He saw this at the Hotel Marguery before the opening of the play. "It wasn't just Red," he remembered. "She was throwing it at everybody when she had too much to drink." And the other dimensions of her jealousy grew. Increasingly, she was "competitive as a writer. She sent parts of her novel to John Ransom, and he was too much of a gentleman to tell her it was worthless." But still she saw herself as a dutiful wife. "She would talk to me, sort of proud of herself that even if he did have the loss of the eye and things like that, that she was still loyal."[31]

Albert could not bring himself to intervene, but Lon felt that he must. From Allen Tate he obtained the name of a psychoanalyst, Lawrence S. Kubie, who had written on the relationship between the artist's creativity and his neuroses. Not only did Lon urge Red to go to him, he visited Kubie to explain the problem. He also found a female psychiatrist for Cinina and visited her. "Red," he told his friend, "this is going to destroy both of you. You go and see him, and get Cinina to see this woman." Both of them subsequently did.[32]

Warren must have felt anxious relief as they prepared to sail for Italy. He had his sabbatical salary and the Guggenheim checks, the movie money from *All the King's Men,* and royalties from his other productions. There were eight months ahead in a country he loved. It was a fine opportunity to work on the novel after all his research, perhaps an opportunity too to work on his marriage.

27

❖

Writing a Novel—from Taormina to Sirmione

So oft as I with state of present time
The image of the antique world compare,
When as mans age was in his freshest prime,
And the first blossome of faire vertue bare,
Such odds I find twixt those, and these which are,
As that, through long continuance of his course,
Me seemes the world is runne quite out of square
From the first point of his appointed sourse,
And being once amisse, growes daily wourse and wourse.
—*Edmund Spenser,* The Faerie Queene[1]

The Associated Press photographer snapped their photo on the deck of the eleven-thousand-ton M.S. *Sobieski* on Tuesday, January 27, 1948: Cinina smiling excitedly, a huge orchid on her dressy black coat, Warren in his old reversible raincoat, a pleased expression on his face and one of his nicotine-free cigarettes between his fingers. The small ship sailed out into rough weather. "Our trip across was a hell of dancing suitcases, chairs that tried to get in bed with us, broken objects, etc.," he told Cleanth Brooks. The company was agreeable, however, and Cinina was in her element, socializing with a member of the Italian Chamber of Deputies who promised political introductions, and with Rysia and Cesare Lombroso, a physician and grandson of his famous namesake, the physician and criminologist. Though the weather cost the *Queen Mary* two days in her crossing, the *Sobieski* docked in Genoa only sixteen hours late.

Cinina found the scene there depressing. "Arrival in Genoa was sad," she told Pier Pasinetti, but then, on the way south toward Sicily, they drove "through glorious Calabria, a combination of Nevada, Colorado, California, and Italy." In Taormina, south of Messina on Sicily's northeast coast, they found "a divine spot" at the Albergo Bel Soggiorno, where the sea was all around them and Etna loomed in the distance. On a picture postcard Cinina told Natalie Davison that the garden was beautiful. It was too cold for swimming, but Warren walked in the hills and found a new spot every day. Once again he had come away to work amid natural beauty. They would be there until early May.[2]

It was a remote vantage point for viewing events at home and abroad. In spite of whatever regrets he might have felt over leaving Lambert Davis and David Clay at Harcourt, Brace, he easily slipped into his new relationship with Albert Erskine, who immediately began helping him on matters literary and otherwise. "I am well into the new novel," Warren reported, "and haven't the slightest idea how it is going. It is not like anything else I have done in method, if anything it resembles Cass Mastern in the double-style business, the over-all narrative and the excerpts from a (fictional) document. I wish I had some comment on it, and I shall send you a batch as soon as I strike a point that seems to make a logical stopping place and can type up a copy." He had been more anxious about cigarettes than critical commentary, however, and he was grateful for Albert's response to his desperate appeal. "I was going wild, or rather I saw that I would soon be going wild when my supply ran out. It ran out about a week ago, but I have been making out on some very light Italian cigarette, which certainly has no nicotine in it but has some rather strong camel dung and sulphur."[3]

It had been a nervous winter in Italian politics, and the spring brought little relaxation of the tension. On January 1 a new constitution had been adopted, but in February a Communist-socialist coalition threatened it. Helen Strauss had accepted an advance from *Life* for an article on the situation, and Warren planned to visit a village for a preliminary look. "I hope the Commies don't shoot us," he told Cleanth Brooks. "But I am being very careful to get letters to the Communist boss as well as to Democristiano boss of the village and maybe they'll shoot each other and not us."[4]

With more crises in Europe and "the war fever at home," *Life* lost interest in the article, but he decided nonetheless to go ahead. (It might still produce income from another magazine.) He made the trip to the village, where a Sicilian-born American anthropologist was doing a book on the island. An Italian professor of mathematics at the University of Messina read Italian with Warren almost every evening and talked with him about Italian politics. And there were long conversations with the local head of the Communist party. Warren's most useful contact was a young socialist lawyer whose father had died in one of Mussolini's prisons. The son owned land back in the mountains, and there he introduced Warren as a friend from the war. "On election day I made the tour with [the local captain of carabiniere] in a Carabinieri truck. Fortunately no grenades were tossed into it." Instead there was hospitality from "*the* Communist in one of the mountain villages, the local school teacher, who took me to his house and gave me cakes and wine and a lecture."[5]

The insights he gained went beyond the political. "There is an awful lot of misery here, and in Sicily at least it seems perfectly clear that the big landowners have had things all their own very brutal and short-sighted way." He was already reading and admiring Alberto Moravia, and these experiences would help provide the basis for friendships with him and others such as Ignazio Silone. The power of these scenes and impressions would be evident in a novel he would publish thirty years later.[6]

His immersion in Italian politics was not interfering with the work, which claimed his mornings as usual. A week before the elections he sent Erskine forty thousand words constituting the first two chapters of his novel in progress. One reason why it was going so fast was that he was working from ample source material. He had vigorously denied that *Night Rider* was a historical novel. This one clearly *was* a historical novel, which drew upon dramatic events in Kentucky in the 1820s and upon dramatic actions by notorious people. Whereas Jack Burden had referred to himself sardonically as a historical researcher and seeker after truth, the nameless and characterless narrator of the new novel appears to try genuinely to seek out and understand the truth, only to conclude, "We have what is left, the lies and half-lies and the truths and half-truths. We do not know that we have the Truth. But we must have it" (p. 345). Burden would have been daunted quite as much as this new narrator. The primary document, *Confession of Jereboam O. Beauchamp,* ran well over a hundred pages. Warren told Erskine some of his concerns about the exposition of the story. "But aside from such mechanical things, I am anxious to get your criticism and suggestion."[7]

His previous novel was on his mind in another context. "One reason I want to get to Rome soon is that Josh Logan (*Mr. Roberts*) has just been here and has approached me with the idea of doing AKM. He has read the novel and claims to be very hot on it. Did not see the play but is sure we can work out something. He wants me to come to Rome to go over the stuff with him." This development produced a different reaction from Cinina. "Red has partito per Roma," she wrote Pier Pasinetti on May 1, "in fretta e furia [haste and rage], yesterday." They were obviously no happier in Sicily than they had been in Louisiana. A month earlier she had told Pier about excruciating sciatic back pain. She was ready to feed herself to the sharks on the voyage home. But her husband was doing well. (He had done 130 pages of his novel and had "a really good superficial knowledge of Sicily. . . .") As for her own writing, she had worked out a new plot despite a bad case of flu, which had put her in bed with penicillin shots. But finally she grew so bored that she got up despite her aches. Even so, when the sirocco came and she heard the donkey bray she felt "that life is not worth living."[8]

In Rome, close to the beautiful Villa Medici, they checked into the Hassler Hotel, perhaps the most elegant and expensive in the Eternal City. They had a fine six weeks there, Warren wrote Pier Pasinetti, "with damned little of the beauties of nature but a lot of the beauties of the interior of Roman trattorias and smoke-filled apartments." They saw a great deal of Italian artists and intellectuals such as Corrado Alvaro and Mario Praz, Elio Vittorini and Alberto Moravia, and "got very chummy with Moravia, who is a hell of a fine guy, full of humor and good sense and wit. We were with him almost daily for the last two or three weeks."[9]

They saw a lot of Eleanor Clark. Early that spring on a ski trail above Davos she had tried a difficult turn and crumpled into the snow with compound fractures of both legs and twisted knees. Her rescuers dragged her in a toboggan for miles down the mountain. Now, finally free of the plaster casts and crutches, she was looking about for a place to live. Her temporary base was a little villa at the American Academy in Rome loaned to her by Frank Brown, the professor in charge of the School of Classical Studies there. She was not only fluent in Italian but had also become a serious student of Roman culture and its architectural monuments. Brown was a brilliant scholar and eloquent raconteur with an enormous presence. Between marriages (to the same wife) he was now romantically interested in Eleanor. His principal project was an important excavation at Cosa, a Latin colony of the Roman Republic from the second century B.C. Warren was in-

terested in classical as well as contemporary Italy, and he offered to
drive the seventy miles north along the coast road to Cosa, on the
Tyrrhenian Sea. Cinina—perhaps impelled by the sciatic pain or pre-
departure depression—was drinking heavily and stayed at the hotel.
So Warren and Eleanor and a friend made the trip. At Cosa they in-
spected the dig and had a picnic lunch. Looking west across the bay
to the small peninsula, Eleanor could see the village of Porto Ercole,
above which, on a clear day, one could see the sixteenth-century
fortress of La Rocca. Not long afterward she would return to rent
rough quarters there.[10]

Albert and Peggy Erskine flew in and joined the Warrens for a
week in Rome. Then the four of them set out in the car for a
leisurely trip northward. Waiting for them at its end were Denis Devlin and his beautiful dark-eyed wife, Caren. "We had a wonderful all-
night binge the first night here," Warren wrote Lon Cheney, "Denis,
Caren, Albert, Peggy, and the Warrens, winding up in an olive grove
on a cliff looking over the lake in the moonlight, tight as ticks, and
full of music. On Jack Daniels, too, by God. We had nursed a bottle
all the way through Italy, and no bottle was ever better used in the
end."[11]

Having resettled in Sirmione, Warren reached what he thought
was his novel's halfway point. "The book is pretty crazy," he wrote
Cleanth Brooks, "but I can't tell yet whether it is crazy-bad or crazy-
good. . . . With luck I'll finish the draft in January." His September
15 reporting date in Minneapolis was already looming. "I am thinking seriously of leaving after this year. BUT THIS IS UNDER THE
HAT. Not because I don't like the place and haven't got the nearly
perfect job for my purposes. But the climate is pretty severe for Cinina. . . . And a couple of propositions have come my way."[12]

Cinina must have been thinking about their return to Minnesota
almost constantly as their Italian days dwindled. Their hotel was
lively, she wrote Pier Pasinetti in late July, with their new friend Tru-
man Capote among the guests. The lake was lovely, but the hotel was
noisy. "I'd like to move, but Red has unpacked and won't budge."
He was hard at work on the manuscript, but at last he had to pack up
as their mid-August sailing date approached. But when they reached
Genoa there was a delay. Then finally, on September 11, she wrote a
note to Albert Erskine on the *Sobieski*'s stationery. They were heart-
broken at leaving, still drinking Chianti Ruffino, "but not for long,
alas."[13]

As the *Sobieski* churned her way west, Warren spent hours at the gradually darkening tale of the two ill-fated lovers of *World Enough and Time,* knowing the pressure and stresses he would feel once he was back in Minnesota. Cinina was apparently feeling stresses too, in addition to her departure depression. By the time they reached New York she was drinking so heavily that Warren was unable to control her. Albert Erskine helped get her to a hospital. Looking back much later, her husband would say, "It was bad. . . . I knew it was hopeless." When Cinina was discharged, not long afterward, the doctor told him there could be a recurrence of this crisis. "Here's my name and number, in case," he said.[14]

28

❖

Premieres and Closings

> . . . time made him think of what old age must be like when
> two people have outlived all their love and hate for each other,
> when they know each other's faults so well that the faults
> no longer have meaning, and old resentments are no more
> than the accustomed pain of a rheumatic joint, part of the
> nature of things, when they can live in peace because neither
> is more than a ghost to the other.
>
> —*World Enough and Time*[1]

Back in Minneapolis they stayed with Hunt and Bid Brown before moving into an apartment in the Hampshire Arms Hotel near the Guthrie Theatre. Warren resumed his walks around the Lake of the Isles with Hunt as the colors changed in that fall of 1948. But then their reentry turned bleak in the snow and ice of early December. "LIFE has been sheer hell," Cinina wrote Pier Marie Pasinetti. She had given in to stomach flu and gone to bed for a week attended by a trained nurse. But all her nurse did was hold her head and empty the pans. "So I got rid of her and suffered in silence." Her husband was at school all afternoon, with 193 students. She suffered internal problems and feared a tumor or cancer, which proved not to be the case. Her back was no better with the return of her sciatica. If she was illness-prone, her husband was injury-prone. "Red fell down and broke a toe and turned his ankle and twisted his knee and leg." Cinina was apparently injury-prone too, and some of her mishaps may well have been alcohol-related. Her husband, with his depth perception lessened by the loss of his eye, may also have been particularly susceptible to the effects of alcohol. Now they both attended the Curative Workshop three mornings a week. "This explains our silence."[2]

Their relationship with Pier had grown steadily closer over the years. As he finished graduate school and looked for a teaching job, Warren supplied letters and advice. The Warrens had also provided a three-thousand-dollar loan, asking only that Pier take out a life-insurance policy in their favor in case he died before repaying it, with Warren paying the premiums. On January 3, Warren tried to fill in the rest of their current picture for him. "We weren't very well prepared spiritually for Christmas. The fall was awful for us both, and we both were about to fall back exhausted with shades drawn and our little hands clutching sleeping pills. Nevertheless, in a modest way, we did enjoy the vacation."[3]

In the fall Robert Rossen had suggested that he and Warren collaborate on a play about Cass Mastern. Rossen planned to produce and direct the play in New York and then make a movie version for Columbia. Now producing and directing the film version of *All the King's Men,* he telephoned in mid-March to say that he wanted Warren in on the editing. So the Warrens planned to go to the Coast as soon as exams were over. It would be a good trade: five degrees above zero in Minneapolis for springtime sunshine in California. And there might be something more. "I am writing to Dixon Wecter, who goes to Berkeley as professor of American History, to see if he can stir something up there." If his friend could manage that, Warren would be prepared. "I shall probably take an indefinite leave a year from this March."[4]

But even if they could change the scene and the weather, they would, as Marlowe's Dr. Faustus observed of himself, take themselves with them. In April, when Cinina learned that Pier's brother had died, she wrote to commiserate. Their family lives had been strangely similar, she said. "You and I are both infinitely lonely & abandoned people." He was a part of their small family, and he should come to stay with them. After their penurious years, they were now in the money. Their Santa Monica house—so roomy that it had four and a half bathrooms—was near the beach, and they would be there until September.[5]

The tenor of their letters prefigured others. "My movie is in its last stages," Warren wrote Frank Owsley on May 11. The editing job would be enormous because "the director shot thousands and thousands of extra feet of film." In this rough version Warren found the characterizations really excellent and some of the atmosphere fine even though the locale had been shifted to the West and the footage shot in Stockton, California. (The closeness of the collaboration would be indicated in the credits: "Written for the Screen by Robert Rossen.") When Warren flew east in late June to receive an honorary degree from the University of Louisville, Cinina had flown north. From her beloved San Francisco, she wrote Pier Pasinetti that she had "relieved myself of many fears & sorrows by returning." She was off alcohol and brimming with "soda pop spirits." These spirits were not, however, contagious. Returning from the "ghastly" heat of Louisville, Warren told Erskine that he had "been on the last few pages of my last chapter for near ten days. Stuck. Rather, everything conspires to prevent my settling down to the last push."[6]

With these letters reflecting the growing tensions between husband and wife, the prospect of visitors to 2034 La Mesa Drive must have been welcome. Pier arrived on July 6, and on July 19, having sent the last of the draft of the novel to Helen Strauss, Warren wrote Albert Erskine, "The thing is too long. I need some help here to get a fresh perspective, especially if the thing is to be ready soon. You see, I'm working part of every day with my collaborator on the play, and that does help to put some artificial distance between me and *World Enough and Time*. . . . I had hope that you might take your vacation out here. As a matter of fact, that would be the only thoroughly sat-isfactory way to do the job fast. . . . I'm asking it of you as a pal and not as an editor. . . . Needless to say, I've got the jitters." Leaving Peggy in New York, Albert departed for Santa Monica.[7]

They worked hard and well, and there was time for some social life. The Warrens had not lacked invitations. One of the pleasantest en-counters was with a man who—Warren later said—worked the same way he did. He was Charlie Chaplin. The actor was preparing for *Limelight,* and he began to tell part of the story and act it out. He was no Charlie Chaplin, Warren hastened to say, but like Chaplin, he liked to tell his stories. "It's self-exploration in a way." Pier Pasinetti loved listening to Warren's stories of Kentucky and Tennessee. "Red is greater as a story-teller than as a writer," he would say.[8]

But there were times when that performing impulse was blocked. Not many months hence, when Allen Tate and Andrew Lytle saw Warren, they would remark on "the mask" that they thought de-scended upon his face as he strove to register no disapproval of things Cinina said or did. But Pier had glimpses behind the mask. He and

Warren would go to the beach to swim for long distances. One day as they walked there Warren said to him, "This can't go on," and for the first time, he spoke of divorce. Looking back years later, Pier would say that by this time Cinina was insane. She was completely unpredictable, and in spite of her avowals to Pier, she had begun drinking again. Erskine thought back to Baton Rouge when she was mixing sleeping pills and liquor. "She was really going down the drain," but Erskine had not fully realized it. Looking back later, he would say, "There was a period of time where I was really gutless about saying to Red, 'Look, I know you feel guilty about this, but you've got to cut it out because it's just not going to work,' but I never did that." So the two went on, taking what comfort they could in the company of old friends. It would not be too long before Warren too was obviously drinking excessively.[9]

Erskine concluded that he had failed, at least partially, as a friend, but he could not think he had failed as an editor. On September 7 Warren wrote him, "I'm certain that no writer could ever hope for a better and more careful piece of editing. . . . I'm damned grateful to you, and no kidding." Warren felt good about his other collaborator too. "The play looks pretty promising," he added. "Or perhaps I've caught Rossen's enthusiasm for it." It could be tried out on the road in late summer, Rossen thought, with a New York opening in October. "AKM is sealed up. It is a superior picture." The release was planned for midfall of 1949 in New York and Hollywood simultaneously.[10]

Now it was time to head east again for his last two quarters of teaching at the University of Minnesota. Hunt and Bid Brown's daughter Chick remembered that "it was a one-man show, breathtaking sometimes. He didn't invite questions, but this may have been because the classroom was always crowded with at least twice the number of students actually registered for the course. There were people standing at the back of the room and in the doorway, sitting on radiators and windowsills. Two amazing performances stand out in my mind. The first was when he recited the whole of 'The Ancient Mariner' and the other was when he recited the whole of 'The Wasteland [*sic*].' He had much to say about the poems, so excited by what he saw and felt that it was as if he himself had written the poems."[11]

November found the Warrens back in New York at the Marguery for the premiere of *All the King's Men*. Cinina told Pier Pasinetti that she liked the film and reported highly favorable reviews and a fine spread in *Life*. Chick Brown would remember the floodlights piercing the December night of the film's Minneapolis premiere. "Red invited a great number of friends to meet him in the lobby of the theater. When he finally turned up he stepped into line at the ticket booth and when his turn came ordered forty-odd tickets." Danforth Ross was a young instructor whom Red had invited along with his wife, Dorothy. As minutes passed and Cinina failed to appear with the movie about to begin, Warren went in and sat beside Dorothy. (They knew that Cinina "was often not around and the rumors were that she had a bad back or that she had a drinking problem or that she had writing ambitions herself and was jealous of Red.") When Cinina finally stepped out of a taxi, Chick recalled her "floating through the crowd in that disembodied way she had, smiling at no one in particular, seeming to expect compliments." Afterward, "I remember catching a glimpse of Red as we left the theater, head down as he hurried Cinina toward the parking lot. I thought he looked embarrassed, if not actually ashamed." The two had lost contact with each other.[12]

In late November, Cinina had told Pier Pasinetti that she was feeling better than at any time in the past two years. She wrote that she had been diagnosed by several doctors as suffering from fungus or virus diseases, but the trouble was actually something else, inflammatory gastritis, which could be cured by diet. A week later she wrote him that she was "zooming around . . . with all the energy in the world." Perhaps it was the diet, or perhaps a manic phase as opposed to the depressive states that helped bring on the drinking. Sam Monk, now chairman of English at Minnesota, reported to Allen Tate, "I have enjoyed Red this fall as never before. He returned in good spirits, and for a while at least Cinina seemed to be making an effort to behave." On January 2 of 1950 she wrote Pier, beginning with a reminder that he owed her a note. Other payments were also coming due.[13]

If she showed the symptoms of a neurasthenic personality, she also had suffered numerous illnesses and accidents such as the bathtub mishap in Rome. In their Minneapolis years many thought of her as "bedridden." During one stretch she took to her bed for more than half a year—because of tuberculosis, she said—and she would receive visitors there dressed in a lacy nightgown. One of the Warrens' friends was Brenda Euland, a wit and rebel, a Greenwich Village intellectual who had come to Minneapolis and enjoyed a career as a

writer, teacher, and editor. Brenda told Cinina that she would bring
a psychic who could tell her how to get well. When the psychic appeared, her first words were "You haven't got TB. Get up and go
out." The visit ended abruptly, and neither woman was ever received
there again. Years later Bid Brown remembered Cinina writing,
"Isn't it wonderful what a recovery I've made? I've just had an x-ray
of my chest and there isn't a scar. It's a miracle!"[14]

But there were psychological scars that were lasting. Cinina felt
that her father had never received the recognition due him. So she
deposited several large boxes of his scores and notebooks in the University of Minnesota Library for safekeeping and study. And she felt
that she as well had never received her due—in Tennessee or
Louisiana or Minnesota. She was not only an Italian whose ancestors,
she said, were mentioned in *The Divine Comedy,* but also a writer and
a sophisticated cosmopolite who spoke languages fluently, played the
piano well, and set a beautiful table. To novelist Frederick Manfred
she had a strong nose and chin and "the spoiled brat girl way of walking and wiggling around." Warren would later say in explanation that
"at home she was treated like a princess, but there [in Minnesota] she
was just a wop." To those who saw her so, she must have fitted a
stereotype—exotic-looking, often loud and voluble, "performing"
Italian with Hunt Brown and given to emotional outbursts. Margaret
Allison came home from college and met the Warrens at her parents'
home. She had heard of Cinina as a semi-invalid, but found her "a
sprightly presence with what could become a rather hectic gaiety. I
remember her pausing as she entered a party at my parents' to toss her
hat up over the crowd onto a cathedral candlestick we kept on a high
shelf." She thought her "quintessentially European—continental, actually, for she was as un-English as she was un-American—and appeared to greatest advantage in the company of other continentals.
Her demeanor, her dress, had that containment, intensity, and
aplomb that are the very opposite of the understated and loose-
limbed style admired in England and the United States. She may have
been disoriented when she observed that the attitudes and skills she
had been trained in from childhood were inexplicably not in demand
in this odd corner of the world."[15]

But her wounds and anguishes could show in livid ways, especially
when they were deepened by alcohol. In that year of 1949, when
Warren was out of town, Cinina invited Margaret and her new husband, George Hemphill, to dinner at Harry's Restaurant. Before the

meal was finished, "to our dismay, she collapsed into what used to be called a crying jag, talking between sobs about her father. I remember our discomfort when she said, 'Red will never be the man he was.' " Needing to be the center of attention, she would interrupt him when he was speaking, calling to him from across the room when he was in another group. She would telephone him at the office to come home and do errands. He rented a room at the Hampshire Arms for a study, and one day when he was helping Chick Brown with a writing assignment, Cinina telephoned him there too, from their apartment on another floor. She knew how her husband impressed people. Isabella Gardner, later to be Mrs. Allen Tate, was struck on first meeting Red "by how tremendously attractive a man he was," with "an extraordinary amount of magnetism. . . ." As time went on, Cinina's jealousy and resentment would surface in increasingly intense ways.[16]

In one of life's ironies, an outside observer might have thought Warren had every reason to be happy. On January 17 William Rose Benét informed him that he had been elected to the National Institute of Arts and Letters in a class that also included Thomas Mann, William Carlos Williams, John Hersey, and Andrew Wyeth. His corrected galley proofs of *World Enough and Time* were at the printers, and the novel would be the July selection of the Literary Guild. Yale University was going to award him an honorary Doctor of Letters degree. *All the King's Men* won the Academy Award for the Best Film of 1949 (his work on the script recognized by the Robert Helzer Award from the Screen Writers' Guild), and he had reason to believe that the Cass Mastern play would go into rehearsal in July for fall production with prospects of a film version. But at the same time, in a pattern Thomas Hardy might not have scorned, fate was incubating a different sequence of events.[17]

On the last day of the month Warren congratulated Frank Owsley on his move to the University of Alabama and told him, "It must be a great satisfaction to you to be back in your home country." Still the Loneliness Artist, he added, "I wish that I could get back in mine more often. But at least I get a glimpse now and then, and in the future I hope to make it more than a glimpse. I've been a DP a long time, but I don't get entirely used to it." There were other reasons for his malaise. "Things with us are sort of half and half. Cinina has been very unwell for almost two years. I'm gloomy but manage to rock along, no aches, no pains. I keep plugging away at my work, teaching and writing, because there isn't much choice I suppose." Writing on February 14 he could be more explicit with Pier Pasinetti. "Cinina has been in the hospital for several weeks, but is steadily improving. . . . But, damn it, we can't sail on April 8, for Ireland. . . ." When Sam Monk asked about Cinina, Warren said, "Her back is giving her less trouble." Monk knew there was more to it than that. He said that Warren had "put her in the hospital in St. Paul away from everybody." During a spring visit from the Warrens, John Ransom would learn that Cinina had been "analysed."[18]

Warren had told Pasinetti, "I am going rapidly mad with work." He was trying to keep up with Cleanth Brooks in their revision of *Understanding Poetry.* "Also I've got one million little bastards in my classes. Unfortunately some of them are very good, and that makes it tougher." When he dashed off a letter to Allen Tate on the twenty-second he was "sunk in the end of quarter confusion. And the situation hasn't been helped much by the fact that I've been ailing and missed a few days." With his work on proofs, the textbook, and examination papers, he was driving himself beyond the limits of his remarkable physical and psychic resources.[19]

Chick Brown had seen something when Warren came to occupy the maid's room in their house while Cinina was in the hospital. One day when he was going over one of Chick's manuscripts with her, he suddenly asked her agitatedly to excuse him because he felt a violent sneeze coming on. He looked as though he might throw up, and she hurried from the room. (Chick's mother, Bid, recalled his breakfasting on a pint of ice cream. They thought he had a stomach ulcer, and it seemed to be getting worse.) By February 15 he was in the hospital being tested for gallstones. After X rays the doctors decided that the problem was his pancreas and prescribed "a mild diet and the water wagon." When this failed to help, there were more X rays and examinations. On March 11 he told Albert Erskine again that he was still on the wagon "but my gut is not going well. . . ." On March 26 he wrote, "I have had another siege abed but am getting up now." In early April, Sam Monk relayed the news to Allen Tate. "Red has been quite sick, as you know, and is not well yet. C[inina], out of the hospital, seems a new woman. I think most of Red's trouble is due to strain, but for a while his doctors took a dim view. They are lingering on here hoping that he'll get his strength back. They sail for Europe in May." Dr. Tom Lowry, physician for the Browns and the Warrens, told Bid that, while he couldn't divulge any details, Warren's marriage was going to destroy him altogether if he didn't remove himself from it.[20]

Cinina's capacity for the unusual had become familiar. When their Japanese maid decided to marry, Cinina staged the wedding in their apartment, with Warren serving as both host and best man. After scanty refreshments, the couple went out to the taxi that was to take them to their honeymoon hotel. Bid Brown remembered the bafflement of the guests and the dismay of the newlyweds when Cinina got into the taxi with them. Her affinity for the dramatic flourished particularly in party situations. In one game of charades, acting out the syllable *syn* in *idiosyncrasy,* she threw herself on the floor, flipped over onto her back, and executed a vigorous series of pelvic thrusts. Saul Bellow, whose appointment in the English department had come through Warren's recommendation, thought their big house at 2725 Irving Avenue looked as if Warren was "indulging Cinina's wish to cut a figure in Minneapolis." The house had an elevator, and Hunt Brown remembered a party when it descended and the door slid open to disclose Cinina, dressed in black, peering out like a figure in a Charles Addams cartoon. At another party Chick Brown heard "a resounding crash down the hall. A table full of glasses had overturned and amidst broken glass Cinina lay stretched out upon the floor. Red, without missing a beat, managed to get her quickly into a bedroom, shutting the door firmly behind him." Whenever a mishap occurred he would offer neither excuse nor explanation. Instead he would show what one friend called "the great stone face." Helen Brennan, the wife of the young novelist Dan Brennan, would try to look after Cinina, but sometimes she was unable to help. Bid Brown knew why. Looking down from over a banister into the stairwell, Bid saw Cinina, standing alone, as she unscrewed the cap on a pint of whiskey, downed a drink, then put it away. By now she had joined Alcoholics Anonymous, but she was fighting a losing battle.[21]

Friends such as Eric Bentley could infer what it was like when the two were alone. For a time he and Warren would have a regular weekly lunch at Bentley's apartment so that they would not be interrupted by business or Cinina, who demanded all Bentley's attention if he visited the Warren household. Bentley knew that it was hard for her to be married to a genius and a brilliant talker who could be, Bentley thought, something of a show-off. But Warren "had such a tremendous sense of guilt over all her troubles" that he abased himself. Aware of her jealousy, "he was always being small to please her.

She inhibited him very, very much because he wasn't supposed to be smarter than she was. She didn't want him to be. So he acted like he had nothing to say very frequently in her presence. It was bondage. It was a bondage he accepted in a highly masochistic way. He let her be a torment to him and almost pretended he liked it."[22]

By now, however, he was distraught enough to confide in Charlie Foster, earlier his student and now his close friend. And so was Cinina ready to confide in Charlie's wife, Doris. Their problem, Cinina said, was that Red wanted to practice birth control and she, because of her Catholic beliefs, refused. But she said there was another problem, and asked Doris to warn her women friends who might be susceptible to Red's charms that he had a bad infection. Doris thought this was simply a ploy prompted by jealousy rather than prophylaxis. Charlie thought he knew what prompted Red's insistence on contraception after the years when, loving children as he did, he had longed for fatherhood: he felt an obligation to protect a sick woman, but also an obligation too to prevent a child's being born into a dysfunctional family. This unhappy wife who boasted of ancestors in *The Inferno* had created one of her own, but she was apparently determined that she should not be its only inhabitant. Years before, Eddie Mims had disparaged Red with the name of the fearsome mythological character Cyclops. Now Cinina sometimes used the name of a grotesque squint-eyed comic-strip character, calling her husband Popeye.[23]

By April they were preparing for a month in Sewanee, and they had more than the prospect of the gentler Tennessee climate to buck them up. Cinina had been translating Elio Vittorini's novel *Il sempione strizza l'occhio al Frejus,* and a portion was published in *Harper's Bazaar.* Also, Dixon Wecter had been planting seeds in Berkeley at Warren's suggestion, and now they gave promise of bearing fruit. And after he finished his work with Rossen on the play, they would visit Denis and Caren Devlin in Ireland. When they drove south late in the month, they went by way of Kenyon. John Ransom told Allen Tate, "We were awfully pleased with Cinina's apparent recovery from her troubled condition; she seemed very much on her best behavior. . . ."[24]

After a week in Sewanee they made plans to leave in time to arrive in New York on the twelfth, where they would stay at the Marguery until they sailed on the morning of the eighteenth. But then the absence of Cinina's support systems—the doctors, perhaps Alcoholics Anonymous—began to tell. In Warren's grim recollection, "she

cracked up." As she grew more violent and he attempted to help her
regain control, she attacked him physically. He telephoned John
Palmer, who came immediately, and in the middle of the night they
drove her "to a booby hatch north of Nashville." She was there for
two days, and though the doctors wanted to keep her longer, they got
in the car again, Cinina more eager than ever to return to Europe,
Warren certain that they would never use the steamship tickets in his
pocket.[25]

In New York, he bought tickets to a play, hoping that the theatre
would divert her. It was May 14. Not long after the curtain went up,
Cinina grew restless and agitated. Then she started talking to the actors on the stage. When he tried to quiet her, she began shouting.
Desperately embarrassed, he got up and walked out of the theatre.
She followed him to the Marguery, shouting at him all the way. Once
in their room, he telephoned Albert Erskine and asked him to pick
up his car and drive it around to the front of the hotel. He telephoned
the doctor who had supplied his number in case of a recurrence of
the earlier breakdown. He arrived promptly and administered a sedative by injection. With Warren he walked Cinina down to the car,
and they got into the backseat with her. Albert drove them twenty
miles north of the city to White Plains. There, at the doctor's recommendation, she unwillingly committed herself to the psychiatric division of New York Hospital.[26]

The next day Warren canceled their passage on the *Mauretania* and
wired the Devlins. He had severed his connection with Minnesota,
though no offer from Berkeley had been officially tendered. He
would stay there in the city, not knowing what her course of treatment would be or how long it would take. In the days that followed
his mood would shift from despair to hope. After she recovered from
this breakdown perhaps they could go to Italy again. Meanwhile, he
would busy himself with promised writing and await the publication
on June 20 of *World Enough and Time*.

29

❖

The Historical Novel

Then I came back into the world, and hope to do my duty still,
whatever it may be and bear with fortitude the ills and losses.
I speak of myself. But do not think I do not know
what you have endured. Could I have made your lot more easy,
I had thrust my hand into the fire.

—*World Enough and Time*[1]

Warren said he meant his book to be "a straight historical novel." His research had gone far beyond the document Katherine Anne Porter had supplied: the thirty-thousand-word *Confession of Jereboam O. Beauchamp* with the accompanying romantically lugubrious verses of the fatal pair plus their epitaph and letters. An eight-page Random House pamphlet, probably written by Albert Erskine, asserted, however, that *World Enough and Time* was to be read as "entirely a work of fiction." The protagonist was named Jeremiah Beaumont, his wife-to-be, Rachel Jordan, and his victim, Colonel Cassius Fort. There was also a coda, which extended their story far beyond that of Jereboam Beauchamp and Ann Cook. "Though the germ came from the Beauchamp story, and though the novel uses much of the framework of the Beauchamp case, it departs from the records freely and is in no sense bound by them. An important aspect of Mr. Warren's narrative method is the quotation of passages from 'documents' of the time—from the hero's own story of his life, from letters, newspapers, diaries, etc.—but these 'quotations' were all invented by the author as an integral part of the novel." The narrative method recalls Jack Burden's treatment of Cass Mastern and his papers. But here the narrator was nameless, a sort of literary anthropologist.[2]

It is a long and complex novel, which demands close attention from even the most sympathetic reader. Orphaned and irregularly educated by eccentric Dr. Leicester Burnham, Jeremiah Beaumont is apprenticed in Colonel Fort's Frankfort law office. There Wilkie Barron tells him about Rachel Jordan, seduced by Fort. Beaumont courts her and breaks with Fort. After Barron introduces Beaumont to Percival Skrogg, an ideologue determined to change the harsh debtor laws, the two co-opt Beaumont into their party and its violence at the polls. When Rachel takes him to the grave of her stillborn child and offers to marry him if he will promise to kill Fort, he agrees. He speculates in land and runs for the legislature in a campaign in which handbills exploit Rachel's seduction. Shocked into a second stillbirth, she urges Beaumont again to kill Fort, who had refused to be provoked into a duel. Beaumont slips into Frankfort by night and stabs Fort to death. After a complicated trial with perjury and contaminated evidence he is convicted, and Rachel, found guilty of complicity, is imprisoned with him. Burnham provides poison, but their double-suicide attempt fails. Rescued by Barron and Skrogg's former bodyguard, One-eye Jenkins, the two flee west escorted by his brother, Lilburn Jenkins. In the horrible swamp sanctuary of La Grand' Bosse, a monstrous old pirate, Beaumont becomes decadent, corrupt, and syphilitic. Rachel goes mad and kills herself. When One-eye appears with the handbill Beaumont needed for his defense, Lilburn prepares to shoot him, only to die when Beaumont interferes and One-eye kills his brother. Setting out with Beaumont for Frankfort in the faint hope of winning a pardon for him, One-eye reveals that both Barron and Skrogg had betrayed him. Beaumont disarms and trusses One-eye, only to be overtaken by him. He and Barron kill Beaumont and take the evidence of his death to Frankfort, where Barron prospers but keeps Beaumont's autobiographical manuscript and eventually commits suicide.

Warren not only chose his title from a poem that would point up his intentions but also supplied an explicit subtitle and a long epigraph. The title came from Andrew Marvell's "To His Coy Mistress," where the poet mocks his lady's ideal of formal and protracted courtly love. The world's encroachments of fleeting time and certain death argue for immediate gratification rather than romantic attitudinizing. Why, then, subtitle the work *A Romantic Novel*? For Warren "romance" had a special meaning here. "It's a story about the young idealist who can't find an object for his idealism," he wrote. "He creates a dream world in which he can play the hero." For an epigraph Warren chose three stanzas from Edmund Spenser's *The Faerie Queene,* where Sir Artegall, the Knight of Justice, seeks his particular grail because the world "growes daily wourse and wourse" whereas in the antique world truth was admired and justice prevailed. Beaumont, Warren said, "wants to find a cause that will justify a violent and heroic act. . . . (The book is, in a way, about the pathology of romanticism.)" Consumed with pride, Beaumont "*must* find a *cause,* in order to justify some of his most secret and destructive [needs]."[3]

The historical milieu supplies a complex background. In the aftermath of the panic of 1819, with many Kentuckians in bankruptcy, the Relief party passed a replevin bill, providing a two-year moratorium on the collection of debts, and met with fierce opposition. Jeremiah blunders into the conflict on the side of replevin rather than entering through political ideology. His particular personal quest—Rachel Jordan's love, and heroism in avenging her honor—comes from a tangle of motives that he does not fully understand. Lacking self-knowledge, he will finally achieve it when it is too late.[4]

Warren provided a gloss of the novel for the *Literary Guild Review.* "I didn't want to leave him monstrous. I wanted to carry him on a journey of redemption, or at least to bring him to awareness." Colonel Fort was to be "a good man who falls from goodness but still loves it, who wants to see justice prevail but knows that justice cannot prevail in the abstract and that in the world justice must somehow work with the facts of the world or it ceases to be justice. He is, in one way, a father figure who carried both the errors and the virtues of the past." Percival Skrogg "is a type of the idealist, the type that puts ends above means so that bad means contaminate even the best ends. He is a parallel to Jeremiah, and it seemed appropriate to me that he should be Jeremiah's betrayer." If Jeremiah is reminiscent of Willie Stark in his fall from virtue, the truly monstrous appears in La Grand' Bosse. "I take him to be, in one aspect at least, the natural man, the monster natural man becomes, void of ideas and ideals."[5]

There are other familiar motifs: the search for identity, the omnipresence of original sin, and the flight to the west in search of redemption. Besides Warren's own particular devices and concerns, the novel echoes those of other writers, not just in a mediating narrator's recording of failings or sins to be expiated, as in *The Scarlet Letter* and *Lord Jim,* but also in individual scenes, as in the prison of the lovers, which suggests the Capulet tomb in *Romeo and Juliet.*[6]

The reactions of Warren's friends were as various as those of the reviewers. Sam Monk thought it "the best he has done. . . . I think he is really non–commercial, and cannot see that this novel is written *for* Hollywood, though it will certainly end there." Some others would feel that, increasingly after *All the King's Men,* his novels were aimed at Hollywood. John Ransom had the most serious reservations. If Jeremiah's sins are scarlet, with adultery and debauchery added to murder, their consequences are melodramatic enough. It was the Grand Guignol violence that Ransom found abhorrent, with Rachel's madness and suicide and Jeremiah's head in a sack swinging from One-eye's saddlebow. The judgment Ransom confided to Allen Tate was moralistic as well as aesthetic. In the collaboration with Cleanth Brooks "Red supplied the ideas; but now it becomes clear, I think, that Cleanth supplied good stern moral principles, and that both of them suffer now that their close relation has been broken up. I think Red's book is pretty horrible. . . ." To Ransom it was full of sententious philosophizing and bad rhetoric. "It's most depressing. How can Red be the soul of honor personally (as I still feel sure he is) and dally with the themes he does in the fictions? . . . I can't but think that Red is going to take a terrible panning from the serious critics."[7]

Ransom was unduly apprehensive. Though a few ridiculed the rhetoric, violence, and romantic excesses, most praised its richness and power. It received a boost with front-page treatment in the Sunday book-review sections of *The New York Times* and the *Herald Tribune,* and the earliest verdicts of "the serious critics" Ransom feared were favorable too.[8]

More than a dozen years later Warren would say, "The novels that seem to have brought the most satisfaction to me are *World Enough and Time, Flood,* and *All the King's Men.*" He concurred in Charlie Foster's analysis of Jeremiah as "a case" but hoped that something more than that was "projected." And he confessed to the kind of trouble creating Rachel Beaumont that he had encountered with Anne Stanton: "She is the weakest thing in the book. The hell of it was that I could find no way to get at Rachel, when the book was really Jeremiah's. But I should have . . . simply done an analysis of R, and chunked it down in the middle and not tried to be so God-damned subtle." Over the years since publication critical opinion has settled down into a balance of familiar pluses and minuses: charges of melodrama ("unconscious parodies of *East Lynne*") on the one hand, and praise for dense intellectual texture and narrative vitality on the other.[9]

By early July the novel was third on the best-seller list. Random House followed the first printing of thirty-seven thousand copies with ten thousand more three days after publication and kept the hardcover in print for the next twenty-four years. (It was ironic, Warren told Pier Pasinetti, that though "the New Yorker review said that the book was deliberately written down to make a movie melodrama," there was no indication of a movie sale.) As Shakespeare had done, he had taken historical sources and shaped them into a powerful and tragic work, but he had loaded onto it an extended coda, which fulfilled some of his intended meanings but dragged on in a way that sapped its power. Over the years no one, finally, would accord *World Enough and Time* a higher place than *All the King's Men*. It would remain his heaviest novel, in its philosophical burden, its length, and its density. He would never consider his work "popular" fiction, and his novels to come would continue to explore philosophical problems.[10]

Though his personal problems were not fatal like Beaumont's, they were acute and debilitating. As Rachel Beaumont had been progressively going mad, so had Cinina. She remained in the hospital in White Plains while Warren went to stay in Albert and Peggy Erskine's summer place in Saugatuck, Connecticut. He had it to himself except for the weekends. "I go into town a couple of days a week & to see Cinina," he wrote his father in late July. "She has finished her translation & the book will appear in Oct. or Nov." He was pressed with the revisions of *An Approach to Literature,* but other matters were hanging fire. Robert Rossen and he had three weeks of revision to do on his Cass Mastern play, *The Wedding Ring,* but Rossen was tied up with a film. The job offer from Berkeley couldn't be tendered until the relation of the regents and the faculty was clarified in the furor over a loyalty oath. He closed with much love to his father and the family, signing himself "Son."[11]

He had ample reason to feel depressed that summer. *The Wedding Ring* would not go into rehearsal. In mid-June, Dixon Wecter had been there for a visit, but a week later, at forty-four, he was dead of a heart attack. "I have counted him one of my really dear friends for twenty-three years," Warren wrote Pier Pasinetti, "and the death left a real hole." Cinina's case followed an up-and-down course. She continually asked him for help with her Vittorini translation, and he faithfully supplied it. Her treatment was costing eight hundred dollars a month, and he was dipping heavily into their reserve. As for his own health, with weather too bad for swimming, he was playing basketball at the YMCA. Then one day he collided with another player and slammed down onto the floor. This painful injury lamed his upper arm and shoulder. The doctor told him that he would have to keep the joint limber, and so he resumed lifting weights, a regimen he would continue for the rest of his life.[12]

So the summer went and the fall came in. From White Plains, in her isolation, Cinina wrote Pier that, on doctor's orders, she had had no contact of any kind with Warren since July 4. Her goal was to leave the hospital in November. It would be six months then, but the doctors thought they should live apart for six additional months, for their relationship was destructive for both of them. She hoped to find a place in New York, take some courses at Columbia, and rewrite her last novel. She was encouraged by Pier's fortitude in his troubles and praised Warren's courage. He had been "very ill and unhappy and is having his own form of rest." She stopped there.[13]

Cleanth Brooks went to his chairman at Yale. "I have this friend," he told him. "I know he's free, not teaching anywhere else. Would you like to pick him up for a time?" Maynard Mack knew Warren's work well, and by October 15 Warren was able to inform Charlie Foster that he was visiting professor of English for the semester, commuting from a New York garret apartment each week from Thursday evening to Sunday morning. He was fortunate to have a salary check coming in again, for Cinina's discharge date had been canceled. But her assessment did not jibe with her doctors'. She thought her health better than it had been since her youth. She told Pasinetti that all the years in bed had benefited her, and in a "perverse sort of way" she was enjoying the experience, especially the fascinating teacher–pupil relationship between the psychiatrist and the patient. Beyond that was this first-ever submergence in "the real elixir of pain." In early December, Warren was able to inform Pasinetti that she "goes out to town a couple of times a week and has even been in to NYC," though there was no date yet for her release. She and her husband did not meet.[14]

As 1950 drew to a close he felt no more sanguine about the world at large than about his own immediate one. "I'm getting mighty little done," he told Pier. "The ambiguity of the present is not conducive to long projects, and I've been distracted by short ones. The world news gets me down. It's just too preposterously awful. [Two weeks earlier, Red China had intervened in the Korean War.] We are entering into a thirty years war, and going in blind. We'll never know the world we grew up expecting to live in. That's a cinch. And one thing, the general picture is so grim that it makes all your ordinary pursuits, the business of literature and so forth, seem trivial in the face of the absolute bestial blankness of the objective world." Against his malaise he employed his habitual antidotes, travel and writing.[15]

The winter proved to be a busy one, "damned full of alarums and excursions, one of the excursions being three weeks in the South, thank God." He had managed, however, to get his Kentucky poem, *Brother to Dragons,* half done, and he would press on until he started teaching again in February. Then, when that was finished in the spring, he hoped to go abroad. He turned down a firm offer from Berkeley because of the insistence on the loyalty oath, which, he told the press, "constitutes not only a threat to academic freedom but, in the end, to ordinary freedom and decency." He knew, however, that there was another job in the offing.[16]

At the Yale School of Drama distinguished playwrights such as Marc Connelly and Thornton Wilder had felt their students didn't know enough and that it would be a good idea to hire someone who could show them something of what a first-rate literary artist did. President A. Whitney Griswold agreed. So did Cleanth Brooks, who knew that he would then get students from the drama school in his twentieth-century literature seminar, where they would study not just Yeats's plays but also his poems and the fiction of Joyce and other moderns. Griswold asked Warren to come and see him and invited Brooks to come along. "We want to hire you," the president told him, "but there's no room in the English department. Do you mind being in the drama school?" Warren would remember that he "didn't feel too crazy about that," thinking all his work would be in drama, but Griswold reassured him. "We'll put you in the drama school officially, but it's right across there, and you'll have another course in the English department."[17]

At the hospital, Cinina's doctors were approaching a decision. Warren had never suggested a separation, although he had thought of one, and he had apparently been attracted to other women, Bid Brown among them. "I think he wanted to get out long before," Cleanth Brooks reflected later, "but he was just too much of a gentleman, probably thinking, 'I cannot abandon her.' " To Eric Bentley, he was "pretending he liked that marriage but it was very obvious to his friends that it was a crucifying process. And we thought at the time that he would never get out, because he had such a tremendous sense of guilt over all her troubles, that it seemed like he thought he should just put up with it." About this time Warren began to see Merrill Moore, his fellow Fugitive, still a prolific sonneteer and now a distinguished psychiatrist at the Boston City Hospital. Apparently he did not see Warren professionally, but as an old friend who cared he helped him to cope with his feelings of guilt. Even earlier in Baton Rouge, others had felt such sympathy that they referred to themselves as "Friends of Red Warren to free him from Cinina." She knew this. Cleanth Brooks had been told that she had passionately declared, "I know they all hate me, but I'll *never* give him a divorce."[18]

In her thick file the psychiatrists must have recorded many symptoms of the fragmented marriage: how she had physically attacked him, how she was frightened of having children, though she had not said so, how she seemed to get sick whenever he published a book. Sympathetic Helen Strauss knew the dynamic between them. Instead of providing security, Warren's "fame and the demands it made on him aggravated and amplified her insecurity and fears, which festered into a constant and crippling emotional malaise." But her physicians had seen gradual improvement, and one day one of them finally told her, "We don't think this marriage you're in is doing you any good. You must get out of it to save yourself."[19]

Then, in late April, Cleanth Brooks had a call from the registrar's office. They had not received from Warren the final grades for his courses. Did Brooks know where he was? Helen Strauss supplied his address and telephone number, in Reno, Nevada. "I didn't know I was coming out here until the last minute," Warren told Brooks, and supplied the grades. He explained that he had received an abrupt phone call from Cinina. "Red," she had said, "get us a divorce."[20]

It was not that quick or easy. Attorney Sam Platt filed the papers, and Warren established residence at the Donner Trail Ranch in Verdi, Nevada, ten miles west of Reno near the California line. Much of the time, however, he would be elsewhere. In early May he wrote to Charlie Foster, now teaching at Grinnell College in Iowa, to ask if he could stay with them for ten days or so. He was working alternately on *Brother to Dragons* and a long introduction to Joseph Conrad's *Nostromo,* and he didn't want Cinina to know where he was. Doris gave him the downstairs bedroom, and Charlie got the books he needed from the college library. But he still could not work without distraction. Robert Rossen was being scrutinized by Senator McCarthy's anti–Communist investigators, and now Warren began to feel that

Gabriel Thomas Penn. Grandpa: source of
stories, poems, and love.
COURTESY OF MRS. ROBERT D. FREY

William Henry Harrison Warren, Jr.
The grandfather he never knew.
COURTESY OF MRS. ROBERT D. FREY

Robert Franklin Warren. Father: would-be
poet, storekeeper, banker, storekeeper again.
To be for years a widower and solitary,
commemorated with admiration.
COURTESY OF MRS. ROBERT D. FREY

Anna Ruth Penn. Mother: doting and dominating, by her son evaded but loved and mourned.
COURTESY OF MRS. ROBERT D. FREY

Robert Penn Warren, age one. His parents' joy and pride, he would re-create their lives in verse.
COURTESY OF MRS. ROBERT D. FREY

The family on their Guthrie front porch, 1910. Mother and Father with Mary Cecilia, Robert Penn, and William Thomas.
COURTESY OF MRS. ROBERT D. FREY

A big event: a sale at Warren's store. The proprietor is at the extreme right.
COURTESY OF MRS. ROBERT D. FREY

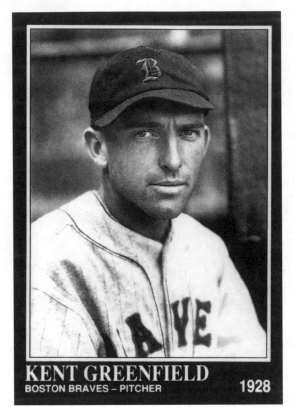

KENT GREENFIELD
BOSTON BRAVES – PITCHER
1928

The friend of his youth: hero, protector, and poetic inspiration.

Clarksville (Tenn.) High School valedictorian, 1920.

In Guthrie, Mother with
Thomas, Robert Penn, and
Mary.
COURTESY OF MRS. ROBERT D. FREY

Behind the Nichols' home in
Nashville, Columbus Day, 1923:
Allen Tate (standing), and Lyle
Lanier, Catherine "Chink" Nichol,
and Robert Penn Warren.
COURTESY OF LYLE LANIER AND CATHERINE
NICHOL LANIER

The Vanderbilt senior.
COURTESY OF MRS. ROBERT D. FREY

Vanderbilt artists: sculptor
Puryear Mims and poet
Robert Penn Warren.
COURTESY OF ELLA PURYEAR MIMS

Surrogate father and surrogate son: John Crowe Ransom, right, and Allen Tate, center, with Charles Coffin.
COURTESY OF HELEN RANSOM FORMAN

Teacher and friend: Donald Davidson, reading a copy of *The Fugitive*.
COURTESY OF MRS. ROBERT H. SULLIVAN

Classmate and friend: Andrew Lytle.
COURTESY OF GEORGE CHAMBERLAIN

Robert Penn Warren and his first wife,
Emma "Cinina" Brescia, in Hammond,
Louisiana.

Warren and Cinina aboard the *Sobieski,* docking in New York, September 21, 1948, after
nine strenuous months in Italy.

Albert Russell Erskine,
Jr., Red Warren's
friend, collaborator,
and editor.
PHOTO BY RALPH ELLISON,
COURTESY OF MRS. RALPH
ELLISON

Outside Random House,
1950, after the publication of
World Enough and Time.
PHOTO BY SALLY ROSS

A young writer in the 1930s:
Eleanor Phelps Clark.

La Rocca, 1952: where the lovers came, and later brought their small children.

Rosanna Phelps Warren and her parents, July 1953, after a difficult and dangerous birth.

WARREN FAMILY ARCHIVE

Two beloved by the Warrens: Rosanna and her godmother, Katherine Anne Porter.

WARREN FAMILY ARCHIVE

Gabriel Thomas, focus of paternal pride and poems.

WARREN FAMILY ARCHIVE

Making a home in Fairfield.
WARREN FAMILY ARCHIVE. PHOTO BY
SYLVIA SALMI

Father and daughter.
WARREN FAMILY ARCHIVE

Father and son.
WARREN FAMILY ARCHIVE

William Styron, skipper, on expedition with the Styron and Warren families, off Martha's Vineyard.
COURTESY OF WILLIAM STYRON

Working professionals: Random House and Pantheon authors, 1965.
REPRINTED BY PERMISSION OF CHASE LTD.

Rewarded for a cultural mission: Robert Penn Warren and William Styron in Egypt, 1967.
WARREN FAMILY ARCHIVE

The writer: vision nearly gone,
but still working, 1970.

Rosanna Warren, painter and
poet: Venice, winter 1977.

At home in Vermont, 1986.

Seventy-fifth birthday honors, October 1980: Cleanth Brooks, Robert Penn Warren,
Phyllis George, Eleanor Clark, and Kentucky governor John Y. Brown, Jr.

Old comrades: Robert Penn Warren and Cleanth Brooks.

Last days, 1989.

Rosanna and Eleanor Warren at the dedication of the Robert Penn Warren Library at Western Kentucky University, April 24, 1994.

they were pursuing him too. It seemed to Charlie that Warren was on the phone to his lawyer every day, uncertain whether he could go back to Hollywood to work with Rossen on the play or should return to the ranch. In mid-May the Associated Press had reported that he was there for a divorce. His election to the American Academy of Arts and Sciences, reported on the tenth, may have seemed to him an ironic commentary on the difference between his professional and personal lives.[21]

On May 23 he wrote Charlie and Doris Foster from the ranch. "It is very nice, a wonderful rushing river, meadow with sheep and horses, mountains in the background, fine hiking and riding, and real quiet for work. The food is good, and they throw in three highballs an evening." There were two or three people there he liked, "a fine, crusty active old lady from Virginia, who charges up the mountains like a goat, and a young lady who is very charming and intelligent and good-looking, and the owner who is a decent enough fellow." There was another kind of pleasure in finishing his Conrad essay and sending it off to Albert Erskine on June 9.[22]

" 'The Great Mirage': Conrad and *Nostromo*"—over five thousand words long, with a biographical note and suggested readings—was one of the best critical essays he would ever write. He called *Nostromo* "Conrad's supreme effort." He named his central themes (so like his own): "themes of isolation and alienation, of fidelity and human solidarity, of moral infection and redemption, of the paradox of action and idea, of 'the true lie,' of the problem of history." He finally provided a general statement on this writer he so admired: "The philosophical novelist, or poet, is one for whom the documentation of the world is constantly striving to rise to the level of generalization about value, for whom the image strives to rise to symbol, for whom images always fall into a dialectical configuration, for whom the urgency of experience, no matter how vividly and strongly experience may enchant, is the urgency to know the meaning of experience." Editor John Palmer would print it in the summer number of *The Sewanee Review*, and it would appear in other places as well.[23]

Meanwhile his impatience with the divorce proceedings was growing. He wrote his sister-in-law that "one difficulty after another keeps emerging," but his time there had not been unpleasant. "The country is wonderful [and I] have met some nice people, especially a very attractive young woman here at the ranch, who goes climbing with me and on sight-seeing jaunts. . . ." At last, on June 28, his divorce was granted, on the ground of cruelty, with Cinina's alimony set at a thousand dollars a month. He had not expected the decree so soon. United Airlines was on strike, and so he took the train to Chicago. He stopped in Minneapolis to take his books and papers out of storage and to visit the Beaches. By early July he was back in his New York apartment.[24]

Cinina had been attending a seminar on Petrarch and Boccaccio in the Columbia University summer session, commuting from the hospital every day for four weeks. At the end of July she emerged at last, alone. She had been completely sober for almost a year and a half. She had been released into the custody of Helen Strauss. That fall, living on her alimony, she would take a small apartment just five blocks north of his. She continued with the novel she had started in the hospital and with her graduate work in order to teach again and make a new life. She and her former husband never met again.[25]

"I shall live in [Yale's] Silliman College permanently as a resident Fellow," he had informed Albert Erskine, finding it "a very satisfying arrangement—no apartment hunting, etc. Also, no rent and 75 free meals a term." He was ready for a holiday, and he showed it. A student remembered seeing him right after the divorce at "a huge gathering of all the *Partisan Review* notables and hangers-on," where "there was a clearing in the center of the huge room with the lectern at which [Arthur] Koestler was giving the big speech, and in that clearing stood a chair, and on it sat a man with a craggy face in the posture of pharaoh, thighs parallel to the floor, hands on knees, head straight up facing straight forward. All alone, surrounded by a circular space. . . . my impression in 1939 that RPW was the great rising star undoubtedly prepared the ground for my amazed contemplation of the Poet Himself in that Hieratic Attitude in 1951."[26]

His preparations that July for a departure for Europe were no more efficient than they had been a quarter of a century before. Commiserating with Pier Pasinetti over his "Kafka-esque" difficulties in obtaining a reentry permit, he told him, "I am involved in one of a milder order, having just emerged from the real thing during the last few months. I have suddenly definitely decided to go abroad, and I have lost my passport. Getting a new one is infinitely complicated. . . . They seem sure I've let mine get into the hands of a Soviet agent or something." A few days later he sailed for England alone, aged forty-six, single again after twenty-two years.[27]

FIVE

Remarriage, Fatherhood, and Renewal

30

❖

A New Life

And you, at the pier edge, face lifted seaward
And toward that abstract of distance that I
Yet was and felt myself to be, stood. Wind
Tugged your hair. It tangled that brightness. Over
Your breast wind tautened the blue cloth, your skirt
Whipped, the bare legs were brown. Steel rang on steel.
Shouts rang in that language.
Later,

The quiet place. Roses. Yellow. We came there, wind
Down now, sea slopping the rocks, slow, sun low and
Sea graying, but roses were yellow, climbing
The wall, it was stone. That last night
Came gliding a track across the gray water from westward.
It came leveling in to finger the roses. One
Petal, yellow, fell, slow.

—"The Faring"[1]

He was at loose ends in this period of healing. By mid-July he had
spent time in London, Oxford, and the country. He spent August on
the Riviera with a friend in "a pleasant spot not far from Nice and
had a very good month." It was an affair that continued during that
year, but one so discreetly managed that the friend's identity seems
unrecoverable, with little to be known other than that she was married and "apparently crazy about him." Later he would look back
upon this period of his life, at his unhappy marriage "and the stopgaps between" it and what was to come. This relationship was one of

the stopgaps. The whole trip had been a pleasant one, and when he returned in September he had six hundred consecutive lines of *Brother to Dragons* to show for it.[2]

Back in Connecticut, he proceeded to settle into his new life. In Silliman College he moved into the Resident Fellow's Suite, so large that it was called "the Gymnasium." He had taken an apartment in New York at 44 West Thirty-seventh Street, where he could go "when the atmosphere of extreme youth gets a little too clammy." For the present, however, the atmosphere was fine. "Red Warren is happily divorced," Katherine Anne Porter informed Eudora Welty in November, "and is a newly-born soul." John Crowe Ransom corroborated the report to Allen Tate. "Red made us a little visit about two weeks ago, just before Christmas in fact; on his way to see his father, who's not very strong. Red is in very fine fettle, evidently relieved of a terrible burden. He is doing a long poem, a real epic of Kentucky; better, I think, than any of his novels unless the first one."[3]

His personal life was undergoing a transformation. The long-blocked emotions had been flowing again, in the mountain-climbing with the young woman above the Donner Ranch and under the Riviera sun with the woman who was crazy about him. The powerful, long-repressed needs continued to make their claims. (Nearly forty years later Bid Brown confirmed for her daughter what had hitherto been only a family rumor—that she had rented a post office box in downtown Minneapolis where Red sent his letters to her, where she read them and then immediately destroyed them. After his divorce, she said, he asked her to elope with him, but in the end she could not make the break from Hunt.) Meanwhile, another relationship was maturing.[4]

He had known of Eleanor Clark before their 1944 Washington meeting from her submissions to *The Southern Review* and her review of *A Southern Harvest,* which he had edited for Houghton Mifflin. When he read it, he might have admired her independence of mind but not her sharp criticism of his introduction and most of the stories. But he had probably also read some of her poems, essays, and stories without knowing much about her life, an unusual and varied one for a young woman born in 1913, who also happened to be a Yankee.[5]

Grandfather John Bates Clark was a Heidelberg-educated philosopher who taught at Carleton College. Grandfather Charles Henry Phelps was an intellectual who joined the migrating forty-niners but managed to stay very poor as editor of the *Californian* and the *Over-land Monthly*. Frederick Huntington Clark was a mining engineer who married Eleanor Phelps and took her along to Guanajuato, Mexico. Their daughter Eunice was born there in 1911. His next job took them to Arizona, where he could indulge in hunting and fishing. But when he began to suffer from an asthmatic heart, they moved to Los Angeles in 1913, where Eleanor was born with her father seemingly on the verge of death. He never fully recovered, but he remained his charming self, a great talker and storyteller, a natural guitarist who could play and sing for hours without repeating himself. But his skills did not include managing money, and when he had it, he was likely to lose his shirt. It seemed to Eleanor as a child that they never had any money. Temperamentally unsuited, he and his wife separated and then divorced.[6]

Eleanor Phelps Clark managed to take her children to Italy, and by the time her namesake was eleven, she and her sister, two little brown-eyed blondes, were in an Ursuline convent school near San Remo where only French was spoken. Their mother left them there for a year while she went home, got a job teaching at Rosemary Hall, and bought a farm in Roxbury, Connecticut. Her own mother had been one of the first graduates of Vassar College, and she registered her two daughters for Vassar at birth. Eleanor finished at Rosemary Hall in three years, but Vassar wouldn't admit her at sixteen. So she spent a year in Italy studying music and Italian, and followed Eunice to college in the fall of 1930.[7]

Eunice and Eleanor bracketed the celebrated class of 1933, whose best-known member, Mary McCarthy, was already making a reputation for herself. They all wrote in the shadow of one student who had graduated seventeen years earlier: Edna St. Vincent Millay. Eunice and Eleanor were talented in languages and music, but their principal gift was for literature. By 1932 Eleanor was working on the school newspaper and writing essays on the work of Eliot, Auden, and other modernist poets and a great deal of poetry. She transferred to Barnard during her junior year but returned to Vassar and graduated in 1934.[8]

She moved to Greenwich Village, supporting herself precariously by freelance writing. Then one day she got up the nerve to enter the office of *The New Republic* and ask Malcolm Cowley for a book to review. He gave her one, and when she finished the review she went out and sold the book for supper money. She continued with her fiction and reviewing, and after two years of living hand-to-mouth she won a residency for the winter of 1936 at Yaddo, a community for artists and composers in Saratoga Springs, where she began work on a novel and made friends with other young writers such as John Cheever and Josephine Herbst. When she returned to the city she landed the job with W. W. Norton where she edited their *New Letters in America,* which included work by Cheever, Richard Eberhart, and a story of her own. She had the summers off, and in 1937, with *New Letters* in production, she wanted to get away from New York to concentrate entirely on her own writing. Her political activities paved the way.[9]

She had allied herself with the Trotskyists, and the year after she left Vassar she met Herbert Solow, a Zionist who had gone to Palestine only to be disgusted with what he saw. Then, before he returned home, a visit to Leon Trotsky in his exile in Turkey changed Solow's life. In 1937, living in a Mexico City suburb, Trotsky founded the Fourth International to propagate his program for world revolution. A circle of followers—secretaries, translators, and bodyguards—assisted him. In New York, the *Partisan Review* had been founded as an alternative to the Stalinist *New Masses.* Herbert Solow became a *Partisan Review* contributor, and Eleanor Clark did too. He recruited sympathetic intellectuals to join the Trotsky Defense Committee and arranged for their travel there. In that summer Mexico City appealed to Eleanor as a place to write among sympathetic friends.[10]

She was invited to Trotsky's home as soon as she arrived, and she returned often. She translated documents in French, which had been translated from Russian by Trotsky's secretaries. She completed short stories and other work begun at Yaddo. During these months she became close to a Czech Trotskyist named Jan Frankel, one of the most important of the secretaries. "I married Jan Frankel just to help him get a visa to enter the USA," she wrote her biographer, "as many were doing around that time (as Auden did for Thomas Mann's daughter Erika)." On their return to New York they were soon immersed in its literary politics, but the events of the summer had provided material for *Gloria Mundi,* a novel she would publish thirty years later. By 1938 she began to realize that she had drifted away from Trotskyist politics. She and Frankel went to Puerto Rico by freighter to stay for a while in a small fishing village. By winter they knew that they had drifted away not only from the radical left but from each other as well. Late in the winter they separated for good.[11]

The constant in her life was her work. Alone in Palisades, north of New York, translating, reviewing, and editing, "living on peanuts," she worked at her fiction. She was there for two and a half years. With America's entry into the war there were new jobs for people with language skills. The Foreign Nationalities Branch of the Office of Strategic Services monitored the foreign-language press and also interrogated European refugees. In the spring of 1943 she moved to Washington to work on the French desk, and later she was moved to the Italian desk. The next year, as Allen Tate's luncheon guest, she met Warren. "She was perfectly beautiful," he said. Tall and athletic with strong classical features, she might have modeled for a statue of Diana. Thinking she was Tate's girl, Warren made only polite conversation. (Ironically, she found Tate very unattractive physically.) She had admired Katherine Anne Porter's work and liked her enormously. When Katherine Anne invited her and Warren to a party there in Washington, they enjoyed each other's company, as they did again at Denis and Caren Devlin's parties.[12]

At the end of the war, with housing in New York tight, she "went and clawed my way into this fourth-floor tenement walk-up." There were two flats to a floor, with a Franklin stove and gas heat in the kitchen, where the bathtub "was a kitchen-sink kind of thing, with a toilet beyond." The location was 223 East Seventy-fifth Street between Second and Third avenues, where there were no buildings to block the view over the East River to the south. The rent was twenty-three dollars a month, and she grabbed it. She had another novel in mind, and so she turned to the Guggenheim Foundation. On her application she listed the novel she had worked on at Yaddo: *The Bitter Box,* of 1946. It told the story of a bank clerk who quits his job to work for the Communist party only to undergo disillusionment shared by many others. It gained several enthusiastic reviews. She received the Guggenheim, sublet the apartment, and booked passage on a freighter for Italy. But once there she was drawn to a quite different subject: a study of Rome and Emperor Hadrian's great villa.[13]

She worked on it through the end of her grant into 1948, not long deterred by the skiing accident that put her on crutches, and glorying in her good fortune when Frank Brown loaned her his *villino* at the American Academy. In that same year she spent time on Monte Argentario, which she had first glimpsed in the distance the day she had gone to see Brown's archeological excavation at Cosa. With the composer Alexei Haieff and the sculptor Isamu Noguchi she shared working quarters on La Rocca, the fort above Porto Ercole, where it was rugged and beautiful and cheap. In Rome her circle of friends had expanded to include Alberto Moravia and Elsa Morante, Ignazio Silone and his wife, Darina, and the scholar-critic Mario Praz. She would return to Italy by freighter again. With her talent and her looks, she made other distinguished friends over these years, Albert Camus among them, and others such as Louis MacNeice and St.-John Perse, who became devoted admirers.[14]

Eleanor and Warren had met again in these years, in Gambier, Rome, and New York. When she returned from Italy to Yaddo in the summer of 1951, she invited him to visit her there. And later, when he began teaching at Yale, "we drifted together." He began taking her to dinner. Still an avid skier, she would drive up to Vermont in her little old Plymouth coupe, and on one trip in early 1952 she stopped to see him in Silliman College. Then, after she checked in at the Green Mountain Inn in Stowe, she sent him an affectionate post-card. A few nights later he called and asked her to have dinner with him in New York. That dinner date was followed by others. When he took her home one early April night, she asked him in, and they walked up the four steep wooden flights of stairs. He sat in the comfortable chair, she on the stool before the little Franklin stove that spread its warmth in the cold room. They chatted and then fell silent. She was staring into the fire. Then he said, "I wonder how it would be if I kissed you." She said, "Well, you could try and see."[15]

The next day they took a subway uptown and then walked across the George Washington Bridge in the sunny spring morning. A week later they went on long walks again when she took him up to Roxbury to visit her mother. Eleanor had taken many boyfriends up there, but this visit was different. Eleanor Phelps Clark liked him at once. When the two returned to New York, he moved in with Eleanor on 223 East Seventy-fifth Street. It was April 11, 1952.[16]

Two days later the reviews of *Rome and a Villa* began appearing. Eleanor was embarrassed because Warren had earlier written a blurb for the book, and she thought some might now think it came from their relationship rather than his objective judgment. She need not have worried. Reviewers praised her brilliant impressionism and verbal polish. She was deeply knowledgeable about her subject, and her poetic prose conveyed the sense of the fountains and sunlight and beauty of the great city and the magnificence of Hadrian's vision. It was a book that would enchant generations of readers.[17]

By now, in spite of his teaching, Warren had three thousand lines of *Brother to Dragons*. He told Andrew Lytle, "I'm trying to raise this gruesome subject to some sort of symbolic and generalized level." Before he could finish, there was a trip he had promised his father. In Mexico City the old man surprised Warren with his vigor and curiosity, and they went on to Cuba. Of all their shared experiences, the son's most persistent recollection would be one of waking about three in the morning and hearing a faint sound from the other bed. In the dimness of the shuttered room Robert Franklin Warren was murmuring lines from "The Burial of Sir John Moore," the favorite he had recited so often in his son's childhood. At the end of the month they returned to Kentucky from this, their last trip together.[18]

Eleanor had been writing faithfully to Warren from La Rocca at Porto Ercole. "I just can't be away from you much longer," she told him. He told her he was flying to London, planning to cross to France on July 4. "I'll meet you at the Channel," she replied. "In fact if there were going to be any more delay beyond July 15 about the car I'd rather come to London than wait anymore for you because I just don't think I can do without you any longer than that. I'm not doing very well at it now." From Paris she took a train at dawn to Dieppe to meet his boat, but "there I was, and no Red." Finally he appeared, the last one off the boat. "It was summer, and the wind was blowing, and I had on a navy dress, and he always went on afterwards about how he'd come off the boat and was entranced by the way my skirt was blowing." They got into a small rented yellow car and drove to "a beautiful little place, Beules-Roses, a pension, with yellow roses." That night they had dinner "on the terrasse of the hotel, under a shower of yellow roses." From there they drove down to the southeast through France then into Italy along the Ligurian coast to Porto Ercole and La Rocca. It was a marvelous summer with the rugged beauty of Monte Argentario about them above the blue translucence of the sea they swam in, warmed by the sun pouring down from the cloudless sky. And she was free now, after the publication of *Rome and a Villa,* to begin new work. Finishing *Brother to Dragons,* Warren found he was able to write lyric poems once more.[19]

Back in their New York walk-up they basked in their happiness and worked at their craft. In late October he sent the bound manuscript of the big poem to Allen Tate, who had happily taken his place at the University of Minnesota. ("I get the largest salary in the department," he wrote Don Davidson, "a boon that I inherit from Red's tenure.") Though Warren was not teaching for the fall term, he was still accepting invitations to give lectures, and he prepared for one in Tennessee in early December. As winter approached Eleanor was feeling less her usual robust self and finally decided to go to the doctor. The reason for her symptoms, the doctor told her, was that she was pregnant. Warren was due to leave the next day, Sunday. He and Eleanor had not talked about marriage, but before he left they went out to Lexington Avenue and bought the ring. They would be married next Sunday, December 7.[20]

"Mother was really heroic on that occasion," Eleanor remembered, "because we just had only one week and she liked to do things rather grandly when possible. We intended to have a justice of the peace, but we couldn't because the JP in Roxbury was a Democrat and my mother wouldn't let him in the house. So we got this Congregational minister. We couldn't get the Episcopalian because we'd been divorced." Albert Erskine, now twice divorced, would be best man, and the matron of honor would be Katherine Anne Porter, now four times divorced—most recently from Albert—whose best man Warren had been. Eleanor drove herself and her groom up to Roxbury. Among the many guests were Tinkum and Cleanth Brooks, who were responsible for a slight delay. Cleanth took their dog, a friendly, impulsive mastiff named Pompey the Great, to the road to relieve himself. Just then Pompey saw something and lunged toward it, carrying Cleanth into an old barbed-wire fence, which cut his face and sent a trail of blood down his shirt. The wedding had to wait while Cleanth borrowed a shirt from the groom. "Mother put on a very nice wedding," the bride said. "I had the best husband in the world and our fulfillment with each other was wonder, glory, joy—non-stop . . . love and luck and joy that fell to me, beyond my merit or expectation." He would record his joy in many poems.[21]

Their honeymoon, interrupted by his classes, was spent in a borrowed house in Westport. As a married man he would no longer be eligible for his quarters in Silliman College. And Eleanor had been informed that the city was going to have her apartment building torn down. They had to find a house and prepare themselves—she at thirty-nine and he at forty-seven—for their new lives and parenthood.[22]

31

❖

Homestead and
Watershed

I had long lived in the world of action and liability.
But now I passed the gate and entered a world
Sweeter than hope in that confirmation of late light.
                                    —*Brother to Dragons*[1]

Shortly after their marriage, Eleanor suggested a trip to Guthrie. She
wanted to meet her in-laws and to find a place where their children
could know the world that meant so much to their father. Thomas
Warren gave a party for his brother and his bride, and it delighted
Warren to see his father and Eleanor seated close together deep in
conversation. But he would take home an unhappy memory too.
Thomas had persuaded his father to take over the office work of his
prosperous business, but the old man refused his sons' offer to build a
little house for him and rented a drab room in town. Now he informed them that he had arranged to go into a "retirement home" in
Clarksville. It was another evidence of his self-control but also, his
elder son thought, evidence of the "crazy pride" that dictated the
lonely meals and solitary walks.[2]

   Though the visit had to be a quick one, they looked at a promising farm, but the whole country had changed too much. The other
search back east was more pressing. They couldn't find anything until
one day when they were driving along winding backcountry Connecticut roads bordered by stone fences at the edges of pastures and
woodland. They had decided to look at a place one of Eleanor's
friends had mentioned in Fairfield County not far from Long Island

Sound. On a brief straightaway along Redding Road they glimpsed it: a barn with a herd of dairy cattle clustered about it. As they passed it they slowed down. "That's it!" they said.[3]

This was not going to be an ordinary remodeling job. The barn, housing thirty dairy cows, had been built in two stages, the first probably in the late 1700s, the second, in the early 1800s. Warren proudly told Lon Cheney, "It is none of your antique ruins. It is a fine upstanding modern barn, tight as a drum and sound as the Metropolitan Life Insurance Company. It is, however, built on an old first-story of stone, wonderful stone work, etc. And the timbers are fine ones, beautifully hewn and pegged, etc. . . . So we combine just enough antiquity without its swaying-in-the-wind inconvenience." They would build their house inside the massive structure. There was the spacious area, supported by beams hewn from single trees, that would become their main floor, and the expanse below, which they reached by climbing down a ladder to the floor, where the stone walls would enclose the kitchen and the long dining room with its wide-mouthed fireplace. There was another barn close by with stalls for horses. These spaces would become their studies, with a whole floor above them for whatever else they devised.[4]

They put down earnest money, applied for a mortgage, and moved ahead as rapidly as they could. An old friend at the Yale School of Architecture agreed to consult with them, and they hired a young local architect to do the design work and supervise construction. In June the mortgage was approved. They set to work chipping off what Eleanor thought was a couple hundred years of whitewash. Then they painted the whole inside, their voices echoing in the huge space upstairs. Ahead was not just the bang and clatter as walls and pipes went in, but more painting and decorating for Eleanor and carpentry for her husband. It was to be a house for work and for pleasure, a house for lifetimes, strong and unique, like the builders themselves.[5]

In the heat of July, Eleanor's bulkiness exempted her from the exhausting labor alongside Warren, but she was busy keeping house in a series of rented cottages. Then, on the twenty-fifth, she began feeling pains. They drove to nearby Bridgeport Hospital, but it proved a false alarm, and after two days she was sent home. On the twenty-seventh Eleanor prepared a late dinner. It was ten-thirty, Warren would remember, when she "had sat down to eat, had then confessed to feeling unwell, and then within something not much longer than Jack Robinson, Rosanna was there." It was "very gory and scary." Disaster was averted as "a neighbor got in just in time to hold Eleanor while I took the baby." At that moment a guest arrived: Andrew Lytle, who remembered Warren's excitement at delivering his own child. When he told the telephone operator in great agitation that it was an emergency and they needed an ambulance now, she told him he was being rude and hung up. Neighbors called the police, and "then the very ignorant little group huddled together on the floor for twenty-five minutes till a doctor, closely followed by cops with an ambulance, arrived." Just then their pediatrician came, and mother and child were hurried off to Bridgeport. On the way the speeding ambulance collided with another vehicle, but the driver made it to the hospital. When Warren pulled up behind, the driver stood leaning against his machine in an attitude of dejection. When Warren asked if everything was all right, he answered, "She'll never be the same." The new father raced inside to check on his family. (One of Warren's LSU students quoted Cleanth Brooks as saying that it was "just God's revenge on Red for writing so many melodramas.")[6]

At the hospital he waited for what seemed two hours without word. It was just as well that he did not know what was happening—and what was not happening. He told Pier Pasinetti that "Eleanor had a very rough time after the event with some hundred stitches needing to be taken as a result of the explosive entry of Rosanna." This took two or three hours, Eleanor remembered, while Red was pacing up and down, watching the door of the maternity ward. Women were ringing for nurses, and nurses, she said, were playing cards. But because Rosanna had been born outside the hospital she was not admitted to the maternity ward. Then, Eleanor learned, "this angel pediatrician decided to check on the baby one more time before he went home and went up to the third floor. She was turning blue, with nobody paying any attention to her." Warren told Pier, "The baby almost died, [but] some two hours of work and then incubation got her around."[7]

Later, with Rosanna Phelps Warren well out of danger, Eleanor remembered her husband "just crowing with glee: 'I'm a father! I'm a father!' " Five days later he told Pier, "she is just out of the incubator and is in fine shape. Very beautiful and well formed, even if a trifle undersized. Eleanor is feeble, but still feels well." He scrawled a postscript: "By the way, fatherhood is not over-rated. I recommend it highly."[8]

Caring for their new baby in their rented cottage, they got on with their work at their desks as well as in their barns, Eleanor on a novel that would eventually bear the title *Baldur's Gate,* and Warren on a variety of projects. And as he wrote his friends in early August describing the arrival of Rosanna, so others were writing about the arrival of his other child, whose gestation had taken nine years. Published in an edition of just under five thousand copies, *Brother to Dragons* ran to over two hundred pages. Like *World Enough and Time,* it was based on bloody events in Kentucky history. It too began with a page of quotation for an epigraph, but then came a foreword, an author's note, and a list of "THE SPEAKERS *in the order of appearance.*"[9]

In childhood he had heard a garbled version of the story: on the night of December 15, 1811, when the cataclysmic New Madrid earthquake hit the Mississippi Valley, Lilburne Lewis and his brother, Isham, murdered a slave in a particularly horrible manner. Warren learned nothing more about the case until the year before he went to the Library of Congress. Then, in 1944, he found references in old newspapers there. Two years later came the automobile trip to Smithland with his father when he climbed up to Rocky Hill for a sense of the physical reality of Dr. Charles Lewis's home.[10]

He found the records in dusty courthouse files, musty rolls of foolscap tied with fading ribbon. But the events were still alive in local memory. So he continued the research begun in the Library of Congress. What caught his fancy now was a philosophical point of entry into this horror story that made it more than simply Grand Guignol: Lilburne and Isham Lewis were nephews of Thomas Jefferson. How did the author of the Declaration of Independence, the "architect of our country and the prophet of human perfectability," react to this atrocity by blood kinsmen? What impact would it have had upon his whole concept of man nourished by his humanist deism? None of the authorities Warren consulted knew of any reference Jefferson made to the affair. Clearly though, he could not have *not* known about his sister's sons and the sequence of deaths they caused. Warren would have to imagine the answers, and therein would lie the heart of *Brother to Dragons.*[11]

He wrestled not only with content—philosophical, psychological, historical—but with form too, through the second visit to Rocky Hill with his father in December of 1951 and on through the revisions of *The Kenyon Review* version a year after that. Early on, when he had thought the poem would resemble "The Ballad of Billie Potts," he wrote three lines in ballad form but abandoned it. Putting the material in the form of a novel would not provide the structure he wanted. As he had done in dramatizing *All the King's Men,* he sought out a collaborator (whose name does not appear in any of his correspondence), but that did not work either. As he had used a chorus in *Proud Flesh,* so he now thought of using Jefferson to comment on the action, but his role loomed disproportionately large. It would have to be a poem in some sort of hybrid form. But what to call it? He settled on *A Tale in Verse and Voices.* He would variously employ blank verse and free verse. The tone and diction would be alternately poetic and literal, rhetorical and colloquial. The line following the list of "Speakers" read simply, "PLACE: *No Place*   TIME: *Any time*" (p. 3). They meet, he explained in his author's note, "to try to make sense of . . . the main body of the action [which occurred] in the remote past." Jefferson would be a speaker himself, not a chorus-commentator. And helping him and the others to understand these actions would be another speaker, "R.P.W.: *The writer of this poem*" (p. 2).[12]

He altered the basic material to meet his needs, omitting some historical personages and inventing fictitious ones. The motivation would be a study in psychopathology appropriate to the horror to come. He made the narrative line clear to support the complexity of philosophical discourse. A physician and planter, Charles Lewis has "fled" from Virginia to the wild frontier, finding the comfortable old world intolerable and seeking in the new world "tension and test, perhaps terror," in an effort to renew "the dear illusion, lost in youth, of being / Some part of human effort and man's hope" (p. 13). But at the outset he admits to Jefferson and to R.P.W. that he had lied to himself and had built the house while concealing his own emptiness. Called mad by some, he tells the two that, if he was mad, in his case "madness is but the cancer of truth, the arrogance / Of truth gone wild and swollen in the blood" (p. 12). Thus two of the prime forces of the drama are introduced: pride, which can corrupt man's actions, and truth, which can help him to understand and to cope with the evil that is a part of the human condition and to retain hope in spite of it.[13]

In effect, Charles Lewis kills his wife, Lucy Jefferson, by uprooting her from her beloved Albemarle and transporting her to Rocky Hill, there in the forest, where her sons grow and change year by year—one into a brutal sadist and the other into an inarticulate lout—and where she languishes and dies, just before the climactic events. If heredity helps to explain to the father the actions of his sons, it can only horrify the uncle, even if he chooses to believe that all of the evil propensities came from Charles Lewis and none from Lucy Jefferson. If nature is at fault in creating the man Lilburne Lewis becomes, so too is nurture. Adored by both his mother and his wet nurse and mother surrogate, Aunt Cat, he is unable truly to give love as opposed to the obsessive, Oedipal-seeming fixation he has upon Lucy Lewis. He turns his loving wife, angelic Letitia, into a neurasthenic invalid. Forcing himself upon her in an unnatural act, he later compels her not only to describe it but also to say that, in part at least, she enjoyed it. (He tells her, "Now I see when angels / Come down to earth, they step in dung, like us. / And like it" [p. 80].) A sometime tavern drunkard, he beats the slave George, sent to bring him home, so brutally that Lucy, unable to fulfill her impulse to pity and succor the victim, dies in the aftermath of this final manifestation of her worst fears: the savage transformation of her son. Then, obsessed with his mother's death and the affronts to her fading memory—not only in the slaves' disrespect for her possessions but even in the encroachment of the grass upon her grave—Lilburne objectifies the guilt and creates the scapegoat for his hatred in the person of the ill-fated George.

Lilburne sends him to the spring with his mother's loved pitcher and a dire threat should anything happen to it. Then, telling Isham to wake the slaves and bring them to the meat house and make a fire, he follows George into the night. When the two return, George holding the handle of the shattered pitcher, Lilburne orders him bound for his fatal mishap and placed on the "whopping tree" in the meat house, where he will suffer a premeditated ritual dismemberment and death. Lilburne harangues the slaves about their offenses, then raises the meat-ax to chop off first the disobedient hands that had made his mother "grieve," then the feet that had once run away from Rocky Hill. Cast into the flames, the butchered body burns until the earthquake sends the chimney collapsing upon the fire. The remains are buried until Lilburne's abused hound unearths the jawbone. Carried to town, it leads to conviction for murder. His madness growing, Lilburne talks Isham into a suicide pact, only to trick him into shooting first and thus becoming his brother's murderer. Like Jeremiah Beaumont, Isham is jailed but escapes and makes his way south, only to die in the battle of New Orleans.

The tale in verse and voices moves complexly, interrupted by argument, commentary, and (in a familiar Warren strategy) two substantial digressions. They are the very personal narrative of R.P.W. reflecting upon the events and their echoes in his own life. He took his biggest risks in the creation of a Thomas Jefferson unlike any other in biography or history. The venerated hero is here presented, according to one Warren admirer, as "a completely, even outrageously, fictional character . . . a man who has systematically repudiated every belief the actual man held in life: [who] speaks like a man on the edge of frenzy."[14]

The poem's title symbolically indicates the underlying causes of Jefferson's anguish. They are the words of Job in the depths of his loss and humiliation: "I am a brother to dragons and a companion to owls" (Job, 30:29). But as one of the poem's best commentators points out, these are words not of self-abnegation but rather of Job's resentment against God in the fullness of his injured pride and anger over unmerited suffering. "Both men lacked, in Warren's estimation, the sense of limitation which is essential to the religious attitude. Both thought themselves freed, by dint of an absolute virtue, from the common human contamination." In "Original Sin: A Short Story," Warren employed the monstrous imagery of nightmare. So too *Brother to Dragons* similarly employs the title's controlling image reinforced by two others both ancient and powerful: the Minotaur and the snake.[15]

In Jefferson's first substantive speech, he employs the image of the monstrous Minotaur in his labyrinth, half man and half bull, as he acknowledges his own pridefulness in the threefold "boast" of the epitaph he composed for himself. He recalls the first boast, his authorship of the Declaration of Independence, but now he thinks of his fellow delegates to the Second Constitutional Convention as men in essence but animals too, each lost in some labyrinth of his own. There "the beast waits . . . He is / Our brother, our darling brother" (pp. 6–7). Revolted at Lilburne's crime ("the death / Of all my hope" [p. 132]) and rejecting his kinship with him, Jefferson is taken to task by both his sister and his cousin, Meriwether Lewis. Lucy tells him that if he "would assume the burden of innocence," he must take Lilburne's hand "and recognize, at last, / That his face is only a mirror of your possibilities. . . ." (p. 191). More crushing words come from Meriwether Lewis, sent by Jefferson with William Clark to open the Louisiana Territory and plot the path to the Pacific. Disillusioned during the expedition by the behavior of both his men and the savages, he becomes governor of the territory, only to be accused of corruption and driven to take his own life in despair. Standing there now, in this Grand Guignol scene, his head gaping from his death wound, he tells his cousin, the great Jefferson, that he was "murdered by your lie. / It

was your lie that sent me forth, in hope" (p. 177). Other acerbic lines
are exchanged as a sharp-tongued R.P.W. argues with a distraught Jefferson about the meaning of the Lewis tragedy.[16]

But there is resolution at the end for both men. After her disquisition on human complicity in evil, Lucy Lewis tells her brother that his
dream was noble, but "there's a nobler yet to dream." And Jefferson
responds, "Without the fact of the past we cannot dream the future"
(p. 193). He utters his last words in a final acceptance: "Nothing we
were, / Is lost. / All is redeemed, / In knowledge" (pp. 195–96).
The resolution for R.P.W. is both more extended and more personal,
with a final affirmation that reinforces that of Jefferson: "The recognition of complicity is the beginning of innocence. / The recognition
of necessity is the beginning of freedom" (pp. 214–15). Reminiscent
of the reborn Jack Burden, he makes his way down from Rocky Hill
toward the parked car. Then: "I opened the sagging gate, and was prepared / To go into the world of action and liability" (p. 215).[17]

Waiting for him there is his father. R.P.W.'s remarks about him
reflect Warren's feeling for the parent preparing now to leave
Guthrie after fifty years to enter the retirement home in Tennessee. A
poignant memory leads to an avowal of love:

> . . . in a café once, when an old friend said,
> "Tell me about your father," my heart suddenly
> Choked on my words, and in the remarkable quiet
> Of my own inwardness and coil, light fell
> Like one great ray that gilds the deepest glade,
> And thus I saw his life a story told,
> Its glory and reproach domesticated,
> And for one moment felt that I had come
> To that most happy and difficult conclusion:
> To be reconciled to the father's own reconciliation.
>
> It is most difficult because that reconciliation
> Costs the acceptance of failure. . . . (pp. 27–28)[18]

R.P.W. supplies a brief portrait of the artist as he might have been
perceived on that first visit:

A fellow of forty, a stranger, and a fool,
Red-headed, freckled, lean, a little stooped,
Who yearned to be understood, to make communication. . . . (p. 26)

A meditation on the second visit, five years later, in December of 1951, reflects something of the artist's emotional history as he thinks of "another year and another winter" and a scene enacted elsewhere:

> I think how her mouth and mine together
> Were cold on the first kiss. Sparsely, snow
> Descended among the black trees. We kissed in the cold
> Logic of hope and need. It was not joy.
> Later, the joy. Or if not joy, the keen
> Appetitive spur and that delicious delusion.

But then comes a tonal change:

> Since then I have made new acquaintance with snow on the brown
> leaves
> Since then I have made new acquaintance with the nature of joy.
> (p. 209)

The reviews that summer and fall—of this demanding two-hundred-page poem costing $3.50—were welcome. In the prestigious newspapers that could make or break a book, it did well. It was called a major work, which showed his mastery of his craft, even his best book. To a few magazine reviewers it was turgid and long-winded, but for others it held echoes of Melville and Dante and constituted that rare achievement, a successful long poem. It clearly represented a turning point in Warren's career, accomplishing for his poetry what *All the King's Men* did for his fiction. It is remarkable for its use of crucial philosophical issues in American history. His attempt to render the sweep of history, which had earlier prompted references to classic ages, focused powerfully now on the American past. At the same time, with its two glimpses of Smithland, in contrast with the grandeur of the land Lewis and Clark traversed, the poem recalled the *Waste Land* view of the modern world. In poetry to come he would take up again themes and motifs explored here: the beckoning West, the violence of the world of frontiersmen and Indians, and the capacity for evil that produced the monstrousness of slavery and incipient genocide. Carrying him further from the formalism of the earlier poetics and giving rein to the dramatic impulse he had felt increasingly, it would bring more flexibility to his poetic style, moving it toward greater openness and personal revelation. His language kept pace with the thematic enlargement. Relying more now upon the polyphony of voices, his verse was capable of a directness that complemented the rhetoric. Added pungency came from explicit sexual language. There was also something at the end not often present in earlier work: hope.[19]

Through the late summer they commuted from rented cottages to Redding Road, where they would take up their tools and work with Rosanna nearby in her basket, the cows licking the salt from the backs of the sweating workmen. As fall came they were hoping to move in by December 21. Warren wrote Andrew Lytle, "We have spent every minute of our spare time working on the place, chopping whitewash, planting trees, painting, etc. We are doing all the interior painting ourselves. It's strictly an economy measure but we both like work like that, and it's fun, too. Rosanna is a most whimsical straw-boss. . . ." He was the most doting of fathers, and for the rest of his life his letters would often contain rhapsodic accounts. "As for our little project," he told Andrew in early December, "she is no longer the little bewildered tomato you saw through the glass. She is over fourteen pounds now, twenty-five inches long, and is a fantastic combination of a steam calliope and divine beauty and diabolic wit. She really is." She had her first Christmas there in Fairfield.[20]

His other project was growing too. In mid-July he had sent Albert Erskine the thirteen-thousand-word first chapter of the new novel, and he finished the second not long after. Just as *Brother to Dragons* connected with other work, so this novel did too, in an even more comprehensive way. One strand led back to *All the King's Men,* perhaps by way of the play he and Robert Rossen had fashioned from it under the title *The Wedding Ring.* In his brief "note on chronology" he wrote that the action in this "historical play" begins in Kentucky the day after John Brown's raid at Harpers Ferry. In this expansion of *All the King's Men*'s Cass Mastern subplot, Warren attempted to broaden the play's relevance through references to slavery and the coming of the Civil War. Then, in the climactic scenes of the third act—in which Phebe, the mulatto maid of Annabelle (now Arabella) Trice, is sold to a slave trader who kills Cass when Cass provokes a quarrel—Arabella's madness rises to a hysteria that suggests an aria from grand opera or the intensity of Elizabethan revenge tragedy.[21]

Another strand also derived from *All the King's Men:* the female slave on the auction block. At the time when he was working on the

Cass Mastern story he learned of another tragic tale from Kentucky, a true one. In the years before the Civil War a wealthy white man sent his two little girls to be educated in Oberlin. They were young women when he died. Returning home to Lexington they learned that all of his assets were seized to satisfy his debts. More than that: They were among the assets. Light enough to pass for white in Ohio, they were in fact part black. The next day they were sold on the block on Cheapside by the courthouse door. The highest bidder, as Warren later wrote, was "a gambler who took them South and sold them to a very 'discriminating' buyer of New Orleans. That is the last we know of them." Their father had never told them of their lineage. "I suppose what made this story stick in my mind for some years was the questions it did not answer. This affectionate father, who had done so much for the happiness of his children, who certainly had never profitted and had no intention of profitting from ownership—why had he not set them legally free? A stroke of the pen would have done it." Warren had determined to write a book that would answer these questions. The imagined analogue for the two nameless girls became Amantha Starr, and her story, *Band of Angels.*[22]

In February the Warrens took their daughter to see her grandfather in Guthrie in time for his eighty-fifth birthday. After their stop in Gambier, John Ransom said, "They are supremely happy, Red is a changed man." Then they decided on a skiing expedition while the Vermont slopes were still good. At Stowe Eleanor went off to the trails while Warren headed for the beginners' slopes. By the time darkness fell he had failed to return to the inn. At last she found that he was in a small hospital some miles away. He had gotten his skis crossed, fallen off the tow rope, and broken his leg. After several days he was permitted to shift into a wheelchair and thence into Eleanor's car for the journey home.[23]

By the last day of April the cast was cut down. "Now with my knee free I can saw wood again," he told Charlie Foster, "and so shall plunge into the shelf-building for the library." They were also working on a room to match Rosanna's "in fond hope of Danny Penn to come along." But they were torn. The available time and money could go to the house—or to a return to Italy, where Eleanor's claim on her place at La Rocca might not last until another year. Italy won, and by June they were on their way.[24]

32

❖

Entrances and Exits

> We have brought you where geometry of a military rigor survives
> its own ruined world,
> And sun regilds your gilt hair, in the midst of your laughter.
> Rosemary, thistle, clutch stone. Far hangs Giannutri in blue air.
> Far to that blueness the heart aches,
> And on the exposed approaches the last gold of gorse bloom, in the
>   sirocco, shakes.
>   — *"To a Little Girl, One Year Old, in a Ruined Fortress (I: Sirocco)"*[1]

Their arrival at La Rocca had something of the quality of films made in Rome's Cinecittà. "When we got there," Warren wrote Edward Davison, "we found that the road up to the fortress was closed and had to walk up . . . up through the precipitous village, then up the near-cliff, toting Rosey-Posey, followed by all the urchins and a lot of baby-loving old women. When we got to the top, there was another gang, all wanting to pinch, poke, dandle, kiss, and scream at Rosey-Posey in a frenzy of the national disease of baby-loving. So Rosanna just up and fainted to escape."[2]

"The Rocca is quite a fine place," he wrote Andrew Lytle.

Philip II of Spain built it, a big fortress on an island connected by a causeway to the mainland. It's on a sea-cliff, sea on three sides, incredible views of sea and distant islands, mountain behind us on the island, lagoons and beaches below, wild flowers all over. We have the watch house for our studies, the highest and most private part, most lately used by the Nazis for the original purpose. It has two rooms, a terrace; so we can work here without disturbing each other. . . . In the next and lower courtyard we have a converted stable (which E fixed up when she first came here) as a salone, a wonderful big beamed and whitewashed room, barred window over the ruined garden full of palm, pine, and oleander. Bedrooms in still lower court. We are surrounded by squalor, and our own life is a combination of three parts Jeeter Lester and one-part technicolor late Renaissance life of ruined princelings.

It was a good place for work. "We are in a very strict routine," he wrote Lon Cheney. "Work nine till two, lunch, swim, dandle baby, a drink before dinner, reading. The only thing wrong is that there's a lot more baby-dandling than I indicate. . . . E has run off twice this morning to do some bootleg baby-dandling when she ought to have been earning the baby's living. I am of sterner stuff."[3]

His poems were flowing once again, and in late July he completed one he might well have read to her. He called it "To a Little Girl, One Year Old, in a Ruined Fortress," and dedicated it *"To Rosanna."* Like Yeats's poems to his infant daughter and son, it was full of harsh images.[4] He set the scene first:

> To a place of ruined stone we brought you, and sea-reaches.
> *Rocca:* fortress, hawk-heel, lion-paw, clamped on a hill.
> A hill, no. On a sea cliff, and crag-cocked, the embrasures
> commanding the beaches, . . .[5]

But then, after a glance at history, he painted a landscape whose rich hues complemented the love in the lines for his child. It was to be the first in a sequence of five poems he would call "Sirocco." The long drought was over in which no lyric poems had flowered. As the mask had fallen from his face, so his heart had been freed of the constriction that had choked them. In the climate of love that he had found with Eleanor, the magic of Italy had helped to produce the flowering.

For all his joy, his fundamental view of the human condition and most human expectations had not changed. He had described a family of peasants living in abject squalor, "crawling with children, one child scabbed and defective, carried around all day by an eleven year old sister who has the face of a saint and a beauty like the dawn." In "The Child Next Door," he described them, how the sister had taught the other to crook a hand in greeting and say *ciao*. The poet

thinks of "the malfeasance of nature" and "the filth of fate," then focuses again on the elder sister in the last lines:

> I think of your goldness, of joy, how empires grind, stars are hurled.
> I smile stiff, saying *ciao,* saying *ciao,* and think: *This is the world.*[6]

This would be the third poem in the sequence. Between it and the
one to Rosanna he would place another called "Gull's Cry." Here the
poet glances at land, sea, and mountain. He hears the defective child,
who cried all night and now squats in the dust. He sees the *gobbo,* the
hunchback, and his wife. Then suddenly his daughter's voice cuts
through this reverie:

> But at your laughter let the molecular dance of the stone-dark
>   glimmer like joy in the stone's dream,
> And in that moment of possibility, let *gobbo, gobbo's* wife, and us, and all,
>   take hands and sing: *redeem, redeem!*[7]

   August was a full month, with visits that brought forth the best efforts of Ernesta, the resourceful factotum of the castle's miserly owner
but also the Warrens' cook. "If it weren't for the cliff and the [deep-
knee] bends and the swimming I'd be a tub," he told Pier Pasinetti.
His daughter was thriving. "She is, I swear it, incredibly beautiful,
gold hair, curly, brook-brown eyes, lovely features, lots of gaiety and
tricks and grins. . . . She'll be distressed to get home and away from
the Italian genius for babies. . . ."[8]
   This ambience and emotion got into the last two poems of the sequence. In "The Flower" the poet carries his child up the hill after
their afternoon at the beach. It is late, but there is still time to pluck
the ritual flower for her hair. The poem's hundred-plus, irregularly
rhyming lines, many of them couplets, provide a loving, elegiac summing up:

> Let season and season devise
> Their possibilities
> Let the future reassess
> All past joy, and past distress,
> Till we know Time's deep intent,
> And the last integument
> Of the past shall be rent

> To show how all things bent
> Their energies to that hour
> When you first demanded your flower.[9]

Then, in "Colder Fire," in thirteen quatrains combining free verse and formal rhyme, the poet speaks to his child, sitting on his knee there in the watchtower above the sweep of their summer land, and tells her,

> I cannot interpret for you this collocation
> Of memories. You will live your own life, and contrive
> The language of your own heart, but let that conversation,
> In the last analysis, be always of whatever truth you would live.[10]

Her parents had accomplished a good deal. Besides the poems, Warren had finished the draft of his novel and Eleanor was well into her novel too. They wanted Pier Pasinetti to visit them there in their special place. "We expect to get back next year unless we get another bambino, or *a*, as we hope. Not yet in sight."[11]

Back in Fairfield in mid-September, Warren had to deal again with the familiar priorities. "I'm now back in the academic harness and find it more galling than usual," he wrote Andrew Lytle. "Now and then I steal a little time for hammering and sawing, but I don't steal any time for the typewriter." He and Eleanor had not been able to do as much planting as they had planned for their three acres, but they had still done a good deal inside and out. It was well that they had, for the late fall and early winter were not only busy, but also a physically and emotionally draining time of ups and downs. As classes came to an end Warren was ready to begin revising *Band of Angels* and preparing a new edition of *Understanding Fiction*. They were expecting Andrew Lytle during Christmas, and sometime during the new year they were expecting Danny Penn, or "Eleanor if it's a girl."[12]

They had a good Christmas, but then the troubles commenced. In late December, while they were lunching with friends in New York, Eleanor felt queasy. She excused herself and went out to the street for some fresh air. When Warren looked out the window he couldn't see her. Outside he found her where she had fallen, hitting her head on a stone stair. Unconscious, bleeding from the nose and mouth, she had suffered a concussion and a skull fracture. The doctor wouldn't touch her "until he had some guarantee of his fee," Warren wrote Arnold Stein. "I could have murdered him." She was hospitalized for several days. Back at home, she had lingering headaches, but still she managed to put on a dinner, three days after New Year's, for the Brookses, Allen Tate, and Randall Jarrell.[13]

When they had visited Kentucky with Rosanna, they had gone to see Robert Franklin Warren in his Clarksville retirement home, and in their last glimpse he was looking out at them from his sitting-room window. By fall, close to eighty-six years old, he had weakened further: "no apparent disease, just giving in." Then, on January 14, Warren was wakened by a call from Thomas. "Father is bad off," he said. He was still alive when Warren reached Clarksville. After Christmas he had remained cheerful in spite of pain and the knowledge that he was dying of prostate cancer. "It developed that he had known of the disease for a year but had not told any of the family, or anybody else for that matter. He was just seeing things out his own way, a very characteristic way, not even taking any drugs until the last few days. I think it is a kind of craziness, but it is a pretty impressive craziness."[14]

They told him what had happened. "He had collapsed the evening before while writing a letter and had fallen from his chair, unconscious. Later, when he became conscious, injections had relieved obviously intense pain. Now unconscious, he occasionally moved. Once, as though by remarkable effort, his right arm slowly rose in the air, and the hand moved as though trying to grasp something." Then the arm fell. Warren watched, his sister clutching his arm, as life ebbed away. After the doctor wrote out the certificate, Warren went into the sitting room where the unfinished letter lay on the desk. Across the sheet was a downward stroke trailing from the last word, apparently made as he fainted and fell. "I looked at the scarcely begun letter. It began: 'Dear Son.' "[15]

Warren returned home to find no surcease from their trials. The day he left for Tennessee, Eleanor had fallen again, and her back was so painful that she could find relief only by lying on the floor. She had wrenched her spine, suffering a slipped disk. By late January, fitted with a brace, she was well enough to receive visitors. One was her father, now in his late seventies but charming and companionable as ever. Frederick Huntington Clark had invested an inheritance from his mother wisely, and now, with the Warrens pressed with the expense of the house and Cinina's alimony, he was able to help them.

When he came from his New York hotel for a visit he and Warren would sit and talk for hours.

With teaching over until September, Warren was doing his usual juggling act with plays and textbook revision. If he needed psychological gearing up for the labor of correcting the galley proofs of *Band of Angels,* the Literary Guild's selection of the book for September provided it. As for the house, "We are trying to get a lot done by midsummer, but feel somewhat like salmon trying to swim upstream in sorghum molasses." But swim he did. The galleys came, and he had them corrected before the end of April. At the same time they were finishing the baby's room and putting additional touches on the guest room. Eleanor's father came to occupy it again. Frederick Phelps was totally unliterary, but he had an extraordinary memory. To Warren's fascination, he could reel off the names of all the sails on famous vessels, such as the Baltimore Clippers. Warren questioned him closely because one of the principal characters in *Band of Angels* captained one of them. On this visit Mr. Phelps fell ill, and when he returned from the hospital he spent his convalescence with them. Eleanor was having problems with help, which she needed doubly now during this pregnancy, for her father as well as her daughter. But still she managed, so that her husband was able to tell the Owsleys, "Eleanor is in the middle of a novel, Connecticut, contemporary, not Rome."[16]

With their trees and shrubs putting out blooms in the spring sunlight, they were looking ahead to the summer. First would come the baby and then, in August, the novel. But in late May they found suddenly that they could not yet breathe easily. "Eleanor had a little scare about Danny Penn night before last," Warren told Lon Cheney, "but all now seems to be in order, and I'm breathing easy again. But crossing my fingers." There were no more premature pains, but by mid-July they had decided to move to a friend's house in New Haven on the twentieth to be close to the hospital.[17]

They waited one day too long. At four o'clock in the morning "Eleanor woke up, complained of a slight indisposition, suddenly decided that it might not be an indisposition but something else. We leaped to the car, and broke all records to New Haven, twenty-three miles away. Ten minutes more and we couldn't have made it. Eleanor hung on, and was awful sick in the car, but just a little more and it would have been a roadside event. But we did make the hospital, and by breakfast time. . . . Gabriel Penn arrived [after less] than twenty minutes in the delivery room. . . . Gabriel Penn is very handsome and healthy and appallingly well behaved." The father and mother had no anxiety about the baby's reception by his sister. They wanted to show him off to their friends, and "speaking of showing things off, Rosanna is the most stupendous beauty of the age, or any age. It is staggering. We begin to get worried. Things go well now with us all reassembled."[18]

Warren's other child, *Band of Angels,* made its formal appearance on August 22 in an edition of twenty-five thousand copies, with ten thousand more to come in late September. Reviews came early so that Warren was able to give Andrew Lytle a report on August 16. "It's getting—as far as you can see at this point—a good start in the world. Lead review (enthusiastic) in Times book Review, cover and lead in Sat Review (review short of enthusiastic), cover and fine review in Chicago Tribune Books. Wishy-washy reviews in Harpers and Atlantic. No indication of daily NY papers yet. Expect a bum review from daily Times. & from Time. and New Yorker." He did not say why he expected the bum reviews.[19]

The donnée of the book—why had Amantha Starr's loving father not provided papers freeing her?—drove the plot, and the question was answered in the novel's last pages, but the writing involved the creation not only of a large cast of characters but of specific nineteenth-century historical milieus as well: abolitionism, slavery, plantation life, the Civil War, Reconstruction, the Gilded Age, and the movement west. His earlier writings fed into this new work, but he had also done research on subjects as diverse as the influence of the doctrine of sanctification at Oberlin College in 1858 and the practice of privateering during the Civil War. It was indeed a historical novel.[20]

Most of the fictional characters, however, are emblematic of a type. Amantha, little Manty, is even more—initially the planter's pampered daughter and then the archetypal victim. The others are easily recognizable: Aaron Pendleton Starr, the prosperous widowed planter; Seth Parton, the Oberlin religious fanatic who is Amanda's first love; Hamish Bond, the slave trader become powerful entrepreneur who buys her on the auction block; Tobias Sears, the zealous, handsome man of ideas who becomes Amantha's husband; Rau-Ru, the slave who becomes an insurgent leader; and the various other black characters: the mammy, the jealous concubine, the lovable old tale-teller, and the wretchedly abused and degraded field hand. By virtue of her tincture of black blood and descent into slavery, Amantha shares aspects of their identity. Like Faulkner's Eulalia Bon in *Absalom, Absalom!* she is "the tragic mulatto" of drama and poetry. But she also serves as a focus for questions that had often troubled her creator.

"Oh, who am I?" These first words (which made some critics wince) signal one of them: the problem of identity. Like Joe Christmas in Faulkner's *Light in August,* she lives alternately as black and white. This problem of identity is shared, though not so self-consciously, by several other characters. Another concern is signaled by the novel's epigraph, A. E. Housman's lines "When shall I be dead and rid / Of the wrong my father did?" Other characters have been wronged by their fathers. The novel's title, taken from the Negro spiritual "Swing Low, Sweet Chariot," signals sympathy for the generations of slavery's victims.[21]

The novel's happy ending—an improbable one for some critics—comes with her ingenious but lame answer to the original question. Aaron Starr "had not been able to make the papers out, or the will, that would declare me less than what he had led me to believe I was, his true and beloved child; he was afraid to hurt me, was seeking, hopefully, some way to . . . see me established in a land far away, and he had not believed that he would die, soon. . . . No, he hadn't betrayed me" (pp. 373–74). No longer a self-pitying victim, she now realizes that she can truly define herself only as an independent person. Her failed marriage revives as her husband goes through a similar revaluation, and the book ends with her description of their conjugal embrace, "with my face pressed into his chest, and the tears running out of me with the awfulness of joy. . . ." (p. 375). If these perfervid lines recall the last ones of *All the King's Men,* they also signify that she, like Jack Burden, now knows surely who she is and where she is going. But the effort to create a thoroughly convincing woman was more ambitious than successful, as Warren acknowledged some fifteen years later when he said, "The narrator is wrong. There's not enough richness and depth in the experience of the narrator—at least it isn't brought out. . . ." The demands made upon her are great, and the handicaps correspondingly severe.[22]

Warren's problems extended beyond Amantha's tone to her character and personality. She is clearly meant to be pitied for her awful plight and admired for her survival, to a large extent on her own terms. But if she was intended to arouse some of the sympathetic emotions Harriet Beecher Stowe intended for Little Eva and Eliza, little Manty suggested to some readers not just Margaret Mitchell's Scarlett O'Hara but also Thackeray's Becky Sharp.[23]

On the positive side, along with the varied and vividly depicted milieus over a forty-year span, Warren employed the poetic with the descriptive, providing his heroine with another capability. The languorous appeal of autumn in New Orleans and the luxuriousness of Bond's Pointe du Loup plantation, the prodigal beauty along the banks of the great river, the enchanted darkness over Lake Pontchartrain—all of these are rendered with sensuous effect. And there are also functional patterns of imagery in the recurrence of dolls, graves, and creatures in flight.[24]

All of these were scrutinized by the novel's commentators. The author was praised for his narrative gift and historical imagination. He was also damned as an unreconstructed Agrarian and, in a marvel of misreading, attacked by Maxwell Geismar for creating "practically an idyll of slavery in the Old South. . . ." The familiar charges of indulgence in melodrama and romance would be repeated, even by the generally sympathetic Leslie Fiedler. He saw again in Warren's fiction an approach to "something not very different from nineteenth-century Italian opera: a genre full of conventional absurdities, lapses of good taste, strained and hectic plots—all aimed at becoming myth and melody," and he felt that the novel could not survive "such a metamorphosis."[25]

Assessments over the years since then, while generally recognizing the importance of the themes, the scope of the narrative, and the admirable effects created in *Band of Angels,* have tended to regard it as an ambitious failure and perhaps the least satisfactory of his novels. In spite of the intricate plotting and fertile imagination supported by immense knowledge and vivid re-creation of the past, this first-person narrative—by a finally unsympathetic heroine who often speaks in clichés—fails to engender belief. But despite the novel's shortcomings, it reaffirmed his presence as a major one on the literary scene, and it provided continuity for further exploration of the issues that had riven the country in the mid-nineteenth century and would come close to doing so again a hundred years later.[26]

33

❖

Political Reportage
and Poetic Frenzy

Moonlight falls on sleeping faces.
It fell in far times and other places.
Moonlight falls on your face now,
And now in memory's stasis
I see moonlight mend an old man's Time-crossed brow.
My son, sleep deep,
Though moonlight will not stay.
Moon moves to seek that empty pillow, a hemisphere away.
Here, then, you will wake to the day.
Those who died, died long ago,
Faces you will never know,
Voices you will never hear—
Though your father heard them in the night,
And yet, sometimes, I can hear
That utterance like the rustling tongue of pale tide in moonlight:
Sleep, son. Good night.

—*"Lullaby: Moonlight Lingers"*[1]

Early September found the family ailing again. Eleanor was in bed with viral pneumonia and later the flu, passed on to her by her daughter and husband. They needed a change, and fortunately Warren's work provided one. He would tell Ralph Ellison that by the time he had returned home after his Oxford years, he could no longer have written his contribution to *I'll Take My Stand*. He had dealt with racial abuses in *Brother to Dragons* within the larger context of evil in human nature. During the time he had been completing *Band of Angels* national attention had been focused on the continuing effects of slavery through the Supreme Court's 1954 decision striking down the separate-but-equal doctrine in public education. One evening when the Warrens were visiting Eleanor's sister, Eunice, and her husband, Jack Jessup, the conversation turned to the court's decision, and Jack suggested Warren do an article for *Life* on desegregation in the South. He quickly agreed. He would take Eleanor with him just as the chill of autumn would start settling over the Connecticut countryside. In October, as they headed south to Washington, Tennessee, and Mississippi—"down home," he called it—he had a lot of thinking to do, not only about his current projects but also about his future.[2]

A planned return trip in January and the writing that would follow may have helped to crystallize a decision. In mid-December he resigned from Yale. "I must say that I feel a little like Lot's wife in leaving the academic scene," he wrote Allen Tate. "A big chunk of my life is invested in it. But I guess the bigger chunk is invested in the typewriter, and the two chunks are becoming more and more incompatible—chiefly because of the kind of teaching I have been doing here. Teaching writing chews up the very part of your energy you want to save for yourself." (Helen Strauss may have helped him make his decision when she sold *Band of Angels* to Warner Bros. for $200,000. The film would have a good cast: Clark Gable, Yvonne De Carlo, and Sidney Poitier.) In late January he would be free.[3]

It was a busy Christmas, with preparations for what would become an annual holiday party. As Warren had always done, he and Eleanor invited many students among the fifty guests. Two of them were Alex Szogyi and Harold Bloom. "Eleanor was so gorgeous," Alex remembered, "just a stunning face, and she had a habit of wearing a red velvet dress so you'd know it was Christmas. I will never forget her coming down the stairs in that gorgeous dress." Then the huge high living room would be filled with buzz and laughter as the drinks went around. "During the years when the Warrens hosted their famous black-tie parties," Ralph Ellison wrote a friend, "Fanny and I were often among their week-end guests. Marked by good food, fine drinks, and live music for dancing, these were pleasurable occasions of a truly rare order. We were introduced to an array of people—writers, artists, curators, publishers, academics—whom otherwise we might not have encountered, [and] as far as we were aware no other writers gave parties that encompassed such a diversity of backgrounds and talent." There would be painters and sculptors such as Peter Blume and Alexander Calder. John Cheever, William Styron, Max Shulman (coauthor with Warren of a dramatic comedy), and their wives would be there. Talented couples like the Warrens themselves—Francis Steegmuller and Shirley Hazzard—would be there. The company would go downstairs to dinner, to the main table in front of the fireplace and the smaller ones. "Eleanor was such a genius at designating the table where you were to be," Alex recalled, "that gradually, over the years, you got to know everybody."[4]

It could not have been easy to leave home in that cold January of 1956 and face not only the hectic pace of traveling and interviewing but also the hostility awaiting him. "My Tennessee license, and Tennessee accent, hadn't been good enough credentials in Clarksdale, Mississippi. But on one occasion, the accent wasn't good enough even in Tennessee." There were of course other kinds of responses. In Guthrie he went to see Hettie Louise Griffey, who had worked for Ruth Warren when he was a boy. The granddaughter of slaves, she had told him stories about slavery times. Looking back over her second career as a teacher she said, "The Negroes that came out of slavery did better than those who have been free all this time." Recording conversations with taxi drivers and tourists, he sought out businessmen, politicians, clergymen, and teachers. He talked with an NAACP official, a self-described "redneck," an aristocrat in the library of his plantation house, a Negro scholar, and a white college student. He encountered goodwill and anger, bitterness and hatred, weary patience and wary hope. He was glad to board the plane for home. "I know what the Southerner feels, going out of the South, the relief, the expanding vistas. . . . But I know what the relief really is. It is the relief from responsibility . . . the flight from the reality you were born to."[5]

Even though the responses he was carrying home were drawn from only four southern states, they ran an enormous gamut. So he devised a strategy to avoid the daunting task of summing up: an interview with himself. Yes, he said, he was for desegregation. But wasn't he a gradualist on this pressing problem? "If by gradualist you mean a person who thinks it will take time, for an educational process, then yes. And I mean a process of mutual education for whites and blacks. And part of this education should be the actual beginning of the process of desegregation." His final response showed how much, despite his relief at leaving, he was still a southerner: "If the South is really able to

face up to itself and its situation, it may achieve identity, moral identity. Then in a country where moral identity is hard to come by, the
South, because it has had to deal concretely with a moral problem,
may offer some leadership. And we need any we can get."[6]

Back in Connecticut, he struggled through February and into
March with a case of the flu and his deadline. He produced twenty
thousand words and then compressed them to eight thousand. "Divided South Searches for Its Soul" appeared in *Life* on July 9. It would
be followed two months later by an expanded version published by
Random House and entitled *Segregation: The Inner Conflict in the
South.* The sixty-six-page book was the place for material too inflammatory for *Life:* the epithets and expletives, the sheer hatred and the
vitriolic anti-NAACP and anti-Negro fulminations. To Albert Erskine, not given to superlatives, the major reviews were "really fabu-
lous." Four weeks after publication sales would pass the six-thousand
mark and orders would continue for a time to come in at a rate of
seventy-five to a hundred a day.[7]

In the busy present he was chairing grants committees, accepting
honorary degrees, and planning a return to Italy. Suddenly the past returned with a jolt. On April 30 his lawyer, Frederick S. Danziger, informed him that Cinina was asking for more money. Now earning
about four thousand dollars a year as an instructor at Columbia, she
wanted to marry a man she had met through a support group. His
family had been New York landowners for generations, but his earn-
ings were small, and Cinina's lawyer feared that if either one of the
couple "should have an 'incident,' she would not have the means for
subsistence," and she might also "publish a book that might be very
damaging to 'everyone.' " Danziger had rejected the proposal and a
subsequent one. Warren agreed: "It is preposterous to expect me to
underwrite the marital adventure in question." He had put behind
him the unhappy childless marriage with its years of self-abnegation.
"I am completely indifferent to any kind of book that Emma B. Warren may write. If, as a matter of fact, she is still harboring her old delu-
sions it might be good for her to return to her treatments."[8]

Her demand prompted positive action in another area. He must
have remembered how Robert Warren came to regret that he had not
provided a better education for Mary Warren. He was determined
that this would not happen to Rosanna and Gabriel. He started a trust
fund for them, and he already had a book in mind to provide the first
deposit.

Another event in mid-May also carried him back into the past. Randall Stewart, the chairman of English at Vanderbilt, and Louis D. Rubin, Jr., the executive secretary of the American Studies Association, succeeded in obtaining four thousand dollars from the Rockefeller Foundation for a three-day Fugitives' reunion at Vanderbilt. As Rubin put it later, "To appreciate the impact of the Fugitives' Reunion, one must grasp the contemporary literary situation. By the 1950s the New Criticism had successfully entered the academy and was forcing even the most benighted pedants to read the actual words used in poems, instead of merely annotating historical, biographical, and philosophical contexts." And here assembled were those chiefly responsible: Ransom, Tate, Brooks, and Warren, and eight more survivors of the group. They gave public papers, poetry readings, and discussed with one another what they had been about those thirty-five years ago. And once again they debated the role of poetry in human life, no more consensual than they had ever been.

When Warren's *Life* article appeared, it would certainly give the unreconstructed Donald Davidson further reason to lament Warren's backsliding from Agrarian principles. Recalling his attempt at the reunion to define what Agrarianism meant to him, Warren confessed that when he had tried to think about it "my mind tended to shut up on the subject. . . . It seemed irrelevant at one stage to what I was thinking and feeling, except in a sentimental way. . . ." But Davidson did not hold this against him. Tate, the featured speaker, looked around him at the formal dinner. There they sat, he said, "all but stuffed." Warren apparently was unprepared for one effect of this journey into the past. At the opening public session he asserted, "I haven't written any verse for a year and a half. I suppose I am here under false pretenses." Looking back three years later, he would tell Davidson that it was this reunion that "got me back to writing short poems." At the time, however, he thought the meetings "crazy enough in conception," finally concluding that they were "pleasant, and sometimes even caught something of the old wrangles." But he was interested in new experience rather than old wrangles, and now Eleanor was busy, with the help of a tall handsome black woman named Isabelle, packing for the voyage that would take them to Italy.[9]

On June 4 Warren gave Albert Erskine a terse summary from La Rocca. "Things go well here. The children thrive this time. Isabelle likes the place. The wild flowers are incredible everywhere. We have the whole quadrangle now to ourselves. Ernesta's cooking remains good. We are at work." The next day they would go to the American Academy in Rome for ten days before returning to La Rocca "for four solid months of work, broken now and then by a visit."[10]

Eleanor had the manuscript of her novel, and Warren had his usual assortment of projects. He had already completed the first two chapters of the book that would provide income for the children's trust fund. It would be called *Remember the Alamo!* and would appear as one of Random House's Landmark Books for younger readers, a special project of Bennett Cerf. In a straightforward style, clear and direct without being simplistic, he moved ahead rapidly. It would be finished long before they returned to Rome in the fall for their second stint at the Academy.[11]

Back at La Rocca the pace of their work accelerated in the fine air above the sea. He was back in the favorite mode he described to Albert Erskine. "I am up every morning and do poetry until the vein runs low, usually about 11:30. Then I get at THE ALAMO until 2 PM or so. I'll keep at the poetry until I recover from the frenzy." A week later he reported that "the poetic frenzy continues unabated. What I now have plus the Rocca poems at the PARTISAN REVUE would now make a book, about 28 poems, some of them quite long, about 1500 lines. . . . When I get to Rome I plan to start the novel, unless poetry keeps urgent. It doesn't matter, just so something keeps urgent." By late August he had typed out the two hundred–plus pages of *Remember the Alamo!* "and as a result have a roaring lot of trouble with my old arm-spine trouble . . . but even so I've had my most productive period in years."[12]

"The seizure continues, hours a day," he told Donald Davidson. "The pieces all belong to one long thing—a kind of suite, I guess you'd call it, which I hope will be unified." In the earliest of the poems he had been celebrating the joy of the children's entry into their lives. Now, in the current poems, he had been mining the past: Civil War stories told by Grandpa Penn, a day's labor on his farm, enforced attendance at a country funeral, the news of murder and suicide heard in the sixth-grade classroom, boyhood fancies and intimations of the future. The poems employed unnamed figures from Italian landscapes and well-known historical figures: Jim Bowie at the Alamo, Lutheran Jakob Böhme's vision of evil manifested in a Kentucky countryside. The inspiration was coming from many sources: from the sight of babes lullabied to sleep and from a macabre vision of the ghostly figures of grandparents in a haunted wood. Within the long suite there were sequences he had already sent to editors. Within the next year a total of forty of his poems would appear in four different magazines. The checks, like the income from the collection he envisioned, would go to the children's trust fund.[13]

So the late summer and early fall went. Then, in the second week of October, the weather began to change. After one cold, wet day there, apprehensive for the children, they left for the American Academy and arrived "in the midst of brilliant sunshine and balmy breezes." In a commanding setting on the Janiculum, Rome's highest hill, it was housed in the Villa Aurelia, "a marble and faded red stucco palace behind tall, ornamental iron gates," which looked as though it had been there since the late Renaissance. In their apartment and studios amidst the Academy's ten villas, set among the boxwood and hedges, the flower gardens and ilex trees, they would do their work, never far from the sound of plashing fountains, with the tawny buildings of the city visible below, framed by the pines of Rome.[14]

One thing the Academy had in addition to these comforts was the society of the residents and visitors. The Warrens enjoyed seeing the Ellisons again, friends since the husbands had met four years before at a publication party for *Invisible Man*. It was in Rome, Ellison remembered, "that we really became friends. For it was there that he became the companion with whom I enjoyed an extended period of discussing literature, writing, history, politics—you name it—exploring the city, exchanging folk tales, joking, lying, eating and drinking. . . . A vigorous man, he damn near walked my legs off as we covered miles of what for him were familiar historical sites, restaurants, and bars. And it was through such pleasurable roaming that any bars to our friendship that might have been imposed by Southern manners and history went down the drain and left the well-known Fugitive poet and the fledgling writer and grandson of Freedmen marvelously free to enjoy themselves as human beings." The Warrens entertained as well as being entertained, and Monroe Spears and his wife, Betty, remembered particularly going to tea in their apartment with the Ellisons and other guests. They were often with old friends too, the Devlins and the Cheevers, and Albert Erskine when he took four weeks of vacation there, "giving the night life of Rome a mansize try with, it seems, some success."[15]

By November the rain had followed them to Rome, and by December, after weeks of it without respite, the children were thinking of home. Warren was entitled to a good conscience as they prepared to leave. By the time they sailed on February 8, his part of the *Modern Rhetoric* textbook was completed. ("One of the things that gives me a bad conscience about this whole book," Cleanth Brooks wrote him, "is my acute realization that your time ought to be going for something better than rhetoric. It has been a case of Pegasus at the plow indeed.") But the teacher's impulses were still strong in Warren. With his encouragement, Agostino Lombardo, a brilliant young teacher at the University of Rome, was putting together a group of essays by Italian scholars and critics on American subjects, which Monroe Spears intended to publish in *The Sewanee Review*. Warren had completed his draft of *Brother to Dragons* in play form and arranged the new poems as a manuscript. Eleanor had reason to feel good too. She had written new chapters of her novel, and after her skiing in the Austrian Alps she had come back "in the pink."[16]

The voyage home on the *Augustus* was a good one. When they were settled in again at Redding Road Warren wrote Agostino Lombardo, "Rosanna is in bliss now with her old toys and her play-yard. We have been in a great confusion getting settled, but life now begins to take shape. I have laid a flagstone terrace and begun my garden, and next week hope to get at a novel." His work was closely observed. Rosanna would recall her father "making, doing, planting pachysandra. He loved to plant trees—digging holes, tamping down the roots, watering them just right—vegetable gardening, especially the strawberries." And she was there for indoor work too. One of her earliest memories was the making of a long table to go before the big fireplace downstairs. It took him weeks, "made of three layers of wood pinned together. I watched him planing and sanding and pinning to get it all right." She and Gabriel were included in the project. "I still have the memory of his showing me how to wrap a piece of sandpaper around a piece of two-by-four, and the varnishing, and getting an ironmonger to make the base. It seemed emblematic to me of what he gave us—the sense of making."[17]

The other kind of making was continuing that summer in the study in the barn. "I finished my book of poems before leaving Rome and now start the novel, God helping me," he wrote Lon Cheney. "Meanwhile, I have laid a flagstone terrace, built a garbage

box, and half painted a study in the barn. I am, as you see, rapidly becoming Americanized." If his ambition needed further fueling, there
was much to encourage it. The *Life* article on segregation received a
five-hundred-dollar prize, and a partnership of theatrical producers in
New York bought his new verse play based on *Brother to Dragons.* It
was scheduled to open in New York in late October or early November. Before that, however, would come another event in mid-
August: the publication of *Promises,* his first book of poems in
fourteen years.[18]

34

❖

Promises Fulfilled—
and Made

And the years go by like a breath, or eye-blink.
And all history lives in the head again,
And I shut my eyes and I see that scene,
And name each item, but cannot think
What, in their urgency, they must mean,

But know, even now, on this foreign shore,
In blaze of sun and the sea's stare,
A heart-stab blessed past joy or despair,
As I see, in the mind's dark, once more,
That field, pale under starlit air.
> —*"Hands Are Paid," in "Boy's Will,*
> *Joyful Labor without Pay,*
> *and Harvest Home (1918)"*[1]

It was a handsome eighty-four-page book, the first thirteen pages consisting of the five poems for Rosanna written at La Rocca, the remaining nineteen poems—under the title "Promises," which gave the whole volume its name—ranging widely from the infancy of Gabriel to the lives of his ancestors. Of these nineteen, five consisted of three or more independently titled segments. Warren dedicated the book to his children. There were three poems addressed directly to Gabriel, but the first poem in this second segment of the book—"What Was the Promise That Smiled from the Maples at Evening?"—takes the poet back to childhood, as several of the rest would do too, and closes with his looking down through the earth for a moment, seeing how,

... agleam in a phosphorus of glory, bones bathed, there they lay,
Side by side, Ruth and Robert: the illumination then spent.

Then he hears his mother calling "Child," and then his father: "We died only that every promise might be fulfilled" (p. 18). This shift, from the literal and nostalgic to the surreal and visionary, served to prepare the reader for such poetic variations as a tale about a monster, a recollection of hanged bushwhackers, and a phantasmagoria about a skeletal grandmother attacked by wild hogs in a dark wood.

In spite of this diversity, there was, for the poet, a thematic unity. "That book is half Kentucky-Tennessee, and half Italy. There's medieval Italy and boyhood—they make a book. It's the long withdrawal from south Kentucky. . . . the book is really on that theme as much as any other theme, the other being father-child, father-daughter, father-son, as infants." His grandfather was there in memory too. "They're all one package—contrast and identity in one package—change and continuity—the human story." And as he had sat there in his study perched above the seventy-foot-deep moats and the sea beyond, writing lyric poetry again after the ten-year drought, "all of this—the place, the objects there, the children, the other people, my new outlook—made possible a new grasp on the roots of poetry for me."[2]

The collection was notable for the shifting of settings in time and space and the fact that almost half the poems were parts of sequences. In "Court-martial," the second of the eighteen poems and the most starkly powerful of them, the speaker, the old Confederate cavalryman, suddenly shifts from scraps of poems to a scene that might have come from Goya's *Desastres de la guerra:* the bodies of summarily executed bushwhackers,

> Each face outraged, agape,
> Not yet believing it true.
> Each hairy jaw is askew,
> Tongue out, outstaring eye, . . .

Angry and defensive at the listening boy's look, the old man tells him, "By God, they deserved it." The poet, remembering tales told at Cerulean by Grandpa Penn, concludes, "The world is real. It is there" (p. 23). It is also there in "Country Burying (1919)," in adult recollection rather than in the boy's impatience at a lost summer afternoon. Even at a physical distance, as in "School Lesson Based on Word of Tragic Death of Entire Gillum Family," the intrusion of the world's madness has the nature of a belated epiphany. The absence of five classmates is explained (in the expertly handled rural dialect), when the news comes that they were murdered by their father with an ice pick. At the end the poet once more meditates on meaning: *"We studied all afternoon, till getting on to sun. / There was another lesson, but we were too young to take up that one"* (p. 36).[3]

The acceptance of the world's grim realities was not new, nor was the attempt to extract meaning from experience. "Gold Glade" and the three-part "Dark Woods" again draw upon boyhood. He is like the Wordsworthian wanderer in beauty, but then, with sunset's dying,

> . . . dark came, and I can't recall
> What county it was, for the life of me.
> Montgomery, Todd, Christian—I know them all. (p. 25)

In that mannerism he would use increasingly, the poet draws the reader into his experience: "You stood, you stood there, and oh, could the poor heart's absurd / Cry for wisdom, for wisdom, ever be answered?" (p. 29). As in earlier poems, there are meanings to be extracted from history, but now, in "Founding Fathers, Nineteenth-Century Style, Southeast U.S.A.," there is also wisdom:

> So let us bend ear to them in this hour of lateness,
> And what they are trying to say, try to understand,
> And try to forgive them their defects, even their greatness,
> For we are their children in the light of humanness, and under
>   the shadow of God's closing hand. (p. 41)

In memory he seeks meaning and blessedness. In the last of the poem sequences, "Boy's Will, Joyful Labor without Pay, and Harvest Home (1918)," time and distance are spanned as the poet feels

> . . . even now, on this foreign shore,
> In a blaze of sun and the sea's stare,
> A heart-stab blessed past joy or despair,
> As I see, in the mind's dark, once more,
> That field, pale, under starlit air. (p. 81)[4]

For some readers the most memorable poems might be the five for Rosanna and the three lullabies for Gabriel, or at the other end of the spectrum, "Dragon Country: To Jacob Boehme" and "Ballad of a Sweet Dream of Peace." The first of these two poems—dedicated to the sixteenth-century German mystic concerned with the origins of evil—hearkens back to *Brother to Dragons* and its evocation of the presence of evil in human life. For Warren's fellow Kentuckian and lifelong collaborator, Cleanth Brooks, that venture into Kentucky history is a "great and moving poem," whereas "Dragon Country," while evoking Kentucky, is also "a country of the mind in which men encounter not human forces merely but principalities and powers." At the same time that the dragon's depredations suggest those of folk-tale monsters such as *Beowulf*'s Grendel, their realistic reportage "reflects the Southern experience, in which evil has an immediacy and reality that cannot be evaded or explained away." In terms of imagery, the creature's foul and violent traces recall the less threatening but no less gruesome figure in "Original Sin: A Short Story." But though the county is now as benighted as the earth was after Hades abducted Persephone, the poet declares that other sections have problems too, and

. . . if the Beast were withdrawn now, life might dwindle again
To the ennui, the pleasure, and night sweat, known in the time before
Necessity of truth had trodden the land, and heart, to pain,
And left, in darkness, the fearful glimmer of joy, like a spoor. (p. 66)

This last stanza, for Brooks, is "no Manichaean celebration of evil" but rather the recognition that "admitting the element of horror in life, conceding the element of mystery, facing the terrifying truth—these are the only actions that can promise the glimmer of ultimate joy."[5]

Most readers seem to have found "Ballad of a Sweet Dream of Peace" (with one of its seven sections bearing the title "Go It, Granny—Go It, Hog!") baffling and bewildering, to be understood if at all only in terms of the surreal or the absurd. Its origin, Warren said, was "the image of a fancifully carved Victorian bureau set in a grove of trees that somehow reminded me of a spot in Central Park." (Its deeper source probably lay in nightmare visions like some in *The Waste Land*.) It came "complete with dialogue" in which one character asks questions and the other supplies answers. In the grandmother's nightly searching of the bureau's drawers, according to the poem's closest student, she is seeking her own past. Spectres from the questioner's past appear too, reinforcing the theme of a lost identity. As the grandmother is devoured each night by the hogs as she goes to feed, so it appears that the questioner will also be consumed by them in his turn. In the seventh poem of the sequence, "Rumor Unverified Stop Can You Confirm Stop," there is a rumor of hope, which presumably prepares for the wondering acceptance of the book's last line, in "The Necessity for Belief": "Much is told that is scarcely to be believed." The metrics also indicated new directions where, in these seven poems and most of the others in the volume, he tended to write in units ranging from quatrains to long verse paragraphs, often in irregular metrical patterns. The boldness predictably elicited strong and divergent reactions from the reviewers that summer and fall. For one of them the book was a failure; for another, his best to date. For the most powerful reactions, however, he would have to wait until the winter and spring.[6]

Meanwhile he was supervising the building of a twenty-by-forty-foot swimming pool and stone terraces, extending the lawn, and planting vegetables. Their typewriters were not clattering at their usual rate. With the needs of the babies and the illness of her mother, Eleanor had not been able to get back to her work. A production of *Brother to Dragons* at Harvard in May convinced Warren that it needed "a drastic rewriting," and by September the New York producers knew that it would have to be postponed until early fall of 1958. If these disappointments prompted feelings of melancholy, there were thoughts about mortality besides those that prompted the children's trust fund. Harriet Owsley had asked Warren's help for a memorial volume for her husband, Frank, now dead a year. Joseph Warren Beach, who had brought Warren to Minnesota, had died in August. And then, learning that Bid and Hunt Brown's eighteen-year-old son, Chris, Warren's favorite as a little boy, was dying of leukemia, he wrote the Browns a long letter of love and grief, revealing some of the things he felt but rarely said. Soon, however, he would have reason to rejoice.[7]

In September, Katherine Anne Porter had said of *Promises*, "I don't know when I have seen anything so whole, and so varied. . . . Bless you." A week later Andrew Lytle thanked him for the "fine book of poems" with their "enlarged sense of the mystery of nature, that is in the woods and natural world, which I find new for you." In the new year institutional voices echoed the personal ones. Mid-January brought the two-hundred-dollar Edna St. Vincent Millay award for *Promises.* Then, on March 11, in the grand ballroom of the Commodore Hotel, he received the thousand-dollar National Book Award for *Promises.* Two months later, on May 5, just a few weeks after his fifty-third birthday, he received the Pulitzer Prize for Poetry for *Promises,* making him the only artist to have won prizes in two genres: fiction and poetry.[8]

In the years since this bouquet of awards, *Promises* has continued to stand as one of his most successful works. He had demonstrated the truth of Tate's assertion that he had what none of the other Fugitives had: power. Moreover, he had given additional evidence of his technical mastery of form at the same time that he was broadening his subject matter. He was using the direct conversational mode where it helped him to ask the fundamental ontological questions that obsessed him. And the fact that he was not just going strong in his sixth decade, but in fact stronger, brought the inevitable comparison. As one practicing poet-critic put it, *Promises* "can only be compared to that last astounding harvest of W. B. Yeats."[9]

This collection was not only a benchmark but also one point in a continuum. Nearly a dozen new poems had by now been accepted for spring publication, and five more would appear in the summer. They were arranged, like most of those in *Promises,* in sequences. Three would appear in *The Sewanee Review* under the title "Prognosis: A Short Story, the End of Which You Will Know Soon Enough." It illustrates perfectly what Warren had meant when he said that he stopped writing short stories because they used up material for poems. This three-part sequence focuses on a woman just informed that she has cancer, then goes on to explore, partly in her own words, not just her relation to her loveless family but her coming to terms with her life and her own humanity. Without the encumbrance of plot, the poet is free here to treat his material at once with economy and poetic intensity. This one might have been set anywhere, whereas "Two Pieces after Suetonius," for the *Partisan Review,* delves into vastly different lives as the poet draws on memories of Capri and the great Roman biographer. Three poems in a sequence in the summer *Yale Review* would be called "Nursery Rhymes." They are different enough from one another to show his abundance of imagination and versatility of technique. Even though nursery rhymes have traditionally included the bizarre and the violent, these infuse familiar images and phrases with an ominous tone bespeaking a tragic view of life. The fourth one for the *Review*'s same issue, "Debate: Question, Quarry, Dream," is another personal one, with the poet hearkening back to Kentucky childhood while his son sleeps. Of the ten that would appear that spring and summer, this is the only one that shows the capacity for joy that had informed several in *Promises*. But there would soon be others in this latter vein.[10]

Warren was not present to receive his second Pulitzer. The winter months had been trying, not just with *Brother to Dragons* but also with the bad luck that had dogged Eleanor. In January she had fallen off a toboggan and broken her leg, her knee swelling so that they could not apply a cast for a week. By March, when she had recovered, they were ready for a change. On the eighteenth Warren wrote Agostino Lombardo, "We are sailing for Le Havre on May 7 and after three or four days in Paris, shall drive to Italy, arriving before the end of May."[11]

Their departure came as a relief. But any expectation of restful quiet was soon dispelled: "We finally got on shipboard, and hit Le Havre the day the Algeria business broke," he wrote Donald Davidson. "We stayed in Paris five days, watching the riot squads and black buses with tommy-guns at every important street corner, and the patrols prowling about, and expecting to be ring-side for a coup d'etat. . . . this is about the grimmest time since June 1940, and I'm gloomier than then—perhaps because I'm older than when I gaily refugeed out of Genoa then. I don't merely mean the possibility of de Gaulle as a new kind of fascism, etc., but something deeper."[12]

His gloom and recurrent pessimism about contemporary history were dispelled in the Roman sunlight, and after a pleasant stop in the company of friends, they headed north for La Rocca. The *signora* was ailing, and they feared this might be their last summer here. "Anyway," he continued, "we are here in our rookery on the cliff and getting some work done, and preparing to celebrate birthdays and going swimming in very blue water. Eleanor is in the middle of a novel. I'm into one, but lately have taken some time off for some verses that keep nagging me." He was freer now to pursue them than he had been, for the work was done on *Selected Essays,* which would appear on June 25.[13]

It may have been his annoyance at the demands of this rather mechanical job that prompted an acerbic note in the preface. "Even our own time, sometimes called, happily or unhappily, an age of criticism, is remarkable, not for a massive and systematic orthodoxy, but for the variety and internecine vindictiveness of voices; and even the 'New Critics,' who are corralled together with the barbed wire of a label, are more remarkable for differences in fundamental principles than for anything they have in common. It sometimes seems hard to find much they do have in common except their enemies." (To the end of his life he would angrily reject the label of "New Critic.") Not a system, he wrote, but "intelligence, tact, discipline, honesty, sensitivity—those are the things we have to depend on, after all, to give us what we prize in criticism, the insight." Though not reviewed widely, the book was generally reviewed well. It displayed all the qualities that made him a superb essayist: clarity combined with eloquence and acute literary sensibility supported by encyclopedic knowledge.[14]

With the familiar sense of freedom and relief La Rocca provided, they dug in: Eleanor to a Random House children's book on Charlemagne's great paladin, Roland, as a warm-up for her novel, Warren to his novel and the poems that kept interrupting. But he was working now at the novel with the kind of emotional intensity that more often came with poetry. In mid-June he had sent Albert Erskine the remainder of chapter 4, adding, "My characters feel pretty good to me, and I have had constant excitement of writing it and thinking about it, just not able to wait for morning to start again, whatever that means. Maybe time to lock me up."[15]

Once again he was drawing on Kentucky lore. In 1925, the entrapment and death of Floyd Collins while exploring Sand Cave (a part of the Flint Ridge system, like Mammoth Cave) had attracted national attention. When Warren began planning the novel he had gone there with Lon Cheney. Then, as usual, he had scrawled notes on single 8½″ × 11″ sheets of paper: questions about theme and event, analyses of motivation, synopses of action, and sometimes paragraphs with dialogue, creating a large cast of characters with lives full of complicated interaction.

By early July, however, he was paying for his long stretches of typing. His shoulder pain was so intense that Eleanor thought he should go to Switzerland for treatment, but he stuck at it for two more chapters. He wrote Albert Erskine, "I think I see it all clear now to the end. For one reason, my damned shoulder has kept me awake so much at night I've had time to think through and dream the whole thing. I hate like hell to interrupt work right now for I feel caught in the drive to the end." But by the next day he knew that he had to give in. Eleanor's old friend Denis de Rougemont set up an appointment with a doctor in Lausanne, and from there Warren went to a clinic in Zurich. "I am being hot mud-packed and massaged and cold-packed and shot full of dope from big needles and generally mistreated. Am anxious to do a few whacks on the book today, but the depressed state of my health after the treatments had its effect, and I gave up." Two weeks later, on the twenty-fifth, he sent the beginning of chapter 8. "This is all I shall do here for tomorrow thank God I blow back to La Rocca. Things have not gone too well, . . . but they think that after two weeks nature may now take over." Eleanor met him at Orbitello and drove them back to La Rocca on the twenty-seventh, Rosanna's birthday. He did not miss Gabriel's party after all, because they had postponed it, and so they celebrated the two together.[16]

After ten days the end of the novel was in sight, though he was experiencing his usual qualms. "I now have its meaning and shape," he wrote Karl Shapiro. "I don't know what I've got. Some days I think my best one, more variety, humor, feeling, some days a pile of shit. But I believe that after a certain amount of suffering, in these matters, we live in the Hand of God, so whack away and pray and keep your bowels open. Which is not hard on an Italian diet." On August 15 he finished the draft and told Erskine he didn't like the tentative title, *The Man Below.* If his mood and ego needed a boost, it had come in another area. "Harvard came back again for the Lowell Professorship," he wrote, "$20,000, 12½% annual retirement fund plus this and that. I declined, without too much backward looking." The last line of his letter suggested that he was rounding into something like his usual fettle again: "I got an idea for a new book."[17]

The superb weather helped his shoulder, though with the shortening September days they had to swim in the morning rather than after the day's work. Then, when the the sirocco began to blow at the end of the month, they packed for a brief return to the American Academy before embarking for home. He could take stock of their Italian sojourn with some satisfaction. The first draft of his novel was finished, and Eleanor thought she was on the home stretch with hers. *Remember the Alamo!* had been published on August 28 with favorable reviews to come, for he had managed to span the audience of juvenile and general readers.[18]

And there was more new work besides *The Man Below.* "When I got through with the novel," he told Lon Cheney, "I plunged back into poems again. I had a lot of half started ones, and now have wound up some of them, which, plus those done since [*Promises*] will about make another volume." Though composed or begun in Italy, all of them drew on Kentucky memories now richly available to him in the continuation of the frenzy.[19]

On Sunday, October 11, 1958, they walked up the *Saturnia's* gang-plank. Two weeks later they would be back on Redding Road, Eleanor to finish the draft of her novel, Warren to buckle down to the "cutting and rewriting and pulling and hauling"—with some help from Lon Cheney's encyclopedic knowledge of Kentucky lore—that would result in the publication of his sixth novel.[20]

35

❖

Twenty Years' Gestation

I must have been six when I first found the cave-mouth
Under ledges moss-green, and moss-green the inner dark.
Each summer I came, in twilight peered in, crept further,
Till one summer All I could see was a gray
Blotch of light far behind. Ran back. Didn't want to be dead.
. . . .
Years later, past dreams, I have lain
In darkness and heard the depth of that unending song,
And hand laid to heart, have once again thought: *This is me.*
And thought: *Who am I?* And hand on heart, wondered
What would it be like to be, in the end, part of all.

And in the darkness have even asked: *Is this all? What is all?*
                                                    — *"Speleology"*[1]

Even though the friends who stayed in the house had left it in good
order, there were a thousand things to do, especially outside, where
their wilderness, as Warren called it, needed all kinds of attention.
He knew that he would have to give the fall and winter to rewriting his novel while doing his part of the revisions on a new edition
of *Understanding Fiction*. So when the opportunity for a brief holiday offered, he took it. He went home for a four-day hunt with
Thomas in the Great Smoky Mountains. "Didn't get a shot but
had a fine time," he reported. The brothers were both raconteurs,
and because of the steady going and coming of customers who
stored their grain in Thomas's silos, there were always new stories of
Guthrie and Todd County to tell. But often, out in the woods, the

two might just sit, wordlessly sharing a companionship that had grown over the years.[2]

The tempo picked up again as soon as he returned home, and it remained rapid as the winter came on. He congratulated Lon Cheney on his new novel and thanked him for his careful reading of *The Man Below*. "I'll get at it this week," he wrote, "and for the moment, anyway, I go at it with hope and new ideas. This is a stage I always have in a book—the moment of reassessing the project and regrouping the forces. Well, pray for me." Another three months of hard work on it lay ahead.[3]

It was not just the novel. He was still writing short poems, still riding the wave that had picked him up those three years ago during his brief time with the Fugitive brothers in Nashville. On a cold mid-March day at the tag end of the winter, he sent Allen Tate the manuscript of a new book of poems. They were a very mixed assortment in both form and content, the most personal and passionate being a five-poem sequence set over a span of seventy-five years and called "Mortmain." This was a day when he had been clearing his desk, and not just of poems. "Since middle November," he told Allen, "I have been in a great sweat of rewriting on my novel, which now, for better or worse, is done, and goes to the printer Monday. I don't know what I've got. Anyway it is very different from anything else I've ever done, and I feel another coming on in the same vein."[4]

The spring brought two brief respites. Near the end of March they went for a week to Vermont. The next month he went to Nashville for a two-day meeting of The Fugitives, lecturing and seeing old friends. He spent some time with Thomas Warren in Guthrie. "We went over for a visit to the state pen at Eddyville," he wrote Katherine Anne Porter. "Very educational." He did not specify what took them there, but the visit would provide useful material for a novel. "I had a longer time with some of the cons at Eddyville than with you all," he wrote Fanny and Lon Cheney on his return.[5]

At the top of his list was gardening, but he was unable to plunge into it immediately. First he had to recover from a case of the measles, brought home from school like the earlier germs of the winter. By May, though, he was attacking several jobs. He approached his gardening enterprise with hope and faith. "I am a rather slovenly but lucky gardener," he confessed to Don Davidson. "Things usually come along for me despite my breaking all the rules or forgetting

them. Except strawberries." True to form, however, he was cultivat-
ing another garden. "I'm moving painfully toward another novel," he
wrote Andrew Lytle. "I have a kind of idea, scarcely an idea, a scene,
a feeling, but I have got the hard germ I always need to start."[6]

July brought the children's birthdays, Gabriel turning four on the
nineteenth, Rosanna, six on the twenty-seventh. They were precocious, and Red was proud of them. Gabriel had discovered a year and
a half before that he could attach proper names to the letters on his
blocks, and Rosanna was writing letters employing both upper- and
lowercase script as she awaited her entry into first grade. Occasionally
Warren would apologize to correspondents for disquisitions on their
achievements, but he usually could not resist sharing them. He told
Lytle, "They are handsome and charming and, often, very good."[7]

There was one infallible way to see that they were good. "Stories
and poems were the warp and woof of our childhood," Rosanna
would say years later, "Greek myths, Civil War tales, family legends."
It was a staple of their lives,

> nightly readings to us, wonderful readings of Twain where he
> would play on the accent, ham it up. All of Tolkien and the Narnia
> books. Even when Gabriel and I were reading to ourselves we still
> continued the out-loud reading, a way to mesh together. He would
> tell us stories about his boyhood, and we would try to imitate what
> he had done. He took us out to meet the six-foot blacksnake in
> Fairfield, that lived in a hole. We were very small, and he took us
> out by the hand to have an evening chat with the blacksnake. And
> I remember this, feeling a distinctive fear but feeling that if Poppy
> was friends with the blacksnake then we could be too. And he
> brought us up on stories of his boyhood, the times he brought
> snakes home, and owls, and populated the house with various crea-
> tures that alarmed his mother, especially.

This telling was all part of a pattern, a mode of living that would
continue into their adolescence. Warren would always say of his
Guthrie family, "We were close, very close," and he would continue
to try—in this different place with these very different children—to
reproduce that remembered closeness.[8]

By August they were ready for a holiday in Maine. After two days
with Jack and Eunice Jessup on their island off the coast, they went
for the rest of the month to visit Bill and Alice Bandy at one of their

cottages on a lake at Wayne, not far from Augusta. They were there when *The Cave* was published on the twenty-third and back in Fairfield by Labor Day, when the reviews were still coming in.

Although some of Warren's habitual concerns inevitably appeared, this four-hundred-page novel was also radically different from its predecessors. It was southern—set in Tennessee—and it drew on history—Floyd Collins's death thirty years before—but it covered a brief time span, lacked a conventional protagonist, and progressed by movement from one point of view to another. The action begins with Jo-Lea Bingham's realization that Jasper Harrick, an admired young Korean War veteran, is trapped in a cave. Discovered earlier by Jasper and Isaac Sumpter, a cynical manipulator, on Sumpter land, and now intended for development as a tourist attraction, the cave becomes the immediate focus of national attention as rescue operations are organized and the entrepreneurial Sumpter publicizes the drama through reports he sends to newspapers, radio, and television in Nashville. As reporters, camera crews, and curiosity seekers converge on Johntown, the principal actors in the drama work through their relationships with one another, ultimately being forced to confront the deeper issues of their own identity and philosophic bases for living. The events and the varied reactions to them reveal something of the nature of Johntown as a community and, in a sense, something of the nature of the human community.

As the cave is the immediate focus of the rescue efforts, so it is the center of a circle formed by the characters. There is the Harrick family, with the novel's most dominant character, the herculean onetime blacksmith, Jack, and his much younger, beautiful, and high-born wife, Celia. Once a prodigious hunter, fighter, lover, and Congressional Medal of Honor winner, Jack is wheelchair-bound with prostate cancer. Celia grieves over him, cherishing his enormous vitality but feeling cut off from him as he struggles silently against pain and approaching death. Their son Jasper has found life in his father's shadow difficult and finally unacceptable. Their other boy, Monty, has found life in their two shadows difficult too, admiring his brother yet jealous of his inherited amatory prowess, afraid that Jasper has taken Jo-Lea away from him when she is actually pregnant with Monty's child. Sexuality permeates the novel, not only in the revealed consciousness of each character but also in the coarse and explicit language of country people who reminded some readers of Erskine

Caldwell's *Tobacco Road*. This quality is there in the subplots at other social levels too.

The central situation is explored through intricate plotting. Because Celia Harrick forbids Monty to risk his life in a rescue attempt, Isaac enters the cave to struggle through tunnels and chambers. Hearing nothing, however, and fearing to go further, he stops short of the dark ledge where Jasper lies pinned by a rock. Assuming he is dead, Isaac emerges to play the hero, carrying back fictitious messages from Jasper. Reentering the cave with food and a heating pad, he takes an envious aspirant, Jebb Holloway, with him, and tricks him into corroborating his fabricated story of Jasper's death. He also enters into a partnership with failed entrepreneur Nick Pappy to sell food to the hordes of curiosity seekers and later to exploit the cave as a tourist attraction. When Brother Sumpter—Isaac's father and Jack Harrick's companion in youth, but now a preacher—enters the cave later and finds Jasper's body still warm, he too corroborates his son's story out of love for him. With Jasper to be entombed in the cave, Isaac departs, angrily repudiating the father he hates and realizing that his future lies in public relations in some big city.

Resolution on the moral level follows as the other principal characters come to a clearer sense of their own identity and the nature of their relationships. Warren's social criticism employs the satiric mode. Brother Sumpter's prayers and exhortations at the cave mouth develop into a kind of old-fashioned revivalist meeting, with confessions of guilt and faith that grow frenetic and hysterical. The arrival of "the media" compounds the extravaganza with its outrageous invasions of privacy and exploitation of tragedy. Ultimately the frenzy of religiosity and drinking produces a saturnalia under the trees and bushes of the mountainside, one that recalls the camp-meeting satire of Mark Twain in *The Adventures of Huckleberry Finn* and the calculated fraud in Sinclair Lewis's *Elmer Gantry*.

The title invited symbolic interpretation, reinforced as it was by the epigraph from Plato's *Republic,* with its allegory of the cave whose occupants, turned toward its wall, mistake the shadows they see there for reality. Warren would later repudiate this allegory-seeking with studied irony. He cited the original title: "*The Man Below,* and the man below is the man inside, of course, inside you. The submerged man in you and the man in the ground. Somewhere along the way this became the point." He had been meditating on this story for twenty years, he said, until he found the proper way to embody it.[9]

What he found was another variation on a favorite theme: fathers and sons at odds. Jack Harrick "can't, will not be a father and take his biological role," he explained. "He has to learn to, well, take a sedative for his pain. He has to learn how to give his [guitar] to the boy. All these things he has to do. But that was quite the very center of the book." This idea, he said, was spelled out in an essay he called "Knowledge and the Image of Man." Through the awareness of life's pathos and the pain of self-criticism man may escape the entrapment of his own ego and achieve a communion with his fellows and with nature.[10]

This kind of vision is achieved in varying degrees by all of the major characters except Isaac Sumpter, whose smart-aleck dialogue recalls that of Jack Burden before his enlightenment in *All the King's Men* and whose cynical self-seeking villainy recalls that of Slim Sarrett in *At Heaven's Gate*. One of the characters here, Timothy Bingham, embodies ideas in Warren's essay. Thinking of his youth, he weeps in the summer night under the blooming moon vine. "The pathos of life possessed him" (p. 398). Through his fear and anguish and exertions he has become more human, rejecting his rigid, moralistic identity as an inflexible banker. Achieving the kind of empowerment that permits him to free himself and his daughter from his terrible wife, he abandons thoughts of procuring an abortion for Jo-Lea in favor of subsidizing her marriage to Monty Harrick and providing a college education for this boy he has fancied an unpromising hillbilly.[11]

Jasper is at peace, achieving in death the freedom from the overpowering presence of his father and all the expectations it brought with a mode of life he had finally found unbearable. He figures in the novel more as a literary device, however, than as the sort of character who normally helps to propel a novel's action. Warren was certainly aware of the risks he was taking with the use of this rather ephemeral central character but obviously felt that his thematic matter would emerge more effectively this way than through an omniscient narrator, as in *Night Rider,* a principal character as narrator, as in *All the King's Men,* or a nameless analytical commentator, as in *World Enough and Time.*[12]

Other aspects of technique are more familiar. Clusters of image and symbol, if not allegorical, are clearly functional. For all his denial of the cave as Platonic symbol other than as a suggestion of the difference between men's perception and actual reality, as licensed by the epigraph, the cave suggests death as its presence hovers over the characters. The situation of entrapment appears in several forms. The novel's intense saturation with sexuality is reinforced by the central image in a powerful Freudian fashion. Several commentators have seen the repeated fetal imagery as recapitulating not only the death of Jack's firstborn but also Jasper's situation and that of Jo-Lea. Womb and tomb are clearly linked. Images of water and images of blood are repeated. One recurrent object is nearly as ubiquitous as Leopold Bloom's cake of soap in Joyce's *Ulysses*. It is Jo-Lea's panties, lowered for dalliance with Monty near the cave's mouth but then jettisoned rather than donned when she realizes that Jasper is trapped and races to spread the alarm. They are the object of lubricious comments and longings by rustics who make Susannah's elders seem tactful. The comments on these symbols of sexuality and surrender, like the occasional four-letter words, are appropriately coarse and vulgar in accordance with the commentators' sensibilities, but there are passages in which a disembodied narrative identity seems the source of them, a voice not quite authorial but at times close to it. And some of these passages are gratuitous, as if they derive from a taste for the ribald rather than the necessities of characterization.

This quality provided a convenient club for those who had no sense of the novelist's fundamental intentions and little appreciation for the versatility of his prose. Reviewers in church-related magazines disapproved sternly. Bawdry and vulgarization, "Bible-slapping" and farce, remarked a representative one. There were many more favorable than unfavorable reviews, though almost all of the former were mixed. A few of the most visible reviews were very favorable, but the book was patronized by more than one as a "popular novel." Warren summarized later for Arnold Stein: "It got the best press I ever had, even with the attack in Time and New Yorker, and has had the best sale. But no book club and no movie." Some of Warren's friends were glad of the financial rewards for him but worried that his concern with movie sales and book-club adoptions would affect the quality of his work.[13]

Subsequent criticism over the years has noted the book's earthy physicality, but while some have remarked on the bleak power of the central symbol of the cave with its existential implications, they have also been aware of the positive thrust of the novel's ending. They have credited the author's taking of stylistic risks with its de-emphasis of the narrative and increasing reliance on the meditative, the philosophical, and the lyrical. With the recognition of the familiar concern with identity and guilt, there has also been praise for the high seri-

ousness of the author's intent, as in the assertion that "none of Warren's novels demonstrates the strenuousness of human effort, the
defining of self through community, quite so insistently as does *The
Cave*." It had been twenty years in the making. In a demonstration of
the persistence of a powerful idea wedded to a powerful symbol, almost exactly twenty years later Warren would publish a poem embodying both.[14]

The passage of time that fall of 1959 was marked for the Warrens by
a keen awareness of both ends of life's spectrum. Their old friend
Denis Devlin had died after a long illness, and Warren was working
with his widow and Allen Tate on an edition of his poems and a
prize in his memory. (Divorced for the second time from Caroline
Gordon, Tate was newly married to the poet Isabella Gardner.) It
seemed that Rosanna and Gabriel were growing faster now, and
their parents were encountering new responsibilities. "Rosanna is in
the first grade and we've been to our first PTA meeting," Warren
wrote Tate, "and Gabriel has made a wooden chair and painted it
red, all by himself. He also makes poems and throws rocks."
Rosanna "is in bliss—reads her head off, paints and draws, loves her
new friends, rides horses. . . ."[15]

Warren had his own poems on his mind and plays as well. At the
Seventy-fourth Street Theatre in New York *All the King's Men* was at
last in its strenuous final rehearsals: "The last ten days have offered me
little sleep, lots of tea, coffee, and booze, train rides at 2 AM, and infinite yammer." Two days after the first performance on October 16 he
wrote Tate, "In 36 hours I have about repaired the damage. The production was extremely good, the lead terrific. . . . I don't know what
the whole press is. . . . but Atkinson in the Times did a very, very favorable review, and the Journal American led off with 'just right' and
a prediction that the play would 'prosper.' The Tribune made a complete, root-and-branch attack—every aspect of play and production.
But the Times counts 80%—and the other papers fill in the difference.—Strange isn't it, a real dictatorship. Anyway, I am *through,* after
20 years." The play closed after a seven-week run.[16]

His name was in the papers again in April 1960 when he was
elected to the American Academy of Arts and Letters, whose fifty
members were chosen for special distinction from among the 250 in
the parent body, the National Institute of Arts and Letters. (Elected
with him were Virgil Thomson and Eero Saarinen.) On December 4

he was inducted with a glowing citation acclaiming him not only as an internationally influential essayist, poet, and novelist but also "as one of the most clear-sighted analysts of our troubled modern America." They also heard "tributes read to the dead of the year," Warren told Arnold Stein, "FL Wright, Berenson, and Maxwell Anderson. Very ghoulish. I succeeded to Anderson's chair. You have your name on the chair. Next you get to put it on a tombstone. It took me two days to get back to the desk."[17]

They had made what time they could for relaxation that fall. In mid-October they had managed a trip to Vermont. In West Wardsboro, twenty miles north of the Massachusetts line and about the same distance west of the New Hampshire line, they found a large cottage that provided rough summer and winter accommodations. Warren went out on snowshoes and explored the area with Stubb Sampson, a man of all work who lived a mile away. Late that month, thinking of the time they had spent in Maine, he wrote Bill Bandy. "Eleanor, inspired by Bandy's camp at Wayne, has just managed to convince me that we need a place in Vermont worse than we need additional life insurance, and so we have just bought it. Very wild and beautiful, near Ski-ing, full of animals, with brawling brook full of trout under the window. We have also bought a four-wheel-drive jeep to get to it. The children have bought some paint to paint themselves up like Indians." They began to make improvements, adding insulation and a porch on the side near the road. They returned in the fall to check on the work and add some furniture to the few pieces left by the former owner. Coming back just before Christmas, they drove the jeep through the roadless ruts up to the Shack, as they called it. "It was pitch black when we got there," Eleanor remembered, "just the two of us and the children, the first time in the winter, with no heat, no water, anything." Just as they got out of the jeep they heard a call from across the brook. They were sure it was a wolf. Their new habitation would occupy a central place in their family, winter and summer, for the rest of their lives.[18]

When he had described the flurry of activities with *All the King's Men* to Arnold Stein, he had added, "Meanwhile I am whacking away at a batch of poems for next summer's volume." Months earlier he had told Don Davidson, "Since I feel a change of mood impending I want to get these out for what they are worth." Many of them would be substantially different from those in *Promises*. In the coming year his readers would be able to judge what they were worth.[19]

36

❖

A Reversal of Fortune

Dawn draws on slow when dawn brings only dawn:
Only slow milk-wash on window, star paling, first bird-stir,
Sweat cold now on pillow, before the alarm's *burr,*
And the old thought for the new day as day draws on.
                                             — *"Obsession"*[1]

Activities in January foreshadowed a busy 1960. Warren continued to work with Allen Tate toward an edition of Denis Devlin's poems and a prize in his name. He agreed to participate in an April symposium in honor of Joseph Warren Beach, and he was working out the legal problems with the Theatre Guild for a new production of *All the King's Men,* the script of which Random House would publish. Before the summer was over *You, Emperors, and Others* would appear, and now with tentative signs of spring dotting the Connecticut landscape, he was working his way into a Civil War novelette called *Wilderness,* which took its name from the series of frightful battles in northeast Virginia in 1864.[2]

With all of his concerns he remained a devoted parent. And now his and Eleanor's vocation was having an impact on Rosanna and Gabriel. Playing Mommy and Poppy, Rosanna threw herself into her role until Eleanor brought her up short. "You can't boss him around all the time," she said. "He has to go out of the house sometimes and go to an office." Rosanna looked at her mother in consternation. "What do you mean, an office?" she asked. "He's a regular Poppy— he's a writer." Warren gave Rosanna an old battered Remington, which she used with great concentration. That night, with the Brookses, the Erskines, and John Palmer at dinner, Gabriel came down to the staircase landing in his pajamas, stuck his head between the bars of the banister, and wailed to John, his godfather, "You tell my mother to give me a typewriter."

Warren's skill and inventiveness as a storyteller provided much of the matter of their childhood. Many of their favorites came from Poppy's own childhood. There were schoolhouse stories, like that of the time he found (or drilled) a hole in the schoolroom floor, hung a bell beneath it by the pretty teacher's desk, and then ran a cord to it so he could ring it while sitting at his desk when she began the lesson. Rosanna was pleased that when she discovered the device she didn't punish him. He fell in love with her. He brought home a dormant snake, which thawed in the warmth of the stove and wriggled across the floor, creating great alarm. He brought home a screech owl and installed it in the sleeping porch, where it woke at night and roused the whole household. There seemed to be endless accounts of such exploits, which sometimes brought retribution. Rosanna didn't want to hear about his being thrashed, but Gabriel wanted all the details of his pants being lowered and his bottom switched. And he loved the one about the time when he notched the switch under the bark so it would break. There was a whole series of Bible stories for times when there was no school bus and Poppy had to drive. "He reinvented them," Rosanna remembered, "reinvented a whole cycle through our childhood, how the little boy Samson brought a lion home, how he conquered the Philistines and brought one home, and his mother told him to come to dinner and then help to wash the dishes. These were much more entertaining than the occasional trips to church."

The stories carried over from listening to playing. "We didn't con-sciously try to recapitulate his childhood," she recalled. "It was just that it was so exciting. He told us how he read about archaeology and made clay figures and buried them for six months and later dug them up. We thought that was great, and so we buried whole cities." He read them books he had loved: *Two Little Savages and How They Grew, Wild Animals I Have Known,* and *Looking for Tracks in the Woods.* Fair-field was fine for imaginative play, but Vermont was even better. That July, remembering the howl of the timber wolf, he told them the story of "Waldo the Good Wolf" and wrote it out for them. Neigh-bors told them their wolf had returned unseen, and by now they may have begun to think of him as a kind of tutelary spirit of the woods.[3]

On one occasion Rosanna called on her father's verbal skills to deal with an obnoxious girl who persisted in kneeing her. "The next time she does it," he told her, "you say, 'You little misbegotten hunk of human gristle, keep your knee under your own behind!' " There were fewer assaults after that.[4]

Though West Wardsboro lacked the sun and sand of La Rocca, it was an all-season retreat. At the end of March Warren told Lon Cheney, "The place is really cut off from the world . . . no electricity, no pump, no telephone, no mail forwarded. Eleanor had a wonderful time skiing—we are close enough to the resort at Mt. Snow. Gabriel is becoming an expert. . . . He has the guts of a lion. I don't need the guts of a lion, for you don't fall very far off snowshoes—and that's the way I spent my afternoons, off into the woods. God, it's a beautiful piece of country." Three months later he told Charlie Foster they were converting "our ski-and-snow shoe place into a summer shack by the simple expedient of sticking on some sleeping porches." They loved the spot: "Deep woods, a fine mountain, a big brook under the window, a lake twenty minutes away for swimming and fishing, nearest neighbor (and a good one) a mile and a half. Eleanor has a work shack off in the woods, and I am building one for myself this week. No telephone, no telegraph station nearer than 38 miles. Two cases of booze in the cellar, one whiskey, one wine. We expect to survive." Theirs was "a fine mountain to look at at drink time, with a sunset over it."[5]

He wrote steadily on *Wilderness* in his "work house in the woods," liking it "better than any place I ever had except the vedetta at the Rocca. I hang out over a little ravine, and watch, and hear, the brook down below. No human sight or sound. It is a beautiful little establishment." By mid-July, he reported to Albert Erskine that he could "see the second half of the thing pretty clearly. And have up a head of emotional steam." Three weeks later he sent him chapter 9. (Happily married for a year now to a tall beautiful contessa named Marisa Bisi, Erskine was basking in the glow of new fatherhood with the arrival of a little girl named Silvia.) As for Warren's own gestation, another week, he thought, would see the completion of chapter 10. "Then the home stretch. Gosh, I don't know what I have, really. I know that some of the narrative is my very best, but I am on thin ice here and there, maybe. *Vedremmo*. I long for your aid and comfort."[6]

Life was planning a six-part series on the Civil War, and editor Jerry Korn hoped Warren would undertake either the first or the last. He replied with some enthusiasm that he would be interested in writing about "the distinction between the historical importance and what might be called the appeal to the national imagination, the symbolic value of the war." He began preparatory reading, discussing the topic with other summer people including philosopher Sidney Hook and art critic Meyer Schapiro. Warren's growing manuscript benefited from their lunches together. The work must have been a welcome distraction. "I have the usual pre-book twitches," he told Andrew Lytle in mid-July. "I have all the hopes and fears and no convictions I can depend on."[7]

On August 31 Random House published *You, Emperors, and Others: Poems 1957–1960* in an edition of four thousand copies. Of the forty-one poems he had published between the spring of 1958 and the summer of 1960, he reprinted all but four, and he added two previously unpublished. He had revised many of them and grouped some together in new sequences. The range was wide in both form and content. He drew upon Kentucky and his childhood as well as his European experiences, though not nearly as much as he had done for *Promises.* He made references to his son, though he appeared much less in this volume and his sister not at all. There were a few poems on an earlier America and a few on the ancient world. The poet dwelled upon his grandfather briefly but devoted a long, powerful sequence to his father. A number of the poems were set in present time, sometimes presenting empty or alienated Americans who sounded like their English counterparts in Eliot's *Waste Land.* There was the quest for truth, often shadowed by the awareness of the brief span of human life and the inevitability of death. But sometimes, as if a continuation of love's exhilaration in *Promises,* there was the attempt to achieve joy through a clear view of life's vicissitudes and the restorative power of nature.

Though there was no epigraph, Warren glossed the title of the book with the first sequence, "Garland for You," and the first of the sequence's eight poems, "Clearly About You." In *Promises* he had spoken sometimes as "I," and sometimes as "you," still speaking in his own voice but also, by implication, drawing the reader into the poem. Now he was quite direct:

> Whoever you are, this poem is clearly about you.
> For there's nothing else in the world it could be about.
> Whatever it says, this poem is clearly true,
> For truth is all we are born to, and the truth's out.

He speaks in "the age of denture and reduced alcoholic intake," a time and mood echoed in other poems. He avoids looking in the mirror, and when finally he does, he sees there a stranger staring at him, and he is aware that "things are getting somewhat out of hand now—. . . ." (p. 3). In the fourth poem of the sequence, "Switzerland" (with material probably gleaned in the Zurich clinic two years before), sickness is pervasive, but at the end the poet prays, "O God of the *steinbock's* great sun-leap. . . . Deliver them all, young and old, to Thy health, named joy" (p. 9). In the sixth poem, "The Letter About Money, Love, or Other Comfort, if Any," the poet (whose life itinerary suggests Warren's own) attempts to find the recipient of this letter, which he has accepted from a shady-looking character for delivery. It appears that the intended recipient, with his often disreputable past, is probably the speaker himself. Finally, he hopes that at the end of his search he will, like a plunging eagle, "bark glory, / and by that new light I shall seek / the way, and my peace with God. . . ." (pp. 13–16). The poem is a metrical tour de force, one single four-page sentence divided into eight stanzas, each adhering to the same eleven-line rhyme scheme. For some readers, the poem's difficulty would obscure its virtuosity.[8]

Next, before another extended sequence, Warren interposed two paired poems from the book's title. "Two Pieces after Suetonius" draws upon the Roman historian's *Lives of the Caesars,* focusing on two of the twelve in "Apology for Domitian" and "Tiberius on Capri." Both men, with their egregious perversions, suffer from some of the same ills that beset the modern men in these poems. To Tiberius, the sea sings, "All is nothing, nothing all," and as he stands on his palace wall in the darkness, diverted by neither his power nor his sex slaves, he rails against "the paradox of powers that would grind us like grain, small and dry" (p. 23). The companion poem builds from Domitian's fears and sadism to his murder, but with the slangy diction Warren often used, he declares abruptly, "Let's stop horsing around—it's not Domitian, it's you. . . ." (p. 21).[9]

"Mortmain," the five-poem sequence that follows, is the most obviously personal. (Twenty-three years after his father's death Warren would write one scholar, "The world never feels the same afterwards. For one thing, you relive the relationship over and over, with many surprises. . . .") The first of the "Mortmain" poems, "After Night Flight Son Reaches Bedside of Already Unconscious Father, Whose Right Hand Lifts in a Spasmodic Gesture, As Though Trying to

Make Contact: 1955," shows the process at work. The newspaper headline–style title, as if to reject the conventional emotion-laden elegy, is reinforced by the graphic details of the sickroom and its moribund patient, only to be reversed in the intensity of the last lines as the hand sinks in death:

> All things—all joy and the hope that strove,
> . . . Were snatched from me, and I could not move,
> Naked in that black blast of his love. (p. 25)

Four of the five following poems in the sequence supply moving vignettes: the father shouldering in boyhood the family responsibilities that deny him the life he wanted, the old Greek grammar he still cherishes in adulthood. The provenance is explicit, as in "A Vision: Circa 1880," the last of the five, where, picturing the father as boy, the poet writes, "That scene is in Trigg County, and I see it. / Trigg County is in Kentucky, and I have been there. . . ." (p. 32). In "Fox-Fire: 1956," the third of the sequence, holding the old grammar in his hand, the poet tries to understand his father's life. He thinks that if he could state, clearly and distinctly, the problem that that frustrated life poses for him, "then God / Could no longer fall back on His old alibi of ignorance" (p. 28). He hears his son, laughing at play in a farther room and puts his father's Greek grammar on the shelf beside his own.[10]

But pathos is not the dominant emotion. In the second poem, "A Dead Language: Circa 1885," he has the memory of his father's stoical courage, reciting a line from the book: "And laughing from the deep of a dark conquest and joy, / Said: 'Greek—but it wasn't for me. Let's get to breakfast, boy' " (p. 27). This mood leads in the fourth poem, "In the Turpitude of Time: N.D.," to a tentatively affirmative conclusion: If "we—oh, could we only—believe / What annelid and osprey know," then in this harmony with nature we might hear the music a star "might sing to our human ear," and wait for the wind's voice to become "our song: / In the heart's last kingdom only the old are young" (pp. 30–31). Then, in "A Vision: Circa 1880," in the whole sequence's last lines, comes an image of affirmation and renewal: "And one high oak leaf stirs gray, and the air, / Stirring, freshens to the far favor of rain" (p. 33). If the title "Mortmain" suggests the past, that past and its claims are now remembered differently, and put to a very different use from that in the very personal poem a quarter century earlier, "The Return: An Elegy."[11]

Guthrie provided material for other poems in the book, those not of emperors but of people from modest walks of life and less, such as Mr. Moody, an albino whose cobbler's bench is his living and his Bible, his obsession. More stark and powerful is the three-poem sequence, "Ballad: Between the Boxcars," based on a death not uncommon in railroad towns where boys hopping freights for fun might pay with death. But this particular death is generalized, as the poet asks if, hearing the cry of our own last moments, "we may know the poor self not alone, but with all who are cast / To that clobber, and slobber, and grunt, between the boxcars?" (p. 48).[12]

Guthrie is also there with a stylistic change of pace in "Some Quiet, Plain Poems." The mood is complex and shifting in the five poems, a mixture of the elegiac, the nostalgic, the hopeful, and even the affirmative. Recalled in Italy, the Kentucky scene is peopled with faces long gone, remembered to the sound of birds calling and rain falling. In the last poem of the sequence, "Debate: Question, Quarry, Dream," recalling longings dreamed in boyhood and on night streets walked in adulthood, the poet concludes,

> Question, quarry, dream—I have vented my ire on
> My own heart that, ignorant and untoward,
> Yearns for an absolute that Time would, I thought, have prepared,
> But has not yet. Well, let us debate
> The issue. But under a tight roof, clutching a toy,
> My son now sleeps, and when the hour grows late,
> I shall go forth where the cold constellations deploy
> And lift up my eyes to consider more strictly the appalling logic of joy.
>
> (pp. 44–45)

These lines about the heart's yearning had a continuing relevance. "I am a creature of this world, but I am also a yearner," he would say later. "I would call this temperament rather than theology—I haven't got any gospel. That is, I feel an immanence of meaning in things, but I have no meaning to put there that is interesting or beautiful." The lines from the poem also employ a tableau the poet will use increasingly: his standing, staring at the night sky, hoping for an answer, which does not come.[13]

There is something of a disjointed effect in the second half, where the poems tend to be very different from one another. They range from "Two Studies in Idealism: Short Survey of American, and

Human, History" (in which a Confederate and a Union soldier reflect on their motives, which led to their deaths) to the three–part
"Prognosis: A Short Story, the End of Which You Will Know Soon
Enough." Unlike the two soldiers, however, the dying woman is
able to love God and the world, and to say, "I have heard the grain
of sand say: I know my joy, I know its name" (p. 60). This is a foreshadowing of a poem that, years later, would put this epiphany more
clearly: this love of the world's beauty can lead to a belief in God.
What might have been a low-key short story becomes instead a
vehicle for an almost mystical insight into life in the presence of
death.[14]

A radical tonal and stylistic disjunction comes in the volume's last
three parts, with end–of–season beach scenes and a sinister sequence
entitled "Nursery Rhymes," in the second of which Little Boy Blue
is cruelly harangued: "You Little Wretch, don't you hear me call!"
(p. 67), and in the last, "The Bramble Bush," where the speaker, having scratched out his eyes in the bramble bush and having scratched
them back again, hears, in the dawn's beauty, "the joy / Of flesh
singing on the bone" (p. 70). The final sequence, "Short Thoughts
for Long Nights," consisting of nine rhymed quatrains, continues
bizarre. "Nightmare of a Mouse" ends as teeth crunch on its skull.
"Nightmare of a Man" ends as his test-tube formula fails and he
weeps for his mother's death. In another, "History, shaped like a
white hen," walks in the kitchen door, consumes a cricket, and walks
out again (p. 77). There are two poems of advice for a little boy to
prepare him for life's disappointments, one on the incommunicabil-
ity of joy, and a final one intended to communicate a large truth
through a small insect. In "Grasshopper Tries to Break Solipsism" the
creature sings all summer long, "For God is light, oh I love Him, love
is my song." He must sing, for should he not, God would weep,
"And over all things, all night, His despair, like ice, creep" (p. 79). If
this was the articulation of something like Yeats's concept in his Last
Poems of "tragic joy" or just another combination of the disarming
and the despairing, only Warren knew.[15]

When the book appeared—and later as well—many commentators
were uncertain about its meanings. From the first the responses were
mixed, with admiration for the excitement and vitality and disdain of
the eccentricity. In the months that followed, the division of opinion
persisted but then began to shift more and more toward the negative.
Warren was caught, as one scholar would later write, in "a massive

shift in national cultural sensibility, away from the highbrow, densely intellectual, formally disciplined style of the high Modern period (best represented in the early Eliot) and toward the loosely structured, transparently readable, Whitmanesque style of the 'New American Poetry,' whose rising prophets in the 1950s were Beat and Confessional poets. . . ."[16]

A number of factors were involved. In his versification, he was no longer interested in the precision of form he had mastered long ago in his Marvellian poems. Increasingly he was using the rhythms of normal speech. Often he was employing long, sometimes Whitmanesque lines. Usually there were rhyme schemes, some of them complex and precise. It was as if he took delight in his facility and demonstrated it across a broad range. To some this seemed virtuosity for its own sake. (The same was true of diction, ranging from classical and philosophical to colloquial and slangy, as if to employ the vocabulary of Jack Burden.) The book has a perceptible structure, with the three-poem sequences dominating the first half and two more the second half. Others also balance one another: the four longer single poems and the two duets: "Two Pieces after Suetonius" and "Two Studies in Idealism." But the effect of the two final sequences, with their nursery rhymes and insects, is to diminish the accreting power of the longer preceding ones.

The book's content demonstrated familiar concerns: the quest for truth, the seeking after identity, and the rites of passage, particularly the loss of innocence and the related necessity of coming to terms with death, especially that of loved ones. There is also the power of love as a mitigating force in the face of the blank indifference of the universe. Some of the poems, however, seem simply to be there, without functional relationship to other poems or major themes, though sometimes employing similar imagery. "Fatal Interview: Penthesilea and Achilles" shows Warren's fondness and facility in adapting classic materials. "Nocturne: Traveling Salesman in Hotel Room" is graphic, resembling a plotless short story in its revelation of loneliness, an invocation of mood with a breath of hope at the end. Demonstrating the variety of his materials—without the richness of the Kentucky poems, for instance—these contribute little to any central effect.

Warren's own judgment since then has done nothing to enhance the book's status. Nine years after publication an interviewer asked him about "fine [overdone] writing." He replied, "I've made some very bad slips, such as in the volume of poems called *You, Emperors, and Others*. . . . I was on the wrong track; I was writing poems that were not on my line, my basic impulse. I got stuck with a lot of side-track poems. I hadn't caught them early enough." He told another that the book "has no real center. I was groping for a center." He became increasingly sure of this judgment, and when, over the years, he published three collections, he kept winnowing until, in his final volume, only three of the original forty-six survived. He had put into the book virtually all of the poems he had published since *Promises*. Years later Albert Erskine would say that Warren was always eager to publish new collections, that he wished his friend would wait and publish them at longer intervals, which would provide more time for seasoning and selection. Whether it was the maker's delight in showing his creations or the familiar writer's conviction that the most recent thing he has done is his best, or the lavish energy and the fierce ambition for success that led to this volume's publication, coming just three years after the phenomenally successful *Promises*, it served his reputation poorly.[17]

Warren must have seen the drift of the reviews as the fall came in. Then, just before Thanksgiving, there was a misfortune in family life on top of the professional one. Rosanna, he told Andrew Lytle, "got thrown from her pony (pretty big creature) and busted two vertebrae and had to get plastered up from crotch to chin, poor baby. But she took it fine. . . . She would have made out all right, I imagine, if it hadn't been for Gabriel, who scared the pony. No harm done, in the end." She was in the cast for seven weeks. A month after that she underwent another rite of passage: the information from classmates that Santa Claus didn't really exist. She wrote him anyway, and the presents she requested were there under the tree on Christmas morning.[18]

The Warrens welcomed 1961 with a party for thirty guests. Albert and Marisa Erskine were there, as were Bill and Rose Styron, and Peter Blume and Hugh Cox and their wives. Warren told Andrew, "We boozed happily till 5 AM and didn't feel too bad the next day and started the year in a very loving frame of mind toward mankind." His feelings about the new year might well have been shadowed by some anxiety. *Life* had accepted his piece on the Civil War, and the short book would follow in due course. He had now settled down to "the grim work of rewriting" *Wilderness*. He might have wondered if, with its publication, his reputation in prose would take a dip like that in his poetry. In a little over four years he would be sixty. He still had his prodigious energy. Still given to meditations on time and decay, whether they turned into poems or not, he must have heard the passage of time even more clearly now.

SIX

Recording History: Literary and Otherwise

37

❖

The War

Mist drifts on the bay's face
And the last of day, it would seem, goes under,
But it's hard to tell in this northern place
If this, now, is truly the day's end, or

If, in a new shift of mist,
The light may break through yonder
To stab gold to the gray sea, and twist
Your heart to a last delight—or at least, to wonder.
                                        —"VII Finisterre"[1]

With the approach of the centennial, C. Vann Woodward had chal-
lenged fellow historians to approach it with fidelity to the facts, so that
they would "flatter the self-righteousness of neither side." (He issued
the injunction in *The Burden of Southern History,* which he dedicated to
Warren.) It was as if Warren heeded the charge in his 109-page study,
The Legacy of the Civil War: Meditations on the Centennial. A short excerpt
came out in *Life* on February 27 and the book itself on March 17.[2]

"The Civil War," he began, "is for the American imagination the
great single event of our history." He traced the old, prewar romantic
unionism and delved into abolitionism and the assertion of the
"higher law" that disregarded the Constitution and prepared the way
for the "irrepressible conflict." As for the war's effects, there was the
change from a mainly agrarian society to one driven by business, technology, and a new financial order. He totaled up its dreadful immediate costs and then focused on longer-lasting effects: "The war gave the

South the Great Alibi and gave the North the Treasury of Virtue. . . . By the Great Alibi pellagra, hookworm, and illiteracy are all explained. . . ." By it the Southerner "turns defeat into victory, defects into virtues" (pp. 54–55). For the Northerner, "the War appears according to the doctrine of the Treasury of Virtue, as a consciously undertaken crusade so full of righteousness that there is enough overplus stored in Heaven" to constitute "a plenary indulgence, for all sins past, present, and future, freely given by the hand of history" (pp. 64, 59).

He traced the war's continuing growth in the national consciousness. "That was our Homeric period, and the figures loom up only a little less than gods. . . ." (p. 82). The moral questions raised are equally portentous: "To what extent is man always—or sometimes—trapped in the great texture of causality, of nature and history?" (p. 100). This crux is most dramatically presented in the question of "the irrepressible conflict." Was the war in fact inevitable? He showed how the affirmative answer was self-exculpating for both North and South. His conclusion was both somber and hopeful. The war was not only a massive tragedy, it was "a crime of monstrous inhumanity, into which almost innocently men stumbled." And its bitter fruits included "the concept of total war, the key to Northern Victory" (p. 16), and ultimately "the secret school for 1917–1918 and 1941–1945" (p. 46). If at the war's end there was "a reconciliation by human recognition" (p. 103) and the catharsis embodied in the Gettysburg Address, there was nonetheless no "instruction" from that catharsis. But there is "an image of the powerful, grinding process by which an ideal emerges out of history" (p. 109).

There was an immediate chorus of praise for the brilliance, insight, and beauty of the work. *The New Republic,* however, published a slashing review convicting him of the biases of *I'll Take My Stand.* Furious, Warren wrote the editor that he wished the reviewer had taken the trouble "to glance at explicit repudiation, some time back, of what I said in 1929." He also supplied a three-point endorsement of civil rights and added, "I think Dr. Martin Luther King a great man, and that the sit-ins conducted according to his principles are morally unassailable and will win." (He did not refer to an impassioned essay he had written, more than a year before, against violence perpetrated upon students seeking lunch-counter integration in Nashville.) *The Legacy of the Civil War* sold steadily, and it would be reissued twenty-two years later.[3]

The Warrens rented their house to Lionel and Diana Trilling and flew to Paris on May 1. In Brittany, where Eleanor had spent a summer as a child, they rented a "Breton farmhouse, redone with les conforts, fine views, perfect seclusion, loads of room and rooms, privacy for work, private beach at the end of the garden, a village a half mile off, delightful countryside and—my God!—cheap, very cheap," he wrote Lon Cheney. "To cap it all, we have a nun's school here where Roposie and Gabriel go very happily." Their new address was "Le Brénéguy, par Locmariaquer (Morbihan)." They could have it until July 1.[4]

They enjoyed their drives about the countryside, the fine beach, and the air full of skylarks and the smell of the sea. "I find that I love the Breton sights. Next to the Rocca, which we have lost, I like this better than any place I ever saw." Its virtues were several. "Eleanor is taking a lot of time to investigate . . . the oyster culture and business here. She is off a lot with the gents of the syndicate, journalists, producteurs, workers, boatmen, biologists and public health officers." Warren was also learning a fair amount from Eleanor's researches. As for his new novel, "I'm not really writing yet," he told Albert Erskine, "just sort of prodding at the amorphous mass which lies on my table like an enormous jellyfish." But by mid-June he had sent him six chapters, and he would send eight more before they left.[5]

In July they moved twenty miles northwest to new quarters. They had a basement apartment in a château surrounded by a fifty-acre park of oak, beech, and chestnut trees and magnolia woods all in bloom. The working conditions were good enough. In mid-July, writing "from the stone ruin where I compose," he told Erskine, "I plug along, with some excitement, between fits of despair."[6]

These had been generally good months. The nuns had kept the children up with their schoolmates at home and given them a quantum leap ahead in French. And there was the usual education at home. "Poppy identified plants and trees and thought of things for us to do," Rosanna would remember. "He gave me French wildflower books, and I set out dutifully to collect and press and draw and tabulate all of them. He didn't force these things on us. They were usually imaginatively proposed. But after about a week I decided I didn't like wildflowers and wouldn't have anything more to do with them. I remember going into a great passion and throwing the notebook down and yelling that I hated wildflowers. My parents looked astonished at this. My mother looked a little worried, and later I was remorseful and went to her in fear and anguish that maybe Poppy wouldn't think I was any good."[7]

By the end of August the solitude was beginning to tell on the children, but there had been compensating factors in their frequent uprooting. The weave and texture of their family culture, reinforced by the stories they heard, grew richer. "We had a very strong sense of continuity between what we imagined to be Poppy's boyhood in Guthrie and what we did in Vermont or Brittany," Rosanna remembered. "So I didn't have much sense of living in Connecticut, because there we didn't live near other children, and our real reality was a version of Guthrie that had been translated to this place." As their Brittany summer drew to a close Warren told Erskine, "Eleanor and I could make out happily . . . in fact we could use some more uninterrupted time with our work, but it won't be too good for the kids." So they made reservations to fly home on September 10.[8]

Life was hectic in the month after their return. Warren had to go to the University of North Carolina in mid-October for a dinner honoring Randall Jarrell. A month later he spent time with another poet, his boyhood idol. T. S. Eliot and his wife Valerie were on their way to the Caribbean, but Eliot needed money, and so a reading was arranged at the 92nd Street YMHA in New York. Warren introduced him, harking back to the appearance of *The Waste Land*. "What we tend to forget is that then there were no exigeses to tell you what the poem meant. But your heart told you, the tingling of your spine told you, your mouth framing the grand syllables, told you. . . . Here was indeed the voice of 'il miglior fabbro.' " He wasn't up to the reception, and so the Warrens sneaked him out a side door to his hotel. There at the Gladstone they had a long pleasant time together in the bar. The reading was Eliot's last public appearance.[9]

Before Warren had completed the first draft of *Wilderness* he had typed up a three-thousand-word summary. The book would run from twenty to twenty-five thousand words, he thought, but then "it began to exfoliate and develop, and the incidental characters began to be more important to me than they had been in the beginning. The ratio of the main character's interest to the incidental characters shifted along the way." The summary had been circulated to the book clubs for adoption. When there was no word from them, he worried because he had overextended himself with investments. Then to his relief the Literary Guild made it their December selection.[10]

The December number of the Literary Guild's *Wings* carried the two pages Warren had sent from France. ("I enclose some crap I have written," he had told Erskine, "at the expense of two days—for their

Wings.") He wrote that his novel (subtitled *A Tale of the Civil War*) was not about the battle though it was "the summarizing image of the blankness, blindness, and brutality, not only of war but of some other kinds of experience as well, and more importantly, of the courage and idealism which enables men to undergo such experience. . . . I hoped to draw the picture of a good man, a man who deeply wants and needs to serve the cause of human freedom. He is Adam Rosenzweig, a young Bavarian Jew, educated by his father, one of the new generation of Jewish humanists and revolutionists who appeared in the 19th century. But the father, who had fought and suffered years of imprisonment for freedom, betrays, in the end, the thing he had fought for; and Adam feels an obligation to fulfill his father's mission." Leopold Rosenzweig is another of Warren's failed fathers. His son also cannot forgive him for another legacy, his deformed left foot. Adam has invented a painful corrective shoe, hoping for acceptance as a Union recruit. Both foot and shoe function symbolically as well as literally in the story.

"His journey begins in New York, in July, 1863," Warren wrote, when "alone in a twilight street, [he] finds a body of a Negro, mutilated, hanging from a lamp post, and then, a few minutes later, is caught up in a howling mob bent on sacking a Negro district in the midst of the atrocities of the Draft Riots." He is saved from death by Mose Talbutt, a runaway slave. He and Jed Hawksworth, driven out of North Carolina for offering testimony for a Negro in court, and now a sutler with the Union army, become Adam's closest companions. Like him, but without his sense of mission, Mose and Jed are groping toward some meaning in their lives.[11]

Through most of the novel Adam is the passive observer, trying to understand the concept of freedom. It is easy to see how Warren decided, while revising, to keep Adam's benefactor, Aaron Blaustein— a onetime peddler become a wealthy man—there in New York and to substitute for him, as sutler-in-the-field, Jed Hawksworth, the renegade North Carolinian. His dialogue and that of Mose gave Warren the opportunity to use the dialect he knew so well. This relationship helped to triple the size of the first draft and also provided climactic events. With Adam and Mose working for Jed, who is sponsored by Blaustein, the scene is set for violence. When Adam finds Jed robbed and murdered by Mose, he blames himself for what he sees as the transferred anger he aroused with a racial epithet. Filled with guilt, he nonetheless feels *"they all betrayed me. . . ."* (p. 303). He covers the evidence and then is caught up in the chaotic confusion of men, animals, and wagons as the battle begins.

Separated from the others, encamped in a solitary glade, he remembers his mother's loving tenderness. Suddenly he leaps to his feet. " 'I came here!' he cried aloud. 'I came here to fight for freedom!' " (p. 288). He has barely time for this thought before famished Confederate infantrymen rush into the glade and overturn the wagon to consume its food. One of them, "the hairy scarecrow," rips the boots from Adam's feet. Soon seven federals appear, and when one of them is set upon by two rebels, Adam picks up a rifle and shoots one of the rebels dead. Swept away into the developing battle, Adam thinks, *"I have killed a man,"* then, *"We always do what we intend"* (p. 300). When the guns have stopped firing and the wilderness is on fire, Adam is alone in a glade where another dead soldier lies.

Sitting there half dazed, he sees among the debris the objects his Orthodox uncle had pressed upon him in Bavaria: a phylactery and the tallith. Thinking of his father's burial, he repeats the traditional prayers. Then he hears the crackling roar of the terrible holocaust that will consume the screaming wounded as well as the silent slain. He feels no remorse but instead conviction. "Yes. . . . he would do it all again. . . . *But, oh, with a different heart*" (p. 310). He prepares to walk out of the wilderness feeling a kinship with the dead. This is the end, Warren wrote in *Wings,* of "the search for a definition of his idealism that can survive the world he has met and the discovery about himself which burst on him in the end."

With its spareness, its hero much more passive than active, and its straight-line progression in space and time, *Wilderness* resembles not at all the earlier novels steeped in history, complexly plotted, and imbued with violence and sexual drama. The war's impact on Adam is conveyed with devices recalling scenes Stephen Crane used for Henry Fleming's baptism of fire in *The Red Badge of Courage.* But in spite of the vignettes—the draft riots, recollections of Pickett's charge, army camp life, and brief infantry skirmishing—the war remains for the most part a curiously remote background. This is a psychological and moral drama in which this thirty-year-old virgin, this Adam in the New World, falls into sin but achieves a kind of redemption, which finally brings a sense of community. Set apart from the others by his foreignness, his crippled foot, and his combined idealism and naiveté, he remains almost as much a symbol as a flesh-and-blood man. The novel—it would be called a parable, an *exemplum*—shows how Adam sees through the falsehoods of Jed and Mose and finally through his own self-deceptions.

It was the misfortune of *Wilderness* to appear close to *The Legacy of the Civil War*. Many reviewers used the virtues of the latter to belabor the deficiencies of the former. Warren was charged with sententious solemnity and mass-appeal sexuality. Some reviewers granted his talent but thought he was overpraised by intellectuals. Worse followed in the balance of the year and on into 1962, when British reviewers outdid their American counterparts. Eight years after *Wilderness* one interviewer told him he thought that novel and *Band of Angels* were his two "most adversely criticized" books and suggested that the absence of irony was in part responsible. Warren agreed but emphasized a technical problem. When the novelette grew, "the development of the central character did not keep pace with the development of the experiences he went through. . . . You have the strange effect of a central *hollowness* with a rich context, with the central character as an observer. He's involved *intellectually* but *only* intellectually."[12]

Warren was well into a new novel by the time he read the reviews. He may not have read all of them, but he must certainly have been aware of *Time*'s attack on him as a gifted artist who "has all too often used his remarkable skill as a novelist with carelessness and cynicism." Success had not been hard for him to cope with, but some others had found it difficult to forgive. Those who knew him best could certainly see his pleasure in the fame his work had brought him, in the rewards steadily accreting. But some saw too that he remained a conscientious artist who applied his strict standards to himself as well as to others, and when he felt that work was less than his best he usually said so. But now he knew that each new one would be carefully scrutinized by those who thought he was no longer the scrupulous artist who had once said that for him, it was poetry or death. He was also a proud man, one who wanted to be like his admired Hardy, to get better with age. His determination must have helped sustain him as he worked at the long, demanding novel now on his desk.[13]

38

❖

Great Expectations

He had never known, he reflected, a writer, not even the
meanest, most time-serving, and most convicted of failure, who
did not, in some recess of his being, cherish the yearning, even
the hope. The disease was in the very medium. He thought of those
things that seemed to promise the craftsman a survival beyond himself:
paint, stone, wood, the chain of notes, the word. He reflected on the
difference between the disease of those who work in this promise of
immortality and the disease of those who do not.

—Flood[1]

Flood had been in progress for a half-dozen years. It was now forty-five
thousand words long, and Warren's overriding concern was to finish it,
but in April he had confided to Bill Bandy, "I flirt with the idea of
going back to a limited teaching schedule. No captive audience in Fairfield. Maybe somewhere else." Maynard Mack, the chairman of English at Yale, inquired if he would be interested in teaching for a term
(despite the fact that some members felt that one member of the Brooks
and Warren duo was enough). He replied that he would join the department only for one term each year. It was agreed that beginning in
the spring term of 1962 he would teach one course on the novel and
another on writing fiction. The classes and the hourlong commute to
New Haven meant two lost days each week from his writing. Travels
further afield did the same, and the family's summer trip, meant to
provide clear time for the novel, would in the end prove costly.[2]

Being a major figure in the literary establishment cost him increasingly varied service. On January 22 he made another of his hectic de-

partures when Eleanor drove him to New York, where he barely caught the plane for a two–week conference with Japanese intellectuals to consider the state of cultural exchanges. The Japanese enjoyed his lectures and memories of his southern boyhood. He enjoyed Japanese PEN officials' taking him on a round of Tokyo's expensive bars. Back home again he carried on his committee duties for the American Academy and the National Institute, and in late March he made a trip to Washington to deliver a birthday tribute for Robert Frost.[3]

In Yale's Silliman College he was teaching Conrad, Dreiser, and Zola, and in his seminar he was showing twelve seniors how to shape their own fiction. In spite of feeling that such writing constituted a "natural process that is promoted by unnatural means," he continued in his familiar way: reading a story aloud, prompting discussion and analysis, and examining students' work with them individually. "Chance to air my opinions," he said. To his colleague Richard Sewall "he was a marvelously fresh, refreshing person in the academic community." Warren told Allen Tate about his satisfaction, "but I begin to look forward to June and solitude with typewriter happily interrupted by family."[4]

On May 27 they left for France. There they drove south to Serres, near Ascain and the resort town of Saint-Jean-de-Luz on the Bay of Biscay just above the Spanish border. Their stay began well enough in "a nice house with a farm next door, surrounded by meadows, view of Spanish mountains out of windows and from garden. We are three miles from the beach, a mile from a lovely little town with superlative food." Rosanna and Gabriel were enrolled at the nuns' school, and their parents were poised for intensive work on *The Oysters of Locmariaquer* and *Flood*.[5]

Then the troubles began. Eager to swim, Rosanna plunged into heavy surf, which knocked her off her feet and broke her arm. For three weeks thereafter she sat forlornly at the water's edge, her left elbow in a cast. Then, the day it came off, she came down with the mumps. By mid-July she had recovered, but soon Gabriel and his father had it. "I am writing this from my bed of ignominy and pain," he wrote Albert Erskine. The doctor was reassuring. Though it could cause sterility, he told his patient not to worry: "Your succession is assured," he said, and fitted him for the same truss he wore himself as president of the local riding club. Ten days later Eleanor's symptoms blossomed, and the doctor administered another injection, for another forty dollars. To Rosanna it seemed that the whole summer was taken up with mumps. There were times when their parents were so sick they couldn't walk to the bathroom. The children next brought home whooping cough, and they would all cough in sequence. By August they felt they could return to Brittany so Eleanor could check details for her book on the Breton coast oyster industry. Warren jumped into the sea as soon as they got there and promptly developed a violent fever that cost him another week in bed. As they prepared for departure misfortune followed them still. "On the way home foolishly ignored the doctor's warblings about fatigue," Warren wrote Tate, "and got backlash which I still have. So I live with antibiotics, morphine for the stummick, nameless pills, etc. . . . Otherwise the summer was OK."[6]

At home again he resumed teaching and put aside his novel. It was November before he could report improvement. "The infection seems about gone, bladder about normal, prostate ditto, but . . . am still on the wagon. Hope to be off by Christmas. . . . I still drag around, and have some of the depression that comes with a prolonged infection, but things are looking up."[7]

In March he finished a thirty-chapter draft of the novel and began his revisions with the help of "a magnificent job of detailed criticism" from Albert Erskine and William Styron. "This is my best one," he declared in early June. "If it isn't I'll change my line of work. I mean this." After the labor of revision it was time for a break. "We leave for Montana this week to give the kids a bit of the Wild West, plus a pack trip. They are delirious. I like the idea myself."[8]

They took the train from New York on June 12 for Bozeman and three weeks at the Elk Horn Ranch. It was, he wrote Allen, "the best thing we ever did. The ranch was magnificent, a high green valley, 7000 feet up, with rushing streams down it and snow caps and forests all around. We had a wonderful pack trip, four days, into the very high mountains, just the family and two wranglers. . . ." The trip had been "complete with snow storm, tent fire, and me being bucked off my horse. . . . Alas, we go away tomorrow." As they sat waiting for the train to move, Rosanna looked out, her head against the window and tears on her cheeks. "Montana is so wonderful," she said. "Let's never come back and ruin it."[9]

When the proofs of *Flood* finally came in October, Warren rewrote a number of scenes. He sent one set to Arthur Mizener, who returned it with heavy annotations and a three-thousand-word critique. He thought the book wonderful, Warren's best since *All the*

King's Men, but he was afraid that many readers would not understand its metaphysical concerns. In a long and grateful reply, Warren said that one friend had thought it was about " 'race' and 'South.' . . . Now there's certainly a lot of my long hassle with the South here, but that's not central. . . ." He was still confident: "I trust that this is my best book . . . because it seemed to me that as I worked I was getting more of myself into it, involving more ratios of things that concern me. I don't mean, God knows, that I am Brad, or that the novel is autobiography. . . ." Before long he would know if others agreed, for they now had a publication date: April 24, 1964.[10]

The new year would see the publication of two more books besides this one: *The Oysters of Locmariaquer* in the summer, and *The Joey Story,* by ten-year-old Rosanna Phelps Warren, in the spring. The previous year of 1963 had begun for her with a trauma. Her dog had been killed by an automobile. His successor was a small sturdy puppy of a camel color and indeterminate origins. Not long thereafter he was joined by a collie they named Aslan. At their camp in Vermont, while her father worked at his desk she worked at hers on the story of her pets. Back in Fairfield she concluded the narrative with Aslan's first birthday. When Warren told Andrew Lytle that Eleanor had finished her book he added, "Rosanna has just finished a book, too—no kidding, but not as long as her Mommy's. Very brilliant and beautiful, too. Sometimes I don't know what to make of her, she's weird and wonderful. . . ." Bennett Cerf liked it too. "She wrote this book for her own private amusement," he recorded, "but when she showed it to me, I was so delighted with it that I persuaded her to let us publish it. . . ." Cerf's account appeared on the dust jacket of the eighty-five-hundred-word story. He celebrated by taking the family to lunch at "21" in New York.[11]

In her book Rosanna had written, "When the children were at school . . . Mommy and Poppy were in their studies in the barn (they are writers). . . ." (p. 15). This year their parents' writing was even more central in family life than before. Eleanor was at last free to return to her long-postponed novel and Warren to his multiple projects, including a book on the civil rights movement and a new novel. By September he had drafts of three chapters of the latter, but then the former began to demand more time. He continued on it into

1964, when they learned that the Literary Guild had taken *Flood* for its May selection.

In April 1931, driving through southwest Tennessee, Warren had seen the house said to have been Ulysses S. Grant's headquarters at Shiloh. The village "was the germ of Fiddlersburg," he would remember. Much later, he started the novel but put it aside. When he took it up again after *The Cave* and *Wilderness,* the idea of people returning to a rural hometown entered in, and on top of that the fate of villages he had seen flooded by the dams of the Tennessee Valley Authority to provide power for rural areas. Then there was more: "I have friends who have arbitrarily attempted to come back and pick up a world by an act of will, and it's never worked. . . ." (He had almost attempted this himself.) And so, he later said, the novel would "deal with the question 'What is home?' Ultimately home is not a place, it's a state of spirit, it's a state of feeling, a state of mind. . . . Your world view in one sense is your home."[12]

His longest book since *World Enough and Time, Flood* follows Bradwell Tolliver's return to Tennessee. Beginning in 1935, it covers more than twenty years and explores the complex lives of many characters through their marriages and divorces, adulteries and murders. There are, unsurprisingly, personal correspondences. Schooled in Nashville and the Ivy League (Darthurst), Brad gains early literary recognition and succeeds as a screenwriter but suffers an unsuccessful marriage. Displaced from the South, he feels a kind of existential loneliness and a yearning for a central core of certainty. The Warren character Brad most resembles is Jack Burden, with his cynicism, his smart-aleck cleverness, and the brusque coarseness of his speech. There are also resemblances in his misuse of his talent, his propensity for harming others, his descent into suffering, and the final clarification of his vision.[13]

The 440 pages teem with so many characters and incidents that they resist brief summary. Brad has been hired by Yasha Jones, an exotic former OSS man, now a film director-producer who has admired his first book, drawn from the life of Fiddlersburg. The film is to show a town's being destroyed by "progress." Brad's white convertible Jaguar XK-150 is a sign of his prosperity from Oscar-winning scripts that have supplanted his abandoned novel about Fiddlersburg. Brad seems on his way to achieving a sense of identity and self-realization as the flood rises to obliterate the town. He realizes that he had failed his first wife, Lettice Poindexter, and that his caveman sexuality had contributed to the sexual surrender of his sister, Maggie Fiddler, to a young man then shot by her husband, Dr. Calvin Fiddler. Now an inmate of the penitentiary above the town, Calvin can no longer bring himself to practice even his permitted medical skills.

After Maggie returns from a trip with Yasha that climaxes their romance, Calvin escapes during a jail break and menaces Yasha with a revolver. Attempting to disarm him, Brad catches bullets in his throat and leg. Performing a ballpoint-pen tracheotomy, Calvin saves his life. By the time of Brad's return to Fiddlersburg, Maggie is happily married to Yasha and pregnant. When Brad visits the prison, Calvin tells him that his memory was restored during the shooting and he is now capable of practicing medicine again. Subjected to the cruelest contemplation of identity in the solitude of his cell, he is more a whole man than Brad is in his lonely freedom. Lettice, having embraced Catholicism and now working in an old people's home, has found joy through praying "to know the *nowness* of God's will" (p. 432). At the end, after observing a memorial service for the town as the waters rise, and knowing "that this was his country," Brad rips up a new producer's lucrative offer to make the movie, feeling "a sudden, unwilled, undecipherable, tearing, ripping gesture of his innermost being toward those people over yonder." A Dantean quester, he thinks, "*There is no country but the heart*" (p. 440).

Some of the subplots and secondary characters are familiar. Lank Tolliver, another of Warren's failed fathers, is a brutal swamp man, a father who must be symbolically slain if Brad is to fulfill himself. Brad's editor, Telford Lott, is a false father surrogate, whereas Izzie Goldfarb, the learned old tailor whose memory helped bring Brad back to Fiddlersburg, had been a true father surrogate, and presumably his values will prove the truest ones for Brad. The novel's range is extended in several ways. One is the Hollywood seen by Brad, the artist manqué. Another is his wartime experience in Spain, where he sought a cause to provide a core of personal conviction. Another is Yasha's service, as M. Duval of the OSS, in aid of the French Resistance. His exotic character—with his scarred bald head, his many skills, his gurulike attributes—would present problems for a number of readers. More effective are the flashbacks to the Fiddlersburg of Brad's youth.[14]

The omniscient narrator's techniques at times seem more a demonstration of technical versatility than a necessity of the material. One admiring critic names the styles: "cinematic landscapes, sardonic commentary, melodramatic dialogue, folk wisdom, epistolary disquisition, and courtroom transcript." (He might have added interpolated Conradian monologues and capsule vitae of Fiddlersburg residents.) The tone is equally varied. There are poetic evocations and portentous philosophizing. The sexual frankness of the earlier novels is surpassed not only in the coarseness of male characters but also in the explicit sexuality, as in Brad's lovemaking with his second wife, Suzie Martine, and the poetic description of her genitalia. And in a combination of erotica and plot development, blind Leontine Purtle, a supposed innocent, readily agrees at a chance meeting with Brad to his spontaneous suggestion of a motel interlude then and there. What shocks him is the discovery that her diaphragm is already in place before the start of the graphically described lovemaking.[15]

Warren supplied his customary epigraph and a subtitle. Both seem at least partly ironic. The former, "And I will plant them upon their land, and they shall no more be pulled up out of their land which I have given them, saith the Lord thy God," is from Amos, 9:15. At the end, preparing to "go wherever it might be that he would have to go," Brad realizes that it was not necessary to move Goldfarb's body as he had intended to do, for he has discovered that there is no country but the heart, and he knows that Goldfarb "was waiting for the waters [to cover all] who had lived in this place and done good and done evil" (p. 439). The last three words of the subtitle, *A Romance of Our Time*, suggest that this is not a romance of lovers' happy endings, or of characters such as the Brontës created, nor of the "legendary mist" in which Nathaniel Hawthorne's men and women sometimes move. If the romance is that of Brad's life, the term can only be ironic, with his failed marriages and tawdry affairs. But with his new vision his feeling is like that of writers such as Washington Irving, valuing the past and regretting its disappearance.

Warren's habitual concerns lie at the heart of the novel: trying to understand the nature of reality, to achieve a sense of personal identity, and to understand and if possible atone for the transgressions arising out of one's personal portion of original sin. The novel is so crammed, however, with plot, characterization, and event that suggested meanings abound. But reviewers had great difficulty determining the author's intention. And no matter what that was, most of them were convinced that he had failed to accomplish it.[16]

The reaction was so vehement that one literary historian was moved to remark, "Every once in a while a novel will appear and provoke among its reviewers contempt, and even fury out of all proportion to its alleged defects. What calls out such a response is something of a mystery." One cause may have been simply disappointment. Expecting a philosophical exploration of changing values with an apocalyptic but potentially cleansing flood at the end, the reader was likely to find these possibilities obscured by melodrama. And whereas work by writers such as Nathanael West, Scott Fitzgerald, and Budd Schulberg had strikingly revealed the emptiness of Hollywood, this novel seemed to have borrowed some of its devices with its prison break, ballpoint-pen tracheotomy, the Yul Brynner–style director, and the Jennifer Jones–style blind country-girl victim who is actually a trollop.

The judgments in *Time* and *Newsweek* were almost unbelievably savage. Arthur Mizener had feared such responses, and in defense he pointed out in *The Sewanee Review* misconceptions about this "philosophical romance," which had a "marvelous, eloquent coherence." But even the admiration Warren usually received in the quarterlies was diminished. And once again, the British reception was worse than the American.[17]

In the first few pages Brad Tolliver had been brooding about reviews. Now, as Warren may have done the same, there were consolations. No matter what the book's general reception, there were opinions he respected. Belatedly, Allen Tate echoed some of Mizener's concerns but confirmed Warren's own judgment: "Flood seems to me your best all round since *All the King's Men*." Of the reviews Tate said, "Well, that happens to everybody." Three years later Warren would still say, "The novels that seem to have brought the most satisfaction to me are *World Enough and Time, Flood,* and *All the King's Men*."[18]

39

❖

Recording the Negro Revolution

I want to make my reader see, hear, and feel as immediately as
possible what I saw, heard, and felt.
                        —*Who Speaks for the Negro?*[1]

The sound of the engine of the first fishing dory dies seaward, Soon
In the inland glen wakes the dawn-dove. We must try

To love so well the world that we may believe, in the end, in God.
                        —*"Masts at Dawn"*[2]

If the reception of *Flood* cast anything like a pall in that spring of
1964, there was a compensatory lift that summer. A year and a half
earlier, Warren had told Andrew Lytle that Eleanor was about to
finish a book. "I can't describe it," he wrote, "it's about Brittany . . . saints, legends, landscape, les calvaires, and, most of all,
about the history of the oyster. Quite literally. Very cranky and
witty and beautiful. You'll love it." So, in due course, did many
readers and reviewers. With the publication of *The Oysters of Locmariaquer* Eleanor would have the rewards not only of her talent but
also for the persistence that kept her at the book while she was raising children, keeping house, and looking after her husband and ailing relatives. Reviewers admired the author's wit and charm and
her novelist's skill. This reception would be crowned by the National Book Award for nonfiction. A year later it would help make
the case for her admission to the National Institute of Arts and
Letters.[3]

After reviewing the proofs of *Flood,* Warren had told Katherine Anne Porter, "Now [I] take to the road on a little piece of journalism in which I have my heart: interviewing the Negro leaders, a way to get out of my box and see the country and clear my mind—or confuse it." *Look* magazine wanted an article based on the interviews and would pay all the expenses. Then Random House would publish the material in book form. At the end of January 1964 he set off for three weeks in Mississippi and Alabama. On his return he wrote Arthur Mizener about his change of pace. "Running around with shotguns in the middle of a Mississippi night is not the same thing as a Yale classroom. Mississippi is a shotgun state right now, no kidding. By the way, the variety of types involved in this business is extraordinary, and as might be expected the younger ones are more interesting than the older 'organizational' types. . . . I wish I could play you some of the tapes I've got." In May he was still interviewing—Adam Clayton Powell one week and Carl Rowan the next. By early August he was near the end of his first draft.[4]

When Professor Evans Harrington invited him to the University of Mississippi Southern Literary Festival on the work of William Faulkner in the spring of 1965, he replied that he would be honored, but he did not see how the university administration could accept him because "I am unequivocally opposed to segregation in any form." He knew the subject would arise, and he thought that "Faulkner is, in the end, quite clear. If he had been alive at the time of the Oxford riots, the mob, had it been both logical and book-reading, would have burned him out." He sent a copy of his letter to the university chancellor, J. D. Williams, who replied that state law forbade the presence on campus of any Negroes other than enrolled students. Warren replied that he had not meant that he would refuse to speak if the audience was segregated, but that he would feel free to discuss race in Faulkner's work as he saw it. With thanks and relief, the chancellor confirmed the invitation.[5]

When he arrived on Thursday, April 22, 1965, a biracial delegation from all-black Tougaloo College was already there. Late that night their car was vandalized while a crowd of five hundred demonstrated outside their dormitory rooms. The next day the delegation's leader lodged a protest before they left, escorted by police. Robert Hamblin, a graduate student serving as Warren's escort and chauffeur, noted his agitation and concern for the Tougaloo students, and when a reporter asked his reaction, he responded, "Shameful!" One of Warren's concerns, Hamblin thought, was that he might "compromise his position as a leading Southern spokesman for racial equality and justice. Of all the festival speakers who were asked to join the Tougaloo group in the walkout . . . Warren had the most to lose in terms of credibility, integrity, and status." (His article based on his interviews, entitled "The Negro Now," had appeared in *Look* on March 23.) After wrestling with the problem, he came to a decision on Friday afternoon; "Dammit, I came here to deliver a speech, and I intend to deliver it." That night he told twelve hundred people that in Faulkner's depiction of blacks' suffering he found "the rejection of the brother, the kinsman, as a symbolic representation of the crime that is the final crime against both nature and the human community." Hamblin sensed a cathartic effect, as though his words, and Faulkner's, "had served as a kind of confession, releasing the anguish and regret of the days, months, and years of racial strife and tension, and positing the hope of a better time to come."[6]

After unforeseen delays, *Who Speaks for the Negro?* was published on May 27, 1965. The 454-page book was the fruit of the thousands of miles Warren had traveled in Mississippi, Louisiana, Tennessee, Georgia, and North Carolina, as well as major northern cities. Its six chapters show his prodigious reading in history, sociology, politics, psychology, anthropology, and, above all, the development of the civil rights movement. For an adequate understanding of the Congress of Racial Equality (CORE), the Southern Christian Leadership Conference (SCLC), and the Student Nonviolent Coordinating Committee (SNCC, or Snick), he also had to know about the Niagara movement, the National Association for the Advancement of Colored People, and the Urban League. Moreover, it was necessary to see proposals such as Whitney Young's Marshall Plan for Negroes and Martin Luther King, Jr.'s, Bill of Rights for the Disadvantaged against the background of Marcus Garvey's Back to Africa movement—and also the split in the Negro leadership over theory and tactics between Booker T. Washington's espousal of accommodation and W.E.B. Du Bois's call for immediate change. All of this and more were necessary for the frank, searching, and intensive discussions with scores of leaders and others in the movement. Also necessary were Warren's energy, persistence, and courage.

Working from masses of transcriptions, he incorporated passages of varying length, supplying scene-setting, vivid descriptions of the people, narrative segments, and italicized passages entitled "Note-books" for various brief vignettes and comments. He introduced each of his subjects with a meticulous description, printed their dia-logue, and then supplied excerpts ("On Violence," "On the Role of the White Liberal"), sometimes followed by a commentary, which might be quite brief. Individuals illustrated the larger issues and dilemmas.

In the most dramatic chapter, "A Mississippi Journal," he sampled opinion in Jackson two days after Byron de la Beckwith escaped con-viction for the murder of Medgar Evers, field secretary of the NAACP, and two days after a riot at Jackson College. It was the sum-mer of the Voter Education Project during which three of the young workers would be murdered and secretly buried in Philadelphia in Neshoba County. Warren rented a car and rode at night across the state with three members of Snick. He watched the speedometer anxiously as the young man driving pushed it up over ninety. Arriv-ing at the home of Dr. Aaron Henry, the president of the NAACP at Clarksdale, Warren interviewed him in a tightly curtained room while a guard with revolver and shotgun sat nearby.

The next chapter, "The Big Brass," focused on the leadership, on nine men and their diverse styles. Warren recorded Congressman Adam Clayton Powell's charm and aplomb. In Black Muslim head-quarters Minister Malcolm X, a man of "ominous dignity," told War-ren that the white race was doomed, and suddenly he discovered "that that pale, dull yellowish face that had seemed so veiled, so stony, as though past all feeling, had flashed into its merciless, leering life. . . ." (p. 255). Warren's strongest, though not uncritical, admira-tion was reserved for Martin Luther King. Warren saw him as "wise and good" (p. 434), and, for some young people with ineffective fa-thers, "the image of the father that might have been" (p. 372).

The succeeding chapters consider "Leadership from the Periph-ery" and "The Young." In the former he turned to black scholars and artists such as James Baldwin. The best segment was a thirty-page di-alogue with Ralph Ellison ranging widely over the literary response to the manifold questions. "No one," Warren wrote, "has made more unrelenting statements of the dehumanizing pressures that have been put upon the Negro. And *Invisible Man* is, I should say, the most pow-erful artistic representation we have of the Negro under these dehu-manizing conditions. . . ." (p. 354). As Warren glanced at his own pronouncements, shades of "The Briar Patch" and *John Brown* were with him still. Again he repudiated the former, but when legal scholar Kenneth Bancroft Clark brought up the name of John Brown, he was as outraged by Clark's sense of Brown as a Christ figure quite as much as he had been by Emerson's encomiums.

At the end of "Conversation Piece" he attempted to sum up: "It would be sentimentality to think that our society can be changed easily and without pain. It would be worse sentimentality to think that it can be changed without some pain to our particular selves—black and white. It would be realism to think that that pain would be a reasonable price to pay for what we all, selfishly, might get out of it" (p. 444).

There were a few reservations among the major reviews, but the response was overwhelmingly favorable. In Warren's reflections there might have been one wry thought. In 1961 he had published *The Legacy of the Civil War* and *Wilderness;* in 1964, *Flood,* and a year later, *Who Speaks for the Negro?* With each brace of books, the nonfiction had been praised, the fiction condemned.[7]

The prospect of summer in Vermont was welcome. Warren had overruled his family's antimodernization sentiments because, on some days, he told Bill Bandy, "I find the primitive charm wearing a little thin, especially the day I carried 27 buckets of water from the spring, 100 yards from the camp, with snow six feet deep to be cut through." Shack One, as they called it, was winterized, and with its old-fashioned tub and two copper wash boilers to fill, it would still be fine for guests who enjoyed roughing it. But Shack Two would provide much better accommodations. Following plans drawn up by the architect who had overseen the construction of their Fairfield home, they erected up on the knoll a large gray wooden structure with sharp angles, a kind of modernistic ski lodge. On the ground level there were bedrooms and baths plus a room for skiing gear. Upstairs were more bedrooms and a huge stone fireplace that heated the spacious living room on one side and the kitchen with its large table on the other. Windows all around gave onto the surrounding forest, and at the western wall was an open porch perfect for observing the mellow sunlight on the mountains at cocktail time. They put in a tennis court, and later Stubb Sampson bulldozed out a great pear-shaped space, which the brook turned into a pond where Warren could swim his mile each morning. Twenty yards from the house he completed his study, the Coop. One half of it enclosed the crude desk he built. The other half was a small screened-in porch. He could work there above the brook in sun and shade, protected from wind and rain by the sheltering trees.[8]

He was feeling a great sense of release. "I am beginning to fiddle with the selected poems, or whatever they will be," he wrote Tate. "It's wonderful to be able to fiddle with a line a half day. While doing WHO SPEAKS, I had damned near forgotten that luxury. . . . Now I am going to indulge myself until I run dry."[9]

Besides the new poems, which came in a flood, he was assessing old ones and revising some for his planned volume of selected poems. He was organizing a collection of critical essays on Faulkner—a favorite since John Gould Fletcher had given him a copy of *Soldiers' Pay* at Oxford—handling the permissions and fees of the thirty-nine contributors without secretarial help. And he was still writing citations and reviewing grant applications for the National Institute and American Academy. "This will be the briefest of notes, I am under great pressure at the moment," he told Lon Cheney in mid-July. But looking back five months later, he would say the summer was "one of the most satisfactory periods in a long time."[10]

Shack Two sheltered numerous guests besides the children's friends. The Styrons came, and the poet William Meredith. Economist John Kenneth Galbraith and his wife, Kitty, would drive over from their place, and they would talk about the follies of American foreign policy and the encroachments of civilization on Stratton Mountain. Often Vann Woodward would be there. ("You were the only person we could think of," Eleanor told Galbraith, "who was bright enough to talk with him.") Robert Brustein came. Like many others, when he first encountered Red's Kentucky accent, "I barely understood a word of what he was saying. . . . But whatever he was saying was witty, as all things he says are—funny, earthy, and outrageous." But Brustein also found him courtly and "one of the kindest and gentlest of men that I know." These visits were always lively. One source was the host's gift for anecdote that would be followed by "a wild and hilarious generalization," and also stories "in the tradition of those tall-tale tellers of the West and the South." These occasions were, in a sense, rewards for the work. One long four-part sequence, entitled "Fall Comes in Back-Country Vermont" and dedicated to Meredith, showed the sense of place and people the camp had given him.[11]

He published one other poem that year after their return to Fairfield, which showed a different kind of awareness. Set a world away, it was entitled "Shoes in Rain Jungle." In early June, Eleanor had spoken before the American Booksellers' convention in Washington, and they had taken the children along to show them "the wheels of government." By this time U.S. planes were flying missions over South Vietnam, and in June twenty-three thousand American advisers had also been committed to combat. Robert Lowell had rejected a presidential invitation to the White House Arts Festival "because of 'dismay and distrust' of American foreign policy." Warren told a reporter that, if he had been invited, he would have had to think carefully about accepting. He told Lon Cheney, "Starting from little we had got ourselves on the verge of a World War without any discussion or debate whatsoever. . . . Either ineptitude or disingenuousness had shrouded the whole thing in a fog. . . . I am for getting some kind of settlement if humanly possible." His poem recalled Napoleon's barefoot soldiers, and Lee's and Meade's troops' quest for shoes that led to Gettysburg. He wrote,

> All wars are righteous. Except when
> You lose them. This
> Is the lesson of history. This—And shoes. . . .[12]

He had found other material for poetry in Washington, and he used it for satiric purposes in "Patriotic Tour and Postulate of Joy." The four-stanza poem begins,

> Once, once, in Washington,
> D.C., in June,
> All night—I swear it—a single mockingbird
> Sang. . . .

The song of the merciless bird penetrates the ears of the president, "every senator available," J. Edgar Hoover, and finally the poet himself, who rises naked in the cold moonlight and cries out in his need "To know what postulate of joy men have tried / To live by, in sunlight and moonlight, until they died." History had been a subject for poems all his life, the Civil War in particular, but these were his first dealing with contemporary politics in more than twenty years.[13]

The holiday season, with Christmas parties in Connecticut and Washington, did not impede his progress. In 1966 he would publish a total of forty-seven poems, all of them to be collected as *Tale of Time: Poems 1960–1966*. This would constitute the first segment of *Selected Poems: New and Old 1923–1966*, to be published in October. During these months of winter and early spring he was sending batches of poems to Allen Tate, John Ransom, and Bill Meredith to be ranked for inclusion. They were helpful and supportive, like Katherine Anne, who had written him the previous fall, "I love your poetry, I have every one you ever published, you have always been to me first of all a poet, best of all your work." He was feeling some degree of urgency to finish this book, for he had a full year off from Yale coming up "and now is the time it seems for the kids to get the most out of a year abroad in school. We cross our fingers, life being what it is, about everything."[14]

On May 27, in another of their hairbreadth departures, they made it to their Norwegian freighter. The food was ample, particularly the smorgasbord, and the hospitable captain invited them up to the bridge, where they flew little Japanese kites. They docked in Le Havre, and by June 6 they were driving south to the port of Le Lavandou, where they took the boat to the Ile de Port-Cros, twenty miles southeast of Toulon on the Riviera.

In mid-June Eleanor wrote Katherine Anne from Le Manoir, once a sanitorium and now a luxurious hotel, that they were "being spoiled to death on this heavenly little island. If I can just get my gritty old Yankee soul to adapt to the luxury, all will be great." Often on the long summer days Warren would read aloud, much from Conrad, whose sea stories fascinated Gabriel. "We've found him a little boat," Eleanor wrote, "and well, altogether, what could one dream of more. Only to be writing something decent, and the Bon Dieu had better do something about that."[15]

If Eleanor had been a believer, she might have seen the intervention of the Bon Dieu one day when Gabriel, with his father for ballast and crew, put out in his reconditioned catboat. Strolling on the cliffs above with her mother, Rosanna watched as a great cloud darkened the sky and the wind rose quickly to near-gale force. Still out there alone was the catboat, now being driven rapidly toward the rocks by the surging sea. They lost control of the sail and bailed furiously as the boat shipped water. (Warren would remember how his son was shouting, like one of Conrad's sailors, "And still the sea came in!") They managed to veer off from the rocks at the last moment, only to founder and then cling to the buoyant cushions until a motorboat rescued them.[16]

They could not have wanted a better place for the alternating work and relaxation. "The island and the hotel are perfect in all ways," Warren wrote Albert Erskine. Eleanor made a workplace in the donkeys' winter stable, and he set up near a stone wall under "a fig tree in a ruined garden far from the hotel." By late August, as they prepared to leave the Ile de Port-Cros, his personal balance sheet was in good order. An essay on Melville was now the introduction to an edition of Melville's poems, and he had finished his work on the Faulkner book. They swam and took long walks with friends such as Francis Steegmuller and Shirley Hazzard. She remembered Warren's swimming "quite far out, for a long time, between two headlands, his elbows methodically rising and sinking" until, after a while, she began to be anxious about him.[17]

By the beginning of September they had moved sixty miles northeast to Magagnosc, a suburb of Grasse (ten miles north of Cannes), where there were schools for the children. They lived in La Moutonne, a three-story farmhouse on eight acres of untended gardens and terraces. It was built against a steep hillside, minimally modernized but commanding a sweeping view of the sea on three sides and the mountains on the other. There was also plenty of room for guests, and so the Styrons and their two daughters came for a visit. The children's pet was a four-month-old goat they called Lily the Kid. They shut her up at night, but she roamed the rest of the day, browsing among the olive trees, and when the children came home from school they would chase each other up and down the terraces, Lily leaping with them. The opening of school had provided a clear field for Warren to start his novel and for Eleanor to work at completing hers.[18]

Selected Poems: New and Old 1923–1966 was published on October 7. "Many of the poems in this volume have been revised," read the prefatory note. "I have tried not to tamper with meanings, only to sharpen old meanings—for poems are, in one perspective at least, always a life record, and live their own life by that fact" (p. vii). Collectively entitled *Tale of Time,* they consist of six sequences. The shortest, containing two poems together entitled "Holy Writ," deals with the lives of Elijah and Samuel. Vividly describing or presaging violence, blood, and death, they are part of the dominant matter of

Tale of Time. The six-poem sequence with the same title, "Tale of Time," recalls Ruth Warren's death. After the numb shock the poet recalls the mad druggist who had listed the people he meant to poison but spared her because he knew ". . . she was too precious to die: / A fact some in the street had not grasped—nor the attending physician, nor God, nor I" (p. 22). The poet's contempt for the people she knew seems to have extended in some fashion to her too, and so he must deal with guilt as well as grief. Older now than his mother was at her death, he concludes the sequence with the fifth poem, "What Were You Thinking, Dear Mother?" Imagining her as a child, lying in the same grass where he later lay, he thinks how she

> . . . found it necessary to live on,
> In your bravery and in your joyous secret,
> Into our present maniacal century,
> In which you gave me birth. . . . (p. 33)

The solution to the problem of coming to terms with the past and living in history is that ". . . You / Must eat the dead." After this kind of eucharistic acceptance of their lives and ways, "Immortality is not impossible, / Even joy" (p. 32).

The most powerful of the other sequences, "The Day Dr. Knox Did It," also draws upon a memory of death, the suicide of a Cerulean Springs dentist just as real as the mad druggist in Guthrie. Warren had even heard the shot fired in the barn loft, and he presumably did what the boy in the poem does: asks his grandfather why the man did it. His reply, "It's one of those things," fails to satisfy, and when the boy persists, his grandfather tells him, almost angrily, "For some folks the world gets too much . . . / . . . For some folks" (p. 62). The poet thinks of the sins and yearnings of his life. He has puzzled long over the events of that day when he fled the sound of the shot, "but toward myself I fled, for there is / no water to wash the world away." Now, he reflects, "We are the world," not guiltless children, and in spite of all "we must frame more firmly the idea of good" (p. 66).[19]

Ten years before, in "The Child Next Door," the poet's response to the horror and poignancy of the "monster" child's existence is to think, *"This is the world"* (p. 149). Throughout *Tale of Time* he returns to this baseline. His daughter screams as her cat's jaws crush the skull of a scampering chipmunk. He thinks of a man in his village, dying of cancer, for whom he can provide no word of comfort. He remembers his father's words after the visit to their dying childhood nurse, *"The world is the world it is!"* (p. 29). There is no way, neither in philosophy nor in religion, to come to terms satisfactorily with the grief and suffering and sin of the world. It is as it is. He can admit that there is the possibility of joy, from love and from beauty, but that is all.

The first and longest segment of *Tale of Time,* entitled "Notes on a Life to Be Lived," confronts the same problems. The poet's voice is like that of others—E. M. Forster, Thomas Hardy, James Joyce—who cannot retain the elements of childhood faith. In "Stargazing," the poet looks up at the black night sky and sees that "The stars are only a backdrop for the human condition. . . ." (p. 3). In another poem of the sequence the world is there and so is guilt: "Have you sat on a hillside at sunset and eaten the flesh of your own heart?" But in the last lines of "Notes on a Life to Be Lived," a tentative, prayerful hope springs from his child in his innocence: "I watch you at your sunlit play. / Teach me, my son, the ways of day" (p. 18).

The book's last sequence, "Delight," enlarges upon this realm of possibility. Delight is unpredictable. It can come in dreams or in the beauty of the rose that perishes. In the uncertain world it cannot be trusted, because "It will betray you" (p. 90). But still, in the frenzy of sea and sun, the scudding of cloud and wind, it can bring joy, and the poet's affirming response is simple: "Give me your hand" (p. 82).

Spanning forty-three years, these poems demonstrate both technical range and continuing experimentation. The earlier style—often convoluted, sometimes densely metaphysical—was giving way to a more nearly fluid clarity. And his revisions and omissions of old work emphasized the new. The reviews and subsequent assessments by no means constituted a chorus of praise. There were complaints of garrulousness and obscurity, but if Warren had worried that this volume might meet the reception accorded *You, Emperors, and Others,* he must have been reassured in the following months at the additional evidence of his increasing stature.[20]

By early November he was back at work. "I have done a long chapter of a novel," he told Erskine, "first draft, and am in agony about it. Wish I could talk it over with you. Read it. And speak your full mind."[21]

He had been uncertain from the start, first entitling it *Call Me Early* and then *So Clear, O Victory.* The fifteen-thousand-word chapter ranged from Andrew Jackson's time to the present in the lives of the Kuttlick and Puckett families of Bolivar County, Tennessee. The shifting point of view from which the story was told added to its diffuseness. He told Francis Steegmuller and Shirley Hazzard that though Eleanor was groaning about her progress, her novel was going splendidly. "I have begun one," he added, "and it is terrible. I have just junked all I have of it, fifty pages, and go moping about. . . . Maybe I started the thing too soon after my seizure of poetry." No matter what the cause, his response was the right one. The discarded chapter was his most unpromising fiction since the unpublished novels thirty-five years before.[22]

But he could not remain idle. Three weeks later he wrote Tate, "I've turned back to a novel I laid aside two years ago. Almost with relief, I'd say. But I haven't yet got retooled." He also enclosed fifteen poems, "the work of the summer and fall." All but one of them would go to make up the first segment of his next book. (Warren was happy for Tate in his new happiness, six months married to Helen Heinz, who would become the mother of his children.) There was still time in December for some concentrated retooling for the novel, which he was calling *Escape,* but not much time. "Have glamorous invitation to go skiing at ski-house of some friends in French Alps," he told the Steegmullers. "Hurrah for us." They would return home to Magagnosc on January 3. He would have reason to work energetically then, for March would see them briefly back in Italy before they journeyed on to Egypt.[23]

40

❖

Garnerings from Under
the Fig Tree and Elsewhere

With the motion of angels, out of
Snow-spume and swirl of gold mist, they
Emerge to the positive sun. At
That great height, small on that whiteness,
With the color of birds or of angels,
They swoop, sway, descend, and descending,
Cry their bright bird-cries, pure
In the sweet desolation of distance.

— *"Skiers"*[1]

Warren said that the trip to Courchevel was a reward especially for Rosanna and Gabriel, who had done well as foreign children in a new school. But one of the rewards for all four of them was the chalet's warmth. La Moutonne had no central heating, and their bedrooms there were like iceboxes. Baudouin de Moustier was a successful industrialist whose family dated back to the twelfth century. His wife, Annie, took pride in the cuisine of the chalet, which, with its tasteful appointments, was suited to the dramatic scenery. Resisting it, Warren alternated in the mornings between the novel and the poems, and it would be afternoon before he took his five-mile walk along the ski trails and in the forest. Then "at night lots of gaiety by the fireside, great food and drink."[2]

As he was proud of Rosanna and Gabriel, so they could be proud of him that winter of 1967. On February 6 *The New York Times* reported that the biennial five-thousand-dollar Bollingen Prize in Poetry, "which many consider the most prestigious in its field," had been awarded to Robert Penn Warren for *Selected Poems: New and Old 1923–1966* with its display of "the full range of an extraordinarily gifted writer's poetic accomplishment."

With his prize, his sheaf of new poems, and more than four chapters of his novel, he had reason to enjoy the respites from routine in the new year. (First called *Escape,* after the predicament of a young Sicilian who gains temporary refuge in the home of a young Tennessee countrywoman, the novel was now *Love in a Valley.*) He took the family with him when he lectured and read poems at the University of Freiburg. Not long after their return to cold La Moutonne, Eleanor took to her bed with the grippe for two weeks. Then, in the rainy spring, they were all down with it. Finally, on March 22, they left for four days of Roman sunshine before they flew to Cairo.[3]

In return for his three days of lecturing and reading at the American University they would have a journey up the Nile. Both Eleanor and William Styron gave readings, so their party comprised four adults and four children. The Styrons were good company. Rose was lively and talented, and so was her forty-two-year-old Virginia-born husband. After attending Duke University and serving in the Marine Corps, he had tried New York publishing. Gambling everything on his writing, he won the Prix de Rome in 1951 with his first novel, *Lie Down in Darkness.* Warren had been an inspiration to him, and the whole first section of his novel contained intentional echoes of *All the King's Men.* After the Styrons moved to Roxbury, they saw the Warrens often. Now his fourth novel, *The Confessions of Nat Turner,* was to be a Book-of-the-Month Club main selection, and Warren wrote a two-thousand-word essay about the book and the author for the July *Book-of-the-Month Club News.*

As Styron would remember their time together, "We gave our lectures and paid our respects to the university, and then spent four or five days on this magnificent trip going up the Nile, fighting fleas and gnats and drinking literally tank cars full of Evian water. And plus a little whiskey on the side." They had enjoyed three days in Cairo, and then the children had ridden camels and real Arabian horses. They saw the Pyramids, Luxor and Karnak, and small towns on the shore as the boat took them up the great river toward Aswan.[4]

Warren stored up his own set of images. "It was stupendous," he wrote Katherine Anne Porter in early April. But now came the letdown. They were exhausted, and there was school for the children and ten days of antibiotics for Eleanor to fight a jaw infection from an old dental problem. "Poor girl. And wonderful girl, she is just literally that, and gets more that way every day."[5]

Their bond with Katherine Anne had grown stronger with each year. She had suffered a series of illnesses, and this may have contributed to an emotional malaise Warren felt. There had been enough without that to bring his melancholy to the surface, for his brother Thomas's wife, Alice, had just died. And so, when he congratulated Katherine Anne on the shower of honors she had received, he told her "such a series of recognitions does a little to restore one's faith in a just and logical order in the universe. But only a little, I fear, for the great machine grinds on." He had been feeling this process in one particular way. Although he took pride in the gusto of Gabriel's assault upon life, Rosanna's growth was a different matter. "I know that she is nubile," he had written the Steegmullers, "or is creeping up on that condition, and I hate all young men, like Yale freshmen, whose minds are in the gutter. . . . In other words, time marches on, and I am not sure that I am prepared for reality." Two months after their return from Egypt Rosanna had gone for a month's visit with friends, and when she returned she was "very much la jeune fille, complete with miniskirt, dear God. Had her delayed 14th birthday party this morning at breakfast. Very beautiful." In the fall, when they would visit potential schools for the following year, he would tell Tate, "I have a bad attack of being the father of a daughter right now." It was no wonder that the theme of time was recurring in his poems.[6]

Rosanna's feelings were mixed as they prepared to go back to Port-Cros for the summer. For Gabriel the island was "a magical place." For her it was a happy time—a time for collecting seashells and gluing them together on scalloped pieces of driftwood as birthday presents—and she felt that for her family it was another Eden. But it was also a time for leaving childhood behind. Their whole life together seemed molded by storytelling, a great mesh of narrative rather than discussion, and she was glad of it. But there was a dark side as well to the encompassing nature of their family. "I felt exiled from the United States as a child," she would remember. "I felt no relation to my classmates. There was nothing we could talk about together." At home there was the reading and storytelling and increasing consciousness of what it meant to be a writer. "As I grew up into my teens and tried to get some sort of sense of my parents not as local gods but as people, I was so aware of these great dark spaces that Pa had inside him, his melancholia." He would rail against Emerson, against "that optimism that he thought cut against reality . . . that God is a very old God, an Old Testament God he hates but respects. One of the very first phrases I heard, or remember, was 'Original Sin.' That was pounded into my ears. He was constantly joking about it, but it meant he believed in it." But she was also "aware of his immense love for us and concern for us." He was never the demanding, domineering parent, exacting emotional tribute from his children, "but we could sense him brooding. Then, he would return to us, with that love, opening up to us again."[7]

Back at Le Manoir, working again under his fig tree, he sent poems to his friends, poems often shadowed by his dark spaces. But on the whole, as Eleanor put it, "it's been a great year in too many ways to mention." On August 28 they sailed from Cannes on the *Raffaello.*[8]

Away for almost a year and a half, they were swamped with tasks at home. When Warren wrote Allen Tate to congratulate him on the birth of his twin sons, he asked about his plans. "My own mind begins to turn to my retirement. I haven't sorted out my feelings or ideas. I found out by many years of not teaching that I miss it." But some aspects of it he had not missed. "It's a sobering experience to have to reread a lot of old notes. And to hear the old voice saying the same God-damned thing." And he needed the time teaching took for planned projects as well as present ones. He had now served as editor or coeditor of fourteen critical books, textbooks, and editions. He and Cleanth Brooks had done their first text because there was none available of the kind they wanted. The money had been particularly welcome in those early years of small salaries. Now, with the acquisition of the two houses and their other ongoing expenses, the royalties were a necessity. There had always been help in the kitchen and the nursery. They had sent the children to the Unquowa School in Fairfield at a cost of seven thousand dollars a year each, and they would soon be going away to prepare for college. But his planning of new work reflected more than just economic necessity. It was also a function of the vital and consuming interest literature had for him. It came too from that prodigious energy and that temperament, which relished creating challenges and meeting them.[9]

But then came a down cycle. On Christmas Day he was "flattened with the flu." His old shoulder trouble had flared up so that he needed a stenographer to deal with his correspondence. The next several months of 1968 were equally frustrating as he missed a conference in Gambier. He tried to be patient. He did make it to Dallas in April for the Southern Literary Festival, where he was able to spend time with Ransom, Tate, and Lytle. They were in the front row for his poetry reading, looking, he announced, like "hanging judges all." One meeting on that trip was a melancholy one. He saw Donald Davidson in the hospital in Nashville, looking frail and feverish. Not long afterward he was dead.[10]

They did what they could to ensure a productive summer when they went to Vermont in mid-June. They brought along David Rosen, one of Warren's Yale undergraduates. He told David, "you will be in the bosom of the family." Rosen found that to be a partially accurate statement, because the family "featured a thirteen-year-old boy who operated at high speed with hammer and saw more than a hundred feet up at tree-top level and a fifteen-year-old daughter who brought easel and library along on long 'wanders' through the woods." He was a licensed swimming instructor and spent time with them in the pool. A fine tennis player too, he taught them and played with Eleanor. When Warren was not at his desk he was cutting old railroad ties for steps down to the pool and laying stone paths and terraces. There was time at the day's end for a combination of the intellectual and the recreational. Rosen would remember "wrangles with Emerson over the question of whether a hard day of work building steps to the pool was its own reward, or whether it merited a glass of bourbon; [and] dinner table questions about a strain of Jonathan Edwards' blood in the family. Red's sense of history was communicated as a part of daily life and was confined to neither tragedy, irony, nor comedy." At his desk he polished the poems for the new book and read proof on them. By early September he was close to the end of the first draft of *Love in a Valley,* begun five years before. Rosanna again provided a reminder of time's flight. "She goes away to school this fall, a fact I find hard to believe and accept, to Milton Academy, at Boston. Gabe goes away next year. So I begin to feel old and lonely, a little."[11]

But soon he was immersed in the fall term at Yale, and on October 16 *Incarnations: Poems 1966–1968* appeared. Although these poems begin temporally where *Tale of Time* leaves off, it is a very different book. It is shorter, consisting of only half as many sequences, dividing into three parts, and depending less on native materials. Its title, with nothing of the narrative implication of its predecessor, is at once suggestive and ambiguous. Although *Incarnations* must inevitably recall "And the Word was made flesh and dwelt among us" (John 1:14), two epigraphs broaden its implication. They refer to the inhumanity of man to man yet also suggest man's dignity and a kind of community shared by all things that live, as well as the element of the divine that can inhere in them.[12]

The three parts provide contrast and balance. Most of the fifteen poems of the first sequence, "Island of Summer," were written under the fig tree by the ruined garden on the Ile de Port-Cros. The connection with the Adamic state after the fall is obvious, but Warren also indulges his taste for history as poem by looking back as far as the ancient Mediterranean world. Grandeur and destructiveness had their place then as well as now. The first poem, "What Day Is," reaches back to the Roman wars. The third poem, "Natural History," begins with the meditation, "Many have died here, but few / Have names. . . ." At a point where Warren had gotten stuck, Gabriel had appeared with a discovery: two Nazi helmets, one bearing entry and exit holes. Shifting from Saracen to modern warfare, Warren describes the helmet and reflects on

> The track of the missile. Death
> Came quick, for history,
> Like nature, may have mercy,
> Though only by accident. (p. 6)

A related meditation suggests a cycle: men and beasts eat figs, they die, and in turn feed the trees. In poems such as the fourth, "Riddle in the Garden," the poet's warning against the dangers of eating a plum suggests God's injunction to Adam and Eve. But this is not didactic allegory. As always, this poet seeks after meanings, though the result is enigmatic:

> You think
> I am speaking in riddles. But I am not, for
> The world means only itself. (p. 7)[13]

The remaining part of the sequence is very different in the striking "Myth on Mediterranean Beach: Aphrodite as Logos." It is a provocative tour de force, juxtaposing the Word of Saint John with the Greek goddess of love incarnated in "an old hunchback in a bikini" (p. 12). She emerges from the foam "in Botticellian parody"

(p. 15). She passes sunbathing lovers, "And passing, draws their dreams away, / And leaves them naked to the day" (p. 16). Even if she is grotesque, the old woman is still a testimonial to the life force, to the persistence of the erotic impulse even though attenuated and disabled. At the same time that the poem is realistic and satiric with its deft rhymed couplets, it suggests more than mere parody. Juxtaposed to the sensual young lovers, she embodies the progression into age, decline, death, and dissolution.[14]

The sequence ends with two majestic poems of acceptance. In "Masts at Dawn" the poet, lying wakeful in the night, "Past second cock-crow," thinks of a strong swell in the nearby sea and how, "if you surrender to it, [you] experience / A sense in the act, of mystic unity with that rhythm." And he ends this line, "Your peace is the sea's will" (p. 22) (a secular variant upon Dante's phrase from the *Paradiso:* "in His will is our peace"). Even if one does not see the white masts as crosses in the dawning, one can see Warren's closest approach to a declaration of faith in the last two lines: "We must try / To love so well the world that we may believe, in the end, in God" (p. 23). The first part of the last poem, "The Leaf," returns to the combined natural and Adamic imagery with overtones of error and guilt. In the next part, lying prone on a high rock, the nesting place of the hawk near the bones of his victims, he feels how "The wide world lets down the hand in shame. . . ." (p. 26). In the next, which is full of echoes of Eliot, he hears his father's voice, and in the last,

> the appalling speed,
> In space beyond stars, of
> Light.[15]

Part II of *Incarnations,* entitled "Internal Injuries," is divided into two sequences. The first sequence, called "Penological Study: Southern Exposure," consists of seven poems. The voice is apparently that of a reporter come to cover an execution. But it is not the condemned who moves him most. It is the principal figure of the first poem, "Keep That Morphine Moving, Cap," a prisoner named Jake dying of cancer, there so long that, after nearly forty years, he cannot now remember why he had cut his wife's throat. He is a figure of desperate courage and pain as he sits there on the toilet, the sweat dripping from his face onto the cement floor. He tells the warden, "Just keep that morphine moving, Cap, / And me, I'll tough it through."

And the warden replies, "You know we're pulling for you, Jake. . . ."
Each of the four stanzas ends, "Oh, in the pen, oh, in the pen, /
The cans, they have no doors. . . ." (p. 31), like a western outlaw ballad. But Jake is neither a ballad hero nor just a crazy old convict,
rather a man in the extremity of human misery whose plight becomes
emblematic:

> . . . let us, too, keep pulling
> For him, like we all ought to, who,
> When truth at last is true, must try,
> Like him, to tough it through. . . . (pp. 31–32)

In the rest of the sequence the poet extrapolates further from Jake's
agony to the human condition. His contemplation of Jake's eventual
death and a scheduled death in the electric chair leads to thoughts of
his own death. In the dawn on the road to the airport he feels mixed
relief and guilt: "Forgive us—oh, give us!—our joy" (p. 42).[16]

The other sequence in part II of the poem as a whole also bears the
title "Internal Injuries," and in these eight poems a death again seems
imminent, as a woman struck by a car lies screaming while the indifferent police await the ambulance. It is a poem like others in which the
poet says, in effect, "This is the world as it is." The tone and diction
again are tough and coarse, but they mask only partly the acute pain
and revulsion the poet-observer feels. He sits in the traffic jam trying
not to seem another gawker, thinking how the victim is black, old, female, poor, alone, just fired from her job, and now sprawled in the
street, and he asks silently, "Merely to be—Jesus, / Wouldn't just
being be enough. . . ." (p. 43). Workers' pneumatic hammers play an
accompaniment to her metronomic scream that rises through this city
where "Penn Station looks bombed-out" (p. 49) and then higher to
where a "jet prowls the sky" (p. 47). He implores his taxi driver to
hurry, for "There comes a time for us all when we want to begin a
new life" (p. 52). He thinks of internal injuries, of "All those fat thick
slimy things that / Are so like a tub full of those things you would
find / In a vat in the back room of a butcher shop, . . ." Then he asks
the driver if he knows what flesh is "and if it is, as some people say,
really sacred?" (p. 54). The driver does not answer, but a dangerous
imminence of something in the air implies anything but incarnation.[17]

The third part of the book, "Enclaves," is the shortest, comprising
two sequences of two poems each. They are very different from their

predecessors, conveying a sense of calm, the presence of love, and even a prayer for knowledge in a world of "Time and Contingency" (p. 61). The first of the four is "The Faring." (In it Eleanor recognized the scene when she waited for Warren on the dock at Dieppe fifteen years before.) If there is a hint of incarnation here, it comes in the imagery in which the poet's beloved, in the sun and wind, suggests the Winged Victory of Samothrace. The companion poem, "The Enclave," picks up the imagery of wind and sun again as day dawns, and the poet asks, "How / May I know the true nature of Time . . . [?]" (p. 59). The reader may choose to believe that here the poet and his beloved create their own enclave, surrounded by the world and all its uncertainties. The last two poems, entitled together "In the Mountains," are dedicated to Baudouin and Annie de Moustier, whose Alpine retreat supplied the brilliant imagery of height and flight, snow and angels.[18]

The book's first two assessments, in journals aimed at the book trade, anticipated the general terms of the responses that would continue through 1969. In the earlier one, two months before publication, *Incarnations* was a well-integrated collection including some of his best work. For the other, a month later, it was an intellectual kind of verse, that of an excellent but minor poet. Although the book was not as widely reviewed as earlier collections, it still achieved some visibility and some high praise, most often in unsigned group reviews. For some, *Incarnations* provided the fulfillment of the promise in *Promises.* Other reviews gave mild to warm approbation, but it would be twenty years before it received the accolade of "greatness."[19]

   The concerns of *Incarnations* are familiar ones. The poet tries to understand the world and explain it to himself. He longs to know his place in it, to make sense of the continuum of history, and to know how to live in time. He is plagued by a sense of guilt, by remorse for parts of his past life that he cannot undo, and he suffers at the tragedy and injustice he sees in the world around him. The antidote is joy. It can come from love, but even so, even immersing himself in the beauty of the world, the poet can only try, condemned to death as all are, to face courageously the truths of life—the tragic aspects of the human condition—and at the same time to hope for the redeeming joy. The style is full of the usual resourcefulness, with the formal and the colloquial equally ready to hand, and with standard metrics quite as available as free verse, and there is the same taste for experimentation. Following the intimation of the book's title, the poems offer meditations on flesh—in the fig, the fish, and the frail human form. But it is protoplasm, not "the word," that is made flesh in this naturalistic incarnation. Warren as "yearner"—the man of religious temperament without religious faith—can manage finally, in these personal, powerful poems, only to tell himself, "We must try / To love so well the world that we may believe, in the end, in God" (p. 23).[20]

41

❖

Two Kinds of Visions

We never know what we have lost, or what we have found.
We are only ourselves, and that promise.
Continue to walk in the world. Yes, love it!

He continued to walk in the world.

—Audubon: A Vision[1]

In the fall Rosanna went off to Boston to the Milton Academy.
Eleanor pressed on with *Baldur's Gate* while Warren resumed his for-
mal teaching in New Haven and his informal teaching elsewhere. In
November he went to New Orleans with Ralph Ellison and Bill Sty-
ron for a panel discussion moderated by Vann Woodward at the
Southern Historical Association meeting. In New Haven Styron
joined him for one of his classes, but by now the atmosphere there
was changing. One observer of the Yale scene wrote that Warren and
Brooks "changed the way literature was taught around the nation."
But for the next generation at Yale "careful reading was not enough.
Many of the scholars who came in the 1960s and '70s had been
schooled in European philosophy, Freudian psychoanalysis, and linguistic theories, especially French structuralist and post-structuralist
ideas. Along with a love of literature and philosophy, they brought a
deep skepticism about the very idea of meaning. . . ." As well versed
as most of this new generation in philosophy and linguistics (and
closer to such influential pioneers such as I. A. Richards), Brooks and
Warren found this denial of fundamental literary values anathema.
Warren was already distanced from the department by his two-day-a-

week commute from Fairfield, and this new trend in the department increased the distance.[2]

There was a difference in the classroom too. His politics were not radical enough for some of his students. "Red gets rather worn out some days," Eleanor told Katherine Anne Porter, "trying to talk honestly to Yale boys who want Dr. Spock and Dick Gregory for President & Vice-Pres.—! Not that he's for this awful mess." To begin seminar discussions he would sometimes ask who could recite a poem or tell the plot of a story, and at times there were only reluctant volunteers. Or he would read a story aloud and then analyze it. Some of his listeners would find this method unprofitable and boring. But there were always students who responded to him. To James Wilcox he seemed "a god from Olympus" with "such an aura of mastery about him, true wisdom, that I couldn't help feel that just being there, in the same room with him, would somehow be beneficial. . . . His mind, razor-sharp, was always engaged with his heart, so that when he spoke, I had a sense of a whole person, not an abstracted intelligence. His sense of humor, his scorn for the spurious, helped sweep many of the Thomas Wolfe–like cobwebs from my writing." David Milch remembered the times they would be invited home for dinner and the way he followed no stiff teacher-student protocol just as he had no time for academic bureaucracy. "He was as pure a democrat as I've ever met," and he possessed "the gift of thinking the best of people, and that somehow made you be your best, or at least want to be."[3]

More than twenty years before, he had read the journals of John James Audubon, immortalized by his science and his art in *The Birds of North America* (1827–38). Not just an illegitimate half-Creole, sometime schoolteacher, and sometime painter, he was rumored to be also the lost dauphin, the son of Louis XVI and Marie Antoinette, and so the rightful heir to the throne of France. "I started a poem on Audubon," Warren later said, "but I got stuck in a trap, a narrative trap. There's no narrative there, as such, to work with. . . . I did write quite a bit, but it wouldn't come together, so I set it aside and forgot about it." But then, "in the summer of 1968 it came back on me." This was one of the roots of his current project.[4]

The other root was in the rich ground of American literary history. A publisher had earlier proposed to him and Cleanth Brooks a text to be called *Understanding American Literature*. The volume would need to draw on a fairly broad range of literary history, and fortunately, one of their colleagues was the critic and scholar R.W.B. Lewis. "So after a certain amount of rumination," Lewis recalled, "they invited me, as a *soi-disant* Americanist, and a colleague and neighbor, to join them as coeditor." Before long they would divide the assignments for two imposing volumes. One of the figures Warren would treat was Audubon. Performing his habitual juggling act again, he plunged into it, leaving *Love in a Valley* still awaiting completion. "Then one day I was helping my wife make the bed, and one line from this old discarded poem . . . came to mind: 'Was not the lost Dauphin,' and suddenly out of that phrase burst the poem. And so a method for doing the whole thing, just like a vision."[5]

Warren had reread the Audubon texts and his own notes. He kept at the poem "by writing at night, going to sleep, and waking up in the morning early—revising by shouting it all out loud in a Land Rover going to Yale. I saw a new way in. Each element of the poem would be a 'shot' on Audubon rather than a narrative. . . . The poem is about man and his fate—all along, Audubon resisted his fate and thought it was evil—a man is supposed to support his family, and so forth. But now he accepts his fate. . . . Audubon was the greatest slayer of birds that ever lived: he destroyed beauty in order to create beauty and whet his understanding. Love is knowledge. And then in the end the poem is about Audubon and me." And so, once a boy studying birds in the woods with Kent Greenfield and making watercolors in the zoo with Sister Mary Luke, Warren now spent eight months portraying the art and mind of John James Audubon.[6]

Returning from Vermont in early February, he told Allen Tate, "One day I have high hopes for it, the next day I'm in the dumps. But when it is done, for better or worse, then I'll take out my novel, on which, after more than four years, I have a half chapter to go. . . ." Three weeks later he had Tate's reaction. The poem was "beautiful and moving," and he added, "I like it better than anything of yours in at least ten years." Howard Moss, the poetry editor of *The New Yorker,* wanted to publish it, but it was too long. So Moss suggested cutting sequences and renumbering the rest. Warren finally agreed to their printing ten of its twenty-seven sections in September. *Harper's* took thirteen for the August number, and the *Yale Review* bought three for the autumn issue.[7]

· · · ·

Monday morning, May 19, was quiet. Warren went upstairs to dress after breakfast while Rosanna and Gabriel sat with Eleanor as she read the *Times.* Suddenly, Rosanna remembered, her mother exploded, and there was turmoil in the house. "Cinina's dead!" she shouted up the stairs. The obituary reported the demise, at sixty-three, of Dr. Emma B. Gardner, survived by her husband, Burton Hathaway Gardner. They had heard nothing from Cinina, even indirectly, for almost thirteen years. (Once, standing at the back of an elevator when Cinina entered, he had stayed there unseen until she left.) Their last contact had been his rejection of her request for increased alimony, continuing the court-decreed payments without complaint though they were a burden in the years when the Warrens were raising their children. Cinina had gone on to finish her Columbia Ph.D. and continued teaching. She also married Gardner, whose family had owned three-thousand-acre Gardiners Island off eastern Long Island since Lion Gardiner had settled it in 1639. Somehow she managed to continue collecting alimony as Mrs. Emma B. Warren. As Eleanor showed the paper to Warren she was still furious. He was shaken but said little. He had acquired too much experience of Cinina's capabilities. And she had not changed, continuing to drain his financial resources as she had so long drained his emotional ones. Years later he mentioned that morning's news to Arnold Stein. Then he said, "I didn't feel a thing." To Stein he spoke with "a tone of muted wonder." Then he said again, "I didn't feel a thing."[8]

Warren had told Tate that life made certain demands that slowed down his writing. His body made some too. In early March he had entered the Harvard University Medical School Hospital for treatment of his shoulder and then continued his recuperation in Vermont. By the time they returned to Fairfield he was able to resume his novel and to await, with his usual trepidation, the publication on November 20 of *Audubon: A Vision,* a thirty-page poem of about 440 lines.

The poem began with a paragraph making it clear that the dauphin legend "did not enter the picture until after his death, in 1851." Sequence I, entitled "Was Not the Lost Dauphin," enlarges on the subject of identity:

> was only
> Himself, Jean Jacques, and his passion—what
> Is man but his passion? (p. 376)

It places Audubon in the cypress swamp observing the great white heron. It places him in nature, there by the bear and the bee, longing to be a part of it as they are: "He leans on his gun. Thinks / How thin is the membrane between himself and the world." Audubon is now acting out a process Warren had described a decade and a half earlier in which man achieves his identity by knowledge, through an image of himself "in the world with continual and intimate interpenetration, an inevitable osmosis of being, which in the end does not deny, but affirms, his identity."[9]

In the rest of the poem, the descriptive merges with the narrative and then the meditative. Sequence II, "The Dream He Never Knew the End Of," is the longest. In its ominous beginning, in a forest clearing at nightfall, Audubon takes shelter in the wretched hut of a witchlike woman who covets his gold watch and connives with her two sons to murder him and an injured Indian. Three travelers burst in to save them, administering frontier justice by hanging the three in the morning. In an unlooked-for experience, the woman's behavior at her death constitutes a kind of epiphany for Audubon. Sequence III is a four-line meditation entitled "We Are Only Ourselves," which encompasses poet and reader as well as Audubon. In what seems almost an evocation of "Masts at Dawn," the poet writes that despite our losings and findings,

> We are only ourselves, and that promise.
> Continue to walk in the world. Yes, love it!
> He continued to walk in the world. (p. 385)

The sections of sequence IV modulate into reflections on Audubon's experience and on the nature of truth and the quest for identity. Audubon lived to be lionized in Europe, to return to his wife, Lucy, before his faculties declined at last, when "he died, and was mourned, who had loved the world" (p. 389). Here the poet's persona becomes more manifest in a kind of preparation for sequence VI, "Love and Knowledge." This short lyric pictures birds in flight, then gives a shot of Audubon, his head bowed over the body in his hand: a bird he has killed in order to immortalize its image. In the last sequence, "Tell Me a Story," the poet completes his identification with Audubon:

> Long ago, in Kentucky, I, a boy, stood
> By a dirt road, in first dark, and heard
> The great geese hoot northward. (p. 391)

Then, in the second and last section, he speaks directly again: "In this century, and moment, of mania, / Tell me a story." He asks for "a story of deep delight," the name of which will be "Time" (p. 392), and a story that, presumably, will encompass the longed-for osmosis of being sought by both John James Audubon and Robert Penn Warren.[10]

Warren explained to Howard Moss that Audubon's story was "in a way, a variant of the fairy tales of the unrecognized princeling, with all those implications—as the story of all of us is, in one way or another, one time or another. Next there is the theme of 'what is man but his passion?' No man is 'real' except in so far as he creates his reality, discovers the true, central passion that may give meaning to his life. . . ." Another fairy tale or folktale variant is suggested in sequence II, "The Dream He Never Knew the End Of." It is entrapment by the wicked witch of the forest. This woman is her embodiment, her face like that of an apparition. She and her brutish sons are part of a world in which nature is not nurturing but red in tooth and claw. Audubon feels himself caught in a tale heard in his childhood that became a never-completed nightmare. He had foolishly displayed his watch, which she covets so much that, wearing it briefly, she becomes shyly beautiful: "Her body sways like a willow in spring wind. Like a girl" (p. 380). Then later, as she defies her captors and the rope, her face is "beautiful as stone." Watching her, Audubon suddenly "becomes aware that he is in the manly state." She hangs

> From the first, without motion, frozen
> In a rage of will, an ecstasy of iron, as though
> This was the dream that, lifelong, she had dreamed toward. (p. 383)

Her glaring face, growing black with rage and congestion, achieves, it seems to him, "a new dimension of beauty" (p. 384).[11]

It has been suggested that Warren felt an affinity with Audubon, whose sense of the land and its exploitation was scarcely less agrarian than his own and that of his friends a hundred years later. There was also Audubon's determination to be defined by that passion, to find his identity in work that provided the kind of interpenetration with that created world that Warren believed one must love. Against his sense of contemporary nightmare, Audubon may have seemed a redemptive figure.[12]

The reviews were good from the start and got better. For some it would be simply his finest poem, a culmination of the long narrative mode developed with "The Ballad of Billie Potts" and *Brother to Dragons*. It was a further step on his journey from formalism to freedom—without rhyme, meter, or stanzaic form, alternating from passages of Whitmanesque long lines to short bursts of dialogue and direct address. The free verse of *Audubon,* saturated with visual effects, links what went before with another long narrative poem to come and something that would appear again in full measure: the imagery of birds.[13]

Warren had every reason to relax and enjoy himself at their annual black-tie party five days before Christmas. The children were home from school with friends, and they all made the trek to Vermont. As usual, he was at work again before the holidays were over. He had his long-deferred novel to finish, a novel whose protagonist would have elicited the sympathy of Theodore Dreiser. And that was another portion on his plate: the Dreiser segment of the anthology. But he also had ahead of him the completion of an edition of another American, a novelist who had also turned increasingly from fiction to poetry in his later years, Herman Melville.[14]

42

❖

American Literature in Two Volumes

> We set out to read the body of our literature, no small part of it by
> some of us for the first time, and to try to divest ourselves
> of preconceptions about it.
> —*American Literature: The Makers and the Making*[1]

Early 1970 brought a measure of frustration and discomfort. Over the years Warren had been making notes for an edition of Melville's poems. Finally it was in production, and at last he plunged into the galley proofs. Describing it on the dust jacket, Albert Erskine would write that *Selected Poems of Herman Melville* "is the most comprehensive selection of Melville's poetry ever presented in one volume. It is introduced by a long and valuable interpretative essay by Robert Penn Warren, who has also provided copious textual and critical notes." As he often did in proof, Warren was rewriting extensively, and it would be summer before he was done. He was responsible for the section on Melville's poetry in the anthology he was doing with Cleanth Brooks and Dick Lewis, and so there was a carryover from one project to the other.

Later Lewis listed Warren's part of the anthology as general introductions to two large sections and fourteen smaller but wide-ranging sections, plus another on the development of fiction in America from the beginnings through Irving and Cooper, Hawthorne, Mark Twain (with Bret Harte); Stephen Crane, Dreiser, and Sherwood Anderson; Hemingway, F. Scott Fitzgerald, Gertrude Stein, and Henry Miller. Much later Tate deduced his other contributions from his style.

Cleanth Brooks reworked another essay of Warren's on John Crowe Ransom. "I thought I knew Red's mind and abilities long ago," he reflected, but he had not realized "how much he knows about American history and the American literature of the nineteenth century." As for their editorial method, "though each always submitted his own work to the other two for suggestions, additions—or cuts—and a general cosmetic treatment, nearly all the introductions are substantially from one pen." For the student of Warren's work these introductions are important. For one thing, they are interrelated, so that his comments on later novelists look back to those on earlier ones, tracing American fiction from the time of pioneers to the moderns.[2]

There was a brief respite in the spring. Warren was to give the Founder's Day address at the University of Virginia on April 12. He replied to Professor Bedford Moore with what sounded like a slightly tipsy letter. "I don't have an academic gown, at least not a presentable one after family charades, nor a mortar board, but my size is about this: height, 5, 10, ordinary suit size 42, hat 7⅛, body well-nourished, teeth good, eyesight fair, hairline receding, religion Protestant and still protesting, solvency, like literacy, fair, and is there anything else you want to know?" After talking on "The Sense of the Past" he enjoyed the ceremonial dinner at Monticello, where Jefferson's favorite wines were served and he had the company of Peter and Eleanor Taylor. As if to make up for the time spent, he completed a draft of *Love in a Valley* and sent it to Lon Cheney in the hope of a reading before he began revisions in the summer.[3]

Returning to the anthology, he had to shift from the Virginia scenes he had seen and the Tennessee landscapes he had created to those of Washington Irving, James Fenimore Cooper, and their predecessors. Popular and honored, adroit in his development of fictional method, Irving was for Warren "our first theoretician of literature," whose great insight was "that to have a national literature the emphasis must be placed on the word 'literature' and not on the word 'national' " (p. 242). But he had even higher praise for Cooper, in one sense, "the founder of American literature," a professional writer with a sweeping body of work, "the first to regard literature as, in itself, a commentary on, and a corrective of, culture, and at the same time the first to create a complex and enduring myth of American life" (p. 285).

Early summer was an auspicious time for the Warrens. *Baldur's Gate* appeared as the July selection of the Book-of-the-Month Club and began receiving generally favorable notices in late June and early July. Then, on the twenty-first, the National Book Committee announced that the National Medal for Literature for 1970 had been awarded to Robert Penn Warren "for the excellence of his total contribution to the world of letters." Previously bestowed on Thornton Wilder, Edmund Wilson, W. H. Auden, Marianne Moore, and Conrad Aiken, it would be presented in Washington on December 2 along with a check for five thousand dollars. He would be able to put this to good use, for he was planning to go abroad next June for sixteen months. In the short term, the news may have provided further impetus to finish up the work on the Melville book, a book on the work of John Greenleaf Whittier, and the anthology, the three books to appear over the next three years in that order.[4]

The rest of the summer went well. Completing the Melville book, he told Tate, "I never would have got into the thing if I'd known how long it would take. Now I am jealous of every minute away from my own writing. You never know, but the last may be the *last*." As he put the thought later, "I feel that I keep on learning something, and want to keep at it. I really don't know any other way of trying to make sense of your life. My life, anyway."[5]

He was feeling the same way about the anthology when the fall term began. "It has become a grind, the last few months. But on the whole the thing has been exciting for me—to read—or reread— American Literature and try to make up my mind about things, . . . [but] it's NEVER AGAIN for me. With this I quit, include me out, I resign." He was anxious to wind up other work. "At last, after seven years of intermittent struggle, my novel is done. It's not like anything before, and certainly not like anything in fashion now. Four people *in extremis,* cut off in a remote and isolated spot in Tennessee."[6]

On November 24 Random House published *Selected Poems of Herman Melville* in an edition of four thousand copies. Warren subtitled it *A Reader's Edition,* "and the reader I refer to is myself" (p. vii). For the selection of Melville's poetry in *American Literature: The Makers and the Making* he had written a five-thousand-word introduction plus headnotes of varying length for each of the poems. He expanded this to nearly seventy thousand words for *Selected Poems of Herman Melville.* The two can profitably be read together.

He had begun his introduction in the anthology, "If we are to understand Melville's poetry, we must see it against the backdrop of his defeat as a writer of fiction, from which he suffered not only the pangs of rejection, but the associated distress of ill health and no doubt, since his father, after failure, had died mad, the fear of madness." But the Civil War gave him "the kind of big, athletic, overmastering subject he always needed for his best work. . . ." (p. 910). He was able to contemplate not only the carnage but also the fact of human annihilation and to deal with this blankness with "a stoicism at once self-assertive and self-denying" (p. 914). Warren went on to explore the poetic devices—paradox and irony, ambiguity and symbolism—and traced Melville's working out of his primary themes from *Moby-Dick* to *Billy Budd*. In his inordinately long poem *Clarel*, Warren saw a "powerful document . . . of the meaning of modernity" and "a forerunner . . . of many works, especially *The Waste Land*" (p. 917).[7]

Many passages in the expanded introduction for *Selected Poems* are relevant to his own work and thought. In Melville's Civil War poems he saw that "there is a doubleness in things. If Nature seems beneficent and beautiful, that is only one aspect [and] such doubleness lies in history, too. Man is doomed to exert will to control events, but even when he seems to act effectively, the process in which his will operates may be only a mask for a secret process of which he has suspected nothing" (p. 18).

"In one sense," he wrote, "Clarel's story is another re-telling of Melville's single great story, which appears in many guises . . . that story of the youth—the Ishmael [*Moby-Dick*'s narrator]—who seeks a way into the world, and an understanding of the world, by seeking a father" (pp. 37–38). In an uncharacteristically Freudian formulation, he declared, "We may take the whole story of Clarel's development as a narrative presenting the stages of the Oedipal conflict and its resolution." And if we accept this, "we see him learning, in the end, that the fate of the mature and self-sufficient man is to live without a father" (p. 41).

Robert Penn Warren was among the most loving of fathers, one likely to err on the side of overprotection. If there was no affinity of guilt between Warren and Melville—an "unnatural father" (p. 80) who alienated the elder and terrified the younger of his two sons—there may have been some affinity of loss. Keenly aware of his father's failed life, if not of his own search for a father, Warren attempted often in his poems to express his love for that quiet man of his childhood. If he did not now feel a special affinity for Melville, and Thomas Hardy, he might well be aware of one later in the way both artists turned their energies to poetry after the public declined their fiction. The response to Warren's fiction had cooled, but he was still a productive novelist whose reaction to harsh critics was, he once wrote Tate, "To hell with them!" When *Selected Poems of Herman Melville* appeared, it was ignored by reviewers, despite the brilliance of the long analysis of the life and work and the scrupulous textual notes—perhaps because it was "an edition," a textbook, and an $8.95 hardcover at that. It was never reprinted.[8]

In mid-January of 1971 Allen Tate wrote Warren that he had liked his *Sewanee Review* essay on John Greenleaf Whittier. "A much longer version is in the introduction to a little selected poems for him," Warren replied. "You see, I try to get a double dip on stuff I have done for the American Lit book." His introduction to the University of Minnesota *John Greenleaf Whittier's Poetry* was half again as long as the anthology introduction. He had told Tate, "If anybody had told me 20 years ago that I'd ever be entranced with Snow-Bound I would have thought him certifiably insane." But there were many reasons why Whittier appealed to him.[9]

It was Whittier's ambition to become the poetic voice of his region. Like Theodore Dreiser, he was possessed by "an almost pathological ambition to take his 'rightful' place in society" (p. 538). He was born into a close-knit family where he read the works of William Penn and learned the Bible well enough to be able to tell its whole story. Encouraged by William Lloyd Garrison, he used his gifts for rhyming in the abolitionist cause, devoting one poem to "the struggle between the proslavery and the free-state forces for the control of 'Bleeding Kansas'" though he wrote an article condemning John Brown's use of violence at Harpers Ferry (p. 545). He was a fascinating neurotic tormented by "some deep inner conflict . . . with fits of self-pity and depression, breakdowns and withdrawals from the world. . . ." (p. 541). The subjects that released his creative energy, Warren proposed, were the "obsessive subjects" of his best poems: "nostalgia for the childhood past" and "the lost girl, a child or a beloved, who may or may not, in the course of the poem, be recovered" (pp. 545–46).[10]

The first of these two subjects finds its fullest expression in the poem that "summarize[s] Whittier's life and work": *Snow-Bound*. A bachelor, he dedicated this autobiographical poem to his family, eight of them, who had lived under the same roof with him. (Many times

Warren would say, "We were a very close family, very close.") Not only did Whittier paint loving portraits, he did so in the context of one of Warren's own obsessive subjects: time, especially loved ones perceived over time. He quoted from the poem:

> O Time and Change!—with hair as gray
> As was my sire's that winter day,
> How strange it seems, with so much gone
> Of life and love, to still live on! (p. 552)

Subtitled "A Winter Idyll," this nostalgic genre piece, lovingly rendering the nuclear family against the brilliantly depicted force of elemental nature, made the poet rich overnight. (Melville's *Battle Pieces,* published at the same time, vanished almost without a sound.) Few shared Warren's qualified admiration, and *John Greenleaf Whittier's Poetry* received no more attention when it appeared on June 2 than had *Selected Poems of Herman Melville.*[11]

Fortunately there was talented help with the anthology. David Milch had taken Warren's fiction-writing course in 1965, and now Warren asked him to join in the work. Soon he was doing research and writing brief biographical sketches of authors. He would say, "In retrospect it always seemed to me that I never really got an education until I began to do that work for them. . . . I think some of my happiest memories are of those several years, which required spending weeks at a time. We would stay in Shack Two, and we would work during the morning, but the early afternoons were saved for his poetry, and then late in the afternoon we would take long walks, and that was a terrific time."

It gave Milch "the opportunity of seeing someone like Mr. Warren, who had been able to fashion a coherent life, and whose commitment to art and to a way of being made sense, but was so extraordinarily humane and inspiriting." He admired the poetry and what seemed to him "a unified sense of composition. It was the sense of a physical readying of the spirit to receive the poem; it's a process of breathing, and it's what I think makes his best and later poetry so almost visceral an experience to read." Warren told him a story. Friedrich August von Kekulé, working toward a theory of the constitution of benzene, dreamed of a snake swallowing its tail. It was a visual model for his closed-chain theory that led to much of modern organic chemistry. A friend remarked that Kekulé was lucky to understand a complicated problem through a dream. But, Warren observed, there would have been no important result without his scientific training. And he quoted Louis Pasteur: "The dream can come only to the prepared spirit." David felt that Warren's whole mode of living was bent toward that end, toward that kind of harmony. He saw the poetry as "an expression of a unified state of being which really is, for Mr. Warren, as close to an exalted state as someone who hasn't God can get."[12]

By early March he had finished his introduction for the Dreiser segment of the anthology and enlarged it to make a book-length study, which Random House had scheduled for August publication. But he still had work to do for the anthology: his 150-page typescript on Hawthorne to cut and polish and his Twain introduction to finish. Once again his treatment of the writer's background and subject matter, skills and obsessions, suggests his own. Both Hawthorne and Warren came from colonial families. Both had dominant mothers. Both went to good colleges where their taste for literature was reinforced. Warren saw polarities in Hawthorne and listed nearly a dozen of them: "He lived in the right ratio—right for fueling his genius—between an attachment to his region and a detached assessment of it; between attraction to the past and its repudiation. . . ." (pp. 432–33).

"The matter is essentially romantic," Warren wrote (he who had called two of his own fictions "romances"), "the mysterious depth of the soul, the scruples of guilt, shadowy and ambiguous psychological and moral issues, but the style he developed was a cool, detached, sometimes portentous art-prose. So in the contrast of matter and style is one more of the vibrant tensions . . . which has made him congenial to the twentieth-century sensibility" (p. 436). And sometimes the soul plumbed in a process of discovery was his own. Besides supplying detailed biographical material, he traced Hawthorne's development from early tales to complex works such as "My Kinsman, Major Molineux." Here he glanced at Freudian criticism with the interpretation of the story's young man enacting "an implicit Oedipal conflict. . . ." This was "one of Hawthorne's central concerns and is, for example, embodied in the recurrent themes of patricide and incest. . . ." (p. 440). But Warren gave emphasis as well to the historical setting and its moral theme involving confrontation with evil. His brilliance at close reading is best demonstrated, however, in a six-thousand-word explication of *The Scarlet Letter,* with a searching exploration of its ambiguities. In his conclusion he emphasized "the obsessive concern of Hawthorne's works: the struggle to achieve self-knowledge."[13]

Driving ahead almost frantically to meet their departure date of August 20, he was aided greatly by James Glickman, one of his students two years before. His job included chores, riding herd on Gabe, playing tennis with Eleanor, and copy-reading Warren's introductions. Glickman saw how he managed to stand the grind, seven days a week. Usually up by eight, he "proceeded to work out with bar weights for about half an hour before going down to the pond to swim a kilometer. Then he came up for breakfast with Eleanor, Gabe, and me, headed for his work cabin out back by about nine-thirty and would not reemerge until one-thirty or so for lunch. After having one sherry and an hour's break to eat, he would head back to his cabin and come back about five o'clock or so. He then would grab a stick, call for Joey and Frodo, and go for a five-mile walk up Mountain Road." Then there would be drinks on the porch as the sun set, dinner at eight, reading, and bed.

In spite of all, he was writing poems, and for Jim it was easy to see at lunchtime how it was going. "When he was in the midst of one, his face took on an extraordinarily meditative quality—cheeks sunken, eyes downcast—and he would be completely absent from whatever was going on around him. Eleanor would sometimes remind him to be polite if someone were talking to him or had asked him something. He would summon himself out of whatever reverie he was in, looking like someone who was swimming to light from a deep watery element, at last breaking the surface, then saying he was sorry, smiling and 'being polite.' A few minutes later, he would be back where he had begun."[14]

In July he labored on his introduction to Samuel Clemens. "The man who was to become Mark Twain was reared," he wrote, "like Hawthorne and Melville, in an atmosphere of fallen gentility, and, as with them, the early death of the father was a shocking fact that conditioned his life and work. For him, too, the past was an obsessive subject" (p. 1261). Like all critics of Twain, Warren applauded his genius in recognizing the riches of American scenes and folklore and making available the native vernacular as no predecessor had done. "Lincoln freed the slave," he wrote, "and Mark Twain freed the writer" (p. 1278).

In just under ten thousand words, a small miracle of compression, he traced Twain's days in Hannibal, Missouri, to his early knockabout life and then the periods of rapid change, which he mined for the material that would make him famous. With the intertextuality that marked all of Warren's introductions, he wrote, "He was like Melville, Stephen Crane, Dreiser, and Hemingway in that he lacked a boldly projective imagination; his imagination had to work on the literal personal experience" (p. 1272). Like Whittier, he profited from "the nostalgia for the simpler world before the Civil War and the rise of the new industrial order and urban complexities. . . ." (p. 1273). It was Clemens's own nostalgia, reinforced when he gathered material for *Life on the Mississippi,* which helped him to complete *The Adventures of Huckleberry Finn.* In a six-thousand-word analysis, Warren saw Huck "as the embodiment of the incorrigible idealism of man's nature, pathetic in its hopeful self-deception and admirable in its eternal gallantry, forever young. . . ." (p. 1285).

He brought the essay to a close with three thousand words on *A Connecticut Yankee in King Arthur's Court,* "the first fictional glorification of the businessman" (p. 1287). He saw "at the visceral level of fable, the same view of history later to be learnedly, abstractly, and pitilessly proclaimed by Henry Adams and to be embodied, redeemed—perhaps—by pity, in the works of Theodore Dreiser" (p. 1290). He quoted Ernest Hemingway's judgment "All modern literature comes from one book by Mark Twain called *Huckleberry Finn*" and William Faulkner's "Twain was all our grandfather" (p. 1274). So the progression was clear in his remaining assignments: Crane, Dreiser, Anderson, Hemingway, and Fitzgerald.[15]

He wrote that if Twain was the grandfather, "Crane was the father." He saw in Crane the same "bleak determinism" he saw in Twain (p. 1637), and in *Maggie: A Girl of the Streets,* anticipations of Dreiser. In something over ten thousand words he explored parallels between Crane's work and that of Hawthorne and Conrad. He wrote that Crane was a realist, even a naturalist, with an impressionistic style, which permitted him in *The Red Badge of Courage* to "leap ahead a whole generation" (p. 1642), which made him, for all his brief life and small body of work, "one of the writers who have turned the focus of action inward. He created for the first time in English, since Hawthorne . . . and for the first time in its modern form, the story of psychological depth and poetic force" (p. 1650).

Sherwood Anderson had befriended William Faulkner and Ernest Hemingway, but other young writers besides these two would benefit from Anderson's example as he "became, in much the same way as

Dreiser, a symbolic figure. Both enacted in their personal lives the drama of their time, the glamour and the failure of the Horatio Alger story" (p. 1923). *Winesburg, Ohio,* Warren wrote, "is as much a return to, as a revolt from, the village and as such represents a release of the burden of memory . . . a poem of Anderson's obsessive theme of loneliness and alienation, [it] struck for the first time a certain deep chord in American experience" (pp. 1925, 1927). A transitional figure as well as a model, he prepared the way for the generation of Faulkner, Hemingway, and Fitzgerald.

He set forth Fitzgerald's story: a midwesterner who could not forget at Princeton that he was a self-styled poor boy in a rich boy's school, a romantic egoist deprived of his dreams of glory in football and the war, an early success both with his art and his pursuit of destructive beauty, a poor custodian of his gift who died early and not quite forgotten. Warren conveyed the tragic glamour, yet he saw defects that underlay it: how Fitzgerald was "spoiled beyond description," how he was handicapped by "his self-indulgence, his somewhat tawdry social ambitions, his small capacity for abstract thought, his painfully limited curiosity about history, politics, and ideas in general. . . ." (pp. 2282, 2284). Warren saw many similarities: Like Twain he luxuriated in the flush times early in his marriage, and like him, he "was haunted by a sense of doom, morbidly haunted by his early Catholicism as Mark Twain was by his Presbyterian conscience. . . ." He was plagued by a duality, by tensions that provided the subject of his work (pp. 2285, 2286).

Warren's four-thousand-word analysis of *The Great Gatsby* is one of the best ever written. Pointing out Fitzgerald's acknowledged indebtedness to Joseph Conrad in structure (in *Lord Jim*) and his thematic indebtedness to Dreiser (in *An American Tragedy*), he saw in the novel's protagonist "the American as the New Adam. In Gatsby, in fact, is the embodiment of the richly ambiguous American story. . . ." (p. 2291). As the novel's basis he saw Fitzgerald's theory that "the secret of life is illusion," a belief shared by other contemporaries besides Dreiser and Conrad (p. 2291). Moreover, Gatsby was "a late exemplar of the romantic individualist, the perverted idealist who earlier appears as Hawthorne's Ethan Brand, Melville's Ahab or Pierre, Mark Twain's Yankee, Dreiser's Cowperwood, and ten years later, Faulkner's Sutpen in *Absalom, Absalom!*" (pp. 2293, 2292). As he wrote, Warren must have thought back to Fitzgerald's bizarre response to his praise of *The Great Gatsby*: "Say that again and I'll hit you." Now he must have understood how any praise of Fitzgerald's masterpiece could have seemed to the neurotic, bedeviled artist a tacit disparagement of his writing since *Gatsby*.[16]

He had gotten a quintuple dip out of the sixteen-thousand-word essay "Hemingway," which he had first published in *The Kenyon Review* in 1947, and he would get one more before he was through with it. Though he devoted most of it to *A Farewell to Arms,* he went on to give a general appraisal of Hemingway's world, of its assumptions and of the style that had given it such an impact. "After Walt Whitman," he wrote, "reportage, documentary fiction, and autobiography more and more tended to merge, as with Richard Harding Davis, Stephen Crane, Dreiser, Sherwood Anderson, and, more recently, Hemingway" (p. 2250). He was the type of writer "who deliberately projects his own personality and life as central to his work," creating a distinctive persona, a seemingly detached observer, "suggesting, by the very intensity of attention and the precision of report, a tightly suppressed emotional force" (pp. 2250–51). As Warren had sought in Fitzgerald's personality a basis for the projection of self into fiction, he traced the self-created Hemingway legend of the virtuoso fisherman, hunter, and connoisseur. Chronicling the career in a surprisingly small space, he also noted "a deep streak of cruelty" and the way, with his success consolidated after *A Farewell to Arms,* "he had become more sadistic and was more and more inclined to indulge fantasies of self-aggrandizement" (pp. 2252–53).

He pictured the violent and often brutal world of Hemingway's art and the stoic-code hero who manages to function in this naturalistic milieu with its bankrupt civilization. Warren demonstrated the fundamental *nada,* the lack of spiritual values. He analyzed the famous style, with its reliance on nouns, "the repudiation of the adjective and the discriminations possible by a range of verbs and by inflections, the simplification of syntax," and beneath this "the need to return to the root of knowledge—the simple sensation or perception embodied in a declarative sentence" (p. 2258). Though Hemingway became "as much a culture-hero as a writer," for Warren he was "incapable of dealing with great tracts of experience" and he "did not try to explore very deeply the dramatic and moral implications of his theme" (p. 2267). Although Hemingway's reputation suffered a scaling-down, Warren predicted a rediscovery of his virtues as "a master narrator" and a "purifier of the language of the tribe" (p. 2270).[17]

Remaining now was all of the book's front matter and back matter. For the introduction the coeditors spelled out clearly the conviction that led them to write a history: the individual writer "exists in a

certain milieu—the political and economic context, the social institutions, the emotional and intellectual climate; and literature, as we
have suggested, represents a continuing dialectic between the individual and his world" (pp. xiv–xv). It would be four months before this
phase of the three-thousand-page book was completed, and then,
three months later, they would begin reading proof. *American Literature: The Makers and the Making* would be published by St. Martin's
Press in May of 1973. Warren must have been as close to exhaustion
as he had ever been when they sailed for Europe on August 20.

43

Two Books and a Crisis

You've toughed it out pretty well, old Body, done
Your duty, and gratified most of my whims, to boot—
Though sometimes, no doubt, against your better judgment,
Or even mine—and are still
Revving over satisfactorily, considering.

Keep doing your duty, yes, and some fine day
You'll get full pension, with your every need
Taken care of, and not a dime out of your own pocket—
Or anybody's pocket, for that matter—for you won't have
Any needs, not with the rent paid up in perpetuity. . . .
—*"Address of Soul to Body"*[1]

"We are in a village a few miles outside of Grenoble," Warren wrote Bill Meredith. "Our apartment is commodious but charmless, but we do have a fireplace, and the house and parc and general surroundings are wonderful." Their address was Furonniere-Stendhal, 38 Claix, "Stendhal's father's country place, where little Henri Beyle stole the dirty books from the library and went hunting. . . . The mountains are splendid, one of them booming right up from our back gate, and in five minutes or less you are in open country. . . ." They were there when the first of his new books was published on August 27.[2]

Asked about his literary preferences when he received the National Medal for Literature in Washington, he had answered, "I think Dreiser is second to none." In *Homage to Theodore Dreiser: August 27, 1871–December 28, 1945 / On the Centennial of His Birth*, he gave his reasons in just under fifty thousand words, more than twice as many as his anthology introduction. He had scrupulously read in Dreiser's manuscripts plus the standard biographies and criticism. The book began, however, with three poems entitled "Portrait." The first, "Psychological Profile," suggested Dreiser's own approach to his characters: compassion and understanding while clearly revealing their defects. It began,

> Who is the ugly one slump-slopping down the street?
> Who is the chinless wonder with the potato-nose?
> Can't you hear the soft *plop* of the pancake-shaped feet? (p. 3)

After sketching his unlovely traits he ended,

May I present Mr. Dreiser? He will write a great novel, someday. (p. 4)

The second poem, "Vital Statistics," gave flashes of his dreary Indiana childhood with its miseries and his terrible needs. The third, "Moral Assessment," asserted not only "his nobility of mind" but also named his gift:

to enact
All that his deepest self abhors, And learn, in his self-contempting
distress
The secret worth
Of all our human worthlessness. (p. 8)[3]

Dreiser's career, Warren wrote in the first sentence of his text, "raises in a particularly poignant form the question of the relation of life and art" (p. 9). Accordingly he set forth Dreiser's early aspirations and jobs, his love affairs, his writing, and always his driving ambition. Incapable of love except for his mother, Dreiser presented his flawed characters—such as the heroine of *Sister Carrie,* "the first of his shadow-selves" (p. 27)—sympathetically, and "under the guise of pity for her, expressing a pity for himself as the ultimate victim" (p. 30). Warren's brilliant thirty-page study of *An American Tragedy* noted deficiencies (chiefly structural) as well as merits. Concerned with the nature of destiny as "root tragedy, it seeks the lowest common denominator of tragic effect, an effect grounded in the essential human situation. It is a type of tragedy based on the notion that, on whatever scale, Man's lot is always the same" (p. 138).[4]

Warren was going against the conventional view that, with his heavy realism shading into dreary naturalism, Dreiser was powerful and compassionate but awkward and tedious. But Warren was frank. "At times I have regarded each of the novels as a total failure and a bore, crudely written and dramatically unrealized" (p. 72). *The Genius* he thought "a crashing bore" (p. 50), the work of a "blundering autodidact" (p. 53). But he called *An American Tragedy* a masterpiece, and the trilogy on the rise of a robber baron—*The Financier, The Titan,* and *The Stoic*—"a massive and passionate daydream of power" (p. 87). Though some sequences were "abominably written" (p. 88), he found himself returning to it not just with admiration but with "commitment" (p. 73). Dreiser was "quite literally, a novelist of the metaphysics of society—of, specifically, the new plutocratic society of the Gilded Age" (p. 32). But as for the charge that he simply could not *write* well, Warren refused "to freeze the question of Dreiser as an artist at the question of prose style" (p. 118). He insisted, instead, on attending to "the rhythmic organization of his materials, the vibrance which is the life of fictional illusion, the tension among elements, and the mutual interpenetration in meaning of part and whole which gives us the sense of preternatural fulfillment. . . ." (pp. 116–18).[5]

Warren must have felt certain affinities. His own prose, though sometimes lyric, depicted life in an essentially naturalistic way, with an emphasis on the power of sex in a world in which individuals, like species, preyed on one another. He defended Dreiser against critics who sneered at him as "the uneducated yearner." As Warren grew older he would repeatedly describe himself as a "yearner," one with a religious temperament but without religious faith. And as he remarked on Dreiser's "frenetic energy" (p. 41), his own psyche must have resonated with Dreiser's in his own tremendous ambition and drive for success. His sympathy for Dreiser, even with his awareness of his wretched personal qualities, also derived from his capacity for understanding Dreiser's misery. When Warren was suffering from the injury to his eye, he said that he felt "maimed." In "Psychological Profile" he had mentioned more than Dreiser's posture, his chin, his nose, his feet—he also wrote, "The left eye keeps squinting backward" (p. 3)— the same eye as his own injured one. Other aspects of Dreiser's life must have had a particular resonance and poignancy for him. Seeking root causes, he wrote, "If a secret drama of Melville's work is the search for the father who died after failure, a secret drama of Dreiser's is the rejection of a father who, after failure, lived" (p. 11).[6]

As the Melville volume had been his own "reader's edition," so this book too constituted a highly personal reaction. An economic but penetrating treatment of Dreiser's major works, it found the sources of his genius in his life and longings. It showed how his vision of life, fumblingly but surely, was translated into art. As in *An American Tragedy,* Dreiser performed the "transliteration of [the logic of character] into a poetry of destiny. . . ." (p. 115). This close analysis of Dreiser's strengths, like Warren's explications of *The Great Gatsby* and *A Farewell to Arms,* showed the accomplished novelist and critic at his most perceptive.

The reviews were all favorable. (The notice in *Time* mixed praise and irony. The book came as a surprise, a wise, "rather grandly plain utterance by a compassionate critic" whose books, like Dreiser's, the reviewer announced, were also now equally unfashionable.) Much later another critic—writing on the Melville, Whittier, and Dreiser books and *Meet Me in the Green Glen*—would entitle his review-essay "Robert Penn Warren's *Annus Mirabilis.*"[7]

Warren remembered the germ of the novel: "On a hunting trip with my brother, in Tennessee, some years ago. . . . We saw the ruins of a nice house in there, and this totally abandoned valley, now a game reserve, a park, began to grow in my mind—this sense of a lost world in that valley." He had, of course, dealt with the Fiddlersburg-Parkerton area in *Flood,* and the process of inundating the past as well as the land. Here the process is to be repeated in Spottwood Valley, a period put to the lives of a small group of characters living at the Corners in this rural area, all but one native Tennessean, and that one an exotic foreigner. Warren introduced three of his principals immediately in a characteristically complicated plot, which requires brief recital.[8]

Cy Grinder shoots a buck, and Cassie Killigrew Spottwood calls on a passing stranger to confirm that it was killed on her land. Cy had been the suitor of her youth until her proud mother had driven him away and brought about her marriage to Sunderland Spottwood, now a helpless stroke victim. Angelo Passetto, on parole from the Fiddlersburg penitentiary and fearing vengeance from other Sicilians, helps to dress the buck and stays on as handyman. Widower Murray Guilfort, lawyer for Cassie and Sunderland Spottwood, tells them their income comes from his managing their investments. It is, however, his own money, and it gives Guilfort the continuing pleasure of seeing his once virile, boastful friend—the only intimate who remembers what a craven weakling boy Guilfort was—now a helpless paralytic. Guilfort also enjoys using Cassie in his erotic fantasies. Having been institutionalized after a breakdown caused by her brutal and unfulfilling marriage, she welcomes the presence of the twenty-four-year-old Angelo, and even her ritualized daily rape.

Each of the characters evolves strategies for coping with personal demons and undergoes profound psychological changes. Angelo devises one chore after another. Then rape becomes seduction as he feeds his sexual fantasies. "You made me pretty" (p. 163), she tells him, and feels reborn, freer of her aberrant perceptions and mental states. Murray Guilfort counteracts memories of a failed marriage with call girls and canny professional advancement. But all changes. Angelo tires of Cassie, seduces Spottwood's mulatto daughter, and outrages town residents. Guilfort tells Cassie that Angelo must leave or face parole violation. When she tells him, his angry rejection of her drives her back toward madness.

At this point, two-thirds of the way through, the book's mode and structure change. It becomes a murder story when Spottwood is found dead, stabbed with Angelo's switchblade. Guilfort finds Cassie's red dress and black underwear and aids in the successful prosecution of Angelo for murder, despite Cassie's assertion that she was the murderer. Angelo's lawyer, Leroy Lancaster, feels himself a failure in the law and his marriage but makes strenuous efforts to get a retrial. Released from the asylum, Cassie persuades Cy Grinder to drive her to the capital in a fruitless attempt to win a pardon. Like the black murderer in *Flood,* Angelo is electrocuted in the Fiddlersburg penitentiary, where Cassie is found unconscious outside the walls.[9]

In the epilogue the valley is now largely under water, a tourist attraction as a state park and game preserve. Cy Grinder is the official in charge. Cassie, calmly mad and recanting her confession, is permanently institutionalized. Murray Guilfort, elevated to the state supreme court but oppressed by the emptiness of his life, drifts into a sleeping-pill suicide. Lancaster's legal career and his marriage have surprisingly turned fruitful, and Cy Grinder, idolizing his daughter, is at last able to feel compassion and something like tenderness for his ugly wife.

Warren supplied two opposed epigraphs from John Clare and Andrew Marvell. The first proposes a tryst in the sweet-smelling green glen. The second describes the poet's love: "begotten by Despair /

Upon Impossibility." The denouement provides no such equilib-
rium, for the fates of the fortunate Lancaster and the hardy Grinder,
played out against a background of uncaring history and remorseless
change, supply the only relief in a tale like one by Hardy or Dreiser.
The varieties of love enacted by Guilfort and Spottwood embody a
kind of commercialized sexuality and aggression rather than romance,
and Angelo's renewal of love in his death cell for the deranged Cassie
requires as much suspension of disbelief as does her earlier acceptance
of his quasi-sadistic dominance.

The nature of the events and the texture of the prose evince the
same sort of dichotomy as the opposing kinds of love. On the one
hand there is the violence coupled with graphically earthy and sexual speech appropriate to the characters. On the other hand there is
the lyrical description of the beauty of the valley. The dominant
motifs of the novel are loneliness, entrapment, and paralysis: Guilfort figuratively in his affluent empty home, Cassie and Angelo literally in prison and asylum, and Sunderland in his hopelessly inert
body.

Two months after the publication of *Meet Me in the Green Glen,*
Warren wrote Erskine, "I took a calculated risk, using the 'cliches' of
Southern fiction and trying to infuse them with a new kind of issue
and a new kind of emotional engagement." For many readers the
perceived "cliches" obscured the attempts at the new. Erskine wrote
him that the novel had received two kinds of reviews: "great and vicious." Warren had told Erskine, "Most reviewers see only 'material'
of course, not what is done with it. . . . And as for the 'cliches' these,
like so many cliches, are really there."[10]

Meet Me in the Green Glen was widely reviewed. At one end of the
spectrum it was a disappointment and a failure, at the other end a
book in which he regained his top form. It was variously a novel
written out of a "holistic vision" and an "exciting novel." Technically
accomplished, it displays all of Warren's literary virtues and vices:
vividly narrated, lyrically embellished, melodramatic with complicated plot twists and a large cast, though without the historical sweep
of *World Enough and Time* or the intense power and philosophical
weight of *All the King's Men.* In the end the American reviews as a
whole just about balanced out. In Britain most reviewers panned it,
but Thomas G. Rosenthal liked it well enough to publish it and sign
Warren up as a Secker & Warburg author. It was the beginning of an
important professional and personal relationship.[11]

. . .

In the other important areas of his life he had reason to be content. It was a period of transition, much more clearly for Rosanna than for Gabriel, and Warren was not fully aware of some of the dynamics of change. He and Eleanor had much to be proud of, and he enjoyed sharing details in his letters. Rosanna had been admitted to Harvard and Yale but opted instead to take the year off to live alone in Italy studying literature and painting. Gabe would enter a lycée, and his father would tutor him for his senior year at Andover, finding it "a pure paternal delight." Rosanna was the natural student. She had been promoted from charcoal to oils at the Accademia di Belli Arti, and except for fits of loneliness she was fine, loving Rome. There was "a little French girl Gabe thinks highly of . . . and a young American who thinks highly of Rosanna. My God, how time races on!" And they were already planning for the summer: "Gabe and Rosanna take off on bikes for a month or so with no old folks, in late June."[12]

Both of the children were keenly aware of his feelings. Rosanna felt moved especially when she read some of his poems, particularly those that pictured the somehow questing poet standing in silence and starlight. She would remember that these poems ended "with a reentry into the human community and the human touch." But at the same time she felt the tension between their own passionate desire to confront life and their parents' wish to keep them safe because of "an increasing sense of horror at the outside world. . . . and we became very impatient with that, and wanted to be out in it and tough it out." And there was something else. "It just went without saying that you had to be excellent at what you did." It was not a matter of competing with others: "It wasn't that anyone said you had to do superb work, it was just assumed that you were doing superb work, and I think this was harder on Gabe than it was on me. . . . he wanted to be a sculptor, and he was sick of living up to academic standards he didn't think were his." So he would ski off the trail in avalanche country and ride breakneck on forty-mile bike trips. It seemed to his sister that it became "a furious throwing himself at the world and out of his family." She continued to excel brilliantly. Later she would increasingly feel the pangs of depression.[13]

But now, in the spring of 1972, the demands of Warren's interior life were growing stronger. In the fall, at the time the reviews were coming in, he had come down with the flu. After antibiotics had knocked it out, he was able to tell Thomas Rosenthal that he would do some revisions before Secker & Warburg, his current English publisher, brought out *World Enough and Time,* but "in recent weeks the idea for a new novel has begun to possess my thoughts and feelings and may demand that I get on with it." By early December he had two chapters. "I live, eat, sleep, and dream it now—the 'voices,' for better or worse, are at work." In early February he had enough—four chapters—to put it aside briefly for perspective. "I've never done anything better," he told Rosenthal, "and rarely as well, I am inclined to say, but I've got to face up to some long-range problems about the basic conception. Pray for my soul."[14]

It did not slacken. "Obsession still prevails," he told Rosenthal, an increasingly important friend and confidant. "In Chapter VI, half way through, I should say. Such speed a new experience for me, but that's the way it now comes." The children remembered the way he dreamed the ongoing narrative. "Each morning we would hear the finished chapter, and it went on day after day. Only just enough so that he could remember all of it and write it down that day, and then go to bed and dream another half an hour of it." He might jot things down, waking in the middle of the night. Sometimes "he would wake up with hoots of laughter," Rosanna remembered. "He would just laugh himself awake, and go right to work." Later he would recount his comic dreams for their enjoyment. At the end of the month he was so possessed by the novel "that I couldn't stop if I tried." But then he had to. The proofs for *American Literature: The Makers and the Making* were due at the end of the month, and they decided to drive to Venice for Easter before he broke to correct them.[15]

They had a fine time in Venice and Milan before they returned home to Grenoble on April 9. But he told Bill Meredith at the end of the month, "I took to my bed immediately on arrival, and have been in poor shape ever since, beginning with flu & relapsed & now something that may be hepatitis." In early May he wrote Tate that it was "a very unpleasant experience, for it begins with a universal & incorrigible itching from head to toe." Eleanor was not ready to accept the local doctor's diagnosis: "There is something abnormal about it," she wrote Albert Erskine, and "he may have to go into a hospital for a day or two for a more thorough liver probe, but if they get to the point of proposing an operation I think we should probably fly home right away & have it there." Gabe's last and most crucial college board examinations were to be given in Geneva on May 16 and 17. Eleanor's old friend Denis de Rougement gave them the name of the best liver specialists in Geneva, and they made an appointment.[16]

After tests at the Clinique Générale, it was concluded that "the hepatitis is over. Itching under control. But it develops that there is a liver blockage. There is some hope that medication may solve this, but less today than yesterday. Which, if no change comes by Monday, means an exploratory operation." They waited with increasing anxiety. Then it became apparent that the treatment was not working. His doctors did not think he had cancer, but he was turning yellow. And there were other symptoms that convinced them that his liver was diseased. They thought he was dying and advised him to return home.[17]

44

❖

In the Midst of Life

Have I learned how to live?
——*"Chain Saw in Vermont in Time of Drouth"*[1]

Cleanth Brooks and David Milch met the plane and drove directly to the Yale–New Haven Hospital with Warren in the backseat, flat on his back, his posture for seven weeks now. When his doctors asked what he had been taking, Eleanor telephoned their landlady in Claix, who called the local doctor. There was nothing harmful in his record of the medication, but Dr. Klatskin, the hospital's top liver specialist, was convinced that the problem was chemically induced. A biopsy revealed obstruction in the liver's bile-duct system and some inflammatory response, probably to medication. They injected a dye and X-rayed it without significant results. There was nothing left but an exploratory procedure. The patient thought they were operating for a stone in the bile duct. The surgeons knew they were looking for cancer.[2]

They found a clear bile-duct system. So they began treatment for hepatitis, and his liver disease began to subside as he convalesced at the Brookses' home in Northford. Allen Tate wrote him a get-well letter. "I want you to live a long time, far beyond my term . . . because, Mr. Warren, you are my oldest continuous friend. And I want you to get the Nobel Prize, sooner than later, so that I can take my own pleasure in it. You are definitely the next American for this. . . ." Warren thanked him, "But I'll have to say how wide of possibility—and even of my deepest caring—your kind wishes about the NP are."

He reported that "a 'natural cure' set in. The liver got back on the job, as it sometimes does . . . merely from the shock of an operation. So I'm mending rapidly." He had lost thirty pounds, but now he was walking four or five miles a day. As the summer wore on, he tired easily, but the signs of jaundice were gone.[3]

There was a sequel. Like most redheads, Warren had sensitive skin—susceptible to burning, rashes, and fungus. His dermatologist wrote him a few prescriptions, and as he accompanied Warren to the door, he asked, "By the way, how have you been?" Warren answered, "I nearly died of hepatitis, but aside from that I'm all right." Eleanor saw the doctor go pale. "Give me that prescription," he said, and tore it up. It was for Griseofulvin, a drug Warren took internally for a fungus infection on his feet. He had continued taking it in France, but he forgot to tell the doctors in Claix and Geneva, and he had forgotten or been unaware of possible side effects. Dr. Klatskin had been right. The itching and the liver problems had been chemically induced.[4]

By August it seemed that things were returning to normal. Eleanor was fine, Warren wrote John Ransom, "and well recovered from the months when she had to run my life and take all the family burdens." A strong woman, she was ready to undertake these responsibilities, though in time she would cross over into areas where Warren insisted on making the decisions himself.[5]

But not always. In 1968 Viktor Golyas's translation of *All the King's Men* had been published in the Soviet Union with enormous success. "You've never seen a book sweep a country as that one did," Golyas told William Styron. "You would see people reading it on the subway." Golyas had also translated some of Styron's work and had spent time with him when Styron and his wife, Rose, visited the Soviet Union. There he gave readings and interviews, and they enjoyed the travel and leisure. Now Golyas hoped Warren would do the same. He had large amounts of blocked royalties there, and he would be welcomed with great acclaim as an honored guest. "Tell him to come," Golyas insisted. Enthusiastic about the idea, Styron did. It would be a free trip, and he was sure Warren would be treated luxuriously, with limousine travel and probably a Yalta vacation too if he wished. Warren liked the idea, and Styron wrote Golyas to set things in motion. Later, when Styron asked Warren about his plans, he smiled and said, "Eleanor refuses to let me go." A passionate anti-Stalinist, Eleanor had published articles against the regime in the *Partisan Review,* and she was sure that if they went, there would be ill feeling. Styron thought they were losing what would be a fine trip because of an imaginary antipathy, but he had to write Golyas to tell him it was off.[6]

Styron had admired Warren long before they met at the end of the 1950s, and he prized his friendship. As he had enjoyed his company in Egypt, so he did in Vermont. Both nonskiers, they would don snowshoes, following the white trails and then swapping stories. But after a time, to Styron's great sadness, the two couples no longer saw each other. Bill thought Eleanor had been offended somehow and that they had been walled out.

One decision had been in the making for some time. Yale had been changing, and the English department now included young luminaries who had helped to create a new milieu in which, according to an article in *The New York Times Magazine*, Robert Penn Warren was "considered something of an anachronism—and even a reactionary—by many of the students as well as a goodly percentage of the faculty, though he is immensely admired here as both a writer and teacher." He would retire at the end of the fall term, and he was also being cautious about new work. In August he had declined the remunerative Charles Eliot Norton Professorship of Poetry at Harvard for 1973–74. He would have had to write six lectures, and his head felt as if it were filled with cold oatmeal. There were other things he wanted to do that fall. He wanted to get back finally to his novel and his poetry.[7]

But the Warrens were hardly through with "the men in white," as he called them. About the time of his surgery he began to notice an intermittent blurring or failing of his vision. Glasses produced a modest improvement, but the blurring continued. Then, in late January, the Warrens were back at Yale–New Haven Hospital, but now the patient was Eleanor. A blood vessel had burst behind her left eye, he told Tate, "giving her blurred vision, nausea, and such things, all very sudden." At Yale the doctors advised waiting in the hope that the blood would be resorbed. "But it's hell on Eleanor, she being such a ferocious reader and auto-driver, and quite incapable of taking any rest." Batteries of tests at Harvard as well as Yale showed no sign of improvement, and by late April it appeared that the vision in the eye had been permanently impaired. But the right eye was fine, and they continued to hope.[8]

It was fortunate that Warren could be at home. He had not said that he would never teach again, but he felt increasingly alienated from the university. There was more to it than just the politicization of the campus. On matters such as student support for groups such as the Black Panthers and issues raised by Students for a Democratic Society, Warren, Brooks, Robert Brustein, and others like them were perceived as conservative and more. And there were new courses in the curriculum. "One seminar last year apparently consisted only of reading contemporary pornography," Warren told a journalist. "I suspect it was the first time in history kids got course credit for reading dirty books." His teaching methods contributed to an estrangement with some of his graduate students. One day he started his seminar with the question "Who can recite a poem?" When no one offered, he asked, "Who can tell the plot of a short story?" Again there was silence. He went around the table, asking each of the ten students in turn if they could recite a poem. When each said no, he rose from his chair, turned, and walked out of the room. It was his last class.[9]

He was making good use of his free time. In the aftermath of his surgery he had told Tate that when he was allowed to go to Vermont he wanted to meditate, "but I don't know what I'll meditate on. Mortality and the brevity of time, I guess. I'd been such a fool that I always assumed, I suppose, that I had forever. Now for a new scheduling of priorities." When they returned to Vermont for Christmas, Warren brought along with him a request to contribute to a book in honor of his old friend I. A. Richards. The result, he said, was the beginning of one of his "seizures of poetry." The new year found him writing varied new poems. The one for Richards, "Time as Hypnosis," drew on the impact of childhood experience on the farm. Others drew on southern and western scenes. The making of this book as he approached seventy would be, amid all the interruptions, his major creative activity in a year that would be far from trouble-free.[10]

During "a confused, driven, and unsatisfying spring" he came down with a streptococcus infection, and in the summer there were "a thousand nuisances, such as sitting in offices of doctors for small matters, such as an infected eye and a sprained knee. God damn it, nothing consequential, just annoying." Writing an introduction to *All the King's Men* for the Secker & Warburg edition, he had run into a problem unusual for him. "I got some kind of block, got gun-shy or superstitious or something, and would sit for hours and stare at the blank page." Finally he sent Rosenthal four thousand words and some Harcourt Brace Jovanovich statistics: the American sales amounted to over 405,000 in hardcover and just under a million and a half in paperback. And there were eighteen foreign translations in print. During this time of frustration he had found a source of satisfaction in politics. "The only bright gleam on the horizon is Watergate. They may get them. What a crew! . . . It's sort of wonderful to see [Senator Sam] Ervin, that piece of Old America, with all its faults and limitations, facing those plastic men. Allegorical."[11]

In Vermont, where he, Cleanth Brooks, and Dick Lewis had labored so long over *American Literature: The Makers and the Making,* he was able to read the reviews. Because it was a textbook, there weren't many. It was called "monumental," "stimulating and sophisticated," with "great reference value." But there were no other printings. The only sequel was a one-volume edition. Brooks wryly observed, "It took us six years, and we didn't make any money on it." But Warren declared, "I'm glad I put those years on it. I feel very different now about my fatherland."[12]

The seizure of poetry was continuing, and by mid-July he knew how he wanted to shape its fruits into a book. He was calling it *Essay Toward the Human Understanding.* Then, in the mood of his musings to Tate, he sacrificed work time. On August 18 the whole family was "going on a canoe trip, portages and all. Gone about ten days, then back here. Pray for our back muscles. We're taking plenty of Sloan's liniment." On their return he reported to John Ransom that "we all headed for North Ontario [and] the wilds, which, alas, aren't quite so wild as they used to be. But we had fine days at the paddle, sleeping bags under the stars, loon calls over the waters, and all the trimmings, including a sound drenching out in the first lake and the problem of setting up camp and making a fire in the storm. Gabe was navigator, with compass and map . . . now we are back to flush toilets and real beds." Weeks later he sent Tate a poem called "Rattlesnake Country," with the comment, "I began it in Ontario, and have just finished it the other day." Later he would get poems from the sights and sounds of this trip too.[13]

The end of 1973 was a time of mixed emotions. In early November at the University of South Carolina Warren received an award wearing a beard, a kind of scraggly imperial he had begun in the wilds. The honorary degrees were piling up. But there was still the worry about Eleanor's vision. Now she, like her husband, had only one good eye. And in mid-December he had been referred to Dr. James D. Kenney "for further investigation of a problem of intermittent blurring or failing of his vision," the blurring "more marked in the past 6 to 8 months, the episodes from seconds to as long as minutes. . . . He also has a sense of ache in the eye associated with this." But there was no glaucoma, and apart from a loss of 12 pounds from his usual 175, "everything else seems OK." As for his weight loss, it was a repetition of the previous medical situation: The doctor was "unable to identify any cause of the symptom of which the patient complained." But they could still be thankful. After the holiday Gabe would be off to France for a month's work as a sculptor's helper. Rosanna was "set on being a painter, and is working ferociously at that at the Yale Art School. Eleanor has just about finished a novelette, which will round out a book of short pieces coming out next fall, I guess. I am overwhelmed by chores now that kill off anything else in my head."[14]

In Vermont he came down with the flu again, and it was fortunate that he had managed to do as much as he had with the new book, for the new year of 1974 would be crammed with activities that would slow down his preparations for another book of poems and delay his return to the novel. Most of this was his own doing. On January 18 the National Endowment for the Humanities announced that he would deliver the annual Jefferson Lecture, which carried a stipend of ten thousand dollars. He also agreed to an expanded version for the Harvard University Press and a fall term as distinguished professor at Hunter College. In addition he would give ten readings during the following spring. He told Tom Rosenthal the reason was "avarice. It is a tough way to make money, but two weeks of that is more than three months of Yale, and the way our economy looks now I think I'd better grab what I can while it's grabable."[15]

In gray February, as he was slogging away at the Jefferson Lecture, Eleanor was busy with her writing. But there was a break coming. "Eleanor is bringing out a new edition of *Rome and a Villa,* and has to go to Italy for a few weeks to do a new essay and a new introduction," he wrote Tate. "I am going along for the ride." Italy was what they needed. "We saw things all over again, quietly and much to ourselves." They stayed in a Roman apartment provided by a friend, "ate some splendid meals," and drank "the best wine in Chianti," provided by another friend, the vintner himself.[16]

Back at home, he had to cut his Jefferson Lecture from forty thousand words to ten thousand. He had returned to classic American writers to see what they said about the nature of democracy and found "a subversive kind of record." Both conservatives and radicals had been profoundly critical. "The earlier writers were warning against the denaturing and dwindling of the self," he said. Santayana feared that the old springs of poetry would be dried up, and moderns such as Bellow and Heller saw it happening. Thinkers such as B. F. Skinner felt man could be engineered to be better, but Warren thought this was an illusion. Institutions such as the church and the family were losing authority, and poetry might help to meet the problem. "We simply have to cling to the concept of a responsible self, to whatever can give a chance of growth to humane values." There were tough times ahead, he said, but "temperamentally I guess I'm a long-range optimist."[17]

Before he gave the first half of the two-part lecture on April 29, he briefed reporters. He spoke again about the concept of the self and described the way it had changed. Jefferson counted on educated men to make democracy work. But now men thought of themselves as more acted-upon than acting, and with the unsureness of personal motives, which was one result of the insights of Freud and Jung, the modern citizen was less likely to feel a responsibility to act as his forebears had done. But poetry would continue as a natural human response, feeding the spirit as bread nourishes a hungry man. Delivered in his habitually rapid, rasping style, it was nonetheless a dazzling display of his historical sense and omnivorous reading, ranging from Saint Augustine and Kierkegaard to Dostoyevsky and Buber, from Adams and Emerson to Twain and Faulkner.[18]

He had discarded the working title, *Essay Toward the Human Understanding* (with its suggestion of John Locke's famous essay), for his new book of poems. On February 1, having read through the manuscript, Tate thought it "a fine collection by any standard. But not *your* best book." (Apparently Warren never asked himself whether this flood of creativity might arouse unhappy feelings in Tate.) He conceived the book as one poem, with individual poems as chapters or sections. The design was carefully crafted, with twenty-four poems differentiated by numbers and typography from eight more, called interjections, placed at intervals among them. In an effort to reinforce the thematic structure, he had drawn seven of the poems from *Tale of Time* and two from *Incarnations.* Then, on October 7, 1974, *Or Else—Poem / Poems 1968–1974* was published in an edition of sixty-five hundred copies.[19]

The enigmatic title, with its threatful air, does not help much in pointing toward the book's meanings. Nor does the epigraph from the fifteenth verse of Psalm 78: "He clave the rocks in the wilderness, and gave them drink as out of the great depths." But his familiar concerns emerge: to understand the nature of time, the tragic element in human life, and, notwithstanding, the possibility of joy. He treats the relationships of past to present and children to parents, using nature as a background for human activity. He ranges from the need to understand experience, even as one apprehends it, to the necessity to live life with an awareness of death. And with poems on Flaubert and Dreiser he assesses the role of the artist in these processes. Though he dwells less than usual on history and politics, they are there too. He draws again upon memory for loved faces and familiar scenes over a life span. He concludes a section of one of the poems with the question "Have I learned how to live?" (p. 31).[20]

As Tate had advised him to do, he led from strength, not so much in the first two poems about time as in the next few derived from the poet's childhood and his reflections on fathers and mothers. In "Natural History" he employed the surreal, much as he had done in "Ballad of a Sweet Dream of Peace." In the new poem, "In the rain the naked old father is dancing, he will get wet." And "the Mother is counting her money like mad, in the sunshine." The father's song "tells how at last he understands," and the mother's money is "her golden memories of love" (p. 5). The poem ends with the poet's resistance to memory: "They must learn to stay in their graves. That is what graves are for" (p. 6). In a further development of this material in the ten-page "I Am Dreaming of a White Christmas: The Natural History of a Vision," the poet's vision, played off against the title's suggestion of a sentimental Norman Rockwell–Bing Crosby Christmas, is not only surreal but bizarre. Against the ominous preliminary injunction—"*No, not that door,—never!*"—the poet enters the long-ago scene. There are the presents for the children, and there sit the parents, eyeless desiccated corpses, bones in tattered clothing. The poet glides from then to now, his memories almost as fresh as the holly on the hearth. He asks,

> Will I never know
> What present there was in that package for me,
> Under the Christmas tree?

> All items listed above belong in the world
> In which all things are continuous,
> And are parts of the original dream which
> I am now trying to discover the logic of. This

> Is the process whereby pain of the past in its pastness
> May be converted into the future tense
>
> Of joy. (pp. 21–22)

He approached the subjects of time and the past again in two other poems about his parents. "There's a Grandfather's Clock in the Hall" invites comparison with "The Return: An Elegy," published forty years before. Whereas this earlier poem contains brief references to the mother, now she is described in her hospital room with specific details that evoke Warren's vigil at her bedside. His pain and anger at her imminent death drive him to vent them on her. Lying there toothless, she asks if he is wearing a new suit; "You say yes, and hate her uremic guts, for she has no right to make / you hurt the way that question hurts." These are the last words she will ever say to him. (As a further hedge against any hint of sentimentality or bathos he uses terms explicitly sexual and vulgar.) As he ranges in time he also thinks of her as a virginal bride. The insight which emerges is that by seizing *"the nettle of innocence . . . every / Ulcer in love's lazaret may . . . even burst into whoops of, perhaps, holiness"* (p. 81).[21]

Following immediately is the seven-page "Reading Late at Night, Thermometer Falling." Most of it constitutes an attempt to recall Robert Franklin Warren vividly, to understand him, and to speak to him across the years. Warren recalls his own youthful discoveries: the photograph of his father that his father immediately tore up, the vanity-press book of poems, containing one by his father, which his father confiscated. He sees him again reading favorite histories and holding the Greek reader, a souvenir of his unfulfilled ambitions. Warren would say he felt he had usurped his father's career. In the poem he says what he had never said in life:

> . . . I live in a profound, though
> Painful, gratitude to you for what
> You could not help but be: i.e., yourself.

The son's love is reinforced by the poignancy of the father's life,

> Who, aged eighty, said:
>
> "I've failed in a lot of things, but I don't think anybody
> can say that I didn't have guts."

Finally comes the eschatological vision: his death at eighty-six after courageous silent suffering from prostate cancer, and

> So disappeared.
> Simply not there. (p. 87)

Whether or not Warren, as yearner, yearned for personal immortality, it was no part of his system of belief. And at the end, his father, like all men, is simply swallowed up in the icy cold of time, as presaged by night and the frigid room where he reads.[22]

One of the father's goals, like that of his son, was "to try to understand how things are, before I died" (p. 83). Concomitant with this is love, another means of confronting the final dominance of time and death. The poet recalls how "every day he walked out to the cemetery to honor his dead. / That was truth too" (p. 85). In *Or Else* Warren also honors the living whom he loves—his children being exposed to intimations of what they will ultimately have to confront: the exigencies of time and the suddenness of death. "Birth of Love" suggests a contemporary rendering of Botticelli's great picture. Here too the poet names no names, but anyone who had seen the pool there in Vermont would not have found it difficult to visualize, and the poet and his wife there too. In this sensuous rendering of the twilight sky reflected in the water from which the nude beloved emerges, the poet cries out in his heart that, if only

> He had such strength, he would put his hand forth
> And maintain it over her to guard, in all
> Her out-goings and in-comings, from whatever
> Inclemency of sky or slur of the world's weather
> Might ever be. In his heart
> He cries out. . . . (pp. 99–100)[23]

One of the two poems Tate liked best, "Ballad of Mister Dutcher and the Last Lynching in Gupton," follows after the book's third "interjection." It is a sardonic poem, based on fact about a small grayfaced anonymous man, a freight handler at the depot. The poet asks if Mister Dutcher isn't entitled

> even to his pride in
> that one talent kept, against the

advice of Jesus, wrapped in a
napkin, and death to hide? . . . (p. 28)

The talent is his ability to make a hangman's noose for a Negro murderer. Like poems such as "The Ballad of Billie Potts," it reveals the
capacity for violence, which, Warren would say, is always there under
the surface of southern life. He revealed it again, as Jack Burden
might have described it, in the last third of the book, in "News Photo
/ (Of Man Coming Down Steps of Court House after Acquittal on
Charge of Having Shot to Death an Episcopal Minister Reported to
Be Working Up the Niggers)" (p. 67). The tragic events he had
treated almost twenty years before in *Segregation* and in *Who Speaks for
the Negro?* were still with him.[24]

He made "Birth of Love" the book's penultimate poem and then
suggested the visual again with "A Problem in Spatial Composition."
Remaining strictly on the literal level, the poem nonetheless is a kind
of summary statement aiming at the infinite. The poet describes the
sunset sky over forest and mountain framed there: ". . . The lintel of
the high window, by interruption, / Confirms what the heart
knows: *beyond is forever*—" (p. 101). Then comes an image that will
become something of a personal symbol. A hawk enters "the composition at the upper left frame," descends (on the page typographi-
cally as well as in the poet's sight), and perches for a moment on the
tip of a bough. Then "The hawk, in an eyeblink, is gone" (p. 102). It
is as if, at one long descending sweeping stroke, the poet has not only
ended both the poem and the book but also intimated a comment on
his own life and human life as well.

Reactions to the book appeared more often in group reviews than
solo ones. And they were predictably mixed, with one of the good
ones appearing, however, in the opinion-making *New York Times.* In
one that must have pleased the author, in the *Library Journal*—a pur-
chasing guide for many librarians—the book was seen as he had intended it, as one long poem, a beautiful one that attempted to answer
the eternal questions. Not bad, he might well have thought, for a man
close to his seventieth birthday.[25]

Over the years he had been working toward longer poetic sequences with increasing flexibility in form. Now, with the interven-
ing accretion of experience, he was casting his net wider. His basic
subject was his own transaction with life, enriched by wife and children, with an attempt to learn more about those who had given him

life. There was no new reservoir of belief. He had gone to Psalm 78 for help, but the water from the cloven rocks was no baptismal font. Life was tragic, but joy was possible through human love and the love generated by the beauty of the earth embodied in the images of partridge and thrush, crow and hawk soaring against mountain and sky, sunset and star. Time, however, was inexorable, and the strongest affirmation he could manage came in the Hardyesque "Interjection #6," where God, blind, "wants only to love you, perhaps" (p. 66).

Critical studies over the years have generally treated the themes and techniques here with perception and respect. In the most admiring estimate, *Or Else* was "a natural fulfillment of *Promises,*" or simply "his best volume." Had he been told this in that fall of 1974, it would have pleased him, but never one to rest very long on his oars, he was already looking forward to the volumes he was planning for his eighth decade.[26]

45

❖

Calamities and Conquests

I want to understand the miracle
of your presence here by my side, your
gaze on the mountain. I want

to hear the whole story of how
you came here, with
particular emphasis on the development of

the human scheme of values.
— *"Vision under the October Mountain: A Love Poem."*[1]

The autumn of his seventieth year was frustrating and often depressing. His love of family would sustain him, and so would his art, when
he could get to it. "I have never been so driven and harried," he
wrote Allen Tate near the end of October, "and every day gets past
me with another thing undone. Hunter College has been demanding
extra days. . . . But the real trouble is 900,000 words of proof which
Cleanth and I are having to do and then collate, for the old *Approach
to Literature.* . . . Meanwhile every thing that I want to do and my
human pleasures and obligations have gone by the board."[2]

Two weeks later the mood had been deepened further by the encroachments of mortality. John Ransom had died at eighty-six. Warren went to the memorial service and then, he wrote Tom Rosenthal,
"down to Sewanee, where I saw Tate, who is in dire straits with emphysema, very feeble." He did not go to Tate's seventy-fifth birthday
party, and when he tried to write a poem for the occasion, "the spirits would not be summoned up."[3]

There were signs of passage at home. Gabriel and Rosanna had endured bouts of mononucleosis. Gabriel was still "furiously throwing himself at the world," as his sister put it, in a way his father admired, but he was finding Amherst no more to his liking than Andover. Rosanna was still performing brilliantly at Yale, but she felt the strain of her intensive work. She was well past her first serious love affair, and now she had brought home "her fine young man," as Warren described him, though other admirers would not receive such favorable reactions. Brother and sister were continuing to assert their independence. Enormously proud of their achievements, their parents were trying to accommodate to the inevitable, but it was not easy. "Gabriel may be studying in Rome all next year," Warren wrote Rosenthal, "and though we wouldn't want to hover over him, we might spend some months in the same country."[4]

In the summer of 1968, Adrian Hall, an imaginative young director with off-Broadway credits, had spent two days at Yale with Warren, who had enthusiastically agreed to collaborate on a dramatic version of *Brother to Dragons*. Now Hall's Trinity Square Repertory Company of Providence was going to videotape it for television. Warren put in a week on the project and then went on location outside Providence. After what he called "a case of carefully applied pressure," he did more than consult. His name was the last of the twenty-two members of the cast—playing his father. In "Reading Late at Night, Thermometer Falling," he had attempted to reproduce his father's speech. Now, momentarily, he assumed his identity. There was other earlier work on his mind too. He had finished revisions on his own dramatization of *Brother to Dragons,* and the Kennedy Center had commissioned an opera based on *All the King's Men.* He was sure of his poetic talent and aching to use it.[5]

He still had the stamina to pursue his multiple projects. Resuming a letter to Rosenthal, he wrote, "At this point I was called to the telephone, then walked the dog for four miles through snow and ice on the coldest night of the year, quite literally." He enclosed a poem but said there would be no more for the present, because "I really feel the need, the compulsion, the appetite to get at the novel." The Warrens looked forward to Rosenthal's visits, and his unstinting admiration for Warren's work had become increasingly important.[6]

Warren was feeling conflicted again, torn between what he wanted most to do and the feeling that he had to make money while he could. Less of his work would appear this year: poems from time to time and *Democracy and Poetry* in July, but the completion of the novel and a collection of poetry was off in the middle distance. In early March he explained his silence to Allen Tate. "I was on, for the first time, a little reading tour set up by an agent. Rather exhausting, but by self-control and God's grace I managed to control the alcoholic intake to a bare minimum (as I do generally now) and got my sleep. I am going out again tomorrow for six days. This depression has scared me enough to take these two trips. My income was hit by the general situation, and I can, as of the present moment, get well paid for my anguish. After two readings in a row I get to feel like a real fool."[7]

Tate continued to supply encouragement. He had told him "Birth of Love" was the finest poem in *Or Else*. Warren had sent him another called "Answer to Prayer." Subtitled "A Short Story That Could Be Longer" and set "in that bad year, in a city to have now no name," it follows a couple walking in the snowy night. The woman abruptly leaves her companion to enter a church. When he asks the purpose of her prayer, she answers, "Nothing much, just for you to be happy." He sees his luck since then as

> answer to prayer long out
> Of phase. And now thinking of her, I can know neither what, nor where,
> She may be, and even in gratitude, I must doubt
> That she ever remembers she ever prayed such a prayer. (pp. 7–8)

Warren would say it was folly to deduce biography from poetry, but anyone who knew anything of his life with Cinina in Minneapolis would see her there. Tate thought the poem "even finer than 'Birth of Love'—if that is possible. It may be your finest of all your poems. . . . *not one word* should be changed." (The *Virginia Quarterly Review* paid $250 for it.) He missed having conversations with Tate about his novel. "Well, I suppose there is no way to make the sedentary trade less lonely." A few months later he would say, "Alas, the literary life gets lonelier and lonelier for me."[8]

But sometimes it was as if past and present activities combined to block the novel. There were three parties to celebrate his seventieth birthday. "Even with three hangovers I felt fine," he wrote Charlie Foster. Then he went to Boston for the Emerson-Thoreau Award. "Well, says I, if Emerson can stand it, I can. And since a check comes with the medal I had an apt quotation from Emerson: 'Money is . . . more beautiful than roses.' "[9]

By late June he was able to send six chapters to Tom Rosenthal, who found the manuscript "one of the most moving and exciting pieces of prose I have read for years. . . . In its rough appearance it could delude the reader into thinking that here is yet another Bildungsroman about yet another southern boy making good, but I find that it is an extraordinary portrait. . . ." Warren replied, "It's not a story 'about Southern boy makes good'—rather about Southern boy making bad by making good." Finishing the first draft in August, he told Tate it was "the best, I swear it!" He would work on revisions in Vermont and then continue in Italy, where John Palmer was lending them his house in the Chianti country, south of Florence, for the fall. They would introduce Gabe to their Roman friends and then head "back to Tuscany to hole up and work like hell."[10]

Their time in Italy started well enough. They walked in the country-side and traveled to Florence once a week for museum pictures and social life. Gabe was thriving at the Temple School of Art in Rome, and Rosanna—headed for summa cum laude distinction with a double major in art and English—came for a needed change. Eleanor told Katherine Anne Porter, "She had been dreadfully sick, with the worst case of mononucleosis I've ever seen or heard of—being fed intravenously for many days when she was already skin and bones, operation for throat abscesses, etc. And then broke up with her young man, a very serious business after a year and a half. . . . I wish we could be more help to her now but it seems just the stage of things when we can be least [sic]. Just stick around, silent loving helpless, and pray, is about it."[11]

Their mood was intensified by their immediate situation. Their villa was cold and miles from a post office, and the help was unsatisfactory. In November they drove the thirty miles to Florence for an overnight visit with R.W.B. Lewis, his wife, Nancy, and their daughter, Emma, Warren's godchild. Warren asked Lewis for help with the manuscript of his novel. Like Warren's protagonist, Dick Lewis had done graduate work at the University of Chicago and also commanded a small mobile intelligence unit on both sides of the lines in Italy in World War II. He was also able to "summarize developments in academic Dante Scholarship" (the protagonist's specialty) and to help tighten the chapter on warfare in Italy. That evening Eleanor sang a comic British music-hall song and her husband read to the children for a half hour from *Uncle Remus* at their bedtime. Another reward was a trip the next day to the rocky summit of desolate La Verna, where, early in the thirteenth century, Saint Francis took the members of the order he had founded four years before. There on a large terrace by the church of Santa Maria degli Angeli in the oldest part of the monastery, they gazed out at the mountain-bordered Casentino Valley, the Warrens, hand in hand, gazing at the sunlit Guidi castle in the distance.[12]

They hoped for improvement in Rosanna's health when she returned to them at Christmas. Staying in a friend's apartment in Venice, her parents worried and waited for her New York flight to land in Milan. Then at last the phone rang. Because of smog the flight had been rerouted to Genoa. The pilot tried twice to land, ran out of fuel, and crash-landed. The fuselage broke in two right in front of Rosanna's seat. Miraculously, no one was killed. A week later, when they went to the Dolomites for skiing, Rosanna slept in her parents' room so that her mother could be there when she woke screaming from nightmares.[13]

The bad dreams lingered, along with her other miseries, after the return home in that January of 1976. "She is working again," Warren wrote Tate. "She has seriously branched out from painting into poems—suddenly terribly good." She was using her studio and special funds, perquisites of the Scholar of the House, in the process of finding what would become her true metier. "Oh dear God," Warren wrote Lewis Simpson, "why should I have two, male & female, children who are artists! I suppose there are worse things, but they do have a hell of a time (they don't know that yet)."[14]

Early in the new year Warren had written Tate, "I had a scare in the fall. . . . My vision began giving me trouble in connection with an eye infection, so I spent a good deal of time with the Yale eye people. I began to feel gloomy and gloomier, and suddenly I realized that I was reliving those times when I was in college, and my sight seemed (or I thought it seemed) to be going worse, and I kept getting deeper and deeper fits of depression, the stuff that led up to my real desperation and dead-endedness in my junior year. Well, the doctors assure me that all is well. But the sense of reliving a period was traumatic. Nothing is ever buried deep enough, I guess." There was more trauma ahead.[15]

In late winter the blow fell. "We are suffering through eye trouble for Eleanor, which may be terrible," he wrote George Core, a friend and editor of *The Georgia Review,* "all we can do is wait & see. Here diagnostics break down." At first it seemed there was reason for guarded optimism. "So we watch & pray, as the hymn says." Eleanor wrote Peter Davison that it was maddening not to be able to read or work or drive a car. "And being so damned healthy in general, maybe arrogantly so, I had no preparation for such a blow. Ah well—the gods used to do as they saw fit. And now?"[16]

A month later Warren told Tate, "The doctors are holding out the slimmest of hope for Eleanor's vision. She will not lose it entirely, and with luck (they'll know in July) they may with mechanical means get her so she can read a good deal. . . . But she won't be able to ski or play tennis, which are life to her. Meanwhile she is stoic and cheerful and takes joy in her children and gives them joy." They were planning a month's trip to Greece, which "gives her a lot of new thoughts and impressions, and comes at a good time. But, Jesus, things aren't as I would have chosen—in so many ways."[17]

Rosanna accompanied them, and Gabe met them there. After Athens and some touring they settled in happily on Crete. "Our normal ideal for travel was just to go somewhere and work," Eleanor said. "This was really dandy." They did a great deal of walking, Warren later recorded, "even taking the hike across the chasm that splits the island, a chasm of almost unbelievable depth and roaring water. Then a little inn at the end to wait for a boat the next day." But the whole trip came to an unexpected end when Rosanna began to show signs of mononucleosis.[18]

At home in mid-June Warren brought Katherine Anne Porter up to date. "Things are not well with us. Eleanor has largely lost her vision—that is, she can't read, though she gets about and even cooks and does such things. . . . but right now everything is up for grabs. Small leakages and ruptures in the tiny veins in the eye ball." The trip had helped somewhat, and Gabriel was a prop for his spirits, working at his sculpture, planning to build a five-ton, thirty-foot schooner in Vermont, and heading for the Rhode Island School of Design in the fall. Warren worked on poems while the novel underwent copyediting. "If only Eleanor were better! But how brave she is and how I love her! I didn't mean to say that. It just popped out." They longed to see her, he told Katherine Anne, and he might use that poor, abused word, love. She replied, "You know that I love you all of you together and each separately and have all these years and shall love you all my life."[19]

The doctors gave their verdict in July. They "despaired of doing anything about Eleanor's vision, and only hope that the loss is now stabilized. Meanwhile she is stoical, but I'll be damned if I am." The sports she loved were gone. "Even now, though, she goes to the court and tries to hit the ball—now and then succeeding. Her very toughness and uncomplainingness are what get me down." It was macular degeneration, which would shrink her vision increasingly. Later that summer she began to work, "using a black [felt-tip pen] and newspaper sheets, then reading what she has done with a big microscope with circular inner illumination. But she can't read yet, so we have a lot of family readings." They started with Homer.[20]

It may have seemed ironic to Warren that his affairs prospered amid so much pain. In the spring he had received the annual ten-thousand-dollar Copernicus Award for "overall achievement as well as the contribution to poetry as a cultural force." Four different versions of *Selected Poems: 1923–1975* would appear in January, one of them a deluxe edition from the Franklin Library with an advance of twenty-five thousand dollars. The same company also paid forty thousand dollars for the rights for one deluxe autographed edition of *All the King's Men,* with an advance of ten thousand. And a movie company had optioned the novel "at a fine figure and with a good contract, with share in profits, *if* the picture is finally made." But he missed things that money could not procure. Sending a new poem, he told Tate not to take it as a burden. "But, oh, how in these last years I have missed your candor and acuteness and, not last, sympathy."[21]

A month before, he told Tate he had been having another of his seizures of poetry, which usually raised his spirits, but he felt unease, and it was partly his own fault, for he had broken another of his resolutions. Robert Brustein had obtained a grant for the Yale School of Drama from the Columbia Broadcasting System Foundation for Play-Writing. Four fellows would receive eight thousand dollars each. One was to come from another field, and Brustein happily appointed Warren. He made it a course in "adapting novels either to the screen or to the stage." Soon he was bored with it, wishing he hadn't undertaken it. The only poem he had done since then was "Loss, of Perhaps Love, in Our World of Contingency." The first of fourteen unrhymed couplets began, "Think! Think hard. Try to remember / When last you had it. . . ." It was followed by a series of images of loss, but then the possibility of joy, with the concluding line "We must learn to live in the world." Seeing it in *The New Yorker,* Katherine Anne Porter wrote him almost immediately. It moved her to tears. It was "one of the most beautiful things you ever wrote." Seven weeks later she wrote again. "Your poem is magnificent and heart-breaking," she told him, "as if the bone marrow had found a voice." But his unease persisted. He told one student of his work, "These days when I finish a poem I always get a little panic that it may be the last, God damn. And my typist now has the novel that has been occupying me off and on for five or six years. We'll see."[22]

He was back at his desk tending to business when they returned from Vermont as the fall of 1976 came on. He had sent his dramatic version of *Brother to Dragons* to George Core for the spring issue of *The Georgia Review.* "I'm just nursing my own little projects along, and now I'm having a little burst of poems." In December he published two whose bleakness may have reflected the emotional strains of the year. The speaker in "Waiting" reflects on natural disasters and then, seeking solace in Catholicism from the pain of a failed marriage, realizes with surprise

> that our Savior died for us all,
> And as tears gather in your eyes, you burst out laughing,
> For the joke is certainly on Him, considering
> What we are. . . .[23]

The other poem was published in *Esquire,* regarded as a "men's magazine," and prized by some readers for its cartoons and voluptuous artwork and by others for its often explicitly sexual fiction. This attribute was shared by "Bicentennial," at nearly 450 lines, one of Warren's longest poems. Its thirty-five stanzas are preceded by the question *"Who is my brother?"* The total effect is something like that in John Dos Passos's trilogy, *U.S.A.,* with crosscutting from one character to another to form a complex picture of society. The characters' lack of personal fulfillment suggests some in the fiction of John O'Hara. Life, it seems, is a matter of chance. Looking ahead to the Fourth of July, the poet cautions against forgetting "the virtues of the old ones who . . . set us free from tyranny." His final stanza adds, "They did not get around to setting us free from ourselves." Contrary to his usual custom, he never reprinted "Bicentennial."[24]

Random House published *Selected Poems: 1923–1975* in an edition of six thousand copies in January 1977. The first segment was called "Can I See Arcturus from Where I Stand? *Poems 1975.*" The ten poems were a varied lot, but all were intended to plumb familiar questions, as the epigraph from "Rattlesnake Country" indicated: "Is *was* but a word for wisdom, its price?" Arcturus, the Pole Star, a bright star of the first magnitude, presumably symbolizes a guide for the process of approaching wisdom, or at least truth, in the course of the journey through life toward death. But it is a difficult process, as "A Way to Love God," the first poem, suggests with its Platonic overtones: "Here is the shadow of truth, for only the shadow is true" (p. 3). Thinking of sheep huddling at midnight, staring at nothing, he muses, "You would think that nothing would ever happen again. / That is a way to love God" (p. 4). Similar imagery concludes "Season Opens on Wild Boar in Chianti," where, the dead quarry lashed to a pole, "the great head swings weighty and thoughtful / While eyes blank in wisdom stare hard," as above "The constellations are steady" (p. 13).[25]

But there is the sense nonetheless of meaning to be sought, and it can come in unexpected ways. "Old Nigger on One-Mule Cart Encountered Late at Night When Driving Home from Party in the Back Country" is a near-death experience "in July, in Louisiana" (p. 14). At the last minute the driver sees the eyes of mule and man blazing in the headlights. Then the poet thinks, as if with clairvoyance, of the old man by his shack in the starlight.

> And so I say:
> Brother, Rebuker, my Philosopher past all
> Casuistry, will you be with me when
> I arrive and leave my own cart of junk
>
> . . . .
>
> To enter, by a bare field, a shack unlit?

holding, he hopes, a "hard-won something," perhaps a "trophy of truth" (p. 17). (To one reader, the old man is "a secret sharer and a man who has learned how to live in the world. . . . a figure of wisdom, much as Wordsworth sees his beggars, hermits, and leech gatherers.") Tate's response to the poem was, "After several readings, no sale. . . ." Warren had thanked him appreciatively nonetheless, for it seemed to him that the older one got the harder it was "to get criticism from a friend. Writing gets lonelier."[26]

If there is pain, as in "Loss, of Perhaps Love, in Our World of Contingency," it is general, as in "Brotherhood in Pain" (pp. 11–12). But at times in spite of fear, there is redeeming joy held precariously in both hands, as in the sight and thought of the beloved, the mother nursing her child, in "Midnight Outcry" (p. 9). There is another kind of summation in "Evening Hawk," where the bird's wing from on high "Scythes down another day," he

> Who knows neither Time nor error, and under
> Whose eye, unforgiving, the world, unforgiven, swings
> Into shadow. (p. 4)

Wisdom lies in seeing the world as it is, as in the hawk's acute vision. Warren had used bird imagery often, but now the talismanic hawk would appear increasingly in other poems besides this brilliant and magisterial one.[27]

More than half of this new book had been written between 1960 and 1975. As he had done in the earlier volume of selected poems eleven years before, he printed the most recent ones first, continuing in reverse chronology. He was inclined to think that his most recent poems best showed the process of development that had brought with it new power, clarity, and subtlety.[28]

Because of the several editions of the collection, reviews began appearing in the specialized journals as early as May 1976, with a few more in the fall. The few that appeared in major publications were good, and they came in good time. For one of his most loyal and prestigious admirers, the book was "the great event in this year's poetry," establishing its author as one of the "giant forms in American poetry," including Emerson, Whitman, Pound, and Eliot, a living poet "comparable in power to Stevens or to Frost." Almost all the reviews accorded him the status of a major poet, in one review even that of the greatest of living poets, and a few marveled that he did not have a larger readership.[29]

Critical opinion since then has supported these judgments, sometimes with the comparison to William Butler Yeats's prodigious late output. Why had the book not made a deeper impression? For one thing there was little in it that was strikingly "new." Instead there was only his impeccable versatile craftsmanship, his profusion of incident, image, and character, and his attempt, at the highest level and with intense personal involvement, to wrest meaning from life through his art.[30]

In her study in the barn Eleanor was at work with her felt-tip pens, her large sheets, her illuminated magnifier, and her courage. She had completed the manuscript of *Eyes, Etc.: A Memoir,* which had been accepted by Pantheon. (She had also cooked for a week for her annual Christmas party with fifty sit-down dinner guests.) "I don't see how she does it," Warren wrote Tate, "except she's iron in the hands and dove-down in the heart." As for himself, now well into his eighth decade, he had ten days earlier declared to his old friend, "Now a novel begins to stir in me and I hope to have more than a stir by June."[31]

SEVEN

*Honors and
Valedictory*

46

❖

The Tenth Novel

You feel like crying out in the emptiness of the house to
demand what—what in God's name—is reality.
—*A Place to Come To*[1]

In January they had ten days in Martinique as guests of the Franklin
Library. Sitting on the hotel balcony overlooking the manicured gar-
den, with the white sands and the brilliant blue Caribbean beyond,
Warren signed the sheets for the limited edition of *Selected Poems*.
Then he worked on new poems while Eleanor revised the typescript
of *Eyes, Etc.*, done with large type on her new machine.

Returning to Fairfield was a return to winter and the claims of the
past. His long introduction to the collection of essays on Katherine
Anne Porter was also a loving tribute. She was now eighty-seven, and
they were looking forward to seeing her when Warren went to Johns
Hopkins to receive an honorary degree in late February. Unexpect-
edly, she entered the hospital the day before they arrived and then
suffered a minor stroke, followed shortly by a more severe one. This
illness deepened this winter of more than discontent. Allen Tate, approaching his seventy-eighth birthday, was increasingly a prisoner of
emphysema and prey to worries over provision for his wife, Helen,
and two small sons. And Eleanor's handicap and her valiant persever-
ance pulled at her husband's heart.

His children were still his main prop. "How I wish I could show
them off to you!" he had written Katherine Anne. Their activities
filled his letters—Rosanna pursuing her two arts in Paris, Rome, and

later New York, and Gabe finishing his degree at the Rhode Island School of Design while he worked at Brown too. Before long he would haul his schooner from Vermont to the coast, where he would fit it out before setting out, at last, to sea. It was as if Warren drew his friends into the circle of his family through Rosanna and Gabriel, and friends like Tom Rosenthal responded. He would not be able to make his mid-March visit to Fairfield coincide with theirs, and "Alas, it is sad that I won't see your magnificent children. . . ."[2]

Warren's prepublication anxiety must have intensified his general malaise, though he told Bill Meredith in the last days of winter that this novel was "the best one I ever did, I'm inclined to think. . . ." He was still writing poems, but when he sent one to Allen Tate, he added, "I've been so generally gloomy of late I haven't done much. . . ." Some of the reviews of his new novel, appearing in mid-March, must have deepened his mood. He would say that *A Place to Come To,* like *Promises,* was "half Kentucky-Tennessee, and half Italy. There's medieval Italy and boyhood—they make a book. . . . It's the long withdrawal from south Kentucky, [but] it's autobiographical only in the deep way that all books are autobiographical." This one, however, was in some of its details the most autobiographical of all his books. It follows Jediah Tewksbury, aged nine, from the death of his father, Buck, in Dugton, Claxford County, Alabama, until he makes a return visit there in his sixties, able at last to think of his birthplace as a place to come to.[3]

Tom Rosenthal's characterization of the first paragraph as "ribald humor" was an understatement if not a misnomer. "I was the only boy, or girl either, in the public school of the town," it begins, "whose father had ever got killed in the middle of the night standing up in the front of his wagon to piss on the hindquarters of one of a span of mules and, being drunk, pitching forward on his head, still hanging on to his dong, and hitting the pike in such a position and condition that both the left front and left rear wheels of the wagon rolled, with perfect precision, over his unconscious neck, his having passed out being, no doubt, the reason he took the fatal plunge in the first place. Throughout, he was still holding on to his dong" (p. 3). Jed mentions both the accident and the prodigious organ often there after, and by the end of the novel the monosyllable has become a kind of motif.

Buck Tewksbury is another of Warren's roaring boys, a celebrated drinker and fornicator hated by his son. Jed's mother is another of Warren's strong women. She is so determined that Jed will escape this background that one night when he returns drunk from his adolescent pursuit of "poontang" she breaks his nose. She often addresses him thereafter as "Old Broke Nose" and never regrets the blow. One of the novel's ironies is Jed's own development into a sexual prodigy.

But that is not his only drive. His compulsion to learn and to make sense of his life carries him from a backwater Bible college to the University of Chicago. Uncouth and awkward, he is redeemed only by his passion for classical languages and his intellectual hunger. *A Place to Come To* sounds many echoes of earlier work. One is Jed's voice, full of irony and the abrasive cynicism of Jack Burden. Another protagonist who seeks a surrogate father, Jed owes his career to Dr. Heinrich Stahlmann, who provides not only housing and employment but a continuing tutorial and friendship. He supplies an alternative to the world's chaos through the life of the mind. But ultimately he fails Jed. With the coming of the Second World War, Stahlmann can no longer live with his past—not only the death of his wife from grief over the Nazis' murder of her mother, but also his failure to take some sort of stand before he fled his country. His description of a rabbit's death beneath a cascade of mountain stones provides a metaphor: "The Great Landslide which was history" (p. 86). It is permanently engraved on Jed's psyche by Stahlmann's suicide as the war begins. In Italy with the Partisans, Jed shows that he is quite as capable of murder as the Nazis, shooting a prisoner he is interrogating. He returns to Chicago to complete his training as a classicist and medievalist specializing in Dante. His marriage to another graduate student (like Jack Burden's) is short-lived, but it inspires the work that makes his reputation: "Dante and the Metaphysics of Death." He feels, though, that he has inadvertently made a kind of Faustian bargain, trading her life for his success.

His continuing account is suffused not only with aggressive sexuality but also near-clinical descriptions of various couplings. Some take place as if in imitation of *Fanny Hill*–style random matings, others through the medium of blue movies, and one is the performance of a blue-blooded stud, Dark Power, who services a mare so dynamically that his matronly owner invites Jed into her bed afterward. He possesses many women variously—in the rain in a forest, in a broom closet during a party, and elsewhere. Orgasms provide the inspiration for a friend's sculpture in stone and metal, and the range of reference extends to masturbation, love bites, fellatio, and defloration. Jed's terminology for bodily parts and actions is often explicit, basic, and colloquial. But this is consistent with his character, like the X-rated dialogue of several others, though much of it seems gratuitous. Clinical description is not always Jed's preferred mode, however. Rozelle Hardcastle is the principal lover in his life, and in one lush description of the rich delta below her mons veneris his imagery is sensuously poetic before it becomes monosyllabic. The description of their lovemaking is a combination of Japanese pillow book and American marriage manual.

This sexuality is most pervasive in Nashville, where Jed takes a teaching job. He thinks of Descartes and "the brilliant formulation which is the basis of our modernity: *cogito ergo sum*. Well, I was to go one step beyond him to a more radical formulation upon which a new era may be founded. Even though I laid no claim to thinking, I still had an argument for my existence: *debatuo ergo sum*. I fuck, therefore I am" (p. 218). When his adulterous affair with Rozelle reaches a dead end, he leaves. "I don't know how much longer I could have lived the life I had been living in Nashville," he confides to the reader, "all the intensities, lies, self-divisions, dubieties, and blind and variously devised plummetings into timeless sexuality" (p. 317).

An atheist unsuccessful in his search for values, he returns to the University of Chicago as a distinguished professor, his chronicle reading as if both he and his creator are weary. "So the years passed. . . . I worked devotedly with my students, more than ever, and even got an award for that. I published articles and books, and got more and more honorary degrees, at home and abroad, for that" (p. 345). Returning to Rome, thirty years after the war, he concludes, "Whatever I had come in search of, I had, clearly, not found. And it might be added, whatever illusions I had started out with I had lost. I had only the old wisdom we all struggle so hard to get and always find we already had: every man has to lead his own life and has little chance of knowing what it means" (p. 356).

But there is some hope at the end of the novel. Jed had resumed an early graduate-school affair with Dauphine Finkel, which had evolved into his second marriage and produced a son before it ended in divorce, leaving him to deal again with his old conviction that he is a deracinated "loneliness artist." He lives his life with the conviction that "the main function of work is to kill time. I mean time with a capital *t*" (p. 361). But he visits Dugton after his mother's death and forms a bond with his simple and affectionate stepfather. He comes to terms with his own identity: "I was I" (p. 396).[4]

A Place to Come To is a long novel that seems longer than it is. This is due in part to the time span and intricate plot, but more than one section asks for compression or deletion. Warren indulges his taste for southern dialect in Jed's mother's letters, whose grammar and phonetic spelling help to characterize her as a tough original but soon become wearisome. Much of Jed's experience rings true, but one late passage, crucial in his changing values, does not. Stabbed while trying to protect an old woman, he watches the mugger escape, and just as he passes out he experiences a kind of epiphany at the grace of the boy's leaping flight. As a protagonist, Jed is neither tragic enough to engage the reader's sympathies nor likable enough to gain his affection. The descriptions of the many scenes are vivid, evocative, and often poetic, but they are overbalanced by the philosophical and metaphysical seeking and undercut by the gratuitous earthiness. The novel was scarcely less vulnerable than some of his others to the familiar charges of melodrama and violence, but there was enough action and romance to make it a Literary Guild selection. And Robert Redford liked it well enough to buy the film rights.

Fretting in London, Tom Rosenthal wrote Julian Symons about the response in the American periodicals: "Yet again the Americans have executed that classic piece of critical camp, namely they have fallen about in agonies of idolatry to praise the poems which were published there in January and have pissed upon the novel from a great height, completely misunderstanding its purpose." Symons had published an enthusiastic piece in the Sunday *Times* about two of Warren's earlier novels, and now Rosenthal begged him to write "a major critical piece on Warren on the occasion of what could easily be his last novel. . . ." Symons did as Rosenthal asked—in part. The book as a whole was "a great deal better than any of Mr. Warren's recent novels, although much inferior to his best work." Moreover, he had never produced "anything fully worthy of his major talent."[5]

American reviewers tended to agree with Symons, if less vehemently. Though Peter Davison gave the book a warmly appreciative review in the *Atlantic Monthly,* the verdicts in the major opinionmakers were generally grim, finding "contrivance," and "portentousness," in a style "ruminative" and "murky." Warren wrote Rosenthal, "Let's lick our wounds," but he also told him that "except for the [*New York*] *Times*" it "had a very good reception, and some 70,000 copies are out. . . . Anyway, the novel made its little fortune before publication. The general misunderstanding, even by reviewers who are favorable, is a disturbing fact however. I thought I had done everything but red-crayon underlining."[6]

The novel's concerns have been clearly perceived: the problem of the deracinated individual seeking a secure set of values in a civilization in decline, the search for identity, and the acceptance of the past. Like the journey of Jack Burden, the far wanderings of Jediah Tewksbury bring him at last a clarification and a return, producing a far more satisfying resolution than that in *Meet Me in the Green Glen,* though this latest one too would suffer by comparison with the earlier ones. But Warren would now see it—together with *World Enough and Time* and *All the King's Men*—as his best fiction.[7]

The spring brought a radical change of pace and scene. With two other couples the Warrens "leased a 70-footer and, according to whim did the Greek islands, a glorious time, with a dash of adventure. . . ." It was a fire at sea, he told Allen Tate, "which brought on the discovery that the fire-extinguishers (certified by the Greek port authorities) were either dead or empty. But the captain and mate were ingenious fellows and got an electrical fire out. . . ." After another mishap in Turkey they spent a week happily on "Rhodes and Santorini (old Thera—'Atlantis'), where we had quite delightful times." Home would offer less exotic delights: "Vermont and the deep woods and our mountain, brook, and pool (25 laps the mile, great for a breakfast appetite)."[8]

It was a productive year. By the time they left for Vermont he had published eleven new poems. There in his coop above the stream he worked on seven more, which would appear before the end of the year. They would serve as the basis for his next volume. By November *Eyes, Etc.,* had come out to a favorable reception and Eleanor was at work on a novel. Rosanna was coming home after months of intensive work on Crete, painting and writing poems, some of them soon to be published. Gabe had taken a semester off, and soon his schooner would be ready for final outfitting. A month later the pace for Warren had increased. Congratulating Allen Tate on the appearance of his *Collected Poems: 1919–1976,* he apologized for his silence: "I haven't had time to breathe with all the preparations for the Christmas party and all sorts of extra work. I've been enslaved by my script writer, then director, and leading man, who are driving on at top speed—but who, at least, are God-damned intelligent and pleasant to be with." He was anticipating a trip to Nashville, where he hoped they would build a set on his property. But a series of difficulties canceled the project.[9]

There was much to occupy him in 1978 even without the movie work. "I have a new book of poems out in August," he wrote John

Stewart. "And in February 1979 a completely rewritten (and some-what cut) version of Brother to Dragons—which I have been work-ing at, off and on, for twenty years. Vastly better poem now, or I kid myself. I plan, with God's help, another book of poems in 1980—at least I've been writing right along and begin to have a thin sheaf." By late April—even with time out to present the National Medal for Lit-erature to Archibald MacLeish in New York and to give a reading in Cambridge—he had finished correcting proof for the new book of poems.[10]

One of the new poems appeared in the *Atlantic Monthly*. The four rhymed quatrains were entitled "Praise," and the first began, "I want to praise one I love, / Instructress in the heart's glory. . . ." The sec-ond took up the phrase again: "I want to praise one who sheds light / In darkness where the foot can find / No certainty. . . ." It was a good summer for the subject of the poem, who by September was approaching the end of her novel. Her husband could not say the same for his own. "I'd been carrying [it] around in my head for years, and morning after morning I'd go out to my workhouse and prop a pad on my knee and stare at a blank page for two hours or so. Then I'd see a hand sneaking a line or two of verse off in a corner. Finally I quit kidding myself and did nothing but poems all summer. . . . if you start a novel you've received a two-year sentence, even with good behavior. But a poem is short—you may live to get it finished."[11]

The ending of *A Place to Come To,* with its protagonist well on toward the end of his life, was probably symptomatic of some of War-ren's deepest feelings. Time's ravages had been in his thoughts all the year—upon Eleanor's vision, Tate's lungs, and Katherine Anne Porter's mind. In two letters, he wrote Tate, she was "tottering on the verge of madness. I guess the damage done by the strokes is irre-versible." Not long after their return to Fairfield he wrote Tate again.

Not a day passes that I don't think of you. . . . It's only natural, I suppose, that I should turn more and more to youthful recollec-tions, but so much of that is associated with you—and a few others like John and Ridley. I had never realized before now how much of a stay, in the fits of depression that led up to my foolish try at sui-cide when the fear of blindness got the better of me, not only in-dividual friendships were but the stay in poetry itself. It was the one thing, it seemed, that could take me out of my fear. Well, the fear had a firm base: an injured eye may bring blindness to the other. But I was afraid to get periodic investigations, and was sure, at the

time, the process had begun. Well, it finally had, and they removed
the injured eye, as you know. Only now, however, do I know into
what a neurotic state the thing had reduced me in the college years.
Well, a little late, thanks.[12]

Though now, at seventy-three, he was still working, still swimming
his kilometer or more before breakfast and walking the trails after the
day's work but feeling changes in his poetic inspiration. "About every
seven or eight years I get that feeling—not a decision, a change in
metabolism or something."[13]

As the year drew to an end he still refused to admit that he was finished as a novelist. "In the back of my mind, I nurse another novel,"
he wrote his old Rhodes classmate Andrew Corry, "but when I tried
to get started on it this summer, nothing but poems would come. So
I guess I'll have another book of short poems in 1980. Then, by God,
the novel. But one happy thing—I don't have to write it unless I want
to. The last one did so well on secondary rights that I can do what I
want." Besides the now familiar comparison of his late poetry with
that of Yeats, there was another comparison. Fellow poet John Hollander, remembering the "positively ludicrous reception" of *Flood,*
speculated that "maybe out of a kind of Hardyan disgust he turned
more to the poems. A return to the early sense of the priority of poetry." His readers were able to judge the results of the return before
the year was out.[14]

47

❖

A New Book of Verse and a New Brother to Dragons

> We have yearned in the heart for some identification
> With the glory of human effort. We have devised
> Evil in the heart, and pondered the nature of virtue.
> We have stumbled into the act of justice and caught,
> Only from the tail of the eye, the flicker
> Of joy, like a wing-flash in thicket.
> —*Brother to Dragons*[1]

Now and Then: Poems: 1976–1978 was published in an edition of five thousand copies in September, though notices had begun appearing as early as July. The first part, called "Nostalgic," consists of ten auto-biographical poems from childhood to maturity. The second, entitled "Speculative," also draws in some of its twenty-seven poems on incidents from the poet's life, but it conveys not only the attempt to understand those incidents but also his persistent concerns: the nature of time, the problem of truth, the meaning of life, and the inevitability of death. As in other books, Warren draws upon the Bible for epigraph: "Let the inhabitants of the rock sing . . . ISAIAH 42:11." But like the poems' occasional references to God, this is no undergirding theme. What is pervasive is the persistent transaction between past and present. In "Sister Water" the poet writes, ". . . 'Now—' / Comes the whisper. But is there a *now* or a *then?*" (p. 47). The questions, and sometimes the tentative answers, are couched in the long lines he favored, loose and conversational, never in metrical patterns and less than half in rigorous structural patterns: five of the twenty-seven in rhymed stanzas and nine in unrhymed couplets.[2]

The book begins with one of its three strongest poems, "American Portrait: Old Style." The principal subject is "K," unmistakably Kent Greenfield. In the first of the seven numbered stanzas the poet recalls their boyhood roaming and imagining beyond the marsh where they found the cracked skull. Then come the vignettes of K as hunter and Big League pitcher:

> and no batter
> Could do what booze finally did:
> Just blow him off the mound. . . . (p. 5)

Returning sixty years later, the poet finds K depleted by time but still showing something of his old prowess without knowing "what makes a man do what he does. . . ." (p. 6). The poet wanders out past the marsh and lies briefly in the six-foot trench they took to be the last sign of one who did not complete the family journey west, looking at the sky and wondering what it would be like to be dead. Then he rouses:

> But why should I lie here longer?
> I am not dead yet, though in years,
> And the world's way is yet long to go,
> And I love the world even in my anger,
> And love is a hard thing to outgrow. (p. 7)[3]

One of the other strongest poems also owes its genesis to Kent. In "Red-Tail Hawk and Pyre of Youth" the boy, with an extraordinary .30-30 shot, knocks the godlike bird out of the sky. "I brought him down with what was a record shot for me," Warren said. "I was then a practicing taxidermist, among other things, and I stuffed the hawk and carried him with me for many years—I used to keep him over my bookshelf." The boy in the poem runs home, the bloody body in his arms, to preserve it in an unintentional parody of the kingly creature it had been. Years later he burns the hawk. Warren confessed, "I lied a little bit there; I didn't burn the hawk, I just threw him away." And he made another confession: "I didn't shoot the hawk. It was Kent. . . ."[4]

Later in the poem he drew on memory again. The years pass,

> And time came
> When my mother was dead, father bankrupt, and whiskey
> Hot in my throat. . . . (p. 19)

Lying on his bed on his last visit home he thinks of the bird's yellow eye staring in vengeance, and wonders "Could Nature forgive, like God?" (p. 20). Waking, he relives the rifle shot and completes the span from *then* to *now;* a suppliant like the Ancient Mariner, he prays that in his last hospital moments he will see again the first moment of the hawk's death plunge

> To bring me the truth in blood-marriage of earth and air—
> And all will be as it was
> In that paradox of unjoyful joyousness,
> Till the dazzling moment when I, a last time, must flinch
> From the regally feathered gasoline flare
> Of youth's poor, angry, slapdash, and ignorant pyre.[5]

A complex poem, it consists—as Warren and Brooks had tried to explain about poems generically in *Understanding Poetry*—not just of statement and idea nor image and symbol, but in the totality of its elements, so that it concerns not just the shooting and preserving of the hawk but also the relationships between man and nature, between past and present, distilling from the transient experience of the man something of the permanence of art, and recalling the paradox of the artist who slays to immortalize, as John James Audubon had done.[6]

The other poems in "Nostalgic" also convey the immediacy of deeply felt experience. Again there is a progression from the back country of the South to the country of the psyche. The last poem in "Nostalgic" links past, present, and future. "Youth Stares at Minoan Sunset" is a word picture of Gabriel Warren on Crete. The first four stanzas place the small human figure against mountain, meadow, and flaming sunset. The boy does not hear his parents' call, but with a Wordsworthian impulse, "He spreads his arms to the sky as though he loves it—and us. / He is so young" (p. 26).

The poet's son is also there in "Speculative." In "Waking to Tap of Hammer" the poet moves from the auditory to the visual. Hearing his son at work on his schooner, he shifts into his son's dreams and then into his own, "In which I, like a spirit, hung in the squall-heart. . . ." Disembodied, he sees his son intently staring through storm spray and rain and then focuses on the boy's face: "I dreamed it was smiling at me" (p. 51). As this section moves toward its close, this image of the disembodied father, glimpsing his smiling son steering in the storm, seems to suggest the future, when the father will no longer be there.

There are no other love poems here after those to Gabriel. The closest comes in "The Mission," with the necessity of understanding "the possibility of joy in the world's tangled and hieroglyphic beauty" (p. 42). "Heat Lightning" might be a description of another coupling in *A Place to Come To*. Metaphorically, heat lightning is to storm lightning as mere copulation is to love's embrace. The encounter is pictured in Warren's later explicit manner: "the business / Banked on a pillow," "the small cry of protest," heels beating on buttocks "in deeper demand." Then, orgasm. "What all exploitation of orifices and bruised flesh but / The striving for one death in two?" Afterward he sees the "glutted, slack look on the face," with "the faintest blood-smear at the mouth's left corner," and later, on his shoulder, two "Symmetrical half-moons of blue marks tattooed. . . ." Finally there is "The newspaper obit, years later, I stumbled on" (pp. 59–60). This poem might be a sequel to "Answer to Prayer" and another transmuted memory of Cinina Brescia.

Here there are no poems such as "Birth of Love." It is as if the presence of time and death had left no room for Eros. This is not surprising. Though Anne Stanton and Jack Burden finally marry, more often in Warren's fiction—*At Heaven's Gate, World Enough and Time*, and *Meet Me in the Green Glen*—love leads to death. And it was death as much as love that he thought of now when he thought of Allen Tate and Katherine Anne Porter. The dark spectre is there in "Departure" as the mistral blows, and the luggage in the hotel corridor knows that "it is going somewhere soon. That is a truth we must all face" (p. 72). In asking the eternal questions Warren uses the vocabulary of a believer, but it is usually undercut, as in "Sister Water." After hearing a garbage truck grinding its contents,

> . . . "God—"
> You think, with a stab of joy, "He loves us all. He will not
> Let all distinctions perish." You cannot pray. But
> You can wash your face in cold water. (p. 48)

That familiar figure, the lone questioner looking up into the starlight, reappears in "Unless," trying to "breathe into the rhythm of stars" (p. 36). But usually, as in "Identity and Argument for Prayer," there is no sound from the "black Spacelessness / Beyond the last stars" (p. 66). Something comes, however, in dreams. "Yes, message on message, like wind or water, in light or in dark, / The whole world peers at us. But the code book, somehow, is lost" (p. 44). This

poem, "Code Book Lost," says it all. There is no Rosetta stone to un-
lock the inscriptions.

The last of the three strongest poems, "Heart of Autumn," ends the
book with the poet watching geese flying south. In majestic lines he
pictures their pathless journey, thinking, "I have known time and distance, but not why I am here" (p. 74). Then, his face again lifted sky-
ward, he feels in his outstretched arms a "process of transformation."

> And my heart is impacted with a fierce impulse
> To unwordable utterance—
> Toward sunset, at a great height. (p. 75)

Like no other poem so much as Yeats's "The Wild Swans at Coole,"
this one draws on the human and nonhuman orders of nature to suggest their intermingling and finally a kind of transcendence in departure.

Now and Then displays continuing technical mastery but no change
in the essential nature of this poet-as-yearner. In some ways changing
constantly, he remains yet the boy he was: loving the world's beauty
while conscious of all the griefs and frustrations in the human lot,
caught in the existential dilemma of seeking transcendence and
knowledge of the *other* and himself, comforted somewhat by the
awareness of love and the possibility of joy, but knowing that for him
the ultimate knowledge, despite dream and intimation, will never be
found in life.

There were fewer reviews of this book of verse than of any since
Incarnations ten years before, only eleven in the year of publication
and only two of these in prominent places. There would be only
eight more reviews in 1979, chiefly in university-based magazines,
but they were favorable. Then, on April 17, in a front-page story, *The
New York Times* reported that "Robert Penn Warren won his third
Pulitzer Prize for his new volume, *Now and Then*."[7]

But now, as the fall of 1978 diminished into winter, the emotional
climate was darkened too. Warren told Allen Tate, "I am not doing
any traveling now, because I can survive without the money, and
Eleanor can't be left alone. The house is isolated and lately there have
been some very bad things in the neighborhood." They made their
preparations for the annual December party and continued with their
nightly readings. Warren went to his study every day, and that fall he
published five new poems, which would appear in subsequent collections. But even so, his feelings about his output were mixed. But he

did not have to wait for new poems to satisfy his impulse always to be at work. There was another poem, an ongoing project that stretched back twenty years, which would carry him into the new year.[8]

It was well that he had such a project in these early months of 1979. Six years earlier, Allen Tate's doctors had predicted his imminent death, but he had carried on, cared for by his wife Helen, and hospitalized periodically. Since 1976, when they had moved from Sewanee, he had been virtually bedridden, receiving guests in his small bedroom, conversing brilliantly when he had the strength, breathing oxygen through the tubes in his nostrils. Walter Sullivan—devoted friend for thirty-five years, well acquainted with his virtues and his faults—would visit often. Tate would talk with acerbity about the visitor just departed, "and you knew that when you left, he would talk about you." Sullivan knew the relationship between Warren and Tate. "He talked about Red Warren, saying that Red's work had suffered because of its popular success, but he was clearly envious of the money Red had made. He kept up with the sales of Red's books and the fees he got for ancillary rights. It seemed unfair to Allen and to Helen that his own writing did not make as much, particularly since, as he put it, Red was already rich and did not need more money. And he complained that Red's letters to him were full of family news and not about literature." Sullivan wrote, "He stayed in his small room, his body growing more frail, his faculties diminishing." On February 9 he died. He was buried with the rites of the Catholic church.[9]

The Warrens stayed with Lon and Fanny Cheney. After the burial they had dinner there with the Bandys and the Sullivans. Then they went into the library, where Allen had often read his work. They talked about friends at the funeral, friends such as Andrew Lytle, there despite his long estrangement from Tate. They relished Andrew's celebrated tale-telling. (Allen had once told Sullivan that "Red had no ear for the spoken language, that he ran his words together and that the rhythms of his sentences were wrong.") They fell silent until Fanny took a book of Warren's from the shelf and asked him to read some of his poetry. As Walter listened, his voice brought back images from the past. When he stopped, they all rose and said their good nights. Later that month Warren told Charlie Foster, "friends become a little more important as they thin out." The day after the funeral they were "back in Washington, at the side of the bed from which K.A. Porter will never rise. . . ."[10]

In memory Warren made the Nashville trip again in early spring. John Egerton came to Fairfield and asked him to take a major part in a large-format, illustrated popular history of Nashville, to be timed for the celebration of the city's bicentennial. He declined but agreed to do a reminiscent essay. Egerton returned on April 1, and for three days he recorded Warren's rambling memories. Egerton rewrote a transcription, and after Warren's changes it would be the concluding portion of the book. He did not need the vintage photographs to visualize the "little Nashville of fifty years ago . . . my first big city [for] I carry the old Nashville in my head, grateful for the friends it gave me and for so much else." Egerton and his colleagues were delighted with the piece, and Warren was pleased with his nine-thousand-dollar payment.

For more than a year now he had been moving toward completing a long-term project: a new version of *Brother to Dragons.* He had never been satisfied with the version of 1953. "In style I had wandered into a trap—too often caught in the trap of blank verse—and that had meant some padding. And I published it without enough of the cooling off process—the last hard look." But it remained very much with him. "I found more and more [what] I wanted to do with it—change pace, change much versification, add and subtract material . . . remove a certain amount of abstraction, etc." The process was intensified by work on the various dramatic versions and a trip in which he followed Adrian Hall's Trinity Theatre company to Philadelphia before the last production in Boston. Working on the script with others, hearing the actors speak their lines, listening for timing and pacing, he did so much reshaping that he began to think of it as a new work.[11]

When Random House published it in September of 1979, the difference from the 1953 version depended on the reader's angle of vision. To some, the changes were slight. To the author, the new manuscript constituted "some 500% improvement." In October, with the book in its shiny black jacket in hand, he told Lewis Simpson, "I nearly broke my back on BTD over the years, sometimes patchily, sometimes six or eight months at a time. Well, I can't do any better. So it's curtains." The poem was now shorter by one-fifth, down to a little more than four thousand lines. It was also divided into seven numbered sections, another reflection of the dramatizations.[12]

He had brought the poem more into line with the historical record, though there were still many discrepancies, he said, because he was writing a poem, not a history. There were striking changes in characterization: R.P.W. is much less the attacking interrogator and more the collaborating inquirer, and so Jefferson's anguish is more protracted as he looks back on his early idealism, comes to terms with man's fallen nature—as exemplified in his nephews' crime—and accepts the consequent purgation. Meriwether Lewis appears earlier and so to greater effect later, when Jefferson sees his own complicity in this surrogate son's tragic suicide, a part of the process of acknowledgment of man's burden of original sin and the awareness of human culpability rather than perfectibility.[13]

And there was more differentiation than that between the two versions in both content and form. For one of the poem's closest students, both the author of *Brother to Dragons* and the character R.P.W. within it stand "in a filial relation" not only to Robert Franklin Warren but also to Thomas Jefferson. Moreover, in this tale full of Dantean echoes, "R.P.W., in his involvement with the story of Jefferson, is telling the story of his own quest as a twentieth-century American poet for a redeeming version of the meaning of history." And one marked difference between the two versions lay in the verse itself. The lines are often shorter, the philosophizing decreased, and the tendency toward the grandiloquent much reduced. He had worked his way out of the blank-verse trap. And contributing to this process, the work on the dramatic versions of the poem had leavened the idioms and passages of early nineteenth-century language with the sounds and rhythms of living speech.[14]

Where the first version had been greeted by more than a half-dozen major reviews, the second drew only one on publication. In those that appeared in the succeeding months, a few would regret the reduction of commentary and sensuous nature descriptions, but more would applaud the reduced didacticism and cynicism. Warren did not waver in his judgment. When asked about people who thought the 1953 version was preferable, he responded, "I would say they are dead wrong." This second version of *Brother to Dragons* would not be reprinted, but he had no time to speculate about its possible permanence. He had done his best to reshape it, to make it sparer and stronger, and like the poems he had been writing over the last few years, it showed his skills now sharper and his creativity unimpaired. If he was a brave ancient, he was also a potent one, with a long essay for *The New Yorker* in the research phase and another book of poems in the final shaping process. And as for a verse epic, he told Lewis Simpson, "I'm vaguely moving—hope to be moving—toward another longish poem. . . ."[15]

48

❖

The Seventy-fifth

Years later, past dreams, I have lain
In darkness and heard the depth of that unending song,
And hand laid to heart, have once again thought: *This is me.*
And thought: *Who am I?* And hand on heart, wondered
What would it be like to be, in the end, part of all.
                                                   — *"Speleology"*[1]

Not long before the publication of the revised *Brother to Dragons,* an
Atlanta reporter had come to West Wardsboro to do an article about
Warren. It would show the rhythm of his life at age seventy-four: the
solitary early breakfast, the workout with the barbells, the long swim
in his creative trance, the work in his coop above Bald Mountain
Brook. "Sitting in his beach chair," Steve Oney wrote, "his thinning,
fading red hair sweat-plastered across his skull and his face flushed
with exertion, he looks like an aged fighting cock." After his five-
hour stint, there is one sherry on the rocks and then lunch prepared
by Eleanor, who has memorized the location of all her utensils and
edibles. "She is a strikingly handsome, green-eyed Connecticut Yankee with high, bold cheekbones and a thick mane of straw blond
hair." As always, their conversation ranges over the children's lives,
politics, and books, but never their own, though her new novel, *Gloria Mundi,* has just come out. After lunch he retires for a nap. Later he
may read and then putter about the place. Or, cane in hand, he may
go for a long uphill hike that takes him for miles to where he can look
out over the glacial lake and rugged mountains.[2]

Oney caught the family dynamics. As the day wanes they move with their guests to the outside porch. A Campari and orange juice in hand, he sits in the fading light, resembling "a statue carved long ago from a clean hunk of rosy sandstone." The dinner-table conversation suggests a marriage "of sweet collaboration wed to a propensity for ceaseless oratorical battle. They disagree on politics, people, literature, psychology and economics. She is the liberal Eastern Brahmin; he is the clodhopper scholar with dung on his boots and poetry in his heart." When Warren blames a weakening of the American fiber on Roosevelt and the New Deal, Eleanor furiously counterattacks. Rosanna intervenes, her hand on her father's shoulder. "You two remind me of those Romanesque carvings," she says, with "a little stone soul being torn apart by a devil and an angel."[3]

Although he writes Tom Rosenthal that he is impatient with the novel that "doesn't seem to come to a head and bust," he is also glad to give priority to poetry because the thought nags him that he may not have enough time left to finish another novel. By the end of the visit, Warren is willing to tackle some of the eternal questions. His speech still comes fast, ideas tumbling over one another in his low-pitched growl. "I think a man just dies," he says. "No heaven. No hell. . . . I'm a naturalist. I don't believe in God. But I want to find meaning in life. I refuse to believe it's merely a dreary sequence of events. So I write stories and poetry. My work is my testimony." He seems almost surprised at some of the things he says. "I take Christianity as a myth. . . . But what I do think is relevant, and what I want to try to emulate now, is the example of Jesus. But any moral human being wants that. I want to give myself in sacrifice of some sort. To participate in the common body of human life. . . . My poetry lets me do that, but that sounds so trite to say." He picks up the manuscript of his new book of poetry and reads from it: "This is an autobiography which represents a fusion of fiction and fact from varying degrees of perspective. As a question and answer, fiction may often be more deeply significant than fact. Indeed, it may be said that our lives are our supreme fiction."[4]

In the late summer mornings he was polishing the book and writing new poems and in the afternoons working on his article for *The New Yorker.* "Jefferson Davis was born in my home county," he wrote John Stewart, "and this past year his citizenship has finally been restored to him. . . . The joke is that Jefferson Davis wouldn't have taken the god-damned citizenship." In his childhood Warren had seen a monument to Davis's memory being built in Guthrie under the sponsorship of Confederate veterans who wanted it higher than the Washington Monument. His own people didn't care much for him, however, and so, Warren remembered, "I grew up in a very mixed state of mind about Jefferson Davis." He started his essay, relying on his memory and the few books there, leaving his reference-checking for later.[5]

In the early pages he used some of the material in his Nashville reminiscence—Grandpa Penn and the war, the Planter's Protective Association, and the events behind *Night Rider.* Then he made the transition to Jefferson Davis, his Todd County birth, and his subsequent career. Comparing and contrasting him with that other Kentuckian, Abraham Lincoln, he found qualities to admire in the "Sphinx of the Confederacy": his "naked energy . . . iron will, self-denial, self-discipline, devotion to principle [and] his conception of honor" (pp. 52–53). And there was sympathy too for "the tall, hollow-cheeked man whose face twitched with neuralgia and whose left eye was bleared in blindness. . . ." (p. 31). Warren followed his ignominious fate in the last days of the war and the persistent gratuitous cruelties Davis suffered from Appomattox until the case against him was finally dropped. Then he traced the long declining years until his death in 1889.[6]

As it happened, the restoration of Davis's citizenship was celebrated along with the Guthrie centennial from May 31 to June 3 in a series of earnest observances. In late August Warren traveled there and stood with his brother and Kent Greenfield among the graves. Perhaps he remembered what he had told Steve Oney about the South: "I love it. My house in the North is really just a big hotel to me. A place I stay. The South will always be my home."[7]

The New Yorker essay came out on February 25, 1980, with the book version following from the University of Kentucky Press. There was a new Random House book out too, *Robert Penn Warren Talking: Interviews 1950–1978,* edited by Floyd C. Watkins and John T. Hiers. It was a part of the gathering momentum for the celebration of his seventy-fifth birthday.[8]

They eased into it with a combination of diversion and ceremony. With friends they sailed from the Gulf up Florida waterways to the Atlantic. In mid-April they flew to Tempe for an Arizona State degree and then to Tucson for a birthday party. He told Tom Rosenthal, "We went to a ranch we know near the Mexican border and spent some days riding in the mountains or on the desert. It is the season of bloom. Quite magnificent." And there was something else besides these pleasures. It was a sense of the West that fed into a "longish poem." He had already done research on an old hero of his, Chief Joseph of the Nez Perce. Here his imagination could superimpose upon these southwestern scenes the Montana landscape where Joseph led his people in their long flight from federal troops. Soon he was more than halfway through the poem.[9]

The tempo of public and private events increased as the spring came on. He told Tom Rosenthal, "Vanity prompts me to say that I get another birthday present on June 9: the Presidential Medal, along with Tennessee Williams, Eudora Welty, and Admiral Rickover . . . the hero of the nuclear submarine against all the older generation. So I half feel that I have been to Annapolis after all. Carter presents the medals at the White House."[10]

Another celebration was taking place in their garden. The engraved card read, "Mr. and Mrs. Hannibal Flores-Jenkins announce the marriage of their daughter, Ana Maria, to Mr. Gabriel Penn Warren, Saturday, the twenty-fourth of May, nineteen hundred and eighty." Dr. Flores-Jenkins and his wife had left Cuba when Fidel Castro came to power, and so Ana had been educated in the United States. Warren had told Charlie Foster, "The girl is a delight to us. She's handsome, charming, extremely intelligent, tough-minded (she'd have to be to live with Gabriel), a painter by trade. Another artist in the family." As Warren heard the marriage ritual, he must have wondered how he would feel when his daughter took this step, further along in her own life, further from the nurturing, protective ambience they had tried to build.[11]

Her career was taking off. She was now publishing in the *Atlantic Monthly,* the *Yale Review,* and the revived *Southern Review.* In May, after winning a prize in a contest for young poets sponsored by *The Nation* and the Poetry Center of the YM-YWHA in New York, she gave a reading there to a full house. She would spend the summer at Yaddo, and before long she would give up painting for poetry. It would have to be an extraordinary suitor who could win her parents' wholehearted approval.

With the August appearance of *Being Here: Poetry 1977–1980* came two articles about him in national magazines. The *U.S. News &*

World Report piece was concerned more with his view of contemporary problems than with his poetry. Dehumanizing technology, he
said, was threatening democracy and human personality itself. If this
was Agrarianism updated, it was also a view now shared by many
other Americans. One week later, a three-page article in *Newsweek*
gave a remarkably compact account of the long career followed with
reflections on its current status: "The New York publishing and literary world, which is still the most important audience for contemporary poets, has remained skeptical—of Warren's Southernness, of his
breadth, which makes him suspect as a 'pure' poet, of his refusal to
join the glittery cocktail circuit," with the result that, "more often
than not, New York has simply dismissed Warren as dated." Paradox-
ically, however, "his themes, such as man's inability to know himself,
would pass the most stringent existential review," and "no other
writer today even approaches Warren's imaginative range and historic
depth." With *Being Here,* the essayist wrote, "Warren has entered his
autumnal phase, the summing up that often crowns a major career,"
but here "at an age when most poets have passed their peak, Warren's
poetry keeps getting better and better." The artist, heavy with honors and awards, "is America's dean of letters and, in all but name, poet
laureate."[12]

Longer than *Or Else* and *Now and Then,* with which it would form
a kind of trilogy, *Being Here: Poetry 1977–1980* had the appearance of
a summation, and he had labored over it as if it was one. He had also
done an uncharacteristic thing. Afraid that the reader might feel "that
a few poems are, in both feeling and style, off the main impulse,
[even] irrelevances," he supplied a commentary explaining that "the
thematic order—or better, structure—is played against, or with, a
shadowy narrative, a shadowy autobiography, if you will. But this is
an autobiography which represents a fusion of fact and fiction [and]
fiction may often be more deeply significant than fact" (pp. 107–8).

As for the book's title, from graduate school he surely remembered
the Venerable Bede, the great eighth-century Anglo-Saxon Latinist,
who wrote that man's life was like the flight of a sparrow through the
hall where the king sat at meat with his nobles. For the moment the
bird is "sheltered from the storm, but after this short while of calm he
flies out again into the cold and is seen no more. Thus the life of man
is visible for a moment, but we know not what comes before it or follows after it." Warren accepted that view. Here he was chronicling
what it had been like to be a man alive—here and now, looking back

in the book's five segments from childhood to years beyond the allot-
ted biblical span—but craving some insight or affirmation, some answer to the questions that had plagued him about the nature of time
and truth, some clue to identity and purpose, what it *meant* to be
here. Dreams, intuition, reflection, and Wordsworthian impulses
from the natural world are the means by which he tries to devise answers to his existential questions.

The forty-eight poems comprising the five sections are placed between a prologue and an epilogue. In "October Picnic Long Ago,"
the poet describes a Sunday in his seventh year, the father bravely
confident, the mother joyously happy in the present, unaware as the
sly shadows

> *Leashed the Future up, like a hound with a slavering fang.*
> *But sleepy, I didn't know what a Future was, as she sang.* (p. 4)

In the last poem, "Passers-by on Snowy Night," set in woodland
darkness, the poet passes a stranger,

> *And each takes the owl's benediction,*
> *And each goes the way he will go.* (p. 105)

Only these poems and two others employ rhyme schemes, and
some of the rhymes here create awkward lines. In most of the poems,
though, his predominant mode is the free verse that he had come to
prefer, now an exceedingly flexible instrument in his hand. He most
often writes in quatrains or stanzas of varying length, sometimes more
than twenty in a poem. His long lines in free verse are not as near
prose as Whitman's, but he often uses the colloquial and conversational. He is equally at home with shorter poems and shorter lines,
but there is little of the experimentation of *You, Emperors, and Others*
and *Or Else.* Some of his effects, however, are so subtle as to be apparent only on close reading.[13]

The imagery is drawn from the animal and vegetable world of
birds, bear and deer, flowers and trees. It ranges from caves to mountains and rivers to oceans, pairing opposites and employing black
upon white for strongest effect, but more persistent than any other is
the imagery of the heavens. One of his most powerful recurring images is still that of the solitary man in the night, as when, in "Snowshoeing Back to Camp in Gloaming," he writes:

So starward I stared
To the unnamed voice where Space and God
Flinch to come. . . . (p. 28)

The imagery is not simply sprinkled through the poems or consistent only within poems. In "Aspen Leaf in Windless World" he asks what image "Will loom at the end of your own life's long sorites?" (p. 87).[14]

He underlined his main thematic concern with not one but three epigraphs, each reflecting on the nature of time. The second one is from a book he had read several times, the *Confessions* of Saint Augustine. If a reader expected conventional religious conviction or even some clear insight into the nature of the divine, he would have been disappointed. The book's dedication indicates instead the familiar reliance on love and wisdom: "To Gabriel Thomas Penn (1836–1920)."[15]

Organized so as to move forward in time while returning to the nucleus of characters and topics, this book constitutes his best collection. There are clusters of poems, not grouped together but spaced throughout the book and linked by subject and type. There is a picture of Grandpa Penn entitled "When Life Begins" (p. 9) and another with similar portraiture, "Safe in Shade" (p. 91), which prompts the poet to wonder where he will find *his* cedar tree when he too approaches his end. All the family is there in memory in "The Moonlight's Dream," as the boy hears their sleep sounds and then walks out as the man will do, under starlight or moonlight, to gaze and wonder. Years later he cries,

Not dead! Though long years now are, and the creek bulldozed dry,
And their sorrow and joy, their passion and pain and endeavor,
Have with them gone, with whatever reality
They were, or are, by sunlight or moonlight—whatever. (p. 18)

Other poems with family models also bridge generations—the poet's son in the snow in "Sila" (p. 37), where his dog has fatally attacked a doe, or in Greek mountains in "Night Walking" (p. 103), unaware that his father, following him, sees him lift his arms to the moonlit sky.[16]

There are poems of incident—one is tempted to call them Cinina flashbacks—in which brooding, threatful imagery supplies meaning: a couple stopping in the mountains for a panorama, the wife taking her headache back to the car while her husband stands gazing, unaware of the mountain lion crouching above him. Here, in "Part of What Might Have Been a Short Story, Almost Forgotten," there is more such imagery before the couple speeds away to whatever other, metaphysical beast awaits:

> Toward what foetal, fatal truth
> Our hearts had witlessly concealed
> In mere charade, hysterical
>
> Or grave, of love. (p. 53)

If this is shadowy autobiography, there may be more in "What Is the Voice That Speaks?" where the man curtly dismisses his lover, only to weep in the night's erotic memory when "I thought of a head thrown back, and the moan" (p. 71).

Warren used the personal past at the beginning and end of the book. In Section I "The Only Poem" recalls a visit with his mother to a neighbor "to see the new daughter / My friends stashed with Grandma while they went East for careers" (p. 19). The poem's focus is Ruth Penn's joy at holding the baby, her eldest son now grown and soon returning to college as time moves inexorably toward her death. The poem that opens Section V, "Eagle Descending," is dedicated "To a Dead Friend." With imagery like that in his hawk poems Warren follows the bird soaring in twilight, riding "the Wind to sing with joy of truth fulfilled" (p. 77). The friend was, of course, Allen Tate.[17]

The subject of death recurs—death as the human lot, the death of those close to the poet, and finally his own. What sustains the poet? Presumably the faithful exercise of his calling so that he too may, like the eagle, soar at the end with the joy of truth fulfilled. In "Night Walking," the next-to-last poem, there is the evocation of love as he thinks of the son who will succeed him. And finally, in the concluding "Passers-by on Snowy Night," he gives his benediction to the unknown other, with a tacit acknowledgment of kinship and common fate, like that of the Venerable Bede's bird, which "flies out again into the cold and is seen no more."

The few major reviews were generally favorable. Along with familiar complaints about repetition and philosophizing was praise for his energy, descriptive powers, and courage in attempting the sublime along with the mystical. And from one of the first of the academic quarterlies to speak came the verdict, "Warren has never written better than he does here in this brilliant and unified volume—brilliant in conception, brilliant in construction, brilliant in artistry." There were comparisons to Hardy, one of them in a long essay in England's prestigious *Times Literary Supplement.* Later judgments of *Being Here* have tended to note individual poems—"October Picnic Long Ago" and "Boyhood in Tobacco Country." If the book is thematically repetitive, it nonetheless shows him mastering the poetics that suited him best in this phase of his work, displaying the sure use of the life experience that was his prime stock-in-trade.[18]

The shoulder pain had worsened in the summer, and when he went for treatment, there was another problem as well. Even before he entered Bridgeport Hospital on October 1 he had presented symptoms frequently presented by men his age. There cystoscopy revealed significant obstruction of the neck of the bladder caused by an enlarged prostate. It was benign prostatic hypertrophy, and the treatment was transurethral resection of the prostate and bilateral vasectomies. (The pathology report noted "evidence of well-differentiated adenocarcinoma of the prostate, involving 4 out of 45 fragments." The notes continued, "The patient was informed of this. At patient's age, 75, it was decided not to treat this further. Bone scans and metastatic series were negative. He will be carefully followed in the office.") He made an uncomplicated recovery while receiving physiotherapy for the shoulder and back pain. On October 18 he dictated a letter to John Stewart. "I am now home, but must spend most of my time in bed, except for a daily trip to a clinic. This sounds much grimmer than it is. It is not serious, just a damn nuisance."[19]

He had been taking an occasional sleeping pill, and now he may have occasionally found one welcome, and not just for his recovery from surgery. Almost exactly a year before, after attending a celebration for Archibald MacLeish in Washington, they had stopped in Maryland to see Rosanna and visit Katherine Anne Porter. They found her weaker, "but mostly bright and clear and much herself. It was very touching to see the meeting, after a long interval in which so much has happened, of KAP and her God-daughter." Warren was deeply moved to see the affection between the young woman, her life before her, and the old woman, her long life approaching its end. He saw her again, but "the last two times were terrible. No recogni-

tion . . . and a constant crying out, 'I want to die, why can't I die?'
Over and over. Too awful." On September 18, 1980, she died, aged
ninety. He could not attend the memorial service, but he agreed to
write the tribute to be given at the American Academy—a tribute to
the artist's "great fictional achievement" and the woman's "unvan-
quishable zest for life."[20]

He was able to hear his own tributes at the Robert Penn Warren 75th
Birthday Symposium at the University of Kentucky. At the opening
ceremonies in Lexington on October 29, Governor and Mrs. John
Young Brown, Jr., were among their hosts. The old friends came
from different parts of his life—Andrew Lytle, Cleanth Brooks, and
Robert Heilman; Vann Woodward, R.W.B. Lewis, and Peter Davison. When it came Warren's turn after the evening's accolades, he
said, "It's very easy in the rapture of assuaged vanity, as this occasion
is for me, to feel that somehow you're worthy of it, in some small way
at least. But I'm enough of a scholar, or at least a reader of literature
and literary history, to know that fashions change." The thing to remember, he said, reciting and then paraphrasing a poem by Yeats, was
that "the joy is in the doing, and not the end of the doing." Although
he looked drawn at departure time, it had been a welcome change
and rather "a jolly time, especially when Eleanor was officially made
a 'Kentucky Colonel' with scroll to prove same."[21]

In the governor's plane they were flown to Nashville for a glittering reception commemorating the fiftieth anniversary of *I'll Take My
Stand*. Warren participated in a panel, chaired by Cleanth Brooks, in
which, with Andrew Lytle and Lyle Lanier, these old Agrarians contemplated their efforts years before against encroaching technology. It
was recorded with television.

They spent Thanksgiving with Eleanor's sister, Eunice Jessup, her
late husband, Jack, very much a missed presence now during the holidays. Then in December, already depressed by the fact that, with the
shoulder injury and the operation, he had done only one poem, he
came down with the flu. But Eleanor sent out invitations anyway.
"We're having a very mini version of Xmas party—all we can handle
after Red's troubled season." The party would not be black tie, with
"a lot of old timers not invited to this little one." But she was not one
to be intimidated by trouble, and with her serving as the guardian of
order and giver of orders, neither was he.[22]

49

❖

Travel and Transition:
At Home and Afar

. . . I want to be real. Dear God,
To Whom, in my triviality,
I have given only trivial thought,
Will I find it worthwhile to pray that You let

The crow, at least once more, call?

—*"Dawn"*[1]

The new year began inauspiciously. It was a "frightful winter," Warren wrote Tom Rosenthal, with "the whole continent under ice."
Eleanor couldn't enjoy the cross-country skiing because of a dog bite
in the leg, and he was having five afternoons of physiotherapy a week
for his shoulder. Then gradually he began to "gather my normal
mean energy." He had written a good many poems before his hospitalization. Twenty-four were published in 1980, and twelve of them
went into the new manuscript, which comprised poems written during 1979 and 1980. By mid-January he had turned it in to Albert Erskine, still his intimate friend as well as editor, whom he consulted
more and more by phone—to New York or neighboring Westport—
rather than by letters. "I felt that *Being Here* was winding up something," he told Rosenthal. "There's a different feel to this one.
Things in common, yes, inevitably, but a real difference in tone, and
more." Publication was planned for October.[2]

In the chill spring he must have thought about Eliot's calling April
"the cruellest month." Caroline Gordon died on the eleventh, and
when Warren wrote Bid Brown, his somber recollections went back

to the infancy of Nancy Tate, left in the care of Caroline's mother so that she and Tate could pursue their careers in New York unhampered by a child. Both the mother and the marriage fared ill. "She was bad news and the news got worse and Allen got in the habit of browsing around in constantly fresh pastures.

"Well, Caroline became generally unendurable, particularly after she undertook to manage the Vatican too and use the blood of Christ for her private pleasure and domain. I am not being sacrilegious—I am describing a human fact.

"For some reason Allen . . . took up marrying as a sort of hobby and the marriages got worse and worse and worse, and worse luck, including the death of a child, kept coming along. It was all too awful. He was an extraordinary fellow of extraordinary gifts—but no luck.

"As for Caroline, a time after Minneapolis and before she went to [Mexico] for good, I happened to see her in NYC on a crowded bus. The next I knew somebody touched an arm of mine. She asked me to get off and go with her to a bar in the neighborhood. (I hadn't seen her for years.) I went. She said she just wanted to say one thing. And said it.

"Would I try to forget the things she had done. She said that she was 'bitterly sorry.' Then she left. I stayed and finished my drink. It was all pretty pitiable. She was in a condition."

At Warren's age increasing awareness of death was natural. After Allen Tate and Katherine Anne Porter, this was one more for the meditations of a man recently informed that there was cancer in his prostate.[3]

But there were reasons too for feeling positive: the Modern Language Association of America's Hubbell Memorial Award, a Book-of-the-Month Club adoption of the Jefferson Davis book, and the club's thirty-fifth anniversary deluxe edition of *All the King's Men.* After writing the introduction, he told Rosenthal, "All I try to write is poems." That was his occupation until the snow gradually melted and the early blossoms began to appear. His celebrated novel was the occasion of the next interruption. It had been made into *Willie Stark,* an opera in three acts commissioned by the Houston Grand Opera and Washington's Kennedy Center and composed by Carlisle Floyd. They went to Houston for the world premiere on April 24. He would have preferred other diversions. "I am tone deaf and don't know an oboe from a flute, and, to be honest, care less. I do go to a lot of operas, just because of Eleanor. I like to see her happy. But I usually scribble on the back of the program." As it turned out, "Eleanor wasn't mad about the music." They went to Washington anyway on May 9 for the beginning of the three-week run. During intermission a tall man made his way to their box to chat cordially. Warren didn't get his name. "He said he was Vice-President," he told Eleanor, "but he didn't say Vice President of what."[4]

Ten days later came a totally unexpected reason for rejoicing. "On the 15th of May, as I sat at the Bicentennial luncheon of the American Academy of the Arts and Sciences, up in Cambridge, I was called to the telephone. Mr. MacArthur managed to communicate to my uncomprehending ears that I had one of their so-called 'Prize Fellowships.' Then I really fainted. It amounts to $300,000 in irrevocable gift—but in installments." The "genius award" changed his life. "Before winning it, I was supplementing my resources by doing readings, writing reviews, that sort of thing. Basically, I've stopped writing anything I don't want to write. Poetry is where my heart is."[5]

Feeling euphoric, he shared his plans with Tom Rosenthal. A trip to Montana would help him complete the Chief Joseph poem after more than a year's work on it. And he would have the time and the means for pure pleasure. "We are talking about going to North Africa in the fall to do two weeks on camel-back among the Berbers." Before returning they would accept an invitation to visit Israel. "There must be something psychic about this, since in my reading to Eleanor, we spent the fall and winter on two readings of the Old Testament, and commentaries." It would be a fruition of his old passion for Melville. "I am going to take the trip Clarel did. . . ." And it would be more than a scholar's holiday, for they would take Gabriel and Ana with them.[6]

His mind was full of his new poem and its hero. "Since my first long stay in Montana in 1935, I have been trapped by his story. Too long to tell. But this was . . . (the tribe that gave Lewis and Clark hospitality and took an oath never to kill a white man.) Well, in the 1870's, after the USA had promised them their sacred land forever in official documents, emigration and miners hit their mountain country. Then began a running war, from Oregon, southwest through Lolo Pass into Montana, then south into now Yellowstone Park . . . then north toward Canada. Over 2000 troops were after them . . . [It] is not just a narrative and actually ends with me on the spot of the surrender. . . . The style is rather different, I may say, from any other poem I've done."[7]

By early July he had published twenty-six poems in that year of 1981, all of them part of the new book, *Rumor Verified: Poems 1979–1980,* which appeared in September. The title poem, "Rumor Verified," is written in Warren's quizzical, ironic, and fanciful mode. Because the rumor has been verified, "you" can disappear from the old life of privilege and try for one of self-sacrifice. What else can you do? "Perhaps pray to God for strength to face the verification / That you are simply a man, with a man's dead reckoning, nothing more" (p. 30). If, as he had said, *Being Here* had closed "an arch of feeling," this new book opened on the declining segment of the arch of life. This volume contains more fear and awareness of death, with a greater acceptance of limitation and sense of closure than any of its predecessors.[8]

The epigraph for the book's eight numbered sections comes from the end of Dante's journey in the *Inferno:*

> I saw something of the beautiful things
> That heaven bears, through a round opening,
> And from there we emerged to see the stars again.

This suggests an answer for the familiar quester gazing at the night sky. But the book's last line (in "Coda") pictures "dark grottoes" in a "caverned enchainment" (p. 97), and this poem's title, "Fear and Trembling," recalls the somber work of the Danish existentialist philosopher Søren Kierkegaard.[9]

There broods here the same threat as the one forty years before in "Terror" and "Crime." And in one poem in this volume, "Nameless Thing" (p. 27), something nameless stalks the house after midnight. In "The Corner of the Eye" even the imagery describing a poem is ominous. The poem "has stalked you all day, or years, breath rarely heard, fangs dripping" (p. 64). When there is an antidote for these poisonous fears and nameless apprehensions, it is provided in the person of the beloved, because of whom the poet is, as one title declares, "Twice Born" (p. 90). This love can be, as another title has it, a "Blessed Accident" (p. 11). It can also be rendered as in "Chthonian Revelation: A Myth" (p. 3), a long poem that follows two swimmers' symbolic journey through darkening Mediterranean waters to a cave where they make love. But in this volume there are also melancholy memories of passionate but passing liaisons, as in "Afterward" (p. 93).

There are gestures of filial love: the recollection, in "What Voice at Moth-hour" of the parental call *"It's late! Come home"* (p. 69). There is a particular poignancy in the father's death scene relived in "One I Knew." Some lines have a complex resonance where the poet writes of that stoical man with his closest companion: "the cancer of which / Only he knew" (p. 17).

Hovering most of all, however, over this volume—with its myriad references, to meditation and sleep, dream and nightmare, cycles in nature and history—is a sense of Last Things. In "Dead Horse in Field" the poet observes the way the unlucky thoroughbred's bones are whitened into "Modern sculpture" and then absorbed under the green benediction of the vine, which "thinks it is God" (p. 60). In "Immanence" the poet thinks how you, "yet yearning," are torn between hope and the fear of being sucked into "the black conduit of Nature's Repackaging System. . . ." (p. 62). In the four-poem sequence "Glimpses of Seasons," an unseasonable October snow prompts the thought "We / Are old enough to know that the world / Is only the world" (p. 74). But we forget this, and still the heart leaps." Like those two other aged poets, Hardy and Yeats, this poet wonders, "Next year will redwings see me, or I them, again then?" (p. 76).

For whatever reason—whether the confessional style was in favor over the philosophical, whether newer names were more attention-getting, whether there was continuing fallout from the Paleface-Redskin controversy—the book was not widely reviewed, and the notices that did appear were drawn out over more than a year. The balance, however, was favorable. Robert Penn Warren's best professional readers apparently knew what to expect from him: the kinds of poems he had been writing since his breakthrough nearly a quarter of a century before with *Promises,* and his technique was even more versatile now.[10]

As usual, he had been moving well ahead in his work, in this instance two books ahead, for he had another collection of poems shaping up in addition to *Chief Joseph of the Nez Perce.* This latter one demanded attention now, 104 years after the chief's surrender. Warren already had eight of the poem's nine sections written and rewritten. But there was one problem. He had carefully followed both cavalry and

Indian accounts, but he still could not see how, in that terrain, fifteen hundred cavalrymen could go undetected until their sudden attack ended the Battle of the Little South Bear Paw Mountains. So he decided to do what he had done for *Brother to Dragons:* see for himself the land where the crucial events had occurred.

Two friends went with him. Stuart Wright was a young teacher at Wake Forest, a book collector who had his own Palaemon press. They flew to Great Falls, Montana, where they were met by David Quammen, Warren's student thirteen years before and factotum in West Wardsboro the following summer. Now a full-time writer passionately attached to Montana, he met the plane and drove them one hundred miles northeast to their motel in Havre and then on to Chinook and the Bear Paw battlefield and monument beyond.

He later wrote, "The battlefield itself is a long sloping meadow that leads down to a hidden swale, where Joseph's people had their camp. It was deserted the day we were there. The grass was brown, the wild rose leaves were rust-colored and the rose hips were ripe and sweet." Soon Warren was deep in thought, making notes from time to time. Then the snow began to drift across the hills, and suddenly they saw what they sought about a mile away. "There was a clear depression," Stuart would remember, "sort of a declivity, and we completely lost sight of the camp itself, which meant that looking in the other direction you couldn't see anything. And there was the answer. That's how the cavalry did it. They were able to slip into that point and actually wait for the attack to begin, because they could not be seen." Stuart said to David, "Look, let's walk up the road and leave him alone." He wandered among the markers of warriors' graves. He would put the waning day into the poem's last lines:

> I turned to my friend Quammen, the nearer. Called:
> "It's getting night, and a hell of a way
> To go." We went,
> And did not talk much on the way. (p. 64)

Now he could complete the poem.[11]

A month later he was in Africa. They had flown to Algiers and then more than a thousand miles due south into that part of the Sahara called the Hoggar—Ahaggar in the language of the Tuareg. It was almost as large as France, but "it constitutes only about the southern quarter of the enormousness that is Algeria, compared to which Tunisia looks on the map about like Luxembourg or Rhode Island." In Tamanrasset, "long a round-up and take-off point for salt caravans heading south to Niger and Chad," their party of eleven checked into the Hotel Tahat, a primitive hostelry, but they were soon out in the desert. Riding the handsomest camel, as the senior female in the party, Eleanor was the *tamrart,* and this gave her book its name.[12]

At first, she wrote, the young ones were doing well, but "for us it's torture." In the rocky terrain at seven thousand feet it was sometimes too difficult for the camels to carry them, but hobbling among the rocks was a "relief on the underside, that's undeniable, we're caked with blood in our underpants and heaven knows when there'll be any washing again. But my darling spouse, never sure-footed at the best of times . . . had to study each step on the level and is utterly hopeless in the descents. He'd rather keep trying than get heaved back up on that damn camel, into the special saddle they had to borrow for him. . . . He grumbles, I scold, we almost quarrel, I use mean words . . . like 'bad sport' and 'spoil-sport.' " She sees herself "grasping, groveling, practically crawling on all fours . . . suddenly turned into an old, very old woman, *tamrart* with a vengeance. . . . the hag in the fairy tale. . . ." With the nights silvered under a seemingly constant full moon, she becomes a "victim of enchantment." There is even a miracle: a sufferer from emphysema, she quits smoking. Anwar Sadat's assassination precluded the visit to Israel, and so they returned, without transition, from the Sahara to southern Connecticut.[13]

A different transition would occur in December. After Rosanna's two years of study and teaching at Johns Hopkins she had taken a tenure-track assistant professorship in September 1980 at Vanderbilt. In spite of teaching new courses she continued to write, and just as she and her father had talked poetry on long walks in Vermont, so now she sent work to him and he sent back comments, mixing tactful criticism and encouragement. In December Stuart Wright was bringing out a collection of her poems, a chapbook called *Snow Day.* Then came a visiting assistant professorship at Boston University. And there was more. She had fallen in love with a young classicist named Stephen Scully, the son of a distinguished art and architectural historian. Warren wrote John Stewart that there was a good reason for Andrew Corry to pay them a visit: "Rosanna gets married in December, here at our house. . . . The very fortunate young man is a professor of

Greek [who] was at J-H on some post Ph.D. grant, but now is back teaching at Boston U." Rosanna's trip to the improvised altar would take place on December 21.[14]

Rosanna heard her father rehearsing for days. "I know I'll say it wrong," he told her. She heard him saying, over and over, "*I do. I do.*" He felt, she thought, a combination of trepidation and pleasure, undergirded by a conviction that these things would work themselves out for them and that they would be carried through by the life force. On Monday of Christmas week the large two-story living room was full of old friends. (One of the most welcome was Isabelle, the children's nurse at La Rocca, handsome and imposing as ever and now Mrs. Isabelle Taylor-Helton, dressed in gold lamé.) At last Rosanna and Steve stood between the two potted pines by the door, the midday sun streaming in through the two full-length windows. Steve's eight-year-old son, Ben, pale and serious in his dark suit, was ring bearer. Cleanth Brooks read a poem by John Donne, and William Arrowsmith read one by Eugenio Montale. The Rev. William Brown— a Baptist preacher in his purple robe, the husband of Florence Brown, the family's cleaning woman—intoned the rest of the service, and they were married. Outside on the terrace the cooks were grilling a freshly killed lamb brought by Steve's architect brother, Dan. Considering the tastes of the bridal pair, this gave a celebratory Greek touch to the festivities. The Warrens treated them to a brief stay at a country inn and then to a week on Saint Martin in the West Indies. It was a good respite before the two young faculty members made their way north toward Boston.[15]

50

❖

A New Book
and a New Baby

Another land, another age, another self
Before all had happened that has happened since
And is now arranged on the shelf
Of memory in a sequence that I call Myself
— "*Covered Bridge*"[1]

At the end of January Warren wrote to Marshall Walker, who was writing a book on his work, that "this has been the worst winter of my recollection in New England. I seem to spend most of my time carrying in logs for our roaring fire in the main dining room. Eleanor seems to spend most of her time going cross-country on skis." There was plenty to do in his study in the barn with its one heater. He had offered two different versions of *Chief Joseph* to *The New Yorker,* but Howard Moss told him that though he and William Shawn were much impressed by its sweep and suspense, it fell "somewhere between being a poem, a document, and an unclassifiable form of journalism. . . ." So it was not for them, but it would appear in *The Georgia Review* in May, and after that Warren would revise it for Random House. The Franklin Library wanted to do a special edition with a handsome advance, but that would have meant delay. "I have another book of short poems already in hand," he wrote Tom Rosenthal, "and I'm getting too antique to wait around for books."[2]

As he approached his seventy-eighth birthday he felt time's acceleration. Just as he had almost always thought his most recent book his best, he must now have felt an additional impulse to make this one his best. So he would apply his most rigorous standards, and doing so he could not wholly tamp down the anxiety he had felt before: How long would the poems keep coming? By early November he had about fifty for the new book.[3]

There were other events with claims on his emotions. Eleanor was working with her felt-tipped pens and magnifying equipment to write a little book on their African safari. He was always amused at her secretiveness—she would say nothing until she dumped a manuscript in his lap—and touched at her courage. He felt pride in Gabe's achievements in his primary vocation as a sculptor and anxiety at the risks of his avocation. He was now sailing his two-masted schooner, and occasionally he would sail a new boat south to be picked up by a purchaser in the Gulf. With one of them, "he got into the worst Atlantic storm in years and lost his radio for three days." Days of anguish for the parents, Warren wrote John Stewart. Another set of powerful emotions had been increasing for some time. There were the pressures on Rosanna, a teacher now at Boston University with a special "presidential appointment" they feared might make her unpopular with her colleagues. And now she was expecting her first child.[4]

Warren conveyed the news with a tone of authority: "We go up for the event in very early December. . . . Since I myself delivered my daughter on the floor—I'd say you can't always depend on the opinion of experts. We go up to Boston to lend a general hand, while her harried husband rushes back and forth to teach Greek." After a protracted labor, Katherine Penn Scully was delivered by cesarean section on December 1. A letter to Rosanna in the summer conveyed something of Katherine's grandfather's feelings: "We hover over every detail of the life you write about that you and Steve have and every little detail of the being of the little angel. . . . We can't wait to see all three, real and not just a lovely dream we have had. Somehow in your letters and poems, you make the little angel seem quite real and immediate even as you make it a dream-child, or dream-baby." The book of new poems would of course be dedicated to her.[5]

April of 1983 saw the publication of *Chief Joseph of the Nez Perce: Who Called Themselves the Nimipu "The Real People,"* dedicated to James Dickey. It marked the culmination of forty years of writing in a nearly extinct form: the long narrative poem. From "The Ballad of Billie Potts" to *Audubon* and *Brother to Dragons,* Warren had taken the material of legend and history to deal with the complexities of human personality, exploring them against the background of a particular culture while infusing the whole with his perennial concerns with original sin against the ongoing process of history. The method of this poem's recounting of treachery and near-genocide is signaled by three epigraphs: Thomas Jefferson's avowal to three Indian tribes of the "wish to live with them as one people," William Tecumseh Sherman's conviction that "they will all have to be killed or be maintained as a species of paupers," and Chief Sealth's assertion that even when "the last Red Man shall have perished [the white man's streets] will throng with the returning hosts that once filled them and still love this beautiful land" (p. ix).

The two-page opening note characterizes the noble, pacific, and hospitable Nez Perce, then quickly relates the series of broken treaties and long retreats, from 1855, when they still dwelled in their traditional homeland, "Wallowa" in northeastern Oregon, to their final confinement fifty years later in northeastern Washington. The principal characters are introduced: old Joseph, the noble and fatefully trusting head of this Nez Perce band; his son, Chief Joseph, who accepts his destiny when President Grant's guarantees are abrogated with the attacks of federal troopers in 1877; and the three competing federal commanders whose outfought and outgeneraled troops leave a trail of blood pursuing the vastly outnumbered Indians.

In the first of the poem's nine numbered sections the poet reveals his strategy: description and narration by a Nez Perce warrior who speaks for his tribe; italicized testimonials from white men (Jean Baptiste le Moyne de Bienville: "They are certainly more like a nation of saints than a horde of savages" [p. 4]); and Joseph's own recollection of his father's signing of the treaty while adamantly refusing to sell Nez Perce land. This method is subsequently elaborated with excerpts from federal documents, from self-convicting army testimonials, and from journalists' accounts of atrocities committed by miners.

The rival commanders of the three federal armies are almost as inimical as the political forces directing them. But these commanders are only instruments of manifest destiny and the precursors of robber barons large and small, when

> Frontiersmen, land-grabbers, gold-panners were dead.
> Veterans of the long chase skull-grinned in darkness.
> A more soft-handed ilk now swayed the West. They founded

Dynasties, universities, libraries, shuffled
Stocks, and occasionally milked
The Treasury of the United States,
Not to mention each other. They slick-fucked a land. (p. 54)

It is Joseph's tragic destiny to survive into this Gilded Age, ultimately accepting not only the friendship of General Nelson A. Miles (once Joseph's pursuer, now commander in chief of the United States Army), but also riding beside a despicable Buffalo Bill in the procession to dedicate Grant's Tomb. Honored by presidents decades later, Joseph is still the hero who had wished to fight to the death, refraining only because of his chiefs' opposition, the man who earned the admiration even of General Sherman, the man who sought in vain for meaning and could only conclude,

The Great Spirit Chief who rules above seemed to be
looking some other way, and did not see what was being
done to my people. (p. 48)

A few years later, sitting before his fire, he fell dead, according to the local physician, "of a broken heart" (p. xii). Throughout, Joseph has felt the eyes of his father upon him, knowing how he "Waits thus in his dark place. Waiting, sees all" (p. 10). The poet, leaving the battlefield at dusk, thinks of the return to the rush of city traffic but of how one might not heed it,

But, standing paralyzed in his momentary eternity, into
His own heart look while he asks
From what undefinable distance, years, and direction,
Eyes of fathers are suddenly fixed on him. . . . (p. 64)

Joseph's love for his father and his concern that he might "find some worth in an act of mine" (p. 52) must have resonated with Robert Penn Warren's own feelings.

The poet took many risks in composing this medley of voices. The reader is prepared to accept the interpolated voices of the large chorus as well as the simulated Nez Perce voice, whether it is that of the warrior who says, "We, too, belong / To the world" (p. 3), or that of Joseph when he says, "I was born at the time of snow. My name— / It was Miats Ta-weet Tu-eka-kas" (p. 5). The poetic idiom of the narrator's voice prevents jangling against the Nez Perce narrative and commentary, but a problem arises when he employs an analytical tone:

> Yes, it would be
> An operation brilliant in textbooks,
> A nutcracker action—depending, of course,
> On information and timing. . . . (p. 30)

For the most part, however, the voices blend. Other risks generally succeed: describing the Gatling gun that "spits bullets like hail" (p. 15), the artillery's "big-bellied belch-gun" (p. 18), and the rifle as "death-tube" (p. 20).

The metrics presented a challenge. Warren generally chose verse paragraphs without rhyme. He did, however, employ alliteration like that of Gerard Manley Hopkins and his Anglo-Saxon models, as when the Indians fire a deadly volley and "the unhived lead hums happily homeward" (p. 36). There are sometimes clearly accented lines, as with one in perfect anapestic tetrameter: "For I stored all I heard for the heart's lonely thought" (p. 20). The imagery is full of the western colors Warren loved and the hawks and eagles who had become totem animals for him. There too is his own archetypal quester, embodied not only in Joseph, remembering his dead, "now lonely under / High stars with no name" (pp. 26–27), but also in the poet who in his "fanatic imagination" (p. 62) sees Joseph both at his surrender and at midnight amid the sleeping tribe, gazing at strange stars, knowing that the eyes of the fathers are fixed on him. This bold and generally successful experiment was little reviewed.[6]

In this spring of 1983, though bucked up by the birth of his first grandchild and himself a survivor now much older than Joseph at the end of his life, Warren was apparently feeling vulnerable. *The New Yorker* had refused two more of his poems. George Core published one of them in *The Georgia Review,* but Warren never reprinted it and no one took the other. In the fall he would refuse an invitation to give a reading "because I've been having a rather unserious but very unsettling infection of the inner ear, grogginess, unsettled innards, uncertainty on stairs, etc. Nothing serious, but slow in leaving." He needed some kind of diversion, and fortunately there was one in the offing.[7]

The eightieth anniversary of the Cecil Rhodes scholarships was to be celebrated in Oxford in June. Warren was to be one of three honorary-degree recipients. They decided on a holiday with Gabriel and Ana, first to Scotland, then to the Western Isles and Orkney, and then back to Scotland. Afterward Warren told Bill Bandy that Gabriel "drove us to every spot he thought of interest . . . never in anything bigger than a small town." They were especially taken with the Orkneys. "Red did pretty well on the trip," Eleanor would later tell Marshall Walker, "went along on about half our archaeological and cliffside expeditions." The people and the place were lovely, she said, "and oh Lord, the sea birds and wildflowers! and cliffs!" Traveling south was different. "At Stonehenge, where we arrived on the day of Midsummer Night," Warren wrote, "we found literally 30,000 idiots encamped, all on drugs or likker, all freaks, with halfshaved heads and hair dyed purple, green, violet. . . . We did not linger long."[8]

Late June found them among 750 other former Rhodes scholars and their guests in Wadham College's manicured garden awaiting the arrival of Queen Elizabeth II and Prince Philip. Dressed in brilliant chartreuse, the queen spoke with the mingled diplomats and politicians, lawyers and journalists from the United States and the Commonwealth who had been Cecil Rhodes's beneficiaries. She could chat with only a few, of course, Warren among them; dignitaries such as Governor Bill Clinton of Arkansas had to be content simply to be in her ambience. Later the honorary degrees were bestowed with all formality. The citations were in Latin, and in keeping with the tradition of humorous allusion, Red Warren, returning fifty-three years after his student escapades, was addressed as "Rufus."[9]

Back in Vermont he experienced ups and downs. John Hersey had asked him for a poem to serve as a preface to a deluxe edition of his celebrated book *Hiroshima,* and he consented. "Work goes fairly well," he told Albert Erskine, "and I am modestly pleased with the recent responses from the New Yorker and the Atlantic. But I do feel that I have somehow run through the impulse of the last 2 or 3 years and am groping for a fresh way in." He sent out only one poem, "Marble," to *The New Yorker,* where it appeared on October 24. It was a long reliving of his mother's death and his father's stoical grief. Although written in present time, the event "is not *then.* / It is *now. . . .*" It is not only mourning but also self-chastisement. He cannot understand why his grief "has not understood its own being" and concludes,

It takes a long time for it to learn
Its many names: like
Selfishness and *precious guilt.*[10]

That November, Eleanor told Marshall Walker some of the reasons why her husband was groping. He was "pretty weak and having more downs than ups right now, keeps working, on several prose jobs, but feels poems eluding him." Having written the introduction to an anniversary volume for the semicentennial of the Academy of American Poets, he felt obliged to attend the celebration at the Library of Congress when they might better have stayed home. They returned to a variety of concerns. Eleanor's sister, Eunice, living alone in a big, isolated eighteenth-century house and suffering from emphysema, had twice needed hospital intensive care. Rosanna was almost completely taken up with her own life. Steve had gone to Greece on a grant to finish his book, and "she and the baby joined him in the remote mountains there and dug with him for stones in remote villages." But the holidays in Vermont prompted the same hospitality as in other years. "Twenty guests bedded down for New Years, some of them on mattresses on the floor when house and guest house spilled them from beds, etc."[11]

He was doing his best to press on, "deep in the job of assembling, assessing, and revising the poems of the last two years, and making selections from previous volumes for what has sort of become my every-tenth year (about) 'New and Selected Poems.' Out late this year or early next. That and a mass of correspondence—mostly not like this, that is to friends. Just stupid odds and ends. Have lost my secretarial help, God damn it." As usual, his estimate of publication dates tended to be on the optimistic side, and the whole year would be fraught with increasing difficulties.[12]

51

❖

The Last Collected
Poems

Yes, stretch forth your arms like wings, and from your high stance,
Hawk-eyed, ride forth upon the emptiness of air, survey
Each regal contortion
And tortuous imagination of rock, wind, water, and know
Your own the power creating all.

—"Delusion?—No!"[1]

It was just as well that he had scheduled only one public event—a poetry reading at Vanderbilt on April 10—for by May he and Eleanor were both ailing. He was now a dozen pounds below his normal 175. He tired easily, with a general feeling of malaise. One finding, however, was specific. He had recently suffered "a minor cerebral vascular accident"—not necessarily a stroke—and he had fully recovered. A chest X ray, bone scan, and metastatic series showed no significant changes. But they did detect a hard nodular area on his prostate, and a biopsy detected cancer. Because of the vascular accident they ruled out estrogen therapy but decided to wait and perform an "orchiectomy if significant symptomatic metastatic disease becomes manifest." It was almost four years since the transurethral resection when the adenocarcinoma had been noted, but neither he nor Eleanor had thought of him as a cancer patient.[2]

The immediate problem was pain from increasingly severe osteoarthritis. There was no sign that the cancer had spread to the spine, but there was "extensive degenerative disc disease and spondylosis throughout the cervical area and also extending throughout the entire spine with moderate scoliosis to the right at the dorso–lumbar junction." He dealt with it with hot wet packs on his shoulders and back, with analgesics such as Tylenol, and "by not paying much attention to the pain."[3]

Summer brought no improvement in his physical condition or his frame of mind. "A lot of grave illness in my family," he wrote Lewis Simpson on July 13. "My brother at death's door, my sister's husband with a paralytic stroke. I'm feeling my years for the first time. I've been visiting from hospital to hospital and nursing homes and funerals." He sent along "Uncertain Season in High Country." Passing a desolate cabin, the speaker says, "I do not stop. I have my own fate. I know it."[4]

The auguries were no better by fall. When Skilly Russell wrote with memories of Berkeley days, he told her, "Am having vertigo. Not serious, but very disabling." He tried always to be optimistic. Five of his friends had had it. "Nothing to do. Just wait for it to go. In every case. Creep around with a stick and become a domestic nuisance. Can't drive. Nor can Eleanor." A national literary conference at LSU was planned for October of 1985 to mark the fiftieth anniversary of the founding of *The Southern Review.* But he feared that he could not attend because he had been forced to cancel a reading and "certainly anything that involves travelling. Speaking is now a problem, whatever causes the vertigo also affects, now and then, unpredictably, enunciation and voice-volume, etc." He was using a recorder, trying to regain normal control. But then, as Christmas approached, he received good news. After further examinations his neurologist rejected the finding of small strokes. Laryngeal polyps had produced a "benign infection" and were removed. The vertigo, Warren said, was gone in twenty-four hours.[5]

There was no corresponding reversal, however, in the way his work was going. At the end of March he had written Peter Davison, "Poetry has gone dead lately" and "new ones won't come these days. . . ." On Independence Day he told Lewis Simpson he would send him a poem if summer was kinder to him than spring had been. It had been dull, he said, with only two poems published plus one promised to *The New Yorker* and another not yet taken. In early October he wrote Rosanna that it had been "my worst summer, poetically, in years. . . . I have thrown away at least a half dozen poems unfinished. All ideas seem to die on me." Then, in February of 1985 he published two poems. In "Re-Interment: Recollection of a

Grandfather" the poet carried his grandfather in his head as his great-grandmother had carried him "in her belly." Now the grandfather's fingers fumble in the poet's skull as he tries to get out. At the end of "Old Photograph of the Future" the child in the picture, now grown into adulthood, stands at his parents' graveside and thinks, "They lie side by side in whatever love survives / Under green turf," and grieves in his guilt "over nameless promises unkept, in undefinable despair."[6]

Over the years, while Thomas Warren's enterprises prospered, he and Alice raised three daughters. He retired at fifty to enjoy the outdoor life he loved. After Alice's death in 1967 he remarried and lived on to survive illnesses and a prostatectomy. He enjoyed his hunting trips, especially those with his brother, until emphysema made walking in the woods too difficult. He survived the death of his eldest daughter, Vivian, who came from her home in France for his seventieth birthday, collapsed on the way back, and died after heart surgery in Houston. In 1984, when Thomas's family saw him failing, his Nashville doctor hospitalized him for tests, which showed not only the respiratory problems but also his stomach as "a war zone of ulcers." Robert Penn came immediately and then wrote to him steadily during the rest of his eight-week hospitalization. They brought him home in mid-August, and six months later, on February 25, he died. The gathered family remembered Robert Penn weeping because he felt he should have been able somehow to protect his younger brother, weeping too at lines from a poem by Housman that someone quoted.[7]

In the next month, *New and Selected Poems: 1923–1985* finally appeared. He called its first, integral, book-length collection of new poems "Altitudes and Extensions: 1980–1984" and divided them into twelve sections marked by Roman numerals. It was his largest collection except for *Being Here* and *Selected Poems: 1923–1943*. A number of the poems are set at altitude—in western mountains, in aircraft, and in skies where hawks fly. The poems show extensions of familiar concerns with individual identity and man's place in the world of nature. But the most persistent images come with the repetitions of "darkness" and "death." And the emphasis on last things ("Last Walk of Season," "Last Meeting," "Last Night Train") suggests an eighty-year-old man preparing his soul. But the epigraph from Saint Augustine is far from funereal, and it subtly extends the nuances of the title:

"Will ye not now after that life is descended down to you, will not you ascend up to it and live?"

The first poem expands the range of reference. "Three Darknesses" depicts three kinds: that of a bear pounding the door of his zoo cave "trying to enter into the darkness of wisdom," that of passengers on an anchored yacht separated from one another in the silence of a dark lagoon, and that of a preoperative patient in his darkened room thinking of moonlit snow peaks floating "in that unnamable altitude of white light." The poet himself, not long since a surgical patient, might well think of God as does the patient in the poem: "God loves the world. For what it is" (pp. 3–4). Then, in "Mortal Limit," the poet sees the hawk spiral into the "downwardness that will restore," perhaps, "the darkness of whatever dream we clutch. . . ." (p. 6). "Immortality over the Dakotas" is what the poet almost feels in his airliner but then thinks of the soon-to-die farmer in his dark field below, staring "at the blackness of sky" (p. 7). In "Far West Once" the poet remembers the last walk of the season years before but recalls too the "redemptive music" heard in sleep, which is still able "to touch the heart, as though at a dawn / Of dew-bright Edenic promise. . . ." (p. 17).

The book's second segment draws on recollections of family and past years. But even in current contentment, as in "Rumor at Twilight," there is unexplained unease, and in "Old Dog Dead," the sense of life as a tragic process. The grief comes not so much from the poignant death of the pet as from the remembered joy of the little girl in his puppyhood and the awareness of how, "little no longer," she will "weep / For what life is" (p. 21). The deeper griefs in "what life is" involve regret and guilt, as in "Marble," here renamed "Doubleness in Time" as the poet relives his mother's death and his father's devastation. If there is any anodyne, it is in the blessedness of love, described in this poet's tenderest poem, "After the Dinner Party," when, guests gone, the couple mount the stairs and "one hand gropes out for another, again" (p. 26).

The third segment comprises one nine-page poem, "New Dawn," occasioned by John Hersey's request for the new edition of his *Hiroshima*. Another of Warren's long narratives, its variety suggests that of *Chief Joseph* though it is vastly different in tracing the single most dramatic event of World War II. It employs a combination of styles in its fifteen parts, ranging from a description of the *Enola Gay*'s takeoff to the bomb's detonation over Hiroshima. In keeping with the precepts of "Pure and Impure Poetry," it employs not just the ugly but also the unthinkably monstrous for poetry.

After the fourth segment's depiction of three kinds of love, the fifth draws heavily on the personal past with memories of Grandpa Penn in "Old-Time Childhood in Kentucky" and "Re-Interment: Recollection of a Grandfather." In the former, the grandfather gives a response to the usually tragic sense of "what life is." When the boy asks, "What do you do, things being like this?" the old man answers, "All you can,"

> . . . Love
> Your wife, love your get, keep your word, and
> If need arises die for what men die for. There aren't
> Many choices.
> And remember that truth doesn't always live in the number of
> voices. (p. 46)

The next segment is the longest in "Altitudes and Extensions." The past is almost always there (as in "Old Photograph of the Future," a guilt-imbued meditation by the man once the infant pictured there with his parents), but there are fewer images of darkness. The principal focus is on problems of identity and self-knowledge, with awareness of the symbolic change of seasons and death's presence never far away. There is lyric joy in "First Moment of Autumn Recognized," where, in the champagne glitter of the air and in a perfection of crystal, you stand, "your being perfected. . . ." (p. 62). But in "Paradigm of Seasons," a rifle shot is followed by another sound:

> The painful bellows of the lungs of an aging man
> Who follows, with a burden of supplies on his back,
> A snow-choked trail. (p. 64)

Drawing to its close, the collection is replete with images of containment, of boxes and cubicles, whether in nocturnal snowfall or the passage of the 3:00 A.M. train or its aerial counterpart. But there is yet affirmation of sorts in "Delusion?—No!" In a kind of mystical experience man becomes hawk and knows that, diving from a crag, he can enter into "that divine osmosis" and be "part of all" (p. 79). Ultimately, in "Is Not Dead," even the rock on which the poet lies naked "in brotherhood," "brooding on our common destinies," is anthro-

pomorphized, not dead but "simply weighty with wisdom" (p. 82).
This poem is followed by "Sunset," with the poet's repetitive plaint
to the night sky's stars that he may know his name, that he may speak
"to your naked self—never / Before seen, nor known" (p. 84).
Then comes the last of the nine segments, a single poem, "Myth of
Mountain Sunrise," at whose triumphant end the sun figuratively
clasps "a girl-shape, birch-white sapling. . . ." (p. 85).[8]

Like its predecessors over the previous decade, *New and Selected
Poems: 1923–1985* received little attention on publication, and its reviews were spread between April and November, but they appeared
in conspicuous places: *The New York Times, The New York Review of
Books, Commentary, Poetry,* and *Library Journal.* The poems were
praised, and for the most part warmly. If they were out of fashion for
some reviewers, for Harold Bloom they confirmed Warren's status as
"our most eminent man of letters." Increasingly he would be judged
on his total achievement, but the continued intensity and the high
level of his craftsmanship in individual volumes such as *New and Selected Poems: 1923–1985* would affirm the earlier comparisons with
the late harvest of Yeats. The other standard comparison would be to
that poet with whom he had felt a special affinity, Thomas Hardy.[9]

Following the *New York Times* review in the same issue was Warren's "Poetry Is a Kind of Unconscious Autobiography." The 3,500-
word essay began with his reply to a woman who had asked if he was
going to write an autobiography: "Hell, no—I've done that already."
In this remarkably condensed version of the experiences that had
made him a novelist and a poet, he recounted successes and failures at
his craft. He asked at the end, "What is a poem but a hazardous attempt at self-understanding? It is the deepest part of autobiography."
"Altitudes and Extensions, 1980–1984" was an extension of the hazardous flights he had been making for almost sixty years. How did it
stack up with the earlier efforts? For the closest students of his poetic
technique, it was the equal of the preceding three volumes. It is,
moreover, a book whose epigraph suggests William Faulkner's pro-
nouncement that the artist's work is his way of "saying No to
death."[10]

Even though more than one of his preceding books had also closed
"an arch of feeling," this collection's basic concerns are the same, as
are the deepest questions. If there is a difference, it lies in the more
pervasive specter of death. But the mode of dealing with it is much
the same: glorying in the beauty of life and the possibility of tran-

scendence; valuing the past and coming to terms with it; hoping for joy and the love that can miraculously proffer it. It is, in fact, what he had said before, repeated now with more assurance, with equal technical dexterity, and with the sense of courage still in the face of death, which might not long be held in abeyance.

As for form, fully one-third of the poems exhibit regular rhyme schemes, and "First Moment of Autumn Recognized" clothes its epiphany in alliterative lines suggesting Gerard Manley Hopkins. But Warren had not reverted to the regularity of his early poems. He explained that, over the years, walking and swimming, he became more aware of "a peculiar physical involvement in the words," with the final result that "it seemed to involve something like the playing of metrical verse against free verse—verse considered more dramatically." The occasional lines of dialogue are appropriately colloquial without the Jack Burden–style sardonicism, and the diction is for the most part formal. This formality is emphasized at the beginning of section VIII in "Milton: A Sonnet," written in free verse but conforming precisely to the rhyme scheme of the classic English sonnet. And it is almost as if this invocation of the blind Milton as old man is meant to add strength to the proclamation that "past and future are intrinsicate," and that they form a present in which the heart may leap in joy like a fish from the "deep wisdom" of the water (p. 75). And overarching all in this collection of linked poems is the recapitulation of the poet's life from childhood to old age.[11]

He continued to work at his craft, but it was a troubled process now. On March 18 *The New Yorker* published a poem in five rhymed quatrains called "The Loose Shutter." It was an irascible recollection of a sleepless night, leaving at morning only the question "What voice? What name? By what thin thread does the past hang?" He wrote Peter Davison, "I haven't written a poem in months. This isn't too unusual for often when I feel that I have finished some phase (as I feel now) I need a fresh look at things (including the self) before I can start again. I've learned not to push it. I hope." His daughter knew how poorly he was faring. As the year wore on, he struggled "with poems he didn't like." She remembered the years when they would take long walks together, how "I felt terrifically grown up to be discussing technically a poem in the making, how he gave you the feeling of being a valued reader, considering seriously what you said, in your middle and late teens." Now when she sent him her poems he would give them the closest scrutiny in four- and five-page letters that were at once professional, deferential, and loving. He was now sending her poems less and less often. When she pressed him he would show her bits, but once he refused because, he said, "They are shit." She was shocked. He hardly ever talked like that. He did manage one poem, however, which would appear in *The New Yorker* in August. It was "John's Birches," in three rhymed stanzas, the last one beginning, "If boyhood is lonely enough, the moss-bearded stone / Communicates wisdom," and ending, "If you are lonely enough, you will never know lonesomeness, / With day full of leaves that whisper, and night never visionless." The thing he had feared for so long had finally happened. These two poems were the last he would ever publish.[12]

But there was one other, unpublished, probably written before both of these, called "A Little Girl, Twenty Months Old, Faces the World: (Photograph, in color: mounted plastic oblong 5 inches high, 7 inches long.)" Its fifteen lines described Katherine Scully on the beach and asked,

Is this the hour
When she discovers the vast world of impersonal beauty and power?

And in that fact the curse, and blessing, of her own identity?[13]

They celebrated his eightieth birthday with a tent on the lawn and dancing after dinner. Peter and Katinka DeVries supplied a lighthearted variation of an A. E. Housman poem, beginning "Now of his three score years and ten / Eighty will not come again." They also supplied another Housman variation to celebrate his forthcoming American Academy and Institute of Arts and Letters Gold Medal for Poetry. It concluded, "Round that thickly laurelled head / Shall flock the friends who called him Red. . . ."[14]

He was able to make the trip into New York on May 15 to receive the medal from the hand of Malcolm Cowley, who called it "a token, no more, of the love we feel for the poet and the man." His best present, not unmixed with anxiety, was very likely the anticipation of the arrival of Rosanna and Steve's second child in the summer. Activities in Fairfield one month after the birthday party were part of another cycle. "Now hell breaks loose," he wrote Albert Erskine, "in getting ready for VT."[15]

52

❖

Poet Laureate—
and Patient

The nurse is still here. Then
She is not here. You
Are here but are not sure
It is you in the sudden darkness. No matter.
A damned nuisance, but trivial—
The surgeon has just said that. A dress rehearsal,
You tell yourself, for
The real thing. Later. Ten years? Fifteen?
        —"Three Darknesses"[1]

When Chiara Scully was born by cesarean section on July 9, her
grandfather was in too much pain to come to see her. The family
couldn't believe that the increasingly troublesome osteoarthritis was
causing this much pain. Then one day the mail brought a medical-
insurance form. Eleanor was shocked at the diagnosis: "prostate cancer." (Both she and Warren had apparently forgotten the content of
the pathology report that led to the resection five years before.)
Eleanor telephoned their old friends Cesare and Rysia Lombroso at
their Vermont summer home. A renowned neurologist, Lombroso
quickly arranged for tests at the Brigham and Women's Hospital in
Boston. At the end of July the Lombrosos drove the Warrens to
Needham, where Rosanna and Steve installed them in their own upstairs bedroom.[2]

 The next day the X rays and bone scans revealed that the adenocarcinoma was no longer encapsulated. It had metastasized widely
into the bones though it had not yet reached the upper spine. They

would have to take measures immediately, but Eleanor insisted that they first return to Vermont. So they got a former student of Warren's to drive them back. Eleanor had increasingly taken over the decision-making process as Warren's problems increased, and this sometimes produced conflict. But often, on the day after a stormy scene, he would say to Rosanna or Gabriel, without preamble, "Eleanor is the best thing that ever happened to me."[3]

After a few days they returned to Needham, and on August 8 Dr. Robert Richie performed the excision of the testes contemplated a year before. With the secretion of male hormones stopped, the spread of the disease should be substantially slowed. Rosanna remembered "a horrendous few days of shock for everybody." It was a particularly difficult time for her, recovering from the cesarean section, caring for a toddler and a new baby, and trying to be a good stepmother to Ben Scully. When Warren returned from the hospital, he and Eleanor stayed in the living room. After a few days, Steve and Rosanna drove them back to West Wardsboro.[4]

Warren dug into the stack of correspondence awaiting him. To his Random House copy editor, Bertha Krantz, he reported, "Another medical session in Boston for a week or so (nothing for me to get excited about). . . . Our house here, and old Shack I, are full of people." Rosanna and Steve were there with Ben and their daughters plus an au pair. Gabriel and Ana would arrive in a few days with "more to come. . . . Maybe they thought there would be a wake. But they got roundly fooled." By late summer he felt fairly well, but he swam less and less.[5]

Guests continued welcome at Shack One and Shack Two. Nearly two years before, a young filmmaker named Ken Burns had interviewed Warren for a documentary on Huey Long. Unable at first to understand a word he said, Burns was terrified, but after a couple of drinks at lunch they resumed and Burns thought the interview phenomenal. Warren's anecdotes about Huey were colorful, and his speech enhanced them with the drawl and the lilt, "like he's speaking in a car that is suddenly plunged down a hill and then up a hill." Burns used the tape at several points in the film where Warren became, to him, a Greek chorus with his comments and readings from *All the King's Men*. Now Burns arrived and showed the first print of the film, to Warren's enthusiastic approval.

When Warren learned that Burns was planning a documentary on the Civil War, he telephoned. "If you're gonna do it right," he said, "you have to talk to Shelby Foote." Because Burns's request had been prompted by Warren, Foote accepted and became the principal commentator in the monumental, much-acclaimed film. Each year thereafter the Burns family would be invited to the Warrens' holiday party. Warren had spent time with Burns's three-year-old Sarah. "She's a wonder, she's a wonder," he would tell her father. Sarah Burns loved Warren. Ken Burns would remember his advice at this phase of his life. "Careerism is death," he told him. Burns already knew that, but even so, he could say of their relationship, "It really changed my life," and later, "His kind of willingness to face the unknown and to face mortality, and most important, I think, to face himself with honesty, was just remarkable."[6]

In mid-September he told Lewis Simpson that he hoped they could attend the LSU conference but "intermittent loss of voice has returned, or voice going to a harsh whisper. When back in Fairfield, I'll go back to my voice machine, etc. . . . Also, long standing is, intermittently, a problem. This makes cocktail parties and lots of other things a problem." For some time now there had been this trouble with articulation complicated by dry mouth and a sensation of closure in his throat. (As for his voice machine—onto which he read passages and then repeated them over and over—the voice he preferred to hear was not his own but Rosanna's. She made tapes for him, reading *The Divine Comedy* in Dante's Italian.) In October, he and Eleanor made the trip to Baton Rouge. In his public reading he got through several poems quite well, but then his voice faded into the hoarse, finally inaudible whisper, and James Olney finished for him. But later he wrote and told Simpson "how much the occasion meant to us. For one thing, just the people we saw from the past. . . . I did hear Eudora read, and fell in love all over again with those stories." He could never forget the demise of the original *Southern Review* and the valuation placed on Mike the Tiger. And he would always think of himself as an exile from the South who had hoped to live the rest of his life there, but this occasion showed the valuation placed upon him and Cleanth by better men than those who had presided over their departure forty years before.[7]

As for his work, he and Albert Erskine had discussed collecting some of his essays, and he had half-agreed to help Harriet Owsley and Bid Brown with special projects. And he continued to write his long, loving, single-spaced letters to Rosanna about her work. He was beginning to sketch out a memoir of his father, and he might have found the holiday visit to Vermont a further stimulus for it, but by November he was not sure that they would be able to go. "I have had some little nuisances that have developed since April 24," he wrote Arnold and Bess Stein. "So plans now tend to be provisional."[8]

By early December, Dr. Bernard Lytton, his urologist, had referred him to James D. Kenney, a New Haven internist. When Dr. Kenney examined him on December 4 his weight had dropped to 144 pounds, and he measured just under 5 feet, 8 inches. His gait was unsteady, and his range of motion was limited by pain across his shoulders and down both arms. A bone scan confirmed metastatic prostate cancer in several sites. At the Yale–New Haven Hospital Dr. Lytton brought in a young Yale-educated specialist. Thomas N. Byrne was a tall, slim neurologist who had undergone fellowship training at Memorial Sloan-Kettering in neural oncology. If Warren's symptoms were caused by the tumor impinging on the spinal cord, he would find it.

He was confronted not only with the pain but also with the ultimate possibility of a pathological fracture of a weight-bearing bone. This could lead to surgery or even spinal-cord compression and paralysis. Dr. Byrne found now that in addition to metastasis into the vertebral column and shoulder blades, there was an enormous amount of severe osteoarthritis. The doctor was surprised to learn that his patient continued lifting weights and doing more than one hundred knee squats a day. On January 19 his three doctors held a joint consultation and concluded that there was no evidence of spinal-cord compression or cancer-caused neuromyopathy. To deal with the degenerative joint disease of his cervical spine, they prescribed ibuprofen, which gave him prompt relief. He was discharged and returned home.[9]

He could not have had better medical supervision. This was the beginning of a long, intimate friendship between him and Tom Byrne. When Byrne saw him again on January 14 he complained of numbness and twitching sensations in his legs. He had also suffered an apparent loss of consciousness on a train returning to Connecticut from New York. He told Byrne of continuing episodes of complete collapse plus difficulty in sleeping and pain in his right shoulder and right foot. In spite of this, he was still doing 120 to 140 squats per day. Byrne found no abnormalities in his cranial nerve examination, no focal weakness, and no atrophy. He prescribed nonsteroidal medica-

tion, and they were able to manage for the most part without nar-
cotics.

Warren formed the habit of writing short bulletins to Kenney. The
substance of the one he sent on February 8 would be repeated: This
was his worst collapse yet, with "pretty complete weakness, unsteadiness, neck giving way to weight of head, shortness of breath, some
uncertainness of memory. Please do not answer. I had merely thought
that you might want to know."

At this juncture, while he was in misery, his name was being applauded in many papers, for on February 26 Daniel J. Boorstin, the
Librarian of Congress, had appointed him "Poet Laureate Consultant
in Poetry." One article began with Warren's declaration "that he took
the post to foster poetry and poets but not to produce verse on demand for official occasions." His duties would consist of consulting
with the Librarian on the poetry collection, giving an October reading, and possibly writing "an essay on the state of poetry sometime
during his one-year tenure." The salary would be thirty-six thousand
dollars.[10]

A few days later he told his niece Tommie Lou Frey his reaction
when he heard about the introduction of the bill in Congress: "Id-
iocy, I thought. . . . Can you imagine some guy being paid for that!
And what fool could take the post." He heard nothing more until
Boorstin telephoned him. It was for only one year, and he had been
poetry consultant before. The new title "is merely tacked on by Congress to the real post." Reactions to the appointment provided an interesting confirmation of his stature as he approached his eighty-first
year. The Irish poet Seamus Heaney said, "If America is to choose a
poet, I don't think it could have chosen better." West Indian poet
Derek Walcott called Warren an artist whose achievements evoked
those of Hardy and Yeats. In his pain he must have felt an added one:
the office came when he could no longer write poems.[11]

He had continued writing to Dr. Kenney through February and
March, as his throat and voice worsened. "Sometimes the closure
simply begins before I can utter any sound *whatsoever*. . . . Am making great efforts to speak slowly and very distinctly." During a house
call, Dr. Williams found that Eleanor had pneumonia in one lung. He
ordered her to bed and arranged for a nurse twice a day. Warren
meanwhile felt himself going steadily downhill. On April 18, suffering extreme pain, he was taken to the Yale–New Haven emergency

room. After three days of exhaustive tests he was given a supply of painkilling Percodan tablets and discharged.

Tom Byrne had told Eleanor to call him at home whenever she needed to, because a standard thirty-minute appointment at Yale translated into a gruelling trip of several hours. As Warren's birthday approached she telephoned to report his increasing difficulty walking. Tom made the hour trip to West Wardsboro, but his examination showed nothing new. "The cancer largely remained confined to the bones; it didn't spread to the lungs or to the liver, or to the brain." Tom was more than a conscientious and compassionate doctor. "I don't know how we developed this very close relationship," he said, "one that I've never had with another patient." The fact was that he admired Warren as an artist and as a man. Tom also listened well. "What he complained of most was that he had no energy, the energy he needed to write, and I think that was his greatest source of sadness. It was the loss of energy, a real sense of weakness and debility. He once called it 'deliquescence.' "

A few months later Dr. Kenney wrote, "The Warrens plan to visit the Orkneys from early June until June 26th." There seemed to be no impingement on his spinal cord, and the amount of calcium in his blood was not excessive, and so "it seems fairest to leave him without additional remedy beyond analgesia and agree to his making the trip." It was "two weeks of pure self-indulgence, with son and his wife on whom we dote. It is one of the most beautiful spots in the world day and night, peculiar light (even at midnight at that latitude.)" At home again he reported to Tom Byrne that he had been able to walk for several miles at a time. But soon he found his gait unsteady again, though he was still able to perform 140 squats each morning. That would be his principal exercise after they made their annual journey to Vermont. He would make his way out to the coop and sit there, where the poems no longer came. No longer could he swim or walk along the rugged paths he had cleared. He was plagued now with the throat problems made more unpleasant by a constant accumulation of mucus though he was drinking an extra quart of water a day. For pain, there was the Percodan.[12]

In Connecticut while the fall colors flamed and faded there was little to lift the mood on Redding Road except for Rosanna's letters and the occasional visits from the children and their spouses and welcome friends. The dying of the year must have deepened the mood evoked by events in lives close to the Warrens. Though Albert Erskine had retired from Random House, he had continued as Warren's editor, financial adviser, and confidant. Thin and angular now, he was still an avid gardener. He was also an inveterate pipesmoker who enjoyed generally good health, but in the spring he had detected something at the base of his tongue. It proved to be cancer, and so in early June, three weeks before the wedding of his beautiful daughter, Silvia, he had begun radiation treatments, and now he was stoically suffering through the long aftereffects and subsisting on broth and milk shakes. The same threat hung over the Brookses, though more immediately and heavily. Cleanth had dedicated the first of his two great critical works on Faulkner to Warren. He had dedicated the other to *"conjiugi dilectissimae."* Tinkum, his charming, witty, and stalwart wife of fifty-two years had been diagnosed with a fast-growing inoperable brain tumor. Warren shared in Cleanth's grief. On October 2 he told Harriet Owsley, "At the moment I can scarcely write a letter." Tinkum's funeral was scheduled for the following day.[13]

At the end of the week, in spite of all, he tried to fulfill his obligations as Poet Laureate, including public appearances. When Bid Brown said she had seen him on television, he replied, "In the morning of Monday there was a frightful news conference, with four blazing TV lights on the patient, and a gang of news people, the most complete idiots I have ever known hired by any newspaper." That evening, frail-looking and walking with a cane, he began his public reading. But after five minutes his throat began to close up, and he handed the poems to a friend.[14]

There was more medical business in December—for both of them. Eleanor had always lived an active life, and she had the scars to show for it, particularly from skiing. Her hip had been bothering her for some time, and in early December her doctor said it was time for a replacement. So they would spend much of January not among the evergreens of their home in Vermont but in the crowded city of New Haven in the doctors' offices of hospital complexes, under the bright lights with the green-clad surgical teams, and in the family waiting rooms while the interminable minutes ticked on.

53

❖

The Inexorable Seasons

The day wore on, and he would ponder,
Lifting eyes from his work, thinking, thinking,
Of the terrible distance in love, and the pain,
Smiling back at the sunlit smile, even while shrinking
From recall of the nocturnal timbre, and the dark wonder.
— *"Midnight Outcry"*[1]

After Eleanor's operation on January 15 she spent three weeks at the Yale–New Haven Hospital. "I had stayed at the Yale Health Center," Warren wrote "Bo" Grimshaw, his bibliographer, "a sort of hospital or something of the sort for mild ailments or for the dying. I belonged in the first category, suffering from what one doctor called an 'incurable disease.' On being questioned at some length, he spelled the word—a word too terrible to mention—A–G–E." He would repeat this diagnosis to other friends, just as he would attribute much of his infirmity to arthritis—never to cancer. Eleanor's recovery went well despite the fact that she "doesn't believe in crutches, and only at gun-point, will use them." At home they were living in the single bedroom on the house's lowest level, but close enough to the big fireplace to benefit from its steady blaze, especially when the fire was built up as snow blew against the windowpanes. Their regular help was supplemented by friends who came and stayed with them.[2]

Emotional sustenance came from the visits of Vann Woodward, Peter and Ebie Blume, and a few others. By April the Warrens were able to go to lunch at the Erskines' in Westport, and a few months later, after the Erskines returned the visit, Warren wrote, "Albert, it revived so much for me when you quoted those great passages of poetry." As his physical activities dwindled, memory played an increasing part. One Sunday he wrote Rosanna, "One of the very first thoughts I had this morning as I woke up was a need to write you. 'Need'—just my deep wish to say to you—that today is the 35th anniversary of the beginning of my great happiness—my constant happiness." It was April 11, the date when he had moved into Eleanor's walk-up apartment in New York.[3]

His memoir of his father appeared as a thirty-page essay in *The Southern Review* entitled "Portrait of a Father," to be reprinted as a book the next year. The rambling, loving, anecdotal recollection began, "My father, as the years since his death pass, becomes to me more and more a man of mystery." He was a man who "had sealed off the past, his own past." There are vivid intermittent vignettes of his life and its uncertain impact on his son, as there are sketches of his Vanderbilt father-surrogate, John Crowe Ransom. At the end his father is still an enigma, dead of the same disease from which his son now suffers. In his persistent obsession—having written a poem about his new granddaughter's discovering eventually "the curse, and blessing, of her own identity"—he muses on his father's identity and his "crazy pride," which dictated the concealment of his own imminent death. Warren was once again trying unsuccessfully to understand the man whose enigmatic personality—paired with the dominating personality of the mother—had shaped him.[4]

Another book would come out that July: *A Robert Penn Warren Reader,* the selections made by Erskine and approved by the author. It presented a five-hundred-page sampling of his fiction, nonfiction, and poetry from more than a half-century's work. The editor's note was graceful and affectionate. Warren supplied material for the dust jacket, full of details about the author's education, his work, his honors, and his family. With amusement Albert would note the number of poems that used the word *fame,* and then, with a smile, quote Milton's *Lycidas:* "Fame is the spur that the clear spirit doth raise / (That last infirmity of noble mind). . . ."[5]

Sitting in his beach chair, the wind shivering the leaves above his tree-house study, Warren wondered about his body, about what was happening to him, as month by month the strength seemed to drain away. He appreciated the expert and compassionate care, as when James Kenney wrote "to reassure you that blood chemistries and blood counts were virtually all normal. It would be intellectually comforting to report a specific disease which explains your symptoms. It is emotionally more comforting to be able to tell you that no such disorder can be discovered." But day by day he felt worse and worse.[6]

His public image remained clearly visible. In the early spring, fifteen established poets with fifteen younger poets in tow marked the end of his term as Poet Laureate. He could not be present for the occasion or for that of his National Medal of Arts. Western Kentucky University decided to buy what would be called the Robert Penn Warren birthplace with the intention of moving it to the Bowling Green campus, fifty miles away, to serve as a center for Robert Penn Warren studies. His response to this plan, to intimate friends, was simple: "Jesus Christ!" In August there was a group visit. "Hell is about to pop here," he wrote Bid Brown from Vermont. "Russian 'critics' who are in the USA for two literary conferences. They and their American keepers. . . . Ten guests altogether—not all sleeping here (just four, I think). Then, thank God, Rosanna and the two babies for a couple of weeks."[7]

Time dragged during the infrequent intervals between guests. But "I spend hours a day reading Dante. Inferno now. I do the Italian [aloud] to myself, then play back my tape of Rosanna reading the same canto. This is a wonderful way of getting [it] right." He told Rosanna, "Dante keeps me from being bored with myself." For years the days had not been long enough for all the writing he wanted to do. Now this anodyne was gone. When his former student Dave Quammen drove up to Fairfield in October, Warren seemed weak but very cheerful. It was a spectacular fall day with the maples in gorgeous color, and they sat for a while in the backyard sipping sherry until Warren said he was getting cold. (Increasingly he would suffer abrupt temperature changes, putting on and taking off his thick sheepskin vest.) After lunch they talked for three hours, the Warrens fascinated by Dave's recent trip to the central Amazon. At last Dave said he did not want to keep them from their work. They both told him that was no longer a consideration. When Dave asked Warren if he was writing any poetry, he replied that occasionally he would put down a few lines on a pad, but that was all. "I haven't written a poem in two years." Sitting straight in his chair he said, with what seemed to Dave a sort of proud resignation, "It's over . . . and I'm glad." Then he amended those last words to "I'm relieved." An hour later, when he slowly walked Dave to his car, he said, "Come back. *Soon*."[8]

.   .   .

Though he was still able, in midwinter of 1988, to start his day with more than a hundred knee squats and then to walk a mile or more in the afternoon, he was subject to sudden feelings of weakness and dizziness and increasing short-term memory loss. His doctors began to worry about the central nervous system, but most of the neurological tests were normal, and so far the bone scans and X rays showed no marked advance of the cancer. Tests had recorded essentially normal pulmonary function, but he complained of shortness of breath, and so he was supplied with oxygen equipment, which worried Eleanor because it cost three hundred dollars a month and Medicare would not reimburse them. (The pulmonary specialist told the primary physicians that "the symptoms far exceed the objective findings.") Warren commiserated with Bid Brown, just home from the hospital. "All I want now is to get rid of this damned hose of oxygen." But then, suddenly, he had to deal with it—hose, cylinder, controls, and all—for the most part by himself.[9]

In June, grieving over the death of her sister in April, Eleanor entered the hospital with a detached retina. Rosanna came with Katherine and Chiara. Warren was shaken with alarm, terror, and grief. Their emotional spaniel, Nino, was almost as frantic as his master. In panic Warren would ask Rosanna over and over, "Where is she?" Rosanna would try to reassure him and distract him with questions. "How did you meet Ma?" she asked. And he told Rosanna how he had met her at lunch with Allen Tate, how ravishing she looked, and how he was afraid to talk to her, thinking she was Allen's girl. Rosanna would drive all of them to the hospital to visit Eleanor, supporting her unsteady father and holding the hand of Chiara, not yet quite three.

"When Ma came home," Rosanna remembered, "it was a classic scene: She was scolding him for using the oxygen nozzle wrong, and he was delighted. He was so happy to be scolded. He and Nino settled down." Eleanor took control with a vengeance. "She seemed to order our lives, what we would eat, how we would eat, when we would wash, all of it." Rosanna had been used to scenes over the years—tirades and the furious firing of servants. But as Eleanor extended her authority into other areas of her husband's life, he became bitterly resentful. Their friends were distressed but powerless. But the family managed somehow to accommodate, and Eleanor was blessed with the friendship of Deanna Hoffman, who had a genius for dealing tactfully with her increasingly dependent, near-blind friend.[10]

In spite of all, they made the annual trip to Vermont. Warren told Arnold Stein of "the joy of Rosanna and her little barbarians" in their Vermont isolation. "Needless to say, there is adequate beauty all over the house—including the mother and grandmother. . . . Rosanna is at my side, writing this letter at my dictation." As always, he thought proudly of his son. "He telephoned from up on the St. Lawrence River that he was sailing down," he wrote Bid Brown on their return to Fairfield. "But no word in a long time. One thing often in my mind—the fact that Gabriel is so often doing things I, as a boy, dreamed about doing. For instance, the sea stuff. . . . How much of life is accident. I still want to be an admiral of the war of 1942." If, as he said more than once, he felt he had somehow stolen the poetic career his father had wanted, he was finding vicarious fulfillment, and perhaps atonement, in his son's achieving things he had wanted for himself.[11]

The days dwindled down with the darkness of autumn. "Nothing goes on here except the shift from day to night and back again," he wrote. "The field out my window has suddenly gone black. It was lit by the last sun a moment ago. But I must add that the shifts from day to night & back again bring their appropriate pleasures." In December he wrote a nostalgic letter about Minnesota days to Chickie Brown Stommel. "I think I'd like to visit old scenes. But now I think not. Not those scenes which have remained so real to me."[12]

Now there was more fatigue, pain, and anemia. In spite of it, Tom Byrne noted, "he remains very witty and insightful." But Tom feared that his patient had "modest advancing dementia." By early November he looked "somewhat pale and frail" to Dr. Lytton, and with the bone scans showing new activity, they ordered two sequences of radiation therapy to guard against pathological fracture and consequent spinal-cord compression and paralysis.

Francis Steegmuller and Shirley Hazzard came to them Christmas Day. Shirley sat with Warren at the far end of the large living room as the sky outside the window turned cobalt blue streaked by slender branches in the still, dead winter light. They looked out together at what seemed a painted scene. She felt that everything for him was intense, distilled to its essence. She thought of Hardy's "The Darkling Thrush" and intoned the lines "Winter's dregs made desolate / The Weakening eye of day." And he, without missing a beat, took up the next line: "The tangled bine-stems scored the sky / Like strings from broken lyres. . . ." But the mood changed at dinner as she sat beside him. He looked down the long table and said, "All the faces of love to see." Shirley said, *"Troppo bello."* Warren said, "No, it can never be too beautiful."[13]

The new year came in. A long time before, writing Allen Tate about a friend whose dying had been prolonged, Warren had said, "I hope I won't linger." But that was what had been reserved for him.

54

❖

Leaf Falling

We live in time so little time
And we learn all so painfully,
That we may spare this hour's term
To practice for eternity.
— *"Bearded Oaks"*[1]

There would be one last book in this new year of 1989. For years Albert Erskine had been keeping a file for a new collection of Warren's
essays. Now he put together four groups, which would total a little
more than four hundred pages. The first and last comprised theoretical
essays that had helped to make his reputation as a critic. In the second
section were his masterful essays on Hawthorne, Twain, Conrad, Hemingway, and Faulkner. In the third came those on the poets: Melville,
Whittier, Frost, and Ransom. These were the artists for whom he had
the profoundest respect (even for the unlikely Whittier), and for some
a sense of aesthetic and even emotional kinship. In Vermont he had
drafted an introduction, but at bottom he felt that the essays should
speak for themselves. In the end he was completely dissatisfied with his
draft, and *New and Selected Essays* was published without an introduction. So they stood by themselves, exemplars of his scrupulous scholarship, critical integrity, and elegant prose. The gifts that had helped to
make *Understanding Poetry* the best and most influential book of its kind
were here displayed in their magisterial range.

At home in Fairfield he would sit in his big chair by the window
with a volume of poetry in his lap or on the floor beside him, the

oxygen cylinder not far away. He would wear jeans and his favorite heavy hunting shirts, and over them the sheepskin vest. Though he would yield to Eleanor's urging that he take his cane and go for a brief walk each morning, it was usually a slow and halting process. He and Eleanor would hold each other's arms, Nino barking and cavorting beside them as best he could on the leash Eleanor held tightly. Inside the house too his gait was slow and uncertain. They were back in their upstairs bedroom, and to ascend the stairs he had first to grasp the stout floor-to-ceiling beam in a full-armed embrace as he moved onto the first step, where he could hold tight to the railing. In spite of his medication this was still a painful process, which brought involuntary explosive cries from his throat.

His correspondence had gradually diminished to short scrawled notes—principally loving letters to Rosanna. But now he wrote even fewer of them, and his days were taken up principally with reading. He enjoyed company, especially dinner guests, and the occasional trip to see close friends such as the Erskines. He was still a genial and witty host, but his speech was now more difficult to understand, and often he would repeat something he had said a short time before. Tom Byrne came from New Haven with increasing frequency. It was hard to know Warren's weight, for he could not support himself, but it could not have been much more than 120 pounds. He was treated for his vitamin B-12 deficiency, but he was eating less, and favorite dishes no longer appealed to him. Dr. Kenney was concerned over his episodes of falling and motor dysfunction, which suggested intermittent ischemic attacks constricting cerebral blood flow. In late February a magnetic-resonance brain scan showed signs of hemorrhages. There was also evidence of cerebral atrophy and possibly atrophy of the brain stem as well. It was what they feared, diffuse brain dysfunction from small strokes, which affected memory and gross motor motion as well. But the radiation therapy, which continued into April, had countered Tom Byrne's fear of spinal-cord compression and resultant paralysis. The family did not know how much time he had left, but they decided to make their annual trip to Vermont as soon as they could.

There they settled into their summer routine as his weakness increased. A childhood friend of Tom's, Dr. Bill Sergeant, arranged for blood transfusions, and Warren stayed overnight in Bennington for two of them. After a third one he showed improvement, and when the children came he was able to enjoy them. To Tom he was a wonderful patient, "willing to put his life in my hands." In spite of the fact that he saw little point in living when he could no longer work, he was still fascinated by what other people were doing with their lives, and his conversation showed the old concern about them. Rosanna knew how, deep down, he grieved at the cessation of his work, but he also seemed to her a great stoic, and she thought that in his father's death he had a model for his own dignity and courage. But he did not imitate his father's concealment. One day in early August, sitting at the long table in the kitchen, he said, quite simply, "I'm dying." Around the corner at the sink Eleanor said, "What did you say?" And he repeated the words very calmly. "Don't be ridiculous," she said. "Of course you're not dying." He replied, "I am dying." Eleanor said, "Well, we're all dying," and that was the end of the conversation.[2]

Sometimes he and Tom talked at length. Warren was not afraid of the progress of his disease or of dying. He had even said that he wanted a stone with his name on it in the family plot in Guthrie. He talked too about a cemetery down the road from their house, near Stubb Sampson's place. When Tom told Warren he was awed by what he had accomplished, he replied, "It's nothing. What counts are family and friends." He never suggested that he thought there was anything beyond the grave, any possibility of personal survival. When Tom asked him directly if he believed, he simply said, "No." He was not dogmatic. He respected the beliefs of others such as Cleanth Brooks in the existence of a personal God. He said his lack of belief might just be a deficiency like his inability to enjoy music. He continued to take joy in his family, who knew that his life was ebbing away in the golden Vermont September. He took joy in them and the world around him. To Tom he seemed a figure of contradictions, his achievements on the one hand and his directness, almost simplicity, on the other. It seemed to Tom that he was able "to fuse things. And I think that's why people loved him so much. There was such a thrill being around him, as he looked at a tree and watched the leaf come down from it, and I thought to myself how it meant so much to Red to have leaves fall from a tree. That was a metaphor for so much. . . ."[3]

Tom would remember his kindness. Rosanna recalled one of the many instances. Steve was there with her, and one rainy evening toward nightfall he answered a knock at the door. A woodcutter had skidded on a curve, and his truck slid into a ditch. He and his helper had walked to the house, and the woodcutter asked to use the telephone. When Steve asked them in, Warren greeted them and invited the helper, a young man in his twenties, to come and sit with him by the fire. Warren gave him his total attention and soon put him at ease. After a while, anticipating the end of the phone call, the helper said, "Well, we'll see you next year." Warren replied, "No, you won't see me next year," and when the boy asked why, he explained quite simply. After hesitation, the boy told him that his mother was in a nursing home with terminal cancer. Warren asked him about her. Before long the visitor went on his way, warmed by the fire and Warren's solicitude.

At times his sense of humor returned in flashes, sometimes in improbable circumstances. Earlier he had been troubled with incontinence. But now, as he took less and less nourishment, bodily functions began to diminish and shut down. But still he would be helped to the bathroom from time to time, and—in the poignant role reversal life sometimes brings—it would be Rosanna who was the helper and encourager. On one successful trip, when she expressed her pleasure for him, he looked up at her with his old, wry grin and said, "Everything I do is blessed."[4]

Tom was preparing them. The energy demands of the cancer, the caloric requirements of the encroaching, enveloping organism, increased to such an extent that he could not support them. It grew by consuming him. And so the process advanced, day by day: cachexia, as the chemicals and waste products of the cancer cells not only suppressed appetite but also redistributed body proteins away from muscle tissue. They inhibited the normal function of heart, brain, and kidneys, causing the general sense of fatigue that gave him the overpowering sense of "deliquescence." Then one day, as Tom was ready to say good-bye, he stood there looking at Warren in his big yellow chair by the fireplace. "He gave me that big smile," Tom would remember. "He looked so frail I just knew I'd never see him again."[5]

He was receiving small doses of morphine, and it was increasingly difficult to move him about and care for him. Deanna Hoffman and John Scully, Steve's brother, came up to help. They had determined they would stay until the end, to deal not only with the illness but also with the strain growing daily heavier on Eleanor, taxing her resources and sometimes producing spasms of impotent rage. In the years since Rosanna's marriage Warren had enjoyed John's company and helped him with his poetry. Now John sat with him as he dreamed and dozed in his chair, rousing from time to time. Rosanna remembered that on one of these days her father dreamed that he was surrounded

by old friends. Cleanth and Vann Woodward came to see him, bringing a copy of Vann's new book with an essay in it on the role of history in Warren's work. Vann read it to him, and later Warren asked
Tom and Deanna to read it to him again. Gabriel was on his way
there, and they told Warren that Ana had given birth to a son, and
that they would name him Noah Penn Warren. He smiled, and they
knew that he had understood.

On a Sunday evening early in September, while he was sitting on
the porch with John in the sunset, he roused and asked him to read
him some poems. He wanted to hear Hardy, and John read "The
Oxen," "Channel Firing," and "The Darkling Thrush." Then John
read Yeats: "The Second Coming" and "The Wild Swans at Coole."
When he read Rosanna's "Painting a Madonna," Warren's face broke
into a beatific smile. A few days later when Albert called, he asked
Rosanna if she had read "Bearded Oaks" to her father. When
Rosanna told him that Albert had called, he said, "Albert," but no
more. The only other words she heard him say as night drew on and
he drifted toward coma were "pain" and "help me." Only now and
then came a glimmer of recognition.[6]

It was Thursday, the fourteenth, and Eleanor slept in the twin bed
opposite his while Rosanna lay on a mattress on the floor between
them so that she could hold his hand. She dozed off, and when she
woke at about one-thirty in the morning he had stopped breathing.

But his daughter's memory of those days would not be dominated
by the brute fact of death.

> Two days before
>
> you died, we saw your death
> funneling in at the eye, your pupil fixed,
> tiny, waking neither
> to light nor to shade
>
> so that your wisdom drained
> inward where only reverberations of our
> voices fathomed:
>
> yet you held us still
> kindly, having foreknown
> the sere flame tasseling
> the roof beam, the palace wall

sinking but invisible
to the chorus; and in the teeth
of our denial
had already greeted

the strange man you alone
saw loitering by the porch,
had wrenched up your
emaciated smile: "Come in! Come in!"[7]

In the center of nearby Stratton, standing above three other frame structures is the old white church, plain and unpretentious, without a steeple and seldom used. There in the early afternoon of Sunday, October 8, family and friends gathered. It was a brief service without a clergyman—first "Jesu, Joy of Man's Desiring" in Carver Blanchard's pure light tenor accompanied by his guitar and Bill Crofut's muted banjo in the cold air of the sparse sanctuary. Then came brief reminiscences from Cleanth, Albert, and Vann, then from Ralph Ellison, Saul Bellow, and Tommie Lou Frey. Next were the voices of four other friends reading poems—one of them his own "Grackles, Goodbye!" The last of Cleanth's brief readings from the Book of Common Prayer died away on the still air: "Then shall be brought to pass the saying that is written, Death is swallowed up in victory."

The procession of cars stopped not far away on the narrow muddy road leading to the graveyard, undisturbed for a hundred years now. In the chill afternoon under gray lowering skies the mourners made their way up the gradual slope to a knoll and a clearing circled by the maples and the oaks and the flat narrow old stones with the names near-obscured by the mosses and stains and the deciduation of the years. When all stood silent in a large circle, Cleanth intoned short lines on the brevity of human life from the Liturgy for the Burial of the Dead. John Hollander read "Bearded Oaks." Lute in hand, Carver stepped forward and lifted his voice in the strains of "Abide with Me." When they died away, Eleanor took the small marble urn of ashes and placed it in the excavation in the greensward. Then, taking up a handful of the dark moist earth, she sifted it down onto the urn. The children followed her, and then the others. As the clouds darkened, the first light sifting of snow began to drift through the branches and onto the clearing and down upon the obscured urn. All slowly departed, leaving the scene to the encroaching night.

Notes

Books by Warren

Published by Random House, New York, unless otherwise noted.

A   *Audubon: A Vision.* 1969.

AHG   *At Heaven's Gate.* New York: Harcourt, Brace and Company, 1943.

AKM   *All the King's Men.* New York: Harcourt, Brace and Company, 1946.

ALMM   *American Literature: The Makers and the Making,* with Cleanth Brooks and R.W.B. Lewis. New York: St. Martin's Press, 1973.

BA   *Band of Angels.* 1955.

BD   *Brother to Dragons: A Tale in Verse and Voices.* 1953.

BD(nv)   *Brother to Dragons: A New Version.* 1979.

BH   *Being Here.* 1980.

BW   *Blackberry Winter.* Cummington, Mass.: Cummington Press, 1946.

CA   *The Circus in the Attic and Other Stories.* New York: Harcourt, Brace and Company, 1947.

Cave   *The Cave.* 1959.

CJ   *Chief Joseph of the Nez Perce.* 1983.

EP   *Eleven Poems on the Same Theme.* Norfolk, Conn.: New Directions, 1942.

F   *Flood.* 1964.

HTD   *Homage to Theodore Dreiser: August 27, 1871–December 28, 1945, on the Centennial of His Birth.* 1971.

I   *Incarnations.* 1968.

JB   *John Brown: The Making of a Martyr.* New York: Payson & Clarke Ltd., 1929.

JD   *Jefferson Davis Gets His Citizenship Back.* Lexington: University of Kentucky Press, 1980.

JGWP   *John Greenleaf Whittier's Poetry.* Minneapolis: University of Minnesota Press, 1971.

LCW   *The Legacy of the Civil War: Meditations on the Centennial.* 1961.

MMGG   *Meet Me in the Green Glen.* 1971.

NR   *Night Rider.* Boston: Houghton Mifflin Company, 1939.

NSE   *New and Selected Essays.* 1989.

NSP   *New and Selected Poems:*
        1923–1985. 1985.

NT   *Now and Then: Poems*
        1976–1978. 1978.

OEP   *Or Else: Poem/Poems*
        1968–1974. 1974.

P   *Promises: Poems 1954–1956.*
        1957.

PTCT   *A Place to Come To.* 1977.

PF   *Portrait of a Father.* Lexington:
        University of Kentucky Press,
        1988, and *SoR,* n.s., 23 (Winter
        1987), pp. 33–67.

RPWR   *A Robert Penn Warren Reader.*
        1987.

RV   *Rumor Verified: Poems*
        1979–1980. 1981.

SE   *Selected Essays.* 1958.

Seg   *Segregation: The Inner Conflict in*
        the South. 1956.

SP   *Selected Poems: 1923–1943.*
        New York: Harcourt, Brace
        and Company, 1944.

SPNO   *Selected Poems: New and Old*
        1923–1966. 1966.

SPHM   *Selected Poems of Herman*
        Melville. 1970.

SP75   *Selected Poems: 1923–1975.*
        1977.

TSP   *Thirty-six Poems.* New York:
        Alcestis Press, 1935.

UP★   *Understanding Poetry,* with
        Cleanth Brooks. New York:
        Henry Holt and Company,
        1938, 1950.

W   *Wilderness: A Tale of the Civil*
        War. 1961.

WET   *World Enough and Time.* 1949.

WSN?   *Who Speaks for the Negro?* 1965.

YEO   *You, Emperors, and Others: Poems*
        1957–1960. 1960.

SELECTED BIBLIOGRAPHY
OF WORKS CITED

"A Note"   Robert Penn Warren. "A
        Note to *All the King's Men.*"

★ For other textbooks see JAG, *Bibliography.*

        SR 61 (Summer 1953),
        pp. 476–80.

Achievement   Justus, James H. *The*
        Achievement of Robert Penn War-
        ren. Baton Rouge: Louisiana
        State University Press, 1981.

Berkeley Campus   Stewart, George R.
        The Department of English of the
        University of California on the
        Berkeley Campus. Berkeley,
        Calif. n.p., 1968.

Bedient   Bedient, Calvin. *In the Heart's*
        Last Kingdom: Robert Penn War-
        ren's Major Poetry. Cambridge,
        Mass.: Harvard University Press,
        1984.

Bibliography   Grimshaw, James A., Jr.
        Robert Penn Warren: A Descriptive
        Bibliography. Charlottesville: Uni-
        versity of Virginia Press, 1981.

Bloom   Bloom, Harold, ed. *Robert Penn*
        Warren. New York: Chelsea,
        1986.

Bohner   Bohner, Charles. *Robert Penn*
        Warren (rev. ed.). Boston:
        Twayne, 1981.

Braided Dream   Runyon, Randolph Paul.
        The Braided Dream: Robert Penn
        Warren's Late Poetry. Lexington:
        University of Kentucky Press,
        1990.

"Briar Patch"   Robert Penn Warren.
        "The Briar Patch," in *I'll Take*
        My Stand: The South and the
        Agrarian Tradition. New York:
        Harper Bros., 1930, reissued
        Baton Rouge: Louisiana State
        University Press, 1977.

Burden   Stewart, John L. *The Burden of*
        Time: The Fugitives and the
        Agrarians. Princeton, N.J.:
        Princeton University Press,
        1965.

Burt   Burt, John. *Robert Penn Warren and*
        American Idealism. New Haven:
        Yale University Press, 1988.

Casper   Casper, Leonard. *Robert Penn*
        Warren: The Dark and Bloody

Ground. Seattle: Washington University Press, 1960.

Clark   Clark, William Bedford. *The American Vision of Robert Penn Warren*. Lexington: University of Kentucky Press, 1991.

Connections   Waldron, Amy. *Close Connections: Caroline Gordon and the Southern Renaissance*. Knoxville: University of Tennessee Press, 1987.

Discussion   Grimshaw, James A., Jr., ed. *Robert Penn Warren's "Brother to Dragons: A New Version": A Discussion*. Baton Rouge: Louisiana State University Press, 1983.

Festschrift   Weeks, Dennis L., ed. *"To Love So Well the World": A Festschrift in Honor of Robert Penn Warren*. New York: Peter Lang, 1992.

Fugitive Group   Cowan, Louise. *The Fugitive Group: A Literary History*. Baton Rouge: Louisiana State University Press, 1959.

"Fugitive 1922–1925"   Tate, Allen. "The Fugitive 1922–1925: A Personal Record Twenty Years After." *Princeton University Library Chronicle*, 2 (April 1942), p. 82.

Fugitives   Rubin, Louis D., Jr. *The Wary Fugitives*. Baton Rouge: Louisiana State University Press, 1978.

Heilman   Heilman, Robert B. *The Southern Connection*. Baton Rouge: Louisiana State University Press, 1991.

Ivy   Conkin, Paul W. *Gone with the Ivy: A Biography of Vanderbilt University*. Knoxville: University of Tennessee Press, 1985.

KAP Letters   Bailey, Isabel, ed. *Letters of Katherine Anne Porter*. New York: Atlantic Monthly Press, 1990.

Literary Correspondence   Fain, John Tyree, and Young, Thomas Daniel, eds. *The Literary Correspondence of Donald Davidson and Allen Tate*. Athens: University of Georgia Press, 1974.

Longley   Longley, John L., Jr., ed. *Robert Penn Warren: A Collection of Critical Essays*. New York: New York University Press, 1965.

Lytle-Tate   Young, Thomas Daniel, and Sarcone, Elizabeth, eds. *The Lytle-Tate Letters: The Correspondence of Andrew Lytle and Allen Tate*. Jackson: University of Mississippi Press, 1987.

Makowsky   Makowsky, Veronica A. *Caroline Gordon*. New York: Oxford University Press, 1989.

Mandarins   Wood, Sally, ed. *The Southern Mandarins: Letters of Caroline Gordon to Sally Wood, 1923–1937*. Baton Rouge: Louisiana State University Press, 1984.

"Matrix"   Robert Penn Warren, "*All the King's Men*: The Matrix of Experience." *YR*, 53 (Winter 1964), pp. 161–67 (repr. in Longley, pp. 75–81).

"Melpomene"   Heilman, Robert B. "Melpomene as Wallflower; or, the Reading of Tragedy." *SR*, 55 (Jan.–March 1947), pp. 154–66.

Memoirs   Tate, Allen. *Memoirs and Opinions: 1926–1974*. Chicago: Swallow, 1975.

Millichap   Millichap, Joseph R. *Robert Penn Warren: A Study of the Short Fiction*. New York: Twayne, 1992.

Nakadate   Nakadate, Neil, ed. *Robert Penn Warren: Critical Perspectives*. Lexington: University of Kentucky Press, 1981.

Owsley   Owsley, Harriet. *Frank Lawrence Owsley: Historian of the Old South*. Nashville: Vanderbilt University Press, 1990.

Parnassus   Cutrer, Thomas. *Parnassus on the Mississippi*. Baton Rouge: Louisiana State University Press, 1984.

Poetic Vision   Strandberg, Victor. *The Poetic Vision of Robert Penn Warren*.

Lexington: University of Kentucky Press, 1977.

Possibilities Simpson, Lewis P., ed. *The
Possibilities of Order: Cleanth
Brooks and His Work.* Baton
Rouge: Louisiana State Univer-
sity Press, 1976.

Reference Nakadate, Neil. *Robert Penn
Warren: A Reference Guide.*
Boston: G. K. Hall, 1977.

"Reminiscence" Robert Penn Warren,
"A Reminiscence." Egerton,
John, ed. *Nashville: The Face of
Two Centuries.* Nashville:
MediaPlus, 1979.

RPWOHP Robert Penn Warren oral
history project, unpublished interviews with Robert Penn
Warren carried out by the University of Kentucky Libraries.

Ruppersburg Ruppersburg, Hugh R.
*Robert Penn Warren and the
American Imagination.* Athens:
University of Georgia Press,
1990.

Snipes Snipes, Katherine. *Robert Penn
Warren.* New York: Frederick
Ungar, 1983.

"*Southern Review*" Simpson, Lewis P.,
Olney, James, and Gulledge, Jo,
eds. *The "Southern Review" and
Modern Literature: 1935–1985.*
Baton Rouge: Louisiana State
University Press, 1988.

Taciturn Text Runyon, Randolph Paul.
*The Taciturn Text: The Fiction of
Robert Penn Warren.* Columbus:
Ohio State University Press,
1990.

Talent Strauss, Helen M. *A Talent for
Luck: An Autobiography.* New
York: Random House, 1979.

TN Watkins, Floyd. *Then & Now: The
Personal Past in the Poetry of
Robert Penn Warren.* Lexington:
University of Kentucky Press,
1982.

TwRPW Watkins, Floyd C., Hiers, John
T., and Weaks, Mary Louise,

eds. *Talking with Robert Penn
Warren.* Athens: University of
Georgia Press, 1990.

Walker Walker, Marshall. *Robert Penn
Warren: A Vision Earned.* New
York: Barnes & Noble, 1979.

Web of Being Guttenberg, Barnett. *Web
of Being: The Novels of Robert
Penn Warren.* Nashville: Vanderbilt University Press, 1975.

Winchell Winchell, Mark Royden.
*Cleanth Brooks and the Rise of
Modern Criticism.* Char-
lottesville: University Press of
Virginia, 1996.

Persons

AE	Albert Erskine
AL	Andrew Lytle
AS	Arnold Stein
AT	Allen Tate
BBC	Brainerd B. Cheney
CB	Cleanth Brooks
CBW	Emma Cinina Brescia Warren
CG	Caroline Gordon
CHF	Charles H. Foster
CTW	Celeste T. Wright
DD	Donald Davidson
EB	Elizabeth W. Brown
ECW	Eleanor Clark Warren
ED	Edward Davison
ES	Elizabeth Stommel
FB	Frederick Bracher
FMF	Ford Madox Ford
FNC	Frances N. Cheney
FO	Frank Owsley
FS	Francis Steegmuller
FW	Floyd Watkins
GPW	Gabriel Penn Warren
HB	Huntington Brown
HO	Harriet Owsley
IOR	Ieda Ogborn Russell
JAG	James A. Grimshaw, Jr.
JB	Joseph Blotner
JCR	John Crowe Ransom
JDK	James D. Kenney, M.D.
JHJ	James H. Justus

JLS	John L. Stewart	*AmR*	*American Review*
JS	Jane Sullivan	*AtMo*	*Atlantic Monthly*
KAP	Katherine Anne Porter	*BMCN*	*Book-of-the-Month Club News*
LD	Lambert Davis	*BotOs*	*Botteghe Oscure*
LDR	Louis D. Rubin, Jr.	*CathW*	*Catholic World*
LL	Lyle Lanier	*ChScM*	*Christian Science Monitor*
LPS	Lewis P. Simpson	*DR*	*Daily Reveille*
MW	Marshall Walker	*Fug*	*The Fugitive*
MWB	Mary Warren Barber	*GaR*	*Georgia Review*
PD	Peter Davison	*HudR*	*Hudson Review*
PMP	Pier Marie Pasinetti	*KR*	*Kenyon Review*
RBH	Robert B. Heilman	*KyR*	*Kentucky Review*
RPW	Robert Penn Warren	*LJ*	*Library Journal*
RW	Rosanna Warren	*MissQ*	*Mississippi Quarterly*
RWBL	R.W.B. Lewis	*NRep*	*New Republic*
SH	Shirley Hazzard	*NY*	*New Yorker*
SW	Stuart Wright	*NYHTBR*	*New York Herald Tribune Book Review*
TGR	Thomas G. Rosenthal		
TLF	Tommie Louise Frey	*NYRB*	*New York Review of Books*
TNB	Thomas N. Byrne, M.D.	*NYT*	*New York Times*
VS	Victor Strandberg	*NYTBR*	*New York Times Book Review*
WF	William Ferris	*PR*	*Partisan Review*
WS	Walter Sullivan	*SatEP*	*Saturday Evening Post*
WTB	William T. Bandy	*SatR*	*Saturday Review*
		SoR	*Southern Review*
		SR	*Sewanee Review*
		SWR	*Southwest Review*

ORGANIZATIONS

		TLS	London *Times Literary Supplement*
JSGMF	John Simon Guggenheim Memorial Foundation	*VQR*	*Virginia Quarterly Review*
RH	Random House, Inc.	*YR*	*Yale Review*
LofC	Library of Congress		

DEPOSITORIES AND COLLECTIONS

OTHER

		LsuL	Louisiana State University Library
[ ]	interpolated note; probable date, illegible notation	LC	Library of Congress
I	Interview (unless otherwise noted, interviews were conducted by JB)	PUL	Princeton University Library Allen Tate Papers Archives of Henry Holt & Co. Caroline Gordon Papers
repr.	reprinted	RHL	Rhodes House Library, Oxford University
		UCal	University of California Library (Berkeley)

PERIODICALS AND SERIES

		UKyL	University of Kentucky Libraries
AL	*American Literature*		
AmPM	*American Poetry Magazine*	UMdL	University of Maryland Library
AmPR	*American Poetry Review*		

UMinnL University of Minnesota Library
USL University of the South Library, Sewanee
UTexL University of Texas Library Harry Ransom Humanities Research Center
UVaL University of Virginia Library
VUL Vanderbilt University Library The Jean and Alexander Heard Library
YUL Yale University Library Beinecke Rare Book and Manuscript Library

CHAPTER 1: THE PARENTS

1. *NSP,* p. 55.
2. *PF,* p. 46.
3. Hopkinsville *Kentuckyan,* 1 Apr. 1890, courtesy of FW.
4. *Local and National Poets of America,* p. 88. The editor, Thomas W. Herringshaw, was a compiler of many directories. See *PF,* pp. 33–35.
5. I: RPW. FW writes that Warren was uncertain whether his grandfather Warren died or simply became unable to support his family in his early fifties. *TN,* p. 50.
6. *PF,* p. 42; I: RPW.
7. William T. Turner, "The Homeland Heritage of a Poet Laureate," unpublished paper, pp. 8–9, courtesy of William T. Turner and Joy Bale Boone.
8. Rowan Claypool, "The Black Patch War," unpublished paper, pp. iii, 6–10, courtesy of Rowan Claypool and Joy Bale Boone. In the late fall large rectangles of fertile soil were cleared to make plant beds. Then, in late January or early February, they were burned to a depth of eight inches to kill weed and grass seeds and insects. Afterward the soil was turned and the tobacco seeds were buried in the beds and covered. In late spring the cleaning process was repeated to prepare crop beds for transplanting of the fragile young plants, which were carefully cultivated for the next two months.

9. See *TN,* p. 32; *Kentucky, A Guide to the Bluegrass State,* Federal Writers' Project of the WPA Administration for the State of Kentucky (New York: Hastings House, 1954), p. 321; I: Melba Smith, Mack Linebaugh.
10. *PF,* p. 10; RPWOHP, no. 10.
11. Turner, "Homeland Heritage," p. 9.

CHAPTER 2: THE CHILD

1. *BH,* pp. 3–4.
2. William T. Turner, "The Homeland Heritage of a Poet Laureate," unpublished paper, p. 10, courtesy of William T. Turner and Joy Bale Boone; *PF,* p. 39.
3. I: RPW.
4. There had been celebrities at the track. In 1868 the James brothers' first success came when they robbed the bank in Russellville, twenty miles northeast of Guthrie. Much later, after Jesse's demise, Frank James showed up one season as a starter at the track. I: Mack Linebaugh. *PF,* pp. 54–55; Rowan Claypool, "The Black Patch War," unpublished essay, p. 1, courtesy of Rowan Claypool and Joy Bale Boone.
5. *PF,* p. 11.
6. *PF,* p. 46; *TwRPW,* p. 302.
7. Courtesy of FW.
8. *TN,* p. 54.
9. *JD,* pp. 1–2, 6–7; I: RPW.
10. *JD,* pp. 3–5, 8–10; I: RPW.
11. Penn Family Genealogy, courtesy of ECW; see *TN,* pp. 26–29; I: RPW.
12. I: RPW; Penn Family Genealogy; *JD,* pp. 4–5; see *TN,* p. 17. Gabriel Thomas Penn's mother-in-law was Mexico Hayes Mitchell, probably named for a kinsman who served in the Mexican War.
13. I: Shelby Foote. Mary Mexico Penn may have erred in supplying this date for the wedding, though that seems unlikely, and she records the fact that her father served under Forrest until the war's end.

14. Martha Jane Stone, *The Warren Family of Trigg County* (Lexington, Ky., n.p., 1990), pp. 66–67, 129, 143.

15. Warren Family Genealogy, courtesy of FW; *PF,* pp. 16–17; see *TN,* pp. 17, 127.

16. I: RPW; Warren Family Genealogy; *PF,* p. 8; *TN,* p. 21.

17. *JD,* pp. 4–5; I: RPW; *PF,* pp. 50–51.

CHAPTER 3: GROWING YEARS

1. *NT,* p. 5.

2. I: RPW by GPW.

3. I: RPW by GPW.

4. I: RPW; see *TN,* p. 35; I: RPW by GPW.

5. I: RPW; Edwin Thomas Wood, "On Native Soil: A Talk with Robert Penn Warren," *MissQ,* 37 (Spring 1984), p. 183.

6. "Robert Penn Warren: A Hometown Symposium," Oct. 15–17, 1987, courtesy of Dept. of Languages and Literature, Austin Peay State University, Clarksville, Tenn.

7. I: RPW.

8. I: RPW; see *TN,* pp. 37–38.

9. I: RPW; see *TN,* p. 37.

10. I: RPW; *PF,* p. 31.

11. *PF,* p. 63; I: RPW.

12. *PF,* pp. 20–21.

13. I: RPW; see *TN,* pp. 36, 54.

14. I: RPW; RPWOHP, no. 15.

15. *PF,* p. 30.

16. I: RPW; *PF,* pp. 12–14.

17. I: RPW; *PF,* pp. 12–14.

18. *PF,* pp. 48–51.

19. *PF,* pp. 55, 68–69.

20. *PF,* p. 56; I: RPW.

CHAPTER 4: HUMILIATION, AMBITION, AND DESPAIR

1. I: RPW.

2. I: RPW by GPW; *TN,* pp. 32–33.

3. William White "brained a [carnival] hand with a tent peg. The carny would have murdered him no doubt. . . ." William was tried for murder and acquitted. See *TN,* p. 33; *PF,* p. 63.

4. I: RPW by GPW.

5. I: Emma Balee Alexander, MWB; *PF,* pp. 54–55, 64. I: Sara Finn Carneal, Virginia McClanahan Owens. One contemporary of RPW said that his mother went before the school board many times to complain of his treatment by the other boys. I: Eloise Hammill Carney. I: Evelyn Hooser, courtesy of FW; see *TN,* p. 52.

6. I: RPW by GPW; see *TN,* pp. 40–45; Millie Ball, "Still America's Dean of Letters," New Orleans *Times-Picayune,* 24 July 1983, Sec. 2, p. 8; I: Eloise Hammill Carney, Mack Linebaugh, notes courtesy of FW; I: Sara Finn Carneal.

7. Word of this episode and others—real and invented—circulated in Guthrie: he was hanged in a well; he was held by his feet and lowered headfirst into the pit of an outdoor privy. "That's a lie," he would later say. "That's a bare-faced lie. . . . This time somebody would have been dead." *TN,* pp. 42–44; I: Laurene Lannon, Mack Linebaugh.

8. Draft of "Reminiscence," p. 20, courtesy of John Egerton.

9. I: RPW by GPW.

10. I: MWB; *TwRPW,* pp. 26–28; Henry Thomas Buckle, *The History of Civilization in England* (London: Longmans Green & Co., 1902).

11. I: RPW by GPW. Warren's experience was curiously similar to that of another brilliant and precocious boy, a writer-to-be whose mind was passionately fixed on a career in a world he had never seen: Joseph Conrad.

12. I: RPW.

13. I: RPW by GPW; notes courtesy of FW.

14. I: RPW, RPW by GPW; Carll Tucker, "Creators on Creating: Robert Penn Warren," *SatR,* July 1981, p. 40; I: MWB; notes courtesy of FW.

15. I: RPW by GPW.

16. I: George Stewart Boone. Mary remembered that he wrote, or acted in, a play called *Parts of Speech*. He wrote one entitled *Dr. Good English and His Patient,* which was presented by the Senior Society, and published several pieces in a student magazine, *The Purple and Gold.* The editor wrote that his stories had "keen description, smooth development, and burning resolution." He also became secretary of the Senior Society. "Robert Penn Warren: A Hometown Symposium," Oct. 15–17, 1987, courtesy of Dept. of Languages and Literature, Austin Peay State University, Clarksville, Tenn.; RPW to Mary Brown, UMinnL.
17. I: MWB; George Barker, "Red Warren, Rebel in the Ivy League," Nashville *Tennessean Magazine,* 27 Dec. 1964, pp. 6–7.
18. I: RPW by GPW; notes courtesy of FW; I: RPW by WF, courtesy of WF.

CHAPTER 5: COLLEGE BOY

1. "Reminiscence," p. 20.
2. Courtesy of FW.
3. *Ivy,* pp. 217, 219.
4. Draft of "Reminiscence," courtesy of John Egerton; RPWOHP, no. 1; transcript courtesy of Vanderbilt University.
5. I: RPW by WF; *Fugitives,* pp. 16–17.
6. For one term paper he did a history of Guthrie, though the subject matter did not interest him much. Draft of "Reminiscence."
7. Born into a well-to-do Tennessee family, AL had been "the Model Cadet" at Sewanee Military Academy before studying in France. He was admitted to Exeter College, at Oxford, but left at the death of his grandfather. I: AL; AL, "A Tribute to Robert Penn Warren," *KyR,* II (1981), p. 15.
8. I: RPW; RPWOHP, no. 1. Except for a B in philosophy in the fall term of his junior year, all the rest of his grades at Vanderbilt would be A's.
9. I: RPW by GPW.

10. I: RPW; privately printed edition, Stuart Wright, 1980, courtesy of SW.
11. Davidson allowed the students to write imitations of authors instead of the usual biweekly critique. Transcript courtesy of VU; RPWOHP, no. 10; draft of "Reminiscence."
12. *Fugitives,* p. 144; I: RPW; "Reminiscence," p. 213; RPWOHP, no. 10.
13. *TwRPW,* pp. 180–81.
14. *TwRPW;* RPWOHP, no. 10; I: AL.
15. "*The Fugitive* 1922–1925," p. 82; I: RPW.
16. I: RPW; AT dated their meeting in Feb. 1923, "*The Fugitive* 1922–1925," pp. 81–82; RPW said he was "small but not feeble" and did not attain full growth until after his senior year.
17. "*The Fugitive* 1922–1925," p. 82; *TwRPW,* p. 359; RPWOHP, no. 15.
18. Draft of "Reminiscence"; RPWOHP, no. 10; *TwRPW,* p. 361; I: RPW; "Reminiscence," p. 208. His poems showed the attraction he felt in the work of Swinburne and the French Decadents. There was also a hint of Yeats together with echoes of Eliot and Pound. See *Burden,* pp. 431–33.
19. *Driftwood Flames,* p. 17; *TN,* pp. 40–41.
20. I: Mrs. Lyle Lanier; I: AL; I: RPW by GPW.
21. I: HO; I: RPW by GPW; "Reminiscence," pp. 212–13.
22. I: Mrs. Lyle Lanier; I: HO.
23. RPW to AT, "Friday" [late spring 1924]; RPW to AT [late May 1924], PUL.

CHAPTER 6: ONE OF THE GROUP

1. *Fug,* 3 (June 1924), p. 69.
2. RPW to DD, 15 Sept. 1923, VUL; *Bookman,* LVII (Aug. 1923), p. 686; *Fug,* 2 (Aug.–Sept. 1923), p. 106; AT to DD, 31 July 1923, as quoted in *Fugitive Group,* p. 128.
3. I: RPW; draft of "Reminiscence," courtesy of John Egerton; "Reminiscence," pp. 211, 220; *TwRPW,* p. 289; RPWOHP, no. 1.

4. *Fugitive Group*, p. 76; *Fugitives*, pp. 13–14; *Fugitive Group*, pp. 4–6; *Ivy*, p. 18; Elliott to Alec Stevenson, as quoted in *Fugitive Group*, p. 4.

5. *Fugitive Group*, pp. 18–20; *Fugitives*, p. 16; John Crowe Ransom, *Poems about God* (New York: Henry Holt, 1919), pp. vi–vii; *Fugitive Group*, p. 27.

6. "*The Fugitive 1922–1925*," pp. 75–79; see *Fugitive Group*, p. 44.

7. *Fugitive Group*, p. xv; *Fug*, 1 (Dec. 1922), p. 66, (Apr. 1922), p. 1; "The Fugitive," p. 79; *Fugitive Group*, p. 47.

8. *Fug*, 1 (Oct. 1922), p. 66; 1 (Dec. 1922), p. 97; "*The Fugitive 1922–1925*," p. 78.

9. "*The Fugitive 1922–1925*," p. 78.

10. I: Mrs. Lyle Lanier; LL to AT, 19 Apr. 1924, PUL.

11. LL to AT, 18 Mar. 1924, 19 Apr. 1924, PUL.

12. I: AL, HO; RPWOHP, no. 1; "Wild Oats," in *Driftwood Flames*, p. 17.

13. RPW to AT, 26 Mar. 1924, PUL.

14. RPW to AT, "Monday" [Apr.] 1924, PUL.

15. RPW to AT, "Tuesday Morning," "Saturday morning," PUL.

16. RPW to AT, "Tuesday Morning," "Saturday morning," PUL. RPW's return address was "The Unstilled Cyclades," islands around Delos including Naxos, where Bacchus wooed Ariadne.

17. RPW to AT, "Tuesday Morning," "Night of Black Friday"; LL to AT, 19 Apr. 1924; RPW to AT [May 1924], PUL.

18. RPW to AT, "Friday"; RPW to AT [May], PUL. The philosophy course for which RPW registered in the winter term of 1923–24 was apparently the one he referred to here as the psychology course. LL to AT, 6 May 1924; RPW to AT, "Friday"; RPW to AT [Spring 1924], PUL.

19. "Three Poems," *Fug*, 3 (Apr. 1924), pp. 54–55; AT to DD, 17 Apr. 1924, *Literary Correspondence*, p. 104.

20. RPW to AT [spring 1924], PUL.

21. I: RPW.

CHAPTER 7: *DE PROFUNDIS*

1. *Double Dealer*, 7 (Oct. 1924), p. 2.

2. Jesse Wills to AT, 22 May 1924; DD to AT [21 May 1924]. LL to AT, 24 May 1924, PUL.

3. Because none of this group of RPW's letters bears a date, it is difficult to determine the sequence of events precisely. I: RPW; DD to AT, 21 May 1924; JCR to AT, 30 May 1924; RPW to AT [May 1924], PUL.

4. I: RPW; BBC. When AT had asked RPW about the reaction of the albatross, he thought she had not been told. RPW to AT [May 1924], PUL; Ruth Warren to AT; erroneously designated by someone as June 1924, this letter was enclosed by RPW with his own letter dated May 1924, PUL.

5. RPW to AT, "Saturday Morning" [early spring 1924], PUL; "Friday" [late spring 1924]. "If these jobs do materialize you must come whatever may be your personal feelings in the matter; I have to have you here." "Friday" [late May 1924], PUL. "Your two delectable letters arrived simultaneously. . . ." "Wednesday" [May 1924]. He apologized for the delay in answering "your numberless and blessed notes. . . ." [early summer 1924], PUL; RPW to DD, "Thursday" [Aug. 1924], PUL; I: Barry Siegel, M.D.

6. Notes courtesy of FW; I: RPW; I: RPW by GPW.

7. I: RPW; Jesse Wills to AT, 22 May 1924, PUL; *TwRPW*, pp. 364–65; RPW to AT [late May 1924], PUL.

8. RPW to AT [late May 1924], PUL; RPW to AT [early summer 1924], PUL; RPW to DD [Monday 1924], VUL; I: RPW by GPW.

9. The Fugitives had voted to publish two of his sonnets about doomed love affairs plus a wry elegy in the Aug. number of the magazine. RPW to AT [early summer 1924], PUL. In each sonnet it was the lady who suffered, and the imagery was also new, with damp fern crushed by

satyr hoofs. *Double Dealer,* 6 (Aug.–Sept. 1924), pp. 191–92; *Double Dealer,* 7 (Oct. 1924); *Fug* 3 (Aug. 1924), pp. 117–18.

10. *TwRPW,* p. 364; RPW to AT [early summer 1924], PUL.

11. RPW to DD, "Thursday" [1924], VUL; AT to DD, 25 Aug. 1924, VUL.

12. CG taught high school for three years (the last of them in Clarksville just before RPW went there) and then worked for the Chattanooga *News* while writing fiction. There she published a history of The Fugitives on Feb. 10, 1923. Surveying little magazines in the South, it was headed, "U.S. Best Poets Here in Tennessee." RPW to DD, "Thursday" [1924], 8 July 1925, VUL; I: RPW; Makowsky, pp. 28–29, 37, 40, 41, 44, 59, 57.

13. AT to DD, 25 Aug. 1924, VUL.

14. RPW to DD, 30 Aug. 1924; RPW to WTB, 9 Sept. 1924, VUL.

15. For 1924–25 RPW registered for two more courses in philosophy, one in English and one in sociology, with another English course for the winter term and physiography (physical geography) in the winter and spring terms. He would earn A's in all of them. Courtesy of Vanderbilt University; I: CB, AL.

16. I: RPW; draft of "Reminiscence," courtesy John Egerton. Saville Clark enlisted in the marine corps and rose to the rank of brigadier general.

17. RPWOHP, no. 1; *TwRPW,* p. 287.

18. I: AL. At one time silver nitrate was widely used as an astringent for treating types of gastritis, especially stomach ulcers.

19. "Praises for Mrs. Dodd," *Fug,* 3 (Aug. 1924), p. 118; "Alf Burt, Tenant Farmer," *Fug,* 3 (Dec. 1924), p. 154.

20. RPWOHP, no. 1; RPW's academic record was comparable to JCR's: Phi Beta Kappa, summa cum laude, and Founder's Medalist.

21. RPW to AT, 11 July 1925, PUL; RPW to AL, "Friday" [26 June 1925], VUL; I: RPW.

22. AL to Mary Greaves Nelson, 6 July 1925, VUL.

23. RPW to AT, 11 July 1925, PUL; "Seventy-Five Years of American Literature: A Panel Discussion," ed. Mary Byrd Davis, *KyR,* II (1981), p. 48; RPWOHP, no. 10; I: RPW.

24. RPW to AT, 11 July 1925, PUL; the new poem was "August Revival: Crosby Junction," *SoR,* 33 (Oct.–Dec. 1925), p. 439.

25. "Easter Morning: Crosby Junction," *Fug,* 4 (June 1925). The other poems printed after this one were "Mr. Dodd's Son," "To a Face in the Crowd," and "The Wrestling Match." This last gives further evidence of his broadened scope, capturing the brutal energy like that in contemporary pictures such as George Bellows's *Stag at Sharkey's.*

26. "August Revival: Crosby Junction." *SoR,* 33 (Oct.–Dec. 1925), p. 439.

27. RPW to AT, 11 July 1925, PUL; RPW to DD, 8 July 1925, VUL.

28. I: RPW by GPW.

CHAPTER 8: THE CALIFORNIA
EXPERIENCE

1. *AmPR,* 8 (Jan.–Feb. 1979), p. 5; *BH,* p. 101.

2. RPW to AL, 8 Aug. 1925, VUL.

3. RPW to AL [14] Aug. 1925, VUL.

4. RPW found the courses he could take "satisfactory," RPW to DD, 21 Aug. 1925, VUL.

5. RPWOHP, no. 1, no. 10; IOR to JB; *The Occident,* 86 (Nov. 1925), p. 13.

6. DD to AL, 16 May 1926, courtesy of FW. Both RPW and AT had appropriated books before, including some from the Vanderbilt Library. AT to DD, 28 May 1926, courtesy of FW; I: AL.

7. AT to DD, 28 May 1926, courtesy of FW.

8. RPW to AT, 6 Feb. 1926, PUL. CG's Guthrie friends knew her as Carolyn.

9. RPW to Saville T. Clark, 17 and 18 May 1926, VUL.

10. During that second semester RPW took a special study seminar with Willard Farnham, an Elizabethan scholar whom he called the best of his teachers there. The other courses included Walter Hart's Chaucer, Guy Montgomery's satire, and *The Faerie Queene,* taught by Thomas Sanford, one of the last of the old guard.

11. Carolyn Anspacher would go on to a brief career acting in New York and working in a film-studio story department before taking a lifelong job with the *San Francisco Chronicle.* Also in the group were Ruth Witt-Diamant, who would later found San Francisco's Poetry Center, and Malvina Milder, later known as a composer and singer as Malvina Reynolds. CTW to JB; RPW to AL [spring 1926], VUL; *San Francisco Chronicle,* 28 Sept. 1979.

12. RPWOHP, no. 1; I: RPW; RPW to AT, 6 Feb. 1926, PUL. RPW told his colleague Bertrand Bronson, "I've just met the most wonderful girl in the world." I: RBH, RPWOHP. CBW's verses, entitled simply "Poems," suggest "a pastiche of several sensibilities popular in 1925: the Imagism of H.D. and Amy Lowell and Sara Teasdale mixed with the more modern practice of Carl Sandburg and Eliot." Laurence Goldstein to JB. Her two short essays were entitled "Music." One was on jazz and the other a defense of opera as an "art-form," both "musically knowledgeable and decently written for an undergraduate." William Albright to JB.

13. IOR to JB; I: AL, RPW.

14. RPW to AT [spring 1926], PUL; RPW to AL [1926], VUL.

15. RPW to AL [1926], VUL.

16. RPW to AT [spring 1926], PUL.

17. RPW to AT [spring 1926], PUL.

18. RPW to AT [spring 1926], PUL; IOR to JB.

19. RPW to AT [spring 1926], PUL.

20. RPW to AT [spring 1926], PUL.

21. RPW to AT [spring 1926], PUL.

22. RPW to AT [spring 1926], PUL; IOR to JB; RPW to Saville T. Clark, VUL; I: RPW, RPW by GPW.

23. I: RPW, RPW by GPW.

24. RPW to Saville T. Clark, VUL. RPW took a seminar in Elizabethan drama from Willard Farnham and a course in aesthetics from a bright young Stanford philosophy teacher named Harold Chapman Brown. Farnham, a "really lovable man and a fine scholar," took a special interest in him and invited him to his home. In the June–July summer session RPW took a course on Browning and his contemporaries. The departmental requirement for an M.A. thesis had been abolished about the time he arrived, but Professor Montgomery had thought his paper on satire was a potential doctoral dissertation. So did DD. RPW to AL [1926], VUL; RPW to DD, 2 July 1926, DD [1926], VUL.

25. RPW went back over his manuscript and wrote a critique of most of the eighteen poems, which revealed an aesthetic distance from them. It also showed, if in the familiarly enigmatic way, that he was trying to look more deeply, and more maturely, into his own psyche. RPW to AL [1926], VUL; RPW to DD, 2 July 1926; RPW to DD [1926], VUL; RPW to AT, 22 May 1926, PUL.

26. RPW to DD, 14 Sept. 1926, VUL; *Fug,* 4 (Dec. 1925), p. 125; RPW to DD, 14 Sept. 1926, VUL.

27. I: RPW by GPW; RPW to DD, 14 Sept. 1926, VUL; *Vacation,* unpublished novel courtesy of Jeffrey B. Russell.

28. He was taking only two courses, half the load of the previous semester: Anglo-Saxon from George A. Smithson and another seminar in Elizabethan drama from Farnham; FB to JB; I: RPW by GPW.

29. RPW to AT, 4 Apr. 1927, PUL.

30. RPW to AT, 4 Apr. 1927, PUL; FB to JB.

31. Domenico Brescia recorded and studied native music in Ecuador, Chile,

Peru, and Colombia. To one acquaintance, Peter Brescia resembled Rudolph Valentino though he was over six feet tall. He became an orchestral conductor like his father, and one musician friend remembered his slightly accented English and his fiery temperament. RPW to AT, 4 Apr. 1927, PUL; I: RPW; I: JS.

32. RPW to AT, 4 Apr. 1927, PUL.

33. "Pro Sua Vita," *NR,* 11 May 1927, p. 333. This poem was never reprinted. See *Burden,* p. 440. RPW to AT, 1 Apr. 1927, 4 Apr. 1927, PUL. "Croesus in Autumn," *SP,* p. 50.

34. *Fugitive Group,* p. 251; *Fugitives: An Anthology of Verse* (New York: Harcourt, Brace, 1928), pp. 153–60; AT to DD, 20 Jan. 1927, *Literary Correspondence,* p. 184.

35. I: RPW; RPW to AT, received 20 Apr. 1927, PUL; see Makowsky, pp. 62–65. Nineteen-month-old Nancy Sue Tate was living in Kentucky in the care of Mrs. Gordon while her parents pursued their literary careers in New York. "My own family will be tractable," RPW continued, "especially since my part of the business will not be floated from the fast dwindling coffers." The time would have to be between the first of July and the middle of August.

36. RPW to AT [spring 1927], PUL.

37. I: RPW by GPW; RPW to AT [spring 1927], PUL. RPW did not disclose who his arch enemy was, possibly Utter, who had taken his name off the list for assistantships at Raymond's request and then put it back at Montgomery's insistence. RPWOHP, no. 1; FB to JB; *TwRPW,* p. 253.

38. RPW to AT, 4 Apr. 1927; RPW to AT [spring 1927], PUL.

CHAPTER 9: NEW YORK AND NEW HAVEN

1. *Fug,* 4 (June 1925), p. 33; *SP75,* p. 325.

2. RPW to AT, "Saturday Night" [June 1927], PUL.

3. RPW to AT, "Saturday Night" [June 1927], PUL.

4. RPW to AT, "Saturday Night" [June 1927], PUL.

5. RPW to AT, "Saturday Night" [June 1927], PUL; RPW to AT, "Tuesday Night" [summer 1927], PUL; RPW to WTB, undated, VUL. It seems likely that the insurance policy had been taken out by Robert F. Warren for his son in his childhood. If so, his signature might have been required on the loan application.

6. *Mandarins,* p. 36; see Makowsky, pp. 58–77.

7. See *Fugitives,* p. 99, and Makowksy, p. 72.

8. I: AL; Floyd Beatty and HO by JS; see *Mandarins,* pp. 33, 60.

9. I: RPW by GPW; RPW to Lewis A. Lawson, 13 May 1968, courtesy of LAL.

10. Makowsky, p. 58; Malcolm Cowley, *The Flower and the Leaf: A Contemporary Record of American Writing since 1941* (New York: Viking, 1985), p. 354; I: RPW by GPW.

11. RPW, "East—Paul Rosenfeld," *The Jewish Journal,* 9 Sept. 1931, pp. 6–7; RPW, "Paul Rosenfeld: Prompter of Fiction," *Commonweal,* 46 (15 Aug. 1947), pp. 424–26.

12. James G. Watson, ed., *Thinking of Home: William Faulkner's Letters to His Mother and Father, 1918–1925* (New York: W. W. Norton, 1991), pp. 141, 144.

13. See Brooks Mather Kelley, *Yale: A History* (New Haven: Yale University Press, 1974), pp. 370–71, 384, 389–90.

14. Like Willard Farnham at Berkeley, Tucker Brooke became a friend and mentor to Warren. He was taking a seminar in early Tudor poetry with John M. Berdan. His other two courses were "English Drama from Dryden to Goldsmith" with George Henry Nettleton and a special course in Old French with Robert James Menner, transcript courtesy of Yale University; AT to DD, 8 Oct. 1927, PUL; *Lytle-Tate* pp. xx, 5–6; I: AL.

15. Between Nov. and the following Sept. he would publish six reviews in *NRep.*

16. His paper dealt not only with Garrick's many roles but also with the whole London theatre milieu. Unpublished RPW essay, UKy. I am indebted to Prof. Ejner Jensen for his comments. RPWOHP, no. 1.

17. Her father had sent her first to Logan Female College. Later she transferred to Kentucky Wesleyan College, where she studied to become a high school teacher. At one point she was offered a fellowship for graduate study at the University of Virginia, but her father persuaded her not to accept it, out of some protective impulse, her brother thought. It was "an old-fashioned idea of a girl's education." Robert Warren later told his son, "I made a hideous mistake with your sister." RPW to DD [1928], VUL; RPWOHP, no. 10; I: MWB, RPW.

18. RPWOHP, no. 15.

19. I: RPW by GPW; I: AL.

20. RPW to AL, erroneously marked "2/12/26," VUL.

21. RPW to AL, erroneously marked "2/12/26," VUL; RPWOHP, no. 1.

22. In the completed sequence, with its imagery of death and echoes of Eliot, the land outlasts men, animals, and crops. See *Bibliography*, p. 185; *TN*, p. 70; *Fugitives*, p. 333; "Pondy Woods," *Second American Caravan*, ed. Alfred Kreymborg, PUL.

23. RPW to AT [spring 1928], PUL; see Makowsky, p. 77; *Fugitive Group*, pp. 255–56.

24. RPW to WTB [spring 1928]; AT to AL, 25 June 1928, *Lytle-Tate*, p. 9.

25. Winchell, p. 43; I: RPW; *TwRPW*, pp. 137, 149–50. Allen Tate's books on Stonewall Jackson and Jefferson Davis were part of a series published by Minton, Balch and Company. Tate had persuaded Earle Balch to encourage AL to do one on General Nathan Bedford Forrest. And for these writers, this was an opportunity for a truthful account of the great conflict, which had been seen primarily through the eyes of northern historians.

26. *Lytle-Tate*, pp. 10–11; I: AL.

27. The first part, which took Brown up to 1855 when he went to Kansas, was completely finished and revised. He was well into part II. Part III would be Harpers Ferry. "There has been a good deal more research than I anticipated," he wrote, "but most of that is behind me now." RPW to W. F. Payson, 8 Sept. 1928, PUL.

28. I: AL.

CHAPTER 10: A SOUTHERNER AT OXFORD

1. *NRep*, 27 Nov. 1929, p. 14; *SP*, p. 98. VS writes, "The most striking part of this poem is its conclusion, where Warren consigns his self-possessed friend into a hell especially designed for sophisticates. Here the suavely indifferent will encounter egotism enough to crush their own," but he does not suggest possible models for the friend. Victor Strandberg, *A Colder Fire: The Poetry of Robert Penn Warren* (Lexington: University of Kentucky Press, 1965), p. 63.

2. RPWOHP, no. 1; records courtesy of Dr. R. A. Fletcher, Rhodes House, Oxford; I: RPW.

3. RPW to AL, 18 Oct. 1928, VUL.

4. See *Memoirs*, p. 46; AT to AL, 28 Oct. 1928, *Lytle-Tate*, p. 13; see Makowsky, p. 79; RPW to AL, 18 Oct. 1928, VUL.

5. Lionel Charles Robbins, "The Mid-Twenties: An Economist's View," pp. 112, 1, 19, and Goronwy Rees, "Memories of New College," in *New College, Oxford: 1379–1979* (Oxford: New College, 1979), p. 121.

6. I: Herbert Woodman.

7. *Handbook to the University of Oxford* (Oxford: Oxford University Press, 1965), pp. 139, 158, 193–96; see also Winchell, pp. 58–61. AT to DD, 24 Oct. 1928, *Literary Correspondence*, p. 217.

8. RPW to AL, 18 Oct. 1928, VUL. Simpson's other works would include *Proof-Reading in the Sixteenth, Seventeenth, and Eighteenth Centuries.* I: CB, Robert H. Super, RPW, Herbert Woodman, Robert H. Martin.

9. I: RPW, Herbert Woodman.

10. RPWOHP, no. 1; I: RPW.

11. I: RPW; RPW to AL, 21 Oct. 1928, VUL. See Winchall, p. 11.

12. John Peale Bishop to AT, undated, PUL; see *Memoirs,* pp. 69–75.

13. Undated ts., RPW to unknown recipient, courtesy of Stephen Donato. RPW dates the incident "December 1928." AT supplies a different date in his description of the incident in *Opinions.* In the letter RPW writes, "If Tate is your authority it won't be the first time his memory got a bit garbled."

14. AT to AL, 21 Dec. 1928, *Lytle-Tate,* pp. 14–15; I: RPW.

15. RPW to AT, postmarked 22 Jan. 1929, PUL.

16. RPW was borrowing from A. E. Housman's poem "1887" for the line "myself I could not save." RPW to AT, 21 Mar. 1929, PUL.

17. RPW to AT, 25 Mar. 1929, PUL.

18. Rhodes reports courtesy of Rhodes House. A later warden of Rhodes House commented that the note "certainly suggests that he had breached some college rule or rules, but the phrase 'kicked out' could just be a rather slangy expression to acknowledge this. The move into digs may have been a compromise." Dr. R. A. Fletcher to JB. Herbert Woodman thought the phrase was just a flippant one RPW supplied when he decided to move into "digs." I: Herbert Woodman.

19. Apparently neither of the first two letters now exists; RPW to AT, 9 Apr. 1929, PUL.

20. Another congenial younger friend who lived in digs nearby was Lionel Handley-Derry, whose grand-uncle had been Gerard Manley Hopkins. A welcome poker participant was Francis "Pinky"

Hill, whose family's money came from South African diamond mines. I: Herbert Woodman, RPW, Lionel Handley-Derry.

21. "Vinegar Hill," *This Quarter,* 2 (Jan.–Feb. 1929), pp. 503–4; RPW to AT, 25 Mar., 9 Apr. 1929, PUL; AT to AL, 16 June 1929, *Lytle-Tate,* pp. 31–32.

22. AT to AL, 4 May 1929, 16 June 1929, *Lytle-Tate,* pp. 26–27, 31–32.

23. AT to AL, 13 May 1929, *Lytle-Tate,* p. 27; RPW to AT, "Wednesday" [1929], PUL.

24. RPW to AT, "Wednesday" [1929], PUL; RPW to AT, 13 May 1929, PUL; notes courtesy of Rhodes House.

CHAPTER 11: CONTRACTS—SECRET AND OTHERWISE

1. *NRep,* 15 Jan. 1930, p. 215; *SP75,* pp. 321–22.

2. RPW to AT [fall 1929], PUL; I: JS, HO.

3. I: RPW, AL.

4. I: JS, Floyd Beatty, RPW.

5. I: RPW. ECW used the word *pudeur* to describe RPW.

6. I: AL. Many years later Andrew Lytle would say he had been told that Cinina had had an affair during RPW's absence and that she thought she was pregnant that summer when he returned from Oxford. Later she showed Lytle a short story she had written about a young woman who thought she was pregnant and seduced another man so that he would marry her. Remembering what he had been told, Lytle concluded that the story was fictionalized autobiography. Tate believed as Lytle did. The Office of the State Registrar of Vital Statistics in Sacramento was unable to find a record of the marriage but informed JB that church marriages at that time did not require state licenses. Warren confided the fact of the first marriage to his longtime friend and editor, Albert Erskine, and also to JB.

7. RPW to AL, 17 Sept. 1929, VUL.

8. RPW to AL, 17 Sept. 1929, VUL.

9. AT to AL, 31 July 1929, *Lytle-Tate*, p. 34.

10. RPW to AT [fall 1929], PUL; I: RPW by GPW.

11. See Edmund Wilson, "The Tennessee Poets," *The Shores of Light: A Literary Chronicle of the Twenties* (New York: Farrar, Straus, 1952), pp. 191–96; RPW, "Kentucky Mountain Farm," *The American Caravan* (New York: Macaulay, 1927), p. 803; see RPW, "Paul Rosenfeld: Prompter of Fiction," *Commonweal* (15 Aug. 1947), p. 425.

12. RPW to AT [fall 1929], 2 Nov. 1929, PUL.

13. RPW to AT [Dec. 1929], PUL; I: CB.

14. RPW to AT [fall 1929], 2 Dec. 1929, PUL; I: WTB.

15. See *Connections*, pp. 74–75; "Tryst on Vinegar Hill," *This Quarter*, 2 (Jan.–Feb. 1930), p. 503; "Empire," *This Quarter*, 3 (July–Sept. 1930), pp. 168–69.

16. See *Connections*, p. 76; I: RPW; DD to AT, 26 Oct. 1929, *Literary Correspondence*, pp. 239, 240, 242, 246–47; see *Mandarins*, p. 49. They counted on AL; Mississippian Stark Young; Frank Owsley, an Alabama historian; and Dixon Wecter, admired by both RPW and AT and considered capable of writing on religion even though he was a Catholic.

17. *JB*, pp. 441–47, 106, 415, 401, 442, 428–29.

18. RPW to DD, 16 Feb. 1920, VUL; *Outlook*, 153 (13 Nov. 1929), p. 427; NY *Evening Post*, 19 Nov. 1929, p. 24; NY *World*, 1 Dec. 1929, p. 11; *NYT*, 12 Jan. 1930, p. 7; *Books*, 12 Jan. 1930, p. 17; Allan Nevins, *NRep*, 62 (19 Mar. 1930), p. 134; *YR*, 19 (Spring 1930), pp. 590–96; *Nation*, 131 (2 July 1930), p. 22; Winchell, p. 464, n. 16.

19. See Daniel Aaron, "The Meditations of Robert Penn Warren," in Bloom, p. 121; see *Fugitives*, p. 336; *JB*, p. 245; see Burt, pp. 21–30.

20. See Ruppersburg, pp. 24–26; *Fugitives*, p. 337; Bloom, p. 2; and Walker, p. 86.

CHAPTER 12: FICTION, FACTION, AND AN OXFORD DEGREE

1. *American Caravan IV*, eds. Alfred Kreymborg, Lewis Mumford, and Paul Rosenfeld (New York: Macaulay, 1931), pp. 3–61; repr. *RPWR*, p. 29.

2. RPWOHP, no. 1; I: RPW by WF.

3. RPWOHP, no. 1; I: RPW by WF; *TwRPW*, pp. 33, 158.

4. JCR to RPW, 20 Jan. 1930, YUL; RPW to DD, 16 Feb. 1930, VUL.

5. RPW to AT and CG, 19 May 1930, PUL; *TwRPW*, pp. 33, 159.

6. *ITMS*, pp. xxxvii–xlviv, 361–410. See *A Band of Prophets: The Vanderbilt Agrarians After Fifty Years*, eds. William C. Havard and Walter Sullivan (Baton Rouge: Louisiana University Press, 1982), p. 161.

7. *TwRPW*, p. 384.

8. *ITMS*, pp. 246–64; RPW to DD, 25 June 1930, VUL.

9. RPW to AT and CG, 19 May 1930, PUL; RPWOHP, no. 1; JAG to JB.

10. JAG to JB.

11. RPW to WTB, 11 June 1930, VUL.

12. RPW to WTB, 11 June 1930, VUL.

13. I am indebted to Professor Ejner Jensen for his comments on RPW's thesis.

14. I: CB.

CHAPTER 13: PROFESSOR WARREN AT SOUTHWESTERN

1. *VQR*, 12 (July 1936), p. 395, repr. *SP75*, pp. 307–8.

2. I: John Thaddeus Wills; wedding announcement courtesy of JTW; I: HO by JS; RPW to DD, 28 Apr. 1931, VUL.

3. I: RPW.

4. I: AE; *RPWR*, p. ii.

5. RPW to DD, 6 June 1930, VUL; DD to AT, 21 July 1930, PUL; LL to AT, 1

Aug. 1930, PUL; I: AL; AT to DD, 22 July 1930; DD to AT, 23 July 1930; DD to AT, "Saturday," PUL.

6. AT, "To the Contributors to the Southern Symposium," 24 July 1930, pp. 406–7; AT to DD, Sept. 1930, pp. 252–53; DD to AT, 5 Sept. 1930, pp. 253–54; DD and JCR to AT, RPW, and AL, 5 Sept. 1930, pp. 407–8, *Literary Correspondence*.

7. See *Fugitives*, p. 222.

8. Thomas Daniel Young and M. Thomas Inge, *Donald Davidson* (New York: Twayne, 1971), pp. 135–36; Paul K. Conkin, *The Southern Agrarians* (Knoxville: University of Tennessee Press, 1988), pp. 69–70; *TwRPW*, pp. 230–31.

9. RPW to DD, 16 Nov. 1930, VUL; RPW to Robert L. Frey and TLF, 10 Apr. 1985, courtesy of TLF; see *Connections*, pp. 81–85. The author is indebted to Hayden and Charlotte Jolly, the present owners, for a tour of Benfolly.

10. *Connections*, pp. 81–85; CG, *The Strange Children* (New York: Scribner's, 1951), p. 142.

11. RPW to AL, 26 Jan. 1931, VUL.

12. Stringfellow Barr to RPW, 21 Apr. 1931, UVaL; RPW to AT and CG, 24 Apr. 1931, PUL.

13. RPW to AL [summer 1931], VUL; RPW to AT, 10 Aug. 1931, PUL.

14. RPW to AT [late summer 1931], PUL.

15. *Poetry*, 41 (Jan. 1933), p. 200.

16. "Watershed," *Poetry*, 40 (May 1932), p. 61, repr. *NSP*, p. 317; "The Return," *NRep*, 15 Jan. 1930, p. 215, repr. *NSP*, pp. 317–18; "The Return: An Elegy," *TSP*, p. 14, repr. *NSP*, p. 311; "Rebuke of the Rocks," *Nation*, 11 Jan. 1928, p. 47, repr. *NSP*, p. 15; "The Return: An Elegy," in *Thirtieth Year to Heaven: New American Poets* (Winston-Salem, N.C.: Jackpine Press, 1980), p. 14. "The Return: An Elegy" and "Letter of a Mother," *TSP*, p. 28, repr. *SP*, p. 89.

17. *Thirtieth Year*, p. 16.

18. *Thirtieth Year*, p. 15.

CHAPTER 14: PROFESSOR WARREN AT VANDERBILT

1. *Encounter*, 26 (Mar. 1960), pp. 20–21, repr. *NSP*, p. 250.

2. I: RPW, TLF, MWB.

3. I: RPW, TLF, MWB; I: George S. Boone; Todd County *Times*, 2 Oct. 1931; *Mandarins*, p. 87; AT to AL, 1 Oct. 1931, *Lytle-Tate*, p. 50.

4. *Thirtieth Year to Heaven: New American Poets* (Winston-Salem, N.C.: Jackpine Press, 1980), p. 15.

5. *PF*, p. 42; I: MWB; AT to AL, 1 Oct. 1931, *Lytle-Tate*, p. 50.

6. *Connections*, p. 107; *Mandarins*, p. 87. See "What Is the Voice That Speaks?" *BH*, p. 71. RPW told FW that "Tale of Time" was not fiction, *TN*, pp. 146–48. For a very different use of these materials see "There's a Grandfather's Clock in the Hall," *OEP*, p. 81, repr. *NSP*, p. 198.

7. *PF*, pp. 42–43.

8. RPW would mistakenly say in later years that his mother died on Oct. 5. The obituary noted that Mrs. Warren "was a member of the Methodist church and was actively interested in the church." Beside these lines pasted in Mary M. Penn's genealogy is the printed comment "NOT TRUE RPW."

9. See *TN*, pp. 145–50; "Tale of Time," *NSP*, p. 248.

10. I: TLF.

11. RPW to LL, 13 May 1931, VUL; *Ivy*, p. 353; Ella Puryear Mims, "My Father Remembered," courtesy of Miss Mims; *Fugitive Group*, pp. 193–96 and *passim*.

12. *Ivy*, p. 353; *Reminiscence*, p. 218; William H. Pritchard, *Randall Jarrell: A Literary Life* (New York: Farrar, Straus, 1990), p. 23.

13. Barr-Warren correspondence, UVaL.

14. CG to Sally Wood, 8 Jan. 1931, *Mandarins*, p. 67; I: AL, CB.

15. CG to Sally Wood, 20 Aug. 1931, *Connections*, p. 102;

16. *Connections*, pp. 107–8, 103; CG to "Dear Coz" [1931], YUL; I: AE.

17. See Makowsky, pp. 107–8.

18. AT to AL, 29 Mar. 1932, AT to AL, undated, *Lytle-Tate,* pp. 52–53; AT to AL, 16 Apr. 1932, *Lytle-Tate,* p. 54.

19. I: BBC and FNC; I: BBC by FW; I: AE; *RPWR,* p. xii.

20. Owsley, pp. 93–94; I: AE, RPW, AL.

21. Owsley, p. 93; I: AE.

CHAPTER 15: TRYING TO BECOME A
NOVELIST

1. Ts., unpublished novel, pp. 16–17, UKyL.

2. Ts., unpublished novel, pp. 16–17, UKyL; I: RPW by WF.

3. Charles A. Pearce to RPW, 26 Aug. 1932, YUL.

4. See Makowsky, pp. 106–12; *Connections,* pp. 113–15.

5. "Reminiscence," p. 215; I: HO; RPW to AT and CG [Nov. 1932], PUL.

6. JCR to AT, 25 Oct. 1932, PUL; AL to AT, 23 Oct. 1932, *Lytle-Tate,* p. 69; RPW to AT and CG [Nov. 1932], PUL; JCR to AT, 25 Oct. 1932, PUL.

7. AT to DD, 10 Dec. 1932, *Literary Correspondence,* pp. 279–80.

8. Addison Hibbard, ed., *The Lyric South: An Anthology of Recent Poetry from the South* (New York: Macmillan, 1928); "A Note on Three Southern Poets," ts., PUL, published in *Poetry,* 60 (May 1940), pp. 103–13.

9. Medical records courtesy of ECW and Vanderbilt University Hospital; I: HO.

10. "Reminiscence," p. 216; DD to AT, 6 Feb. 1933, PUL; *Connections,* p. 123.

11. See *Connections,* pp. 123–25; Malcolm Cowley, *The Flower and the Leaf* (New York: Viking, 1985), pp. 355–56; *Literary Correspondence,* p. xlviii.

12. RPW to FO, 25 Aug. 1933, VUL; I: JS; RPW to AT, 24 Aug. [26 Aug.], 1933, PUL; RPW to FO, 25 Aug. 1933, VUL.

13. RPW to FO [Sept. 1933], VUL; JCR to AT, 28 Sept. 1933, PUL; I: JS, WS;

Charles A. Pearce to RPW, 18 Oct. 1933, YUL.

14. *Literary Correspondence,* pp. 410–11; "When the Light Gets Green," *SoR,* 1 (Spring 1936), pp. 799–806, repr. *CA,* pp. 88–95.

15. RPW to AT [Oct. 1933], PUL.

16. See *Connections,* pp. 135–36; *Mandarins,* pp. 157, 159.

17. RPW to AT [Oct. 1933], PUL.

CHAPTER 16: DOORS CLOSING AND
DOORS OPENING

1. *AmRv,* 3 (May 1934), p. 239, repr. *SP,* p. 41.

2. Neither of the existing readers' reports is dated. The covering letters from Chambers to RPW are dated 20 and 29 Mar. 1935, following the submission of his second novel. Though they relate primarily to the rejection of the second novel, Chambers went into detail to compare it with *God's Own Time.* D. L. Chambers to RPW, 20 Mar. 1935, YUL.

3. D. L. Chambers to RPW, 20 Mar. 1935, YUL.

4. Medical records courtesy of ECW and Vanderbilt University Hospital.

5. I: RPW; see *Bibliography,* pp. 187–88.

6. I: Walter Sullivan, BBC; CB; CB, RPWOHP; see *Parnassus,* pp. 6–12, 31.

7. *Parnassus,* p. 31.

8. I: HO, JS, CB.

9. *TwRPW,* p. 272; I: RPW, JS, CB.

10. CG to AL [spring 1934], VUL; *The "Southern Review" and Modern Literature: 1935–1985,* eds. LPS, James Olney, and Jo Gulledge (Baton Rouge: Louisiana State University Press, 1988), p. 36.

11. CG to AL [spring 1934], VUL; AT to AL, 17 Aug. 1934, *Lytle-Tate,* p. 91; I: Shirley Barber Ring.

12. I: CB; CB, RPWOHP, no. 1.

13. RPW, "The Fiction of Caroline Gordon," *SWR,* 20 (Winter 1935), pp. 5–10; I: CB.

14. CG to SW, 1 Oct. 1934, *Mandarins,* pp. 165–66; CG to AL [24 Oct. 1934], VUL.

15. Owsley, p. 73; "Matrix," pp. 161–62.

16. CBW to HO, 24 Sept. 1934, VUL; Heilman, p. 5; CG to AL [24 Oct. 1924], VUL.

17. "Matrix," p. 164; I: CB.

18. RPW's courses could hardly have suited him better: a survey of modern English prose and poetry, creative writing, Shakespeare, and nondramatic Elizabethan literature; EBW to HO, 2 Oct. 1934, VUL.

CHAPTER 17: HUEY'S UNIVERSITY

1. *BD,* p. 11; *BD* (nv), p. 10.

2. "The Unvexed Isles," *The Magazine,* 2 (July–Aug. 1934), pp. 1–10, repr. *CA,* pp. 163–69. "Her Own People," *VQR,* 11 (Apr. 1935), pp. 289–304, repr. *CA,* pp. 175–89; LD to RPW, 11 Sept. 1934, UVaL; *TwRPW,* p. 178.

3. RPW, untitled novel, UKyL.

4. I: RPW, Mack S. Linebaugh, FW; notes on Kent Greenfield courtesy of FW.

5. I: TLF.

6. I: AE, RPW.

7. I: CB; *Connections,* p. 131; CBW to HO, 23 Sept. 1934, VUL; AT to AL, 17 Aug. 1934, *Lytle-Tate,* p. 91.

8. J. A. Thompson to JB; RPW to AT, 8 Nov. 1934, PUL; EBW to HO, 1 Nov. 1934, 11 Dec. 1934, VUL.

9. LD to RPW, 15 Nov. 1934, 13 Dec. 1934; RPW to LD, 17 Dec. 1934; LD to RPW, 18 Dec. 1934, 21 Dec. 1934, UVaL; "History," *VQR,* 11 (July 1935), pp. 353–56, repr. *SP75,* pp. 294–96; "Resolution," *VQR,* 11 (July 1935), pp. 352–53, repr. *SP,* pp. 63–64.

10. RPW to AT, 8 Nov. 1934, PUL; *Parnassus,* pp. 32–34, 39–43; RPW to AT [autumn 1934], PUL. RPW solicited manuscripts for *SWR* from KAP, John Peale Bishop, Randall Jarrell, and several Agrarians.

11. AL, in *Connections,* pp. 144–45; Makowsky, p. 131; *Connections,* p. 145; *SoR/Original Series, 1935–1942: A Commemoration, 1980* (pamphlet; Baton Rouge: Louisiana State University Press, p. 15); CG to Dorothy Dey, as quoted in *Connections,* p. 145; AL, *Ibid.*

12. *Parnassus,* pp. 43–49.

13. RPW to AT and CG, 4 Feb. 1935, PUL; CBW to HO, 2 Feb. 1935, VUL; RPW to FO, 11 Feb. 1935, VUL.

14. RPW to FO, 11 Feb. 1935, PUL; "Goodwood Comes Back," *SoR,* 6 (Winter 1941), pp. 526–36, repr. *CA,* pp. 108–19; RPW to AT and CG, 4 Feb. 1935, PUL.

15. D. L. Chambers to RPW, 20 and 29 Mar. 1935, YUL; novel ts., UKyL.

16. The stories deriving from *God's Own Time* are "Testament of Flood," *The Magazine,* 2 (Mar.–Apr. 1935), pp. 230–34; "Christmas Gift," *VQR,* 13 (Winter 1937), pp. 73–85; and "The Love of Elsie Barton: A Chronicle," *Mademoiselle,* Feb. 1941, pp. 161, 282–90, repr. *CA,* pp. 163–69, 96–107, 143–62.

CHAPTER 18: *THE SOUTHERN REVIEW*—AND OTHER PROJECTS

1. "History," *VQR,* 11 (July 1935), pp. 353–56, repr. *SP75,* pp. 294–96.

2. I: RPW, AE, CB; *Parnassus,* pp. 9, 50; CB and RPW, "The Origin of the *Southern Review,*" in "*Southern Review,*" pp. 34–35; RPW to AT, 20 Mar. 1935, PUL.

3. RPW to AT, 20 Mar. 1935, PUL; "Wessex and Louisiana," *Time,* 10 June 1940, as paraphrased in *Parnassus,* p. 239.

4. See *Parnassus,* p. 53; EBW to HO, 21 Mar. 1935, VUL.

5. *Parnassus,* pp. 54–60, "Conference on Literature and Reading in the South and Southwest," intro. by Thomas W. Cutrer, "*Southern Review,*" pp. 38–78; FMF, *The Great Trade Route* (New York: Oxford University Press, 1937), pp. 151, 271; "*Southern Review,*" pp. 52, 66, 76–77; "Some

Recent Novels," *SoR,* I (Winter 1936), p. 632, as quoted in *Parnassus,* p. 60.

6. Huey P. Long, "Politics and Education," ed. Charles East, *"The Southern Review,"* p. 79.

7. RPW as quoted in *Parnassus,* pp. 64–65, 72–73; Charles East to JB.

8. CBW to AE, 15 June 1935, courtesy of AE.

9. RPW to AE [summer 1935], courtesy of AE; I: PD; RPW to DD, 9 July 1935, VUL.

10. I: CB; *Parnassus,* p. 66.

11. See *Parnassus,* p. 66; Charles East, "The Death of Huey Long," in *"Southern Review,"* pp. 82–84; Heilman, pp. 5–6.

12. Charles East to JB; CG to AL, 16 Sept. 1935, VUL; RPW to LD, 8 Nov. 1935, UVaL; RPW to AT [autumn 1935], PUL; RPW to LD, 13 Nov. 1935, UVaL.

13. Herbert Agar and AT, eds., *Who Owns America* (Boston: Houghton Mifflin, 1936), pp. vii–x, 268–79; *Parnassus,* p. 126; CG to Robert Logan Lytle, 13 Jan. 1936, VUL; *Connections,* pp. 156–58.

14. I: CB; see JAG, "Cleanth Brooks and Robert Penn Warren: Notes on Their Literary Correspondence," *MissQ,* 48 (Winter 1994–95), p. 94.

15. *Poetry,* 49 (Nov. 1936), pp. 106–7, repr. *SP75,* pp. 314–15.

16. I: RPW; see VS, *A Colder Fire: The Poetry of Robert Penn Warren* (Louisville: University of Kentucky Press, 1965), p. 72. RPW and Robert Frost had gotten along well during the Colorado writers' conference. When DD showed RPW's book to Frost, he liked the first poem he read. Then, as he read further, his antipathy to Eliot flaring up, he muttered, "but he's fallen among thieves."

17. Ruth Lechlitner, *Books,* 16 Feb. 1936, p. 10; *Nation,* 142 (25 Mar. 1936), p. 391; Robert Lann, *NRep,* 87 (15 July 1936), p. 304; Morton Dauwen Zabel, *Poetry,* 48 (Apr. 1936), p. 37.

18. "Picnic Remembered," *Scribner's Magazine,* 99 (Mar. 1936), p. 185, repr. *SP75,* pp. 309–11; "Monologue at Midnight," *VQR,* 12 (July 1936), p. 395, repr. *SP75,* pp. 307–8.

19. See Randolph Paul Runyon, "Repeating the 'Implacable Monotone' in *Thirty-Six Poems,"* *MissQ,* 48 (Winter 1994–95), pp. 39–56; EBW to HO, 30 Oct. 1935, VUL; I: AE.

20. Joseph Brewer to RPW, 14 May 1931, YUL; CBW to AE, 29 July 1936, 6 Aug. 1936, courtesy of AE.

21. Andrew Turnbull, *Thomas Wolfe* (New York: Scribner's, 1967), p. 220. RPW, "A Note on the Hamlet of Thomas Wolfe," *AmR,* 5 (May 1935), pp. 191–208, repr. *SE,* 170–83. At a meeting of the Modern Language Association later that year Wolfe met the other Agrarians and got along equally well with them.

22. AT to RPW, 4 Dec. 1935, YUL.

23. T. J. Wilson to RPW, 22 July 1936, PUL. Ever since RPW's Oxford days he had been interested in the kind of work done by pioneers such as I. A. Richards. In 1935 he had offered to write an essay for the *VQR* on Richards—the teacher of William Empson and F. R. Leavis—as linguistics scholar, critic, and semanticist. I: John Palmer, RPWOHP.

CHAPTER 19: GETTING IT
WRITTEN—AMONG OTHER
PROBLEMS

1. *Poetry,* 51 (Oct. 1937), pp. 10–11, repr. *NSP,* p. 306.

2. I: RPW by WF.

3. I: RPW by WF. "I didn't research it," he said of the novel. "I just went and talked to people." One was a federal judge tried for night riding and acquitted. RPW to FO, 22 Mar. 1937, VUL; RPW to AT [spring 1937], PUL.

4. See Thomas Daniel Young, *Gentleman in a Dustcoat: A Biography of John Crowe Ransom* (Baton Rouge: Louisiana State University Press, 1976), pp. 263, 268–69, 283, 286.

5. Young, *Gentleman,* pp. 287–91.

6. RPW to KAP, 26 May 1937, UMdL; AT to CB, 24 June 1937, YUL.

7. CB to AT, 28 June 1937, YUL.

8. CB to AT, 28 June 1937, YUL.

9. RPW to·Ms. Garcia, 13 Dec. 1981, VUL.

10. VS notes the similarity here of the "Death By Water" of Phlebas the Phoenician in *The Waste Land, Poetic Vision 52.* Acknowledging the poem's influences, RPW would later call it "a modernistic metaphysical poem. . . ." RPWOHP, no. 10. But there may have been more at work. The lover's meditation in "Bearded Oaks"—"Ages to our construction went, / Dim architecture, hour by hour"—recalls the dark and sinister imagery of Hardy's "The Convergence of the Twain."

11. Mildred Bronson to JB; RPWOHP, no. 15.

12. RPWOHP, no. 15; CBW to AE, 8 Aug. 1937, courtesy of AE.

13. CB to AT, 1 Dec. 1937; RPW to AT, 2 Nov. 1937, PUL.

14. I: RPW; RPW to AT, 2 Nov. 1937; CB to AT, 1 Dec. 1937, PUL.

15. RPW to AT [Dec. 1937], PUL.

16. Cecile Starr to JB; I: Leonard Unger.

17. I: Leonard Unger; RPWOHP, no. 1; Norton Girault, *Texas Writers' . . . Newsletter,* Nos. 31–35.

18. I: CB; CB to AT, 27 Mar. 1938, PUL.

19. AT to CB, 30 Apr. 1938, YUL; CB to AT, 27 Mar. 1938, PUL.

20. RPW to AT, 10 Mar. 1938; RPW to AT, 12 Mar. 1938; RPW to AT [spring 1938], PUL.

21. Real estate records courtesy of Charles F. McMains, Jr.; real estate information courtesy of Charles East and LPS; RPW to Charles F. McMains, Jr., courtesy of Mr. McMains.

22. *Mandarins,* p. 214; see *KAP Letters,* pp. xix–xxiii, 163; I: AL; Makowsky, p. 144.

23. CB to AT [summer 1937], PUL; AT to CB, 30 Apr. 1938, YUL; CB to AT, 20 June [1938], PUL; I: AE.

24. RPW to CG [1938], PUL; CB to AT, 20 June [1938], PUL.

25. RPW to AL, 23 Aug. 1938, VUL.

CHAPTER 20: *NIGHT RIDER,* AND A NEW BEGINNING

1. *SoR,* 59 (Summer 1951), 363–91, repr. *SE,* pp. 31–58.

2. RPW to AL, 23 Aug. 1938, VUL.

3. RPW to AL, 23 Aug. 1938, VUL; RPW to AE [1938], UMdL; CBW to HO, 23 Sept. 1938, VUL; RPW to AL, 23 Aug. 1938, VUL.

4. RPW to AE [1938], UMdL; RPW to AL, 23 Aug. 1938, VUL.

5. CG to Phelps Putnam, 14 Sept. 1938, quoted in *Connections,* p. 182.

6. RPW to H. A. Moe, 17 Oct. 1938, courtesy of JSGMF; "How Willie Proudfit Came Home," *SoR,* 4 (Oct. 1938), pp. 299–321, repr. *RPWR,* pp. 56–76.

7. In RPW's files were five pages of transcribed testimony about the night riders' raid on Hopkinsville on Dec. 7, 1904, and eleven typed pages of newspaper accounts of horsewhippings, shootings, attempted dynamitings, and raids in force, UKyL; Rowan Claypool, "The Black Patch War," unpublished papers, courtesy of Rowan Claypool and Joy Bale Boone.

8. See *TwRPW,* p. 137. See *Fugitives,* pp. 337, 350; Snipes, pp. 34, 38; Clark, pp. 74–75; and Basil Davenport, *SatR,* 19 (18 Mar. 1939), p. 6.

9. RPW had started reading Conrad at fifteen and owned almost all the volumes of Doubleday's Malay Edition. He would write one of his best essays on *Nostromo,* which Conrad called his largest canvas and Warren called his "supreme effort." " 'The Great Mirage': Conrad and *Nostromo,*" *SE,* pp. 32, 37, 55; *TwRPW,* p. 28; *Burden,* p. 474; Alvan S. Ryan, "Robert Penn Warren's *Nostromo:* The Nihilism of the Isolated Temperament," *MFS,* VII (Winter), repr. Longley, p. 55.

10. The old man was a natural raconteur, and his speech patterns were much like those of Andrew Lytle and John Donald Wade in their celebrated stories. If RPW needed a literary model, there were several. "I'm sure Faulkner had a hand in it," he would say later, "in this beginning of writing fiction." The language of Mississippian Anse Bundren in Faulkner's *As I Lay Dying* (1930) is very close to Willie Proudfit's except for his slight Tennessee variants. RPW to AT [late 1938], PUL.
11. *SE*, p. 58; RPW to JSGMF, 14 Mar. 1939, courtesy JSGMF; *NY*, 15 (18 Mar. 1939), p. 84; *SatR*, 19 (18 Mar. 1939), p. 6; *NYTBR*, 19 Mar. 1939, p. 6 and 19 Mar. 1939, p. 2; *Nation*, 148 (29 Apr. 1939), p. 507; *NRep*, 99 (31 May 1939), p. 108.
12. RPW to H. A. Moe, 14 Mar. 1939, courtesy of JSGMF.
13. CBW to HO, 20 May 1939, YUL.
14. RPW to Kenneth Burke [summer 1939], 13 Nov. 1939, YUL.

CHAPTER 21: ITALY, THE PLAY, AND THE WAR

1. *Poetry*, 57 (Feb. 1941), pp. 285–88, repr. *SP75*, pp. 284–86.
2. RPW to FO [14 Aug. 1939], VUL; EBW to KAP [15 Aug. 1939], UMdL.
3. See Joseph R. Millichap, "A Special Kind of Complex Eden: Robert Penn Warren's Italy," *Southern Quarterly*, 34 (Winter 1996), 65–71.
4. RPW to AT, 31 Aug. 1939, PUL; RPW to Kenneth Burke [fall 1939], YUL.
5. Huey P. Long, quoted in *Parnassus*, p. 215; see also pp. 213–30; I: CB; RPW to FO [14 Aug. 1939], VUL.
6. RPW to AL, 14 Nov. 1939, VUL; RPW to BBC, 13 Nov. 1939, VUL.
7. RPW to BBC, 13 Nov. 1939; RPW to AT, 28 Oct. 1939, PUL.
8. RPW to AT, 14 Dec. 1939, PUL.
9. I: Mary O'Connor, RPWOHP; RPW to Kenneth Burke [fall 1939], YUL.

10. *Proud Flesh*, ts., PUL; fragment of Highway Patrolmen's Chorus, YUL. Analyzing Anne Amos's early rejection of Strong's marriage proposal, the Chorus Leader attributes it to sentimentality, to her domination by her brilliant and erratic brother, to her lack of a sense of meaning in life, and to the absence of any "emotional experience of any fundamental intensity." The problem with Anne's motivation would persist.
11. JCR to AT, 9 Nov. 1939, PUL.
12. RPW to H. A. Moe, 11 Jan. 1940, courtesy of JSGMF. "Terror," *SP75*, pp. 284–86. See *Achievement*, p. 56; *Poetic Vision*, p. 148; *Fugitives*, p. 345; RPW in Kimon Friar and John Malcolm Brinnin, eds., *Modern Poetry: American and British* (New York: Appleton-Century, 1950), pp. 542–43.
13. "Love's Parable," *KR*, 2 (Spring 1940), pp. 186–88, repr. *SP75*, pp. 311–13; RPW to AT, 2 Apr. 1940, PUL.
14. RPW to KAP, 20 Feb. 1940, UMdL.
15. RPW to CB, 7 Mar. 1940, YUL.
16. EBW to HO, 12 Mar. 1940, VUL; RPW to ED, 12 Mar. 1940, YUL.
17. RPW to AT, 2 Apr. 1940, PUL; *TwRPW*, p. 367.
18. RPW to AT, 2 Apr. 1940, PUL; *TwRPW*, p. 367; RPW to AL, 30 Apr. 1940, VUL.
19. RPW to FO, 11 May 1940, VUL; I: PMP.
20. RPW to AE and KAP, 12 June 1940, courtesy of AE; LSU *Daily Reveille*, 18 Sept. 1940; I: RPW.

CHAPTER 22: THE LONELINESS ARTIST

1. *Nation*, 7 Mar. 1942, p. 286, repr. *SP75*, pp. 297–98.
2. RPW to CB, 8 June 1940, YUL; RPW to AE and KAP, EBW postscript, 12 June 1940, courtesy of AE.
3. Ibid.

4. RPW to FO, 27 Aug. 1940, VUL; I: PD, RPWOHP.

5. I: Helen Ransom Forman.

6. CB to AT, "Monday" [autumn 1940], PUL; RPW to KAP, 25 Apr. 1941, UMdL.

7. I: Leonard Unger, RPWOHP; RPW to AE, 16 Feb. 1941, courtesy of AE.

8. Wallace Fowlie, *Journal of Rehearsals: A Memoir* (Durham, N.C.: Duke University Press, 1977), pp. 79–80; I: Wallace Fowlie.

9. Francis Fergusson to RPW, 1 Mar. 1941, 9 May 1941, PUL.

10. I: Wallace Fowlie; Fowlie, *Rehearsals*, p. 80.

11. RPW to AE, 16 Feb. 1941, courtesy of AE; I: AE.

12. JCR to RPW, 24 June 1941, YUL; CB to AT, 30 Jan. 1941, PUL.

13. CB to AT, 30 Jan. 1941, PUL; *Parnassus*, pp. 4–5, 8–9, 238–39.

14. RPW to AT, 1 Sept. 1941, PUL; Alexander and Jean Kern to JB.

15. RPW to AT, 1 Sept. 1941, PUL; "End of Season," see note 1.

16. See *Parnassus*, p. 39.

17. LPS, "The Loneliness Artist: The Image of the Writer in Robert Penn Warren's Fiction," *SR*, XCIX (July–Sept. 1991), pp. 337–400; Charles East to JB; I: CB.

18. RPW to KAP, 3 Nov. 1941, UMdL; CB to AT [summer 1941], YUL.

19. *Daily Reveille*, 30 Oct. 1941, p. 1.

20. RPW to AL, 3 Nov. 1942, VUL. One voting for the *SoR* was Col. Troy H. Middleton, a fair-minded country boy who knew little about literature and, called to active duty not long afterward, would perform brilliantly in the invasion of Sicily and emerge from the war a three-star general and future president of Louisiana State University. Brooks's judgment was a generous one: "General [Hodges] has been very fair and sympathetic," he wrote Tate. "I think that he honestly regrets the loss of the *Southern Review*." CB to AT, 20 Dec. 1941, PUL.

21. CB to AT, 20 Dec. 1941, PUL.; Charlotte Goodman to JB; *TwRPW,* p. 298.

22. I: LD.

23. James Gray, *The University of Minnesota, 1851–1951* (Minneapolis: University of Minnesota Press, 1951), pp. 81, 137–39, 200–1, 428; Doris Taft Hedlund, "Joseph Warren Beach, The Professor Who Didn't Retire," *Minnesota Daily,* 14 Oct. 1957, pp. 110–14; I: CB.

24. RPW to KAP, 24 Mar. 1942, UMdL; RPW to AT, 23 Mar. 1942, PUL.

25. Documents courtesy of the LSU English department; I: CB, Thomas A. Kirby.

26. I: RPW, CB, Thomas A. Kirby; CB to AT, 15 Apr. 1942, PUL.

27. Jewel Claitor, "Robert Penn Warren: Minnesota's Gain, L.S.U.'s Loss," *Daily Reveille,* 9 May 1942.

28. LPS, "Loneliness Artist," p. 400; *PTCT,* pp. 93–94.

Chapter 23: In the Northland, at Fame's Door

1. *NYRB,* 16 July 1981, p. 40; repr. *RV,* pp. 33–34.

2. I: Mary O'Connor, RPWOHP; "Original Sin: A Short Story," *KR,* 4 (Spring 1942), pp. 179–80, repr. *SP75,* pp. 288–89.

3. JCR to RPW, 4 Sept. 1942, YUL. See P. M. Jack, *NYT,* 26 Apr. 1942, p. 4; *NY,* 18 (9 May 1942), p. 80; Frank Jones, *Nation,* 155 (16 Sept. 1942), p. 277.

4. CG to AL, 19 May 1942, VUL.

5. Ernest Sandeen to JB.

6. RPW to DD, 29 Aug. 1942, VUL. In what may have been Warren's last detailed recounting, he wrote, "Now it seems that the LSU business was a squeeze-out. Four times Cleanth and I were put up for promotion by the head of our department, and the administration blocked the move every time. . . . Then,

they offered a raise, but did not match the Minnesota figure—and matching the figure would not have broken some of their own precedents. . . . Then Frey told the President that they had matched the Minnesota offer and that I had simply gone because I wanted to. I don't know why I should rehearse this stuff, but I'm still pretty sore about it and about the way they handled the SR. . . ."

7. RPW to FO [summer 1942], VUL. The author is indebted to Prof. Kent Bailes for a guided trip to RPW's Minneapolis residences.

8. RPW to FO [summer 1942]; RPW to BBC, 16 Dec. 1942, VUL.

9. RPW to BBC, 16 Dec. 1942, VUL; I: Mary Wyville. She was enrolled in Warren's graduate writing course in which he used his new textbook, *UF.* She remembered his raspy voice reading Edwin Arlington Robinson's "Mr. Flood's Party" with great effect. He saved his critiques of students' work for individual conferences, and he held up high standards for them.

10. After a B.Litt. at University College, Oxford, HB returned to Harvard for his Ph.D. before coming to the University of Minnesota in 1937. His special interests were Shakespeare and Milton, but he ranged fluently over French, Italian, and German plus some Hebrew and Japanese as well. His accent was impeccable when he and CBW "performed" Italian in rapid animated conversation. EB to JB; RPW, introduction to a projected volume of letters of EB; I: ES.

11. I: ES.

12. RPW to FO, Christmas Day, 1942; I: RPW.

13. RPW to KAP, 6 Apr. 1943, UMdL.

14. "Memories of Red," Alexander and Jean Kern to JB, 12 May 1989.

15. See John Berry McFerrin, *Caldwell and Company: A Southern Financial Empire* (Chapel Hill: North Carolina University Press, 1939), reissued by Vanderbilt University, pp. 169, 103, *passim.* Elected U.S. senator in 1911 and then denied reelec-

tion, Luke Lea organized an artillery regiment in the First World War, led it with distinction, and nearly earned a court martial by attempting to kidnap the kaiser with a view to presenting him to President Wilson at the Paris Peace Conference. In the Caldwell debacle Luke Lea and his son were convicted of conspiracy in North Carolina and allowed to return to Tennessee on bond, only to see the state supreme court adjudge them fugitives to be returned to serve their sentences.

16. McFerrin, *Caldwell;* I: RPW; RPWOHP, no. 15. BBC had worked for a Caldwell company until a friend warned him that its activities constituted "the Indian rope trick." He resigned and went to work for the *Banner.* Sergeant York had been reared on a back-country farm with religious principles that did not, however, prevent him from killing 20 German soldiers and capturing 132 more while taking a strongly defended hill.

17. *Louisiana Leader,* VII (Oct. 1940), p. 5, as quoted in *Parnassus,* pp. 159–60; see Clark, p. 81; *Achievement,* pp. 180–81; *Taciturn Text,* p. 43. RPW, intro. to *AKM* (New York: Modern Library, 1953), p. iii. Longley writes, "in the same general classification with this [seventh] circle are lumped together a grouping of sinners which seems heterogeneous and nonsystematic to the modern mind: suicides, usurers, sodomists, soothsayers, magicians, and diviners. Under the system of theology in Dante's own time, however, this grouping was entirely logical: all these sins are sins of violence: violence against man, against nature, or against God. Thus, all the characters in *At Heaven's Gate,* except for the two or three who represent the wholeness and harmonious development of humanity, are violators of nature." Longley, p. 61. Dante's strong attraction for RPW went beyond the artistic and the moral. He would later say, "I am a man of [religious] temperament in the modern world who hasn't got any reli-

gion. Dante almost got me at one stage, but then I suddenly realized, 'My God, Dante's a good Protestant—he was! Where have I gone?' " *TwRPW,* p. 243; see *Parnassus,* p. 198.

18. I: RPWOHP, no. 1.

19. RPW wrote Leonard Casper that the title derived from "no Shakespearean source exclusively," but Casper makes a strong case for sonnet XXIX, p. 187. When RPW published the Wyndham testament separately seven years later, he provided a gloss on it: "First, the story provides one of the various views which are contrasted in the novel, the naive religious view at one end of the scale. Second, the story serves a purpose in the over-all organization of the plot. Ashby is driven out on his pilgrimage by two forces: by the effect, even in his remote corner of the world, of the financial speculation and corruption in the city, and by his own repentance and vision. When he finally reaches the city, he, in his innocence, brings down the house of cards which is Bogan Murdock's empire." *Statement of Ashby Wyndham,* in *Spearhead: Ten Years' Experimental Writing in America* (New York, 1947), pp. 415 and ff.; RPWOHP, no. 15.

20. I: RPWOHP, no. 10; RPW, "Pure Poetry and the Structure of Poems," retitled "Pure and Impure Poetry," in *SE,* pp. 3–31. See Snipes, pp. 42, 44. She writes that RPW has said that Sarrett " 'was almost a portrait of a person I knew, the closest portrait I've ever done in a piece of fiction.' If Sarrett was not a Mr. Hyde that Warren imagined in himself, then I suspect the real model exemplified what Warren most feared to become—the intellectual without heart. . . . It is curious that a character so close to having the convictions of his author (and incidentally rather like him in appearance, perhaps) should be so convincingly evil."

21. See *Taciturn Text,* pp. 41–58.

22. See the Springfield *Republican,* 1 Aug. 1943, p. 7e; *Commonweal,* 38 (6

Aug. 1943), p. 398; *SatR,* 26 (21 Aug. 1943), p. 6; *NYT,* 22 Aug. 1943, p. 4; *NRep,* 109 (23 Aug. 1943), p. 258; *Nation,* 157 (28 Aug. 1943), p. 243; *Library Journal,* 68 (Aug. 1943), p. 625; *Christian Century,* 60 (1 Sept. 1943), p. 991; *AtMo,* 172 (Sept. 1943), p. 131; *YR,* 33 (Autumn 1943), p. xii.

23. AT to FO, 18 Nov. 1943, PUL; JCR to RPW, 7 July 1943, YUL; *Weekly Book Review,* 22 (Aug. 1954), p. 5.

CHAPTER 24: IN THE SERVICE OF THE STATE

1. *PR,* 11 (Winter 1944), pp. 56–70, repr. *NSP,* pp. 287–300.

2. RPWOHP, no. 10; "Siesta Time in Village Plaza by Ruined Bandstand and Banana Tree," *SP,* pp. 51–52; "The Mango on the Mango Tree," "Butterflies over the Map," "The World Comes Galloping: A True Story," and "Small Soldiers with Drum in Large Landscape," appeared in *Poetry,* 62 (June 1943), pp. 121–27, repr. in *SP75,* pp. 302–7 as "Mexico Is a Foreign Country: Four Studies in Naturalism." See *Bibliography,* p. 460. See also *Achievement,* p. 5.

3. I: RPW, AS. Some commentators would say that the story is archetypal. RPW said he had heard it from "an old lady who was a relative of mine." To his great-aunt Anna Mitchell in Cerulean, it was not a folktale but a story she had heard as a young girl. See *TwRPW,* pp. xvi, 296–97, 342–44.

4. It was "the question of the man who goes to the West to become a different man—redeemed—prospers and comes back. . . . He doesn't know why he wants to come back. He comes back to his true 'human' father—he dies by his own blood—and name. Now when they kill him he accepts from his father's hand the natural gift. He's a sacrifice this time. But he's returned. He's performed the human cycle." *TwRPW,* 342–44. "The Ballad of

Billie Potts," *PR*, 11 (Winter 1944), pp. 56–70; *NSP*, pp. 287–300.

5. I: RPW, ECW.

6. RPW to DD, 25 Apr. 1944, VUL. Leo Kennedy, *Book Week*, 16 Apr. 1944, p. 6; Louise Bogan, *NY*, 20 (22 Apr. 1944), p. 85; Willard Thorpe, *NYTBR*, 7 May 1944, p. 4; Elizabeth Drew, *Weekly Book Review*, 25 June 1944, p. 11; Frederick W. Dupee, *Nation*, 159 (25 Nov. 1944), p. 660. Now an established poet, Randall Jarrell could be as critical of Warren's poems as he had been as a Vanderbilt student. After reading *Selected Poems* he wrote one friend, "The world and everything in it, in them, is so purely Original Sin, horror, loathing, morbidness, final evil, that to somebody who knows Red it's plain he manages his life by pushing all the evil in it out into the poems and novels. All his theory says that the world is nothing but evil, whereas the practice he lives by says exactly the opposite." William H. Pritchard, *Randall Jarrell: A Literary Life* (New York: Farrar Straus, 1990), p. 149.

7. RPW to Douglas Newton, 14 July 1944, UVaL. He described plans for a collection of his stories, which would become *CA. TwRPW*, p. 333.

8. RPW to FO and HO, 14 July 1944, VUL; *TwRPW*, pp. 42, 72.

9. RPW to FO and HO, 14 July 1944, VUL; *TwRPW*, pp. 42, 72; I: RPW; "Cass Mastern's Wedding Ring," *PR*, 11 (Fall 1944), pp. 375–407, repr. *RPWR*, pp. 98–130. Except for six lines deleted from chapter 4 in the novel, the versions are identical.

10. KAP to Barbara Wescott, 23 July 1944, *Letters of KAP*, p. 285; RPW to AT, 8 Aug. 1944, PUL; EB to JB; RPW to HB and EB, 23 Aug. 1944, UMinnL; KAP to Glenway Wescott, 27 Aug. 1944, *Letters of KAP*, p. 287; I: RPW.

11. RPW to HB and EB, 23 Aug. 1944, UMinnL; RPW to Douglas Newton, 14 July 1944, UVaL; RPWOHP, no. 1; RPW to KAP, 9 Nov. 1944, LC.

12. RPWOHP, no. 1; Norton Girault to JB.

13. RPW sent out letters in furtherance of the idea for poetry recordings. He was also arranging for Edgar Lee Masters to record his poetry, and he was trying to obtain literary materials of Edwin Arlington Robinson and Sherwood Anderson.

14. RPW to AL, 23 Nov. 1944, VUL; RPW to AT, 1 Jan. 1945, PUL.

15. RPW to AL, 23 Nov. 1944, VUL; RPW to AT, 1 Jan. 1945, PUL; I: RPW; CBW to EB, 24 Jan. 1945, UMinnL.

16. RPW to AT, 31 Jan. 1944, 16 Jan. 1945 ["late Jan early Feb 1945"], PUL.

17. AT to RPW, 9 Feb. 1945, YUL.

18. "Pure and Impure Poetry," *KR*, 5 (Spring 1943), pp. 228–54, repr. *SE*, pp. 3–31, *NSE*, pp. 3–28. "A Poem of Pure Imagination: An Experiment in Reading," repr. *KR*, 9 (Summer 1946), pp. 391–427 (see *Bibliography*, p. 236), *SE*, pp. 198–305; *NSE*, pp. 336–423. Page citations refer to this last version.

19. RPW wrote, "The rejection of the relevance of the 'moral' " by scholars such as Earl Leslie Griggs and John Livingston Lowes was based on a total misreading of the poem. *NSE*, pp. 336–40.

20. *NSE*, pp. 341–42.

21. *NSE*, pp. 351–65. Of Coleridge Warren wrote, "He lived into the guilt of opium long before the Mariner shot the Albatross; he knew what guilt is. . . ." (p. 359). In this essay he ranged afield from Maud Bodkin's archetypal criticism to Poe's discussion of a similar crime against an animal in "The Black Cat." In the essay's final, book-length form, these sixty-odd pages would be supplemented by notes, twenty more pages of evidence and argumentation.

22. RPW to CB, 31 July 1945, YUL.

23. RPW to KAP, 30 June 1945, UMdL; RPW to AT, 29 May 1945, PUL.

24. RPW to KAP, 30 June 1945, UMdL; *KAP Letters*, p. 306.

25. RPW to AT, 3 Sept. 1945, PUL; RPWOHP, no. 1.

CHAPTER 25: *ALL THE KING'S*
MEN—AT LAST

1. "Matrix," pp. 161–67, repr. in Longley, pp. 75–81.
2. Minnesota *Daily,* 10 Oct. 1945. "Since
coming here," the account continued,
"Warren has been the idol of a growing
cult of devotees. Students say he makes
them understand literature as they never
have before."
3. RPW to AT, 22 Dec. 1945, PUL.
Tate added, "It is a vindication of the va-
lidity of a critical procedure which we all
share but which you have developed further than any of the rest of us." AT to
RPW, 13 Feb. 1946, YUL.
4. Noel Polk, "Proposal for a New Edition of Robert Penn Warren's *All the
King's Men,*" courtesy of Noel Polk. I:
LD; I: RPW; LD to RPW, 19 Nov. 1945,
23 Nov. 1945, YUL.
5. Ibid.; RPW, "Lambert Davis: The Book
Editor, 1938–1948," in "A Statesman of
the Republic of Books" (Chapel Hill:
University of North Carolina Press, 1970),
no p.; RPW to BBC [Nov. 1945?], VUL;
I: LD, RPW. RPW took his epigraph from
the Third Canto of Dante's *Purgatorio.*
"Mentre che la speranza ha fior del verde,"
which may be translated "[Man is not so
lost that eternal love may not return] / so
long as hope retaineth ought of green."
They are the words of Manfredi, a murderer killed in battle against the papal army
and buried in unhallowed ground. Explaining his presence there in Purgatory
rather than in Hell, Manfredi tells Dante
that no pope could deny him repentance.
"I was pretty sure that when the novel was
finished," Warren explained, "people were
going to misread the meaning of my main
character." So, he reasoned, "the epigraph
says that there is always that little bit of
green, of hope. . . . Willie Stark's deathbed
reversal of feeling is like Manfredi's." So
RPW pointed up the spiritual dimension
added to the political, philosophical, and
ethical ones of the book.

6. *AKM* ts., YUL. Noel Polk found
hundreds of variants between the typescript and the first edition. One change
was to make Burden's speech less racy
and more speech-sophisticated. Noel
Polk to JB.
7. I: PMP.
8. KAP to RPW, 5 Jan. 1946, YUL.
9. See JHJ, "The Mariner and Robert
Penn Warren," *Texas Studies in Literature
and Language,* 8 (Spring 1966), pp.
117–28, repr. Nakadate, pp. 126–37; see
TwRPW, p. 58. RPW volunteered another life model: "Cass Mastern's story
had a germ. A lot of the details are historical—it's based on the Jefferson Davis
story. His father, Sam, came to Kentucky,
to our country, where Jeff was born."
TwRPW, p. 334.
10. Compare *AKM* with Hamilton
Basso's *Sun in Capricorn* (1942), John Dos
Passos's *Number One* (1943), and Adria
Locke Langley's *A Lion Is in the Streets*
(1945). Of these three protagonists and
Willie Stark, Hamilton Basso wrote, "He
may not be intended to represent Huey
Long, but it is hard to see how he could
represent anybody else." "The Huey
Long Legend," *Life,* 9 Dec. 1946, p. 108.
"A Note," pp. 476–80; see *TwRPW,* p.
69; Ladell Payne, "Willie Stark and Huey
Long: Atmosphere, Myth, or Suggestion?" *American Quarterly,* 20 (Fall 1968),
pp. 580–95, repr. in Nakadate; "Matrix,"
p. 80. Payne's argument is based on detailed resemblances between the early
legal and political careers of Stark and
Long, upon physical resemblances, upon
speeches, and upon gubernatorial tactics.
Resemblances are also argued between
supporting characters and living models.
11. *TwRPW,* pp. 57–58, 366, 72, 78, 73;
"Matrix," pp. 75, 77. On Rose Long:
RPW to Mr. Culbert, 28 Jan. 1985,
courtesy of LPS. JAG discusses Shakespearean sources for *AKM* and proposes
Coriolanus as a neglected and likely one in
"The Other *All the King's Men,*" unpublished essay.

12. Burden takes refuge in a denial of consequentiality and responsibility, epitomized in the tic in a hitchhiker's cheek. (The result of neither emotion nor intention, the tic is merely a neurological disorder, a phenomenon which Jack generalizes under the rubric "The Great Twitch.") When he faces the fact that actions can be not only consequential but also fatal, he overreacts with his theory of entrapment, for short, "The Spider Web": "He learned that the world is like an enormous spider web," and inevitably the spider injects "the black, numbing poison under your hide" (p. 200). RBH writes, "As the consciousness of an age, Jack also embodies its philosophic searchings. Jack appears first as an idealist," but then he "plunges into pragmatism, but it is a drug and never a very efficient one; under the pressure of pain he falls into mechanism—the Twitch theory. But eventually he rejects the world as idea, the world as act, and the world as mechanism; these are the half-truths of a disintegrating order. What he envisages is a saving union of the idealist and pragmatist impulses of modern man. . . ." "Melpomene," pp. 154–66, repr. in Longley, pp. 94–95; *TwRPW,* p. 108. See also Norton R. Girault, "The Narrator's Mind as Symbol," *Accent,* VII (Summer 1947), pp. 220–34.

13. Casper, pp. 122, 130; *Taciturn Text,* p. 63; *Achievement,* p. 199.

14. RPW wrote DD, "You have put your hand on a real problem when you talk about the point-of-view business in regard to the ethical reference. Almost always the personal, limited view will break down, either for mechanical or other reasons. It broke down badly for me in AKM in the problem of presenting Anne Stanton. I couldn't for the life of me figure out a way to give a proper rendering of her relation to the Boss in terms of the narrator. So I finally did what I did—simply threw that matter on the reader's mercy. I know the limitations of the

treatment in general, but I couldn't find any other way into this particular book. The first-person narrative may be what Allen once called it, the great alibi of the novelist. But I tend to find more and more that I write best when I write with a very formally defined sort of mask, another person's self. My next novel, I fear, will be of the same sort, but with a very different narrator." RPW to DD, 9 Oct. 1946, VUL.

15. See Burt, p. 171.

16. See "Melpomene," pp. 93–94.

17. RPW and CBW to KAP, 16 Mar. 1946, UMdL. On Sept. 10 12,500 more copies of *AKM* were printed and 8,727 more on Oct. 15, *Bibliography,* p. 37.

18. J. P. Wood, *SatR,* 29 (17 Aug. 1946); George Mayberry, *NRep,* 115 (2 Sept. 1946), p. 265; Diana Trilling, *Nation,* 163 (24 Aug. 1946), p. 220; Henry Rago, *Commonweal,* 44 (4 Oct. 1926), p. 599. As for the charge of melodrama, Eric Bentley wrote, "The worst thing you can truthfully say about *All the King's Men,* is that the almost Hollywoodian thriller which is Warren's vehicle is all too easily separable from his theme . . . Warren's brand of theatricality obviously owes more to the screen than to the stage." "The Meaning of Robert Penn Warren's Novels," *KR* 10 (Summer 1948), pp. 407–24. See E. F. Walbridge, *LJ,* 71 (Aug. 1946), p. 1051; Orville Prescott, *YR* 36 (Autumn 1946), p. 192; Robert Gorham Davis, *NYT,* 18 Aug. 1946, p. 3; LDR, Jr., "All the King's Meanings," *GaR,* VIII (Winter 1954), pp. 422–34; see Basso, "The Huey Long Legend," *Life,* 9 Dec. 1946, pp. 106–8.

19. "A Note," p. 480; "Melpomene," pp. 85–89; Bill Moyers, in *TwRPW,* p. 206; RPW to TR [Aug. 1973], courtesy of TR.

20. E. H. Dexter, *Time,* 48 (26 Aug. 1946), p. 98; see *TwRPW,* p. 395. To LDR, however, "there is a visceral feeling that Anne would not be interested in Willie and that she takes up with him be-

cause Red had to round out the plot." I: LDR. See Lucy Ferriss, "Sleeping with the Boss: Female Subjectivity in Robert Penn Warren's Fiction," *MissQ,* 43 (Winter 1994–95), p. 154.

21. RBH, "Robert Penn Warren at LSU: Some Reminiscences," *KyR,* 2 (1981), p. 36.

22. William Faulkner to LD, 25 July 1946, YUL.

23. William Faulkner to LD, 25 July 1946, YUL; Payne, "Atmosphere," p. 89.

24. "Matrix," p. 80; Jonathan Baumbach, "The Metaphysics of Demagoguery: 'All the King's Men,' " from *The Landscape of Nightmare* (New York: New York University Press, 1965), repr. in Bloom, pp. 80, 66; Snipes, p. 70; Walker, pp. 97, 99. See JB, *The Political Novel* (Westport, Conn.: Greenwood Press, 1955, 1979), *passim.,* and *The Modern American Political Novel: 1900–1960* (Austin: University of Texas Press, 1966), *passim.;* Burt, p. 141; "A Note," p. 480; "Melpomene," pp. 83, 91; Arthur Mizener, "Robert Penn Warren: 'All the King's Men,' " *SoR,* 3 (Summer 1967), pp. 874–94, repr. in Bloom, pp. 92, 96.

25. Mizener, *All the King's Men,* p. 81; I: LDR.

CHAPTER 26: PRIZES AND
PERFORMANCES

1. *AKM,* p. 103.

2. CBW to PMP, 25 Apr. 1946, courtesy of PMP; RPW to AL, 11 July 1946, VUL; RPW to BBC, 6 May 1946, VUL.

3. RPW to AL, 11 July 1947, VUL; *PF,* p. 63; *BD* (nv), p. xi. One of his essays was a review of the Viking *Portable Faulkner,* published under the title "Cowley's Faulkner," *NRep,* 12 Aug. 1946, pp. 176–80 and 26 Aug. 1946, pp. 234–37, repr. *NSE,* 197–215. As Joseph R. Millichap writes, "Literary historians have credited Cowley's edition and Warren's review of it as the turning point in Faulkner's critical reputation." See

"Robert Penn Warren and Regionalisms," *MissQ,* 43 (Winter 1994–95), p. 32.

4. *TwRPW,* pp. 351, 348.

5. RPW to ED, 12 Aug. 1946, YUL; RPW to DD, 26 Aug. 1946, VUL; I: ECW, Helen Ransom Forman, RPW.

6. I: LD.

7. *Talent,* pp. 127–35.

8. *Talent,* pp. 127–35.

9. "New Best Seller," Minneapolis *Sunday Tribune,* 13 Oct. 1946.

10. RPW to BBC, 10 July 1946, VUL. On the story's publication many in Hopkinsville found Bolton Lovehart almost indistinguishable from John Wesley Venable, Jr., and some resented the way they thought the author had taken advantage of a shy but friendly recluse with a harmless pastime. See RPW, "Writer at Work: How a Story Was Born and How, Bit by Bit, It Grew," *NYTBR,* 1 Mar. 1959, pp. 4–5, 36, repr. "Blackberry Winter: A Recollection," *Understanding Fiction,* eds. CB and RPW (Englewood Cliffs, N.J.: Prentice-Hall, 1959), pp. 377–82, 378; Joy Bale Boone, "A Circus at the Top," Louisville *Courier-Journal Magazine,* 4 June 1978, pp. 10–15, 13.

11. More than just a symbol, the circus in its context "makes it universal, a symbol of an imaginative, creative, and romantic vision of life, where it recalls the central symbols of Hawthorne's tales and romances of art and artists." Millichap, p. 12. The story achieves effects much like those in Faulkner's "Miss Zilphia Gant" and "A Rose for Emily" and Sherwood Anderson's "Adventure" and "Loneliness." Though Bardsville is larger than Anderson's Winesburg, there is in RPW's story the same hearkening back to an earlier time. Walker, p. 74.

12. Boone, "Circus," p. 15.

13. *Talent,* p. 130; "The Circus in the Attic," *Cosmopolitan,* Sept. 1947, pp. 67–70 and ff., repr. *CA,* pp. 3–62.

14. Millichap, p. 17; RPW, "Writer at Work," pp. 378–79; see Walker, pp. 76–78.

15. RPW, "Writer at Work," p. 379; Millichap, p. 25.

16. RPW to AL, 8 Sept. 1948, VUL; *Time,* 51 (26 Jan. 1948), p. 101; Orville Prescott, *YR,* 37 (Spring 1948), p. 575; Granville Hicks, *NYT,* 25 Jan. 1948, p. 5; John Farrelly, *NRep,* 118 (26 Jan. 1948), p. 32; Richard Match, *NYHTBR,* 25 Jan. 1948, p. 4; *NY,* 28 (24 Jan. 1948), p. 80.

17. *TwRPW,* p. 238; *UF,* p. 381.

18. *Talent,* p. 130; Eric Bentley, "The Meaning of Robert Penn Warren's Novels," *KR,* 10 (Summer 1948), pp. 407, 423–24.

19. Arthur Mizener to AT, 5 Dec. 1946, PUL; *Talent,* p. 130.

20. RPW to KAP, 24 Feb. 1947, UMdL; AL to AT, 5 Mar. 1947, *Lytle-Tate,* p. 209; RPW to Peter Taylor, 7 Mar. 1947, courtesy of SW; RPW to AL, 24 Feb. 1947, VUL.

21. RPW to CB, 10 Feb. 1947, YUL; I: CB.

22. ECW also received a thousand-dollar grant from the American Academy and the National Institute to support her writing.

23. RPW and CBW to KAP, 19 July 1947, UMdL; I: AE.

24. I: Eric Bentley, RPWOHP; RPW to Robert Hivnor, 18 July 1947, courtesy of Robert Hivnor; RPW to KAP, 19 July 1947, UMdL.

25. RPW to AL, 8 Sept. 1947, VUL; I: Eric Bentley, RPWOHP.

26. Bennett Cerf, *At Random: Reminiscences of Bennett Cerf* (New York: Random House, 1977), p. 235; I: LD; *Talent,* p. 130.

27. "Theatre Off Broadway: Experimental Groups Are Having an Exciting, Successful Season," *Life,* 24 (Mar. 29, 1948), pp. 82–83. RPW to CB, 20 Feb. 1948, YUL. "The revolving stage, the treadmill, the light projections, the characters who pop up out of the audience, all these can distract at times from the story they are trying to tell." *Time,* 19 Jan. 1948; I: AE. "The story is told in flashbacks, encompassing twenty-three scenes, as two characters on the apron of the stage debate the nature of the Stark phenomenon. When you consider that the [President

Theatre's] stage is about the size of a handball court, it is especially remarkable what fluidity Erwin Piscator has achieved in the production." *NYT,* 19 Jan. 1948, p. 19.

28. CBW to PMP, 18 Nov. 1947, courtesy of PMP.

29. CBW to PMP, 18 Nov. 1947, courtesy of PMP; I: Helen Ransom Forman.

30. I: HO, HO by JS.

31. I: Richard Wilbur, BBC, AE.

32. I: BBC. Dr. Kubie published a Freudian analysis of Faulkner's *Sanctuary* in 1934 and several books, including *Neurotic Distortion of the Creative Mind* (Lawrence: University of Kansas Press, 1958).

CHAPTER 27: WRITING A NOVEL— FROM TAORMINA TO SIRMIONE

1. Edmund Spenser, *The Faerie Queene,* Book V, quoted in *WET,* p. vii.

2. CBW to PMP, 1 May 1948, courtesy of PMP; CBW to Natalie Davison, 8 May 1948, YUL.

3. RPW to AE, 18 Mar. 1948, courtesy of RH.

4. RPW to CB, 20 Feb. 1948, YUL.

5. RPW to AE, 18 Mar. 1948, courtesy of RH; RPW to PMP, 29 Apr. 1948, courtesy of PMP.

6. Ibid.

7. An edited bibliographical description of the title page suggests its scope and variety: "THE CONFESSION / OF / JEREBOAM O. BEAUCHAMP. / WHO WAS EXECUTED AT FRANKFORT, KY. / ON THE 7th OF JULY, 1826. / FOR THE MURDER OF / *Col. Solomon P. Sharp,* / *A Member of the Legislature and late Attorney General of Ky.* / WRITTEN BY HIMSELF, / And containing the only authentic account of the murder, and / the causes which induced it. / TO WHICH IS ADDED, / SOME POETICAL PIECES, WRITTEN BY MRS. ANN BEAUCHAMP, / *Who voluntarily put an end to her existence,*

on the day of the ex- / ecution of her hus-
band, and was buried in the same / grave with
him. / BLOOMFIELD, KY. /
PRINTED FOR THE PUBLISHER /
1826." Warren may well have had more
source material than this account edited
by various interested parties. And he had
read some of the five plays and six novels
based on the tragedy. The complexity was
such that one editor of the *Confession*
concludes that Warren's narrator, remark-
ing on the lies and half-lies, the truths
and half-truths, and the ignorance of the
truth, "echoes the confusion of anyone
who ever studied the facts. . . ." *The Con-*
fession of Jereboam O. Beauchamp, ed.
Robert D. Bamberg (Philadelphia: University of Pennsylvania Press, 1966), p.
14; see also *The Kentucky Tragedy: A Prob-*
lem in Romantic Attitudes, ed. Loren J.
Kallsen (Indianapolis: Bobbs–Merrill,
1963); and Walker, pp. 132–33. RPW to
AE, 12 Apr. 1948, courtesy of RH.
8. RPW to AE, 12 Apr. 1948, courtesy
of RH. Joshua Logan had just adapted
and produced Thomas Heggen's immensely successful novel, *Mr. Roberts,* on
Broadway. CBW to PMP, 1 May 1948,
courtesy of PMP; CBW to AE and Peggy
Erskine, 2 Apr. 1948, courtesy of AE.
9. RPW to PMP, 8 July 1948, courtesy
of PMP.
10. RPW to BBC, 5 Aug. 1948, courtesy of BBC.
11. RPW to PMP, 8 July 1948, courtesy
of PMP.
12. RPW to CB, 15 July 1948, YUL.
13. CBW to PMP, 27 July 1948, courtesy of PMP; CBW to AE, 11 Sept. 1948,
courtesy of AE.
14. I: RPW.

CHAPTER 28: PREMIERES AND
CLOSINGS

1. *WET,* p. 211.
2. CBW to PMP, 6 Dec. 1948, courtesy
of PMP.

3. I: PMP; RPW to PMP, 3 Jan. 1948,
courtesy of PMP.
4. Ibid. Three years younger than RPW,
Rossen had fought his way up from New
York's Lower East Side. From avant-garde
theatre he had gone on to scripts at
Warner Bros. that often reflected his
strongly leftist politics. RPW to PMP, 14
Mar. 1949, 17 Jan. 1949; CBW to PMP,
18 Mar. 1949, courtesy of PMP. Some
readers of the novel objected that Jack
Burden was missing from the film. RPW
served as consultant and participant in
Ken Burns's documentary film on Huey
Long. Burns comments, "In a feature film
it was too much to handle. Because you
have one story and the compelling figure
is Willie Stark. The literary figure is Jack
Burden." I: Ken Burns. For a detailed discussion see Joseph R. Millichap, *"All the*
King's Men, Photography, and Film," in
Festschrift, pp. 149–57.
5. RPW to PMP, 22 Apr. 1949, courtesy
of PMP.
6. RPW to FO, 11 May 1949, VUL;
CBW to PMP, 14 June 1949, courtesy of
PMP; RPW to TLF, 5 July 1949, courtesy of TLF.
7. RPW to AE, 19 July 1949, courtesy
of RH.
8. I: PMP; I: RPW by Alexander S.
Crouch, courtesy of Mr. Crouch.
9. *Lytle-Tate,* pp. 222–23; I: PMP, AE.
10. RPW to AE, 7 Sept. 1949, courtesy
of RH; RPW to CB, 12 Sept. 1949,
YUL.
11. ES to JB, 6 Dec. 1988.
12. CBW to PMP, 28 Nov. 1949, courtesy of PMP; ES to JB, 6 Dec. 1988; Danforth Ross to JB, 4 June 1992.
13. CBW may have been diverted by a
zoology course she was taking, which,
she told PMP, was "nice & orderly & abstract." CBW to PMP, 28 Nov. 1949, 3
Dec. 1949, courtesy of PMP; Samuel
Monk to AT, 23 Nov. 1949, PUL; EBW
to PMP, 10 Oct. 1949, 2 Jan. 1950, courtesy of PMP.
14. I: HB and EB, RPWOHP.

15. I: RPW; Margaret Allison Hemphill to JB.

16. Ibid.; ES to JB, 6 Dec. 1988; I: Isabella Gardner, RPWOHP.

17. Broderick Crawford, as Willie Stark, won the award for best actor, and Mercedes McCambridge, as Sadie Burke, received the best supporting actress award.

18. RPW to FO, 31 Jan. 1950, VUL; RPW to PMP, 10 Feb. 1950, courtesy of PMP; I: Samuel H. Monk, RPWOHP; JCR to AT, 3 June 1950, PUL.

19. RPW to PMP, 10 Feb. 1950, courtesy of PMP; RPW to AT, 22 Feb. 1950, PUL.

20. I: ES; RPW to AE, 15 Feb., 11 Mar., 16 Mar., 26 Mar. 1950, courtesy of RH; Samuel H. Monk to AT, 4 Apr. 1950, PUL.

21. ES to JB, 6 Dec. 1988; I: ES, HB, and EB, RPWOHP; Mark Royden Winchell, "An Extended Family," *SoR,* 31 (Spring 1995), p. 199; I: Saul Bellow; ES to JB; Dan Brennan to JB.

22. I: Eric Bentley, RPWOHP.

23. I: Doris Foster and CHF; I: Saul Bellow.

24. JCR to AT, 3 June 1950, PUL.

25. RPW to PMP, 3 May 1950, courtesy of PMP; I: RPW, CB.

26. I: RPW, AE.

CHAPTER 29: THE HISTORICAL NOVEL

1. *WET,* p. 147.

2. By the time RPW was writing in California in the spring of 1949 he had an extensive bibliography of factual and fictional treatments of Beauchamp and his love affair with Ann Cook, which came to be called "the Kentucky Tragedy." A year later his supply of materials had grown, with the help of the University of Kentucky Library, to a mass of maps, photostats, portraits, and engravings. See *The Confession of Jereboam O. Beauchamp,* ed. Robert D. Bamberg (Philadelphia:

University of Pennsylvania Press, 1966), and *The Kentucky Tragedy: A Problem in Romantic Attitudes,* ed. Loren J. Kallsen (Indianapolis: Bobbs-Merrill, 1963). See also RPW, "Background of a Novel: *World Enough and Time,*" (New York: Random House, n.d.), 7 pp.

3. *The Faerie Queene,* prologue to the Fifth Book. *TwRPW,* pp. 187, 261.

4. See Burt, p. 180.

5. RPW, "A Confession." *Wings: The Literary Guild Review* (New York: July 1950), pp. 6, 8.

6. See Clark, p. 105; Burt, p. 197; *Achievement,* pp. 226, 234.

7. Samuel Holt Monk to AT, 23 Nov. 1949; JCR to AT, 3 June 1950, PUL.

8. See A. B. Guthrie, *SatR,* 33 (24 June 1950), p. 11; Brendan Gill, *NY,* 26 (24 June 1950), p. 89; *Time,* 55 (21 June 1950), p. 99; Elizabeth Janeway, *NYTBR,* 25 June 1950, p. 1; Malcolm Cowley, *NYHTBR,* 25 June 1950, p. 1; C. J. Rolo, *AtMo,* 186 (July 1950), p. 86; Paul Pickrel, *YR,* 39 (Summer 1950), p. 765.

9. *TwRPW,* p. 92; RPW to CHF, 21 July 1950, courtesy of CHF; Casper, p. 148; Snipes, p. 84; Joseph Frank, "Romanticism and Reality in Robert Penn Warren," in Bloom, pp. 60, 62; RBH, "Tangled Web," in Nakadate, pp. 117, 119, 125; Walker, p. 116; Leslie A. Fiedler, "No!" in *Thunder: Essays on Myth and Literature* (Boston: Beacon Press, 1960), pp. 123, 126; *Achievement,* pp. 222, 225.

10. RPW to PMP, 7 July 1950, courtesy of PMP; *Bibliography,* pp. 58, 66. There were two special limited editions, two book-club editions, English editions, and a paperback edition twenty-nine years after the original publication.

11. RPW to Robert Franklin Warren, 28 July 1950, courtesy of TLF; RPW to CHF, 21 July 1950, courtesy of CHF.

12. RPW to PMP, 7 July 1950, 8 Aug. 1950, courtesy of PMP; I: MWB, RPW.

13. CBW to PMP, 24 Sept. 1950, courtesy of PMP.

14. I: CB; RPW to CHF, 9 Oct. 1950, courtesy of CHF; RPW to DD, 6 Nov. 1950, VUL. CBW to PMP, 24 Sept. 1950, courtesy of PMP; RPW to Alice Warren, courtesy of TLF; RPW to PMP, 7 Dec. 1950, courtesy of PMP.
15. RPW to PMP, 7 Dec. 1950, courtesy of PMP.
16. RPW to PMP, 8 Jan. 1951, courtesy of PMP.
17. RPW to WTB, 24 Mar. 1951, VUL; I: JLS, RPWOHP; Minnesota *Daily,* 18 Apr. 1951; I: CB, RPW.
18. I: CB, Eric Bentley, RPWOHP.
19. *Talent,* p. 132.
20. I: Mary O'Connor, RPWOHP; I: CB.
21. Minneapolis *Star,* 18 May 1951; I: CHF; RPW to BBC, 11 May 1951, VUL; Minneapolis *Dispatch,* 10 May 1951. Perhaps Warren had taken some comfort from the action of the National Institute of Arts and Letters in adding his name, with those of eleven others, "to its list of those whose works the institute regards likely to achieve a permanent place in American culture." Minneapolis *Dispatch,* 2 Feb. 1950.
22. RPW to CHF, 23 May 1951, courtesy of CHF; RPW to AE, Saturday afternoon [9 June 1951], courtesy of RH.
23. *NSE,* pp. 140, 160; see *Achievement,* p. 237.
24. RPW to AE, 19 June 1951, courtesy of RH; RPW to Alice Warren, 19 June 1951, courtesy of TLF; RPW to PMP, 3 July 1952, courtesy of PMP. The Associated Press item on the divorce noted their actual marriage date of 1929, probably derived from court records.
25. CBW to PMP, 27 Sept. 1951, 6 Oct. 1951, courtesy of PMP.
26. RPW to AE, 19 June 1951, courtesy of RH; Mrs. Karl Shapiro to JB.
27. RPW to PMP, 3 July 1951, courtesy of PMP.

CHAPTER 30: A NEW LIFE

1. *I,* pp. 57–58.
2. RPW to CHF, 18 Sept. 1951, courtesy of CHF; I: ECW; *TwRPW,* p. 337.
3. *TwRPW,* p. 337; I: Matthew Bruccoli, RPWOHP; RPW to AL, 15 Apr. 1952, VUL; KAP to Eudora Welty, 8 Nov. 1951, *KAP Letters,* p. 407; JCR to AT, 11 Jan. 1952, PUL.
4. ES to JB.
5. I: ECW; ECW, "No More Swans," *PR,* 4 (Mar. 1938), pp. 56–58.
6. I: ECW.
7. I: ECW.
8. I: ECW, Victoria T. Miller (hereafter VTM). See her dissertation, "The Literary Achievement and Reputation of Eleanor Clark" (Ann Arbor: University Microfilms, 1991).
9. VTM, "Literary Achievement."
10. See VTM, pp. 14, 20; Alan Wald, *The New York Intellectuals: The Rise and Decline of the Anti-Stalinist Left from the 1930's to the 1980's* (Chapel Hill: University of North Carolina Press, 1987), p. 248.
11. VTM, p. 21; ECW to VTM, 12 Mar. 1992, courtesy of VTM; ECW, *Gloria Mundi* (New York: Pantheon, 1979). See ECW, *Dr. Heart: A Novella / and Other Stories* (New York: Pantheon, 1974), pp. 78, 80, 85. ECW to VTM, 14 Feb. 1989, 12 Mar. 1992, courtesy of VTM; VTM, pp. 24–25, 28.
12. I: ECW; VTM, p. 29; I: RPW.
13. I: ECW. Eleanor Clark, *The Bitter Box* (New York: Doubleday, 1946). James Laughlin called Clark "a very fine new writer," placing her in the company of Eudora Welty, Carson McCullers, and Jean Stafford (*Book Week* 14 Apr. 1946, p. 16); Diana Trilling called the novel "a work of unquestionable moral-political taste," (*Nation,* 27 Apr. 1946, p. 514); and Rose Field wrote that she would be hailed as a "find," (*Weekly Book Review,* 14 Apr. 1946, p. 5).
14. I: ECW; see Donald Stewart, "An Italian Anchorage," *NYT Magazine,* "The Sophisticated Traveler," part 2, 20 May 1990, p. 51; I: RW. See Jon Stallworthy, *Louis MacNeice* (London: Faber & Faber, 1995), *passim.*
15. I: ECW.

16. I: ECW.

17. *Time,* 59 (14 Apr. 1952), p. 120; *NY,* 28 (14 Apr. 1952), p. 120; *NYT,* 13 Apr. 1952, p. 3.

18. RPW to AL, 15 Apr. 1952, VUL; *PF,* pp. 64–65; I: RPW.

19. RPW to HB, 27 May 1952, UMinnL; ECW to RPW, 12, 19, 20, 27 June 1952, courtesy of ECW; I: ECW.

20. AT to DD, 27 Oct. 1951, *Literary Correspondence,* p. 355; I: ECW.

21. I: ECW; ECW to VTM, courtesy of VTM.

22. I: ECW; RPW to BBC, 4 Mar. 1953, VUL.

CHAPTER 31: HOMESTEAD AND
WATERSHED

1. *BD,* p. 215.

2. Notes courtesy of FW; *PF,* pp. 62, 65.

3. RPW to DD, 5 Mar. 1953, VUL; I: ECW.

4. I: ECW; RPW to BBC, 4 Mar. 1953, VUL.

5. RPW to BBC, 4 Mar. 1953, VUL.

6. RPW to AE, "Thursday" [1953], courtesy of RH; I: ECW, RPW, RW; I: AL; Arthur H. Scouten to JB.

7. I: ECW, RW; RPW to CB, 1 Aug. 1953, YUL; RPW to PMP, 1 Aug. 1953, courtesy of PMP.

8. I: ECW; RPW to PMP, 1 Aug. 1953, courtesy of PMP.

9. RPW was coediting *Short Story Masterpieces* with AE (New York: Dell, 1954), which would be followed by two more collaborations: *Six Centuries of Great Poetry* (New York: Dell, 1955), and *A New Southern Harvest* (New York: Bantam, 1957). Following the text of BD were fourteen pages of notes, including letters and various legal documents on the historical bases of the poem.

10. *TwRPW,* pp. 339–40. RPW corrected "Lilburn" to "Lilburne" in the second version of the poem.

11. *TwRPW,* pp. 339–40; *Burden,* p. 510; RPW, "The Way It Was Written,"

NYTBR, 23 Aug. 1953, pp. 6, 25, repr. in *Discussion,* pp. 1–3.

12. *TwRPW,* p. 43. The three lines written in ballad form would become the only ones given to the murdered slave. See Casper, pp. 149, 188; *Discussion,* p. 2. RPW did not name the collaborator but said that "a friend from the theater" had suggested the play form (*Burden,* p. 510). It might have been Robert Rossen, Francis Fergusson, or perhaps a member of the Yale School of Drama. JAG suggests David M. Clay as a possible collaborator. JAG to JB. Later Adrian Hall worked with him on a play version of the poem.

13. At one point RPW omits the presence of Dr. Charles Lewis, who had brought the family to the frontier from Albemarle County in Virginia, and any mention of his son Lilburne's first wife and children but invents a brother for the second wife, Letitia, and a mammy, Aunt Cat, who had nursed Lilburne as an infant. "I have undertaken to fill in the gaps of action and motivation," he told the reader, "for instance, in the personal story of Laetitia and Lilburn" (p. xi).

14. Burt, p. 200.

15. Victor Strandberg, "Theme and Metaphor in *Brother to Dragons,*" *PMLA,* LXXIX (Sept. 1964), pp. 498–508, repr. *Discussion,* pp. 81–82. Cf. Robert Frost's thirty-page poem about Job, *A Masque of Reason.*

16. In the list of speakers, Jefferson's epitaph is given in full, the other two achievements listed being his authorship of the Statute of Virginia for Religious Freedom and his founding the University of Virginia (p. 2); see Burt, p. 201, and Neil Nakadate, "Voices of Community: The Function of Colloquy in Robert Penn Warren's *Brother to Dragons,*" in *Tennessee Studies in Literature,* XXI (1976), pp. 114–24, repr. in *Discussions,* p. 116.

17. RPW described his intention. "I don't want to set it as a historical poem. . . . I want a modern man, myself . . . and my father. . . . And this is all a fantasy . . . a kind of dream situation.

And . . . the special relation with my father that I had is also tied in the poem." *TwRPW,* p. 348. RPW made these comments not long before the publication of the 1979 revised version of the poem, but they probably represent his feelings about the 1953 version as well.

18. See *TwRPW,* p. 348.

19. Leslie Fiedler wrote that RPW had handled bombast and melodrama with "skill and poignancy," pursuing "a difficult, improbable, heartbreaking rhetoric." "Seneca in the Meat-House," *PR* (Mar.–Apr. 1954), pp. 208–12, repr. in *No! in Thunder,* pp. 127–31. For the Chicago *Sunday Tribune* reviewer it was "a major book of literary quality" (23 Aug. 1953), p. 3; for Babette Deutsch in the *NYHTBR,* it was masterful across a whole range of effects, (23 Aug. 1953), p. 3. In the *NYT,* Randall Jarrell called it his best book, sometimes cruel, crude, and obsessed, but "always extraordinary" and a great event (23 Aug. 1953), p. 6. The reviewer for *Time* accused him of producing "a bogus air by putting long-winded rationalizations in Jefferson's mouth," 62 (24 Aug. 1953), p. 82. Hugh Kenner found Jefferson unconvincing, the poetry full of echoes of T. S. Eliot and on the whole "strained and declamatory." *HudR,* 6 (Winter 1954), pp. 605–10. See *Bibliography,* p. 4; *Burden,* p. 513; Ruppersburg, p. 78; George P. Garrett, "The Recent Poetry of Robert Penn Warren," in Longley, p. 227; and *Achievement,* where JHJ remarks on the poem's "resourceful balancing of the original and the traditional. The gravity of the subject is announced by invocations and apostrophes and rendered in basic unrhymed iambic pentameter, a pattern that is nevertheless lightened by frequent metrical irregularities characteristic of his poetry from the time Warren first read Dante in 1938" (pp. 61, 63–64).

20. I: ECW; RPW to AL, 3 Dec. 1953.

21. *The Wedding Ring,* copyright 24 July 1951, UKyL. RPW expanded the roles of Gilbert Mastern, Duncan Trice, his wife, Arabella, and her maid, Phebe, and created other characters, but most of the plot remains essentially the same. There are also echoes of *NR* and *WET.*

22. RPW heard this story from a Kentucky writer, book collector, and farmer who had done research for a book to be called *Slavery Times in Kentucky.* His research included an interview with an old judge who recalled the story of the two girls being sold into slavery. RPW, untitled, unpublished ts., UKyL; J. Winston Coleman, Jr., *Slavery Times in Kentucky* (Chapel Hill: University of North Carolina Press, 1940); see *TwRPW,* pp. 261–62.

23. JCR to AT, 26 Mar. 1954, PUL; I: ECW.

24. RPW to CHF, 30 Apr. 1954, courtesy of CHF.

CHAPTER 32: ENTRANCES AND EXITS

1. *PR,* 23 (Spring 1955), p. 171, repr. *NSP,* p. 269.

2. RPW to ED, 25 July 1954, YUL.

3. RPW to ED, 25 July 1954, YUL; RPW to AL, 9 Aug. 1954, VUL; RPW to BBC, 18 June 1954, VUL.

4. William Butler Yeats, "A Prayer for My Daughter" and "A Prayer for My Son."

5. *NSP,* p. 269.

6. *NSP,* pp. 269–70.

7. *P,* p. 4.

8. RPW to ED, 25 July 1954, YUL; RPW to PMP, 14 Sept. 1954, courtesy of PMP.

9. *P,* p. 9.

10. *P,* pp. 12–13.

11. RPW to PMP, 14 Sept. 1954, courtesy of PMP.

12. RPW to AL, 28 Oct. 1954, VUL; RPW to KAP, 26 Jan. 1955, UMdL.

13. RPW to KAP, 26 Jan. 1955, UMdL; RPW to PMP, 4 Aug. 1955, courtesy of PMP; RPW to AS, 3 Oct. 1966, courtesy of AS.

14. RPW to PMP, 4 Aug. 1955, courtesy of PMP; see *PF,* pp. 78–79.

15. *PF,* pp. 78–79.

16. RPW and BBC were in the planning stages for a script of a play or a motion picture, and RPW and CB were working at the textbook revision at the same time that he was completing the poetry anthology with AE. RPW to CHF, 24 Mar. 1955; RPW to FO and HO, 28 Apr. 1955, VUL.

17. RPW to BBC, 28 May 1955, VUL; RPW to FO, 22 June 1955, VUL; RPW to CHF, 24 Mar. 1955, courtesy of CHF.

18. RPW to PMP, 4 Aug. 1955, courtesy of PMP.

19. RPW to AL, 16 Aug. 1955, VUL.

20. He had used not only Coleman's book "and Canot's autobiography, but also . . . memoirs of officers on slave patrol, hearings in the British Parliaments, and other documents from the Brown University and Yale Collections." Casper, p. 188.

21. The familiar RPW motif of western migration appears in the series of removals Amantha and Tobias make in the last twenty years of her tale.

22. *TwRPW,* p. 162. Born apparently in 1842, Amantha leaves Kentucky for Ohio at nine, returns and is sold into slavery at sixteen, and concludes her story in Kansas at forty-six in 1888. Her accents suggest those of the heroines she may have encountered in novels: "Oh, who would save me?" (p. 74). "Oh, my life was nothing" (p. 345). At the same time, her narration must bear the burden of explaining the Louisiana Constitutional Convention and describing its culmination in the New Orleans riot and massacre of 1866. She must also handle RPW's favorite device of the interpolated story, relaying to the reader Hamish Bond's twenty-seven-page account of his life.

23. Conscious of her charms' effect on Bond, who is "aware of the whiteness of my small hands laid decorously together at my waist" (p. 119), Amantha suggests shrewd Scarlett O'Hara. Her narration—

telling her story with the knowledge that the reader is listening—sometimes shades into a direct address to the reader. In fairness, however, at times when she speaks in her most melodramatic tones she is describing how she felt rather than what she actually said: "Oh, who am I? For so long that was, *you might say,* the cry of my heart" (p. 3) [italics added]. See *Bibliography,* "Warren's Later Poetry: Unverified Rumors of Wisdom," *MissQ,* 37 (Spring 1984), pp. 165–66.

24. *Achievement,* pp. 239, 241. For imagery including scraps of paper and "the fetal mummy that haunts Warren's novels" see *Taciturn Text,* pp. 133–34, 140.

25. For an enthusiastic review see Arthur Mizener, *NYT,* 21 Aug. 1955; Maxwell Geismar, *Nation,* 1 Oct. 1955, p. 287; Leslie Fiedler, *NRep,* 26 Sept. 1955, p. 30, repr. *No! in Thunder,* p. 133. Gore Vidal wrote a savagely clever review in the voice of one "Marian" delivering a report to members of her book club. "Book Report," *Zero,* 2 (Spring 1956), p. 98. By this time the book had been purchased for filming, which must have reconfirmed hostile critics' belief that it had been written for the movies. For a refutation of some hostile reviews, see F. Cudworth Flint, "Mr. Warren and the Reviewers," *SR* 64 (Autumn 1956), repr. in Longley, pp. 125–39.

26. Snipes, p. 124; *Burden,* p. 517; *Achievement,* p. 237.

CHAPTER 33: POLITICAL REPORTAGE AND POETIC FRENZY

1. *SP75,* p. 256.

2. I: ECW.

3. RPW to AT, 8 Jan. 1956, PUL; Strauss, p. 131.

4. I: Alex Szogyi; Ralph Ellison to Nathan A. Scott, Jr., courtesy of Ralph Ellison.

5. *Seg,* in *RPWR,* p. 236; I: Hettie Louise Griffey; RPW, "Divided South Searches for Its Soul," *Life,* 9 July 1956, p. 111.

6. "Divided South," p. 114.

7. See note 5.

8. Frederick S. Danziger to RPW, 30 Apr. 1956, 10 May 1956; RPW to Frederick S. Danziger, 16 May 1956. Cinina's friend was Burton Hathaway Gardner. A form of his family's name occurs in Gardiner's Bay and Gardiner's Island at the eastern tip of Long Island.

9. LDR, p. 672; *TwRPW*, pp. 19–20; CG to Stark Young, 17 May 1956, in *Connections*, p. 337; RPW to DD, 11 Mar. 1959, VUL; RPW to JLS, 28 June 1956, courtesy of JLS.

10. I: ECW; RPW to AE, 4 June 1956, courtesy of RH.

11. RPW to AE, 4 June 1956, courtesy of RH.

12. RPW to AE, 27 July, 5 Aug., 26 Aug., 28 Sept. 1956, courtesy of AE.

13. RPW to DD, 23 Aug. 1956, VUL. For sources of "School Lesson Based on Word of Tragic Death of Entire Gillum Family," see *TN*, pp. 95–99. RPW to AE, 22 Dec. 1956, courtesy of AE; *Brother to Dragons: A Play in Two Acts*, was finally published by GaR in 1976; *Bibliography*, p. 232.

14. See Russell Lynes, "An Academic Presence in Rome," *Architectural Digest*, May 1987; RPW to BBC, 20 Sept., 15 Oct. 1956, VUL.

15. Ralph Ellison to Nathan A. Scott, Jr., 17 July 1989, courtesy of Ralph Ellison; RPW to BBC, 22 Jan. 1957, VUL.

16. RPW to AT, 22 Jan. 1957, PUL; RPW to Agostino Lombardo, 10 Mar. 1957, courtesy of Agostino Lombardo; JAG, " 'A Singular Association': The Brooks-Warren Literary Correspondence," *SoR*, 31 (Spring 1995), p. 244.

17. *SoR*, 31 (Spring 1955), p. 244; I: RW.

18. RPW to BBC, 14 Mar. 1957, VUL.

CHAPTER 34: PROMISES FULFILLED—
AND MADE

1. *SP*, p. 266.

2. *TwRPW*, pp. 280, 332, 239.

3. *SP75*, pp. 228–32; *P*, p. 19; see *TN*, pp. 80, 95–99, *passim*, for other source material.

4. See *Achievement*, p. 42.

5. CB, *The Hidden God* (New Haven: Yale University Press, 1963), pp. 100, 109, 111.

6. Despite the fantastic characters and events, there was enough of an inner consistency to this vision, with its obscure logic of a nightmare, for Warren to recast it a few years later with a chorus that "announces at the beginning the expected coming of a saviour" so that the "poem-play thus frames the nightmarish activities in the forest with the expectation of resurrection and salvation. . . ." See William Finley, "Warren's 'Grotesque' Nightmare: 'Ballad of a Sweet Dream of Peace,' " in *Festschrift*, pp. 171–88. Like *The Waste Land*, this poem includes not only a young woman of easy virtue but also a man who is something like a Quester Knight and must withstand his own ordeal in this woodland version of Eliot's Perilous Chapel among the mountains. See George Garrett, "The Recent Poetry of Robert Penn Warren," in Longley, p. 228. See W. J. Smith, *NRep*, 137 (14 Oct. 1957), p. 18; *SatR*, 40 (9 Nov. 1957), p. 15; Dudley Fitts, *NYT*, 18 Aug. 1957, p. 6; James Dickey, *SoR*, 66 (Spring 1958), p. 307; M. L. Rosenthal, *Nation*, 186 (18 Jan. 1958), p. 57; Morgan Blum, *KR*, 21 (Winter 1959), pp. 97–120; Babette Deutsch, *NYHTBR*, 25 Aug. 1957, p. 4; Paul Engle, Chicago *Sunday Tribune*, 8 Sept. 1957, p. 2.

7. The other demands on his time included writing citations and membership nominations to the National Institute of Arts and Letters for artists such as John Cheever, S. J. Perelman, Flannery O'Connor, and W. S. Merwin. RPW told the Browns that "before he goes Chris may have had a deeper and clearer experience of what it is to be a human being than those of us who waste and hurry through year after year of the wild

chase to evade what the human self-consciousness was really put down here to discover. . . . I do not think there is any such thing as an obscure, or a short, good life; there isn't any time where a loving life is concerned, nor any quantity when it comes to the eternal ideas, loving kindness and beautiful things or actions, nor do I think death can defeat them; I feel as loved by my mother as when she lived, and find myself caught up with gladness that we can be delivered from the self-engrossed body that tries so hard and never succeeds in sharing perfectly in these eternal realities, and be made part of the very eternal things themselves and be fulfilled at last. My ideas of what people refer to as immortality are dreadfully unconventional but of the eternity of the light we have little glimmers of and reflect so faultily, I just do not doubt; there is just too much proof around of how good and lovely things do not die. . . ."[*sic*]. He wrote them another eloquent letter of condolence on 8 Dec. 1957 after Chris's death. RPW to HB and EB, n.d., courtesy of ES.

8. KAP to RPW, 26 Sept. 1957, UMdL; AL to RPW, 2 Oct. 1957, YUL; *NYTBR,* 17 Jan. 1958, p. 27.

9. Garrett, "Recent Poetry," in Longley, p. 230; see *Burden,* p. 530; *Achievement,* pp. 31, 71.

10. See *Bibliography,* pp. 198–99.

11. RPW to Agostino Lombardo, 18 Mar. 1958, courtesy of Agostino Lombardo.

12. RPW to DD, 9 June 1958, VUL. Right-wing generals including Jacques Soustelle had led a secret army organization to put down the Algerian insurrection and appeared to threaten a military coup against France's Fourth Republic.

13. RPW to DD, 9 June 1958, VUL; RPW to Agostino Lombardo, 12 Apr. 1958, courtesy of Agostino Lombardo. To make up *SE* RPW had added to the essays on Faulkner and KAP from his other writings about them. His praise for

Thomas Wolfe's fiction and Herman Melville's poetry was still heavily qualified, but his admiration for Conrad, Hemingway, and Frost was as undiminished as it had been in the reviews and special editions that had originally elicited the pieces. The other two essays of the ten that made up the three-hundred-page book were "Pure and Impure Poetry" and the long study of *The Rime of the Ancient Mariner.*

14. *SE,* pp. xi–xiii.

15. EC, *The Song of Roland* (New York: Random House, Legacy Books, 1960). See *Bibliography,* p. 200; RPW to AE, 28 June 1958, courtesy of AE. Six of these poems would appear in the fall, as varied as the ten that appeared or would appear in spring and summer magazine numbers, with settings ranging from ancient Greece to Switzerland and Kentucky.

16. RPW to AE, 6, 12, 14, 21, and 25 July 1958, courtesy of AE.

17. RPW to AE, 3 and 5 Aug. 1958, courtesy of AE; RPW to Karl Shapiro, 13 Aug. 1958, courtesy of Karl Shapiro; RPW to AE, 1 Sept. and 15 Aug. 1958, courtesy of AE.

18. Emily Maxwell, *NY,* 34 (22 Nov. 1958), p. 214. RPW had used the same material when he sold "How Texas Won Her Freedom" to *Holiday* magazine for March 1958, pp. 72–73, 160, 162–67.

19. RPW to BBC, 1 Oct. 1958, VUL; RPW to AE, 7 Oct. 1958, courtesy of RH.

20. RPW to BBC, 1 Oct. 1958, VUL; RPW and ECW to KAP, 20 Sept. 1958, UMdL.

CHAPTER 35: TWENTY YEARS' GESTATION

1. *BH,* pp. 31–32.

2. RPW to KAP, 2 May 1959, UMdL; I: RPW.

3. RPW to BBC, 4 Jan. 1959, VUL. BBC had published two earlier novels,

Lightwood (1939) and *River Rogue* (1942). *This Is Adam* was the first of a trilogy, which would be completed with *Devil's Elbow* (1969) and *In Pursuit of Happiness* (1974).

4. RPW to AT, 19 Mar. 1959, PUL. The manuscript included the sixteen poems he had published the previous spring and summer plus a score more, which would appear in the coming spring and summer in *BotOs, VQR,* and other magazines.

5. RPW to KAP, 2 May 1959, UMdL; RPW to FNC and BBC, 2 May 1959, VUL.

6. RPW to DD, 11 Mar. and 10 July 1959, VUL; RPW to AL, 21 June 1959, VUL.

7. RPW to AL, 21 June 1959, VUL.

8. I: RW.

9. RPW had been dissatisfied with the title, and when the book was ready for the printer, AE said it was terrible and urged RPW to find another. "Oh hell," he remembered saying, "call it *The Cave* and be done with it." They found a copy of *The Republic,* located the passage in Book VII, and typed it into the setting copy. "Stuck it on like that. Impulse. Last minute. . . . That's the story of the notion of this deeply plotted allegory from the start." *TwRPW,* pp. 136–37.

10. "Knowledge and the Image of Man," *SR,* 62 (Spring 1955), pp. 6, 25, repr. in Longley, p. 241.

11. Though the vision achieved by the other characters also produces new relationships with one another, the most complex is that between Jack and Celia after they have worked their way through their various guilts. The deepest is that of Jack, who is finally able to admit to Brother Sumpter that he loved Jasper but wanted him to die, because, as he is finally able to tell himself, "*somebody always has to go in the ground. If he was there I would not have to go*" (p. 385). The description of Isaac's affair at the university with wealthy Rachel "Goldie" Goldstein suggests memories of Carolyn Anspacher

at Berkeley. The dialogue of Isaac's newspaper employers recalls that of the newsmen in *AHG* and *AKM.*

12. Jasper is what one critic, referring to Faulknerian characters such as Caddy Compson and Addie Bundren, calls an "absent presence." Other modernist novels offer characters who influence others when they themselves are no longer there: Mrs. Moore in E. M. Forster's *A Passage to India* and Mrs. Ramsay in Virginia Woolf's *To the Lighthouse,* to name only two. RPW's knowledge of modernist techniques appears here in other ways. Like Joseph Conrad in *Victory* and Faulkner in *As I Lay Dying,* he chose to present the action as perceived sequentially by many characters ranging from the reflections of sensitive Celia Harrick to the inane vulgarities of adolescent yokels and hillbillies. See André Bleikasten, *The Most Splendid Failure: Faulkner's "The Sound and the Fury"* (Bloomington: Indiana University Press, 1976), and *The Ink of Melancholy: Faulkner's Novels from "The Sound and the Fury" to "Light in August"* (Bloomington: Indiana University Press, 1990).

13. "This is one of the country's finest novels in years," wrote Paul Engle, "by one of its finest writers in years," *Chicago Sunday Tribune,* 23 Aug. 1959, p. 1. The novel would be popular, Granville Hicks wrote, because, like RPW's earlier popular novels, it would be a best-seller "deliberately designed to seize upon and hold the interest of the general reader," *SatR,* 22 Aug. 1959, p. 13. This quality would disturb some students of contemporary literature, wrote Riley Hughes, but they would be missing something. "All his skill as a story-teller—his mastery of narrative form, his wonderfully racy style—serves his real purpose. He is concerned with the deepest realities of the human spirit. . . ." *Catholic World* (Nov. 1959), p. 127; see also Melvin Maddocks, *Christian Science Monitor,* 24 Sept. 1959, p. 9. RPW wrote, "The picture Ace in the Hole

[Paramount, 1951, directed and co-written by Billy Wilder, with Kirk Douglas, Porter Hall, and Jan Sterling], which I never saw and which E says is great[,] killed the movie off. The picture, despite international awards, was a total flop, and caves are out for good and all." RPW to AS, 7 Dec. 1959, courtesy of AS.

14. *Achievement,* p. 274; see *Web of Being,* pp. 100–1; Casper, pp. 154, 158, 186.

15. RPW to AT, 9 Oct. 1959, PUL; RPW to AS, 7 Dec. 1959, courtesy of AS.

16. RPW to AT, 18 Oct. 1959, PUL.

17. Citation courtesy of the American Academy of Arts and Letters and the National Institute of Arts and Letters, *Proceedings,* Second series, no. 11 (New York: 1961), p. 13; RPW to AS, 7 Dec. 1959, courtesy of AS.

18. RPW to WTB, 26 Oct. 1959, VUL; I: RPW and ECW. For the Vermont purchase Warren presumably was able to use funds from a new book published September 28: *The Gods of Mount Olympus* in RH's Legacy imprint for younger readers.

19. RPW to DD, 10 July 1959, VUL; RPW to AS, 9 Dec. 1959, courtesy of AS.

CHAPTER 36: A REVERSAL OF FORTUNE

1. *YEO,* p. 75.

2. *Selected Poems by Denis Devlin* would be published by Holt, Rinehart and Winston in 1963 with a preface by RPW and AT.

3. I: RW. Some have voiced doubts that wolves had lived in these woods in recent times, but there are eastern coyotes, which do howl.

4. I: RW.

5. I: ECW; RPW to BBC, 31 Mar. 1960, VUL; RPW to CHF, 24 June 1960, courtesy of CHF; RPW to AL, 15 July 1960, VUL. Sophia Loren and Carlo Ponti bought La Rocca only to be scared off after one night by local boys wailing like ghosts. Ultimately it would become an expensive condominium. I: ECW.

6. RPW to AE, 13 July, 3, 7, and 8 Aug. 1960, courtesy of RH.

7. I: ECW; RPW to AL, 15 July 1960, VUL; RPW to CHF, 20 Sept. 1960, courtesy of CHF.

8. Repr. *SP75,* pp. 191–92, 196–97. VS sees this poem sequence as "divided almost evenly between *you* and your old adversary, the undiscovered self," a kind of corollary of the opposition between the bankrupt conscious ego and the healing unconscious. *Poetic Vision,* pp. 165–66.

9. Repr. *NSP,* pp. 261–64.

10. RPW to MW, 22 Nov. 1978, courtesy of MW; in *NSP* Warren reprinted only the first of the five sequences, pp. 263–64.

11. Repr. *SP75,* pp. 203, 205. Cf. the concluding lines of "In the Turpitude of Time: N.D." with those of Yeats's "Sailing to Byzantium" and the last lines of "A Vision: Circa 1880" with those of *The Waste Land.*

12. Repr. in part in *SP75,* pp. 212–14. Cf. A. E. Housman's "To an Athlete Dying Young."

13. Repr. *SP75,* p. 210; *NSP,* p. 265; *RT2,* p. 243. "Debate: Question, Quarry, Dream" had unusual antecedents. When ECW's friend Samuel Barber sent tickets to the opening of one of his operas, RPW went with her. At the reception afterward, he said, "Sam, thank you for inviting us. I got a pretty good poem written during the performance." One can only conjecture how a poet so sensitive to tonal qualities of language could have such a disinclination to listen to music. When ECW first took him to an opera he said he'd rather be in Sing Sing. But she persisted in Rome, Milan, and Paris, and in later years he could listen to Vivaldi with some pleasure. I: ECW. CB remembered Warren's singing, with his son, songs such as "The Wreck of Old Ninety-Seven" with a country-music

twang. I: CB. Later he collaborated in scoring "Ballad of a Sweet Dream of Peace" for music. See below.

14. Repr. *SP75*, pp. 51–53. Cf. "Prognosis" and "Masts at Dawn," *Encounter,* 29 (Oct. 1967), p. 7, repr. *I*, pp. 22–23, *NSP*, 236–37.

15. See "The Gyres" in Yeats's *Last Poems.*

16. See Paul Engle, *Chicago Sunday Tribune*, 4 Sept. 1960; John Holmes, *NYHTBR*, 16 Oct. 1960; Dudley Fitts, *NYTBR*, 23 Oct. 1960; Kenneth Koch, "Fresh Air," in Donald M. Allen, ed., *The New American Poetry* (New York: Grove Press, 1960), p. 231. VS writes that RPW's reputation suffered as a result of "the Paleface-Redskin controversy" described by Philip Rahv. RPW's friend and editor of the *Partisan Review,* Rahv posited two schools of American literature: that in the tradition of English literature, exemplified by writers such as Hawthorne, and that in the native American, exemplified by writers such as Twain. "Paleface and Redskin," *KR,* 1 (Summer 1939), pp. 251–56.

17. *TwRPW,* pp. 128–29; I: AE; see *Achievement*, p. 33; VS, "Warren's 'Worst' Book," *SCR,* 23 (Fall 1990), pp. 74–83. This reassessment argues that the volume includes some of Warren's best poems, interrelates with his major achievements, and possesses a kind of unity of its own.

18. RPW to AL, 11 Jan. 1961, VUL.

CHAPTER 37: THE WAR

1. *SPNO,* p. 91.

2. RPW to AL, 11 Jan. 1961, VUL. "A Mark Deep on a Nation's Soul," *Life,* 17 Mar. 1961, pp. 82–89; C. Vann Woodward, *The Burden of Southern History* (Baton Rouge: Louisiana State University Press, 1960), p. 87; *TwRPW,* p. 265.

3. *RPWR,* p. 270; Richard Harwell, *Chicago Sunday Tribune,* 23 Apr. 1961; *NY,* 37 (29 Apr. 1961), p. 150; Charles Poore,

NYT, 27 Apr. 1961, p. 19; David Donald, *NYTBR,* 14 May 1961, p. 3; Edmund Wilson, *Patriotic Gore: Studies in the Literature of the American Civil War* (New York: Oxford University Press, 1962), p. xxxi; Peter D'A. Jones, *NRep,* 142 (15 May 1961), pp. 16–17; RPW, *NRep,* 145 (14 July 1961), p. 31. *LCW* was reprinted (Cambridge, Mass.: Harvard University Press, 1983). RPW wrote "Episode in the Dime Store" on 1 Apr. 1960. It was published under that title in *SoR,* 30 (Autumn 1994), pp. 654–57; see James A. Perkins, "Notes on an Unpublished Robert Penn Warren Essay," *SoR,* 30 (Autumn 1994), pp. 650–53.

4. RPW to BBC, 19 May 1961, VUL.

5. RPW to BBC, 19 May 1961, VUL. See Eleanor Clark, *The Oysters of Locmariaquer* (New York: Alfred A. Knopf, 1964), p. 99. RPW to AE, 13 May 1961, courtesy of RH. Working on *Flood,* the new novel, RPW asked BBC for details of the parole system in Tennessee and Kentucky, perhaps recalling their trip to the Eddyville penitentiary in 1959. RPW to AL, 25 May 1961, VUL; RPW to AE, 13 May 1961, courtesy of RH.

6. RPW to AE, 14 July 1961, courtesy of RH.

7. I: RW.

8. I: RW; RPW to AE, 27 Aug. 1961, courtesy of RH.

9. Untitled carbon ts., UKyL; I: ECW.

10. RPW, "Battle of the Wilderness (or The Wilderness) / Summary of a novelette by Robert Penn Warren," UKyL; *TwRPW,* p. 114. In that fiscal year RPW had been able to put $18,000 into investments but confessed "I'm on thin ice." He had forgotten $3,000 he had borrowed from RH to buy the Vermont property. RPW to AE, 6 July 1961, courtesy of RH.

11. RPW to AE, 12 June 1961, courtesy of RH; "RPW tells about *Wilderness,*" *Wings: The Literary Guild Review,* Dec. 1961, n.p. RPW said the only battle he ever saw was a sham battle his father took

him to see in Nashville where Confederate veterans reenacted scenes from the war. I: RPW.

12. Orville Prescott, *NYT,* 15 Nov. 1961; Samuel Hynes, *NYTBR,* 19 Nov. 1961, p. 58; Granville Hicks, *SatR,* 44 (18 Nov. 1961), p. 19; *Time,* 78 (17 Nov. 1961), p. 93; J. N. Hartt, *YR,* 51 (Dec. 1961), p. 304; R. N. Hertz, *NRep,* 145 (18 Dec. 1961), p. 23; Coleman Rosenberger, *NYHT,* 3 Dec. 1961, p. 4. For citations of other reviews see *Reference Guide,* pp. 170–82. See also Walker, p. 253, repr. *TwRPW,* pp. 160–61, 114–15. See CB, *The Hidden God: Studies in Hemingway, Faulkner, Yeats, Eliot, and Warren* (New Haven: Yale University Press, 1963), p. 121.

13. *Time,* 78 (17 Nov. 1961), p. 93.

CHAPTER 38: GREAT EXPECTATIONS

1. *F,* p. 56.
2. RPW to WTB, 16 Apr. 1961, VUL; I: CB, ECW.
3. *NYT,* 22 Jan. 1962; Shoichi Saeki to JB.
4. RPW to BBC, 19 July 1962, VUL; RPW to AT, 8 Mar. 1962, PUL; Peter Wallace, "Robert Penn Warren: 'Just the Process,' " *Yale News,* 26 Apr. 1962, pp. 1, 8; I: Richard B. Sewall.
5. RPW to AE, n.d. [June 1962], courtesy of RH.
6. RPW to AE, June 1962, 31 July 1962, courtesy of RH; I: RPW, RW, ECW; RPW to AT, 30 Sept. 1962, PUL.
7. RPW to AT, 25 Nov. 1962, PUL.
8. RPW to BBC, 27 May 1963, VUL. RPW was still making public appearances. Taking the podium at Princeton after a scholarly discourse by Bernard Malamud, he seemed "a tart old slyboots" to *Newsweek*'s reporter, and when he began with a quip, "the audience, almost hysterical with gratitude, went berserk with laughter" and later rewarded his "superb piece of showmanship" with "thunderous applause." *Newsweek,* 6 May 1962, p. 69. RPW to AT, 10 June 1963, PUL.

9. RPW to AT, 17 July 1963, PUL; I: RPW and ECW. Predictably, RPW had been enjoying literature as well as nature, reading Henry James all this summer as he had devoted the previous one chiefly to Émile Zola.

10. RPW to Arthur Mizener, 26 Nov. 1963, VUL.

11. RPW to AL, 10 Nov. 1963, VUL. Rosanna Phelps Warren, *The Joey Story* (New York: Random House, 1964). At about this same time Rosanna made a booklet of eleven pen-and-ink sketches with watercolors entitled "The Joy of Being Owned by a Dog." On the cover she wrote "Happy Birthday Poppy!" Courtesy of RW. I: ECW.

12. *TwRPW,* pp. 111–13. See these pages for sources for the names Fiddler and Maggie.

13. There are also less obvious connections, which function in a symbolic way: a dramatic figure in the plot who has suffered the loss of an eye and Brad's near-obsession with the blindness of Leontine Purtle, the innocent-seeming Fiddlersburg seductress. He asks her, "What's it like to be blind?" (p. 232).

14. There is the subplot of Pretty-Boy, the Negro murderer awaiting execution and finally brought to repentance. And there are characters who function not only through their actions but also through the strength of their portrayals: "Boots" Budd, the tough deputy warden; Brother Potts, the preacher dying of cancer determined to live long enough to read his poem about the church at its last service; Brother Pinkney, the admirable Negro minister who has quietly started an NAACP chapter; Blanding Cottshill, the old-family lawyer who has quietly lived lovingly with a black woman most of his life and will undertake a desegregation case when he relocates to a nearby town.

15. Nakadate, p. 117.
16. Bohner, p. 142.

17. See Bohner, p. 139; *Burden,* p. 531; *Time,* 83 (24 Apr. 1964), p. 106; *Newsweek,* 63 (4 May 1964), p. 93; *NYHT,* 26 Apr. 1964, pp. 6, 10; *NYTBR,* 31 May 1964, p. 18; *Chicago Sunday Tribune Books Today,* 3 May 1964, pp. 6–7; *SoR,* 72 (Oct.–Dec. 1964), pp. 690–98.

18. AT to RPW, 17 Oct. 1964, PUL; *TwRPW,* p. 92.

CHAPTER 39: RECORDING THE NEGRO REVOLUTION

1. *WSN,* p. ix.

2. *I,* pp. 14–15.

3. RPW to AL, 12 Jan. 1963, VUL. See *NYTBR,* 28 June 1964, p. 28; *NYRB,* 2 (30 July 1964), p. 7.

4. In Nov. 1963 RPW had attended a conference on nonviolence at Howard University. RPW to KAP, 18 Jan. 1964, UMdL.

5. RPW to Evans Harrington, 20 Aug. 1964, courtesy of RH. In Sept. 1962, by court order, James Meredith, accompanied by federal marshals, registered as the university's first black student. A campus riot on the night of the thirtieth, despite the presence of the Mississippi National Guard, left two dead and scores injured. To keep the record clear, Warren noted in his letter that he had spoken in the spring at Tougaloo, one of Mississippi's black colleges. Besides this, he had a book coming out on the subject in the winter, and "by spring I might be even less welcome than now."

6. RPW, "The Negro Now," *Look,* 23 Mar. 1965, pp. 23–31. Robert W. Hamblin, "Robert Penn Warren at the 1965 Southern Literary Festival: A Personal Recollection," *SLJ,* 22 (Spring 1990), pp. 53–61. RPW published his lecture "Faulkner: The South, the Negro, and Time," in a volume he edited: *Faulkner: A Collection of Critical Essays* (Englewood Cliffs, N.J.: Prentice-Hall, 1966), pp. 251–71.

7. See *Newsweek,* 7 June 1965; *NRep,* 152 (22 May 1965), p. 21.

8. RPW to WTB, 12 Jan. 1963, VUL; RPW to BBC, 23 May 1963, VUL; I: ECW.

9. RPW to AT, 18 July 1965, PUL.

10. RPW to BBC, 20 July, 1 Dec. 1965, VUL.

11. I: John Kenneth Galbraith, ECW; I: Robert Brustein, RPWOHP.

12. "Fall Comes in Back-Country Vermont," *NY,* 23 Oct. 1965, pp. 56–57, repr. *SPNO,* pp. 52–57; "Shoes in Rain Jungle," *NYRB,* 11 Nov. 1965, p. 10, repr. *SPNO,* pp. 50–51; Washington *Evening Star,* 7 June 1965, p. A-10. Commenting at length to BBC, RPW added, "I am not a pacifist, and I am strongly anti-communist." RPW to BBC, 14 Jan. 1966, VUL.

13. "Patriotic Tour and Postulate of Joy," *NY,* 22 Jan. 1966, p. 28, repr. *SPNO,* pp. 9–10. In the third stanza the heroes in Arlington Cemetery stir and meditate on the bird's message, recalling one of Thomas Hardy's best poems, "Channel Firing."

14. KAP to RPW, 18 Nov. 1965, UMdL; RPW to AT, 15 Jan. 1966, PUL.

15. ECW to KAP, 17 June 1966, UMdL.

16. I: RW.

17. RPW to AE, 17 June 1966, courtesy of RH; I: FS and SH; RPW, *Selected Poems of Herman Melville: A Reader's Edition* (New York: Random House, 1970).

18. I: RPW, ECW; I: William Styron, RPWOHP.

19. For material from RPW's Kentucky childhood in these poems, see *TN,* pp. 94, 105–7.

20. LDR, *NYTBR,* 9 Oct. 1966, p. 4; Louis L. Martz, *YR,* 56 (Winter 1966), pp. 275–79. Analyzing the revisions, Martz noted the ninety pages of new poetry, fifty pages from *YEO* (a third of it excluded), virtually all of *P,* and three-quarters of *SP.* Hayden Carruth, *HudR,* 19 (Winter 1966), pp. 689–700; Walker, p. 156; PD, *AtMo,* 218 (Nov. 1966), p. 163;

William Stafford, *Chicago Sunday Tribune Books Today* (9 Oct. 1966), p. 10; Joseph Slater, *SatR,* 49 (31 Dec. 1966), pp. 24–25. VS writes that RPW had shifted over to the metrics of "the new American Poetry" so much so that "most of the book resembles the Eliot-Pound-Williams free verse strain as opposed to the Yeats-Auden-Thomas discipline of the high Modern period." *Poetic Vision,* p. 261.

21. RPW to AE, 14 Nov. 1966, courtesy of RH.

22. *So Clear, O Victory,* UKyL; RPW to FS and SH, 14 Nov. 1966, courtesy of SH.

23. RPW to AT, 9 Dec. 1966, PUL; RPW to FS and SH, 14 Nov. 1966, courtesy of SH.

Chapter 40: Garnerings from Under the Fig Tree and Elsewhere

1. *I,* p. 61, repr. *SP75,* p. 236.

2. RPW to FS and SH, 28 Feb. 1967, courtesy of SH; I: RW.

3. RPW to AS, 17 Feb. 1967, courtesy of AS.

4. I: William Styron, RPWOHP; I: Rose Styron and William Styron.

5. RPW to KAP, 8 Apr. 1967, UMdL.

6. RPW to KAP, 8 Apr. 1967, UMdL; RPW to FS and SH, 28 Feb. 1967, courtesy of SH; RPW to AT, n.d. [fall 1967], PUL.

7. I: RW, GPW.

8. ECW to William Meredith, 31 May 1967, VUL.

9. RPW to AT, 27 Sept. 1967, PUL; I: GPW. Besides finishing *Love in a Valley* he wanted to do essays on Tate, Cooper, Faulkner, and Dreiser and a collection of essays on KAP's work like his Faulkner volume.

10. RPW to AT, 7 May 1968, PUL; LPS to JB.

11. David Rosen to JB; RPW to AE, 2 Aug. 1968, courtesy of RH; RPW to HO, 3 Sept. 1968, VUL.

12. The noun in the title is plural rather than singular, and the standard definition provides a broader compass: "a living being embodying a deity or spirit . . . the assumption of human form or nature, as by a divine being." *American College Dictionary* (New York: Random House, 1958), p. 612; see *Achievement,* p. 82. However, the first of the book's two epigraphs retains the religious context while pointing toward the social by quoting from Nehemiah 5:5—"Yet now our flesh is as the flesh of our brethren"— which is the people's outcry against exploitation by greedy officials. The second epigraph, from a folk ballad—"John Henry said to the Captain, 'A man ain't nuthin but a man' "—gives voice to the pride of the legendary hero defeated at driving railroad spikes when pitted against the nonhuman steam drill.

13. GPW had also provided material for the previous volume's "Little Boy and Lost Shoe." I: GPW.

14. See *Achievement,* pp. 81–82.

15. See Bloom, pp. 196, 10, 6. He writes that in part C of "The Leaf," which rings changes on "The fathers have eaten a sour grape, and the children's teeth are set on edge," (Jeremiah 31:29–30), RPW is both disavowing and surmounting the influence of Eliot and replacing it by the poetic voice he has achieved in the vocation denied to his father. Bloom, p. 8.

16. Sending the poem to AT, RPW explained, "Some years ago when I was hanging around the Eddyville penitentiary, I saw, in the infirmary, an old coot on the can. He was dying of gut cancer, I was told, but had the half-delusion that if he could crap it out he would be cured. So he spent all the time possible there, groggy with morphine. The dialogue between him and Warden is reported in the poem." RPW to AT, 30 July 1967, PUL. The poem is dedicated to BBC and FNC. As a reporter BBC, accompanied by FNC, had witnessed an execution. Writing the segment about electrocution,

RPW could not remember how much voltage was required, and BBC told him: 2,300 volts.

17. See Ruppersburg, pp, 101, 107, 110.

18. See Bohner, p. 121; *Poetic Vision*, p. 241.

19. See *Publishers Weekly*, 194 (19 Aug. 1968), pp. 71–72; Bill Katz, *LJ*, 93 (15 Sept. 1968), p. 3145; *Time*, 94 (12 Dec. 1969), p. 107; GC, *MissQ*, 22 (Fall 1969), pp. 313–26; Louis L. Martz, *YR*, 58 (June 1969), pp. 596–98; Bloom, pp. 5, 10, 195.

20. RPW's concern with spatial relationships would lead him, during a reading, to hold up a page to show the arrangement of the words. See *Poetic Vision*, p. 241.

CHAPTER 41: TWO KINDS OF VISIONS

1. *A*, p. 19; *RPWR*, p. 385.

2. Marc Wortman, "Shattering the Urn," *YR* (Dec. 1990), pp. 32–34.

3. ECW to KAP, 17 Jan. 1968, UMdL; I: Gregory L. Lucente; James Wilcox to JB; I: DM.

4. *TwRPW*, pp. 333, 244; RPW to KAP, 19 Oct. 1969, UMdL.

5. RWBL, "Warren's Long Visit to American Literature," *YR* (Summer 1981), pp. 568, 570; I: RPWOHP, no. 1.

6. *TwRPW*, pp. 334, 244, 358. RPW had praised Welty's "A Still Moment," in which Audubon is one of the three principal characters, and had written one scholar that her story was "in all likelihood the germ" of *Audubon*. M. Bernetta Quinn, "Robert Penn Warren's Promised Land," *SoR*, NS (new series) 8 (Spring 1972), pp. 329–58, repr. Nakadate, p. 292. See Lesa Corrigan, "Snapshots of Audubon: Photographic Perspectives from Eudora Welty and Robert Penn Warren," *MissQ*, 47 (Winter 1993–94), pp. 83–91.

7. RPW to AT, 2 Feb. 1969, PUL; AT to RPW, 25 Feb. 1969, YUL. See Anthony Szczesiul, "Robert Penn Warren's *Audubon:* Vision and Revision," *MissQ*,

47 (Winter 1993–94), pp. 3–14.

8. I: ECW, RW. CBW had headed the Italian department at C. W. Post College and then the foreign-language department at Mitchell College, *NYT*, 13 May 1969, p. 47; AS to JB.

9. RPW to Howard Moss, 24 Mar. 1969, YUL; RPW, "Knowledge and the Image of Man," *SoR*, 62 (Spring 1955), p. 187.

10. Page numbers for *A* are from *RPWR*. In *ALMM*, RPW provided a headnote of a little less than 2,000 words to introduce excerpts from Audubon's *Ornithological Biography* of 1839, most importantly the 1,800-word selection, "The Prairie." In writing the poem Warren altered or omitted several elements in the headnote. One was a catalog of Audubon's failings. In "The Prairie" Audubon is alert and not passively bemused as the witch woman prepares to attack him. In his headnote Warren also omits any specific information about the punishment meted out to the three, much less specifying that they were hanged and that he was sexually aroused at the spectacle of her death. *ALMM*, pp. 1061–62.

11. RPW to Howard Moss, 24 Mar. 1969, YUL. See *Bibliography*, pp. 215–18. The largest structure that can be seen behind much of the poem is the Adamic myth, with Audubon experiencing untouched places in the New World. See Burt, pp. 99–100; Clark, p. 146; *Poetic Vision*, pp. 242, 250; Ruppersburg, p. 89; Bloom, p. 205; Bedient, pp. 144–45; MW, p. 173.

12. Each critic supplies his own explanation of Audubon's sexual arousal, from the contention that it is the transfiguring power of her defiance of death that provides her beauty and his arousal to the suggestion that this is "sadistic sexuality."

13. Laurence Goldstein calls attention to an essay in which "Warren notes that America has exhausted the political and military figures commonly associated with a nation's development. . . .

Audubon might be read as Warren's recommendation for a national myth, his sacred book." RPW, "Dearth of Heroes," *American Heritage,* 23 (Oct. 1972), p. 4. Goldstein, "Audubon and Robert Penn Warren: To See and Record All Life," *Contemporary Poetry,* I (Winter 1973), p. 51. His next volume of poems would include "Interjection #4: Bad Year, Bad War: New Year's Card, 1969" (*OEP,* p. 35). It is an ironic poem, implying not only the hostilities in Vietnam but also a broader sense of collective guilt.
14. *Time,* 94 (12 Dec. 1969), p. 107; Thomas Lask, *NYT* (13 Dec. 1969), p. 33; Chad Walsh, *Chicago Tribune Book World,* 3 (16 Nov. 1969), p. 3; Louis L. Martz, *YR* (June 1970), pp. 551–69; Norman Martien, *PR,* 38, No. 1 (1971), p. 122; Harry Morris, *SoR,* 79 (Apr.–June 1971), pp. 301–9; Ruppersburg, p. 2, Bedient, p. 3; Bohner, p. 126; *Poetic Vision,* p. 264. See Burt, pp. 103–6; Goldstein, "Audubon," p. 47.

CHAPTER 42: AMERICAN LITERATURE IN TWO VOLUMES

1. *ALMM,* I, p. xi.
2. RWBL, "Warren's Long Visit to American Literature," *YR* (Summer 1981), p. 571. See also RWBL, *Literary Reflections: A Shoring of Images 1960–1993* (Boston: Northeastern University Press, 1993), pp. 277–78. CB to AT, 21 July 1973, PUL. The three editors had agreed not to publish any of their own essays. RPW as poet and novelist "was a different matter," so they "finally beat down his objections" and printed *A.*
3. RPW to Bedford Moore, 1 Apr. 1970, UVaL.
4. *Baldur's Gate* (New York: Pantheon, 1970) is set in New England and focuses on a sculptor modeled on a man Eleanor knew when she began the novel at nineteen. Her parents served as models for

minor characters. ECW to KAP, 12 Feb. 1970, UMdL.
5. RPW to AT, 7 Aug. 1970, 15 Oct. 1970, PUL.
6. RPW to AT, 15 Oct. 1970, PUL. RPW's estimate of the time spent on the anthology was nine years. CB said it took them six years. I: CB, RWBL. See RWBL, "Warren's Long Visit," p. 568.
7. Page references for Melville material run from 910 to 917 for *ALMM* and from 18 to 81 for *SPHM.* RPW here invoked another of his masters: "In general, Melville and Hardy have much in common—their thirst for ultimates and their metaphysical cast of mind, their stoicism and irony, their combination of compassion and grudging 'meliorism,' their collocations of compassion and conventionally poetic elements, their wrenching rhythms, their idiosyncratic vocabularies. . . ." (p. 79).
8. "Art is often confessional and penitential," RPW wrote, "and self-criticism, even self-denigration, can be as central a dynamic in literature as self-justification" (p. 81). He saw this especially in Melville's later work.
9. RPW to AT, 20 Jan. 1971, PUL. The Whittier book came to the University of Minnesota Press through RPW's service as an adviser for their American Writers Series.
10. Whittier quotations from *ALMM* run from pp. 538 to 554; those from *John Greenleaf Whittier's Poetry* from pp. 3 to 61.
11. *John Greenleaf Whittier's Poetry,* dedicated to Doris Foster and CHF, contains 140 pages of Whittier poems. In Whittier's "Ichabod," RPW saw a thematic parallel with Hawthorne's "My Kinsman, Major Molineux," where both concern "a betrayal by the father" and "deep ambivalences of the son toward the father."
12. I: David Milch.
13. He would achieve a "double-dip" when he reduced the introduction to produce "Hawthorne Revisited: Some

Remarks on Hell-firedness," for *SR*, 81 (Winter 1973), pp. 75–111.

14. James Glickman to JB.

15. *NSE*, p. 112; RPW to AE, 13 Aug. 1971, courtesy of RH. Much reduced, the essay would appear as "Mark Twain," *SoR*, NS 8 (Summer 1972), pp. 459–92, and under the same title in *NSE*, pp. 103–36.

16. As in his other essays, RPW drew here on much scholarship and criticism.

17. RPW would reprint his early Hemingway essay in *NSE*, pp. 163–96; for other appearances see *Bibliography*, p. 236.

CHAPTER 43: TWO BOOKS AND A CRISIS

1. *NY*, 11 Sept. 1971, p. 46; *SP75*, pp. 64–65. Cf. W. B. Yeats's "A Dialogue of Self and Soul," *The Collected Poems of W. B. Yeats* (New York: Macmillan, 1959), pp. 230–31.

2. RPW to William Meredith, 17 Dec. 1972, UKyL.

3. Numbers in parentheses refer to pages in *HTD*. I: RPW, *Washington Post*, 2 Dec. 1970, p. C2.

4. For criticism of the novel's structure, see *HTD*, pp. 127–28.

5. But how to reconcile this enthusiastic response, as LDR put it, from RPW, "the conscious artist, the highly skilled critic-craftsman," to Dreiser "the blunderer"? Part of the answer was that he "envied Dreiser's ability to deal with the forces of life and desire in a brutal, competitive, modern industrial society" and his "tremendous capacity for recognizing and delineating the deeper psychological drives of modern life." LDR, "Dreiser and *Meet Me in the Green Glen*: A Vintage Year for Robert Penn Warren," *Hollins Critic*, IX (Apr. 1972), pp. 5–6.

6. Noting Dreiser's youthful affair with a Jewish actress in the Little Theatre of Chicago, RPW may well have remembered again Carolyn Anspacher in

Berkeley's Little Theatre group. *HTD*, p. 153.

7. LDR, "Vintage Year," p. 10; *NY*, 47 (2 Oct. 1971), pp. 131–32; *Publishers Weekly*, 200 (26 July 1971), p. 46; *SatR*, 54 (4 Sept. 1971), p. 30; *Time*, 98 (30 Aug. 1971), pp. 55–56; *SoR*, 10 (Spring 1971), pp. 504–16; JAG, "Robert Penn Warren's *Annus Mirabilis*," *SoR*, NS 10 (Spring 1974), pp. 504–16.

8. *TwRPW*, p. 163.

9. JAG told Warren that "textually the murderer is never really pinned down" and so there are four possibilities. Surprised, RPW answered, "Of course Cassie killed her husband." From his notes JAG continues, "there was no question in his mind that Cassie is guilty and of course what he is doing and what he was trying to set up, and has in so many of his books, is to suggest [the complexities of southern society], how they exist and how they can be misinterpreted." JAG to JB.

10. RPW to AE, 2 Dec. 1971, courtesy of RH. LDR and others note the similarity of the Angelo-Cassie relationship and that between Joe Christmas and Lena Grove in Faulkner's *Light in August* (1932), LDR, "Vintage Year," p. 5. In *Requiem for a Nun* (1950) Faulkner supplied statistics on his Yoknapatawpha County and Mississippi. In Flannery O'Connor's "The Life You Save May Be Your Own," one-armed Tom T. Shiftlet works as Lucynell Crater's unsalaried handyman before he decamps. Warren also used both devices.

11. *NYRB*, 17 (2 Dec. 1971); *AtMo*, 228 (Nov. 1971), p. 152; *NYT*, 6 Nov. 1971, p. 29; *NYTBR*, 7 Nov. 1971, p. 6; *SatR*, 54 (9 Oct. 1971), pp. 31–32, 35–37. LDR refuted the charge that RPW's fiction fell off after *WET* because he was writing too much. The reason for any falling off was that "those ideas which in the early fiction gave such profound definition to the documentation of the world of action began taking on so much im-

portance in their own right that they grew abstracted from the felt experience of the stories. Instead of the ideas evolving out of the people and events, the process was reversed and Warren took to creating the people and events primarily to fill out a philosophical structure." LDR, "Vintage Year," pp. 3, 10; see *Achievement,* p. 264. RPW wrote John W. Aldridge, in response to his *SatR* review, "I have never in my life encountered such a precise and detailed account of my hopes and intentions in a novel as you have done for *Meet Me in the Green Glen.*" RPW to John W. Aldridge, 4 Dec. 1971, courtesy of John W. Aldridge.

12. RPW to AT, 24 Apr. 1971, PUL; RPW to AT, 8 Mar. 1972, PUL; RPW to AL, 25 Mar. 1972, University of the South.

13. I: RW.

14. RPW to TGR, 17 Oct., 5 Dec. 1971, 3 Feb., 9 Mar. 1972, courtesy of Secker & Warburg; RPW to AT, 8 Mar. 1972, PUL. From 1940 to 1962, RPW was published in England by Eyre and Spottiswoode. In 1964 Collins published *Flood,* and in 1970 W. H. Allen published *I.* Beginning in 1972 with *MMGG,* Secker & Warburg became RPW's English publisher.

15. RPW to TGR, 9 Mar. 1972, courtesy of Secker & Warburg and TGR; RPW to AT, 8 Mar. 1972, PUL; I: RW, GPW; RPW to WTB, 28 Mar. 1972, VUL.

16. RPW to William Meredith, 27 Apr. 1972, VUL; RPW to AT, 5 May 1972, PUL; ECW to AE, 12 May 1972, courtesy of AE.

17. I: ECW; RPW to RW, 19 May 1972, courtesy of RW; RPW to AT, 20 May 1972, PUL.

CHAPTER 44: IN THE MIDST OF LIFE

1. *OEP,* p. 31, repr. *SP75,* p. 39.
2. I: CB, ECW, JDK.

3. AT to RPW, 8 June 1972, PUL; RPW to AT, 20 June 1972, PUL.

4. I: ECW. Griseofulvin, a penicillin derivative, at certain levels produced liver tumors in mice and, among adverse reactions in humans, skin rashes and hives. The first precaution listed was "Patients on prolonged therapy with any potent medication should be under close observation. Periodic monitoring of organ system function, including renal, hepatic, and hemopoietic, should be done." Ortho Pharmaceutical Corporation product information.

5. RPW to JCR, 4 Aug. 1972, courtesy of SW.

6. I: William Styron.

7. Thomas Meehan, "The Yale Faculty Makes the Scene," *NYT Magazine,* 7 Feb. 1971, p. 52.

8. I: JDK; RPW to AT, 23 Jan. 1973, PUL; RPW to TGR, 24 Apr. 1973.

9. Meehan, "Yale Faculty," p. 51. Gregory Lucente writes JB, "Warren paid a great deal of attention to formal / organizational matters in our writing. But his most consistent interest in discussing our work was not so much with technique as with meaning. . . ." At the end of each writing course he would offer to speak about his own experience, and "there would come a moment in which he would look away and say, very quietly— much more quietly than usual—that writing was a way of spending time alone, a lot of time alone. I don't know if I'd call it a look of sorrow or quiet satisfaction, but it seemed to be something he was still coming to terms with."

10. "Time as Hypnosis," in *OEP,* p. 7; RPW to AT, 20 June 1972, PUL; RPW to I. A. Richards, 23 Nov. 1973, courtesy of Magdalen College, Cambridge University.

11. RPW to TGR, 14 July 1973. RPW was one of three American writers who had offered to turn over their Russian royalties to Aleksandr Solzhenitsyn, who was said to be short of funds. *NYT,* 21 Dec. 1972, p. 28.

12. *CEA Forum,* Oct. 1973, p. 10; Michael J. Hoffman, *American Literary Scholarship: An Annual 1973* (Durham, N.C.: Duke University Press, 1975), pp. 425–26; *Reference Service Review,* Dec. 1973, p. 10; I: CB; RPW to AT, 21 July 1973, PUL.

13. RPW to AT, 9 Aug. 1973, PUL; RPW to JCR, 27 Aug. 1973, courtesy of SW.

14. RPW's history noted that he was allergic to pork, beef, coffee, and nicotine. He had quit the latter thirteen years before. I: JDK; RPW to TGR, 14 Jan. 1974; RPW to AT, 9 Jan. 1974, PUL.

15. *NYT,* 19 Jan. 1974, p. 64, 15 Mar. 1974, p. 39; RPW to TGR, 16 Nov. 1974.

16. RPW to AT, 8 Mar., 2 May 1974, PUL.

17. Patrick O'Sheel, "Companion to Owls," *National Endowment for the Humanities,* IV (Feb. 1974), p. 8, repr. *Washington Post,* 28 Apr. 1974, pp. F1–3.

18. See Henry Mitchell, "Choosing the Big Horizon," *Washington Post,* 30 Apr. 1974, pp. B1, 3.

19. AT to RPW, 1 Feb. 1974, PUL. LDR writes, "Red was an *innocent . . . ;* he was naive, easily flattered; he didn't sense resentment or jealousy, possessing neither of these traits himself. Here he's sending Tate new poem after new poem, and never sensing for a moment that Tate, who had run bone dry creatively, might be in any way envious!" LDR to JB.

20. RPW wrote, "Many of the poems are based on actual episodes which I can date; for instance 'Folly on Royal Street' clearly belongs to a time when C and M and I knocked around N.O., back in the 1930's. But written long after. And 'The True Nature of Time' deals with an event (quite literally) that occurred about 1952. 'Sunset Walk . . .' deals with an event which literally happened probably in the early spring in Vermont, in 1973, and the last two poems with events of the following summer. 'Rattlesnake Country' deals

with various stays on Western ranches over a period of some years." RPW to Tom Parker, courtesy of Tom Parker.

21. "The Return: An Elegy" in *TSP,* p. 51. See the account of Ruth Warren's death above, and also "What Is the Voice that Speaks?" *BH,* p. 71.

22. Though RPW reiterated his lack of religious belief, the name of God recurs often in his poetry. But his version of the deity was very like that of Thomas Hardy's in poems such as "Hap," where, if God exists, he has created the world and then forgotten it. Here, in *"Interjection #6: What You Sometimes Feel on Your Face at Night,"* the reference is to "God's blind hand" (*OEP,* p. 66).

23. I: RW, GPW.

24. See *TN,* pp. 71, 77. RPW glossed some of the work for Haward Moss, the editor of *NY.* He had sent him a three-page poem called "Forever O'clock," which begins "A clock is getting ready to strike forever o'clock. / I do not know where the clock is, but it is somewhere." The sound the clock makes "trying to make up its mind is purely metaphysical." In the poem's second section a near-naked "little two-year-old Negro girl-baby" playing in a deserted farmyard is seen by a man driving "a beat-up old 1931 Studebaker. . . . I watch the car that I know I am the man driving as it recedes into / distance and approaches the horizon." (He is describing a car he owned.) In the third and last section, the watching poet wonders "if it will ever get there" (pp. 37–39). When Moss wrote that the poem seemed effective but they wondered what it actually meant, RPW replied in two single-spaced pages: "The poem is, in the most general way, about time, or rather, about kinds of time and their relations and about identity (how I loathe that word now!) Involved in this background (and in the poem) is the notion of two kinds of memory—or two views of time. The first kind of 'sequential,' and the second 'archetypal.' " He

went on to define these in detail. It was the kind of explication that he and CB had done in *UP,* though much more detailed. The poem was finally published by *YR,* 63 (Summer 1974), pp. 545–47. Howard Moss to RPW, 5 Oct. 1973; RPW to Howard Moss, 10 Oct. 1973, YUL.

25. *Washington Post Book World,* 8 Dec. 1974, p. 3; Peter Meinke, *NRep,* 171 (7 Dec. 1974), pp. 29–30; Robert F. Clayton, *LJ,* 99 (15 Oct. 1974), p. 2607; Anatole Broyard, *NYT,* 24 Oct. 1974, p. 39; J. P. McClatchy, *YR,* 64 (Spring 1975) p. 427.
26. Walker, p. 176; Bohner, p. 131; Bloom, pp. 5, 202.

CHAPTER 45: CALAMITIES AND CONQUESTS

1. *OEP,* p. 62, repr. *SP75,* p. 59.
2. RPW to AT, 30 Oct. 1974, PUL.
3. RPW to TGR, 16 Nov. 1974; RPW to Edwin Stirling, 13 Nov. 1974, YUL.
4. I: RW; RPW to TGR, 14 Nov. 1974.
5. Angela Solomon, publicity release, courtesy of Frances L. Egler, Great Performances.
6. RPW to TGR, 18 Jan. 1975.
7. RPW to AT, 9 Mar. 1975, PUL.
8. *SP75,* pp. 7–8; AT to RPW, 9 Feb.; RPW to AT, 7 Aug., 7 Sept., 1975, PUL.
9. RPW to CHF, 15 May 1975; Julius Novick, *NYT,* 16 Feb. 1975, p. 27; RPW to CHF, 6 Mar. 1975. Two other projects had been maturing. For his part of a tribute to CB, RPW had decided to interview him. By late May the collaboration had produced more than a hundred pages of intellectually intimate, stimulating, and wide-ranging interchange between two of the brightest minds of their long generation. RPW, "A Conversation with Cleanth Brooks," *Possibilities,* pp. 1–124. In July the Harvard Press brought out the hundred-page *Democracy and Poetry.* After mixed reviews, the book excited little further comment.

10. TGR to RPW, 7 Aug. 1975; RPW to TGR, 10 Aug. 1975; RPW to AT, 7 Aug., 7 Sept. 1975, PUL.
11. ECW to KAP, 13 Feb. 1976, UMdL.
12. RWBL, *The City of Florence: Historical Vistas and Personal Sightings* (New York: Farrar Straus Giroux, 1995), pp. 6, 8, 73–79, 233.
13. RPW to LPS, 5 Nov. 1975, courtesy of LPS; I: ECW.
14. RPW to AT, 5 Feb. 1976, PUL; RPW to LPS, 5 Nov. 1975, courtesy of LPS.
15. RPW to AT, 3 Jan. 1975, PUL.
16. RPW to GC, 23 Mar. 1976, courtesy of SW; RPW to TGR, 6 Apr. 1976; ECW to PD, 22 Apr. 1976, YUL.
17. RPW to AT, 20 May 1976, PUL.
18. I: ECW; RPW to AT, 20 May 1976, 14 June 1976, PUL.
19. RPW to AT, 14 June 1976, PUL; RPW to KAP, 15 June 1976, UMdL; KAP to RPW, 22 June 1976, UMdL.
20. RPW to TGR, 2 July 1976; RPW to AT, 25 July 1976, PUL; RPW to TGR, n.d.
21. *NYT,* 10 May 1976, p. 29; RPW to TGR, 30 Aug. 1976; RPW to AT, 13 Aug. 1976, 4 Sept. 1976, PUL.
22. I: Robert Brustein, RPWOHP; RPW to AT, 5 Feb. 1976, PUL; KAP to RPW, 11 Sept. 1975, UMdL; KAP to RPW, 31 Oct. 1975, LC; RPW to JLS, 14 Feb. 1976, courtesy of JLS.
23. RPW to GC, 8 Nov. 1976, courtesy of SW; "Waiting," *AtMo,* Dec. 1976, p. 47, repr. *NT,* pp. 39–40.
24. *Esquire,* Dec. 1976, pp. 132–35, 200–1.
25. As Warren explained the Arcturus reference to Robert Brustein, the latter saw a resemblance: "that he's bear-like. He has that kind of wonderful huggy quality about him. Yet he has that wonderful chest that juts forward and that marvelous eagle-like head. So I think of him more as a bear than an eagle, but he surely looks more like an eagle than a bear." I: Robert Brustein, RPWOHP.

26. *Poetic Vision,* p. 114; RPW to AT, 7 Sept. 1975, PUL.

27. For Harold Bloom, the hawk is the poet's "personal emblem" as well as "the inevitable sign of the truth" in other poems to come as well as in this one, "surely one of his dozen or so lyric masterpieces, a culmination of forty years of his art. . . ." "Sunset Hawk: Warren's Poetry and Tradition," in Walter B. Edgar, ed., *A Southern Renascence Man* (Baton Rouge: Louisiana State University Press, 1984), pp. 74–75.

28. But his beginnings were clear in the last segment with twenty-three of the forty-two poems having appeared in the earlier volume. The longest of them, "The Ballad of Billie Potts," marked the turning point in his career. He reprinted only half of *YEO.* He included all but ten from "Tale of Time," four from *I,* and one from *OEP.* A. L. Clements writes that in the last segment of *SP75* there are reminders "of his association with the Fugitives, of the Ransom and Tate manners, of the Metaphysicals (particularly Donne and Marvell), and Eliot-like devices and diction remain, besides his own distinctive signature." "Sacramental Vision: The Poetry of Robert Penn Warren," *South Atlantic Bulletin,* 43 (Nov. 1978), pp. 47–65, repr. Nakadate, pp. 302–20; see especially pp. 303–4 and 311. For titles of poems omitted see *Bibliography,* pp. 142–43.

29. "Harold Bloom on Poetry," *NRep,* 20 Nov. 1976, pp. 20, 22–23, 26.

30. See *Poetic Vision,* p. 115; Bloom, "Sunset Hawk," p. 75; Paul Mariani, "Robert Penn Warren," in Bloom, pp. 222, 221.

31. *Eyes Etc.: A Memoir* (New York: Pantheon, 1977); RPW to AT, 17 Dec., 8 Dec. 1976, PUL.

CHAPTER 46: THE TENTH NOVEL

1. *PTCT,* p. 180.

2. RPW to KAP, 15 Feb. 1977, UMdL; TGR to RPW, 4 Mar. 1977.

3. RPW to AT, 16 Mar. 1977, PUL; RPW to William Meredith, 28 Jan. 1977, VUL.

4. Able at last to pity his natural father, Jed daydreams of showing his own son the scenes of his youth. Acting on this fantasy, he writes Dauphine asking her to rejoin him so that the three of them can be together. Warren meant the story to have a wide reference. It was "about the Southerner who hates (or is ashamed of) the South [and] such a Southerner, even if a great success in the world, is always a 'placeless' man—so we come back to the 'modern man'—in his motel room and his TV program." *TwRPW,* p. 280. In one of the correspondences between fiction and life, Dugton, like Guthrie, is a place to be "from." Among others, Dauphine Finkel resembles RPW's Berkeley lover, Carolyn Anspacher, and Agnes Andersen's death resembles Ruth Penn's and leaves Jed with strong feelings of guilt over the failed marriage.

5. TGR to Julian Symons, 14 Mar. 1977; *TLS,* 29 Apr. 1977, p. 507; see Paul Theroux, London *Times,* 2 May 1977, p. 11.

6. *AtMo,* 239 (May 1977), p. 96; *NYTBR,* 13 Mar. 1977, p. 4; *NY,* 53 (11 Apr. 1977), p. 139; *NYRB,* 24 (17 Mar. 1977), p. 4; *Time,* 74 (14 Mar. 1977), p. 109.

7. *Achievement,* p. 266; Bohner, p. 154.

8. Bohner, p. 154; RPW to AT, 5 July 1977, PUL.

9. RPW to AT, 9 Dec. 1977, PUL; RPW to TGR, 9 Jan. 1978. In 1994 Sidney Pollock recalled that the screenplay was the problem. He thought the story very moving, but he and Julian Barry found more in the novel than they could pack into the script. They wanted Jane Fonda for the part of Rozelle, but she didn't like the story, and finally Robert Redford and Pollock shut down the project. I: Sidney Pollock.

10. RPW to JLS, 6 Feb. 1978, courtesy of JLS.

11. "Praise," *AtMo* (June 1978), p. 45; RPW to FW, 2 Dec. 1978, courtesy of FW.

12. RPW to AT, 16 Nov. 1978, PUL.

13. RPW to AT, 1 Feb., 16 Nov. 1978, PUL; RPW to TGR, 5 Sept. 1978. Paul R. Lichter, M.D., writes, the initial injury to the left eye "was a blunt injury [with] no penetration of the eye. This eliminates the chance of . . . sympathetic ophthalmia wherein certain ocular lacerations in one eye can actually affect the other eye as well. . . . Likely, the injury to the left eye resulted in development of a cataract that probably became hypermature or, in some other way was related to the development of glaucoma in the left eye. . . . the development of glaucoma secondary to the cataract could account for all of the eventualities that led to the removal of the left eye . . . , It is possible that, by swimming in salt water, the already damaged cornea of the left eye developed increasing swelling that could have accounted for even further decrease in vision. Most likely, the secondary glaucoma resulted in marked elevation of intraocular pressure. This, in turn led to the severe headaches and even the nausea suffered by the patient." Paul R. Lichter, M.D., to JB.

14. RPW to Andrew Corry, 29 Nov. 1978, courtesy of JLS; RPW to TGR, 14 Aug. 1972; I: RPWOHP.

CHAPTER 47: A NEW BOOK OF
VERSE AND A NEW *BROTHER TO
DRAGONS*

1. *BD*(nv), p. 131.

2. "Sister Water" may be a reference to Saint Francis's hymn "Canticle of the Sun," which persists in Quentin Compson's stream of consciousness in Faulkner's *The Sound and the Fury.*

3. Cf. the end of "Masts at Dawn" in *I*, p. 23.

4. RPW said that Harold Bloom "wrote a review for *The New Leader* in which he

talks about the place that hawks occupy in my poetry. . . . And so I thought about the fact that I had killed a hawk, a red-tail, in my woodland boyhood." RPW dedicated the poem to Bloom. *TwRPW,* pp. 239–40, 296; I: RPW.

5. *TwRPW,* p. 296.

6. Bloom, pp. 207–8, first published as "Sunset Hawk: Warren's Poetry and Tradition," in W. B. Edgar, ed., *A Southern Renascence Man: Views of Robert Penn Warren* (Baton Rouge: Louisiana State University Press, 1984), pp. 59–79.

7. Bloom wrote that "the quality of achievement is consistent almost through-out these poems. Like Hardy, Yeats, and Stevens, Warren is at his strongest past 70." *NRep,* 179 (30 Sept. 1978), p. 34. The other national publication was *LJ,* 103 (Aug. 1978), p. 1516, where William Logan noted "garrulous energy . . . pleasing complexity [and] old-fashioned philosophy. . . ." See *Bibliography,* pp. 361–62.

8. RPW to TGR, 28 Sept. 1978, erroneously dated 1979; RPW to AT, 16 Nov. 1978, PUL.

9. I: WS; WS, *Allen Tate: A Recollection* (Baton Rouge: Louisiana State University Press, 1988), pp. 1, 96, 105.

10. WS, *Allen Tate,* p. 113; RPW to CHF, 25 Apr. 1979.

11. *TwRPW,* p. 337; RPW to FW, 18 July 1977.

12. RPW to TGR, 6 Feb. 1979; RPW to LPS, 22 Oct. 1979, courtesy of LPS; Richard N. Chrisman, "*Brother to Dragons* or *Brother to Dragons, A New Version?* A Case for the 1953 Edition," in *Discussion,* p. 212.

13. See Boynton Merrill, Jr., *Jefferson's Nephews: A Frontier Tragedy* (Princeton, N.J.: Princeton University Press, 1976); *Discussion,* pp. 283–93.

14. Lewis P. Simpson, "The Poet and the Father: Robert Penn Warren and Thomas Jefferson," *SR,* 104 (Jan.–Mar. 1996), p. 60.

15. See Burt, p. 199. For detailed analyses of the poem's genesis and the differences between the two versions see VS's "*Brother to Dragons* and the Craft of Revision," in *Discussion,* pp. 200–10, and in Margaret Mills Harper's "Versions of History and *Brother to Dragons,*" in *Discussion,* pp. 229–30 and 232–39. I am grateful to Sam Prestridge for his unpublished, exhaustive study, "Warren's Craft of Revision in *Brother to Dragons.*" Harold Bloom thought that Warren was "still dreadfully unjust to Jefferson," but he "does seem to me the best poet we have now, and the enormous improvement in the poem's rhetorical force is evident upon almost every page." *NRep,* 181 (1 Sept. 1979), p. 30, repr. in *Discussion,* pp. 181–83; *LJ,* 104 (1 Sept. 1979), p. 1703; *NYRB,* 21 Feb. 1980, repr. in *Discussion,* pp. 184–90; *TwRPW,* p. 339; RPW to LPS, 22 Oct. 1979, courtesy of LPS.

CHAPTER 48: THE SEVENTY-FIFTH

1. *BH,* p. 8.
2. Steve Oney, "A Southern Voice," *Atlanta Journal & Constitution Magazine,* 16 Sept. 1979, pp. 13, 52; Eleanor Clark, *Gloria Mundi* (New York: Pantheon, 1979), reviewed *NYTBR,* 16 Sept. 1979, p. 12; *Time,* 11 (3 Sept. 1979), p. 72. Set in New England mountain country, it follows numerous characters, the conflict between residents and outsiders bent on developing ski resorts and condominiums, with passions that lead to murder.
3. Oney, "Southern Voice," pp. 13, 52, 14.
4. Oney, "Southern Voice," pp. 14, 55, 13, 58; RPW to TGR, 12 Jan. 1980.
5. RPW to JLS, 16 Feb. 1980, courtesy of JLS; *Bibliography,* p. 244; I: RPWOHP.
6. *JDCB,* pp. 31, 52–53; for one of RPW's sources see Shelby Foote, *The Civil War: A Narrative* (New York: Random House, 1974), Vol. 3, pp. 957–1060.
7. "A Reporter at Large: Jefferson Davis Gets His Citizenship Back," *NY,* 2 (Feb.

1980), pp. 44–52 and ff.; *JD,* pp. 113–14; Oney, "Southern Voice," p. 55.
8. *SoR,* 89 (Summer 1981), p. xcv.
9. RPW to TGR, 18 May 1980; RPW to FW, 8 Apr. 1980, courtesy of FW.
10. RPW to TGR, 18 May 1980; *NYT,* 18 Apr. 1980, p. C25.
11. RPW to CHF, 3 Mar. 1980, courtesy of CHF.
12. "A Conversation with Robert Penn Warren: Can Democracy Survive in a World of Technology?" *U.S. News & World Report,* 18 Aug. 1980, pp. 64–65. Annalyn Swan, "America's Dean of Letters," *Newsweek,* 25 Aug. 1980, pp. 65–68. She wrote, "Lionel Trilling, so the story goes, once said, 'Red, you know, he'd have gotten a lot further if he'd only come and lived in New York,' " p. 66.
13. JHJ writes, "There are couplets, triplets, quatrains, octosyllabics; magisterial verse paragraphs recalling Wordsworth and Arnold; and irregular stanzas in which line lengths and stanza lengths are determined by the intensity of experience they recount." *Achievement,* p. 108. Bohner writes that this book and *NT* "reveal the same inventiveness of language, particularly striking compounds, and unexpected ellipses and shifts in word order. The diction is occasionally tortured and convoluted, descending at times into a kind of telegraphese." Bohner, p. 162.
14. A logical argument built on a chain of syllogisms, sorites is a device in which "each subject is the predicate of the one that went before." It is for Runyon the dominant mode of RPW's imagery. Thus, for example, *glitter* will link two poems, *deadfall* two others, *heart* two more, and so on through the book. *Taciturn Text,* p. 21. For the sorites above, see pp. 52–53, 36–37, and 66–67.
15. "Bless snow! Bless God, Who must work under the hand of / Fate, who has no name. God does the best / He can. . . ." "Function of Blizzard" (p. 45).
16. Peter Stitt writes that the five-part structure "loosely parallels the structure of

life. . . ." "Robert Penn Warren: Life's Instancy and the Astrolabe of Joy," *GaR,* 34 (Winter 1980), pp. 711–31.

17. The friends were AT and CG, the baby, their daughter, Nancy. Several other poems draw on Guthrie incidents. See *TN,* pp. 103–5.

18. R. B. Shaw, *Nation,* 231 (8 Nov. 1980), p. 476; Paul Breslin, *NYTBR,* 2 Nov. 1980, p. 12; James Dickey, *SatR,* 7 (25 Aug. 1980), p. 56, repr. *Night Hurdling* (Columbia, S.C.: Bruccoli-Clark, 1983), pp. 52–55; Stitt, "Robert Penn Warren," p. 731; Helen McNeil, *TLS,* 28 Nov. 1980, pp. 1363–66. See *Poetry,* 138 (May 1981), pp. 107–9; Bohner, p. 162; Bloom, p. 206; *Achievement,* pp. 101–2.

19. Medical reports courtesy of ECW; RPW to JLS, 18 Oct. 1980, courtesy of JLS.

20. RPW to PD, 11 Oct. 1979, courtesy of PD; RPW to Margaret Mills, 23 Sept. 1980; RPW, "Katherine Anne Porter: 1890–1980," *Proceedings of the American Academy and Institute of Arts and Letters,* Second Series, no. 31, pp. 57–60, courtesy of the American Academy.

21. J. A. Bryant, Jr., "Robert Penn Warren's 75th Birthday Symposium: Introduction," *KyR,* 2 (1981), pp. 3–29, 47–60; RPW to HB, 16 Nov. 1980, UMinnL.

22. ECW to William Meredith, 1 Dec. 1980, VUL.

CHAPTER 49: TRAVEL AND TRANSITION: AT HOME AND AFAR

1. *RV,* p. 80.
2. RPW to TGR, 20 Jan. 1981; RPW to George Core, 3 Jan. 1981, courtesy of SW.
3. RPW to EB [1981], UMinnL.
4. Although not impossible, it seems unlikely that RPW did not recognize George Bush, but it made a good story. RPW to TGR, 2 Mar., 30 May 1981; Donald Henahan, "Opera: Floyd's 'Willie,' " *NYT,* 27 Apr. 1981, p. C21; I: ECW; about the opera RPW wrote, "I objected to some oversimplification and missing of theme, but audience couldn't have cared less. . . . It's not my baby, anyway. All I care about is cash, if any." RPW to MW, 25 Nov. 1981.

5. RPW to TGR, 30 May 1981; *NYT,* 27 Mar. 1983.
6. RPW to TGR, 30 May 1981.
7. RPW to TGR, 30 May, 2 July 1981.
8. The working title of *RV* had been *Life Is a Fable.* ECW had persuaded him to change it, to AE's approval. RPW to TGR, 2 July 1981.
9. See *Braided Dream,* p. 90 and *passim* for linked images. Cf. Kierkegaard's companion work, *Sickness unto Death.*
10. See L. S. Marcus, *LJ* (Aug. 1981), p. 1548; Donald Hall, *NYTBR,* 8 Nov. 1981, p. 13; Irvin Ehrenpreis, *AtMo,* 248 (Dec. 1981), p. 88; Jay Parini, *TLS,* 29 Jan. 1982. For the Paleface-Redskin controversy see chap. 36, n. 16.
11. SW to JB; David Quammen to JB; RPW to TGR, 23 Oct. 1982.
12. RPW to Owen Laster, 23 Nov. 1981, courtesy of Owen Laster; Eleanor Clark, *Tamrart: 13 Days in the Sahara* (n.p.: Stuart Wright, 1984), pp. 2, 4, 7.
13. Clark, *Tamrart,* pp. 12–13, 57, 59; RPW to ES, 30 Jan. 1982, UMinnL.
14. RPW to TGR, 20 Jan. 1981; RPW to RW, 20 July 1981; RPW to TGR, 17 Oct. 1981; I: RW. ECW had been put off by Stephen Scully's taking RW to a professional basketball game which RW enjoyed.
15. I: RW; RW to JB.

CHAPTER 50: A NEW BOOK AND A NEW BABY

1. "Old Covered Bridge," *SoR,* 19 (Spring 1983), pp. 342–43, repr. *NSP,* pp. 47–48.
2. RPW to MW, 30 Jan. 1982; Howard Moss to RPW, 19 Jan. 1982, YUL; RPW

to TGR, 23 Oct. 1982. No new work of his would appear until the *GaR* published *CJ* in the summer number. During the rest of 1982 only seven new poems would appear, but this did not mean that the poems were not coming. In 1983 he would publish twenty-eight poems, though he would exclude a quarter of them when he finally published the collection. His daughter would speculate that he was discarding a fair amount of new work. As usual, he was doing his own submissions, and he had formed close relationships with editors such as George Core at *The Sewanee Review* and Stephen Berg at the *AmPR*. A few times he lost track of poems—which magazine had them, or whether or not they had been published—but the editors sorted them out. He contributed "Remark for Historian" to *The Motive for Metaphor: Essays on Modern Poetry,* eds. Frances C. Blessington and Guy Rotella (Boston: Northeastern University Press, 1983), p. xi; RPW to TGR, 27 Sept. 1982; I: RW.
3. RPW to Stephen Berg, 17 June, 7 Nov. 1982, courtesy of SW.
4. RPW to JLS, 19 Nov. 1982.
5. RPW to JLS, 19 Nov. 1982; RPW to PD, 1 Dec. 1982, YUL; RPW to RW, 1 Aug. 1983, courtesy of RW.
6. Almost exactly a year later the *TLS* called it "a skilful performance" but "an anachronism" harking back to the nineteenth century. Literary criticism in the decade that followed has been sparse and split, with objections on the one hand to "a paleface's ventriloquism" and "Indian ugh-talk" and acclaim on the other hand for "a brilliantly polyphonic example of the author's characteristic dialogism. . . ." Eleven years after the poem's publication, an account of belated recognition for Chief Joseph—the inclusion of the Little South Bear Paw battlefield in the Nez Perce National Historical Park—appeared in *The New Yorker,* but it included no reference to *CJ.* See Rhoda Donovan, *LJ,* 108 (15 Apr. 1983), p. 828; Nicolas Tredell, *TLS,* 27 Apr. 1984, p. 454; Bedient,

p. 87; Mariani, in Bloom, p. 222; Clark, p. 128; Mark Stevens, "Chief Joseph's Revenge," *NY,* 8 Aug. 1994, pp. 26–33.
7. "Personal History During Nocturnal Snowfall," published as "Personal History," *SR,* 91 (Fall 1983), p. 565. "Instant on Crowded Street" remained unpublished.
8. RPW to WTB, 16 Jan. 1984, VUL; ECW to MW, 14 Nov. 1983; RPW to William Heyen, 13 Sept. 1983, courtesy of William Heyen.
9. *NYT,* 30 June 1983, p. 2; I: ECW.
10. RPW to AE, 1 Aug. 1983, courtesy of AE; "Marble," *NY,* 24 Oct. 1983, p. 46.
11. ECW to MW, 14 Nov. 1983; RPW to WTB, 10 Jan., 27 Jan. 1984, VUL.
12. RPW to WTB, 16 Jan. 1984, VUL.

CHAPTER 51: THE LAST COLLECTED
POEMS

1. *NSP,* p. 79.
2. RPW to RW, June 1984, courtesy of RW; "To Whom It May Concern," Elwood F. Ireland, Jr., M.D., 4 Dec. 1984; Jerome P. Richie, M.D., to Bernard Lytton, M.D., courtesy of ECW; I: ECW.
3. "Bone Scan," J. A. Creatura, M.D., 29 May 1984, courtesy ECW; I: TNB.
4. RPW to LPS, 13 July 1984, courtesy of LPS.
5. RPW to IOR, 24 Nov. 1984, courtesy of RH. The LSU conference would also mark the 25th anniversary of the review's refounding, and the 125th anniversary of the founding of the university. RPW to David Colbert, 2 Dec. 1984, 28 Jan. 1985, courtesy of LPS.
6. RPW to PD, 31 Mar. 1984, courtesy of PD; RPW to LPS, 4 July 1984, courtesy of *SoR;* RPW to RW, n.d., courtesy of RW. "Re-Interment," *AtMo,* Feb. 1985, p. 48, *NSP,* p. 49; "Old Photograph," *Encounter,* 64 (Feb. 1985), p. 23, *NSP,* p. 55.
7. TLF to JB.
8. "Here the fusion of light and Eros constitutes Warren's wholly original 'myth' of sunrise (as he confirmed in a

phone conversation with me). . . ." VS, "Poet of Youth: Robert Penn Warren at Eighty," in *Time's Glory: Original Essays on Robert Penn Warren,* ed. JAG (n.p.: Central Arkansas, 1986), p. 103.

9. Harold Bloom, *NYRB,* 32 (30 May 1985), p. 40; George P. Garrett in Longley, p. 230; VS, "Poet of Youth," p. 104.

10. William H. Pritchard, *NYTBR,* 12 May 1985, pp. 8–9; RPW, " 'Poetry Is a Kind of Unconscious Autobiography,' " *NYTBR,* pp. 9–11; VS, "Poet of Youth," pp. 91, 96.

11. Pritchard, p. 10; see *Taciturn Text,* p. 211.

12. "Loose Shutter," *NY,* 18 Mar. 1985, p. 42; RPW to PD, 23 Apr. 1985, courtesy of PD; I: RW; "John's Birches," *NY,* 12 Aug. 1985, p. 26.

13. Courtesy of RW.

14. Courtesy of RW. A birthday greeting from the White House began, "Nancy and I want to send our congratulations on your 80th birthday" and extolled his central role in reaffirming "our connection to both the past and the future." He sent a copy to TLF and wrote on it "Jesus Christ!" Courtesy of TLF.

15. Courtesy of the American Academy and Institute of Arts and Letters; RPW to AE, 31 May 1985, courtesy of AE.

CHAPTER 52: POET LAUREATE—AND PATIENT

1. *NSP,* pp. 4–5.

2. I: ECW, RW, Stephen Scully.

3. I: ECW, RW, Stephen Scully.

4. I: ECW, RW, Stephen Scully.

5. RPW to Bertha Krantz, 9 Aug. 1985, courtesy of RH; RPW to RW et al., 23 Aug. 1985, courtesy of RW; medical notes courtesy of ECW.

6. I: Ken Burns.

7. RPW to LPS, 15 Sept., 12 Oct., 22 Oct. 1985, courtesy of *SoR.*

8. RPW to RW, 27 Nov. 1985, courtesy of RW; RPW to AS and Bess Stein, 7 Nov. 1985, courtesy of AS.

9. I: ECW, JDK, TNB.

10. Don Shannon, *Los Angeles Times,* 28 Feb. 1986.

11. RPW to TLF, 2 Mar. 1986, courtesy of TLF; Shannon, *Los Angeles Times;* Derek Walcott, Seamus Heaney, and Christopher Lydon, *PR,* 4, 1986, pp. 606–12; *Newsweek,* 7 Mar. 1986, p. 127; see also John C. Broderick, "The Poet Laureata of the United States," *Dictionary of Literary Biography Yearbook,* 1986, pp. 30–38.

12. RPW to James Olney, 27 June 1986, courtesy of *SoR.*

13. RPW to HO, 2 Oct. 1986, courtesy of HO; RPW to EB, 10 Oct. 1986, UMinnL.

14. RPW to EB, 10 Oct. 1986, UMinnL.

CHAPTER 53: THE INEXORABLE SEASONS

1. *NSP,* p. 169.

2. RPW to JAG, 12 Feb. 1987, courtesy of JAG.

3. RPW to AE, 1 June 1987, courtesy of AE; RPW to RW, 11 Apr. 1987, courtesy of RW.

4. *PF,* pp. 7, 15, 70.

5. I: AE.

6. JDK to RPW, 16 Mar. 1986, medical materials courtesy of ECW.

7. RPW to EB, 6 Aug. 1987, UMinnL.

8. RPW to EB, 6 Aug. 1987, UMinnL; RPW to RW, 10 July 1987, courtesy of RW; David Quammen to JB.

9. Frederick L. Sachs to JDK and TNB, 24 May 1988; RPW to EB, 25 Mar. 1988, UMinnL.

10. I: RW.

11. RPW to AS, 4 Sept. 1988, courtesy of AS; RPW to EB, 30 Sept. 1988, UMinnL.

12. RPW to AS [n.d.], courtesy of AS; RPW to ES, 14 Dec. 1988, courtesy of ES.

13. I: SH.

CHAPTER 54: LEAF FALLING

1. *NSP,* pp. 306–7.
2. I: RW.
3. I: TNB.
4. I: RW.
5. I: TNB.
6. John Scully to JB.
7. RW, "Two days before," *GaR,* 46 (Summer 1992), p. 357.

Genealogy

PENN

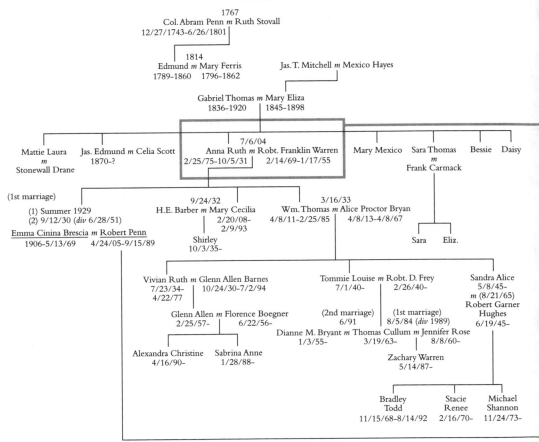

1767
Col. Abram Penn *m* Ruth Stovall
12/27/1743–6/26/1801

1814
Edmund *m* Mary Ferris   Jas. T. Mitchell *m* Mexico Hayes
1789–1860 1796–1862

Gabriel Thomas *m* Mary Eliza
1836–1920   1845–1898

Mattie Laura   Jas. Edmund *m* Celia Scott   7/6/04   Mary Mexico   Sara Thomas   Bessie   Daisy
m   1870–?   Anna Ruth *m* Robt. Franklin Warren   *m*
Stonewall Drane   2/25/75–10/5/31 │ 2/14/69–1/17/55   Frank Carmack

(1st marriage)   9/24/32   3/16/33
(1) Summer 1929   H.E. Barber *m* Mary Cecilia   Wm. Thomas *m* Alice Proctor Bryan
(2) 9/12/30 (*div* 6/28/51)   2/20/08–   4/8/11–2/25/85   4/8/13–4/8/67
Emma Cinina Brescia *m* Robert Penn   2/9/93   Sara   Eliz.
1906–5/13/69   4/24/05–9/15/89   Shirley
                                          10/3/35–

Vivian Ruth *m* Glenn Allen Barnes   Tommie Louise *m* Robt. D. Frey   Sandra Alice
7/23/34–   10/24/30–7/2/94   7/1/40–   2/26/40–   5/8/45–
4/22/77   *m* (8/21/65)
                                                                      Robert Garner
Glenn Allen *m* Florence Boegner   (2nd marriage)   (1st marriage)   Hughes
2/25/57–   6/22/56–   6/91   8/5/84 (*div* 1989)   6/19/45–
                              Dianne M. Bryant *m* Thomas Cullum *m* Jennifer Rose
                                 1/3/55–   3/19/63–   8/8/60–
Alexandra Christine   Sabrina Anne
4/16/90–   1/28/88–   Zachary Warren
                                                  5/14/87–

                                          Bradley   Stacie   Michael
                                           Todd   Renee   Shannon
                                      11/15/68–8/14/92   2/16/70–   11/24/73–

WARREN

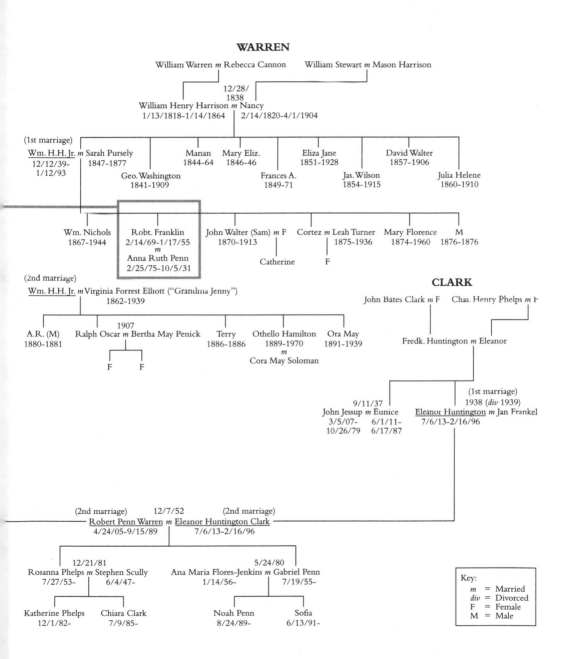

William Warren *m* Rebecca Cannon   William Stewart *m* Mason Harrison

12/28/
1838

William Henry Harrison *m* Nancy
1/13/1818-1/14/1864   2/14/1820-4/1/1904

(1st marriage)
Wm. H.H. Jr. *m* Sarah Pursely
12/12/39-   1847-1877
1/12/93

Geo. Washington
1841-1909

Manan   Mary Eliz.
1844-64   1846-46

Frances A.
1849-71

Eliza Jane
1851-1928

Jas. Wilson
1854-1915

David Walter
1857-1906

Julia Helene
1860-1910

Wm. Nichols
1867-1944

Robt. Franklin
2/14/69-1/17/55
m
Anna Ruth Penn
2/25/75-10/5/31

John Walter (Sam) *m* F
1870-1913

Catherine

Cortez *m* Leah Turner
1875-1936

F

Mary Florence   M
1874-1960   1876-1876

(2nd marriage)
Wm. H.H. Jr. *m* Virginia Forrest Elliott ("Grandma Jenny")
1862-1939

CLARK

John Bates Clark *m* F   Chas. Henry Phelps *m* F

A.R. (M)
1880-1881

Ralph Oscar *m* Bertha May Penick
1907

F   F

Terry
1886-1886

Othello Hamilton
1889-1970
m
Cora May Soloman

Ora May
1891-1939

Fredk. Huntington *m* Eleanor

9/11/37
John Jessup *m* Eunice
3/5/07-   6/1/11-
10/26/79   6/17/87

(1st marriage)
1938 (*div* 1939)
Eleanor Huntington *m* Jan Frankel
7/6/13-2/16/96

(2nd marriage)   12/7/52   (2nd marriage)
Robert Penn Warren *m* Eleanor Huntington Clark
4/24/05-9/15/89   7/6/13-2/16/96

12/21/81
Rosanna Phelps *m* Stephen Scully
7/27/53-   6/4/47-

5/24/80
Ana Maria Flores-Jenkins *m* Gabriel Penn
1/14/56-   7/19/55-

Katherine Phelps
12/1/82-

Chiara Clark
7/9/85-

Noah Penn
8/24/89-

Sofia
6/13/91-

Key:
m = Married
div = Divorced
F = Female
M = Male

Acknowledgments

My first thanks must go to the late Robert Penn Warren and then to his family: his wife, the late Eleanor Clark; their children, Rosanna Phelps and Gabriel Penn; his sister, Mary Cecilia Warren Barber; and his niece, Tommie Louise Warren Frey, all of whom have helped me with great generosity, supplying documents, photographs, and memories. My warm thanks go also to Robert D. Frey, Stephen Scully, John Scully, and Ana Maria Flores-Jenkins Warren; to John Burt, Robert Penn Warren's literary executor; and to Owen Laster, his literary agent. Warren's many friends have helped me, chief among them the late Cleanth Brooks and Albert Erskine, and to them I am especially grateful. In a special place is my wife, Martha Cortelyou Allen. I truly cannot thank her enough.

For support, I am indebted to the University of Michigan, generous in all ways but particularly through the Department of English Language and Literature, the Office of the Vice President for Research, the Faculty Assistance Fund, the sabbatical-leave and retirement-furlough programs, and the Information Technology Division, including the invaluable loan of equipment and general consulting assistance. My gratitude goes too to the National Endowment for the Humanities, the American Council of Learned Societies, and the American Philosophical Society for grants that were vital to the completion of my work.

I have also been very fortunate in those other friends of scholarship, the libraries and librarians. The latter are acknowledged by name below, and they helped me at the following institutions: Emory University, University of Kentucky, University of Western Kentucky, University of California (Berkeley), Library of Congress, University of Maryland, University of Minnesota, Princeton University, Vanderbilt University, University of Virginia, and Yale University. The Graduate Library of the University of Michigan purchased materials I needed, and the Reference Division saved me countless hours by answering many queries, most of them by telephone. All of these institutions courteously and efficiently provided copies of documents. I am particularly grateful for access to letters and to special collections and archives, all identified here and in the notes.

There were other invaluable sources that require special mention: the forty-four interviews carried out and recorded, and most of them transcribed, under the University of Kentucky Robert Penn Warren Oral History Project, part of the Warren Collection and identified as RPWOHP, also the hospitality there of the Gaines Center for the Humanities. At Emory University, I was made welcome in the Floyd C. Watkins Manuscript Collection, and at Wake Forest University in the personal archive of Stuart Wright, through his courtesy. At Vanderbilt University, I worked in the Jean and Alexander Heard Library and made particular use of the collection of Agrarian materials, especially letters, identified as VUL. The University of Maryland Library (UMdL) gave me access to their collection of Katherine Anne Porter papers. The Princeton University Library (PUL) made available Warren material in the archives of Henry Holt and Company, the archives of Charles Scribner's Sons, selected papers of Harper & Brothers, the archives of *Story* magazine and Story Press, the Caroline Gordon Papers, and the Allen Tate Papers. At the Beinecke Rare Book and Manuscript Library of Yale University (here YUL), I was able to work with the resources of the Robert Penn Warren Papers, the Cleanth Brooks Papers, the Edward Davison Papers, and the Peter Davison Papers. The University of Virginia Library (here UVaL) generously made its resources available to me, especially those of the Library Reference Division. Rhodes House at Oxford University provided records. The American Academy and Institute of Arts and Letters, the American Academy in Rome, and the John Simon Guggenheim Memorial Foundation provided valuable and voluminous materials. The collection of Warren materials with which I started came from the files of Random House, here identified as RH.

I wish to make special acknowledgment to Professor John Burt for permission to quote from Robert Penn Warren's unpublished writings; to Professor John Michael Walsh for permission to quote from Cleanth Brooks's unpublished writings; to Mrs. Robert H. Sullivan for permission to quote from letters of Donald Davidson; to Mr. Peter Davison for permission to quote from letters of Edward Davison; to Mr. John Egerton for permission to quote from "A Reminiscence" in *Nashville: The Face of Two Centuries;* to Mrs. Ralph Ellison for permission to quote from a letter of Ralph Ellison; to James Glickman for permission to quote from his letter to me; to Mrs. Nancy Tate Wood for permission to quote from letters of Caroline Gordon; to Mrs. Margaret Allison for permission to quote from her letters to me; to Mrs. Lyle Lanier and Mr. L. Gene Lemon for permission to quote from the letters of Lyle Lanier; to Mr. George Chamberlain for permission to quote from letters of Andrew Lytle; to Mr. Samuel H. Monk II, for permission to quote from letters of Samuel H. Monk; to Barbara Thomson Davis for permission to quote from letters of Katherine Anne Porter; to Mrs. Helen Ransom Forman for permission to quote from letters of John Crowe Ransom; to Mr. David B. Rosen for permission to quote from his letter to me; to T. G. Rosenthal for permission to quote from letters to and from him; to Professor Louis D. Rubin, Jr., for permission to quote from his letter to me; to Mrs. Elizabeth B. Stommel for permission to quote from her letters to me; to Mr. Owen Laster for permission to quote from Helen H. Strauss's *A Talent for Luck: An Autobiography;* to Mrs. Helen H. Tate for permission to quote from letters of Allen Tate; to Professor Floyd Waykins for the use of his notes and permission to quote from letters to him; to Mr. James Wilcox for permission to quote from his letter to me; and to Mr. William Ridley Wills II for permission to quote from a letter of Jesse Wills.

Special and heartfelt thanks are due to these friends who read the manuscript of this book, in whole or in part, and in various stages: John W. Atkinson, Carl Brandt, John Burt, Cleanth Brooks, Rev. Andrew M. Greeley, James A. Grimshaw, Jr., Louis D. Rubin, Jr., and Lewis P. Simpson. I cannot begin to thank them adequately. For the work of my editor, Robert D. Loomis, any expression of thanks would be inadequate. Benjamin Dreyer was superb as production editor.

I have received so much kindness at so many hands that it is difficult even to describe the forms it took. Not the least of them was hospitality, especially from the Warrens, but from many others as well. The names here include interviewees (I list all Oral History Project contributors, those I did not interview personally as well as those I did) and correspondents, who sometimes sent books, photographs, and copies of Warren letters as well as their own. Some friends conducted interviews for me. Other friends provided expertise in special areas. The help I had from scholars and critics appears in the notes and bibliography, but most of their names are here as well. Research assistants and typists expedited the work greatly. To all of those below I offer again my everlasting thanks: Daria M. Ague, William Albright, John W. Aldridge, Marnie Alicia Allen, Frank Anthony, James Atlas, Kent Bailes, William T. Bandy, Martin Beadle, Daniel M. Becker, M.D., Ralph Bellamy, Eric Bentley, Wendell Berry, Wesley Berry, Raymond F. Betts, Gregory A. Beyer, Beverly D. Bishop, Staige D. Blackford, John Blades, Carver Blanchard, Philip Bonham, George S. Boone, Joy Bale Boone, William Boozer, John C. Broderick, George Bornstein, Michael Bott, Cecile Starr Boyajarian, Enoch Brater, Dan Brennan, Mildred Bronson, Elizabeth W. Brown, Heidel Brown, Huntington Brown, Matthew Bruccoli, Robert Brustein, Jackson Bryer, Marjorie Bryer, Ken Burns, Thomas N. Byrne, M.D., H. Don Cameron, Carolyn Carroll, Ross Chambers, Brainerd B. Cheney, Frances N. Cheney, Bart Clark, Karen Clark, John Coleman, Paul Collinge, Norman Coliver, Ray Colvig, Becky Conekin, John Constable, Duncan B. Cooper III, George Core, Muriel Cowley, Alexander Crouch, John G. Cross, Jody Crudin, Isabella Davis, Lambert Davis, Peter Davison, James Dickey, Linda Dietert, Stephen Donato, Denis Donoghue, Howard Dubin, M.D., Charles East, Blanche T. Ebeling-Konig, Richard Eberhart, John Egerton, Ralph Ellison, Marisa Erskine, John Ervin, F. Robert Fekety, Jr., M.D., William Ferris, Edith Fitzell, R. A. Fletcher, Joseph M. Flora, Shelby Foote, Helen Forman, Charles H. Foster, Doris Foster, Wallace Fowlie, Anne Freudenberg, John Kenneth Galbraith, Isabella Gardner, George Garrett, Mark W. Garrett, Arthur Geffen, Sue Gibson, Susan Gilman, Norton R. Girault, Lawrence Goldstein, Steven Griffin, Robert B. Hamblin, Barbé Hammer, Rick Hart, Richard Harteis, David Havird, Shirley Hazzard, William Hegen, Robert B. Heilman, Margaret A. Hemphill, Cathy Henderson, Robert Hivnor, Daniel Hoffman, Deanna Hoffman, John Hollander, Carol Hollinshead, Robert A. Hull, M. Thomas Inge, Dorothy Jeakins, William Marshall Jenkins, Jr., Ejner Jensen, Jane Johnson, Nancy Johnson, Steven Jones, Eleanor Joseph, James Justus, Bruce Kawin, Alfred Kazin, James D. Kenney, M.D., Cynthia G. King, Thomas A. Kirby, Pat Knight, John Knott, John T. Knowlton, Robert Hoppelman, Penelope Kosch, Bertha Krantz, Sydney Krause, Frederick W. Kreye, Catherine Lanier, Lyle Lanier, Betty Leighton, R.W.B. Lewis, Paul R. Lichter, M.D., Mack Linebaugh, A. Walton Litz, Darcy Litzerman, Agostino Lombardo, Cesare Lombroso, M.D., John L. Longley, Jr., Strawberry Luck, R. D. Luckett, Claire McCann, Austin MacLean, F. Charles McMains, Sr., F. Charles McMains, Jr., Scott McPhail, Veronica Makowsky, Frederick Manfred, Gale Marlin, Leo Marx, Michael

Mewshaw, David Milch, Christie Miller, Victoria Thorpe Miller, Joseph R. Millichap, Ella Puryear Mims, Clay Moldenhauer, William Moss, G. Mary Nelson, Carol O'Brien, Mary O'Connor, Harriet Owsley, John Palmer, Jay Parini, Marvin G. Parnes, P.M. Pasinetti, James A. Perkins, Leo Pflaum, Rosalind Pflaum, Sidney Pollock, Jean Preston, Sam Prestridge, David Quammen, Patrick F. Quinn, William Riggan, William M. Roberts, Thomas G. Rosenthal, Danforth Ross, Randolph Paul Runyon, Hugh Ruppersburg, Ieda Russell, Jeffrey B. Russell, Anne Sadowski, Patrick Samway, S.J., Ernest Sandeen, Judith Sandridge, Robin Sarris, Judy Saunders, Katie Scott, Arthur H. Scouten, Edgar F. Shannon, Jr., Kate Sharp, Margaret M. Sherry, Howard Shevrin, Daniel R. Shulman, Barry Siegel, M.D., Calvin L. Skaggs, Don C. Skemer, Dave Smith, Elinor Smith, Monroe Spears, Zaro Starr, Francis Steegmuller, Arnold Stein, James Stein, George R. Stewart, John L. Stewart, Elizabeth B. Stommel, Eric Stover, Victor Strandberg, William Styron, Jeffrey Suchanek, Jane Sullivan, John Sullivan, Theresa Sullivan, Walter Sullivan, Robert H. Super, Peter Taylor, John A. Thompson, Gregory J. Turner, Brenda Ueland, Thomas A. Underwood, Leonard Unger, Martha Vicinus, Gore Vidal, Marshall Walker, Floyd Watkins, Robin D. Wear, Mary Louise Weeks, Randy F. Weinstein, Robert Weisbuch, Mark Weishahn, René Wellek, Maxine Wells, Eudora Welty, Richard Wilbur, James Wilcox, Joel Williamson, Patricia C. Willis, John Thaddeus Wills, Linda S. Wilson, James A. Winn, Marice Wolfe, J. Howard Wolmer, Nancy Tate Wood, Thomas Wood, Herbert Woodman, C. Vann Woodward, Celeste T. Wright, Stuart Wright, Delbert Wylder, Mary Wyville, Emily Zinn, Lynn Zollmer.

My last statement of indebtedness is to those who have helped me and not found their names here: to them, my apologies along with my gratitude.

Index

Grateful acknowledgment is made to the following for permission to reprint both published and unpublished material:

Atlantic Monthly Press: Excerpts from *Letters of Katherine Anne Porter*, edited by Isabel Bailey (Atlantic Monthly Press, 1990). Reprinted by permission of Atlantic Monthly Press.

Estate of Cleanth Brooks: Excerpts from letters of Cleanth Brooks to Allen Tate, housed in the Cleanth Brooks Archive at Beinecke Library, Yale University. Used by permission of The Estate of Cleanth Brooks and Beinecke Library, Yale University.

John Burt, Literary Executor for Robert Penn Warren: Excerpts from the letters of Robert Penn Warren. Used by permission of John Burt, Literary Executor for Robert Penn Warren.

John Egerton: Excerpt from "A Reminiscence," by Robert Penn Warren, from *Nashville: The Faces of Two Centuries, 1780–1980*. Reprinted by permission of John Egerton.

Fanny Ellison: Excerpt from a letter of Ralph Ellison to Nathan Scott. Used by permission of Fanny Ellison.

Helen Ransom Forman: Excerpts from letters of John Crowe Ransom to Allen Tate, housed at Princeton University Library, and to Robert Penn Warren, housed at Beinecke Library, Yale University. Used by permission of Helen Ransom Forman.

James Glickman: Quotes from James Glickman. Used by permission of James Glickman.

Margaret Allison Hemphill: Excerpts from letters of Margaret Allison Hemphill to Joseph Blotner. Used by permission of Margaret Allison Hemphill.

Mrs. Lyle Lanier: Excerpt from a letter of Lyle Lanier to Allen Tate. Used by permission.

The Literary Estate of Katherine Anne Porter: Excerpts from letters of Katherine Anne Porter to Robert Penn Warren, housed at the Beinecke Library, Yale University, the University of Maryland Library, and the Library of Congress. Used by permission of The Literary Estate of Katherine Anne Porter.

Louisiana State University Press: Excerpt from "The Briar Patch," by Robert Penn Warren, from *I'll Take My Stand: The South and the Agrarian Tradition*, by Twelve Southerners. Copyright © 1962, 1977 by Louis D. Rubin, Jr. Reprinted by permission of Louisiana State University Press.

Estate of Samuel Holt Monk: Excerpts from three letters of Samuel Holt Monk. Used by permission of The Estate of Samuel Holt Monk.

The William Morris Agency: Excerpts from "October Picnic Long Ago," "Swimming in the Pacific," "Passers-by on Snowy Night," "Snowshoeing Back to Camp in Gloaming," "Aspen Leaf in Windless World," "The Moonlight's Dream," "Part of What Might Have Been a Short Story," "The Only Poem," "Eagle Descending," "Speleology," and "Commentary," from *Being Here,* by Robert Penn Warren. Copyright © 1978, 1979, 1980 by Robert Penn Warren. Excerpt from *Brothers to Dragons,* by Robert Penn Warren. Copyright © 1953 by Robert Penn Warren. Excerpts from "The Faring" and

position," from *Or Else,* by Robert Penn Warren. Copyright © 1966, 1968, 1970, 1971, 1972, 1973, 1974 by Robert Penn Warren. Excerpts from "School Lesson Based on Word of Tragic Death of Entire Gillum Family," "Gold Glade," "Dark Woods," "Boys Will, Joyful Labor without Pay, and Harvest Home," "Original Sin: A Short Story," "The Flower," and "Colder Fire," from *Promises,* by Robert Penn Warren. Copyright © 1955, 1957 by Robert Penn Warren. Excerpts from "Psychological Profile," "Moral Assessment," and 228 words of prose from *Homage to Theodore Dreiser,* by Robert Penn Warren. Copyright © 1971 by Robert Penn Warren. All material reprinted by permission of Random House, Inc.

David B. Rosen: Excerpts from David B. Rosen's recollections of Robert Penn Warren and his family. Used by permission of David B. Rosen.

Louis D. Rubin: Various quotes by Louis D. Rubin. Used by permission of Louis D. Rubin.

St. Martin's Press: Excerpt from *American Literature: The Makers and the Making,* by Robert Penn Warren with Cleanth Brooks and R.W.B. Lewis. Copyright © 1973. Reprinted by permission of St. Martin's Press, Inc.

The Sporting News: *The Sporting News* Conlon Collection baseball card No. 617. Reprinted by permission of *The Sporting News.*

Elizabeth B. Stommel: Excerpts from letters of Elizabeth B. Stommel to Joseph Blotner. Used by permission of Elizabeth B. Stommel.

Mrs. Robert H. Sullivan: Excerpts from letters of Donald Davidson to Allen Tate. Used by permission.

The University of Georgia Press, Helen Tate, and Mrs. Robert H. Sullivan: Excerpts from *The Literary Correspondence of Donald Davidson and Allen Tate.* Reprinted by permission of The University of Georgia Press, Helen Tate, and Mrs. Robert H. Sullivan.

The University Press of Kentucky: Excerpt from *Portrait of a Father,* by Robert Penn Warren. Copyright © 1988 by The University Press of Kentucky. Reprinted by permission of the publishers.

University Press of Mississippi, Helen Tate, and George Chamberlain, Literary Executor for Andrew Lytle: Excerpts from *The Lytle-Tate Letters: The Correspondence of Andrew Lytle and Allen Tate,* edited by Thomas Daniel Young and Elizabeth Sarcone. Reprinted by permission of University Press of Mississippi, Helen Tate, and George Chamberlain, Literary Executor for Andrew Lytle.

James Wilcox: Excerpt from a letter of James Wilcox to Joseph Blotner. Used by permission of James Wilcox.

William Ridley Wills II: Excerpt from a letter of Jesse Wills to Allen Tate, housed in the Allen Tate Papers at Princeton University Library. Used by permission of William Ridley Wills II.

Nancy Tate Wood: Excerpts from letters of Carolyn Gordon to Andrew Lytle, housed at Vanderbilt University Library, and one letter beginning "Dear Coz," housed at the Beinecke Library, Yale University. Used by permission of Nancy Tate Wood.

About the Author

JOSEPH BLOTNER was born and raised in New Jersey. He lived and taught in the South for fifteen years. Educated at Drew, Northwestern, and the University of Pennsylvania, he interrupted his education to fly with the 8th Air Force in England during World War II. He then taught at the Universities of Idaho, Virginia, North Carolina, and Michigan. At Virginia he was a member and later chairman of the Balch Committee, which brought William Faulkner to the university as its first writer-in-residence. His work on Faulkner includes *Faulkner in the University* (with Frederick L. Gwynn); *William Faulkner's Library: A Catalogue; Faulkner: A Biography* (in two volumes and an updated one-volume edition); and *Selected Letters of William Faulkner* as well as *Uncollected Stories of William Faulkner.* He edited four novels in the *William Faulkner's Manuscripts* series, and three volumes of Faulkner novels (with Noel Polk) for the Library of America. His other books are *The Political Novel, The Fiction of J. D. Salinger* (with Frederick L. Gwynn), and *The Modern American Political Novel: 1900–1960.* Twice a Guggenheim Fellow and twice a Fulbright Lecturer at the University of Copenhagen, he has been a visiting professor at Trinity College (Connecticut) and the Universities of Mississippi, Arizona, and Rome. He is Professor of English Emeritus at the University of Michigan. The father of three daughters, he lives with his wife, Marnie, in Charlottesville, Virginia.

About the Type

This book was set in Bembo, a typeface based on an old-style Roman face that was used for Cardinal Bembo's tract *De Aetna* in 1495. Bembo was cut by Francisco Giffo in the early sixteenth century. The Lawston Monotype Machine Company of Philadelphia brought the well-proportioned letter forms of Bembo to the United States in the 1930s.